ADVERTISING
THE PROCESS AND PRACTICE

McGRAW-HILL SERIES IN MARKETING

Consulting Editor
CHARLES SCHEWE
University of Massachusetts

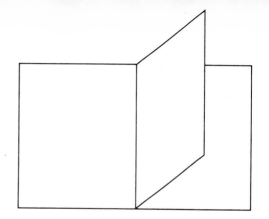

ADVERTISING
THE PROCESS AND PRACTICE

Jack Engel
Iowa State University

McGraw-Hill Book Company
New York   St. Louis   San Francisco   Auckland   Bogotá   Hamburg
Johannesburg   London   Madrid   Mexico   Montreal   New Delhi   Panama
Paris   São Paulo   Singapore   Sydney   Tokyo   Toronto

This book was set in Souvenir Light by Black Dot, Inc.
The editors were John F. Carleo, Michael Elia, and M. Susan Norton;
the developmental editor was Susan Friedman;
the designer was Joan E. O'Connor;
the production supervisor was Charles Hess.
The photo editor for the four-color insert was Inge King.
The cover, part- and chapter-opening illustrations were drawn by Liam Roberts;
all other drawings were done by Fine Line Illustrations, Inc.
R. R. Donnelley & Sons Company was printer and binder.

ADVERTISING: THE PROCESS AND PRACTICE

1 2 3 4 5 6 7 8 9 0 D O D O 8 9 8 7 6 5 4 3 2 1 0

Library of Congress Cataloging in Publication Data

Engel, Jack.
    Advertising, the process and practice.

    (McGraw-Hill series in marketing)
    Bibliography: p.
    Includes index.
    1.   Advertising.   I.   Title.
HF5823.E7   659.1   79-26656
ISBN 0-07-019511-0

To Eleanor,
my wife and best friend

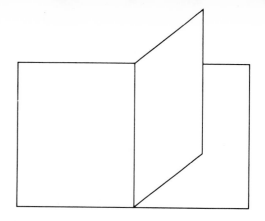

ABOUT THE AUTHOR

Currently an Associate Professor at Iowa State University, JACK ENGEL has been on the advertising agency firing line for twenty-five years. His interests and work experience cover the entire advertising spectrum: marketing, creativity, public relations, media, traffic, account supervision, production. His background includes manufacturing, wholesaling, and retailing experience, sales and market research. He has created and supervised ad campaigns to retailers and manufacturers, both consumer and industrial and has interviewed thousands of package goods consumers. He holds a graduate degree from Columbia University and did additional graduate work at Case Western Reserve University.

Along the way he has won over 40 readership and other awards for his creative and marketing skills. From all of this experience, and from his years of teaching advertising to professionals and to college students, has come an insider's view of the real world of advertising, a practical and understandable overview of this fascinating and competitive field.

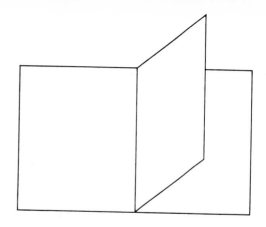

CONTENTS

Unit 7
CAREERS IN ADVERTISING

PREFACE

If this book were attached to a routing slip, I'd want it to go first to college students, then to company officials, both with and without advertising responsibilities, and then to advertising professionals. You are the people I had in mind when I first decided to write this manuscript. You are my target audience.

My interest in this project began to take shape after several of my young friends said that they had been surprised by their first jobs in advertising. Expecting one thing, they found another—quite different from that outlined in their college texts. Expecting large budgets, they found small ones. Expecting to find themselves part of a sophisticated team of specialists, they found *they* were the entire team. *They* were wearing all the hats: doing research, sales promotion, art direction, copywriting, media management, and more. Having once been surprised in this way early in my own career, I wondered out loud to my wife why someone hadn't written a book about all types of advertisers, large and small, retailer and manufacturer, consumer-oriented, and industry-oriented. She pointed to a desk, passed me a pencil, and said, "With twenty-five years' experience in every phase of the business, from retail, wholesale, manufacturing, market research, sales, and copywriting to media and agency management, and now teaching, *who else* could write it better?" Wifely bias aside, that's where it all began.

What do I mean by "all" advertisers? I certainly mean the big ones, the Procter & Gambles and the General Motors and the top national companies and their advertising agencies, who spend $5.5 billion of the total ad expenditures of $27 billion in a given year! But I also mean to introduce and discuss problems of small businesses, a community of independent business people and approximately one million enterprises. The media strategies relevant to a Procter & Gamble (P&G) are often irrelevant to a small company. One P&G national television commercial at $60,000 would wipe out an entire year's ad budget for most businesses! Although these businesses also depend on the sales stimulation provided by advertising, their specialized needs have been virtually ignored, except by the trade press. I hope to correct this oversight.

I was also concerned that retail, industrial, trade, professional and international advertising were not receiving their fair share of attention from authors of advertising textbooks and hope to fill this gap, as well.

The language in this book is down to earth. It is designed to communicate with graphic examples and illustrative parables. For example, describing the business goals of people in advertising shows you their problems intimately and on a human scale.

Students and professionals should find new ideas and presentation techniques within these pages to mirror the rapid changes taking place within our mobile society. There is new information about test-market theory, locations, and practices and new data from psychological sources on advertising readership. Cooperative advertising, an expanding horizon, is presented.

International advertising is growing in importance for foreign businesses as well as for American ad agencies, multinational corporations, and small- to medium-sized exporters. I have outlined the general state of international advertising with important similarities and differences that exist between countries.

In organizing the text, I've begun with the well-understood and visible consumer. From there I've progressed to the relatively unknown industrial, professional, and trade buyer. Then I've moved to the language of advertising in which the reader sees subjective theory and technique balanced by research. This evenhanded approach will almost assuredly bring a few howls of protest from purists. But advertising is a business, and if research can demonstrate that one creative approach is more effective than another, the reader deserves to know about it.

At the very outset, I admit to a bias in my approach to teaching. I like to work from the known and the specific to the unknown and the general. If you are involved with a specific retailer's problem, it is easier to move from *that* to the operation of the manufacturer than the other way around. Throughout this text, I have used this approach to encourage learning and knowledge and to discourage rote memorization.

Above all else, this book is a workbook designed to help anyone who wants to engage in this quite mad but wonderful business of advertising. I hope that the reader will keep it as a ready reference long after the quizzes and exams are forgotten!

ACKNOWLEDGMENTS

John Donne said it for all of us back in the seventeenth century: "No man is an island, entire of itself; every man is a piece of the continent, a part of the main. . . ." Surely he meant this in reference to the debt authors owe the world they live in. I, for one, find that the substance of this book can be traced to contributions made by the people I have met within and outside the advertising business. To single each one out would be an impossible task; yet their knowledge and wisdom are evident in each chapter. Among those who were most helpful are Henry Platek, Howard Baird, Bill Weber, Bob Rosser, Bill Kido, Bart Panettiere, and Jack Kinley.

My most recent debt, however, is owed to those scholars who reviewed the drafts of this manuscript, making constructive comments and recommending improvements. They are, in alphabetic order, Professors Anson H. Gordon, Bernard V. Katz, William Nickels, Milton Richards, Charles D. Schewe, and Nathan Weinstock.

I am also grateful to a top-notch publishing company for recognizing that twenty-five years of assorted advertising experiences could yield an updated approach to the business, and for backing this judgment by assigning a creative professional, senior editor, Michael R. Elia, to advise me and to keep me on course. He was aided by Susan Norton, who orchestrated the editing. But my special thanks must go to Susan Friedman, the editor most intimately concerned with the word-by-word presentation. Her vision and advice, and her honesty, all played a major role in the structure of this new advertising text.

Jack Engel

P.S.   For those who feel that the history of advertising is less exciting than what is going on *now*, skip the introduction and move into Chapter 1.

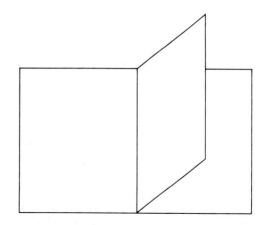

INTRODUCTION:
THE EVOLUTION
OF ADVERTISING

To know where we are today in the world of advertising, we should consider where we were yesterday. Quite often we learn that ideas we consider and praise as "new" are not new at all. Neolithic people (circa 5000 B.C.) required food, shelter, and clothing and traded for them with others. We can only guess whether they advertised. But if we define advertising as a method of delivering a sales message, they may well have done so.

During the New Stone Age, pottery and weaving became established crafts in settled villages, which were visited by wandering farmers, animal herders, and hunters. Goods were bought or bartered, and probably both villagers and travelers passed the word along about particularly good craftspeople. The first advertising was what we now call "word of mouth."

The history of advertising from 5000 B.C. to A.D. 1450 is generally

FIGURE I-1
An artist's rendering
of what some early
ads might have
looked like hewn by
chisel on stone.
(Courtesy Institute
of Outdoor
Advertising.)

fashioned from a few surviving written records and artifacts. They allow us to conclude that:

1 until Gutenberg invented the printing press with movable type in A.D. 1450, most of the advertising (except store signs and wall posters) was "word of mouth";
2 most people, even in the upper classes, could not read, although they could identify signs and markings;
3 the advertiser had to resort to verbal communications: hawking, shouting, and "crying" to reach an essentially illiterate populace[1] (Figure I-1).

PAPYRUS AND WALL POSTERS

The introduction of papyrus and reed pen meant that a sales message could be kept and reread. One 3000-year-old Theban papyrus still advertises for a

---

[1]Frank Presbrey, *The History and Development of Advertising* (New York: Doubleday, Doran & Co., 1929), p. 11. Merchants in ancient Egypt used criers to announce ship and cargo arrivals. To this day in certain African villages, traveling merchants walk around crying their wares to a rhythmic drum beat. So formalized did crying become in the Middle Ages that in the province of Berry, France, twelve criers organized a company.

runaway slave. Lost-and-found ads on papyrus were common in Greece and Rome. From writing on papyrus, it was an easy step to wall posters. (Excavations in the ruins of Herculaneum and Pompeii uncovered wall posters announcing gladiatorial events.) The Romans undoubtedly used wall posters in England, Gaul, and Persia and on all major thoroughfares within the Empire (Figure I-2).

STORE SIGNS

Merchants in the larger cities and towns were already using signs over their shops at the time of the Caesars. During the early Middle Ages, signs were probably the major advertising medium (Figure I-3).

Here is Macaulay in his *History of England:*[2]

> The shops were therefore distinguished by painted signs, which gave a gay and grotesque aspect to the streets. The walk from Charing Cross to Whitechapel [in London] lay through an endless succession of Saracen's Heads, Royal Oaks, Blue Bears and Golden Lambs which disappeared when they were no longer required for the direction of the common people.

[2]Thomas Macaulay, *The History of England*, Butler's ed. (Philadelphia: E. H. Butler & Co., 1856), vol. 1, p. 107.

FIGURE I-2
A representation of a Roman wall poster. (Courtesy Institute of Outdoor Advertising.)

FIGURE I-3
Typical of
merchants' signs
throughout western
Europe in the
Middle Ages are
these in a
reconstructed village
in Aarhus, Denmark.

AFTER GUTENBERG

Like many inventions, Gutenberg's press was widely ignored, except by some church visionaries and a few fellow printers. No business people, it appears, came beating on his door to ask him to print advertisements of merchandise. Advertisers used the tried and the true: store signs and criers. And Macaulay suggests another medium:

> London was a labyrinth of narrow alleys between houses; goods were conveyed about the town on small trucks drawn by dogs.[3]

It is more than likely that in the 1680s enterprising tradespeople painted their business signs on dog-drawn wagons, much as they were to do with horse-drawn wagons 200 years later.

Handbills

The printing press eventually caught on. Print could reproduce a page of words and illustrations in relatively large quantities and more cheaply than

[3]Macaulay, op. cit., p. 107.

handcopied messages. The printing art spread throughout western Europe, and William Caxton, a missionary printer, brought England its first "modern" press. After he had printed a volume of church law in 1477, the clergy let him tack a handbill (advertisement) about the volume on the church doors. Although the posting of handbills on church doors was no novelty, Caxton's was the first posted notice to have been printed on movable type.[4]

The Weekly Papers

Once ambitious people recognized that the printing press could be used to distribute the news, it was only a short time before newspapers and advertising became closely associated. The first regular English weekly, *Weekly Newes*, appeared in 1622. Just three years later, this ad appeared, one of the first in a periodical:

> An excellent discourse concerning the match between our most gracious and mightie Prince Charles, Prince of Wales, and the Lady Henrietta Maria, daughter of Henry the Fourth, later King of France . . . with a lively picture of the Prince and Lady cut in bronze.[5]

In 1653, *Mercurius Politicus* was created for Cromwell's army. It ran this ad in 1658:

> That excellent and by all Physicians, approved China drink, called by the Chineans, Tcha, by other nations Tay alias Tee, is sold at the Sultaness Head Coffee-House, in Sweeting's Rents, by the Royal Exchange, London.[6]

By this time, the word *advertisement* had come to be used as a heading for commercial announcements in newspapers. Most of the ads were for books, which were increasingly affordable by a widening circle of literate people. (Semiliterates bought books to impress friends.) But many of the ads were for medicines, because it was the time of the plague. Handbills and newspapers carried ads for cordials, antipestilential pills, and royal antidotes. Coupled with news stories, the ads left no doubt about the severity of the great plague, in which 68,596 persons died.

In eighteenth-century England, some journals were already refusing to accept "quack" ads. This attitude owed something to improved diets and the availability of hot water for washing body and clothes. As bad complexions

---

[4]Turner relates the excitement to be found in a typical fair handbill: "There is to be seen a strange and monstrous child, with one body and one belly, and yet otherwise it hath all the proportions of two children, that is two heads, two noses, two mouths, four eyes, four ears, and four leggs, four hands and four feet. The monster is of the female kind, it was born at Fillips Town on the Twenty Ninth of April, 1699. The father of this child is present where it is to be seen." E.S. Turner, *Shocking History of Advertising* (New York: E.P. Dutton Co., Inc., 1954), p. 23.

[5]Turner, op. cit., p. 23.

[6]Turner, op. cit., p. 23.

and other ailments got washed away by soap and hot water, the need for pills and unguents diminished. Then, as now, advertising could only sell what was needed.

The Coffee Houses

The coffee house, the seventeenth-century "intellectual cafe," was a gathering place for discussions and the news of the day. It is important to the history of advertising because it sold London, provincial, and selected foreign newspapers. Many of the coffee houses accepted classified ads, too. One ad turned up some 218 years later under curious circumstances: On February 22, 1741, the Spanish ship *Nuestra Señora de los Milagros* ran aground and sank off the Yucatan coast. In 1959, some of her goods were recovered. Among them was a gold, double-cased English watch. The watchmaker had used a snippet of newspaper as a shim between the works and the inner casing. The snippet of newspaper contained a classified notice of a timber auction (Figure I-4).

The American Classifieds

Meanwhile, across the sea, American advertising simply aped the English. In April 1704, the first issue of *The Weekly Boston* Newsletter contained

FIGURE I-4
This English watch revealed a shim fashioned from a classified ad of the times. When the watch was recovered from a sunken Spanish ship in 1959, the ad was still legible. (From Mendel Peterson, "Reach for the New World," *National Geographic*, December 1977, p. 746. Courtesy of Pablo Bush Romero Collection.)

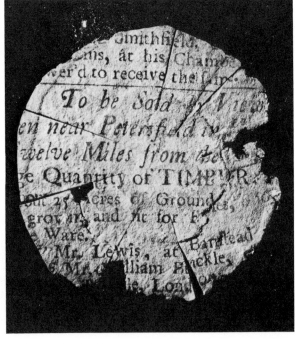

classified ads. This early colonial newspaper had a grand circulation of 300 or fewer.

Colonial printers ran off advertising handbills on a wide range of subjects. The availability of land was a typical handbill subject. Supporters of the English king, speculators, and developers like William Penn often had handbills printed to encourage people to settle on their lands. Some developers even offered no rent for five years as an inducement.

Fundamentally, however, the colonials thought of advertising in connection with classifieds, most of which, like their British counterparts, promoted plasters, potions, surgery, and pills.

The Penny Press

In the 1800s in the United States, a newspaper selling for 6 cents (as many did), was out of reach of the poor. When the first successful penny paper was begun in 1833,[7] it led the way for a series of lively penny newspapers in Chicago, New Orleans, Atlanta, San Francisco, Kansas City and Portland (Oregon). The papers brought a wider set of potential buyers to the advertisers. But they also introduced some of the wildest circulation wars and publicity stunts in American journalism. (It was *The New York Herald* that sent Stanley into deepest Africa to find Dr. Livingstone.) Increased circulation meant advertising dollars for the papers from manufacturers and merchants. Businesses began to recognize that even poor people could buy something (Figure I-5).

Early Outdoor Signs

Intellectual critics of advertising quite early saw it as self-serving puffery and flattery. And when newspaper-sized ads ballooned into large roadside signs, these critics had further cause for irritation. Yet advertising was undeniably successful in increasing the sale of merchandise. Between 1850 and 1900, a steady procession of advertised products made their debuts on posters, on brick walls and chimneys, in handbills and newspapers: Bovril bouillon, Armour and Swift meats, Heinz horseradish sauce, Lipton tea, Singer sewing machines, Remington typewriters, condensed milk, gramophones, player pianos, furnaces, water closets, and of course, the ever present stomach remedies. "Chew Mail Pouch" ads graced the picturesque red barns of rural America, as they do to this day. It was a time of unregulated, unplanned, worldwide growth and expansion. Too often, exuberant advertisers both

[7]Just one year after the founding of *The New York Sun* in 1833, a Frenchman, Alexis de Tocqueville, arrived in New York and made this observation: "A glance at a French and an American newspaper is sufficient to show the difference that exists in this respect between the two nations. In France, the space alloted to commercial advertisements is very limited, and the news intelligence is not considerable, but the essential part of the journal is the discussion of the politics of the day. In America, three-quarters of the enormous sheet are filled with advertisements and the remainder is frequently occupied by political intelligence or trivial anecdotes." Alexis de Tocqueville, *Democracy in America*, Henry Reeve text, ed. Bradley (New York: Alfred A. Knopf, 1948), vol. 1, p. 185.

FIGURE I-5
New Yorkers of the
1880s saw ads like
these in *The New
York Times,* which
began life as a
penny paper.

here and abroad ignored the sensibilities of the very customers they were trying to reach. Their excesses, then as now, became one of advertising's major social problems.

LITERACY AND ECONOMIC GROWTH

Many people have wondered why advertising reached its highest state of development in the United States. There are a number of reasons. One answer is that this was a relatively new, unpopulated country that attracted people seeking a better life. As people arrived by the thousands, they attracted industry and capital, which began to satisfy their needs with existing as well as new products. All these products required retailers and wholesalers to satisfy the unceasing demands of people with money to spend. A new land meant new business opportunities for many people, unhampered by either government or established manufacturing monopolies. A manufacturer of a wood-burning cook stove, for example, might introduce the product in New York only to have it copied in several dozen other localities by other ironworkers. Advertising stimulated both the production and distribution of goods. It was able to do this because advertising requires a literate audience. It found one in this country because of the national system of public education for all children. In 1869, over 50 percent of our five- to seventeen-year-olds were enrolled in school; in 1900, this figure had risen to 80 percent. Nothing is more responsive to advertising than a literate, ever-moving society that is financially capable of buying merchandise.

Big-Store Advertising

The late nineteenth century in the United States was a time of merchandising excitement. Several innovative store owners were experimenting with a new idea: the department store, a place for the whole family to buy everything it needed under one roof. Although the department store concept originated in France, Americans adopted it, embraced it, and developed it under Jordan Marsh of Boston, John Wanamaker, and R. H. Macy, men whose stores still bear their names. From the first, these new-fangled stores aggressively advertised in newspapers, magazines, and handbills (Figure 1-6).

At about this same time, A. Montgomery Ward of Chicago initiated the first general mail-order house in the country. He was followed by the largest, Sears, Roebuck, in 1886. The mail-order houses provided delivered goods to farmers and rural citizens. Products ranged from a $1.50 horse clipper to the $14.95 Acme American Range (Figure 1-7).

Emergence of National Magazines

In Great Britain during the nineteenth century, one widely circulated newspaper could cover England and thus afford an advertiser a national market. But no single American newspaper could do this, because of the problems of printing in one location and then delivering papers to a vast land. But national coverage was possible for a publication that did not depend on day-to-day events for its editorial lifeblood: the magazine. When *Godey's Lady's Book* arrived on the American scene in the 1830s, it afforded national advertisers an eager, responsive, and widespread market.[8]

Magazines were successful in the United States for several reasons: First,

---

[8]*Godey's Lady's Book* was followed by Harper's in 1850, *Atlantic Monthly* in 1857, and *Scribner's* in 1870. Although *The Saturday Evening Post* was founded in 1821, it didn't achieve prominence until later. Three rural magazines were also begun in this period: *Prairie Farmer*, *American Agriculturist*, and *Southern Planter*. The first two remain strong farm publications.

FIGURE I-6
Calling itself the "most magnificently appointed" department store in America, Chicago's Burley & Company explains how the new store is divided into "apartments." Ad appeared in *Harper's* Magazine, September 1893.

LIGHTING THE PATH TO ECONOMY

Is a Saving of $50⁰⁰ Interesting to you?

ARE you *using* this Catalogue. Do you and your family use every opportunity for saving money that this book has brought into your home?

Try This Plan for Saving

Every time you need to buy anything for your own personal use, for the family or the home, look it up in Ward's Catalogue. Take advantage of the saving.

Then keep a list of everything you buy and the amount you saved. Thousands of our customers do this, and frequently they write us, "My savings in buying at Ward's amount to at least $50.00 cash each season."

How Ward's Low Prices Are Made for You

Sixty million dollars' worth of goods have been bought for this book—bought for cash in large quantities to get the lowest prices. Frequently we buy 100,000 pairs of shoes in one order to get a lower price.

And at Ward's the savings made by our big buying, through our buying for cash, these savings are yours—always yours.

Always Compare Quality as Well as Price

In gathering our vast assortments of merchandise, our buyers search the markets of the world for low prices. But only for low prices on goods of standard quality. We never buy goods to offer you unless they are the kind of goods that will stand inspection and use—the kind that will hold your good will. At Ward's "we never sacrifice quality to make a low price." We offer no "price baits."

Use Your Catalogue— Save Money Every Month

You have a copy of this Catalogue. Use it for everything you need to buy. Ordering each month from Ward's means a monthly saving. $50.00 in cash will soon be saved if you use your catalogue for everything you buy.

Your Orders Are Shipped Within 24 Hours

Your order will be shipped within 24 hours. We appreciate your orders at Ward's and we give your orders immediate attention.

But more than this—one of our six big houses is near you. Just consider how much less time it takes for your letter to reach us—how much less time for your goods to get to you and how much less the cost of transportation. It is quicker and cheaper to order from Ward's.

ESTABLISHED 1872

Montgomery Ward & Co.

The Oldest Mail Order House is Today the Most Progressive

Chicago   Kansas City   St. Paul   Portland, Ore.   Oakland, Calif.   Fort Worth

FIGURE I-7
Mail-order
advertising copy
has long been
considered an
excellent example of
the art of motivating
people to buy. If the
picture and the copy
failed to extract an
order, sellers had no
other way to move
their goods.

FIGURE I-8
Post-Civil War
advertisers were as
proud of their
factories as some
moderns. Three
Hood wrappers
would get you this
jigsaw puzzle, a fad
of the times as well
as an advertising
gimmick. (Courtesy
Rockwell Gardiner
Collection,
Stamford, Conn.)

Congress approved low postage rates, which allowed magazines (and newspapers) to be economically distributed by mail. Second, some Americans felt that magazines would be the vanguard of culture. And finally, American intellectuals expected that magazines would build a truly native American culture in a land peopled by immigrants from many nations. Earlier American magazines had failed at the latter goal by being too imitative of the English. However, one imitation that was very successful was the jigsaw puzzle. (Figure I-8).

The Ad Agency in America

Before the Civil War, some big-city newspapers had solicited advertising from merchants and manufacturers through street salesmen (Figure I-9). Some salesmen soon learned that they could earn more commissions if they represented not one but several newspapers and, later, magazines. Some also contracted annually with certain publications and, in effect, became brokers of advertising space.[9] One of the most effective post-Civil War advertising agents was a former bill collector for *The Boston Globe*, George Rowell. He systematically drew up a list of 100 newspapers he considered superior to the rest; he even approximated their circulations. He offered his clients an inch of space per month in all 100 newspapers for $100! He also declared a policy that won him the hearts of all 100 publishers: he guaranteed payment. Francis Wayland Ayer, another advertising giant, reasoned that he should

[9]"How it was in advertising: 1776–1976," *Advertising Age*, April 19, 1976, p. 41.

discover what his customers wanted *before* they advertised. Common today, a market study was truly unique 100 years ago (Figure I-10).

The Commission System

The American Newspaper Publishers Association ended the space-brokerage business, because some advertisers were shut out by brokers who were unfamiliar, unfriendly, or inaccessible or who were handling a preferred, competitive account. The newspapers that belonged to the association agreed to end the domination of the broker-agents. They decided to pay a commission to advertising agencies for the business they placed. Any bona fide advertising agency was eligible to receive a commission of 15 percent of the total of all advertising space it bought on behalf of a client. This move by the newspapers restored the ownership of the space to the medium. At the same time, it recognized that agencies were performing a valuable service to the advertiser and newspaper alike.

The Age of the Auto and Plane

In 1915, only seven years after Henry Ford introduced his Model T, the automobile industry was already spending $4 million a year in advertising. In short order, body shops in the industrial heartland of the country began to produce vehicles with brand names that splashed across magazines and newspapers from coast to coast: the Peerless, Hupmobile, Willys-Knight, and Pierce-Arrow (Figure I-11). Advertising began to acquire a reputation for flamboyant, creative devices and strategems. With millions of people four-wheeling down the highways, captive in a confined space, companies

FIGURE I-9
Volney B. Palmer is accorded the honor of being the first advertising agent in America. He had offices in Boston, New York, and Philadelphia.

FIGURE I-10
Two pioneer advertising agents of the post-Civil War era whose visions persist in the agencies that bear their names: J. Walter Thompson (left) and Francis Ayer (right). (*Advertising Age*, April 19, 1976.)

THE YEAR'S OUTSTANDING VALUE

Experienced motorists who know the smoothness, flashing activity, silent power and rugged stamina of the *patented* double sleeve-valve engine are quick to acknowledge the Willys-Knight Standard Six as the year's greatest value. ¶At the lowest price in history, Willys-Knight's beauty of design and superiority of performance are now enjoyed by thousands of new owners. ¶The sweeping success of the Standard Six has made 1928 Willys-Knight's biggest year. Quality was never as high—prices were never as low—sales were never as great. ¶Most emphatically, it will be well worth your while to give the Standard Six your closest inspection. And the more exacting your scrutiny, the greater will be your appreciation that this beautiful car possesses everything that wins you to a fine Six—from the fundamentals of design and construction to the smallest details of appointment. ¶A demonstration of the Standard Six reveals the ease of control, quick starting, comfortable riding and sustained brilliance which have won the praise of more than 325,000 enthusiastic Willys-Knight owners. ¶And years of service—with remarkable freedom from carbon troubles and repairs—will bring you a new conception of the economy with which a truly fine car may be operated.

BEAUTIFUL STANDARD SIX NOTABLE FOR WILLYS·KNIGHT'S TYPICAL SMOOTH-NESS AND POWER

5 PASSENGER SEDAN
$1095

COACH ... $995
TOURING   995
ROADSTER   995
COUPE ...   1045

Prices f. o. b. Toledo, Ohio, and specifications subject to change without notice. Willys-Overland, Inc., Toledo, Ohio. Willys-Overland Sales Company, Ltd., Toronto, Canada.

WILLYS · KNIGHT SIX

FIGURE I-11
In 1928, this five-passenger sedan sold for the advertised price of $1,095. The average American working for industry then earned about $1,500 a year.

took to advertising on roadside billboards. The little-known Burma Shave Company, for example, soon turned the driving public into connoisseurs of nonsensical doggerel.[10]

In 1927, a single-engine plane flown by an unknown, solo air mail pilot took off from Roosevelt Field on Long Island, New York. When it landed without refueling in Paris 33½ hours later, Charles Lindbergh had electrified the world. When Lindbergh returned to the United States, he was besieged with requests for advertising endorsements. His only public testimonials were made to repay his backers, among them an oil company and a manufacturer of spark plugs. However, Lindbergh did fly from one end of the country to the other to promote air travel. The "Lindy" seal of approval meant thousands, even millions, of dollars in extra sales for almost any product he endorsed. He was supported in promoting air travel by airplane manufacturers who, as the largest investors in airline advertising, sold "comfort and speed" in the hope that their own customers, the fledgling airlines, would benefit (Figure I-12).

The Crash and the Depression

With the stock market crash in 1929, the prosperity of the 1920s ended. Advertising and business plunged into the depths of the worst depression America has ever known. Advertising billings dropped $2 billion in 1930. In 1933, with over 14 million people unemployed, goods remained on grocers' shelves, appliances remained unsold, factories closed. For most people, there was little money to spend.

Because advertising reflects society and the times, Depression ads emphasized money, ways to earn it, and ways to save it. About one-third of the labor force was out of work. Those who worked in the factories lived on an average cash income of less than $100 a month. Under President Franklin Roosevelt, the Federal Emergency Relief Administration spent $1 billion for direct relief in 1933. Government agencies provided public assistance and conservation and public works jobs to help the unemployed. Slowly the country recovered. By the late 1940s, factories were humming again, people had more money to spend, and advertising was telling them how to do it.

Recovery at Midcentury

Between 1940 and 1975, most advertisers' budgets increased dramatically as they rushed into the Age of Affluence.[11] All the genius of the advertising industry was put to work selling suburban living, second cars, second homes, exotic vacations, and a mind-boggling parade of new products (Figure I-13). Even the shortage of vital materials does not seem now to deter the American

[10]"He played the sax;/ had no. B.O.;/ But his whiskers scratched/ so she let him go/ Burma Shave."

[11]Despite temporary reductions due to three major wars, World War II (1941–1945), Korea (1950–1953), and Vietnam (1965–1973).

FIGURE I-12
Early air-travel
ads—and air cargo
service—were often
sponsored by plane
manufacturers who
attempted to create
a market for flying.
This type of
advertising strategy,
in which a
manufacturer tries to
influence customers
of its customers, is
common today.
Boeing and
Lockheed are two
prime users of the
strategy.

HARBORS
AND PHANTOM
PORTS

WHILE Chambers of Commerce labor earnestly for deeper river channels to bring them closer to the seaboard, and political wars are waged bitterly over preferential railroad rates that may jeopardize the markets of inland and isolated towns, *a thousand dry-land ports have suddenly appeared with wharves open to business from all the world!*

A thousand communities have at least sensed the opportunity for a place of importance upon the new map being drawn of channels and harbors that open to the sky. It is significant that upon these charts many great coastal harbors are conspicuously absent. For the ships of the air, following laws that have always governed the development of permanent transportation systems, *are being drawn only to the most efficient terminals.*

At whatever hour of the day or night this message reaches your eyes, somewhere above the United States planes are carrying commercial cargo at a hundred miles an hour to scheduled destinations. *These planes must have suitable landing fields.*

In the early days of automobiles, the stigma "bad roads" stuck to communities that failed to grasp the need for better roads to smooth the way for the new machine. "Bad harbor facilities" have ruined many a promising seaport town. "Inefficient railway service" has hampered the development of cities that might have become important commercial centers. And now that a new and revolutionary leap forward is being taken in transportation, the towns and cities of today are going to be powerfully influenced by the degree of attention they pay to air-ports.

There are still less than 250 municipal airports worthy of the name. There are almost as many commercial and private ports. There are somewhat less than a hundred maintained by the Army and Navy. *More than 3000 "phantom ports," improperly equipped, are of use only as emergency landing fields.*

Few American air-ports can yet compare to the European "world-ports" of Croydon, LeBourget, Tempelhof. Great cities like New York are awakening to the full significance of this; though it still takes as long to get from a New York flying-field to the heart of the city as it does to fly from New York to Philadelphia. The really notable American air-ports

are being built in inland cities such as Detroit, Cleveland, Chicago, Wichita and Cheyenne.

What does all this mean to you? If you are a man of broad industrial and commercial interests, your traffic managers, forwarding departments and general sales managers can answer you best. *It is of vital importance in American business to promote and maintain efficient municipal air-ports!*

When the New York-Atlanta Air Mail was inaugurated in May, instead of one, two ships were required to take 32,000 pieces of mail from New York and Philadelphia. Business men had realized at once the value of a night mail service that would insure delivery in Atlanta at the same time as in New York.

Those who hesitate to employ the airplane will do well to recall that there are still many old-timers who refuse to ride in automobiles!

The great Ford all-metal, tri-motored planes, carrying millions of pounds of freight, transporting scores of thousands of passengers, flying on extended missions from the tropics to Arctic seas, *have known no accidents to passengers!*

FORD MOTOR COMPANY

FIGURE I-13

Familiar ads of the last two decades pointed the way toward greater creativity. They and other ads also reflect American priorities.

people from listening to advertisers or advertisers from persuading (Figures I-14).

As we enter the last two decades of the twentieth century, can we expect advertising to continue relatively unrestricted by government? Will new techniques and technologies further improve ad effectiveness? Will more businesses become socially accountable for their advertising? An intelligent answer to any of these questions should logically begin with our first section, "Consumer Advertising."

IN SUMMARY

1 Until Gutenberg's printing press, most advertising was verbal. It took the form of "crying" from the fishing wharf, from the market stall, from the dusty roadside. Exceptions were crude wall posters and store signs.

2 The popularity of handbills for promoting goods and services was a direct result of the invention of the printing press with movable type. Printers could print large quantities compared to what was possible with traditional hand-copying operations.

3 The printing press led to the creation of weekly newspapers that featured classified advertising. The word "advertisement" was used as a heading for commercial announcements.

4 Coffee houses, seventeenth-century gathering places for intellectuals, sold newspapers to their patrons. The proprietors often acted as classified-sales agents for the newspapers.

5 The first American newspaper, *The Weekly Boston Newsletter*, followed the lead of English newspapers by accepting classified advertising.

6 The penny press of the 1830s made it possible for even the poorest to buy a newspaper. Manufacturers were thus exposed to a new audience.

7 Advertising found fertile ground in the United States because of a growing, literate population; a large, rich land attracting thousands of immigrants; and new opportunities for industry and capital, unhampered by government restrictions or established business monopolies.

8 Department stores in the United States have from their very beginnings been regular, large-volume advertisers.

9 The national magazine finally permitted manufacturers to reach a nationwide audience economically. With their debut, ad budgets began to expand dramatically.

10 Mail-order selling by catalogue opened the rural markets of America to the advertiser. The first general mail order house was Montgomery Ward.

11 Advertising agencies emerged as a form of business in the 1860s when "space" salesmen for certain newspapers began to provide some creative services in addition to their knowledge of the effectiveness of selected media.

12 The launching of the advertising agency system as we now know it began when newspapers stopped the practice of brokering space and began to pay agency commissions. This action restored ownership of the space to the publication.

13 By the 1920s, many automobile manufacturers were competing for the public's favor. The industry's ad expenditures hit a high of over $4 million a year.

A probability report.

The Sierra Club doesn't say that our planet is likely to go under at any moment through our heedlessness. The composite photograph above merely depicts a possibility.

The probability is fairly remote.

Every day, however, we are making environmental changes with consequences we still don't understand or even suspect.

Take heat, for example.

Everytime we build a city block of high-rise buildings, we change the wind pattern so there's less wind to carry the heat away.

Everytime we heat or air-condition these buildings, use an electric appliance or light, drive a car or manufacture a product, 100% of that energy eventually winds up in the environment as heat.

And it's not only cities.

We know that when we clear a forest, the land beneath absorbs more heat. And this also happens when we plow fields, defoliate veg-etation or take the life out of the soil. (One acre of grass, for example, has a potential cooling effect up to that of a 10-ton air conditioner.)

We are eliminating natural cooling systems and creating urban heat islands where the climate is hotter, rainier, cloudier, more humid and, of course, dirtier, too. These artificially created climates, called "micro-climates" are already altering their immediate surrounding environment. And, if we create enough of them, we might alter the temperature of the entire earth.

One day as we approach the global heat limits, the polar ice caps could begin to melt, flooding some cities of the earth.

There are limits to the alterations we can make on our ecosystem. We would do well to slow the pace of change so we can determine these limits scientifically, before we discover them accidentally.

Sierra Club
Mills Tower San Francisco

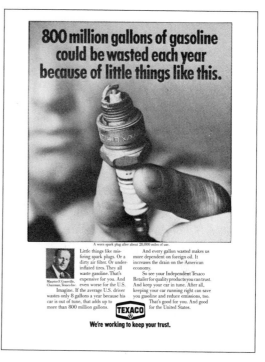

FIGURE I-14

Behind these advertising headlines of the late 1970s, a historian could detect a society threatened by a scarcity of natural resources.

14 When business plunged into the depths of America's worst depression, advertising expenditures plummeted also. The new ad theme for those stark years was "how to make and save money."

15 Between 1940 and 1975, a period of great affluence for most Americans, advertising budgets grew dramatically. During this period, advertising introduced the greatest array of new products the world had ever seen.

Unit

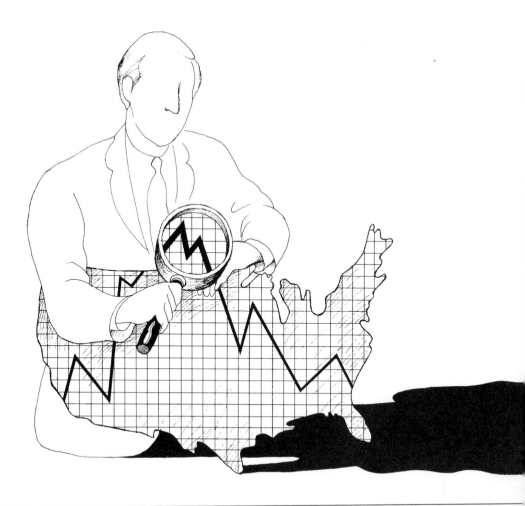

1

CONSUMER ADVERTISING

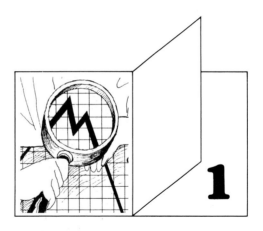

NATIONAL ADVERTISING

National consumer advertising in the United States is a relatively recent phenomenon. It began during the mid-1800s when the circulation of popular media grew large enough and covered a wide enough geographical area to justify an investment in advertising by companies looking beyond their immediate localities. Today, national consumer advertising is a directed effort to influence masses of consumers coast to coast. National advertisers want to promote the sale of goods, their services, and ideas. Although most sales will eventually take place at local retail stores served by local media, the major promotional messages of these national advertisers are carried by any or all of the national media: television, radio, magazines, billboards, transit (buses and cabs), direct mail (advertising sent through the mails), and a few Sunday magazine supplements (picture-story inserts) sent to metropolitan newspapers.

The messages reach the residents of small-town Osceola, Iowa and Chagrin Falls, Ohio at the same time that they reach the residents of high-rise apartments in San Francisco, Boston, and Atlanta. National advertising is less an end in itself than a tool to serve the needs of people who make and consume things. As a tool, it informs people and encourages sales. The end results of this paid-for communication are to stimulate competition among advertisers and keep prices down and production up. Thus advertising can claim credit for helping provide jobs.

Obviously it costs money to reach millions of consumers through the mass media. Procter & Gamble, the soap conglomerate, spends over $221 million advertising on national television and $21 million advertising in national magazines each year.[1] But advertising is just as vital to smaller companies. The important thing for us to recognize is that national media, with their vast circulations, are often less expensive *per consumer reached* than the thousands of local broadcast stations and newspapers we would need to reach the same consumers. During the Super Bowl XII football game, a $250,000 one-minute television commercial was estimated to have reached 80 million households. Total cost per household came to less than a half-cent. But not all 80 million households will buy what you have to sell. Therefore although the cost of reaching them may be under a half-cent, the actual cost of selling to those interested will be higher. How much higher is difficult to determine, because not everybody buys within a measured period of time. If a viewer of your television commercial buys your product six months later, how can you tell it was your Super Bowl advertisement that made the sale?

Because of the difficulty of determining exactly what sales response advertising brings, many companies relate the cost of advertising to the number of units sold. They simply divide the number of units sold into what it cost to advertise them nationally. Thus the advertising cost of an average carton of cigarettes is approximately 12 cents; of a case of beer, approximately 6 cents.[2]

IS ADVERTISING NECESSARY?

Some theorists believe that advertising more than pays for itself because it helps to increase sales. And increased sales, according to economic theorists, make it possible for manufacturers to lower prices, reduce profits per unit, and still flourish. Many examples prove this to be true. Black & Decker, the innovative mass merchandiser of low-cost power tools, is a case in point. Immediately after World War II, the first Black & Decker electric drill sold at retail for $16.95. Thirty years later, a far more sophisticated unit sold for under $10. (Figure 1-1).

What caused this drastic reduction at a time when the cost of hourly factory machine labor had moved from under $1.80 to $4.40 and the cost of materials had risen by 40 percent?[3] The reduction was due to a basic

[1]*Advertising Age*, August 28, 1978, p. 180.
[2]"Ad costs for beer, ale, malt liquor," *Advertising Age*, September 26, 1977, p. 112.
[3]Bureau of Labor Statistics, U.S. Department of Labor, 1975.

#7004

¼" ELECTRIC DRILL

4 Days Only **$7**

Double insulated, single-speed drill for light duty; uses accessories.

FIGURE 1-1
Woodworkers throughout the country saw this discount chain store's direct-mail ad featuring Black & Decker's electric drill and responded to it. The listed price is considerably lower than that of comparable drills thirty years ago. Black & Decker relies on planning, mass production, and mass national advertising for its corporate success.

marketing strategy of company officials. First they dedicated themselves to developing the finest low-cost drill possible. Once the design was set, they invested millions of dollars in updated and automated machinery, which increased productivity per worker and the number of drill units or parts created and assembled. Having attained their goal of large-volume production at a lower labor cost per unit, Black & Decker managers were able to reduce the wholesale and retail cost per drill. They then turned to national advertising to generate the demand they required. Black & Decker was the first manufacturer to advertise power tools on network television. (Figure 1-2).

There can be little doubt that Black & Decker's national advertising has proved to be a benefit for the consumer. But what happens if reduced prices fail to deliver more sales? The company cannot maintain those reduced prices for long without endangering its financial stability. And what happens if advertising fails to materially increase sales? Then its ineffectiveness quite often adds to the price of the product.

SOCIAL VALUES

Advertising benefits society in ways other than lower prices. From an economic point of view alone, the small, middle-sized and larger Black &

MAN: I was asked to talk about the incredible Black & Decker Workmate.

There's almost nothing it can't hold.

But the Workmate is so incredible, I'm gonna let it do the talking.

(MUSIC)

(MUSIC)

(MUSIC)

(MUSIC)

(MUSIC)

(MUSIC)

(MUSIC)

(MUSIC)

(VO): The Workmate, from Black & Decker and nobody else.

FIGURE 1-2

Success of its low-priced electric drill propelled Black & Decker into making and selling an entire line of electric and air-powered tools: drills, screwdrivers, impact wrenches, air hammers, sanders, saws. These frames from a television commercial sell the benefits of a relatively new product, a portable workbench. The thirty-second commercial ran on national television.

Deckers of this country directly employ millions of workers; purchase large quantities of steel, chemicals, machinery, and supplies; and so on. Their purchasing power provides jobs in the private sector and tax dollars for the public. In addition, company advertising budgets provide jobs for artists, advertising agencies, photographers, printers, and a wide variety of media personnel. National advertising stimulates competition among companies. Competition results in more merchandise, a greater choice of goods, and a constant parade of new and improved products. It also encourages the creation and development of work-saving devices and appliances, all of which permit people to invest more of their time in leisure and social activities.

Advertising also informs and educates millions of people about health, disease, cultural affairs, and other important topics. Advertising has become a basic part of our information-gathering system. Many people enjoy advertising as much as they do entertainment and news. "There is a positive consumer demand for advertising as useful information," declares Leo Bogart of the Newspaper Advertising Bureau.[4] His observation is supported by numerous surveys[5] that show that people want to be exposed to advertising.

WHO DOES THE ADVERTISING?

Although most people are familiar with the giant national advertisers who spend enormous sums for media advertising, it would be hard to find a nationally oriented consumer goods company that did not advertise in some manner. Table 1-1 shows the huge sums spent by some of the nation's most visible advertisers. But giant corporations are only the tip of the iceberg. Thousands of medium and small companies also rely on national media to reach their audiences. Their financial health depends on the effectiveness of their advertising.

Manufacturers

Best known of all national advertisers are the manufacturers of consumer products such as appliances, deodorants, foods, clothing, candy, soft drinks, cars, and gasoline. These companies depend on advertising to move their goods through the channels of distribution (from manufacturer to wholesaler to local retail stores), to develop consumer loyalty to their brands and dealers, and to reduce the effects of competition. They need volume to keep their factories operating efficiently, profitably. To get volume sales, they turn to advertising.

---

[4]Newspaper Advertising Bureau, Report of the Director, 1975.
[5]B. Sindlinger study, reported in *Research Memo*, Newspaper Advertising Bureau, April 1975.

TABLE 1-1
IN MEASURED MEDIA ONLY, GROUPED BY INDUSTRIES; AD DOLLARS IN THOUSANDS

100 LEADERS' MEDIA EXPENDITURES COMPARED IN 1977

Rank Company	Total	News-papers	Genl mags.*	Farm pub.	Spot TV	Net TV	Spot radio	Net radio	Out-door
					% of total dollars				
Airlines									
87 American Airlines	$25,153.0	47.3	8.4	--	23.7	0.3	18.9	—	1.5
89 Delta Air Lines	23,553.6	63.3	5.1	—	7.0	0.4	19.2	—	5.1
84 Eastern Airlines	25,722.8	45.9	12.3	—	24.4	2.6	10.2	—	4.7
85 Trans World Airlines	26,389.6	47.4	6.1	—	29.3	—	14.6	—	2.6
79 UAL Inc.	27,971.8	28.7	10.5	—	25.4	26.6	8.5	—	0.3
Appliances, TV, radio									
36 General Electric Co.	56,610.3	14.6	18.6	—	20.6	42.8	0.8	2.3	0.3
80 North American Philips Corp.	27,931.1	5.7	7.3	—	42.8	42.8	0.5	0.8	—
32 RCA Corp.	59,258.0	24.2	28.3	—	18.8	27.2	0.8	0.1	0.6
Automobiles									
67 American Motors Corp.	31,486.9	22.6	11.3	—	16.9	47.4	1.3	0.3	0.4
13 Chrysler Corp.	97,400.0	2.5	18.4	—	18.2	33.9	2.0	1.0	0.5
7 Ford Motor Co.	157,306.2	17.1	15.8	1.2	17.8	42.0	4.8	0.6	0.7
3 General Motors Corp.	235,346.1	20.2	18.7	0.7	11.4	38.5	6.8	1.2	2.5
96 Honda Motor Co.	20,574.5	7.1	32.0	—	6.7	49.7	4.5	—	0.1
40 Nissan Motor Corp.	49,354.2	12.8	15.5	—	26.0	33.5	11.7	—	0.4
52 Toyota Motor Sales U.S.A.	41,675.9	14.8	14.5	—	31.9	29.1	6.0	—	3.7
47 Volkswagen of America	45,474.9	9.2	28.2	—	21.1	40.1	1.1	—	0.3
Chemicals									
62 American Cyanamid Co.	34,925.7	0.8	22.4	12.6	15.2	46.8	2.1	—	—
99 Union Carbide Corp.	19,227.8	10.5	9.5	2.3	3.3	70.1	1.9	1.0	1.4
Drugs, toiletries, and cosmetics									
8 American Home Products Corp.	156,965.1	1.4	3.8	0.2	22.5	69.1	1.4	1.8	—
88 Avon Products	24,455.4	—	14.5	—	11.8	73.3	0.3	—	—
71 Beecham Group	29,779.2	0.2	6.1	—	12.7	81.0	—	—	—
81 Block Drug Co.	27,698.8	—	12.7	—	24.7	62.3	0.2	—	—
5 Bristol-Myers Co.	164,100.8	1.8	14.2	—	11.5	69.7	2.7	—	—
55 Chesebrough-Pond's	40,106.6	4.0	9.4	—	18.4	68.2	—	—	—
29 Gillette Co.	64,444.0	0.8	8.7	—	18.5	72.0	—	—	—
26 Johnson & Johnson	66,428.6	1.7	15.9	—	6.6	73.1	2.7	—	—
60 Miles Laboratories	32,990.5	0.2	2.9	—	18.5	73.9	0.2	1.7	2.5
66 Noxell Corp.	32,400.3	—	20.2	—	11.8	67.1	0.9	—	—
91 Pfizer, Inc.	22,831.1	0.4	30.3	5.5	5.1	57.3	1.3	0.1	0.1
53 Revlon Inc.	41,040.7	2.6	20.5	—	30.4	44.1	1.0	1.4	—
44 Richardson-Merrell	48,027.7	0.4	7.6	—	16.6	71.4	3.2	0.8	—
83 A. H. Robins Co.	25,856.3	0.9	14.5	—	84.6	—	—	—	—
42 Schering-Plough Corp.	48,618.2	2.7	19.0	0.4	13.6	53.8	1.6	5.6	3.3
86 SmithKline Corp.	25,177.2	1.1	3.0	1.8	4.7	65.5	6.1	17.2	0.7
23 Sterling Drug Co.	70,128.8	1.0	8.9	0.3	12.5	70.2	2.7	4.2	0.2
72 Squibb Corp.	29,512.4	0.5	3.6	—	15.9	70.1	10.0	—	—
15 Warner-Lambert Co.	89,719.9	1.0	0.9	—	22.5	69.2	1.0	4.7	0.7

Rank Company	Total	News-papers	Genl mags.*	Farm pub.	Spot TV	Net TV	Spot radio	Net radio	Out-door
				Food					
76 Beatrice Foods Co.	28,580.8	12.2	10.7	2.8	51.9	13.9	8.0	0.3	0.2
51 Borden Inc.	43,240.7	9.7	9.1	0.6	40.3	28.8	9.3	1.0	1.2
63 CPC International	34,271.7	3.2	9.8	0.7	37.8	45.7	1.5	0.7	0.7
56 Campbell Soup Co.	40,053.0	9.5	11.6	—	19.6	50.2	5.8	1.2	2.2
73 Carnation Co.	29,353.1	9.5	0.5	0.9	25.1	62.6	1.3	—	—
97 Consolidated Foods Corp.	20,360.2	10.2	9.8	—	46.6	23.4	9.5	—	0.5
41 Esmark Inc.	49,073.0	4.1	5.1	—	20.6	69.7	0.4	—	0.1
2 General Foods Corp.	252,717.1	2.5	11.5	—	28.5	56.7	0.4	0.3	0.1
9 General Mills	151,918.5	2.4	10.4	—	29.1	54.3	3.1	0.6	—
59 H. J. Heinz Co.	37,845.1	6.7	2.2	—	13.9	76.4	0.7	—	—
27 Kellogg Co.	66,289.6	4.7	4.6	—	26.0	62.8	1.8	—	—
20 Kraft Inc.	77,363.7	7.1	19.1	—	36.6	27.3	6.0	3.1	0.8
12 McDonald's Corp.	98,567.4	—	0.3	—	59.2	37.9	0.9	—	1.7
65 Morton-Norwich Products	33,281.9	0.2	11.3	—	12.3	73.7	0.2	2.3	—
18 Nabisco Inc.	82,744.7	3.5	5.3	—	14.6	76.2	0.4	—	—
22 Nestle Enterprises	70,808.5	14.8	3.0	—	30.7	50.4	1.1	—	—
28 Norton Simon Inc.	66,067.6	8.7	22.5	—	18.9	44.6	1.4	0.3	3.6
30 Pillsbury Co.	62,867.8	4.3	6.2	—	24.7	63.4	0.9	—	0.5
43 Quaker Oats Co.	48,220.5	7.2	18.4	—	35.2	37.4	1.8	—	—
19 Ralston Purina Co.	78,475.9	3.5	12.9	0.8	14.7	63.9	3.1	0.1	1.0
78 Standard Brands	28,029.2	8.8	15.3	—	18.5	45.9	8.3	0.3	2.8
				Gum and candy					
57 Mars Inc.	$39,177.0	6.3	5.6	—	46.3	40.6	0.8	0.4	—
68 Wm. Wrigley Jr. Co.	30,486.1	12.8	1.7	—	62.9	2.3	7.2	4.5	—
				Oil					
74 Exxon Corp.	29,170.8	6.2	16.9	0.4	13.1	54.1	8.2	—	1.1
45 Mobil Corp.	47,500.7	12.3	8.5	2.5	58.6	15.4	2.2	·0.4	0.2
92 Shell Oil Co.	22,224.3	13.5	21.5	10.0	12.0	49.1	1.5	2.9	0.2
				Photographic equipment					
37 Eastman Kodak Co.	55,471.8	6.9	31.7	—	4.7	54.9	0.5	0.7	0.6
75 Polaroid Corp.	28,835.5	6.5	26.7	—	1.8	64.9	0.1	—	—
				Retail chains					
82 K-Mart Corp.	27,425.3	—	18.1	—	55.2	19.1	—	7.7	—
61 J. C. Penny Co.	37,296.6	—	6.1	—	41.7	50.8	—	0.9	0.5
10 Sears, Roebuck & Co.	148,874.1	—	27.8	—	14.8	53.9	—	3.5	0.1
				Soft drinks					
33 Coca-Cola Co.	58,981.9	5.9	5.8	—	46.2	30.7	7.2	0.8	3.4
16 PepsiCo Inc.	83,676.0	2.0	1.8	—	48.1	42.0	5.3	—	0.8

100 LEADERS' MEDIA EXPENDITURES COMPARED IN 1977

Rank Company	Total	% of total dollars							
		News-papers	Genl mags.*	Farm pub.	Spot TV	Net TV	Spot radio	Net radio	Out-door
Soaps, cleansers (and allied)									
54 Clorox Co.	40,774.3	1.6	15.0	—	12.6	69.7	1.1	—	—
14 Colgate-Palmolive Co.	95,425.9	1.7	6.6	—	36.5	53.6	1.4	0.2	—
58 S. C. Johnson & Son	38,860.5	1.7	17.5	—	10.3	67.2	2.7	—	0.7
1 Procter & Gamble Co.	355,557.7	1.5	5.7	—	30.4	62.3	0.1	—	—
11 Unilever	115,344.4	3.1	6.2	—	31.1	59.3	0.2	—	—
Tobacco									
25 American Brands	68,110.5	32.8	42.6	—	4.4	7.7	1.2	0.2	11.2
21 B.A.T. Industries	76,253.8	32.0	42.3	—	7.3	0.9	—	—	17.5
31 Liggett Group	61,692.4	38.3	30.1	—	10.2	10.6	0.7	—	10.1
4 Philip Morris Inc.	168,321.6	31.6	28.7	—	6.2	18.9	1.4	—	13.4
6 R. J. Reynolds Industries	162,236.1	36.4	36.7	—	3.0	3.2	0.1	—	20.7
Telephone service, equipment									
17 American Telephone & Telegraph Co.	83,220.2	12.0	12.6	—	34.0	34.8	5.8	—	0.9
39 International Telephone & Telegraph Corp.	51,275.3	—	11.0	—	52.8	30.5	2.7	2.1	0.9

Reprinted with permission from *Advertising Age,* August 28, 1978. Copyright © 1978 by Crain Communications, Inc.
General magazines refers to large-circulation magazines such as *Playboy, Better Homes and Gardens,* and *Outdoor Life,* as opposed to lesser-known business or trade publications. *Spot television* is a class of television commercial purchased for and viewed in a specific

Large Retail Chains

Sears, Roebuck & Company ranks among the nation's largest advertisers. But it has a number of giant retail-chain competitors: J. C. Penney, Montgomery Ward, Western Auto, Ace Hardware, and others. These chains control enough retail outlets to justify the use of national media. Sears, for example, supports its 858 stores and 2,918 other catalog sales outlets[6] with an umbrella of national advertising. So do large food chains such as A&P, Safeway, and the fast-growing group of franchise restaurants: McDonald's, Burger King, Jack-in-the-Box, and Pizza Hut, among others. But there are other ways to advertise nationally. Some retail hardware chains provide all

[6]Gordon L. Weil, *Sears, Roebuck, U.S.A.* (New York: Stein and Day, 1977), p. 2.

Rank Company	Total	News-papers	Genl mags.*	Farm pub.	% of total dollars Spot TV	Net TV	Spot radio	Net radio	Out-door
Wine, beer, and liquor									
35 Anheuser-Busch	58,687.2	3.5	5.1	—	17.4	54.8	14.6	3.1	1.5
100 E. & J. Gallo Winery	19,020.7	1.4	13.2	—	28.4	53.6	1.0	—	2.4
24 Heublein Inc.	68,491.5	6.6	21.6	—	29.8	29.9	2.2	0.4	9.5
49 Jos. Schlitz Brewing Co.	43,928.8	2.6	1.7	—	14.1	77.0	4.5	—	0.1
50 Seagram Co.	43,862.2	16.0	61.7	—	2.7	—	0.1	—	19.5
Miscellaneous									
94 ABC Inc.	21,232.6	26.9	48.7	—	22.0	—	0.2	0.6	1.7
77 American Express Co.	28,483.4	10.2	15.2	—	17.9	50.0	6.4	—	0.3
46 CBS Inc.	47,164.5	25.9	49.6	—	21.9	—	0.4	0.8	1.2
90 Goodyear Tire & Rubber Co.	23,136.7	—	9.8	1.9	28.0	56.4	0.7	2.6	0.6
70 Greyhound Corp.	30,144.1	9.7	20.1	—	12.2	43.3	3.1	9.5	2.2
95 Gulf & Western Industries	21,038.5	9.3	14.7	—	39.1	34.6	1.2	0.3	0.8
69 Hanes Corp.	30,303.6	3.5	18.1	—	7.1	67.6	1.8	1.9	0.1
93 Kimberly-Clark Corp.	21,976.6	6.3	13.3	—	24.7	55.7	—	—	—
38 Loews Corp.	53,939.4	39.5	34.8	—	0.1	—	0.7	—	24.9
64 Mattel Inc.	34,011.8	0.5	3.5	—	63.2	32.4	—	—	0.4
98 Scott Paper Co.	20,276.9	7.7	2.3	—	66.7	21.7	1.5	—	0.2
48 Time Inc.	44,718.7	10.3	42.4	—	40.8	3.1	0.9	2.5	—
34 U.S. Government	58,740.0	14.5	39.6	—	—	29.6	11.2	—	5.0

market area such as Baltimore, San Diego, and so on. *Network television* is a class of commercial purchased for and seen by all stations affiliated with the network, coast to coast. (The definitions of spot radio and network radio are similar to those of spot and network television.)

their independent dealerships with colorful catalogs for distribution via the mails. Some insert full-color supplements and brochures in metropolitan newspapers.

A major problem of large retail chains is how to divide the advertising budget between national and local efforts. When a greater share of the advertising is national in origin, local retail outlets often feel they could use the money to better advantage. On the other hand, when retail outlets control the local ad budgets, they may divert the money to other uses. Because of these different advertising budget philosophies, it is not uncommon for retail chain advertisers to move abruptly from centralized to decentralized budget control. For the past few years McDonald's, with 5,000 retail outlets, has spent approximately one-third of its total ad budget on national advertising. The rest has been used in local and regional promotion.

Service Organizations and Special-Interest Groups

Very much a part of the national advertising scene are the many service and special-interest organizations. Messages promoting scouting, medical research, international relief, and the like are run as free public service announcements by the media. Privately owned media, newspapers, magazines, billboards, and transit systems are under no compulsion to provide free advertising space to anybody. Broadcasting stations, however, which operate on public airwaves and are subject to federal regulation, are required by federal law to devote time to nonprofit good works and consumer education.[7]

Commercial Marketing Associations

A relatively recent national advertiser is the *commercial marketing association*, a group of like-minded producers of a commodity. Currently active associations include The American Dairy Association, The National Pork Producers, The Beef Council, The American Egg Board, The Wool Growers, The Cotton Council, Florida Citrus Growers, and California Almond Growers Exchange. As a single producer, no one farmer or small cooperative could consistently afford to reach millions of consumers. As part of a large association, however, the individual producers now enjoy the same opportunities as other national advertisers. Their greatly increased financial base often permits them to hire an advertising agency to create and place their advertising in national media.

The Federal Government

Government has come to appreciate the power of national advertising. In 1972, it joined the ranks of the top 100 advertisers. Federal advertisers include the Environmental Protection Agency, the Veterans Administration, the Department of the Treasury (for savings bonds), even the Postal Service. Largest advertisers of all are the military services, who recruit men and women. The Army, for example, recently budgeted $32 million[8] for magazines, billboards, and newspapers in just one year. The Navy, also a heavy user of magazines and billboards, budgeted $16 million[9] in the same year. Media expenditures by the major United States government advertisers for a typical year appear in Table 1-2.

As Table 1-2 indicates, in 1976 the United States government spent over $112 million in advertising, making it the seventeenth-largest national advertiser that year.

---

[7]The Federal Communications Commission (FCC), a governmental regulatory agency, has the power to revoke, renew, and modify broadcasting licenses throughout the United States.

[8]Bruce Mulock, *U.S. Government Advertising Expenditures*, The Library of Congress, Congressional Research Service, January 16, 1978, p. 2.

[9]Mulock, op. cit., p. 2.

TABLE 1-2

GOVERNMENT ADVERTISING EXPENDITURES (NATIONAL MEDIA 1976)

Medium	Expenditure
Magazines	$20,365,000
Newspapers	5,031,000
Spot television	3,919,000
Network television	5,576,000
Radio	3,472,000
Outdoor (billboards)	9,832,000
Total measured media	48,195,000
Total unmeasured media*	64,801,000
Estimated total	$112,996,000

*Estimated total includes at least $6 million in ad funds spent by local and regional recruiting commands; amounts for preparing, printing, and distributing public service print and broadcast ads; printed posters and brochures and billboard materials; and college and other institutional publications.

Political Parties

Every four years, the presidential campaign comes to America. This is not new. What *is* new is the use of national media to influence voters of the fifty states simultaneously. Some people, those who head political parties among them, feel that national advertising, notably television, has forever changed the face of politics in the United States. In the recent general election campaign, Jimmy Carter spent over $10 million for television and other media. In the 1972 election, the Democratic National Committee spent over $1.75 million on a national telethon on the eve of the nominating convention promoting Senator George McGovern and the Democratic Party to the country. The Committee to Re-elect President Nixon directed a nationwide direct mail effort among registered Republicans to raise money. (Some of these funds were later used in the unsuccessful attempt to cover up the Watergate break-in at Democratic headquarters.) National media used during presidential campaigns include television, direct mail, billboards, radio, and magazines.

Before 1974, the money for presidential advertising came primarily from wealthy individuals and labor unions. This dependence on relatively few people and power groups propelled Congress to pass the 1974 Federal Election Campaign Act. Under this law, congressional candidates receive matching federal grants for individual contributions of $250 or less. Major party presidential candidates receive lump sum grants from the United States Treasury. During the Carter–Ford election campaign, each major party nominee received $21.8 million. With these large sums available, it's not surprising that skilled writers, songsmiths, filmmakers, and marketing experts line up on one side or the other to use national airwaves, billboards, and magazine pages to sell their candidate to the people (Figure 1-3).

He sees it your way.

President Ford is a President who sees the issues pretty much the way most Americans see them.

He believes that the only way to maintain the peace of America is to maintain the military might of America, and that he has done.

He opposes big spending and higher taxes, so he's vetoed many of the costly bills passed by the liberals in Congress, saving the taxpayers 9.2 billion dollars.

He says "yes" to more *quality* in education, but "no" to forced busing as a means to achieve that quality.

He takes a tough view of crime, backs the death penalty in specified instances of murder, and wants to put more teeth into local law enforcement agencies.

He says the Vietnam draft evaders can return if they're willing to work at earning back their good citizenship, but he will not offer them any blanket pardon.

He wants to cut down the size of big government and beef up the authority of local government, so that local people can have more control over their own neighborhoods.

He attaches such importance to neighborhoods, and is so concerned with their future, that he's ordered the development of a federal plan to create a climate in which neighborhoods can survive and flourish.

He supports welfare assistance for the truly needy, but thinks all able-bodied recipients should be put to useful work.

He is angered by court decisions that strip the authority of parents to guide their minor-aged children in such sensitive areas as abortion and the use of contraceptives.

He doesn't regard hard work and clean living as old-fashioned, and even his opponents have credited him with conducting an open, honest Administration.

If you're among those who sees the issues the way President Ford does, you should be among those who vote on November 2nd to keep him right where he is.

THE PRESIDENT FORD COMMITTEE.
JAMES A. BAKER III, CHAIRMAN. ROYSTON C. HUGHES, TREASURER.

FIGURE 1-3

These ads were paid for in large part by the people during the 1976 presidential election. Most of the ads and other campaign expenses were paid for by the United States Treasury in accordance with the Federal Election Campaign Act of 1974.

IF YOU'RE BLACK, THE ODDS ARE ONE IN FOUR YOU'RE DYING FROM HIGH BLOOD PRESSURE.

High Blood Pressure is like a time bomb ticking away, ready to kill or cripple at any moment.

Right now this time bomb is inside one out of every four Black people. In fact, High Blood Pressure is a leading contributor to death among Blacks.

Every year, tens of thousands of Blacks of all ages die from heart disease, from stroke, from kidney failure. Caused by the time bomb inside them. And your blood pressure needn't be very much above normal to be a threat to your life.

What's worse, you could be dying from High Blood Pressure and not even know it. Usually there are no symptoms. You *feel* fine, but all the while the bomb is ticking away. Until, suddenly, it explodes.

Your Blood Pressure can be measured in 30 painless seconds.

Any medically trained person can check your blood pressure, easily. And painlessly. In less than half-a-minute. But the results could add years to your life.

With treatment, you can live a normal, healthy life.

Treatment is usually as simple as taking a pill every day. Take care of your High Blood Pressure and you can lead a longer, healthier life.

So find out *if* you have it. See a doctor. Soon. Find out if you are the one in four.

A Public Service of this Magazine & The Advertising Council

HIGH BLOOD PRESSURE. Treat it...and live.

The National High Blood Pressure Education Program, U.S. Department of Health, Education, and Welfare.

HIGH BLOOD PRESSURE EDUCATION CAMPAIGN
MAGAZINE AD NO. HBP - 2471 - 76 — 7" x 10" (110 Screen)
Volunteer Agency: DKG, Inc.   Volunteer Coordinator: Sanford Buchsbaum, Revlon, Inc.

B-64

FIGURE 1-4
One of a continuing series of print and broadcast ads designed to alert Americans to the dangers of high blood pressure. Time, space, and talent are freely donated by Ad Council members.

THE ADVERTISING COUNCIL

Both public service and special-interest group advertising have a unique relationship with an organization created during World War II, the Advertising Council. The council contributes ideas, artwork and writing talent for public service campaigns. Council members include advertising agencies, national advertisers and advertising media companies. The familiar council symbol (logo) has appeared on ads urging Americans to conserve natural resources, promote our democratic way of life, and the like. Between 1966 and 1978, the Council estimated it had contributed over $6 billion in creative services, advertising space, and time (Figure 1-4).

HOW MUCH PROFIT IS NEEDED?

With the exception of political parties, government, service organizations and special-interest groups, most national advertisers must make a profit on their operations to remain in business. A poll among the general population[10] revealed that those surveyed estimated average American net corporate profits at over 30 percent. The true figure is more like 5 percent,[11] which means that for every dollar of income in the average company, only 5 cents is profit.

No company can afford unlimited investments of money in advertising! Yet there are no hard-and-fast rules about how much of a national advertiser's profit should go for national advertising. The traditional way is to budget according to *sales* and not profit. Thus ad budgets range from 7 percent of sales for candy companies to less than 2 percent for big retailers. Industry practice suggests an ad budget benchmark of 3 percent of gross sales, and most companies tend to hover at that level. This fixed percentage allows the actual budget to rise and fall with the business cycle. But highly successful companies spend much more than 3 percent—up to 23 percent—and many spend less. Block Drug Company (maker of Nytol and other products) invests almost 23 percent of its gross sales in advertising. Procter & Gamble, with sales of over $8 billion, invests 5.7 percent. (This 5.7 percent translates into $460 million,[12] a sum that awes competitors. In previous years, P&G's ratio of advertising to sales has fluctuated between 5 and 8 percent (Table 1-3).

THE PLACE OF ADVERTISING
IN THE MARKETING MIX

We have so far minimized the aspect of advertising as one component in the domain of marketing. *Marketing* includes the activities of all those who are

[10]Roper Reports, 76–1, December 1975.

[11]"Profits of Manufacturing Corporations by Industry Groups," Federal Trade Commission, *World Almanac & Book of Facts* (New York: Newspaper Enterprise Association, Inc., 1977), p. 140.

[12]"100 leaders' advertising as per cent of sales," *Advertising Age*, August 28, 1978, p. 29.

TABLE 1-3

COVERING TOTAL 1977 AD EXPENDITURES, INCLUDING MEASURED AND UNMEASURED MEDIA

100 LEADERS' ADVERTISING AS PERCENT OF SALES

Ad rank	Company	Advertising	Sales	Adv. as % of sales
	Airlines			
92	American Airlines	$ 28,875,000	$2,379,117,000	1.2
97	Delta Airlines	25,700,000	1,870,347,000	1.4
84	Eastern Airlines	32,500,000	2,035,893,000	1.6
95	Trans World Airlines	26,490,600	3,393,473,000	0.7
91	UAL Inc.	30,310,200	3,267,282,000	0.9
	Appliances, TV, radio			
25	General Electric Co.	112,210,300	17,518,800,000	0.6
75	North American Philips Co.	44,000,000	1,916,761,000	2.3
19	RCA Corp.	124,000,000	5,100,000,000	2.4
	Automobiles			
86	American Motors Corp.	31,486,900	2,236,896,000	1.4
17	Chrysler Corp.	127,100,000	16,708,000,000	0.7
8	Ford Motor Co.	184,000,000	37,841,000,000	0.4
2	General Motors Corp.	312,000,000	54,961,300,000	0.5
99	Honda Motor Co.	23,574,500	1,201,959,784	1.9
61	Nissan Motor Co.	57,000,000	10,030,000,000	0.6
68	Toyota Motor Sales U.S.A.	49,175,900	10,872,000,000	0.5
63	Volkswagen of America	52,700,000	11,522,857,824	0.5
	Chemicals			
33	American Cyanamid Co.	96,000,000	1,600,000,000	6.0
72	Union Carbide Corp.	46,100,000	7,036,100,000	0.7
	Drugs, toiletries, and cosmetics			
10	American Home Products Corp.	171,000,000	1,972,000,000	8.7
62	Avon Products	55,000,000	959,227,000	5.7
90	Beecham Group	30,779,200	1,576,300,000	1.9
88	Block Drug Co.	31,000,000	135,919,000	22.8
6	Bristol-Myers Co.	203,000,000	2,191,433,000	9.3
50	Chesebrough-Pond's	67,260,000	807,997,000	8.3
37	Gillette Co.	90,044,000	1,587,209,000	5.7
35	Johnson & Johnson	91,800,000	1,713,583,000	5.3
71	Miles Laboratories	46,500,000	479,129,000	9.7
83	Noxell Corp.	33,255,500	137,628,000	24.2
79	Pfizer Inc.	37,500,000	945,700,000	3.9
43	Revlon Inc.	80,000,000	809,810,000	9.9
13	Richardson-Merrell	148,771,000	836,004,000	17.8
77	A. H. Robins Co.	38,793,500	306,713,000	12.6
54	Schering-Plough	63,000,000	940,859,000	6.7
60	SmithKline Corp.	57,585,000	780,337,000	7.4
80	Squibb Corp.	37,100,000	1,341,583,000	2.8
46	Sterling Drug	72,000,000	687,853,000	10.5
7	Warner-Lambert Co.	201,000,000	2,542,728,000	7.9
	Food			
21	Beatrice Foods Co.	123,000,000	6,318,888,000	1.9
58	Borden Inc.	59,340,700	3,481,278,000	1.7
64	CPC International	51,000,000	1,132,500,000	4.5
57	Campbell Soup Co.	60,000,000	1,769,132,000	3.4
85	Carnation Co.	31,853,100	2,300,000,000	1.4
96	Consolidated Foods Corp.	25,900,000	3,500,000,000	0.7
3	General Foods Corp.	300,000,000	5,380,000,000	5.6
12	General Mills	160,500,000	3,243,000,000	4.9
52	H. J. Heinz Co.	65,800,000	2,150,027,000	3.1
48	Kellogg Co.	69,804,300	1,533,442,000	4.6
30	Kraft Inc.	99,000,000	5,238,807,000	1.9
22	McDonald's Corp.	122,157,600	3,241,477,000	3.8
81	Morton-Norwich	36,102,000	609,303,000	5.9
31	Nabisco Inc.	96,400,000	2,073,278,000	4.6
47	Nestle Enterprises	71,300,000	1,250,000,000	5.7
	Food			
17	Norton Simon Inc.	127,115,000	1,755,958,000	7.2
39	Pillsbury Co.	85,800,000	1,700,000,000	5.0
55	Quaker Oats Co.	60,800,000	1,551,348,000	3.9
42	Ralston Purina Co.	80,673,900	3,760,000,000	2.1
64	Standard Brands	51,000,000	2,124,311,000	2.4
	Gum and candy			
64	Mars Inc.	51,000,000	790,000,000	6.5
88	Wm. Wrigley Jr. Co.	31,036,900	397,941,000	7.8
	Oil			
82	Exxon Corp.	$35,270,800	$58,458,000,000	0.06
15	Mobil Corp.	142,772,470	34,442,935,000	0.4
93	Shell Oil Co.	26,800,000	10,193,685,000	0.3
	Photographic equipment			
40	Eastman Kodak Co.	85,471,800	4,763,500,000	1.8
76	Polaroid Corp.	38,864,000	1,061,945,000	3.7
	Retail chains			
5	K-Mart	210,000,000	9,941,398,000	2.1
29	J. C. Penney Co.	100,000,000	9,369,000,000	1.1
4	Sears, Roebuck & Co.*	290,000,000	17,224,033,000	1.7
	Soaps, cleansers (and allied)			
70	Clorox Co.	47,875,000	872,800,000	5.5
23	Colgate-Palmolive Co.	120,000,000	3,837,204,000	3.1
69	S. C. Johnson & Son	48,860,500	450,000,000	10.9
1	Procter & Gamble	460,000,000	8,099,687,000	5.7
14	Unilever	145,000,000	1,355,072,000	10.7
	Telephone service, equipment			
16	American Telephone & Telegraph Co.	131,968,200	36,494,806,000	0.3
27	International Telephone & Telegraph Corp.	104,699,000	16,688,000,000	0.6
	Tobacco			
41	American Brands	83,921,350	4,616,390,000	1.8
36	B.A.T. Industries	91,253,000	1,478,777,800	6.2
49	Liggett Group	68,357,400	943,248,000	7.2
9	Philip Morris Inc.	184,000,000	5,201,977,000	3.5
11	R. J. Reynolds Industries	164,686,100	6,363,100,000	2.6
	Wine, beer, and liquor			
45	Anheuser-Busch	75,437,000	2,231,230,000	3.4
100	E. & J. Gallo Winery	22,020,700	435,000,000	5.1
26	Heublein Inc.	106,459,200	1,620,112,000	6.6
59	Jos. Schlitz Brewing Co.	59,128,800	1,134,079,000	5.2
44	Seagram Co.	78,000,000	2,184,263,000	3.6
	Miscellaneous			
93	ABC Inc.	26,800,000	1,616,872,000	1.7
73	American Express Co.	46,000,000	3,446,229,000	1.3
31	CBS Inc.	96,379,000	2,776,311,000	3.5
53	Esmark Inc.	65,000,000	5,280,160,000	1.2
34	Goodyear Tire & Rubber Co.	93,862,700	6,627,800,000	1.4
67	Greyhound Corp.	50,825,000	3,852,525,000	1.3
28	Gulf & Western Industries	100,610,984	3,642,998,000	2.8
56	Hanes Corp.	60,278,000	414,158,000	14.6
87	Kimberly-Clark Corp.	31,076,600	1,725,500,000	1.8
51	Loews Corp.	66,114,000	3,237,888,000	2.0
78	Mattel Inc.	38,511,800	436,645,000	8.8
98	Scott Paper Co.	25,502,000	1,520,226,000	1.7
74	Time Inc.	45,951,000	1,249,816,000	3.7
24	U. S. Government	116,235,954		—

*Percentage shown would be more than doubled if Sears' $360,000,000 in local advertising were added to the $290,000,000 national total. The ad totals for the other retail chains also do not include local spending.

Note: All ad totals are domestic. Whenever possible, AA has reported the company's domestic sales figure in this table, although only a worldwide sales total was available for some companies.

Reprinted with permission from *Advertising Age*, August 28, 1978. Copyright © 1978 by Crain Communications, Inc.

involved in the transfer of goods from producer to consumer. Briefly, those activities often referred to as the marketing mix concern relationships among product, brand, distribution, pricing, sales, and advertising policies. Without a good product, advertising is of little avail. In fact, one of the fastest ways to kill a poor product is to advertise it extensively. Without a brand to promote, advertising lacks a recurring symbol for quick identification. Without a competitively priced product, advertising must struggle under a severe handicap. Without the product support of meaningful warranties and guarantees and adequate profit margins for the trade (wholesalers and dealers), advertising has major hurdles to overcome at the trade as well as at the consumer level. Without good product distribution, advertising is weakened.

In fact, of all the elements that go into making up the marketing mix, distribution plays a uniquely critical role. (Distribution is expensive. It's estimated to cost 20 cents of each sales dollar as opposed to 3 cents for advertising.) It is the one major component not rigidly controlled by the manufacturer. The manufacturer cannot compel any independent wholesaler to stock goods or retailer to sell them.

However, once all the components of the mix are in harmony, we can expect advertising to work in any or all of the following ways:

1 Create and retain goodwill for a product or complete line of products (Figure 1-5).
2 Generate store traffic and sell merchandise for local dealers (Figure 1-6).
3 Promote new uses for an established product (Figure 1-7).
4 Deliver helpful information to consumers (Figure 1-8).
5 Provide offers, coupons, and samples (Figure 1-9).
6 Emphasize a trade name (Figure 1-10).
7 Keep and maintain customer interest *after* the sale (Figure 1-11).
8 Attract new dealers and distributors (Figure 1-12).

WHY ADVERTISING SPENDING VARIES

Competition among a group of manufacturers of similar products is one important reason why they devote a higher percentage of their sales to advertising than they might otherwise do. But it is by no means the only reason. We will examine this reason and some others:

1 Degree of competition.
2 Availability of appropriate media and costs.
3 Advertising cycle of the product.
4 Supply and demand and nature of the product.
5 Provide offers, coupons, and samples (Figure 1-9).
6 Emphasize a trade name (Figure 1-10).

Degree of Competition

If only one company made toothpaste, it would only have to tell people so infrequently. Its advertising investment as a percentage of sales would be

I couldn't count my duty done
With twenty kinds. Oh, no sir!
I'll carry all the twenty-one
As long as I'm your grocer.

"21 Kinds for my Customers"

There are twenty-one kinds of Campbell's Soups, a soup for every taste and every occasion. These delicious, appetizing kinds, all prepared in Campbell's famous kitchens, have become a necessity in almost every household. They are made from selected meats and poultry, blended with the most luscious and inviting vegetables.

Campbell's Tomato Soup
The pure juice of choice vine-ripened tomatoes, blended with butter, sugar, herbs, spice and seasoning. Used not only as a soup, but in many tempting sauces for meats, fish, spaghetti, rice, etc. America's leading favorite.

Campbell's Chicken Soup
A rich broth obtained from selected poultry, combined with blanched rice, celery, parsley, tender chicken meat, herbs and seasoning.

Campbell's Vegetable Soup
The broth from selected beef contains diced white potatoes, sweet potatoes, carrots, sweet red peppers and golden turnips, besides peas, lima beans, corn, tomatoes, okra, celery, parsley, Dutch cabbage, pearl barley, onion, leek, bay leaf, spices and alphabet macaroni.

Campbell's Ox-Tail Soup
The broth is prepared from medium sized ox-tails and blended with puree of whole tomatoes, diced carrots and sweet yellow turnips, barley, beef marrow, onions, leeks, herbs, spices and seasoning.

Campbell's Bean Soup
Choice hand picked Michigan beans are cooked, strained, blended with a puree of carrots and celery, a flavoring of other vegetables, and temptingly seasoned.

Campbell's Asparagus Soup
Fresh asparagus cut on the Campbell farms, is made the same day into a rich, creamy soup, with milk, butter and seasoning. Tender asparagus tips add to the inviting appearance and flavor. A favorite during the Lenten season.

Campbell's Chicken Gumbo
Selected poultry is used for a broth which is blended with a puree of whole tomato, celery, parsley, herbs, spices in Southern style and seasoning, together with blanched rice and sliced okra.

Campbell's Pea Soup
The carefully selected peas are cooked, strained and blended with milk, creamery butter and seasoning to a delicious, smooth quality specially appropriate for luncheons and exceptionally pleasing to vegetarians and observers of Lent.

Campbell's Vegetable-Beef Soup
Unusually rich broth from the shins of beef, whole tomato puree, diced potatoes and carrots, green peas, onions, pearl barley and cubes of solid beef make up this tasty and very filling soup—a meal in itself.

Campbell's Celery Soup
Crisp, tender stalks of celery, field-blanched to a perfect whiteness, are made into a puree and blended with milk, creamery butter and seasoning. A refreshing delicacy, peculiarly appropriate during Lent.

Campbell's Mock Turtle Soup
Cubes of delicate meat from selected calves' heads are used in a rich beef broth blended with whole tomato puree, in which celery, herbs, spices and specially high seasoning give the flavor enjoyed by epicures.

Campbell's Mutton Soup
Specially prepared mutton broth, diced potatoes and carrots, barley, celery, parsley, tender fresh mutton, sweet red peppers, flavored with a touch of leek. Salt and pepper may be added to taste. A splendid strength-building food for all children and invalids.

Campbell's Vermicelli Tomato Soup
Puree of fresh, whole tomatoes is used with vermicelli, full cream cheese, parsley, onion browned, spices and flavoring. An Italian dish Americanized.

Campbell's Bouillon
Strong, rich meat broth made from fine beef and slightly flavored with the essence of celery, onions, leeks, parsley, herbs and seasoning.

Campbell's Consomme
Made from high-grade beef, and perfectly clarified by fine straining. Delicately flavored with the essence of carrots, onions, celery, parsley and spices, with careful seasoning.

Campbell's Tomato Okra Soup
The pure juice of selected, vine-ripened tomatoes is blended with creamery butter, sugar, herbs, spices and seasoning, and made additionally tasty with fresh sliced okra.

Campbell's Julienne
A banquet soup of clarified broth from high-grade beef in which carrots, white turnips, celery, Savoy cabbage, lettuce and leeks are shredded. Whole small peas and a flavoring of onion, parsley, spices and seasoning are added.

Campbell's Pepper Pot
The stock made from choice beef contains tripe, salt pork, potatoes, onions, hot peppers, choice whole red peppers and seasoning. The most highly seasoned of all soups.

Campbell's Beef Soup
Selected beef is used for the broth. Diced solid beef, diced carrots and yellow turnips, celery, leeks, barley, spices and seasoning make it a most substantial food.

Campbell's Mulligatawny Soup
Chicken and rice are skilfully combined with puree of carrots, yellow turnips, apples, leeks, onions, chutney, garlic, fresh citron, candied orange peel, cocoanut, fresh fruits, sugar, fine seasonings and curry, in the manner of India.

Campbell's Printanier Soup
Made of beef broth blended with carrots and white turnips cut in small fancy shapes, sliced celery, Savoy cabbage, leeks, whole small peas, parsley, herbs, spices and seasoning.

Your grocer can easily get all these kinds for you. If you have any difficulty send his name to Campbell's Soup Company, Camden, N. J., and we will see that you are supplied.

All the same price   15 cents a can

Campbell's Soups
LOOK FOR THE RED AND WHITE LABEL

FIGURE 1-5
This 1926 Campbell Soups ad helped to familiarize readers of *The Ladies Home Journal* with its wide variety of soups.

FIGURE 1-6
Wolfschmidt ad employs humor to build traffic for dealers, state liquor stores, bars, and restaurants.

FIGURE 1-7
Proclaiming the egg as a key ingredient in innumerable recipes, this ad aimed at homemakers illustrates several ways to use the product.

It was two of those fellers from the city come up the road in a big green car, asked me if I wanted some new boots. I didn't. Already had boots, had 'em for seven years. But they talked and we drank some, and then we looked at the boots some, and I tried 'em on. Now, I have to say, they did seem to have my size. So I walked 'em about for maybe a week, and once I went over and stood in Orville Wade's creek, just to see if they were waterproof, which they were. When those boys came back from the city, this is what I said. One, I said thank you for the fine boots, which are warm and dry as a hen's bottom. Two, I'd like a pair of 13-wides for Cousin Luther, double-wide on the left foot where the tractor run it over.

If you can't find a dealer near you, please send two dollars for a catalogue full of good boots, sound advice and general recollections. The Timberland Company, Newmarket, N.H.

Timberland

A whole line of fine leather boots that cost plenty, and should.

FIGURE 1-8

The traveler weary of foot and short of breath finds good news in this excellent Timberland ad. One of advertising's important social values is delivering information to people.

FIGURE 1-9

Coupons and offers are a common characteristic of food processors' advertising strategy. This small section of an advertising supplement is typical. The supplement included offers from Sanka Decaffeinated Coffee, Ken-L Ration dog food, Quaker cereals, and a few other companies. The supplement was sent to a number of the nation's newspapers in order to help move merchandise. (The coupons as reproduced will not be accepted).

extremely low, more than likely under 1 percent. But in the drug and cosmetic industry, stiff competition is normal. There are hundreds of products to choose from. Each competitor attempts to increase its share of market at the expense of the others. It may resort to new products, new packaging, and massive doses of advertising. In a less competitive arena, the entrance of even one new company into a market can greatly increase everyone's advertising

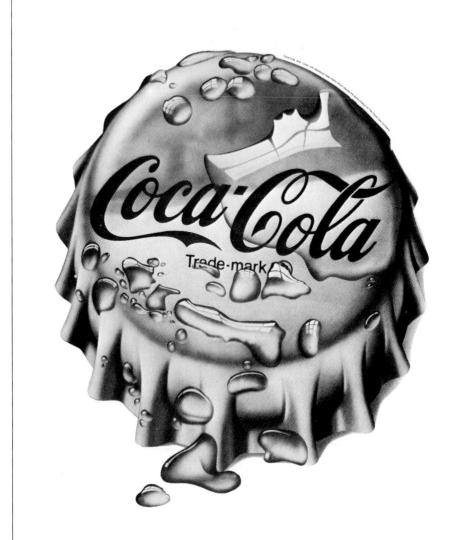

Refreshment.
165 million times a day.

FIGURE 1-10
A trade name is valuable as an identification symbol. The Coca-Cola Company took this national ad to explain why. Reproduced with permission of the Coca-Cola Company.

BMOC

McDonald's

We do it all for you.

"TWOALLBEEFPATTIE SSPECIALSAUCELETT UCECHEESEPICKLE SONIONSONASESAM ESEEDBUN."

ISU - you just said a mouthful. In fact it takes a whole bunch of mouthfuls to eat a Big Mac. Beautiful, isn't it?

FIGURE 1-11

Luscious "Big Mac" reinforces customers' attitudes toward a product already purchased. Colorful posters, developed by McDonald's national headquarters, were inserted in selected newspapers throughout the country. Many ended up decorating walls and dormitory rooms.

budget. Before 1976, for example, an Iowa dairy dominated the newly discovered yogurt market in central Iowa. But when national competitors entered the battle in 1976, the company responded by increasing the frequency of its yogurt advertising. It's a familiar story, repeated wherever competition becomes heated.

Availability of Appropriate Media and Costs

Most people recognize that national network television is expensive. They would be amazed if they knew how few companies can actually afford to invest regularly in the medium. As a case in point, consider that an average prime-time network television commercial costs $50,000.[13] If the price of a national television spot is our sole criterion for determining buyers, we can state without reservation that companies with sales under $5 million need not apply. Even under the happiest of circumstances, the average $5 million company could not afford more than five thirty-second, prime-time spots a year.[14] (If it could be content with less expensive television time, it could afford more commercials.)

But cost is not the only criterion for those who buy national media. Media must also suit an advertiser's needs and wishes. Some companies prefer not to use billboards because of their restricted message area and because of their ecological implications. Others feel that a reasonable sales message cannot be delivered (and absorbed) in thirty to sixty seconds of television time. Similarly, companies may find that suitable magazines are limited. The manufacturer of a wood saw who aims for the do-it-yourselfers has a small number of magazines to choose from: *Workbench*, *Family Handyman*, *Mechanix Illustrated*, *Furniture*, *Popular Mechanics*. Compare this restricted selection to that open to an automobile manufacturer, for whom practically every national medium is a reasonable investment and nearly every adult a potential sales target.

Advertising Cycle of the Product

Products and services—and companies, too—go through life much as humans do, with a beginning, a middle, and an end. Newly born products need a good, healthy start in order to thrive and grow. Without wide promotion, sales decrease, dealers drop the line, and death comes early. Marketers divide the life of products and companies into three cycles: pioneering (when the product is introduced), competitive, and retentive (when the product has settled into maturity). Most advertising dollars go into the first two cycles. We can see this by examining the tire industry's ad

---

[13]*Broadcasting Yearbook*, Broadcasting Publications, Inc., 1977, p. A-2.
[14]Assuming an ad budget of 5 percent of $5 million in sales, the company has $250,000 available for the year's advertising. Five 30-second spots would eat up the entire budget!

FIGURE 1-12
Typical Pioneer seed corn ad does double duty. It sells farmers but also attracts new dealers, most of whom are farmers.

investment as a percentage of sales and comparing it to the more dynamic soaps and cleansers industry.

Tire companies seem to be in the retentive cycle, content to promote the name of the company and little else. There are few new tire products, an unfailing characteristic of companies in the retentive cycle. Tire companies move into the competitive cycle only when they introduce a newly formulated cord fabric for building tires or a radical change in tread design.

But within the competitive soaps and cleansers industry, new technologies and formulas are percolating all the time. Many of the new soaps and detergents, for example, need thorough explanations. Each manufacturer attempts to show why the results of its technology are superior to everyone else's. They do this in frequent and widespread advertisements that consume a larger percentage of the soap than tire industry sales. On the other hand, few people need to be sold on what new things a tire can do (Figures 1-13).

FIGURE 1-13
Large advertising budgets are necessary for soap manufacturers to explain new products and formulas to the public, via print and broadcast. In a recent issue of *Better Homes and Gardens,* there were twelve ads for soaps and cleansers.

Supply and Demand and Nature of the Product

Some companies gauge their advertising budgets according to public demand for their products. Spices, for example, are less likely to be on a weekly shopping list than meat and vegetables. To increase demand for oregano, you would spend more to promote it. You'd have to sell the overall advantages of oregano and then sell your specific brand. Contrast oregano with meat. Demand for meat is typically and constantly high. No one needs to promote it unless one segment of the industry (lamb producers) wishes to gain a larger share of the market at the expense of the others (producers of beef and pork). The point is that high demand often keeps down the dollars invested in advertising as a percentage of sales.

Another factor that keeps advertising percentages low is the supply of the product. Coors beer is an example. Company policy is to restrict production and distribution. Demand for the beer where it is sold is high, and high demand permits the company to spend less on advertising. Of fourteen top brewers in the nation, Coors' ad cost per case is 1 cent. Compare that to

Miller Brewing Company with nationwide distribution and an ad cost per case of 11 cents.[15]

Quality of Distribution

Imagine that you are trying to influence chain supermarket buyers to stock your new soft drink. Your sales agents tell you that the chain supermarkets want you to create consumer demand. In effect, they want you to invest in national advertising *before* they'll stock your merchandise. But if you advertise extensively, people asking for your product are likely not to find it. This causes unhappiness for the consumer and lost sales for the bottler. The best of all distribution situations occurs when your ad encourages millions of people to look for your product in their stores—and find it there.

The *manner* of distribution, too, can play a part in how much money a company invests in advertising. Direct selling companies, like Avon and Scott & Fetzer (makers of Kirby vacuum cleaners) spend less on consumer advertising than competitors like Revlon and Hoover, traditional marketers. Direct selling companies justify this policy because they pay a large percentage of the door-to-door business as commissions to their salespeople.

Company Financial Strength

A company that is undercapitalized (without enough money to pay creditors on time) or in severe financial trouble will have difficulty budgeting an adequate percentage of its sales for national advertising. This places it at a disadvantage in a market full of well-capitalized competitors. Few companies are willing to borrow money for the purpose of advertising. They'll borrow for machinery, personnel, and materials, but they'll balk at applying the same business logic to advertising. Some experts claim that this attitude is shortsighted and reflects badly on a company's marketing skills.

PUBLIC ATTITUDE TOWARD ADVERTISING

By and large, people believe the advertising they see and hear. If they did not, they would cripple business. But there *is* public resistance. Organized groups such as The Educational Council have brought a desensitizing program to many schools. Students are taught to be critical of all advertising and to recognize puffery. Women's groups regularly take advertisers to task for treating women as sex objects. Racial, ethnic, and religious groups protest ads that portray unfair stereotypes. Others criticize advertisers as unfeeling, inhumane, money-grubbing machines.

Advertisers need to examine these complaints. They are real. Whether

[15]"Ad costs for beer, ale, malt liquor," *Advertising Age*, September 26, 1977, p. 112.

they belong on the doorstep of the advertising industry is another matter. But what specifically are these complaints? And what should we do about them?

Children and Junk Foods

Many complaints arise from the television advertising of so-called junk foods (sugared cereals, potato chips, pretzels, pizzas, candies, and soft drinks) to gullible children. One group proposed a ban on television ads that used toys and prizes as inducements to get children to buy cereals. The proposal was dropped because the Federal Trade Commission concluded there was insufficient evidence that such ads were deceptive. Those involved with these complaints are still trying to come to grips with the competing claims of public health and free enterprise.

Violence and Advertising

The steady increase in television violence has multiplied the number of advertising critics. Their claim: Without sponsors' support, few programs would dramatize violence. A growing number of national companies are responding to these social and economic pressures. Metropolitan Life Insurance Company has instructed its advertising agency to avoid purchasing time on violent television shows. Kraft and other advertisers are following suit.

Opponents of the use of pressure tactics claim that the First Amendment of the Constitution covers advertising and that pressuring advertisers is a form of censorship that will grow worse if it's allowed to go unchallenged. The answer to violence, they state, is for the parents to exercise judgment and supervise which TV programs their children watch.

Other Complaints

Television alone is not solely responsible for complaints against advertisers. The public also charges the abuse of other media. Frequently mentioned is unsolicited mail, often called "junk mail," and phone calls by unknown parties to solicit business. Both, critics claim, are an invasion of household privacy.

Church groups and others regularly condemn sexually suggestive ads that appear in magazines and newspapers and on billboards. Perhaps most damaging of all complaints is the widespread opinion that one must be skeptical of *all* advertising claims.

THE ADVERTISERS' RESPONSE

People who make their living from advertising claim that its extreme visibility makes for all the criticism, and they like to point out advertising's benefits to the public. From advertising, people learn about grocery products and prices, new foods and ways to cook, clothing and medicines, new movies, television and radio programs, even how to reproduce important papers and documents. Although people may resent having to share their television picture or radio speaker with approximately sixteen commercials an hour, they appear willing to accept these distractions in exchange for entertainment, music, and education. Less resentment is evident among magazine and newspaper readers, who can skip ads,[16] than among audiences of other media.

But how do advertisers react to skepticism about their claims? Most agree this is a serious problem that, individually or collectively, they have tried to solve. They point to the sum of their efforts as proof of their good intentions: Better Business Bureaus, Truth in Advertising campaigns, National Advertising Review Board, (a self-regulatory group to prevent and correct misleading advertising). Unfortunately, not all advertisers comply with industry efforts to eliminate misleading ads. There are those who justify extravagant claims by pointing to competition in the marketplace. How to curb *their* excesses without stifling competition is the challenge business now faces as advertising approaches the twenty-first century.

IN SUMMARY

1 National advertising is a sales presentation of goods, services, and ideas to a mass market through national media.
2 At its best, advertising increases demand for goods, which in turn permits the efficient manufacturer to reduce or hold the line on prices. Advertising also can take some credit for providing jobs.
3 Major users of national advertising are manufacturers, large retail chain stores, service organizations and special-interest groups, commercial marketing associations, government, and political parties.
4 Without an adequate profit, a company will find it impossible to advertise for very long.
5 Traditionally, a rule-of-thumb figure for advertising of 3 percent of sales has won wide acceptance.
6 Advertising works in many ways. Most important, it helps sell goods by developing traffic for a manufacturer's retail outlets.
7 Of the five elements of the marketing mix (value of the product itself, brand identity, distribution, pricing, sales and advertising policies), the distribution system is the only one not controlled directly by the manufacturer.
8 Investments in advertising by companies and organizations vary widely depending on any or all of the following: competitive situation, the advertising cycle, quality of distribution, availability and cost of the proper media, supply and demand and nature of the product, and financial strength of the company.
9 Public skepticism of advertising claims may be the most serious problem business has to face.

[16]In a magazine readership study by Gilbert Youth Research for *Seventeen* magazine, three of five girls read the magazine, advertising, and editorial material, from cover to cover. (Magazine Readership Survey, *Seventeen*, 1974, p. 6.)

CASE STUDY   Wendy's Hot 'n' Juicy

R. David Thomas, founder and board chairman of Wendy's, started out in the food service business at seventeen as a bus boy. Today his quick-service family restaurant chain of over 1400 units and $800 million in sales is one of the major success stories of the 1970s. In seven years, sales rose from $2 million.

"The image of the hamburger must be predominant," says Thomas. "If you want roast beef, don't come to Wendy's."[17] Wendy's makes no attempt to appeal to children but is interested in the family unit, which includes anybody who loves a hamburger. Fast-food chains, notably McDonald's, invest heavily in advertising aimed at children. Wendy's simple, unadorned menu is the same as it was when the first unit opened in Columbus, Ohio: a single, double, or triple quarter-pound hamburger, fries, chili, a Frosty Dairy Dessert, and the usual selection of soft drinks.

The target audiences consist of adults, mostly business people, professionals, and secretaries (ages eighteen to forty-nine), and the Wendy decor and interior design emphasize their attempt to please this clientele: old, antique-appearing table tops, carpeting, paneling. To reach this market, Wendy's spent $5 million in 1977 on network television ads (but over $20 million in total expenditures throughout the United States), not an outstanding sum compared to the standards of its rivals, McDonald's and Burger King. Television ads show adults and a few children enjoying Wendy's "hot 'n juicy" hamburgers to a comic musical background beat.

[17]"Skeptics watch as Wendy's sales soar from $2MM to $400MM," *Institutions/Volume Feeding Magazine*, February 1, 1978, p. 50.

FIGURE 1-14
Demonstration, one of television's most convincing sales techniques, is Wendy's way of getting more from its limited ad dollars. In the commercials, customers wipe "juicy" hamburger stains from happy faces. "Hot'n Juicy" is the campaign that helped move the company from $2 million in sales to $800 million in seven years.

Although national television spots reach many areas where there are not yet any Wendy's units, management believes this total approach predisposes potential new markets to Wendy's and creates demand and traffic when a unit does open (Figure 1-14).

QUESTIONS NEEDING ANSWERS

1 Do you agree with Wendy's management's decision to use national advertising even though Wendy's is not represented in many areas? Why?
2 Does it makes sense to concentrate most of Wendy's advertising on its hamburgers instead of on other items sold? Explain.
3 Do you think a preponderance of children eating at a fast-food restaurant discourages business people from eating there? Explain.
4 Would the success of other fast-food franchises help or hinder Wendy's expansion plans? Explain.

STUDENT PROJECT

Contact the owner-manager of a local franchise of a nationally known fast-food restaurant. Try to discover which national franchise fast-food restaurant chains provide the greatest national advertising support for their franchise holders. Find out what the local franchise holder thinks of Wendy's advertising as opposed to that of others.

QUESTIONS ABOUT THE PROJECT

1 Does the competitive franchise holder think Wendy's television ads are effective or not? Explain.
2 What percentage of total sales of the local franchise holder goes to national advertising? Explain. Do you think it should be increased or decreased and why?

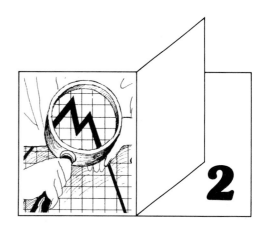

RETAIL

Update Up to this point, we've reviewed national consumer advertising. But retailers also direct a substantial amount of advertising at the ultimate consumer. We call this *retail advertising*. It uses local media and generally serves geographic areas that are important to retailers who sell goods to people like you and me. Although national companies may occasionally advertise on a specific local medium—a radio station, for example—we call this *national spot advertising* and not retail advertising.

Retail advertising is a method of informing consumers of a specific region about the availability or cost of the merchandise at a nearby retail store. It is paid for by a retailer and is a cost of doing business just like rent or wages to clerks. (It is also tax deductible, which means the retailer's cost of advertising is taken off income tax obligations. Without this tax write-off, it is quite

possible that many retailers would drastically reduce their advertising outlays.)
If national consumer advertising must sell a product, service, or idea, then
local retailer's advertising must make the buying take place *in the retailer's
store.*

IMPORTANCE OF THE RETAILER

As retailers will agree, their job is to warehouse specific types of merchandise,
to communicate the news that these are available *at their stores*, and to sell
the merchandise when customers arrive.

The retailer's importance to the general economy is recognized by the
Small Business Administration, which estimates that 1,215,000 retailers
account for over $700 billion in gross sales each year.[1] They employ 21
percent of all workers[2] in the nation. Without retailers, "instant goods" at the
grass roots level would not be economically feasible for the manufacturer nor
available for the ultimate consumer. Typically, channels of distribution run
from manufacturer to distributor to retailer.

Without local financial support, most media would have severe problems. The commercial broadcast media, television and radio, are totally

[1]"Establishments, Employees, and Payroll by Major Industry Groups: 1976 and 1975," *County
Business Patterns*, Bureau of the Census, 1976 and 1977.
[2]County Business Patterns, 1976, Table 1A.

TABLE 2-1

ESTIMATED ANNUAL U.S. NEWSPAPER ADVERTISING EXPENDITURES 1973-1977 (IN
MILLIONS OF DOLLARS)

	1973	1974	1975	1976	1977
National	1,111	1,194	1,221	1,502	1,680
Local	6,484	6,807	7,221	8,408	9,390
Total	$7,595	$8,001	$8,442	$9,910	$11,070

Source: McCann-Erickson, Inc.; NAB estimates for classifieds 1973—1977.

TABLE 2-2

WHERE THE MONEY* COMES FROM TO KEEP WEEKLY NEWSPAPERS ALIVE—1977 (BY CIRCULA-
TION GROUPINGS)

Circulation	Total ad income (%)		Total income (%)		Circulation income
	Local	National	Local	National	as % of total income
Less than 3,000	80.25	5.28	43.29	2.95	8.49
Less than 5,000	82.76	3.55	47.88	2.03	7.41
Less than 7,000	81.36	5.85	40.0	3.56	7.76
Less than 10,000	87.67	2.62	41.81	1.21	8.66
Over 10,000	70.22	14.80	37.90	7.79	8.98

*Other income includes commercial printing, classified advertising, and public notice advertising.
Source: *National Weekly Newspaper Cost Study*, National Newspaper Association, Washington, D.C., July
1977.

subsidized by advertising, much of which comes from local business people. Newspaper and magazine readers are informed and entertained at "subsidized" rates (Tables 2-1 and 2-2).

If we average circulation income for weekly newspapers throughout the country (see Table 2-2), we discover that it comes to 8.26 percent. In other words, readers pay less than 10 percent of the total cost of the newspaper. The local retail advertiser pays the major portion of the total cost of both weekly and daily newspapers.

THE ADVERTISING LESSON FOR THE RETAILER

Most successful retailers advertise consistently. Because of their advertising, their volume and profits are larger than smaller competitors' or competing nonadvertisers'.[3] Some retail store analysts contend that advertisers bounce back more quickly from recessions. Although this claim has not been proved by irrefutable research, owners of media like to point out that local investments in advertising have grown steadily over the years. Between 1967 and 1975 throughout the country, local radio advertising has increased 123 percent, local newspaper 78 percent, local outdoor 84 percent, and local television 190 percent. Media owners consider this proof positive that advertising pays off for retailers! Although these figures should be tempered by media rate increases over the years, the advances are real and appear to be continuing[4] (Table 2-3).

Although retailers account for over $9 billion[5] in newspaper advertising alone, some advertise very little and some not at all. If we were going to develop a checklist of reasons why some merchants don't advertise, we might come up with the following:

1 **No faith in advertising.** Retailer knows from previous experience that advertising won't work.
2 **Small payoff.** Some retailers fail to set advertising objectives for their ads. When the returns are in, they may be disappointed. Others don't know what to expect, although they are convinced that they can't afford the newspaper or radio advertising rates.
3 **Lack of faith in local media.** When retailers believe that local media advertisements aren't worth the investment, they won't advertise. They may be suspicious of the circulation figures of the local newspaper. They may feel that the local FM radio station or Yellow Pages reach too few of the right people. They may have no confidence in direct mail or pass-out circulars.

---

[3]"Eighty-two percent of all food shoppers refer to the newspaper . . . before they do their marketing," *Selling News*, October 1975, p. 1.
[4]*Advertising Age*, August 27, 1973, p. 187; December 29, 1975, p. 34.
[5]*Advertising Age*, December 29, 1975, p. 34.

TABLE 2-3

AVERAGE PROFIT AND ADVERTISING INVESTMENTS*
AS A PERCENTAGE OF SALES FOR SELECTED RETAILERS

Retail type	Profit margin	Amount invested in advertising (%)
Automobile dealers	16.46	1.42
Department stores ($5—$10 million yr)	38.64	3.65
Combination food stores (over $200,000/yr.)	19.29	1.00
Jewelry stores (under $100,000 yr)	43.9	3.2
Hardware stores	34.06	1.66
Florists	55.48	2.16
Furniture stores ($500,000—$1 million yr)	40.90	4.92
Pharmacies ($180,000—$200,000 yr)	37.0	1.7
Motels and motor inns (11—20 units)	54.51	2.66
Apparel stores	39.0	1.53
Cocktail lounges and taverns	47.0	0.75
Appliance and radio and television dealers	27.0	2.5

*Some of monies listed as advertising were actually spent in printing and stationery.
Sources: *Expenses in Retail Business,* NCR Marketing Education and Publications (Dayton) 1978, 1974; *Cost of Doing Business Survey,* National Appliance and Radio-TV Dealers' Association (NARDA), Chicago, 1976.

4 *Concern for the future.* Retailers worry about unemployment, availability of money for expansion, and the overall mood of consumers. If they sense difficult business conditions, they may not wish to invest in what they consider a speculative venture—advertising.

On the other hand, retailers who do advertise regularly generally expect their investment to pay off in any or all of the following ways:

1 *Increase in store traffic.* An increase in customers is probably the easiest way for merchants to tell that their advertising is working. Customers who come to buy an advertised item not only justify the cost of the ad, they also see the other items in the store. Shopping center advertising, for example, aims primarily at delivering customers to a large, central location (Figure 2-1).

2 *Liquidation of surplus merchandise.* Retailers use the potent word "sale" to clear their shelves of goods not sold during regular operations. Sales are an element of inventory control (Figure 2-2).

3 *Tie-in with a fashion trend or fad.* Few retailers can predict the life of a trend or fad. Yet even frivolous fads make money for retailers if their advertising strikes "while the iron is hot." The proper time is generally after the product has been introduced nationally and has received acceptance by important national, regional, or local personalities.

4 *Enhanced reputation.* The ingredients that go into building a retail reputation are many: quality merchandise, good repair service, prompt delivery, reasonable prices, friendly and well-informed clerks, interest in customers' needs, extensive

FIGURE 2-1

The Staunton Plaza in Staunton, Virginia is one of thirty-five shopping centers in six eastern states using this copyrighted ad format, the creation of Musheno Associates of Lebanon, Pennsylvania. The format is designed to attract customers to the mall. In recent years, shopping centers and malls have appeared throughout the nation and have introduced more sophisticated and better-financed local advertising.

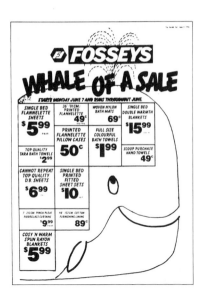

FIGURE 2-2
Sales can be presented in a variety of ways. Fosseys' store approached the event with banners flying and trumpets blaring four-and-a-half-page newspaper "whale" of an advertising spread. Gimbels tried a different tack: all copy, no illustration, no nonsense.

Be here saturday 10 a.m.

One terrific day in the great tradition of Gimbels One-day sales. Be here early.

LINENS, DOMESTICS

Cannon's Royal Family percale sheets, 50% off
Sale: 2 for $7 Orig. $7 ea.
Bright floral on white. $8 fulls.
2 for $8, $12 queens, **2 for $12**,
$15 Kings. **2 for $15**. Dept. 231.
Cases also priced.

20%-45% off Comet blankets, twin, full sizes one price
Sale: $8 Orig. $10-$15
Machine wash and dry acrylics in it.
blue, yellow, brown hunter, navy.
Dept. 250

45% off standard size goosefeather pillows, now
Sale: $8 Reg. $15
Soft, medium or firm. Filled with whole white goosefeathers. Cotton tick.
Dept. 251

50% off discontinued vinyl place mats. Regularly $2, Sale: **.99**
Dept. 221

Entire stock art needlework department. Kits, yarn, more. **50% off**
Dept. 171. Not at Echelon, Moorestown

BATH SHOP
Save 20% on entire stock of wall-to-wall bath rugs
Sale: $32

HOME NEEDS SALE

Selected tea kettles on sale, Your choice of seven kinds
Sale: 33% off
Reg. $11 to $18, Sale: **7.34-11.99**.
Aluminum. Stainless steel. More.
Dept. 670

Save $5 on Proctor's 2-10 cup beverage brewer
Sale: 19.99 Reg. $25
Makes coffee or tea. Boils water for instant soups, cocoa.
Dept. 671

Save $6 on Proctor's lightweight steam/dry iron
Sale: 9.99 Reg. $16
29 steam vents. Mirror sole plate.
Easy to read fabric control.
Dept. 671

Faceted old-fashioned or hi-ball glasses from Italy
50% off
Choose: Manhattan, reg. $1 ea. **4 for $2** or Oxford, reg. 1.50 ea. **4 for $3**
Dept. 665

Imported ceramic ashtrays, pencil cups, desk organizers
25% off
Orig. 2.50-$25, Sale: **1.89-18.75**
Great assortment of desk-toppers.

SAVE ON FURNITURE

Save 25% on Kroehler's sofa/loveseat ensembles
Sale: $675 Orig. $1050
Coil construction. Striped rayon velvet covers. Super savings!
Dept. 608. Not at Upper Darby

Save 50% on handsome sofas with nylon covers
Sale: $249 Orig. $500
Contemporary and traditional looks.
Be early. Quantities are limited.
Dept. 608. Not at Upper Darby

Velvet living room chairs now 40-50% off and more
Sale: $119 Orig. $200-$250
Wing. Swivel rockers and high backs in soft, cushy velvet. Be early.
Dept. 601. Not at Upper Darby

Brass-finish tables and etageres, 33%-37% off
Tables: $119 Orig. $190
Cocktail and sofa tables. Rush Etageres, orig. $300. **Sale: $199**
Dept. 602. Not at Upper Darby

30% off planked pecan-look entertainment center
Sale: $70 Orig. $100
Holds your stereo, tapes, small TV.
Top doubles as serving center.

SLEEP CENTER

Sealy Back Saver mattresses, box springs
Sale: 33% off
Every size, every firmness, ours alone. Reg. 99.95-619.95, **$66-$399**
Dept. 610

$220 savings on Sealy sleep sofas, four styles
Sale: $499 Reg. 719.95
Double your space in home or apartment with a comfortable sleeper.
Dept. 615

Save $22 on sturdy steel-frame cots, foam mattress
Sale: $88 Reg. 109.95
Great for your home or summer home, or child's room.
Dept. 615

Save $100 on hi-risers that open to sleep two
Sale: $199 Orig. $299
Another space stretcher. Great for small home or apartment.
Dept. 615. ($10 deliv.)

FLOOR COVERINGS
Save $80-$200 on worsted wool oriental-design rugs

stock, good credit policies, and so on. People will travel long distances to patronize merchants who fulfill their expectations. Telling the greatest number of potential customers about any or all of a retailer's strengths is a job for advertising.

Advertising that develops a distinct store personality can pay off especially well for the retailer. No law of advertising or business says that retailers should look or act alike. But often they do. Take a quick glance at any Wednesday or Thursday newspaper in the country. The pages are filled with virtually interchangeable ads. Astute business people try to avoid this follow-the-leader mentality by designing distinctive ads. Others provide strong, persuasive reasons in their ads for consumers to buy. Ads being different and being persuasive surely help the customer to decide among stores. In a day when many shoppers think nothing of driving more than ten miles to go shopping,[6] the unimaginative retailer is at a serious disadvantage. Shoppers are no longer heavily dependent on the hometown retailer, who must now create an identity in the face of unrelenting competition from both Main Street and the shopping center mall.

Retailers should ask themselves some basic questions: What is my strong point? Is it the extent of the line I carry? Is it unusual, hard-to-find merchandise? Is it price alone or is it price and value combined? Is it superior service, knowledge, competence? Is it early and late store hours every day of the week? (Several national grocery store franchises are in operation whose major claim to an identity is the fact that they remain open when major supermarkets are closed. Typical of this group are White Owl Stores, Convenience Food Marts, 7-11 Stores, and Lawson's.) Is it repair facilities, one-stop shopping? What is it that makes me different, retailers should ask themselves, that makes my personality (Figure 2-3)?

One large Midwestern food chain runs a weekly consumer advice column that promotes economical meal planning and applauds nutritional labeling (Figure 2-4). Another provides attractive ads with recipes. A New England retailer teaches consumers how to buy beef by describing four available grades. These retailers are responding to surveys that indicate that consumers are looking for value, nutrition, and variety in their meal planning. A hardware retailer might run ads featuring ways to repair and maintain roofs, gutters, siding, electrical appliances, and the like. Real estate brokers might experiment with an advertising series on how to prepare a home for quick sale or on answers to ten common questions asked by home buyers. Result: an advertised personality people can relate to (Figure 2-5).

Department stores have a unique identification problem because they are the most visible advertisers in daily newspapers. The way they arrange the graphic elements in their ads leads consumers to rate them on an economic scale. Consumers identify cluttered ads as the trademark of an archaic and behind-the-times store. Bold, strident headlines with an emphasis on price

---

[6]*Shoppers on the move* (a report), Newspaper Advertising Bureau, August 1975.

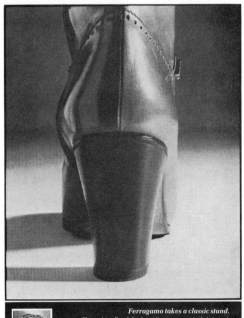

FIGURE 2-3

The common denominator among these retail ads is a devotion to building a reputation for a specific characteristic: MacHugh for quality haberdashery in the East; Neiman-Marcus for a wide variety of high-priced, unusual merchandise in Dallas; Bishops' restaurants for wholesome, appetizing food in the Midwest; Medick-Krieger, a Ford dealer, for customer service in Columbus, Ohio.

FIGURE 2-4

Food Day ads for Sipes Stores in Tulsa, Oklahoma, show an image change. According to Cecille Bates, director of the stores' advertising and public relations, this and other ads were designed to provide nutritional information. A few years later, a market study showed that Sipes was perceived as a high-priced store, so management embarked on a campaign to prove that Sipes is also a store with a world of low prices. (Courtesy: Sipes Food Markets).

FIGURE 2-5
Many car dealer ads tend to become invisible because they look alike, but these small classified ads stand out. Classified ads generally cost less than the more conspicuous display units.

say, "This is a discount store." Unusual, dramatic ads seem to identify a progressive store with prices ranging from modest to high. Uncluttered ads with large, stark illustrations suggest exclusive and expensive merchandise. Saks Fifth Avenue in New York, Halle's in Cleveland, Younkers in Des Moines, Marshall Field in Chicago, and Neiman-Marcus in Dallas are some of the nationally known stores that fit this last description.

Perhaps no other retail store has fixed on certain employees whose performance depends on the effectiveness of advertising as has the department store. Buyers for each department, for example, have primary responsibility for the sale of merchandise in that department. Therefore, they work closely with the advertising staff of the store to generate traffic and sales. In effect, the personality of the store reflects what these buyers wish to convey to customers (Figure 2-6). Ads that don't communicate the buyers' standards of quality, style, and taste raise doubts in customers' minds, make them wonder about the price of merchandise, and confuse them about the personality of the store. And, of course, goods that fail to satisfy customers' needs remain unsold, with or without advertising.

COOPERATIVE ADVERTISING AT RETAIL LEVEL

One reason department stores are so visible in local advertising media is the practice of *cooperative advertising*. As the name implies, two parties to an advertising agreement cooperate. The agreement, whether written or implied, is between a manufacturer and a retailer who agree to divide the cost of promoting the manufacturer's product at the local level. The retailer generally places the ad after consultations with sales representatives of the print and broadcast media. As a rule, most of the ad is given over to the product itself, because most manufacturers send complete camera-ready proofs, prerecorded tapes and records for radio, and videotape or film for local television. *Camera-ready* is the term used to describe an ad when it is in its final form and ready for the printing reproduction process.

Why Retailers Like Co-op

Retailers who use co-op funds set aside by manufacturers can expand their advertising budgets. Without these funds, some retailers could not advertise at all. Estimates for retail advertising support through manufacturers' cooperative programs run between $3 to $4 billion a year.[7] Here's how a typical co-op program works.

First, let us assume that a department store handles American Tourister luggage. According to the co-op agreement, the store is permitted a total of 2

[7]Interview with Frank Hennessey, bureau vice president for cooperative sales, *Selling News*, March 1976, p. 1.

FIGURE 2-6
Kick-off ad in a series for Halls department store in Kansas City tied in with a concurrent jazz promotion run by the Crown Center Shopping Mall. Dramatic use of headline and white space directs the readers' attention to some of the specialized areas within the store. Buyers for each department work closely with the advertising and sales promotion staff of the store for all campaigns.

percent of its yearly net sales (of American Tourister) as an advertising allowance with a 50/50 joint dollar participation in each ad. Thus, if it purchased $10,000 worth of luggage during the year, the store is eligible to receive $200 (2 percent) from the manufacturer *if it spends $200*. The co-op system is set up so that the retailer must always invest a percentage (usually 50 percent) of the store's own money. The rationale of the manufacturer is that retailers who are spending their own money will tend to invest it wisely.

Some manufacturers specify what media retailers may use to be eligible for co-op funds. Others specify whether their product—under the arrangement—may appear with other merchandise or only with noncompeting items. To receive co-op funds after the ad has run, retailers must submit copies of the reprinted ad, proof of broadcast (usually delivered in writing by the station), and paid invoices to the advertising department of the cooperating manufacturer. Logic explains how retailers with large sales volumes (such as department stores) are able to enjoy substantial cooperative advertising support from manufacturers (Figure 2-7).

Dealer Combinations

Some retailers simply do not purchase enough merchandise from one manufacturer to qualify for very much under the co-op advertising program. They can therefore do very little individual advertising. One solution is to follow the lead of a group of nine hardware store dealers in the Milwaukee area. They banded together to run a small two-column ad featuring a Stanley

FIGURE 2-7
Typical data made available to local media as a sales aid for calling on retailers. Co-op funds, once aggressively pursued only by local newspapers, are now fair game for radio, television, and some magazines. Source: Newspaper Advertising Bureau.

-5-

NEWSPAPER ADVERTISING BUREAU - December, 1977

MFG/BRAND	PRODUCT(s)	PROGRAM/ MARKETS	ACCRUAL BASED ON...	PARTICIPA- TION	OTHER MEDIA	REMARKS/EXP. DATE	HOW TO GET PAID
RAM Golf Corp. 1501 Pratt Blvd. Elk Grove Village Illinois 60007 312/956-7500 (retail)	golf equip- ment	all	2% of net shipments from 8/1/77 thru 7/31/78	50/50	radio,TV catalog, flyers, direct mail, circular	ads must prominently feature RAM & speci- fied brand names of RAM equipment ---	send full page tearsheet with newspaper invoice to: RAM Golf Co-op c/o The Advertising Checking Bureau, Inc. P.O. Box 1919 Memphis, TN 38101
Red Devil Inc. 2400 Vauxhall Rd. Union, NJ 07083 (retail)	paint sundries	all	3% of pur- chases made during pre- ceding cale- ndar quarter	50/50	radio,TV	must include brand name 'Red Devil' -- no competitive ads -- art & copy materials available -- no production costs covered	send full page tearsheet & newspaper invoice within 30 days from date ad is run to: Sales Promotion Coordinator Red Devil, Inc. 2400 Vauxhall Road Union, NJ 07083

hammer retailing at $4.99. The ad named all nine dealers and cost them each ⅑ of the total, of which 50 percent was picked up by Stanley under its co-op plan.

An aggressive group of Mobil service stations combined recently in a cooperative $65,000 promotion on tires. The results: a 73 percent increase in sales, a 90 percent tire revenue increase over the previous year.[8]

Setting Up a Co-op Program

By and large, the supervisory time devoted to co-op advertising depends on the volume of the store's business. The Revco Discount chain, headquartered in northern Ohio, requires a full-time manager and staff to cope with the paperwork generated by their yearly sales of $658 million.[9] A medium-sized furniture or department store can probably handle all the details with existing staff.

Here is a plan by which a typical retailer can design a co-op program for the store:

1 Check purchase orders and list major suppliers according to their sales.
2 Contact these key suppliers or their distributors.
3 Determine the amount of co-op monies available based on purchases and the manufacturer's ground rules.
4 Plan to use the co-op monies to reinforce overall sales and advertising objectives.
5 Request appropriate reproducible advertising material from key co-op suppliers. Sometimes the manufacturer's distributor may warehouse these items.
6 Determine which materials will fit store plans and *use them*. Tailor the rest to store needs. Ask help from media sales representatives, the store's own qualified employees, advertising agency or a freelance consultant. (Be sure to ask about the cost of this assistance.)
7 After the ads have been aired or run, be sure to collect from the co-op manufacturers (Figure 2-8).

OTHER ADVERTISING ALLOWANCES

Some retailers, notably food store chains, receive advertising allowances based entirely on the number of cases of any product they purchase. Known as "per case allowances," these monies may be spent as the retailer wishes. The retailer may not even have to use the money for advertising at all. Automobile manufacturers have evolved a system of their own called "per unit allowances" to support dealers. Each dealer is required to contribute to a special cooperative fund—perhaps $9 per car—based on the number of cars purchased from the manufacturer. In turn, the auto maker contributes a set amount per car—perhaps $3—to the fund. The funds are spent at the local

[8]*Co-oportunities* (a report), Newspaper Advertising Bureau, March 1976.
[9]*Annual Report* of Revco D.S., Inc., 1977, p. 3.

```
REQUEST FOR CO-OP INFORMATION FROM _____
                                    (dealer's name & address)
                                    _____
                                    _____
Name & address of manufacturer      _____
                                    _____
                                    _____

        To help us in setting our ad-
        vertising program for the year,
        would you please indicate the
        terms of your cooperative ad-
        vertising allowances.
    1. Do my purchases meet your requirements for a co-op allowance?
            ____YES         ____NO (If NO,kindly return form.)
    2. How do you compute co-op funds for my store?
        _____
        _____

    3. How long a period may I use to base accrual of co-op funds?
        ____calendar year(Jan. 1-Dec. 31) ____a year from first purchase
        ____my fiscal year               ____other_____
    4. Based on my purchases to date, how much do I have avail-
       able to spend? $_____
    5. What is the extent of your co-op participation: ____50/50
       ____75/25    ____100% paid    ____other
    6. What proof do you require that ad was run?_____
        _____
    7. How do we get paid?_____
    8. Are all media eligible for co-op? ____newspapers ____radio
       ___TV    ____direct mail    ___circulars    ____billboards
       ___yellow pages    ___ newspaper classified

                    Please return this form with the
                    signature and title of a person in
                    authority. Thank you.

                    _____
                              name
                    _____
                              title
                    _____
                              phone
```

FIGURE 2-8
A coop form to
assist retailers in
arranging for
advertising materials
and financing from
their suppliers.

level under the direction of the automaker but in consultation with dealers. This fund is separate from the automakers' national advertising budget.

A variation of the automakers' plan operates in franchised fast-food restaurants. In fact, many of the national chains (McDonald's, Burger King, Kentucky Fried Chicken) will not sell a local franchise to an investor without an advertising allowance built in as part of the agreement. The average percentage hovers near 3 percent of gross sales. These advertising funds plus a corporate contribution are divided according to both national and regional demands.

Some dealers spend hardly any time developing their own advertising plans. They depend almost entirely on their suppliers for suggestions. There is a certain amount of logic to this course of action in most cases, because suppliers know the best selling seasons for their products. Yet retailers should make the ultimate decisions about where and when to advertise. They should offer advice on the relative effectiveness of local media. They should also try to spend ad dollars when people are ready to buy.

Figure 2-9 dramatizes an unplanned and a planned system. Note that under one arrangement (planned), the retailer spends money when buying is taking place; under the other (unplanned), spending lacks any relationship to sales. Retailers who don't plan do a disservice to their employees by failing to support them when they need help the most. They also fail to support them and the business if they make no recommendations to manufacturers on the relative worth of local media. By and large, suppliers appreciate local input.

Astute retailers often plot monthly sales and advertising expenditures on a graph to see how closely they relate to each other. The resulting pattern is used to give direction to their ad budgeting. Here is a typical system.

Budgeting and Timing Plan

1 Check the store's sales ledgers, and write down the amount of last year's sales by months. Add all the figures to determine the store's annual sales.

2 Determine what percentage of annual sales occurred in each month. To do this, divide total annual sales **into each month's sales.** This figure indicates the percent of the year's sales each month represents. For example, if annual sales were $300,000 and December accounted for $30,000, then the percentage of annual sales represented by December would be $30,000 ÷ $300,000, or 10 percent

3 On a piece of graph paper with twelve boxes across representing January through December and twenty boxes vertically representing percent of sales from zero through twenty, plot the monthly percentages. Use a straight line to connect points.

4 Then follow the same procedure for advertising expenditures, by month. Plot these on the graph, and connect with a dotted line.

FIGURE 2-9
In the planned graph, the retailer has coordinated sales and advertising. In the unplanned graph, monthly advertising expenses have little to do with the actual sales activity of the store. Thus, advertising fails to provide the proper support at the right time.

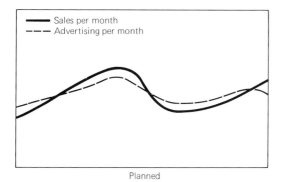

Planned

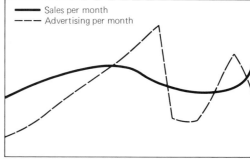

Unplanned

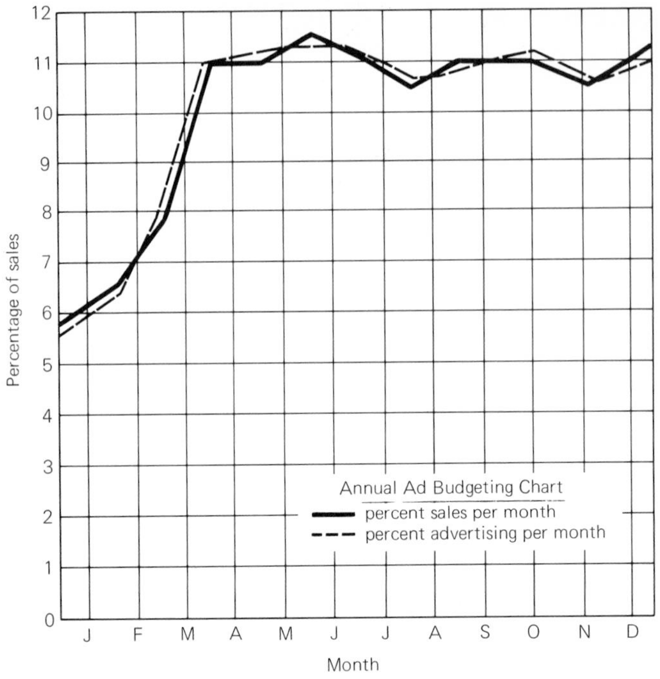

FIGURE 2-10
The annual ad
budgeting chart fixes
a specific percentage
of the budget to
coincide with
expected monthly
sales.

5   If both lines, dotted and straight, are fairly close to one another, the store's
advertising and sales are well-matched. If not, changes should be made to increase
effectiveness of ad timing. (Figure 2-10).

WHEN NOT TO ADVERTISE

There are times when the retailer would be wise not to advertise:

1   When the product is mediocre. In this case, advertising merely moves the
merchandise into the hands of the disgruntled "round-trip" customer—out of the
store and back! The "roundtripper" can cost the retailer time, money, anguish,
and worse.
2   When personnel are ill-prepared, untrained, or ill-disposed. To boast of good
service under these conditions is to court irritation.
3   When the advertised products are in short supply. People tend to take out their
frustrations on both the retailer and the manufacturer when the advertised goods
are not at hand. They may buy a competitive product, perhaps at a different store.

Advertising is not a cure-all. It can't hide the fact that the retailer's
personnel are surly and more concerned with coffee breaks than with serving
customers. It cannot gloss over the fact that merchandise is old, stained, out of
style. It can't make amends for an inflexible bookkeeping system that
constantly insults customers by sending them dunning letters. It cannot make

FIGURE 2-11

These retail ads are part of a cooperative promotion kit created and prepared by the manufacturer. The ads arrived at the retail stores in the form of glossy reproductions called "slicks." Slicks are handed over to the local newspapers with the request: "Put my name at the bottom of the ad and make it BIG."

a success of a poor manager. To expect advertising to right all these wrongs is naive and costly. Only when retailers help make these problems disappear does advertising stand a chance of proving its effectiveness in bringing customers into stores, and in having them return (Figure 2-11).

WORD OF MOUTH—AN ADVERTISING CONSEQUENCE

Word-of-mouth advertising is a welcome bonus for any retailer. This kind of advertising occurs when one customer tells another good things about a given store. It is, in effect, a testimonial by an independent party. As an unpaid testimonial, word of mouth carries far more weight than any ad. Wall Drug Store in the Black Hills of South Dakota presents an example of word of mouth at its best. The story began when Ted and Dorothy Hustead placed small billboards along the highway advertising free ice water. But the ice water wasn't all the visitors enjoyed. They also appreciated the low-cost meals and the hundreds of souvenirs. Over the years, customers spread the word about the unusual drugstore. Today, Wall Drug Store handles up to 10,000 people a day during the tourist season. The Husteads spend $100,000 a year on advertising signs whose job is to get visitors to stop so they, too, can carry their good impressions to friends and neighbors (Figure 2-12).

Some retailers who do not advertise say they rely on word of mouth for their success. Although it may work in some cases, word of mouth, despite its virtues, is slower than the proverbial rheumatic turtle. Advertising speeds the good word along!

FIGURE 2-12
There is nothing unusually clever or unique in these highway signs telling motorists to stop at Wall Drug. But there is good common sense evident. Along one 45-mile stretch of interstate, there are fifty-three signs. In fact, two men with a truck work nine months of the year servicing signs, while new signs keep two professional painters busy. Advertising has paid off in a big way for this "remote" retailer.

IN SUMMARY

1 Retail advertising informs consumers about the cost and availability of merchandise. It is a necessary part of a retailer's cost of doing business.

2 Without retailers, most people would not find goods readily accessible because it costs too much for manufacturers to sell direct to the ultimate consumer.

3 The money invested by retailers in media helps defray all or part of the true cost of radio and television programming and magazines and newspapers. Readers, for example, pay for less than 10 percent of the total cost of weekly newspapers.

4 Retailers who don't advertise generally give the following reasons: disbelief in advertising's effectiveness, lack of faith in local media, pessimism about unemployment and general economic conditions, unavailability of money for growth, and the mood of consumers.

5 Retailers who do advertise expect an increase in store traffic. They find that advertising helps liquidate surplus merchandise, ties in with trends and fads, and builds reputations.

6 Astute retailers try to avoid a follow-the-leader mentality by designing distinctive ads. These frequently depend upon the retailer's strong points: extent of the line, type of merchandise, price and value of goods, service, knowledge, competence, store hours, repair facilities, and so on.

7 Department stores are usually heavy advertisers in local newspapers and other media. These stores can convey a definite personality by the way they design their ads.

8 Cooperative advertising is an agreement between a manufacturer and a retailer who agree to divide the cost of promoting the manufacturer's product at the local level.

9 Retailers like co-op funds because they allow them to expand their ad budgets. The system is set up so that retailers must always invest a percentage of their own money in the local ads.

10 Retailers can set up a co-op program by contacting their suppliers and determining the monies they have available to them based upon past purchases. A typical formula: 2 or 3 percent of total purchases with 50/50 participation.

11 Other advertising allowances open to some retailers are per case allowances, per unit allowances, and an advertising franchise based upon a percentage of gross sales.

12 Retailers should plan to time their advertising to coincide with actual sales activities.

13 Some conditions militate against advertising: poor product, poor personnel, and inadequate supplies of the advertised product.

14 Although good word-of-mouth advertising is effective as a testimonial from an independent party, paid advertising helps speed the good word along.

CASE STUDY   A Woman's Bank in the Big Apple

On October 16, 1975, the First Women's Bank of New York opened for business. The opening was an adventurous move into a business dominated by men. Like many other retailers—and a bank is a retailer of money—banks know that they need an identity to stand out from the pack. The First Women's Bank is no exception. We turn to Jane Trahey of Trahey Advertising, who handles the account, for the details.

"In an effort to be amusing, the designer of the bank stuck up a huge $1 bill on the barricade which surrounded the bank in its building stage. In place of George Washington on the face of the dollar bill, the designer had substituted Mona Lisa. It created a lot of talk. When the vice president for marketing of the bank and I decided to design our ad campaign, we lifted Mona off the buck and slapped her into every ad we ran.

"The result was high visibility and a constant reminder that no woman had ever graced a buck before. We used it on our annual report, we used it on mailing pieces, we used it to launch ads and follow-ups. It was a very talked-about campaign, considering that we had very few dollars to play with.

"The first ad series ran in the *New York Times.* We ran fifty ads or the equivalent of four full pages on opening day. We used all our important corporate depositors to give the bank instant credibility" (Figure 2-13).

"We then moved to a retail campaign and used real depositors and their pictures plus Mona Lisa" (Figure 2-14).

Currently, the First Women's Bank is using only newspapers to reach the people working, shopping, or living within the bank's immediate area. A special feature of the bank is its "working people's hours," including late evening and Saturday banking. The bank boasts that it "doesn't keep banking hours!"

FIGURES 2-13, 2-14 (p. 77) Women traditionally experience difficulties in obtaining mortgages, loans, and credit cards. Recognizing the need for a bank that would cater to women—as well as to men—the First Women's Bank of New York City adopted Mona Lisa as its identifying symbol and aggressively went to work advertising itself.

"Some of us try to hold
on to positive feelings
about New York—and once in a while, an
enterprising organization helps to cheer those
feelings on. That's what The First Women's
Bank does. It's a bank that doesn't
keep banking hours! Their
tellers are ready and waiting
when you need them,
Saturdays from noon till
four, Mondays and
Thursdays till 5:30 PM.
That's a big plus for
New York City
and for you!"

THE FIRST WOMEN'S BANK

111 E. 57th (at Park) N.Y. 10022 phone 212-644-0670

ARLENE FRANCIS BANKS WITH US.   MEMBER FDIC

QUESTIONS NEEDING ANSWERS

1 Do you think a women's bank will get the support of women? Why? Why not? How about men?

2 If you were the president of the bank, would you restrict your advertising to newspapers? Explain.

3 If it could be proved that money enters and leaves a bank according to a prescribed pattern (during holidays and vacations and at income tax time), would it make sense to prepare a budgeting plan so that advertising and sales (incoming money) are closely matched? Explain.

4 Where a new bank is dominated by several larger, better-known competitors, would it be better not to advertise until you had accumulated enough funds to make a big advertising splash?

5 Would it make any sense for officers of the bank to personally call on small businesses in the area and make bank services known?

STUDENT PROJECT

To see if there is indeed a lack of identity in many retailers' newspaper ads, students might clip several such ads from their weekly or daily newspaper. See how many fail to convey a definite feeling or mood about the store. Then visit the managers of these stores and interview them. See if perhaps there *is* something that is unique about the store that the advertising fails to portray and could.

QUESTIONS ABOUT THE PROJECT

1 After interviewing managers or owners of retail stores, do you get the feeling that they are sensitive to any unique characteristics they might have?
2 How interested do you think retailers are in their advertising? How many paste their ads on windows, counters, or cash registers?
3 What do the retailers you have contacted think of coop funds from the manufacturer? How many of them get involved with coop programs?
4 If you were appointed advertising manager of the stores you visited, what changes would you make in your advertising? Why?

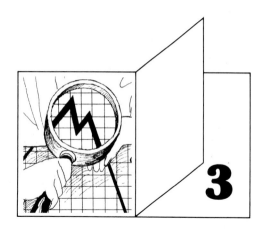

3

BACKGROUNDING:
SETTING THE STAGE

Update The manufacturer and the retailer seldom have the same problems, yet both look to advertising as the magic that makes dreams come true. In the first two chapters, we surveyed the separate and unequal worlds of the national and the local retail advertiser. In this chapter, we take a look at how business people gather information vital to their advertising.

THE MARKET SITUATION

The term "market" is one of the most flexible in advertising! To company advertising managers, it means market identification: who buys or is a prospect for the product. To the sales manager, it means all that plus changes that occurred in the market during the past few years and those expected in the next five. To the market researcher, it means all *that* plus *demographic information* about consumers: age, income, education, sex, and social class.

Business people who talk about a market could mean any or all of the above. They could also mean geographic locations such as the Philadelphia market or the Southwestern market. As we can see, market has many meanings. But the word serves a function for both retailers (local advertisers) and manufacturers (national advertisers).

THE DEALER LOOKS AT THE MARKET

Imagine that several business people have just bought an automobile dealership. As new retailers they are vitally interested in their market. Unfortunately, the men, women, and young adults who make up this market are not theirs exclusively. Other, established car dealers claim the same market and show very little inclination to share the business. They challenge the new dealers with full-page ads in the local paper.

The newcomers' simplest course of action is to respond with ads of their own. But there is a better way: research. The dealers need to discover everything they can about their market. Research may take time, but it is essential for avoiding costly and perhaps fatal surprises.

Sources of Information

American business people are blessed with an abundance of valuable information. It is stored in both likely and unlikely places. A quick check will reveal the following sources of data:

> United States Census
>
> State, county, and municipal records (car ownership documents, voter registration rolls, and the like)
>
> Mailing list rental agencies (listed in the yellow pages)
>
> Local media (newspapers, radio, billboards, and television)
>
> City, professional, and business directories
>
> Telephone books
>
> Trade associations

United States Census　The United States Census is a treasure chest of data. Conducted every ten years, with auxiliary studies in between, the census covers every metropolitan area, city, town, and rural locality. All census material is available free or at token cost from the Superintendent of Documents, Government Printing Office, Washington, D.C. 20402. Volumes available include: most recent population figures, per capita and per household income and sales, automobile ownership per household, savings per household, and employment.

State, County, and Municipal Records　Municipalities, counties, and states require licenses for some products, services, and businesses. Automobile

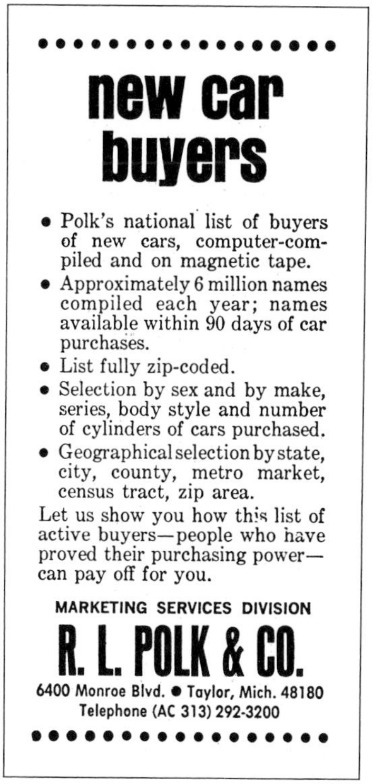

new car buyers

- Polk's national list of buyers of new cars, computer-compiled and on magnetic tape.
- Approximately 6 million names compiled each year; names available within 90 days of car purchases.
- List fully zip-coded.
- Selection by sex and by make, series, body style and number of cylinders of cars purchased.
- Geographical selection by state, city, county, metro market, census tract, zip area.

Let us show you how this list of active buyers—people who have proved their purchasing power—can pay off for you.

MARKETING SERVICES DIVISION

R. L. POLK & CO.

6400 Monroe Blvd. ● Taylor, Mich. 48180
Telephone (AC 313) 292-3200

FIGURE 3-1
Retail car dealers can rent lists of car owners in order to mail advertising literature and special offers. Most major city phone books carry Yellow Page advertisements of rental list brokers.

owners must have state-authorized (and recorded) licenses in order to operate their vehicles. Boat and motorcycle owners must also apply for licenses. Municipal governments regularly issue operator permits to restaurants and bars, licenses for dogs, and the like. The lists containing these records are open to public scrutiny and often become the basis for mailing lists used by retailers and manufacturers.

Mailing List Rental Agencies Companies such as R. L. Polk and R. H. Donnelley rent names and addresses of many specific groups of people such as doctors, educators, and realtors. They and others could provide our new automobile dealership with gummed mailing labels or cards for every car owner within specified areas according to make of car and year (Figure 3-1).

Local Media Local media are usually the most up-to-date sources of customer information. Most large metropolitan daily newspapers have active research departments that develop specific information for both their editorial staff and their advertisers. The broadcast and outdoor media often provide the same valuable information. The Scripps-Howard newspaper chain, for example, conducts inventories of consumer food items on householders' shelves within its markets (Figure 3-2). Grocery stores, for example, could determine what brands to order or avoid. The Newspaper Advertising

FACIAL TISSUE

(% of Net Homes Reporting)

BRANDS	1977	1976	1975	1974	1973
Kleenex	41.7	39.9	39.9	49.9	41.4
Puffs	35.3	36.4	33.6	22.5	27.0
Scott					
Scotties	13.0	14.5	12.8	16.8	22.5
Lady Scott	1.2	.7	1.0	.7	1.0
Heritage House (Fisher-Fazio)	5.0	6.4	5.6	5.5	4.5
Edwards	1.9	2.4	–	–	–
Northern	1.0	1.8	1.5	–	–
Other Brands	7.4	5.4	12.2	11.3	12.8
No Brand Stated	1.2	1.8	1.8	2.2	.4

FIGURE 3-2
A grocer can see at a glance what brands customers and prospects prefer. Scripps-Howard Pantry Studies, conducted in fourteen major cities in the United States, are available to the chain's advertisers and prospects.

Bureau, Inc.,[1] in representing newspapers across the country, provides its membership with up-to-date news of consumer buying trends. Its reports are particularly valuable for determining which months are best for advertising and selling specific merchandise, from automobiles to girdles.

City, Professional, and Business Directories City directories are usually available in municipal libraries, airports, and bus stations. Alphabetically arranged, they provide names and addresses of all the people in the community. They also indicate type of employment. Directories of lists of members are usually available from business and professional organizations such as advertising clubs, Rotary societies, dental societies, chambers of commerce, and the like. Members usually share some common characteristic, be it high income, love of sports, or community interests.

Telephone Books Reissued every year, telephone books reduce an advertiser's percentage of incorrect names and addresses. In some areas, the

[1]485 Lexington Avenue, New York, N.Y. 10017.

first three digits of a phone number help locate names for phone and mail contact. Postal ZIP Codes are a further source of aid.

Trade Associations Normally of greater interest to manufacturers than to retailers, many trade associations are small offices staffed by an executive secretary and several assistants. Funded by dues from members, they function to protect the economic welfare of their own group. There are trade associations devoted to hardware, recreational vehicles, rubber products, food chains, and discount stores. Often they can provide per capita information about consumer purchases and buying trends as well as the best-selling lines of merchandise by month—in short, a buyer profile. Some trade associations report average profit margins and the typical dealers' ratio of assets to liabilities; others provide advertising-to-sales percentages, a most helpful statistic. Gale Research Company's *Encyclopedia of Associations* has detailed information about 13,000 trade associations, professional societies, labor unions, and patriotic organizations.

Miscellaneous Sources The Midwest Farm Paper Unit, Chicago, Illinois— the administrative arm of five state magazines aimed at farmers in Illinois, Indiana, Wisconsin, Iowa, Nebraska, the Dakotas, and Minnesota—publishes an annual buyers' intentions survey (Figure 3-3). Over a hundred items are featured by state in each study. Enterprising retailers in these states can learn what the farmers in their areas are planning to buy. Not only farm implement dealers but also hardware, appliance, auto, and truck dealers and even travel agencies can get a feel for this rural market and plan accordingly. *Survey of Buying Power* is an annual that provides retail sales per household and per person in every county and metropolitan area in the country. The list includes sales of food, general merchandise, apparel, furniture and appliances, automotive supplies, gasoline, drug, lumber, building materials, and hard-ware.[2]

THE MANUFACTURER LOOKS AT THE MARKET

The sources of ready information available to the consumer products manufacturer are even more extensive than those for the retailer. The most accessible are:

Governmental departments and executive agencies.
Media data and research (magazines, newspapers, billboards, television, radio).
Industry and association studies.

---

[2]"Survey of Buying Power," *Sales and Marketing Management Magazine*, New York.

1978 Dakota Farm Buying Intentions

SURVEY METHOD—In October, 1977, THE FARMER wrote to 1,150 Dakota farmers, asking them what building they would do and what equipment they would buy in 1978. These farm families were asked to place a check mark after each item in the questionnaire that they planned to buy in 1978. They were asked to check only the intended purchase of new items except where "used" items were specified. Men were asked to answer the questions on farm buildings and equipment; women were asked questions related to the house, home furnishings and home equipment.

Names of those to whom questionnaires were mailed were computer selected by perfect random sampling from THE FARMER's circulation list so as to assure a valid cross-section of Dakota subscribers. Replies were received from 452 women and from 464 men.

Based on this sample, potentials for each item were estimated by multiplying the percentage figures by the 82,500 Dakota farms.

ITEMS FOR THE FARM HOME and FAMILY LIVING

HOME

Plan to build new home	4.9	4,010
Plan to buy new mobile home	.4	363

Paint Home:

Inside	34.3	28,289
Outside	35.4	29,197

General Improvements to Home:

Air conditioning—		
Central system	2.7	2,186
Room unit(s)	4.4	3,663
Carpeting	19.5	16,055
Floor tile	6.6	5,470
Heating system—		
Electric heating system	2.7	2,186
Furnace	4.0	3,284
Heat Pump	1.5	1,271
Room or space heater	3.8	3,102
Solar heat	1.3	1,089
Wood or combination wood	6.6	5,470
Insulation	15.3	12,590
Linoleum	12.4	10,214
Roofing	10.6	8,753
Siding	7.1	5,833
Water heater—		
Electric	7.3	6,023
LP gas	.9	726
Oil	.7	545
Wall paneling	14.4	11,864
Water softener	5.1	4,191

APPLIANCES and HOME FURNISHINGS

Clothes dryer—electric	7.5	6,204
Clothes dryer—LP gas	.9	726
Food freezer	6.2	5,107
Dehumidifier	2.2	1,823
Humidifier	5.1	4,191
Kitchen equipment—		
Dishwasher—built-in	4.4	3,663
Dishwasher—portable	2.7	2,186
Range—electric	8.6	7,112
Range—LP gas	2.4	2,005
Microwave oven	10.4	8,572
Refrigerator	6.9	5,651
Organ	1.8	1,452
Piano	1.8	1,452
Sewing machine	8.0	6,567
Television set—black & white	4.2	3,465
Television set—color	10.0	8,209
Washing machine—automatic	9.7	8,027
Washing machine—wringer type	3.1	2,549

FAMILY VACATIONS

Vacation trip(s) in 1978	59.5	49,096
Spring	5.3	4,373
Summer	24.6	20,254
Fall	15.3	12,590
Winter	17.5	14,413
Vacation out of state	51.5	42,521
Vacation out of continental USA	5.8	4,744

Vacation & Recreation Equipment:

Airplane	1.1	908
All terrain vehicle	1.1	883
Boat	1.3	1,089
Minibike	.4	355

Motor home	1.5	1,271
Motorcycle	1.5	1,238
Outboard motor for boat	.4	363
Pickup camper	3.8	3,102
Rifle	4.1	3,374
Shotgun	2.2	1,774
Snowmobile	3.4	2,838
Swimming pool	.7	545
Travel trailer	1.1	908

FARM BUILDINGS and EQUIPMENT

New Buildings and Improvements:

Dairy Barn and Equipment—		
Confinement building	.2	173
Free stall with milking parlor	.2	173
Loafing shed with milking parlor	.4	355
Stanchion type	.6	528
Automatic silage feeding system	.4	355
Barn cleaner—mechanical	.2	173
Manure stacker	—	—
Milking system—		
Bucket type	.2	173
Pipeline—parlor	.4	355
Pipeline—stanchion barn	1.1	883
Portable—stanchion barn	.2	173
Stanchions	.2	173
Milk House and Equipment—		
New milk house	.9	710
Milk cooler, bulk—new	.4	355
Milk cooler, bulk—used	1.3	1,064
Space heater—electric	.4	355
Water heater—electric	1.5	1,238
Water heater—LP gas	.2	173
Water softener	.2	173

First figure is round percentage of replies; second figure is projection to number of Dakota farms.

FIGURE 3-3

Reports like these are issued annually by some bimonthly farm publications. They can be a definite means of securing business for retailers in farm belts. They can also alert manufacturers to the need to concentrate advertising in specific states.

Directories and reference works.

University research.

Governmental Departments and Executive Agencies There are over seventy-five governmental departments and executive agencies at the federal level. They include the Bureau of Labor Statistics; the Bureau of the Census; the Bureau of Manufacturers; the Bureau of Alcohol, Tobacco and Firearms; the Council of Economic Advisers; the National Park Service; the Marketing and Consumer Services; and the Bureau of Mines. The information these agencies house is vast. From the various bureaus within the Department of Agriculture alone, for example, a manufacturer can learn about choosing the components that go into designing a country kitchen, laying out a septic system, or discovering what percentage of disposable income Americans spend for food. From the National Park Service, a business can learn about the trends for camping by vehicle or backpacking. From the Department of Commerce, manufacturers can receive pamphlets concerning census figures, specific product use, new inventions available for licensing, and even specific opportunities to sell certain products overseas. Departments within state governments, too, often have information of value. Lists of available publications from governmental agencies and bureaus are sent to citizens upon request from the Superintendent of Documents. Pamphlets are either free or modestly priced.

Media Data and Research There are over 3,000 industrial, trade, and professional publications within the United States. Nearly all develop information about their own specialized fields. For example, the business publication *Hardware Age* prints frequent profiles of hardware store operations. The studies indicate store size, average profit margins, what type of merchandise sells best and most frequently, and the average retail advertising budget. These data can be used by any manufacturer selling to the market. For example, data that reveal that small, portable appliances are beginning to sell well throughout the year instead of only at Christmas time can lead to a completely new promotion and advertising strategy.

Manufacturers can request most studies directly from the appropriate magazines. Generally, the studies contain information not available through public libraries, universities, or chambers of commerce.

Consumer publications from *Woman's Day* to *The New Yorker*, although fewer in number than business publications, provide indispensable research about their readers, listing age, income, education, what they buy, and what they don't. A recent study by *Better Homes and Gardens*, for example, indicated that families eat chicken approximately once a week and hamburgers more frequently. Fish is served perhaps once every two weeks. This type of basic information aids manufacturers of small appliances and operators of franchised fast-food restaurants, among others.

From *Seventeen* magazine[3] come data reflecting what apparel young

---

[3]"Back-to-School Study," *Seventeen*, New York, 1977.

MOST CALLED FOR BRANDS

TABLE WINES

Today, more and more emphasis is placed on gracious living in homes of urban Black consumers. Especially those families who own their own homes, or have designer-decorated apartments. A tastefully decorated home is still the prime "status" achievement of upscale income Black families. Urban Black consumers are good prospects for vintage table wines. "Good" wine served with soul food is a natural.

PREPARED BY THE MARKETING DEPT.

EBONY · JET · Black Stars

Brand Names	Total %	N.Y. and N.J. %	Phila- delphia %	Balti- more %	Wash- ington, D.C. %	At- lanta %	Cleve- land %	De- troit %	Chi- cago %	St. Louis %	New Orleans %	Los An- geles %	San Fran- cisco %	Hous- ton %	Gary %	Pitts- burgh %
Taylor	22.1	23.5	38.8	14.7	37.0	27.1	4.9	9.7	22.7	36.0	50.4	14.3	3.5	30.9	.7	13.6
Manischewitz	14.9	20.1	8.4	30.8	8.1	33.6	4.2	6.3	6.8	3.3	–	33.4	33.2	7.4	–	29.7
Gallo	11.7	11.2	1.7	.9	5.1	2.3	–	29.8	22.1	7.8	19.5	2.3	–	7.4	37.6	2.7
Mogen David	10.3	1.6	1.6	23.0	1.2	10.1	11.1	20.1	15.3	15.3	6.6	1.3	–	13.2	35.4	5.0
The Christian Brothers	8.2	2.2	5.3	5.7	22.7	2.1	–	8.0	12.2	–	5.5	8.5	7.2	6.2	14.6	–
Harvey's	6.1	3.8	21.9	.6	–	1.4	57.6	.1	11.8	10.0	1.3	–	–	–	11.7	12.6
Italian Swiss Colony	6.0	9.8	3.3	1.7	5.3	3.9	–	6.3	6.2	–	1.1	20.1	3.1	7.7	–	8.4
Almaden	3.6	.8	.3	1.3	5.1	1.6	–	1.2	.1	–	5.5	10.0	17.8	10.2	–	–
Dubonnet	3.2	3.4	1.0	.4	.3	5.7	2.8	.3	–	–	–	2.0	31.9	.5	–	.2
Duff Gordon	2.0	5.1	12.2	1.0	.8	.2	–	–	.8	–	1.8	–	3.3	.5	–	2.2
Lancer's	1.4	.8	–	1.2	1.5	3.9	–	.6	1.6	3.7	–	–	–	8.8	–	–
Cadillac Club	.9	–	–	–	–	–	–	9.1	–	–	–	–	–	–	–	–
Paul Masson	.7	.4	.7	1.5	2.4	.9	–	.1	.3	–	–	.5	–	2.3	–	.7
Cask	.6	–	–	–	–	–	–	5.9	–	–	–	–	–	–	–	–
Bardenheier's	.5	–	–	–	–	–	–	.2	–	10.4	–	–	–	–	–	–
Mateus	.5	.2	–	1.2	3.7	–	–	–	–	–	–	–	–	1.1	–	2
Brillante	.5	4.4	.1	–	.4	–	–	–	–	–	–	–	–	–	–	–
Gold Seal	.3	.3	.3	–	.6	1.4	–	.2	–	–	3.3	–	–	–	–	.7
All Others	6.5	12.3	4.6	16.1	6.0	5.7	19.5	2.2	.2	10.2	8.2	7.5	.1	3.9	–	23.7
Total Respondents	100.0	100.0	100.0	100.0	100.0	100.0	100.0	100.0	100.0	100.0	100.0	100.0	100.0	100.0	100.0	100.0

FIGURE 3-4

Using research as a tool, the editors of *Ebony*, *Jet*, and *Black Stars* magazines prove the importance of metropolitan blacks to the consumption of nationally known wines. The purpose of the report is to influence media buyers. In the *Better Homes and Gardens* reader profile, note how often chicken is served in the home. Background information of this type helps advertisers.

CHICKEN

How often do you serve chicken in your home? (Base 869)

53.0%	Once a week
10.9	Once a month
28.9	Twice a month
5.5	Seldom
.6	Never
1.1	No answer

In which ways do you purchase chicken? (Base 869)

64.2	Fresh whole chicken
65.7	Fresh chicken parts
9.9	Frozen whole chicken
13.9	Frozen prepared parts
4.3	Barbecued whole chicken
21.5	Take-out fried chicken parts

women are buying. Clothing manufacturers evaluate this information and try to anticipate trends that they can adapt in both advertising and sales. From *Sports Afield*, manufacturers of fishing lures can sense customers' attitudes through research and statistics. *Ms.*, *Time*, and *Ebony*, just to name a few, all carry specific profiles of their readers, essential reading for manufacturers who advertise. Most consumer magazines offer these studies at no charge to manufacturers (Figure 3-4).

Industry and Association Studies   Often a complete industry made up of competing companies will join together to promote the welfare of all members. The National Electrical Manufacturers Association is such an organization; Automotive Accessories Manufacturers of America is another. These and other groups, manufacturers of products or producers of bulk commodities, study their industry and customers frequently. They pass their findings on to their membership. As an example, the Pan-American Coffee Bureau, funded by international coffee producers, periodically surveys the North American market. When study revealed that staleness significantly affected consumers' pleasure in coffee, the industry developed the pressurized vacuum coffee can and a host of advertising appeals based on freshness. A study also revealed inconsistency of brewing techniques among coffee lovers. This finding inevitably led to the introduction, supported by heavy advertising, of at least a half-dozen automatic brewing machines.

Through its association, the recreational vehicle industry constantly analyzes production and records general consumer interest and sales trends. Toy Manufacturers of the United States, the Potato Chip Institute, The Cotton Council, and many other similar organizations perform comparable research. All this information can improve intelligent decision making *before* advertising begins (Figure 3-5).

Directories and Reference Works   Many states and municipalities publish data on worker productivity, average household income, and percent of home and telephone ownership. *Ayer Directory of Publications* (Newspapers and Periodicals), *Editor & Publisher International Year Book*, and the various *Standard Rate & Data Services* publish valuable consumer demographics each year. Most of these sources are available at public, school, and university libraries. And while you're in the general reference section of the library, it might be wise to check *Readers' Guide to Periodical Literature* and *The Industrial Arts Index* for specific articles of interest that have appeared in recent magazines, both consumer and business. Even *The World Almanac & Book of Facts* has information of value to the manufacturer. For example, among other vital items, recent editions contained major food commodities consumption for the last twenty years, total net income per farm by state, motor vehicle registrations by state, occupational earnings in selected cities, hourly earnings in manufacturing industries, and rankings of United States Standard Metropolitan Statistical Areas (SMSA). The latter can be very

THE LITTLE ENGINE THAT COULDN'T.

Small hands need a big train.

A small child fumbling with a tiny, HO-gauge train is a heart-rending sight. He can't set it on the track, can't hook the cars together, and can't keep it running. That's why Lionel has always made big O-gauge trains ...the big Lionel is scaled right for a youngster's coordination. Because he can handle it with ease, your child will enjoy a big Lionel more than a tiny train that thwarts him at every turn.

Built to last a lifetime.

Small-scale trains are fine for

finicky hobbyists. But when it comes to youngsters' toys, only the strong survive. That's why

Lionel builds a strong, rugged train...for the way young kids play. We build a train that shrugs off train wrecks and derailments...a train that will endure and grow into an absorbing adult hobby.

Don't be misled by price.

A small, fragile train that spends its life in the closet is no bargain. Look for the train that will give your youngsters a lifetime's worth of enjoyment...a big, rugged Lionel.

LIONEL®
Big Trains for Small Hands.

Division of Fundimensions. A division of the General Mills Fun Group, Inc., Mount Clemens, Michigan 48043

As appearing in:
Time
Newsweek
Sports Illustrated
Field & Stream
Outdoor Life
Popular Mechanics
Popular Science
Mechanix Illustrated

FIGURE 3-5
Studies by the Toy Manufacturers of the United States as well as its individual members help develop advertising themes. Lionel ran this ad for parents of children six to eleven.

helpful for selecting marketing and advertising objectives based on raw population figures.

One of the finest one-volume publications, available in most libraries, is *The National Atlas of the United States of America* published by the Department of the Interior. This is a veritable warehouse of statistical information that has been converted into special, individualized maps based on sociocultural patterns: population changes, crime and law enforcement trends, minority and ethnic population pockets, religious preferences and trends, and educational achievements, among others. The secret of finding information is knowing where to look for it; a good place to start is with a pertinent reference.

University Research Research goes on almost at every university and college, and reports on it are usually available for the asking. If sociologists, psychologists, political scientists, home economists, nutritionists, clothing and textile experts, statisticians, and journalists are operating in a nearby university or college, the chances are excellent that business people can locate new research findings on a variety of subjects that can shed further light on the consumer.

SURVEYS

Whenever meaningful information is not readily available to retailers or manufacturers, advertisers may have to search it out. Surveys are one tried and true method for finding things out. Simply put, a reliable survey is an investigative procedure whereby one or more interviewers question selected individuals on a given subject. By questioning a relatively small but well-chosen group, it is possible to determine how large groups—even millions of people—feel about products, services, and ideas. The survey technique of properly selecting the smaller group so that it is representative of the larger group is known as *sampling*. The larger group, in the language of the researcher, is often called the *universe*. Thus a major advantage of the survey is economy; it costs less to query 100 persons than 10,000! And the small sample will represent the larger group if the following conditions are met: everyone in the large group (universe) must have an equal chance of being selected, and every member of the small group must be selected at random.

The Theory and the Practice

Let's say we want to learn what percentage of all students (grade school through college) drink milk with their meals. We could select our small sample at random from students aged six to twenty-two. If we needed a nationwide survey, we'd have to select students in proportion to the distribution of their sex, place of residence, community size, race, religion, and family income among all students. Any or all of these conditions may have a bearing on what our survey uncovers. Our resultant sample group should be an accurate, proportional representation of all students in the fifty states. Whatever this small sample group reveals about drinking milk should hold true for the total student population.

On the other hand, if we are only interested in college students in West and East Coast universities with an average population of over 20,000, then our universe is narrowed considerably. In this case, our sample must be chosen at random from all universities conforming to our qualifications. Samples of this type, a subgroup of a larger, more diverse universe, are called *stratified samples*, but they, too, must be selected at random if their conclusions are to be both sound and valid. If we wished to survey heavy beer drinkers, we'd select our sample from a universe composed of young male adults. We know we should use them from previous studies,[4] and so we stratify our sample by ignoring women of all age groups and older men.

One of the dangers of the random sample technique lies in researchers' overlooking important subgroups who may not be typical of the population at large. If we use our beer example, we can see that a survey of *all* people would include many who do not drink beer at all. The nondrinkers reduce the numerical importance of questions directed to the real beer drinkers. This could divert marketing and advertising strategists away from their prime sales prospects.

Are Surveys Accurate?

Since the early days of national polling, skeptics have criticized the applicability of the random sample. How, they wonder, can a survey of 150 households in, say Cook County, Illinois, tell us what 140,000 households in that county think? Or, how can the carefully designed nationwide sampling poll taken by researcher Elmo Roper accurately reflect the opinions of over 210 million people when his interviewers only contact 1250 households? The answer is that they can, if the polls are set up to meet three major objectives:

A proper sample size based on diversity of respondents

A proper set of questions

An acceptable margin of error (This is important because some advertisers are willing to make decisions if they feel their samples show a 90 to 95 percent accuracy.)

For example, just a week before the presidential election of 1976, the Roper poll and other polls showed that the major candidates were too close to each other in popularity for them to be able to predict a winner. The final vote did, indeed, prove the general accuracy of the polls. Carter received 51.1 and

---

[4]"A History of Packaged Beer and Its Market in the United States" (New York: American Can Company, 1969), p. 28.

TABLE 3-1

HOW LARGE A SAMPLE?
(HOMOGENEOUS POPULATIONS)

Sample size or n	Probable error (%)
100	7
250	5
500	3
1000	2
2000	2

If you want to base your decisions on results that are at least 90 percent accurate, here is a breakdown used rather extensively in the polling business. Accuracy means that the results of your survey will not vary by more or less than the percent of probable error.

Ford 48.9 percent of the popular vote,[5] a scant 2.2 percent difference. Since there is always a built-in error in sampling surveys, this error should be understood right from the beginning. Usually the larger the sample, the smaller the degree of error (Table 3-1).

On occasion, human error can make polls wrong. In the 1948 presidential election, all the leading polls were wrong in predicting that the Republican candidate, Tom Dewey, would defeat Harry Truman. Their predictions were based on a poorly timed final round of interviewing and faulty interpretations of responses. In general, if a survey is properly designed and executed, the chances that the probable error could exceed certain stated percentages are less than 10 chances in 100 (Table 3-1).

Industrial advertisers may discover that the diversity of industry by product, technology, and size of plant may make a reliable sample more difficult to come by. Yet it is still important that the sample be drawn accurately, and that it be large enough.

Survey Methods

There are four popular survey methods: mail, phone, face-to-face, and focus groups. Despite increasing postage rates, the mail survey is still the most economical (Table 3-2). You can select every nth name from a phone book, directory, or other source, provided they make up an appropriate universe for your study. (Nth means any serial number you wish: every third, every ninth, and so on.) The major disadvantage of a mail survey is the characteristically low rate (20 to 40 percent) of questionnaire returns. Respondents have to go through the mechanics of completing and mailing the form. Some research companies can increase returns by enclosing inducements such as pencils, ballpoint pens, rulers, coins, teabags, and even small packets of coffee (Figure 3-6).

[5]"Election Statistics," *World Almanac & Book of Facts*, (New York: Newspaper Enterprise Association, 1977), p. 42.

Family Products' Information Service
Box 286
Spring Park, MN   55384

Dear Mother-to-be:

We have been asked by a manufacturer of baby supplies to get
the opinions of Mothers-to-be about the three products described
in this envelope.

The enclosed quarter dollar is a token of my appreciation for
your time in reading and responding to this request.

Here's what I'd like you to do.

    (1)   Open this envelope and read the descriptions of
           the three different products. Please do this now.

    (2)   After reading the materials, please put all three
           pages back in this envelope.

    (3)   In about a week, an interviewer will telephone to
           ask for your opinions about products for the baby.
           <u>Please keep this envelope (with the materials inside
           it) near the phone</u> so that you can refer to it when
           the interviewer calls.

You will receive a gift for your new baby in return for your
assistance. This gift will be mailed to you shortly after the
telephone interview.

Thank you for your assistance. Please be assured there is no
selling in any way associated with this request - we are only
interested in your frank opinions about baby products.

                Cordially,

                Ruth Edwards

                Ruth Edwards

RE/cb

FIGURE 3-6
Market researchers use many techniques to help clients arrive at sound advertising strategies. This letter served to introduce an ad from each of three competitive paper diaper manufacturers. The objective of the research was to discover which advertising approach attracted the majority of the mothers-to-be. The 25¢ piece was designed to increase the number of responses. (Courtesy Frevert & Hall Research Associates.)

TABLE 3-2
COMPARISON OF SURVEY METHODS

Mail	Phone	In person
Most economical	Next most economical	Most expensive
People most accessible	People relatively accessible	People least accessible; may require other visits
Easy and cheap to reach wide areas	Relatively easy and cheap to reach wide areas	More difficult and costly to reach wide areas
Respondent rapport* least acceptable	Respondent rapport relatively good	Best rapport of the three methods
Least complete or usable returns	Better returns	Most complete and usable returns
Reasoned responses are relatively thoughtful and considered	The nature of the method leads to reasoned responses that are the least thoughtful	Reasoned responses are adequate but not quite as good as those of the mail questionnaire

*In interviewing industrial buyers and specifiers, rapport may be more difficult to establish between respondents and interviewers because of their uncommon level of technical understanding. Also, the place of contact is usually the workplace, not the home.

Phone surveys are usually the fastest to conduct. Decided assets in phone interviewing are a personable voice and an ability to gauge the sincerity of the respondent. Phone surveys have the disadvantage of contacting respondents who may say anything just to be rid of the questioner. Local phone surveys done by local people are usually the second most economical kind of survey. WATS (wide area telecommunication service) lines are available to large-volume users of the telephone who pay a specific bulk rate for unlimited (or limited) calls. WATS, characterized by the 800 area code number, has become a popular way to interview people coast-to-coast from one central location (Table 3-2).

Face-to-face interviews are the best and most expensive survey method. Interviewers question only those people selected in the sample. (A mailed report could reflect opinions of others in a household.) Also, skilled interviewers can make sure questions are properly understood and answered. Off-the-cuff comments by respondents can prove extremely valuable to advertisers if they are recorded by the interviewer. Some national firms who regularly conduct research estimate a professional face-to-face interview at $16 or more per respondent (Table 3-3).

Focus group surveys are becoming increasingly popular with advertisers. Groups can range from five consumer panels of 160 people each, as when Gillette tested its Trac II razor system,[6] to ten or twelve homemakers judging a shopping center. Advertisers discover these advantages in focus groups: (1) immediate responses, (2) respondents who can build on one another's comments, and (3) respondents who often express real in-depth feelings on a

[6]"Gillette's Trac II: The steps to success," presentation by William G. Salatich, vice chairman, Gillette Company, to business students at Boston University, November 12, 1971.

TABLE 3-3

INTERVIEWING COSTS BY SURVEY METHODS

Method	Cost per interview
Mail	$ 8.00
Personal	16.00
Phone (wide area telephone lines, WATS)	21.00*

Costs include data processing and analysis and are based on a twenty-minute interview of 300 persons.
Source: B.R. Panettiere, Director, Marketing Research Services, General Foods Corp., White Plains, N.Y.
*Local phone survey costs are estimated to be considerably less expensive than WATS.

wide range of pertinent subjects. The major disadvantages are that one or two talkative panel members may dominate the session, and that the panel may not be at all representative of all shoppers.

Pretesting

Once the researcher has formulated the questions, it is wise to pretest them in a few interviews with the types of persons to be included in the survey sample. This precaution helps to fine-tune the wording of the questions and to make other revisions.

Businesses don't have to confine themselves to random samples. They can ask readers to answer and return questionnaires printed in newspaper or magazine ads. They can pass out questionnaires in stores or question customers directly. A built-in disadvantage of these methods is that the results cannot be accurately extended to the whole population. However, if a survey is what businesses require, they need to know how to construct one.

THE SURVEY MODEL

The purpose of a survey is to get meaningful results (Figure 3-7). Questions that antagonize respondents so that they lie or refuse to answer detract from the value of the survey. A good technique for encouraging meaningful responses is to begin with nonthreatening questions after interviewers have introduced themselves (in a personal interview) or provided reasons for the survey (in a mailed questionnaire). In a food or personal care study aimed at women, interviewers might ask a respondent whether she lives in the city or country, whether she likes sports, and so forth. If researchers are surveying men to learn about deodorant-buying habits, an easy lead-off question might be, "Where do you buy most of your soaps and other personal health products? At a grocery store, a drugstore, or some other place?" Opening with a question about deodorants can create hostility.

A follow-up survey question might be, "Which of the following personal health products do you seldom buy at a drugstore: soap, detergents, deodorants, toothpaste?"

With deodorants introduced as one of several products, it is now safe to move ahead and ask the basic questions, "How often do you buy deodorants? Once a week? Once a month? Once every two to three months? Never?"

In all cases, the developer of the survey should try to avoid creating a biased question that will influence the response. Congressional representatives are often guilty of asking biased questions such as "Do you favor godless socialism?" (Table 3-4).

HOW LARGE MANUFACTURERS DO RESEARCH

With their larger resources, national manufacturers can usually afford to hire an outside research company or do the work with an expanded staff. Many

```
                    Sample Consumer Survey

                                       Cottage Cheese

        Male_____   Female_____


        1. Do you eat cottage cheese?  Yes____   No____

              Occasionally?____   Frequently?_____

        2. Do you eat it for diet reasons?____   Or taste?_____

              Nutrition?____   Weight Control?___  Convenience?____

        3. What brand do you buy regularly?_____

        4. Why do you choose this brand?_____

        5. Have you tried other brands?_____

        6. Do you prepare it   as a salad?_____   as a filling

              in cakes or pastries?____   as another way?_____

        7. When do you normally eat cottage cheese?_____

              With meal?_____   As a snack?___ _____

        8. Is there anything you don't like about cottage cheese?

              _____

                           Thank You.
```

FIGURE 3-7
A typical one-page consumer survey questionnaire. The questions are easy and pose no threat to the respondent.

TABLE 3-4

SAMPLE RETAIL SURVEY (HARDWARE)

To our customers: The purpose of this survey is to discover your hardware needs for the coming year so we can serve you better. Would you take a few minutes to fill out the questionnaire? Thank you.

1. Do you live in (name city or town)? _____ Yes _____ No _____ Other _____
2. How many years have you lived here? _____ 0–1 _____ 1–3 _____ 3–5 _____ 5–10 _____ over 10
3. How often do you purchase (type of goods) for yourself or your family in all stores?
   _____ once a week _____ every other week _____ once a month
   _____ other _____
4. How often do you buy gift items (small appliances, sporting goods, etc.) in *all* stores?
   _____ once a week _____ every other week _____ once a month
   _____ other _____
5. Which of the following items do you plan to buy in the next six months?
   _____ Hand tools _____ Power tools Type _____
   _____ Paint _____ Nails, screws, bolts
   _____ Lawn mower _____ Snow blower _____ Vacuum cleaner
   _____ Plumbing supplies: washers, faucets, toilet tank accessories
   _____ Electrical supplies: wire, switches, sockets, bulbs
   _____ Sports equipment for: _____ tennis _____ racketball _____ baseball
   _____ football _____ basketball _____ badminton _____ fishing _____ sledding
   _____ ice skating _____ other _____
   _____ Small appliances _____ automatic coffee maker _____ hair dryer
   _____ hamburger maker _____ french fryer _____ electric shaver _____ slow cooker, crockpot type _____ pizzamaker _____ other _____

6. Please rate this store *compared to other stores of its type.* (The farther you check to the right, the better you think it is; the farther to the left, the poorer.)

SERVICE

Poorest   Best

GOODS IN STOCK

Poorest   Best

BRANDS AND QUALITY YOU PREFER

Poorest   Best

PRICES

Poorest   Best

7. Please complete this sentence: I WISH HARDWARE STORES WOULD

_____

_____

Note: This prototype survey can be altered easily to suit almost any kind of retail business. The function of the rating scale is to assign a numerical weight to each box. Very low equals 5; very high equals 100. Each box after the first increases in value by 5. The function of open-ended Question 7 is to uncover specific problems and grievances of customers.

FIGURE 3-8
Procter & Gamble's classroom approach trains its market researchers to conduct valid and reliable interviews. The company feels there is an art to asking questions, and that a good research-designed survey means nothing if the execution is inadequate.

large companies support permanent market research staffs. According to the American Marketing Association, manufacturers of consumer goods spent $1.072 million as the yearly mean marketing research budget.[7] As an example, one extremely large food processor and distributor, spends over 0.7 percent of sales for its marketing research. Procter & Gamble, with sales over $8 billion, employs over 200 men and women in learning about the needs of the American consumer (Figure 3-8). During the course of an average year, Procter & Gamble turns out about 900 individual advertising/marketing/consumer research reports, which entail interviews with close to 2 million respondents—homemakers, children, teenagers, career men and women, doctors and other professionals—from every state and every demographic stratum.

For other companies with smaller sales volumes, independent consultants are available. Home Testing Institute[8] is a typical research service. Its carefully selected panel of 40,000 families represents all incomes, geographical areas, educational levels, races, and religions. Such services will pretest acceptance of new foods, new and old package designs, even advertising appeals. There are services that record on a national and regional level the daily purchases of goods among selected samples of women. McCollum/Spielman & Company[9] of Great Neck, New York, pretests consumer

[7]"687 Companies spent $325 million for marketing research in 1978," American Marketing Association, 1978.
[8]Home Testing Institute, Garden City Park, N.Y.
[9]"Advertising Control/Television," McCollum/Spielman & Company, Inc., Great Neck, N.Y.

FIGURE 3-9
A carefully selected studio audience records its reactions to a battery of television commercials. Often, when audience reactions toward the commercial are unfavorable, it will be altered and made more palatable. Considering the high cost of purchasing television time, pretesting commercials makes good sense. (Courtesy McCollum/Spielman & Company.)

reactions to television commercials, as does Audience Studios, Inc. of Los Angeles (Figure 3-9).

In-Store Sales Testing

Some manufacturers regularly place new products on selected grocers' shelves. Not only are the products themselves up for study, but so are the label designs. On occasion, even supporting placards, displays, and banners—which we call *point-of-purchase advertising*[10]—are studied. In other cases, manufacturers do no supportive advertising in order to see how well the product will move without it.

HOW ADVERTISERS RESPOND TO MARKET RESEARCH

Once the research has been completed, tabulated, and summarized, it is time to act on it. Advertisers must ask themselves whether the results are plausible. Will they conflict with previous company philosophy? If so, how should the

---

[10]"Point-of-purchase advertising" refers to the material displayed in a retail store to stimulate sales.

company reconcile opposing points of view? If the company's latest studies show its major target audience as women eighteen to twenty-four, where once it was women twenty-five to thirty-five, this information should be relayed to the advertising department so it can tailor ads to that age bracket. If company studies show that most people install their own auto air filters instead of relying on auto dealers and service stations, then the company must face the fact that advertising *solely* to tradespeople is no longer an intelligent course of action. (Advertising to tradespeople will be discussed in a subsequent chapter.)

How advertisers respond to the information uncovered by market research says a lot about the company's commitment to progress. Some companies and institutions will initiate surveys at a moment's notice but never act on what they find. Dismissing these, there are innumerable examples of how research proved to be the catalyst for more effective advertising. Two will make the point. The United States Department of Health, Education and Welfare (HEW) had learned through research that one in ten Americans has high blood pressure. Their studies also indicated that only 29 percent of this group were being adequately treated. The Advertising Council, with the encouragement of HEW, took on the job of informing the American public that high blood pressure is a major cause of death. Within a relatively short period, mortality rates of hypertension related to cardiovascular disease declined sharply (Figure 3-10).

Here's another example. Government and business statistics have documented the emergence of the emancipated man and woman (under thirty-five) and their social relationships. These relationships have developed into a variety of lifestyles that represent good sales opportunities for, among others, a chain of forty-three department stores spread throughout five Western states, The Broadway. The Broadway's advertising is directed away from the conventional because it recognized the changes going on in the marketplace. According to The Broadway's advertising manager, "The ads show people in activities that use the products we are promoting. We're featuring live-action photography and a sort of colloquial copy so that this special group will identify with the ads and The Broadway. We have what they need and we want them to know it. The ads all incorporate the slogan 'We know who you are. We know where you live because we live there, too!' " (Figure 3-11).[11]

CONFLICTING RESEARCH STUDIES

Sometimes it's hard to act on market research because of conflicting results. In a recent promotional bulletin, *Ebony* magazine[12] reminded potential

[11]Interview with Claire Segal, promotion manager, *Selling News*, February 1978, p. 1.
[12]"Urban Black Consumer Market," Market Research Report, *Ebony*, 1972, p. 2.

FIGURE 3-10

A recent ad campaign to fight the tragedy of death because of high blood pressure came about when research pointed out the high incidence of high blood pressure among Americans. (Courtesy The Ad Council.)

Use the Shredding Blade for:
Vegetables and fruits for salads.
baked goods, and to grate
semi-soft cheese
and chocolate

Use the Plastic Mixing Blade for:
Sauces, dips, spreads,
mayonnaise, baked goods.
eggs, whipped cream.

Use the Slicing Blade for:
Fruit, cooked meat, raw meat,
French-cut beans, Julienne
cut vegetables.

Use the Chopping Blade for:
Vegetables, fruits, nuts. Or grate
hard cheeses with it. Use it
to crumb bread, chop meats
(cooked and raw), for
whipping, mixing.

Farberware's new Food Processor shreds, slices, blends, chops, mixes. For just $140.

Watch the flashing blades, watch 'em. It's Farberware's new kitchen cut-up and it's almost as fast as the speed of light. And it's so versatile, it's scary. Like it slices red, raw meat quickly for wok cookery. It purees green tomatoes for Green Sauce over Mexican chicken in a flash. And it mixes up the best brownies you've ever put a tooth to. Plus it whips, crumbs, grates, mashes, grinds. What a fantastic machine. Bowl, cover, 3 stainless steel blades, 1 plastic blade, cookbook included. Small Electrics, 95.

See this Food Processor demonstrated from 11:00 to 4:00
Grossmont, February 4; Chula Vista and Fashion Valley, February 5

The Broadway

Monday thru Friday 10am-9pm, Saturday 10am-6pm, Sunday Grossmont & Fashion Valley 11:30am-5pm, Chula Vista 12 noon — 5 pm
Grossmont Center, La Mesa 465-1121; Chula Vista and H 427-1161; Fashion Valley, 275 Fashion Valley Road 291-6011

FIGURE 3-11
Cutaway drawings, reasons-why copy, and how-to-do-it information are all part of the enticing ads this chain of Western department stores put before special customer groups that research identified as the new style setters.

advertisers that "black Americans are the heaviest per capita U.S. consumers of distilled spirits and other alcoholic beverages." In a similar report for *its* advertisers, *U.S. News & World Report*[13] stated that household heads who completed one or more years of college drank or served more liquor at home than those without college. It also stated that household heads making $15,000 a year or more are likelier to serve liquor at home than those making less. Blacks comprise a minority among college students and among those who earn $15,000 a year or more. Are the key words "drank or served liquor

[13]"The Market for Liquor," Market Research Report, *U.S. News & World Report*, 1975.

at home?'' No doubt *The U.S. News & World Report* study is accurate for its audience of mostly white professionals and business people. But it apparently neglects liquor consumption by blacks, an important omission to a distiller.

Conflicting market research studies require an evaluation and judgment. Ask these questions: Does the research have specific application to my problem? Do the conclusions appear logical? Who conducted the study? Are they competent and reliable? Is there an obvious bias? Is the sample representative? Does it include groups besides the ones I'm interested in and in what proportion? Do the questions ask what I really want to know?

Answers to these questions will make decision making easier. They permit advertisers to use insights of research to move ahead, to plan meaningful advertising, to select the proper media, to determine when to schedule their ads. Most of all, the answers to these qualifying questions about a company's market research will help advertisers avoid serious errors.

IN SUMMARY

1 The term ''market'' has many meanings. It can identify a geographical location, customers, and prospective customers. It can also concentrate on specific demographic items such as age, income, education, sex, and social class. ''Market'' is often more directional than precise.

2 Some of the best sources of information for both retailer and national advertiser are governments: local, state, and federal.

3 Trade and professional publications as well as local media often develop specific research of vital interest to the communities they serve.

4 Trade associations are found in many product categories, both at the manufacturing and at the retail levels. The associations offer members data that can play an important part in formulating advertising strategies.

5 Often overlooked by businesses are the ongoing research activities at colleges and universities, which could prove valuable in tracking and understanding the consumer.

6 When research is not available, many advertisers develop their own through investigations and surveys.

7 The survey technique of properly selecting a smaller group so it is representative of a larger group is called *sampling*. A major advantage of sampling is economy.

8 One of the dangers of the random sample technique is for researchers to overlook important subgroups whose opinions and buying behavior may be at variance with the universe or larger group.

9 Survey sampling is accurate if studies contain three major elements: (a) a proper sample based on the diversity of respondents, (b) a proper set of questions, and (c) an acceptable margin of error.

10 Four common ways to run a survey are by mail, by phone, by personal interview, and by focus groups. The most dependable, although the most costly, is the face-to-face interview.

11 Advertisers discover these advantages in focus group interviewing: respondents build on one another's comments; there is immediate response; and in-depth exploration of opinions takes place.

12 Pretesting any questionnaire before a full-scale study is an essential part of developing a reliable survey instrument.

13 Survey questions should be carefully worded in order not to antagonize or prejudice respondents.

14 Questions you must ask when making an evaluation of market research are: (a) Does the research have specific application to my problem? (b) Are the conclusions logical? (c) Who conducted the study? Are they competent, reliable? Is there obvious bias? (d) Is the sample representative? Does it include groups besides the ones I'm interested in? (e) Do the questions ask what I really want to know?

CASE STUDY   A Business Publication Surveys the World of Shopping Centers
In June 1976, *Shopping Center World* began the long and painstaking process of taking a census of its industry.[14] Sources of information for the publication's researchers included the U.S. Department of Commerce, the Bureau of the Census, various chambers of commerce, the publication's own files and surveys, and other listings. The report revealed the overwhelming size of the new retail status symbol and its gross annual sales. There are over 18,800 shopping centers in the United States, occupying some 2.565 billion square feet. The United States shopping center industry does an estimated $245 billion in annual retail sales.[15] That is greater than the national income of any industry other than manufacturing.[16]

How can retailers and manufacturers use this research? For the new retailer, it suggests geographical areas in which to locate. For the franchise fast-food or service company, it directs attention to an area that may require additional advertising support because of new outlets and competition. Main Street merchants need to redirect their sales and advertising plans, their present and their future physical locations. Once a shopping center enters an area, retail sales for everyone change. Manufacturers need

[14]"Shopping Center Census," *Shopping Center World*, January 1977 (5:12), pp. 15–17.
[15]"State of the Industry," *Shopping Center World*, January 1978 (6:12), pp. 33–35.
[16]"National Income by Industry," *World Almanac & Book of Facts*, (New York: Newspaper Enterprise Association, 1977), p. 117.

TABLE 3-5

SHOPPING CENTER MATH

Average size of all centers in United States: 133,437 sq. ft.

$$\text{(A football field} = 57,600 \text{ sq. ft.)}$$

Average annual gross sales per sq. ft.: $93

Percent of total retail business in United States (all centers): 36.3

Leading regions in established centers:

Northeast	3,795 centers
South	2,707 centers
Far West	2,706 centers

Source: *Shopping Center World*.

TABLE 3-6

LEADING SHOPPING CENTER STATES

	Number of centers	1976 Sales (in millions of dollars)
California	2,044	$23,452
Texas	1,470	15,328
Florida	988	13,260
New York	868	13,278
Ohio	737	12,011
Pennsylvania	730	11,081
Illinois	628	10,129
Georgia	587	5,942
Massachusetts	544	6,570
Virginia	493	6,102

Source: *Shopping Center World.*

to evaluate the changing traffic patterns in communities into which new shopping centers have moved. Will the majority of their sales in an area now be concentrated within one or two stores? Will they have to call on the large volume buyers only and let their distributors call on the smaller stores? Will their anticipated increase in cooperative advertising permit them to reduce their national media exposure? These are but a few of the many questions that research reveals to marketers and advertising strategists (Tables 3-5 and 3-6).

QUESTIONS NEEDING ANSWERS

1 How can a group of Main Street merchants in California employ focus group surveys to combat the many shopping centers in that state? What questions would you ask of respondents?
2 If you were a developer of a shopping center, would it be important for you to know how many other shopping centers are in existence or in the planning stages adjacent to your selected site? Why?
3 The average annual sales per square foot of shopping centers is $93 (Table 3-5). What attraction does this fact have for retailers seeking cooperative advertising funds from suppliers? Does it have any implications for the type and brands of merchandise carried by the shopping center retailers? Explain.
4 Name some of the kinds of businesses that would be interested in moving into a shopping center. How can advertising help generate traffic for a shopping center?
5 Would it make sense for a shopping center to hire a well-known television personality in order to bring people to the grand opening? Why? Can you name an appropriate one?

STUDENT PROJECT

Select a nearby shopping center, and talk to the manager about developing a survey to determine attitudes of the persons who shop there. By working in groups, you can interview the retailers in order to determine the make-up of

the questions. Prepare a survey, pretest it, and then conduct it by mail, by
phone, by personal interviews, or by focus groups. At the conclusion of the
study, write a brief synopsis of your findings.

105

BACKGROUND:
SETTING
THE STAGE

QUESTIONS ABOUT THE PROJECT

1 Do people resent being interviewed? Why? Why not?
2 Prior to your contacting the manager of the shopping center, had he or she or
  anyone else conducted a study similar to yours? If so, did your conclusions mesh
  with those of the earlier study?
3 Did your study uncover any serious weaknesses that might lose customers for the
  shopping center? If you were the manager of the shopping center and had access
  to your study, what courses of action would you take?
4 Why wouldn't a study of customers of a New England shopping center tell you
  about the same thing that a similar study would if it were conducted in Texas?
  Explain.

QUICK REFERENCES FOR ADVERTISERS

Standard Rate & Data Service. Includes reader profiles, advertising, cost,
circulation coverage, and informative data about business, consumer publications, radio and television stations, and direct mail lists.

Edwin T. Coman, *Sources of Business Information*, rev. ed., University of
California Press, 1964. Lists of useful materials by subject.

Directory of Newspapers, Magazines, and Trade Publications, N.W. Ayer & Son.
An annual with publications arranged geographically, names of management
officials, addresses, advertising rates, mechanical data.

Buying Intention Survey, Midwest Unit Farm Publications (Iowa, Wisconsin,
Indiana, Illinois, Minnesota, Dakotas, Nebraska). A yearly indication of what
farm families in these states intend to purchase the following year, from field
equipment to kitchen appliances.

Editor & Publisher Yearbook, an annual. Provides names, addresses, rates, and
circulations on all United States and Canadian daily and weekly newspapers.

Advertising Age, a weekly tabloid filled with news and statistics of the advertising
business, advertising expenditures of the nation's top 100 advertisers and others,
cases and campaigns of companies and ad agencies throughout the country.

Dun & Bradstreet Middle Market Directory, an annual. Provides names and
addresses, type of business, number of employees, sales, officers.

Encyclopedia of Associations, 6th ed., 2 vols., Gale Research Co., 1970.
Detailed information about 13,000 trade associations and professional societies.

Fortune Directory, the 500 largest United States industries, published annually.

Poor's Register of Corporations, Standard and Poor annual. Contains list of firms
and business and economic histories.

Television Factbook, 2 vols., Television Digest. Annual. Includes statistics and data on United States as well as foreign broadcasting stations.

Thomas Register of American Manufacturers, 11 vols., annual. Includes firms arranged by products, also trade names.

Who's Who in Finance and Industry, Marquis, biennial. Over 25,000 business persons with biographical material.

Business Statistics, U.S. Department of Commerce.

County Business Patterns, U.S. Bureau of Census, annual. Provides employment and payroll data by county and industry.

Survey of Buying Power, Sales and Marketing Management Magazine, annual. Up-to-date income and spending data per capita and per household for metropolitan areas and counties.

U.S. Industrial Outlook, U.S. Department of Commerce, annual. Describes over 125 major industries.

Standard Industrial Classification Manual, U.S. Bureau of the Budget. A government code system that assigns companies numbers according to what they manufacture. Provides a systematic way to develop mailing lists as well as an analytical tool for evaluating industrial media and distributor territories.

Test Market Profiles, a service of A. C. Nielsen Company. Provides media marketing information for each of 199 Designated Market Areas (DMAs) including population, total households, effective buying income, and demographic characteristics.

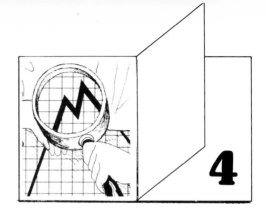

CHANGING PROFILE
OF THE MASS MARKET

Update Taking an advertising position without knowing the situation is a risky business. As we've seen, vast quantities of research data are available to advertisers for minimizing risks and maximizing success. Without this background data, advertising tends to depend solely on the decision maker's limited, personal experience. In a fast-changing economy, advertisers need to know *more* about the consumer, not less; that is the subject of this chapter.

THE EVER-MOVING CONSUMER

If *ever* an economy boasted change as a common denominator, it is ours. Approximately 20 percent of us pick up and move each year.[1] Industry media claim 20 percent of their circulation changes every year as personnel move in,

[1]"Moving? Here's what you should know," *Good Housekeeping*, August 1977, p. 208.

up, or out. Decision makers must constantly adapt their strategies to the changeable marketplace. Who would have guessed that men would desert barber shops in droves in the mid-1970s only to return to hair stylists five years later? Who would have guessed that over 11 million cars and trucks would sport civilian band (CB) radios? As if perplexed business people didn't have enough problems, they are beset by other startling developments: (a) only one quarter of American families can afford a median-priced house whereas twice as many could afford one in 1973,[2] (b) both spouses in the typical American family now work to provide the income they need,[3] (c) a new baby boom is predicted to begin in the 1990s and to peak about the year 2000,[4] and (d) there are even indications that the shopping center—that symbol of picture-window suburbia—is returning to the city.[5] Foley Square, in downtown New York City, recently became the site of a 28,000-square-foot center that houses twenty retailers. Chicago's Water Tower Place covers a block on northern Michigan Avenue in the city itself. One hundred retailers do business there. Whether retailers return to the city or expand in the suburbs, they simply follow the consumer, who is the boss when it comes to influencing the actions of advertisers. Difficult as it is to anticipate change, advertisers have to include it as another variable in their plans.

Where Are the Markets?

Keeping track of the American consumer is an important part of an advertiser's job, whether the company produces consumer, farm, or industrial products. In 1966, there were 196.56 million of us, and over 72 million were employed. Twelve years later, with a population of over 215 million, our employed population had risen to over 99 million. Thus, while the population grew at a 10 percent rate, the work force jumped 27 percent. What happened? For one, women joined the work force in growing numbers and for a variety of reasons: (a) to maintain a standard of living threatened by inflation; (b) to perform better-paying work formerly withheld from women; and (c) to use time that had been spent caring for children.

But there are other important changes. Life expectancies have risen.[6] The average age of people has risen in some categories, fallen in others. Certain sections of the nation such as the Southeast and the Southwest have enjoyed an influx of people and industry at the expense of other states and regions. Young people are marrying later, and many more women are therefore in the labor force. In 1960, for example, 28 percent of all women twenty to twenty-four years old were single, compared to 45 percent in the 1970s.

[2]Housing Report: Massachusetts Institute of Technology & Joint Center for Urban Affairs, 1977.
[3]Department of Labor, 1977.
[4]Prediction by Professor Ronald D. Lee, University of Michigan, 1977.
[5]"Is retailing moving downtown?" Newspaper Advertising Bureau report, *Selling News*, November 1976, p. 4.
[6]Statistical Abstract of the United States, U.S. Department of Commerce, 1978, Population: XIV.

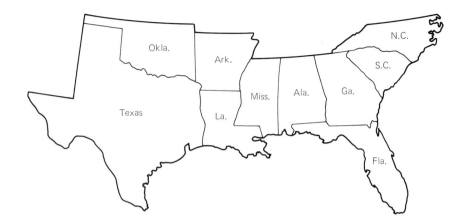

FIGURE 4-1
Outstanding growth has been taking place within these states over the past decade. The influx of people and businesses opens new opportunities to advertisers.

Almost half the 7 million unemployed Americans are twenty-four and younger. Unemployment among teenagers has been on the rise for twenty years and the rate is now about one in five.[7] Among black teenagers, unemployment fluctuates between 25 and 31 percent (it is 18 percent for whites of the same age). Are the good things in life as advertised by American companies beyond the reach of these youthful consumers? Is it more than coincidental that the majority of shoplifters are adolescents?

Geographical Winners and Losers

The South has risen! Next to the western states, the largest population switch in the past decade has taken place in the southeastern half of the United States, often called the Sun Belt (Figure 4-1). This area has recorded outstanding growth and economic progress. One reason is the weather. People who dislike cold weather have descended on these states, either to retire on a pension, or to work in new or expanded plants. Another reason for growth is industry's desire to find locations where taxes are lower and the business climate more favorable to higher profits. Georgia is a case in point. Between 1960 and 1975, manufacturing employment throughout the nation grew 9.2 percent; in Georgia, it rose 27 percent. Nationwide, retail sales during this same period rose 145 percent. In Georgia, the figure was 242 percent. In one recent year, more than 10,000 new jobs were created among the industrial private sector alone.[8] Many of these jobs came from plants migrating from the North. A magazine survey[9] of migrating plants which had moved all or part of their operations from North to South found these

[7]Ibid. p. 408.
[8]J. Michael Robertson and Martin Shartar, "The Center of the Sun Belt," *Atlanta* magazine, May 1977.
[9]*Industry Week Magazine*, February 28, 1977.

TABLE 4-1

FASTEST GROWING METROPOLITAN CENTERS IN THE 1970S

Metropolitan market	Percent of gain in population, 1970–1976
Fort Myers, Fla.	57.0
Fort Lauderdale-Hollywood, Fla.	42.9
Sarasota, Fla.	41.3
Anchorage, Alaska	40.2
Fort Collins, Colo.	39.6
West Palm Beach-Boca Raton, Fla.	37.7
Killeen-Temple, Texas	37.6
Pensacola, Fla.	34.0
Tucson, Ariz.	25.0
Orlando, Fla.	32.7
Tampa-St. Petersburg, Fla.	31.1
Brownsville-Harlingen-San Benito, Texas	30.1
Bradenton, Fla.	30.1
Phoenix, Ariz.	29.7
Tallahassee, Fla.	28.9
Bryan-College Station, Texas	28.3
Reno, Nev.	28.1
Santa Cruz, Calif.	27.3

METROPOLITAN CENTERS IN DECLINE IN THE 1970S

Metropolitan market	Percent of loss of population, 1970–1976
Cleveland, Ohio	5.3
Jersey City, N.J.	4.6
Pittsburgh, Pa.	4.0
New York, N.Y.	3.7
Newark, N. J.	3.3
Pine Bluff, Ark.	3.2
Duluth-Superior, Minn.	2.7
Akron, Ohio	2.3
Pittsfield, Mass.	2.1
Buffalo, N.Y.	2.0
Philadelphia, Pa.	0.8
South Bend, Ind.	0.7
Detroit, Mich.	0.5
Rockford, Ill.	0.4

Metropolitan population		Net change in population. 1970-1976 (in thousands)	Percent of change
2 million or more	Industrial Belt	− 475.4	− 1.2
	Sun Belt	+ 212.1	+ 1.7
1-2 million	Industrial Belt	+ 130.7	+ 1.8
	Sun Belt	+2170.3	+18.1
500K-1 million	Industrial Belt	+ 191.6	+ 1.5
	Sun Belt	+1337.5	+13.4
250K-500 K	Industrial Belt	+ 231.0	+ 2.9
	Sun Belt	+1459.7	+13.9

Source: Sales & Marketing Management, 1977.

reasons: lower labor costs, tax advantages, lower land costs, favorable climate, availability of energy supplies, and access to new markets. In the area of new shopping center openings, the Sun Belt states top the list.[10]

The losers, by and large, are the larger industrial cities of the North— Philadelphia, Chicago, Detroit, Providence, and Cleveland (Table 4-1).

The noticeable population shift from the city to the green belts surrounding the cities is even more dramatic. Suburbia has attracted industry, and the excellent freeways that bring employees and suppliers right to the factory door are called "the new Main Streets" by community planners. Wherever these freeways intersect major highways, clusters of apartments, commercial office buildings, shopping center plazas, and industrial plants have taken root. The movement to the suburbs has diminished the once-dominant market power of the central city.

A quick look around the country confirms the transfer of marketing power from the central city to the suburbs. In fact, in only eight of fifty of the

[10]"State of the Industry," *Shopping Center World*, January 1978, p. 35.

TABLE 4-2

SELECTED MAJOR MILITARY MARKETS IN THE UNITED STATES

County	Military percent of county retail sales
San Diego, Calif.	7.1
Bexar, Tex.	7.2
Cumberland, N.C.	15.9
Virginia Beach, Va.	17.4
El Paso, Colo.	9.5
Norfolk, Va.	7.7
Onslow, N.C.	31.4
Monterey, Calif.	7.9
Bell, Tex.	15.9
Chattahoochee, Ga.	12,236.2
Charleston, S.C.	8.4
El Paso, Tex.	6.1
Hardin, Ky.	30.3
Harrison, Miss.	13.4
Comanche, Okla.	18.3
Okaloosa, Fla.	19.4
Richland, S.C.	5.3
Sarpy, Neb.	38.4
Pulaski, Mo.	40.4
New London, Conn.	5.6
Montgomery, Ala.	5.3
Escambia, Fla.	5.6
Dale, Ala.	51.2

Source: *Sales & Marketing Management,* July 23, 1973, p. A-34.

largest cities do the populations of the central cities outnumber those of the suburbs.[11]

The rapid growth of the South and some western states was also helped by government expenditures. Monies poured into federal projects, military bases, space centers, and coal research projects all create employment. Some observers believe the Sun Belt has gotten more than its share of federal funds. But the arguments over equity aside, it is important that advertisers know about federal spending (Table 4-2).

Demographic Decision Making

Advertisers must make decisions based on their understanding of *demographics*. Demography concerns statistics of human population: number, ages, income, education, sex, and other factors. Some of these essential factors change from day to day. Because marketers cannot possibly alter plans on a daily or even weekly basis, their primary concern is to look for trends upon which to build a long-range plan, a *strategy* (Figures 4-2, 4-3, and 4-4).

A strategy is not a temporary solution to an event. A tactic is. For example, if the Near Eastern oil producers curtail shipments to the United States and cause a gasoline shortage, it might be a good tactic for a mass-transit system to drop fares temporarily. The system will pick up goodwill as well as additional revenues. But this is tactical advertising, a short-term solution to an immediate problem. To be successful over the long term, advertisers need a strategy geared to the continuing, basic needs of the marketplace. Much of the material for developing a strategy will come from the advertisers' knowledge of their buying audience as they are affected by the fertility cycle, the age revolt, the sexual revolution, racial and ethnic awakening, the new life styles, and the educational launching pad.

The Fertility Cycle   Since the early 1970s, fewer and fewer women in the United States have been having children. Just to keep the population at replacement level, a goal of the zero population growth (ZPG) movement, requires women of childbearing age to have 2.1 children each. But in 1975, the birth rate was 1.8, well below replacement level, and three years later, it had moved upward only slightly.[12] The implications of this faltering fertility rate are enormous. At first, the cycle will affect manufacturers of products for infants and children. As fewer children reach school age, the teacher population will shrink and schools will close for lack of students. Textbook publishers will shift some of their capacity to other markets. Toy manufacturers, cereal processors, and soft drink bottlers will feel the pinch. Marginally

[11]Thayer C. Taylor, "How to uncover high-growth markets in low-growth periods," *Sales & Marketing Management Magazine*, July 25, 1977, pp.A-7–A-24; "Suburbs: Third force in marketing," *Sales and Marketing Management Magazine*, July 23, 1973, A-26–A-28.
[12]Statistical Abstract, of the United States, U.S. Department of Commerce, 1978, Population: XIV, p. xiii.

FIGURE 4-2

The long-range strategy of the American Dairy Association is to tie in with the milk drinkers who now consume fast-food treats. Representing the dairy farmers of the country, the association promotes its "Milk is a natural" theme in all media.

FIGURE 4-3
Hormel's "short
orders" recognizes
the increasing
number of persons
living alone and
attempts to satisfy
their taste for good
food without
leftovers.

successful businesses that depend on children may simply go out of business. And so on throughout the entire economy.

Generally, the early signs of demographic change are faint. Only when the change is well underway do most of us take heed. It goes without saying that the longer strategists ignore demographic changes, the more difficult and costly their ultimate adaptation to new market conditions.

The Age Revolt Age is one common way for advertisers to segregate audiences, *if people act their age.* Many people don't. Consumers in their fifties buy motorcycles. Plastic surgeons reshape faces, breasts, and bodies as men and women seek to prolong their youth. What strategists are witnessing today is a revolt of all age groups. While those in the under-five-year-old age group have declined in numbers between the 1960s and the late 1970s, and

FIGURE 4-4

Aiming at the millions of young people looking for a vocation without attending college, the advertiser zeroes in on the traditional correspondence schools' audience: young men.

five- to seventeen-year-olds have barely held their own, eighteen- to twenty-four-year-olds have almost doubled in numbers (Table 4-3). Members of this group know the taste of money and the responsibility of driving—if not owning—cars, boats, and motorcycles. They buy stereos and records and have high expectations of enjoying the affluent life early in their careers.

Particularly significant to the advertising strategist is the increase of singles among the traditionally married twenty- to twenty-four-year-olds. Is this a trend toward more people's delaying marriage or remaining single throughout their lives? We see that one of the nation's fastest-growing markets, the live-alones, are increasing four times faster than any other kind of household. Will the six-pack become the two-pack as manufacturers adapt to these one-person households? Is the fact that young people are earning more now than young people have ever earned before contributing to the desire to remain single?[13]

New attitudes among many married couples in the thirty- to sixty-year-old group are also worth noting. Fewer today intend to make the sacrifices of earlier generations for their children's higher education or their parents' retirement home. They protest the huge sums it takes for them to support an ever-swelling social security system. They worry less about going into debt because they know new bankruptcy laws allow them to shed their creditors. They avoid the clothing their parents wore as an unmistakable sign of middle age. What message do these thirty- to sixty-years-olds send to the advertiser? Sell me the *unusual*, the *bizarre*, the (for most persons) *unattainable*, and I'll buy it!

If the young and their parents aren't behaving in their traditional roles, surely *their* parents, slowed by age and infirmities, can be counted on to perform as the elderly have traditionally done in fact and in fiction. Even here, we sense a spirit of revolt. There are almost 23½ million men and women living today who are sixty-five years of age and older. Over 5 million of them live alone. Community programs all across the nation are encouraging these older citizens to leave their isolated routines and participate in the outreach services of senior centers. Some experts look upon these centers as holding a place in an older person's life similar to the role played by schools in the lives of children. The National Council on Aging, in Washington, D.C., lists over 500 senior centers and clubs in the United States. But other institutions cater to the elderly. For those in reasonably good health, there are retirement homes and villages where the more affluent can live and enjoy the good life. Many of these facilities are located in quiet, small towns near major metropolitan centers.

Why do the elderly in centers, in isolation, or in retirement villages interest the advertiser? Most have an income. Approximately 30 percent receive $5,000 a year or more.[14] Of the family units whose members are

[13]*Prices and Earnings Around the Globe*, Union Bank of Switzerland (Zurich), October 1976, pp. 28–29: see U.S. cities.

[14]Bureau of the Census, *Money Income and Poverty Status of Families and Persons in the United States*: 1975 and 1974 revisions, September 1976.

TABLE 4-3

CHANGES IN POPULATION FROM 1970 TO 1976

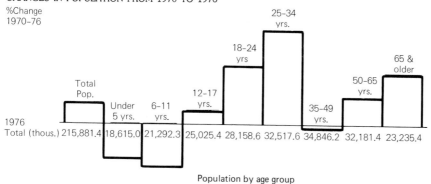

Population by age group

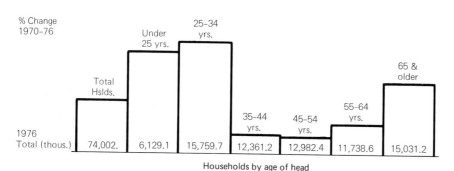

Households by age of head

Source: *Sales & Marketing Management's 1977 Survey of Buying Power.* ©Sales & Marketing Management.

sixty-five years and older, 5.5 percent have incomes of $15,000 a year and over.[15] But the spending habits for our older citizens are not the same as those of others. For example, food, approximately 16 percent of an average family's budget, is 30 percent for the average retired couple with a budget of $6,465 annually.[16] Do older couples eat out more often, or eat better, or is there some other explanation? These are questions restaurant and food store managers, as well as food processors, need answers to. Some fast-food restaurants have attracted senior citizens by providing them with a discount. One small midwestern restaurant gave away 3,000 discount cards in only a few weeks, with all the advertising done by word of mouth (Figure 4-5). The elderly enjoy gardening, arts and crafts, golf, gourmet cooking, taking college courses, and traveling. Companies and institutions providing equipment and services for these avocations might do well to look at this market in a new way—from the point of view of an older person. Travel agencies and banks should find the older citizen a new source of business and profit. Advertisers need to abandon the myth that elderly customers aren't worth cultivating.

[15]Ibid.
[16]"Three budgets for a retired couple," news release, Department of Labor, August 19, 1976.

FIGURE 4-5
One of many special discount inducements
now part of an advertiser's approach to
the elderly.

FIGURE 4-6
Stereotypic ad of the average homemaker is meeting opposition from some women's groups. Advertisers need to be
aware of changing attitudes.

The Sexual Revolution No one need do more than attend the average movie, witness young unmarried couples hitchhiking throughout the country, or be aware of the skyrocketing divorce rate to know there is a sexual revolution going on. The Census Bureau estimates that 1.3 million people, both young and old, live together without being married. In 1975, the annual number of divorces passed the million mark. Since 1960, the divorce rate has more than doubled.[17] And the move for women's rights has been pervasive. Early militancy has given way to firm pressure by millions of women seeking better jobs and equal pay for equal work. And the business community is responding. There is also growing opposition to the stereotyping, in print and broadcast advertising, of women as sex objects or happy-to-be-waxing-the-floor homemakers (Figure 4-6).

The true importance of the sexual revolution is a redefining of sex roles. Because the vast majority of them hold jobs outside the home, women want to see themselves portrayed in professional situations. Advertisers should show them for what they are: intelligent, hardworking, vital members of society. Instead of always being "my girl Friday," women want to be shown as bosses. As more women move into executive positions, smart advertisers will be quick to reflect this new condition (Figure 4-7). Advertisers are also recognizing that men are playing a growing role in the running of the household, from diapering the baby to washing the dishes and scrubbing the floors. Their ads are beginning to reflect this reality and, in a sense, establish housework as a legitimate province for men also (Figure 4-8).

The Racial and Ethnic Awakening During the 1950s and 1960s, ads showing blacks anywhere but in black magazines were rare. Even people of Slavic, German, Italian, Scandinavian, and Oriental heritage seldom appeared as heroes or heroines in advertisements. Only the Anglo-Saxon population had widespread exposure, the implication being that it was most desirable to be white and English, Scottish, or Irish. Today the stereotype of using a Pole as a foundry worker, a black as a waiter, and an Irish person as a police officer is fast disappearing. The emphasis is on individuality.

Advertisers are beginning to sense that although some products appeal to many different people, the way to reach those people has changed. Advertisers now see the racial, the ethnic, and even the religious submarkets as requiring more than one universally appealing advertising message. The ideal approach, some marketing experts contend, is to have both specific racial or ethnic messages and a universal one. The ethnic messages will touch a responsive chord among those who feel a strong, unifying bond of ethnic and racial culture. The universal approach will serve to meet the expectations of everyone as long as ethnic and racial groups are represented. Social scientists claim that there is a greater similarity between whites and blacks of

[17]Statistical Abstract of the United States, U.S. Department of Commerce, 1978, Population: XIV, p. 13.

The last feminine hang-up

You've come a long way . . . at least, that's what they tell you.

And, in a lot of areas, that's true.

As far as marriage is concerned, you're making up your own mind—saying "yes" if that's what you really want. And "no" if it's not.

As far as a career is concerned, you're looking a lot beyond typing 80 words a minute. And, even if you do decide to have babies some day, there's a lot else you want to accomplish, too.

Fantastic. Every bit of it.

But there's one area you may not have turned around yet. One area where the old ideas about how a "woman should think" may still be hanging you up. But good.

That's the area of the world. Not just your corner of it. The whole big, wide world. From politics to the environment. From science and medicine to the jobless rate.

When the conversation turns to matters like these, are you ready to jump in with opinions of your own? And facts to back them up?

Or does that modern, liberated woman suddenly revert to a respectful silence? A silence which is broken mainly by the sound of some man's opinions?

That's easy enough to change.

Some of the women's revolutions were hard. Luckily, this one is easy.

To change your sex ideas, you may have had to turn your head inside out.

To change your career ideas, you may have had to convince a lot of people who've stood in your way.

From parents to teachers to personnel directors.

But to become so well-informed that no man, ever again, will talk you down or try to talk down to you?

Simple. All it takes is an hour or so a week (an enjoyable one at that) and 50¢ a week.

PLAYBOY is a man's magazine. TIME is not!

TIME is simply this: the easiest, clearest, most complete, best organized way to keep up with everything important.

Every week, you get it all. In one place. Not frantic bits and pieces. But the whole, smoothly thought-out (and entertainingly written) story. The background you need to understand it. The beginning, middle and end. What's likely to happen next. Why it all went the way it did.

All placed neatly there in front of you. Divided into more than 20 departments so you don't miss a thing you want to know.

By reading TIME, you catch up quickly. And you keep up. No matter what subject comes up.

Not bad for a fascinating hour or so of reading.

Save half the newsstand price.

Whether you just want to understand what's happening—or be part of the forces that make it happen—this is the moment to try TIME.

Try it at our subscription rate of 50¢ a week. That's half the newsstand price and you can have it for as long as you want, from 25 weeks to 100.

But mail the postpaid card now.

And your TIME will come.

Try TIME at half the newsstand price

— — — Just write in the number of weeks you want, detach, and mail — — — —

Send me____weeks of TIME for only 50¢ a week and bill me later.

Minimum: 25 weeks. Maximum: 100 weeks. (TIME is $1.00 a copy on newsstands, so you save half.) Send no money now. You will be billed later.

Mr./Ms. _____ (please print full name)

Address _____ Apt. No.

City _____

State _____ Zip

Signature _____

If college student, please indicate ☐ undergraduate ☐ graduate.

Name of College/University _____

Year studies end _____

Rate good just in U.S. _____ T11672

FIGURE 4-7
This selling message is aimed at the emancipated woman by advertising strategists who have recognized that the traditional role of women has changed.

At State Farm, our life insurance computer will tell you when enough's enough.

How else can you really be sure you haven't bought too much? Or too little? Or the wrong kind?

At State Farm, we make sure you get just what you need. We do it by computer. Our impartial Matchmaker computer service figures not only what kind of life insurance you need, but also what amount.

You see, we take your financial needs and limitations and feed them into our computer. A computer programmed to compare your needs with a vast storehouse of insurance information. Information about the kinds and amount of insurance people like you have been able to afford in the past. Information backed up with national and industry statistics, and years of State Farm experience.

The result is an objective life insurance program computed to match your needs, as well as your budget.

See a State Farm agent soon about his free Matchmaker computer service.

He can show you just what you need.

The Matchmaker.

State Farm is all you need to know about insurance.

STATE FARM LIFE INSURANCE COMPANY. In New York and Wisconsin, non-participating life insurance is offered through State Farm Life and Accident Company. Home Offices: Bloomington, Illinois.

FIGURE 4-8

Will this standard insurance ad come to be known as American Gothic? As the fortunes of women rise in our society, advertisers worry whether the "homebody family" stereotype still holds true. They worry whether as many men will consider insurance necessary, since so many women are proving they can make it on their own.

similar incomes, for example, than between all classes within one racial or ethnic community.[18]

Once, the tactic of publicly advertising oneself as, say, a Swede, might have been considered a poor way to win friends and influence people. This attitude is slowly changing. People are proudly proclaiming their heritage, and advertisers are quick to respond (Figure 4-9).

The New Life Styles   *Life style* is defined as the way in which people conduct themselves within their environment. Once persons were more concerned with what people thought of them. These persons might have inwardly rebelled against accepting the establishment's code of conduct, but outwardly they conformed. The late 1960s saw an end to "blind conformity" by many people. Where the behavior norm was to finish school, marry, have children, and become "pillars of the community," people are now backpacking around the country without any thought of settling down, or adopting the gypsy life in motor homes, or abandoning careers to begin new ones. In a democratic country of over 215 million devoted to education, a free press, and free expression, it is somewhat surprising that it took so long for people to flaunt unconventional life styles. Take the case of communal living. Certainly no stranger to this country, the communal life style of working and sharing receives far greater acceptance today than it ever did in the late nineteenth century. A life style has developed around the sports of skiing, tennis, boating, and golf. Here, the sport becomes the focal ingredient in a family's activities. In fact, for some families, it has supplanted the socializing role of the church.

Most dramatic—and most interesting to advertisers—of all life styles is the desire of a sophisticated people to do things with their hands, once considered beneath their dignity. Millions are becoming do-it-yourself carpenters, plumbers, masons, electricians, auto mechanics, and gardeners. The overriding appeal is a desire not so much to economize as to feel the joys of accomplishment. Census figures for homebuilding indicate how strong this urge has become. Over 18 percent of single-family housing starts in 1976 (164,000) were of the owner-built variety.[19] "People who have never built anything before are looking for alternatives to buying a conventional house," reports The Shelter Institute in Maine, where, during a two-year period, some 600 people paid $250 for sixty hours of construction lessons. How does a manufacturer or retailer advertise a $200 table saw to a couple who has never built a house before? Do these advertisers rely on the use of professional plumbers as spokespersons for a plumbing tool, or do they find some amateurs who did the job for themselves?

The new life styles have spawned or revitalized manufacturers, retailers, and advertisers of mobile homes, auto vans and pickups, motorcycles, backpacking and sporting equipment, interior decorating and garden sup-

[18]Leonard Reissman, *Inequality in American Society*, (Glenview, Ill: Scott, Foresman and Company, 1973), p. 102.
[19]Bureau of Census, 1976.

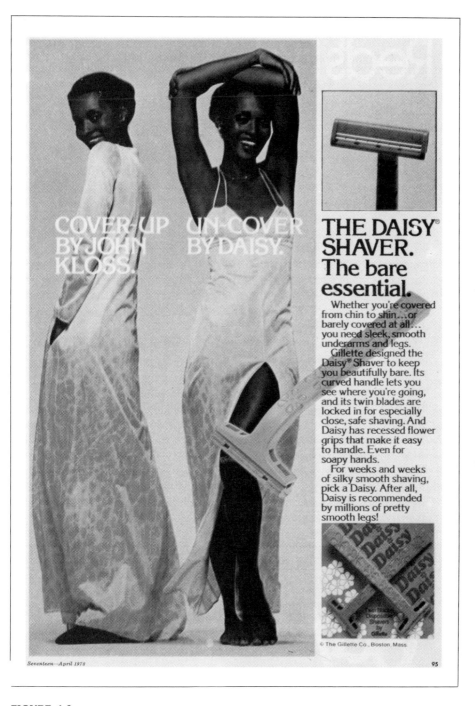

Seventeen—April 1978   95

FIGURE 4-9

Recognizing that minority groups may rebel against tokenism in advertising, major companies are approaching these target audiences with candor and devoting entire ads to minority groups alone.

plies, furniture, audio systems, and more. They have encouraged retailers to specialize in the products that appeal to the unconventional buyer. In short, they offer new communications opportunities to the advertiser.

The Educational Launching Pad   Education is another of the vital statistics that bears on what people will buy. Many studies reveal that college-educated consumers, for example, spend their money differently from the way others do. More of them read professional magazines. More of them take overseas vacations. They join racket, health, golf, and yacht clubs. They become involved with community affairs because they can afford to. College graduates, aside from teachers, earn more per capita than those without college. Yet they tend to be more skeptical of advertising claims. Some advertising strategists feel that advertisers should upgrade the intellectual level of their ads.[20] Opponents of this viewpoint say that many products and services have little bearing on one's educational achievements. In fact, they caution, the average annual increase in the number of persons enrolled in institutions of higher education has been sluggish.[21] They point to the 80 percent of the population who have not gone beyond high school. "These are the consumers," they warn, "who can make or break businesses, not the elite." To back their statement, they point to well-paid blue-collar workers, many of whom earn as much as or more than white-collar college graduates. But formal education alone does not tell the whole story. Community adult education courses have been growing in popularity. People of all ages are being exposed to new information. To the degree that they accept these new thoughts, they become different people and different consumers.

Advertising strategists cannot avoid dealing with the startling transformations brought on by exposure to new ideas, concepts, and knowledge and the pride of age, sex, race, and culture. They need to look for help in perceiving these demographic changes. As in the past, this help will come from government and business statistics, the media, and continual awareness of the changes going on in the United States and around the world.

HOW ADVERTISING APPLIES BEHAVIORAL SCIENCES

To this point, we have taken a look at *where* and *who* consumers are. In a less complex world, that may have been all an advertising strategist needed to know. Today, in a competitive arena in which, in one year, the A.C. Nielsen

[20]Stephen A. Greyser, "Businessmen look hard at advertising," *Harvard Business Review*, May/June 1971, pp. 18–26; 157–165.
[21]Statistical Abstract of the United States, U.S. Department of Commerce, 1978, Population: XIV, p. xv.

Company[22] recorded 1,154 new-product introductions in the grocery, health, and beauty aids fields alone, advertisers must know more about the makeup of their target audiences. And to learn about the ever-changing consumer, advertisers turn to the behavioral sciences, which explain human behavior in terms of *psychology*, *sociology*, and *anthropology*. An individual's behavior, unless it is representative of a larger universe, is of little interest to a manufacturer of a mass-produced product. But the behavior of groups, their desire to conform or dissent, their willingness to accept or reject the new or the old, are matters that advertisers need to know.

If psychology is the study of the mind, then the *psychology of group behavior* is the study of many minds bound together in some communal way: by geography, by interests, by vocation. Advertisers are interested in the ways groups of people receive messages, selecting some, rejecting others. They are interested in how some words and pictures cause people to desire a product, while other words and pictures leave them unimpressed. Advertisers are interested in analyzing how their spokespersons (presenters) come across in their ads to the general mass audience. Among other interests, they also wish to discover whether buying responses of groups exposed only to verbal and visual messages differ from those of groups who actually get to use the product. Psychological studies like these are run by researchers working for universities, advertisers and their ad agencies, government, and private industry.

When masses of people respond to the McDonald's appeal "You deserve a break today" by eating at a McDonald's, psychologists may come forth with a series of explanations: (1) People are reminded of the hard work of running a house and wish to please their spouses and children. (2) People feel they have earned time off from meal preparation and look upon eating out as a type of reward. (3) People wish to avoid cleaning up. (4) Spouses feel a change of mealtime scenery improves married life. (5) Singles feel that eating out is both a reward and an adventure (who's that stranger eating alone?). But when we begin to analyze how the McDonald's theme attracts people according to their income, education, or other specific criteria, we enter the domain of *psychographics*.

Psychographics can be explained as an in-depth, motivational study of people's real wants and the reasons behind them. Returning to our McDonald's example of a person's desire to please spouse and children, a compilation of psychographic explanations could reveal that some people want to play the role of the family "good guy," to be loved and esteemed because of the eating pleasures they provide for the family. Others' psychographic motivations may be the same but could also include the desire

---

[22]The A.C. Nielsen Company, besides its research on household television and radio usage, reports on the market movement through retail stores of food, drug, beauty, and health care products.

1. (Singers VO) You, you're the one.

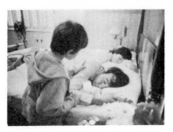

2. (Music under) KID: Dad! Dad! It's bike time. (Singers VO) Your morning... DAD: O.K. I'm up. (Singers VO)... sun's awake. KID: Come on.

3. (Singers VO) Now the weekend's here. MOM: I'll fix your breakfast. DAD: Oh, we'll take care of that.

1. (Music under) TERRI: Come to McDonald's this weekend for a good hot breakfast...

2. ...and you'll be off to a good headstart.

3. GIRL: I'm going to a parade!

FIGURE 4-10a

(Top) Family situations in which Mom or Dad play the "good guy" role are typical of McDonald's television commercials. In this introduction to a 60-second sequence, Dad treats the family to breakfast at McDonald's and then helps his son learn how to ride a two-wheeler without training wheels.

FIGURE 4-10b

(Above) When we analyze why people respond to a McDonald's appeal, we can learn from psychographics, the in-depth study of people's real wants. In each of the illustrated commercials, the head of the family is told over and over what a great guy he is for taking his family out to eat. Their love and affection is his reward. (Courtesy McDonald's Corporation.)

to prove that their families can afford to go out to eat on a regular basis (Figure 4-10).

Geraldine Fennell illustrates the ambiguous meanings of words that consumers use—in simple surveys—to describe reasons for buying:

> Three motorists may say power is important to them. But Consumer A may want power because his habitual driving pattern makes it necessary to be able to enter fast-moving traffic; B, because owning a powerful car is associated with his masculine self-image; C, because he enjoys the sensory experience of driving a powerful machine.[23]

Psychographics goes beyond the who and asks *why*. Coupled with traditional

[23]Geraldine Fennell, "Consumer perceptions of the product-use situation," *Journal of Marketing*, April 1978, p. 39.

psychological inquiry, it reduces the possibility of an advertiser's drawing incorrect conclusions.

Psychology of the Buyer

The things people want have no limit. Economics may limit acquisitions, but it doesn't limit desires. The basic human psychological needs are: *to be important*, *to be loved*, and *to be protected*. From these basic psychological needs, various authors have postulated the existence of others. Hattwick[24] specifies some of them as follows: desire for information, desire to be clean and fresh-smelling, desire for convenience, desire for profit and wealth, desire for economy, desire for efficiency. Sometimes these supplemental wants can be as magnetic in their psychological appeal as the basics from which they come. Examples of these more sophisticated and changing needs are abundant. The beginning wage earner who once thought life would be complete with a four-bedroom house in the suburbs now sees life as unfulfilled without a condominium in Hawaii, a second house on Lake George, and a membership at an exclusive Memphis racket club.

Some psychologists argue that these secondary wants are simply an updated restatement of the three basic needs. Why would anyone want to be clean if it weren't to be loved or admired by the opposite sex, they argue? Why would anyone want to be efficient in anything if it couldn't be flaunted before others? This position borrows heavily from the works of an army of psychologists from Aristotle to Hobbes, from Freud to Watson.[25] Some psychologists disagree with how the advertising industry has extended the theory of three basic psychological needs to embrace other needs such as a desire for information. These critics point out that there are deeper motivations involved. Some even challenge the validity of the basic needs as we have outlined them. Be that as it may, the basic-need theory has been accepted and practiced by advertisers for over a hundred years; it remains the foundation of the great majority of all ads bombarding (and informing) the public.

Advertising Recall

A major objective of advertising is to implant brand names in the minds of consumers. This isn't too difficult if you have the money, the creative messages, and minimal competition. But when many similar products scream for attention, a problem arises. It stems from the fact that the human mind may not want to retain, in the short run, more than five to nine items in one

[24]Melvin S. Hattwick, *How to Use Psychology for Better Advertising* (Englewood Cliffs, N.J.: Prentice-Hall, Inc., 1956), p. 109.
[25]The *De Anima* of Aristotle is considered to be the first work defining the field; Hobbes—in the seventeenth century—is considered to have laid the foundations of modern psychology; Freud gave it new directions, while J.B. Watson's *Behaviorism* played an influential role in American thought.

category. This is the studied and researched conclusion of Harvard psychologist George A. Miller.[26] James J. Jenkins' laboratory studies discovered further that:

> Recall is not just a function of what the outside world presents but is also a function of what you do with the events as you experience them.[27]

Jenkins' conclusion: words or instructions that focus on meanings give excellent recall; words that focus on the form or abstract concept of a word are difficult to remember.[28]

According to some advertising agency specialists,[29] the mind is like a memory bank except that "as a defense mechanism against the volume of today's communications, [the mind] screens and rejects much of the information offered it."[30] Yet the average mind is exposed to more than 500,000 ad messages in one year[31] (Figure 4-11).

Anthropology Anthropology's contribution to advertising stems from its analysis of human cultures and the living patterns of Americans of European, African, Asian, and Hispanic descent. *Culture* is the customs, ideas, and attitudes shared by groups and passed along from generation to generation. Cultural values and codes of conduct have a bearing on what members of a culture eat and wear and on members' relationships within and beyond their own group. In a society dominated by the Protestant work ethic, for example, one way for the individual to advance is to produce to the best of his or her ability and to be rewarded. This work ethic has been important among certain immigrant groups in this country. On the other hand, many young people feel it is wrong for one person to attempt to outdo another. Advertisers will have to be aware of both points of view and their relative importance in society (Figures 4-12, 4-13, 4-14, and 4-15).

Cultural Innovators Every group has a small nucleus of adventuresome risk takers. Some behavioral scientists call them *innovators* or *opinion leaders*. Advertisers recognize them as vital cogs in the machinery of making advertising work. What percentage of the population are innovators is hard to determine, but some experts claim it hovers around 3 percent. Innovators are more vocal, more impetuous, or more motivated than others. They can

[26]George A. Miller, "The Magical Number Seven, Plus or Minus Two: Some Limits on our Capacity for Processing Information," *Psychological Review* 1956, vol. 63, pp. 8–97.

[27]James J. Jenkins, "Language and Memory," in *Communication, Language, and Meaning* ed. George A. Miller. (New York: Basic Books, Inc., 1973), pp. 162–163.

[28]Ibid.

[29]Jack Trout and Al Fries, "The positioning era cometh," *Advertising Age*, April 24, 1972, pp. 35, 38.

[30]Ibid.

[31]Ibid.

In fact, Ban® Roll-On is more effective at stopping wetness than all leading aerosols.

FIGURE 4-11

To test the memory recall of advertising brands according to the theory that the mind may not want to remember more than five to nine items within one category, ask your friends how many deodorants they can name, or detergents, or margarines. Reproduced with permission of the copyright owner Bristol-Myers Co. © 1977.

FIGURE 4-12
Some states still point to the work ethic of their cultures as a reason for industry to move there. This ad appeared in *Fortune*.

How we sweetened the melting pot.

We all pitched in. That's how we sweetened the melting pot called America.

Like a big family coming together for a festive meal, each immigrant group has added its contribution. The world's best skills, talents, minds, hearts, music, children, customs, that's what's gone into America.

We've put them all together and they've nourished the greatest nation in the world.

And the best thing is, we haven't stopped pitching in.

Today 9½ million American workers invest in their country by buying U.S. Savings Bonds.

You can too. Sign up for the Payroll Savings Plan where you work. It's an easy, automatic way to sweeten your life while you sweeten your land by taking stock in America with U.S. Savings Bonds.

Series E Bonds pay 6% interest when held to maturity of 5 years (4½% the first year). Interest is not subject to state or local income taxes, and federal tax may be deferred until redemption.

Take stock in America.

 A public service of this publication and The Advertising Council.

SP-1678

FIGURE 4-13
Ethnic and cultural diffusion within our country may produce an ad like this.

FIGURE 4-14
Recognizing one culture's dietary laws as a means of dramatizing product superiority to a non-Jewish audience, this television frame uses Uncle Sam as a spokesperson for kosher hot dogs. Courtesy Hebrew National Kosher Foods

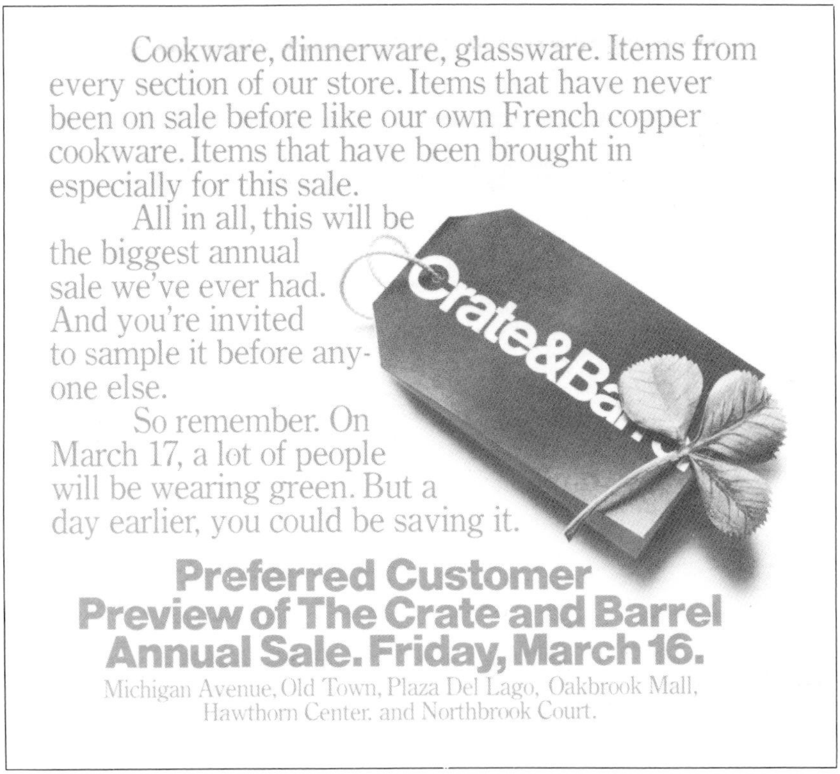

Cookware, dinnerware, glassware. Items from every section of our store. Items that have never been on sale before like our own French copper cookware. Items that have been brought in especially for this sale.

All in all, this will be the biggest annual sale we've ever had. And you're invited to sample it before anyone else.

So remember. On March 17, a lot of people will be wearing green. But a day earlier, you could be saving it.

Preferred Customer Preview of The Crate and Barrel Annual Sale. Friday, March 16.

Michigan Avenue, Old Town, Plaza Del Lago, Oakbrook Mall, Hawthorn Center, and Northbrook Court.

FIGURE 4-15
On St. Patrick's Day in the United States everyone becomes Irish. The rivers run green and so do the printing presses, as they pour out advertising whose ultimate function is to get "the green." Crate & Barrel uses the Irish theme to introduce a preferred customer direct-mail promotion.

hasten the acceptance of most products and services simply by being among the first to buy or use them. In the early 1950s, for example, the risk takers in many communities invested in something called television. It wasn't at all necessary for the innovators to actively sell the experience to their neighbors. Their mere ownership made television attractive to their neighbors.

Unfortunately for advertisers, a person who is an innovator for one product may not be for another. Determining who the innovators are for a specific product requires study and evaluation. Three criteria must be met for a group to be tagged as innovators:

1 Are the selected innovators truly leaders—by vocation, heritage, education, community rank, acknowledged abilities?
2 Will the mass market easily recognize these persons as appropriate innovators of a specific product?
3 Is it probable for the innovators to be associated with such a product?

If the innovators fulfill these requirements, advertisers must define who they are, locate them, and attempt to influence them and their friends early in the game (Figure 4-16).

"My Sunstream solar systems save me money and energy. I'm a believer." *Jor L 7. Maxworthy, J, M.D.* *Odessa, Tex.*

"We installed our Grumman Sunstream solar systems to help heat the water we use for baths, showers, washing dishes, clothes—and the water in our whirlpool bath.

"Using the sun's rays to conserve energy and lower my electric bill makes all the sense in the world to me."

Sunstream™ is a product of Grumman technology, which landed Americans on the moon. Grumman stands for reliability in Gulfstream executive jets, Grumman trucks, canoes, and Pearson yachts.

Sunstream solar systems carry a five-year limited warranty supported by a national dealer service network.

For more information on domestic water, space and pool heating, write Grumman Energy Systems, Inc., Dept. H920, 4175 Veterans Memorial Highway, Ronkonkoma, NY 11779.

GRUMMAN *Sunstream*

The reliable source

FIGURE 4-16
Clever Grumman ad copy recognizes that solar heating innovators are better educated, more affluent than the average, and live in sunny western states. Innovators can be found in most cultural groups. They enjoy recognition and the follow-up advertising that tells them how wise they were to get on the bandwagon early.

Sociology of Groups   Because social group behavior in all classes forms a recognizable pattern, it is of acute interest to advertisers. Even where common sense dictates one approach, social pressures within a group may dictate another. Because social inequality is universal in human societies, every individual has a particular *socioeconomic status*, a place within the group based on actual or perceived economic standing. Our socioeconomic status exerts an enormously powerful effect on us, and every advertiser should know the social pressures and expectations of particular social groups. Such knowledge means effectively positioned advertising. The publisher of birth control information, for example, should not expect massive sales within the social groups that expect members to marry and produce three to five children. Those advertisements would be much more effective if they reach the social groups that expect members to limit their family size or to delay childbearing.

The point is that by learning and applying principles of the sociology of groups, advertisers can be effective and efficient. We will discuss some of the topics that advertisers should know about.

The Youth Market   Contemporary advertising has attentively wooed youngsters, particularly the more than 12 million fourteen- to nineteen-year-olds. And no wonder. Twenty-two percent earn anywhere from $1,000 to $20,000 a year. As a group, they respond more often to peer pressure than to family pressure. And while many of them complain about a lack of money and work[32] (47 percent have no stated income), they do account for a startling degree of spending (Table 4-4 and Table 4-5).

Advertisers have to consider how to treat sexual subjects and products in ads for teenagers. Traditionally, advertisements have shown teenagers as more mature preteens, eating pizzas and hamburgers, drinking soft drinks, dancing with the opposite sex—at arm's length. Some sociologists see this portrayal as society's refusal to recognize the maturity of the teenager. Alfred Kinsey is one:

> This failure to recognize the mature capacities of teenage youth is relatively recent. Prior to the last century or so, it was well understood that they were the ones who had the maximum sexual capacity and the great romances of literature turned around the love affairs of teenage boys and girls . . . Helen was twelve years old when Paris carried her off to Troy . . . Tristan was nineteen when he first met Isolde. Juliet was less than fourteen when Romeo made love to her . . .[33]

Advertisers have been changing their appeals to these "affluent" teenagers.

[32]George Gallup Youth Study, May 1977.

[33]Alfred C. Kinsey, *Sexual Behavior in the Human Female* (Philadelphia: W. B. Saunders Co., 1953), pp. 13–21; 101–126.

TABLE 4-4

PURCHASING BEHAVIOR OF
CROSS-SECTION OF *BOYS' LIFE*
READERSHIP

Types of Athletic Footwear Owned	
Footwear	**Percentage**
Jogging/running shoes	50.7
Training or "all purpose" shoes	46.3
Hiking shoes or boots	43.8
Basketball shoes	42.4
Tennis shoes	35.0
Baseball/softball shoes	24.5
Football shoes	24.3
Soccer shoes	14.0
Bowling shoes	6.5
Golf shoes	3.3
No answer	0.4

Note: Percentages add to more than 100% due to multiple response.
Source: *Boys' Life* National Reader Panel, May 1979.

TABLE 4-5

PURCHASING BEHAVIOR OF HIGH SCHOOL GIRLS IN ONE YEAR

	Number purchasing	**Number purchased**	**Total expenditures**
Total buying coats	3,397,000	5,020,000	$235,825,000
Total buying jackets	2,814,000	4,188,000	137,011,000
Total buying suits	4,001,000	7,067,000	236,870,000
Total buying dresses	4,530,000	11,917,000	324,359,000
Total buying skirts	4,539,000	9,409,000	147,817,000
Total buying sweaters	5,533,000	30,182,000	518,937,000
Total buying tops	4,293,000	27,001,000	238,350,000
Total buying pants	7,018,000	36,351,000	641,360,000
Total buying footwear	6,974,000	21,827,000	423,618,000
Total buying boots	1,747,000	1,945,000	72,676,000
Total buying hosiery	6,604,000	115,209,000	171,857,000
Total buying bras	5,312,000	17,296,000	99,107,000
Total buying jewelry	4,840,000	39,085,000	300,901,000
Total buying watches	1,158,000	1,224,000	41,734,000
Total buying cameras	516,000	588,000	22,698,000
Total buying record players	411,000	420,000	94,590,000
Total buying sewing machines	292,000	303,000	72,180,000
Total buying portable televisions	252,000	285,000	52,830,000
Total buying tape recorders	240,000	261,000	11,321,000

Source: *Seventeen's* Back-To-School Study, 1977.

TABLE 4-6

GALLUP YOUTH SURVEY (SELECTED QUESTIONS)

What do you consider to be the key problems facing young people today?	
Drug use and abuse	27%
Getting along with parents/communication	20%
Alcohol use and abuse	7%
Finding employment/earning money	6%
Peer problems/pressure	5%
Job boredom	3%
Career doubts	3%
Smoking	3%
Immaturity	3%
Economic problems	3%

Source: George Gallup, *Des Moines Tribune,* May 19, 1977.

They are recognizing them as young men and women, and they are sending them frank and direct messages:

> Smitty did it.
> Smitty. It's the spirited, sexy
> new feeling in fragrance.
> It's exhilarating. It's
> exciting. And only
> Smitty does it.
> Smitty by Coty.[34]

A minibike manufacturer puts it this way:

> Lean. Tough.
> Hungry. Mean.
> The rest is up to you . . .
> This is some kind of cycle you're eye-balling . . .[35]

Today's teenagers are far more sophisticated than their predecessors. They are influenced by the wide-ranging eye of television. Their concerns, as recorded by the selection in Table 4-6 from a Gallup study of over 1,000 teenagers, go far beyond simplistic ideals.

The interests of teenagers and their acceptance into family councils make them extremely attractive to the advertiser. For instance, according to *Product Management Magazine,*[36] 14.5 million teenage girls own 10.5 million record players, 5.5 million television sets, and 6.5 million tape recorders. In homes with working mothers, 36 percent of teenage girls select the toothpaste and deodorant brand for the family while 80 percent do the weekly shopping. The

[34]Advertising copy for Coty's Smitty in *Seventeen,* April 1978.
[35]Advertising copy for Rupp minibike in *Boys' Life,* 1972.
[36]"The teenage market: where less is more," *Selling News,* Newspaper Advertising Bureau, October 1976, p. 4.

changing roles played by family members pose new opportunities for advertising strategists. How do you reach teenagers? What do you say? Will testimonials of middle-aged movie stars turn them on or off (Figure 4-17)?

The Elderly Marketing will be profoundly affected when society recognizes that age sixty-five is hardly the end of the road. As the population grows older, and as able-bodied senior citizens are integrated into the activities of society on the same terms as any other group, traditional target marketing will change. Already universities throughout the country are extending the teaching age of professors from sixty-five to seventy as more and more healthy senior citizens choose to continue working. It is expected that in the not-too-distant future the mandatory retirement age of sixty-five in most businesses and industries will be raised also. This is not too surprising, since many retired people believe that working hard to get ahead is more important in life than doing the things that provide for personal satisfaction and pleasure.[37] Advertisers should recognize that the older householder is more likely to be a home owner and spend more time around the home than younger people. The older householders have different informational needs and will read local newspapers and magazines on a more regular basis than members of other age groups.[38] Time magazine, for example, defines almost 11 percent of its circulation as householders sixty-five years of age or older.[39] Unfortunately, television research studies such as Arbitron do not reflect the numbers of viewing households with family members over sixty-five years of age. These statistics, like those of other age groups, should be of great interest to certain industries and businesses: restaurants, food manufacturers and retail food stores, banks, recreational equipment manufacturers, and travel agencies and resorts. Proof of retired citizens' love of travel can be seen in the following headline taken from *Blue Beret*, a monthly magazine sent mostly to older-aged owners of a unique travel trailer:

Airstream Plans Caravan to Panama.

Cost of the three-month tour limited to 300 units was $3,000 for travel expenses only. Owners of these travel trailers are organized into regional clubs, and as many as 4,000 have descended on one locality for a rally and fun: parties, square dances, and the like. Estimated income to retailers at cities playing host to the national rally runs into several million dollars.[40]

The Question of Class Class distinctions are very much alive in this country. Class influences what jobs we take, what we consume, whom we

---

[37]Daniel Petersen, "Iowans pick pleasure over work," *Des Moines Register*, March 18, 1979, p. 3B.
[38]"Young people and newspapers," a survey by Yankelovich, Shelly, and White (New York), 1976.
[39]*Time* National Subscriber Study, p. 3.
[40]*Blue Beret*, May 1977, p. 5.

81

FIGURE 4-17
Most mass advertising caters to the young and handsome. With most of our population in age groups under sixty-five, that kind of appeal makes sociological sense. It makes psychographic sense as well, because in our culture, adults prefer to be young forever. (Courtesy Institute of Outdoor Advertising.)

marry, where we go to school, what books we read (if any), how we dress, where we live, and how we select our friends. There are those who refuse to believe that the United States has social classes, but it does. Loosely defined, class implies a social organization of like-minded people at a particular economic level who have similar material wants and values. This organization enables class members to develop and cope with their surroundings. As Kurt B. Mayer points out:

> In a class system, the social hierarchy is based primarily upon differences in monetary wealth and income. Social classes are not sharply marked off from each other nor are they demarcated by tangible boundaries. Unlike estates, they have no legal standing, individuals of all classes being in principle equal before the law. Consequently, there are no legal restraints on the movement of individuals and families from one class to another. The same is true of intermarriage which, while it may be frowned upon and discouraged, is not prevented by law or insuperable social pressures.[41]

Advertisers need to recognize that products and services appealing to lower-income families should stress price and value, since these are uppermost in importance to the purchasers. Ads aimed at middle- and upper-income classes can forego price and dramatize other values and exclusivity (Figure 4-18). Ads showing rich Americans using a "grease cleaner-upper" won't convince middle-class suburbia as well as presenters who look and act like suburban homemakers. Advertisers need to recognize also that for decades, the middle and upper classes have had fewer children than the lower classes (Figure 4-19).

Interestingly, there are groups of middle-class white-collar workers who identify with the upper and upper-middle class, although their incomes are not much higher than those of manual workers. They read magazines like *Better Homes and Gardens* and embrace upper-class values as best they can. Discovering who these people are, where they live, and what motivates them is one of the constant challenges facing advertisers.

The Black Middle Class   The upward economic mobility of blacks within the past decade has been dramatic. The median money income of black and other families, for example, has tripled from 1960 to 1977.[42] The number of blacks in the professions has more than doubled,[43] and many others are moving from low-income into higher-paying jobs.[44] In marketing terms," 40 percent of blacks must be considered middle-class or better (and that 40 percent controls 70 percent of the black income)."[45] Marketing people see

---

[41]Kurt B. Mayer, *Class and Society*, (New York: Random House, 1955), pp. 7–8.
[42]Statistical Abstract of the United States, U.S. Department of Commerce, 1978, Population XV.
[43]Kevin Hall, "New market: Among blacks, the haves are now overtaking the have-nots," *Advertising Age*, February 11, 1974, p. 35.
[44]Ibid.
[45]Ibid.

FIGURE 4-18
Using a blend of handwritten and typed copy, this Poughkeepsie, New York, specialty fashion store aims its ads at middle-class buyers. Guess whom the Neiman-Marcus ad is aimed at? Often the sheer drama of an ad layout will register a subtle price in the minds of the reader.

this growing black market as a new group of motivated achievers and are gearing ads at their rising expectations (Figure 4-20).

The Hispanic Market   Just as dramatic as the economic visibility of blacks is the emergence of the Hispanic or Latino populations in this country. Demographers believe that in the 1980s this Spanish-speaking group of an estimated 30 million people will exceed any other minority in size. Advertisers need to know that 60 percent of this group live in the Southwestern states and are generally of Mexican heritage. An additional 20 percent have their roots in Puerto Rico and live in and around New York, Pennsylvania, and New Jersey. The next largest segment, with ties to Cuba, live in Florida. Despite the fact that 25 percent of all Latinos live in poverty, it is estimated that this fast-growing minority spends $31 billion each year.

Conclusion

The mass market, as we have seen, can be both large and segmented. For some products, such as toothpaste, the potential for sales embraces everyone; for other products, such as denture cleansers, the potential sales opportunities are narrowed by factors of age, sex, class, race, or religion. The importance to advertisers of identifying and analyzing their target audiences cannot be overly emphasized, because without this vital information, intelligent selection and use of media is not possible.

Big Farmer Tours presents. . .

Switzerland, Austria, West Germany and Liechtenstein. . .
Added attraction — Hungary

This trip was designed especially for YOU. It is planned for a small group of travelers to the places you have dreamed about. We will visit farms specializing in corn, wheat, vegetables and vineyards, and also in raising beef cattle, dairy cattle and hogs.

It is tremendously exciting to talk to the farmers in other countries to get their ideas on imports and exports, machinery, fertilizer, and animals. Wives enjoy talking to the housewives and seeing their homes and how they live.

In Budapest you will get insights into one of the largest hog operations and biggest corn-producing systems in Hungary. Also, the Raba Tractor Plant will give many ideas on tractor maintenance that enables Hungarians to operate their tractors over 10,000 hours.

In beautiful Vienna you'll hear the Vienna Boys' Choir and visit the birthplaces of Strauss, Beethoven and Schubert. Afterwards, enjoy a boat trip down the Danube and sightseeing in the Wachau Valley with its ancient castles. . .Then on to Salzburg, Mirabell Gardens and the famous water fountains of Hellbrunn Castle.

We'll take short trips into West Germany to see Berchtesgaden, Linderhof Palace and the beautiful Alps. We'll visit a typical Austrian dairy farm located along the Inn River near Innsbruck, and then we'll travel through fertile areas to Liechtenstein.

On to magnificent Switzerland—Lake Constance, the Rhine Falls at Schaffausen and a bus trip to Luzerne—before meeting with a Swiss banker who will tell us about those 'numbered' bank accounts, investing in Swiss francs and the price trends of gold. Now, on to Interlaken where we'll visit an outstanding Simmental herd and to Gruyere to sample their famous cheese.

Write us today for our colorful brochure. Departure date is June 21, 1978 with 14 nights and 16 days. Circle Reader Service No. 142.

We develop our tours to fit the farm family; they are custom-made; your time is planned. . .truly a worry-free vacation!

BIG FARMER, INC.
131 Lincoln Highway
Frankfort, IL 60423
or call (815) 469-2163

FIGURE 4-19

Once looked upon as a class near the bottom of the economic ladder, farmers have shot to the top in recent years. As a dramatic example of class mobility, the farmer class has few equals. The ad promoting a foreign tour quickly won response from farmers all over the country. (Courtesy *Big Farmer* magazine.)

FIGURE 4-20
Stride Rite shoes for children have always carried a quality appeal, and a higher-than-normal price. The company's latest catalog cover indicates that it is aware of the rising affluence of blacks.

IN SUMMARY

1 People and families change geographical locations, interests, and buying patterns. Successful advertisers must keep up with them.

2 Women have joined the labor force in growing numbers. They have a variety of reasons, chief of which is a desire to maintain a standard of living threatened by inflation.

3 The Sun Belt states are the chief beneficiaries of a population and industry emigration from other regions of the country. The Sun Belt's marketing importance has risen accordingly.

4 Proper demographic knowledge of the consumer means better decision making by advertisers. Important demographic factors are size of population and peoples' age, sex, racial and ethnic characteristics, income, and education.

5 An advertising strategy is a long-term commitment that can be shaped by a nation's fertility rate, attitudes toward traditional roles of age and sex, racial and ethnic attitudes, and levels of education.

6 The fact that the average American's life expectancy has increased substantially has had and will continue to have a profound effect on some aspects of advertising.

7 The true importance of the sexual revolution is a redefining of sex roles; women want to see themselves portrayed in professional situations, and as intelligent, competent members of society.

8 Advertisers turn to the behavioral sciences of psychology, sociology, and anthropology to help explain human behavior. Advertisers are interested, among other things, in how people receive or reject a message.

9 Psychographics is the term applied to motivational reasons for people's real wants.

10 The basic human psychological needs are to be important, to be loved, and to be protected. These remain the foundation of most advertising appeals.

11 Research studies prove that advertising recall depends on how the message is presented, and whether the mind will want to retain the message.

12 Anthropology's contribution to advertising is its analysis of people's customs, attitudes, and ideas.

13 Innovators or opinion leaders can hasten the acceptance of many products and services. This is the reason they are sought out by advertisers.

14 When advertisers know the socioeconomic status of groups, they are better able to position their advertising to appeal to these groups, whether they be young or old and lower, middle, or upper class.

15 Marketers see the growing black middle class as a new market controlling at least 70 percent of the black income.

16 The Hispanic market is rapidly becoming an important sales outlet, particularly in certain sections of the country.

CASE STUDY   Carol Wright Keeps Pace with
the Ever-Changing Mass Market   Carol Wright is a creation of
one of the nation's top marketing companies, Donnelley Marketing. Under her name
(fictitious), millions of American consumers receive batches of cents-off coupons.
Carol Wright knows all the right people, *who* they are, *where* they live, *where* they
buy, and *what* they buy. "She" reaches them by direct mail, with an envelope filled
with twenty to twenty-five noncompeting coupon offers and occasionally samples.
One of the purposes of the coop mailing, as it is called, is to reduce the high cost of
postage to individual manufacturers; the other is to divide the cost of handling millions
of folders, brochures, and coupons, inserting them into proper envelopes, affixing
mailing labels, and actually carting the mail sacks to the post office. One Carol Wright
mailing placed more than $127 million into the hands of American consumers.
Postage alone for such a mailing runs in excess of $2 million. With a redemption rate
that often reaches 16 percent of the total number of mailed coupons, retailers and
manufacturers exchange more than $20 million from this one mailing.[46]

The right users, to Carol Wright, are the heavy users of national brands such as
General Foods, Procter & Gamble, the Nestlé Company, and others. Heavy users,
according to Donnelley, are often worth three to four light users. They're the
households that change with growing children, the ones that add rooms or move
every few years. These users are part of the overall 65-million-household Donnelley
data base (approximately 88 percent of all households in the United States). From
demographic data from the U.S. Census and its own tailored lists further refined to
include 614 selected counties in the country with high supermarket density, Donnelley
compiles its Carol Wright mailing to 18 million households four times a year. Almost
55 percent of its Carol Wright mailing is sent to households earning $15,000 to
$25,000 or more. Further research indicates that 82 percent of recipient homemakers
make buying decisions immediately upon the receipt of the mailing. A typical Carol
Wright mailing can mean 4 million sales in just three weeks. Clairol Herbal Essence
was one of many products promoted through a Donnelley coop mailing. A foil-packet
sample plus coupon was mailed to the entire list. The product immediately achieved a
major share of the shampoo market. (Source: Donnelley Marketing.)

QUESTIONS NEEDING ANSWERS

1   It has been said by housing experts that only 25 percent of American families can
afford a median-priced house whereas twice that number could afford one five
years earlier. How will this development affect the following products and services:
tennis club memberships, rental apartments, paper diapers?

2   Who stands to benefit more from the 33 million social security checks sent out
each month, food manufacturers or fast-food restaurants?

3   With over 38 million women at work, will there be more day-care centers for
children and greater alienation between working parents and their children?

4   Why would an appliance advertiser seeking to reach the black market prefer one
state over another?

[46]"The 1977 Carol Wright heavy-user mail couponing program," *Donnelley Marketing News*,
December 1976, p. 8 (Stamford, Conn.: Donnelley Marketing).

5 Describe the repercussions in business if men and women lived an average of 85 years instead of 72.

6 The South and the West received $33 billion more in federal spending than they paid in taxes, according to *The National Journal* (June 1976 issue). In what specific ways can this information be of value to the advertiser?

7 In 1960, there were approximately 16 million eighteen- to twenty-four-year-olds. By 1977, the figure had almost doubled. How do these figures relate to any or all of the following? (a) Sales of vans and pick-ups. (b) Increases in advertising by lesser-known law schools. (c) Popularity of backpacking and traveling in national parks. (d) Sales of stereo components.

8 If you were the paid professional advertising counselor for a manufacturer of men's socks treated to combat foot odors, would your advertising strategy concentrate on the need not to offend or on the desire to be clean and fresh-smelling?

9 Describe the cultural innovator you'd select for the following products: (a) Gasoline additive that increases mileage 25 percent. (b) Device that creates a square hardboiled egg. (c) Antipickpocket device for a man's wallet. (d) Artificial-eyelash kit.

STUDENT PROJECT

To test Professor George A. Miller's research on the capacity of the mind to store and recall five to nine brand names on a short-term basis, survey three students from another class. Ask them to name as many brand names as they know for the following product categories: skis, detergents, deodorants, fast-food restaurants, headache remedies, gasolines, CB radios.

QUESTIONS ABOUT THE PROJECT

1 Is there a relationship between the amount of advertising for a particular product line and the number of brands recalled?

2 What role does point-of-purchase advertising, such as service station and restaurant signs, play in this situation?

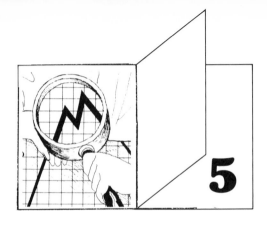

NATIONAL TELEVISION AND RADIO

Update Pursuing the elusive consumer is hard work. Once advertisers complete their research, they are ready to select a medium or vehicle to reach the target audience. We begin our discussion of national media with the broadcast twins, television and radio.

TELEVISION

National network television is no place for a half-hearted commitment. It costs too much! For example, in 1978, the average cost of a thirty-second commercial during network prime time was $50,000.[1] Consider that two of these television spots would immediately exceed the yearly advertising

[1]"A short course in broadcasting: 1978," *Broadcasting Yearbook*, 1978, p. A-2.

budgets of most American businesses. Of course, a prime-time announce-ment brings the advertiser 21 million viewers, or, if the advertiser happens onto a smash hit, as many as 36 million.[2] Table 5-1 shows some figures that illustrate the impact of television. For the particular study in Table 5-1, each rating point represents 730,000 households. It may go up or down, depending on the number of sets in operation. If advertisers ran commercials during a situation comedy (rating 20.1), they'd have reached 14.67 million households in one fell swoop. If they could afford them, that is the kind of commercial time they would buy. But, as we'll explain, it isn't as easy as that even for those who have the money.

The Basic Media Decision

As we investigate the reasons why advertisers select television instead of some other media, we must keep in mind that some of the reasons pertain to commercial radio as well. But first we need to understand what we mean by the basic media decision. This term refers to the specific communications vehicle—television, radio, print—that will carry the major responsibility for communicating advertisers' paid messages to target audiences. In this chapter, the first basic media decision of national advertisers concerns television.

Commercial television came to a radio-adoring public in 1939. Like radio, television is entirely supported by advertising. Within ten years of its debut over the American airwaves, it surpassed radio in popularity. For the

[2]"Roots II," Arbitron rating, February 1979.

TABLE 5-1
NETWORK TELEVISION PROGRAM RATINGS

Program type	Rating	Television households Number (in millions)
News		
Today (7:30 A.M.–8:00 A.M.)	4.2	3.06
CBS News (7:15 A.M.–8:00 A.M.)	2.3	1.68
Daytime		
Drama	7.1	5.21
Quiz and audience participation	5.3	3.87
All 10:00 A.M.–4:30 P.M.	6.3	4.58
Evening information	13.0	9.45
Evening		
General drama	16.8	12.28
Suspense and mystery	17.9	13.04
Situation comedy	20.1	14.67
Variety	17.0	12.36
Feature film	19.8	14.47
All 7:30 P.M.–11:00 P.M.	19.0	13.88

Source: A. C. Nielsen, November 1977, *World Almanac & Book of Facts,* 1979, p. 426.

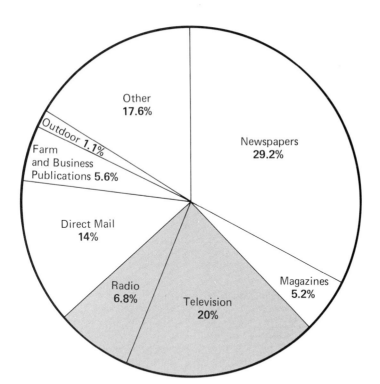

Other
17.6%

Outdoor 1.1%

Farm
and Business
Publications 5.6%

Direct Mail
14%

Newspapers
29.2%

Radio
6.8%

Television
20%

Magazines
5.2%

FIGURE 5-1
Major media share
of ad dollars.

national advertiser, the greatest advantage of television is its broad reach, through the networks. This breadth is one reason, among others, why television is something different for the national advertiser from what it is for the local or regional advertiser.

The larger the advertising budget, the more often the national advertiser can advertise. The money gives more options: a choice of networks, participation in specials, first crack at new programming. In short, for the national consumer goods manufacturer, television is always worthy of consideration. But advertisers must evaluate any medium according to three criteria: *reach, frequency,* and *continuity.*

Reach *Television reach* reflects the number of unduplicated households receiving a particular broadcast over a specified time period. (In context, unduplicated is the same as separate, individual households). The same definition applies to radio. Within the industry, this is generally a four-week period. Sometimes reach is called a "cumulative audience" or "cumes" for short. People also use the word "circulation." For example, if the *same* 15 million households watch "Happy Days" each week for four weeks, the total *audience* is 60 million (4 × 15). But the total *reach* (cumes) is still 15 million separate households. Total reach is important to advertisers who need to know how many different households—and persons—see their messages.

Media competitive to television claim that the same people see the same shows time after time. This criticism only holds true if shows fail to attract additional viewers.

Frequency   *Frequency* concerns the number of times advertisers wish to contact their audiences. Frequency is measured over short time periods, not longer than three months. Many advertisers measure the frequency with which their ads are seen by selected audiences as a period of six to thirteen weeks, often called "flights." For an advertiser who decided on a television blitz, frequency could be measured over a single weekend. The idea is to concentrate enough ads in a short time period so that most viewers will be aware of what the advertiser is selling.

Continuity   When advertisers run commercial messages over the long run, they are using the strategy of *continuity*. Continuity can support one creative strategy or several. In essence, it reveals top management's long-term commitment to advertising. The most familiar television advertisers believe in the benefits of continuity: Gillette, General Foods, Procter & Gamble, and General Motors, to name a few. Mindful of the ability of the human mind to recall only a limited number of brand names easily, they are in no mood to allow a competitor to displace them. This raises major problems for smaller companies. Because it costs big money to do a reasonable job on national television, advertisers must honestly assess their financial capability to sustain a television promotion. If they recognize that they can't afford to do more than a token job, they must either select another medium or pick and choose individual television stations and not use the entire network. It is a sad admission, but a true one, that most companies cannot take advantage of this powerful national selling tool, either because of lack of money or because of the limited number of good national spots. To understand the reasons, we need to look at the medium itself.

Television: Past, Present, Future

Today over 73 million homes have one or more television sets. That's 98 percent of all homes in the United States. Most are color sets. Thirty years ago, the competing media believed that the newcomer would be essentially a metropolitan medium, because it depended upon a short-range signal, from horizon to horizon, of roughly forty to fifty miles. The competitive media believed that the people of rural and small-town America would never see a television broadcast in their homes because of this limited signal. They were mistaken, because they did not foresee the coming of microwaves and low-power translator stations by which signals could be picked up and boosted from horizon to horizon until television reached every nook and cranny in the country. In 1948, there were 400,000 sets in use; they already presented an accurate vision of things to come. A May 1948 *Pulse Radio Survey* showed that whenever a better-than-average television show was

FIGURE 5-2
Eighty-nine percent of all homes watched the Kennedy-Nixon debates over television; just sixteen years later, slightly more than one-half of all television set owners took the time to watch the Carter-Ford debates. Television had lost its novelty.

broadcast, "hardly any TV-equipped homes tune in on the Fred Allen and other top-notch [radio] comedians."[3]

Today there are 961 television transmitting stations, of which 253 are educational and carrying no commercial advertising. The commercial stations carried over $7 billion in advertising during 1976[4] (Figure 5-2).

We can only guess at what television will be like tomorrow. Screens may be larger and thinner. All transmission may be by communication satellite rather than by telephone lines and cables. The 1980 Olympics in Moscow, to be broadcast by Moskva Intelstat satellite and through the NBC television network, is a case in point. NBC paid over $72 million to the Soviet Union for the commercial rights to the sports extravaganza. *Videodisc systems* may hurt television broadcasters. These systems—now moving into limited commercial production—permit customers to buy their own copies of popular movies, sporting events, even pornographic films and play them through their sets. Broadcasters assume that the videodiscs will be played during prime time, and they may change the nature and the price of commercials bought at that time. A great deal will depend on the price of both the individual discs and the videodisc apparatus and on the quality of the reproduction. Conceivably, lending libraries, commercial or public, may have a role to play if videodiscs become widely accepted.

[3]B. B. Smith, "Television, there ought to be a law," *Harper's*, September 1948, pp. 34–42.
[4]"A short course in broadcasting: 1978," *Broadcasting Yearbook*, 1978, p. A-2.

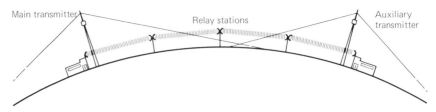

FIGURE 5-3
Television transmission waves travel in straight paths; relay stations and auxiliary transmitters or translator stations are therefore required. [*The Way Things Work*, (New York; Simon and Schuster, 1967), p. 123.]

UHF and VHF Transmission Television stations are divided into two broad categories, commercial and educational. Within the commercial category, there are two main types: UHF (ultrahigh frequency) and VHF (very high frequency). Most network stations are VHF. Since short-wave television signals only travel in a straight line, they require tall antennae at their transmitter stations and additional antennae spaced on hills or tall towers in order to provide good coverage throughout a region (Figure 5-3). The major difference between UHF and VHF is carrying distance. VHF waves are sent out between 54 and 216 million times a second; UHF between 470 and 890 million. The more frequently the wave is sent out (UHF), the *shorter* the distance it covers. Major commercial interests obviously prefer the VHF stations because their waves go out farther, reach more households, and require fewer costly auxiliary transmitters and antennae. National advertisers are not particularly interested in UHF stations unless they are unable to buy good time slots on the more powerful, popular stations (Figure 5-4).

Cable Transmission Cable television or community antenna television (CATV) systems are developed in response to such obstacles as tall buildings, forests, and mountains, which prevent normal television signals from reaching viewers. Because many hard-to-reach localities are sparsely populated, conventional stations prefer not to build costly transmitters and antennae nearby. Cable television moved to take advantage of this vacuum.

With cable service, private interests build community antennae on a hill or tall structure to pick up near and distant signals from conventional television stations. The cable company does not pay for the pickup. It delivers signals by means of a wire or cable to homes that subscribe to the service. Some cable signals are better than conventional signals. Yet, even where conventional television signals are strong, cable companies have moved into the area because they see a business opportunity, and because they can offer subscribers an average of six to ten clear channels instead of the usual three.

At first, it was a rocky road for many cable companies. Subscriber turnover was high and their installation costs substantial. But cable companies have prospered as they have begun selecting their locations based more on the ability of households in an area to pay $6 to $10 a month (average subscriber *fee*) than on weak signals from established VHF stations. Like providers of all other services, the owners of cable television have learned that there is *no market* where there is no ability to pay! In 1971, the Federal Communications Commission (FCC) urged cable systems to initiate their own programming.[5] Some 67 percent have done so, averaging 23 hours weekly. In 1978, it was estimated that 18 percent of all television set owners enjoy cable.[6] Supporters of cable believe that growing numbers of viewers

[5]Warner Cable Corporation reports through newspaper stories impressive successes with a sophisticated pay-television cable system called Qube in Columbus, Ohio. Qube offers thirty channels of programming, and subscribers can also "talk back" by means of an electronic console. Other cable promoters dream of a two-way electronic system by which subscribers could shop for goods in the comfort of their homes. Some even hope that facsimile newspapers can be run off the television set and tied into a printing device.

[6]"A short course in broadcasting: 1978," *Broadcasting Yearbook*, 1978, p. A-2.

FIGURE 5-4
Satellite communications overcome the terrestrial straight-path limitation on television transmission waves and beam pictures and sound around the world. This ad appeared in *Broadcasting Yearbook*.

will pay for the privilege of having a greater choice of channels. However, there is another side to cable, as this report from the ABC Network points out:

> Park County, Montana, is a pertinent example of what cable TV's fractionalization of audience can do. Park County with its 4100 TV homes is adjacent to the Missoula-Butte and Billings marketing areas . . . and geographically remote from Salt Lake City which is 500 miles away . . . 65 percent of these Park County homes are on cable. The result . . . over the full broadcast day, the three imported Salt Lake signals take 42 percent of the audience . . . leaving only 20 percent and 30 percent shares for the local stations in Missoula-Butte and Billings. The cumulative effect . . . is obvious. The local free TV station with reduced audiences suffers reduced revenues. This can mean a reduction in its ability to provide the kind of news and public affairs coverage the local community requires.[7]

The implied threat is that cable television may weaken free television because as its economic power grows, it may also buy off the major sporting events, comedy shows, and so on. Already, cable companies buy new movies and other programs from the producers for their subscribers. Dubbed "Home Box Office," "pay as you go TV," or "subscription TV," this enterprise is expanding rapidly, leading some cable systems to advertise "without cable, all you have is TV." But the idea of subscription television is not new. All during the 1960s, it had been debated in Congress. The "pros" painted a picture of unlimited cultural programs from all around the world brought into the living room of every American family. They also pointed to the business community's love affair with the "free enterprise system" of capitalism as justification for permitting pay-as-you-go television to flourish. The "cons" argued just as vehemently that the relentless law of supply and demand would soon swing in favor of the cable systems because they would be able to pay more for entertainment than the established networks. When that time came, they said, free television would have little of general interest for the masses, and each family would have to pay if it wanted entertainment on its television screen. Without a definitive ruling from the federal government on this controversy, it appears that marketplace forces will continue to operate: both cable and established television meeting head-to-head in competition. Already some experts anticipate cable to be in nearly 30 percent of American homes at the end of the 1980s.[8] (Figure 5-5.)

The Networks and Affiliates

There are three major television networks within the United States today: the National Broadcasting Company (NBC), the American Broadcasting Company (ABC), and Columbia Broadcasting Company (CBS). They own[9] or are

---

[7]*Television—Medium at the crossroads*, American Broadcasting Company, 1977.
[8]*Cox looks at the future*, a report (Atlanta: Cox Broadcasting Corporation, 1975), p. 56.
[9]Federal Communications Commission (FCC) regulations restrict any one station from owning more than five others.

FIGURE 5-5

"Dayton's best value in the world of entertainment" is what Viacom Cablevision of Dayton guarantees subscribers. In addition to Dayton's conventional television channels, the cable company offers 24-hour-a-day satellite service from Atlanta, sports from Madison Square Garden in New York City, Christian Broadcasting Network programs, stations from Cincinnati, Indianapolis, and Columbus, plus other special-channel programs devoted to live coverage of the House of Representatives, a video flea market (where viewers phone in items for sale), review of stocks and sports, video music, 24-hour news, community bulletin board, and so forth. (Courtesy Viacom Communications, Inc.)

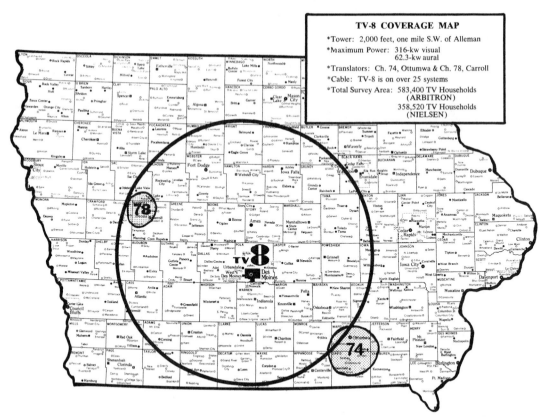

FIGURE 5-6

A CBS affiliate's coverage area in central Iowa helps a media buyer make buying decisions. Eastern and western Iowa receive programming from Illinois and Nebraska CBS affiliates; northern Iowa from a Minneapolis CBS affiliate. Comparable coverages are available from the other major networks, thus providing national advertisers with coast-to-coast coverage.

affiliated with stations in all major markets. Their programming is the common thread binding network and affiliate. The network depends on its *affiliates* (locals) to distribute its product: news, information, sports, and entertainment. With coverage of all major markets assured, the network can attract national advertisers to buy commercial time. In exchange, the affiliate depends on the network for exciting shows with which to hold an audience. In 1978–1979, the networks shaped up as follows: CBS-TV, 198 stations; ABC-TV, 190 stations; NBC-TV, 212 stations. In addition, 91 independent stations are not affiliated with any national network. There are also lesser networks that service specific regions: The Alaska TV Network, Cal-Oregon Broadcasting, Hughes TV Network, and others. Although advertisers don't have to buy each and every affiliate station when making a "network buy," it makes sense because these are generally the top markets with greatest audience reach and sales potentials.

The way the networks and affiliates divide advertising dollars is complicated. In theory, the affiliate stations make part of their broadcast time available to the network. In practice, it is the major portion. The networks pay for this time with ad revenues, with exact amounts determined primarily by an affiliate's audience ratings. The network pays approximately 12 to 25 percent of each advertising dollar to the affiliates and keeps the rest to pay for its large staff of trained news gatherers, on-camera persons, writers, producers, directors, maintenance staff, and outside talent. A hit program like "The Mary Tyler Moore Show" cost the CBS Network over $150,000 a week to air.[10] Affiliates make most of their income by selling advertising spots adjacent to network programming. They may sell them to national advertisers who want extra coverage or to local businesses. The sales are made by the station's own business staff or through national representative organizations. The national network sales office sells network commercial time and obtains affiliate clearances (Figure 5-6).

The Rating Game

Anyone who checks the daily selections of the television menu served up by the networks knows how fiercely they compete. If NBC runs a famous film at 8 o'clock, ABC and CBS will try to entice viewers away from the film. At stake are millions of viewers who translate into millions of dollars of revenue: in 1978, over an estimated $8 billion from advertisers. How do advertisers know who has won the hourly battles for the viewers? They're informed by commercial survey companies, who have slowly become the most powerful institutions in the broadcast industry. Chief among these is the originator of the ratings system, A. C. Nielsen. His company measures the television and radio coverage of national and local markets. One Nielsen study, for example, indicated that the average household ran its television set 6½ hours a day (Figure 5-7).

Basically, Nielsen's system is a demographic random sampling of television households. He uses phone interviews, personal diaries, and electronic devices such as an *Audimeter* (Figure 5-8). This unit, about the size of a large toaster, attaches to the television set and records when the set is on. The Nielsen Company gathers this information in a computer at its Florida headquarters and sells the results to broadcast stations, advertising agencies, and advertisers. Other rating services, the most familiar being Arbitron (earlier known as ARB), provide similar information. This information determines

[10]Jerry Thorpe, veteran television producer of "Kung Fu" and "Harry O", states that "the cost of a one-hour series episode has gone from $130,000 to around $200,000." Al Stump, "When a star is hit by a coconut," *TV Guide*, June 5, 1976, p. 27.

Here's how to keep your TV Diary:

In columns 1, 2, 3 . . . at the right, **please fill in the NAMES, AGE and SEX** of all household members (whether they watch TV or not). Include persons temporarily away, such as on trips or vacations. See Example below for typical entries. If no Man or Lady of House, write NONE in that column.

If you have several TV's, you probably received several diaries. Please write names in same order in each diary, and keep one diary with each TV. (If you didn't receive a diary for each TV, see instructions inside back cover.)

(A) WHEN THE TV IS "OFF"
Draw a line down the "OFF" column for all quarter-hours the TV is off.

Important: If your TV is broken, or won't be used at all in the diary week, **please answer the questions** on the next page . . . and return your diary immediately.

(B) WHEN THE TV IS "ON"
- Put an X in the "ON" column for each quarter-hour the TV is turned on for six minutes or longer. Please be especially sure to show all **late-evening** TV use.
- Write in Station Call Letters, Channel Number, and Name of Program. For Movies, please write "Movie" and Name of Movie. (See Example, below.)
- Put an X in the column under the name of each person watching six minutes or longer during each quarter-hour the TV is "ON."

(C) If an entry in a column does not change from one quarter-hour to the next, DRAW A LINE down that column to show entry did not change. (See Example, below.)

(D) If the TV is "ON" but no one is watching, fill in the station and program information and put "O" in the first person column.

(E) If you have a visitor watching this TV, write "VISITOR" in one of the blank name columns along with visitor's age and sex. (If exact age is not known, put in approximate age.) If you do not have room to write in any more names, write in the **number** of other persons watching in the column marked "OTHERS."

FIGURE 5-7

Using a diary technique, A. C. Nielsen Company receives weekly reports from a sample of television viewers. These reports become part of the famed Nielsen ratings. Prior to the receipt of the diary, each respondent is phoned and alerted to the fact that the diary is coming. Then, a postcard reminder is sent to encourage the respondent to return the diary quickly.

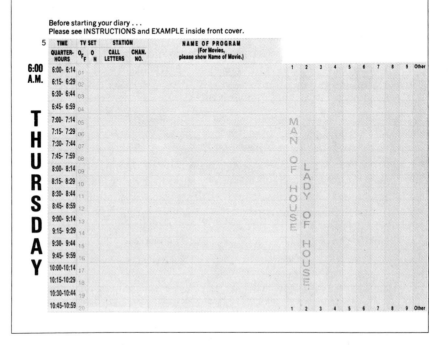

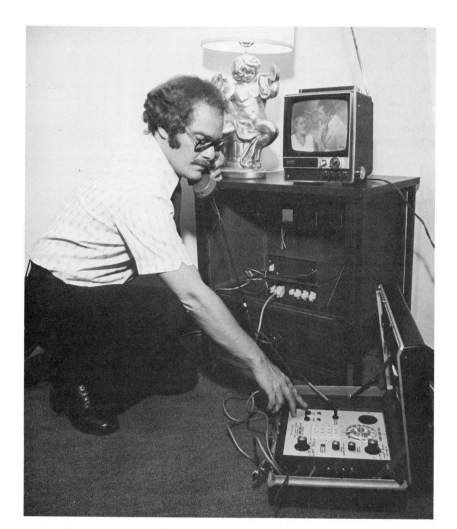

FIGURE 5-8
This is the
Audimeter (inside
cabinet) installed by
A. C. Nielsen
Company. It records
television viewing
and transmits data
to the Florida-based
Nielsen computer.

important media-purchasing decisions. Advertisers in particular are anxious to discover whether their commercials are being seen by a large share of the audience. They assume that the program that attracts a majority of viewers will also be the best for their announcements (Figure 5-9).

The Price Structure of Television Commercials

Networks usually sell their television commercial time to a group of participating advertisers. During the course of one Super Bowl football game, for example, twenty-seven brand names flashed across the screen. Although most network programming is purchased by several participating sponsors per show, some advertisers do not wish to share the prestige with any other

How to get to the heart of your competition.

Today your best source of more spot dollars is what's being spent in newspapers.

But you're probably losing sales because your ADI is bigger than the newspaper circulation area.

And you're losing more because the marketing areas of your prospects —banks, fast food chains, and retail stores don't correspond to either your Metro, ADI, or TSA.

We have the solution— Arbitron Information on Demand!

Now you can show a local advertiser just how many of *his real prospects* you reach. Arbitron Information on Demand (AID) makes it possible because it can pull together audience data for whatever county or combination of counties you need.

So stop giving your competition an even break. Join the other television stations that are getting new money away from newspapers.

Get in touch with your Arbitron Television representative right away.

Arbitron Information on Demand

ARBITRON TELEVISION

New York (212) 262-2600. Chicago (312) 467-5750. Atlanta (404) 892-7866.
Los Angeles (213) 937-6420. San Francisco (415) 391-1702. Dallas (214) 522-2470. Washington (301) 595-4644.

FIGURE 5-9
Hard-hitting research company's ad directed toward television sales managers encourages them to go after newspaper advertising dollars. (Courtesy Arbitron Television)

company. These individual sponsors, such as Xerox and Hallmark, often are associated with a show, an advantage they feel is well worth the additional costs. Individual sponsors can underwrite innovative or unique programs consistent with their corporate image. Individual sponsorships also lend themselves to distributor-dealer promotions, often a major consideration with any television buy.

In the early days of television, single sponsorship was usual. But fierce competition for top-rated spots as well as escalating costs have forced advertisers to share the expense.[11] Costs are also a major reason most commercials run for thirty seconds instead of sixty. Some advertisers cram two of their products into one thirty-second spot. These thirty-second spots range from $6,000 in major markets to $5 in the smallest markets. The price structure for popular network program commercials is quite unstable. In some ways, it resembles an auction in that people bid against others who want the available spots. Because only a limited number of commercials are available during a broadcast day, when there are too many buyers, the price goes up, a classic example of the law of supply and demand.[12] For the past thirty years, the price of network television, like that of other media, has been on an escalator going up. During most of that time, audience size has also been going up.

Pricing Commercials

Television commercials are sold under a variety of conditions: *preemptible*, *immediately preemptible*, and *fixed*. A *fixed* spot is the costliest, because it cannot be displaced by another advertiser's commercial. Only a major station crisis or an event of great importance can supplant it. *Preemptible* spots are bought with the understanding that if another advertiser will pay more, the original advertiser will be preempted. But when this happens, the station gives the original advertiser enough notice so that they can work out another arrangement. Cheapest of all spots is the *immediately preemptible*, which permits the station to move spots as it sees fit. Stations do not have to give the advertiser prior warning. Since the introduction of the preemptible spot, the paperwork in advertising agencies and broadcast stations has become awesome. Advertisers don't want to pay for commercials that have never run or are being delayed:

> Our clients' advertising is carefully planned and bought, to reach a specific target audience at a particular time with a particular commercial . . . We check every invoice, line for line, against every line on our buy sheet before the bill is paid. . . . Unless it is a true emergency, don't pre-empt without telling us in

[11]The term "spot," through time and sloppy usage, has developed a number of meanings. To a time buyer, it is the purchase of time on a market-to-market basis and also an ad placed between programs. To creative people, it's the word that indicates any television or radio commercial. Purists insist that a commercial placed within a program is a participation, but most people still call it a spot.

[12]Price is a function of need, scarcity, and the satisfaction the item brings to individual purchasers.

advance and don't schedule a *make-good* without our prior approval or the changes won't be in our buy sheet even if they are on your bill. . . . J. Walter Thompson volume in spot creates a tremendous amount of paper—800,000 spots per year, 42,000 invoices per year, $75,000,000 spot TV and radio billing.[13]

In addition to the three-tiered pricing structure, *package deals* and *plans* are negotiated between advertiser and network. The price depends on the programming, the ratings, and the amount of money the advertiser is willing to commit to television over a specified time period.[14] (All these are related to the way the television industry sells time, in segments called *dayparts:* daytime, 6:00 A.M.–4:30 P.M.; early fringe, 4:30 P.M.–7:30 P.M. prime time, 7:30 P.M.–11:00 P.M.; and late fringe, 11:00 P.M.–1: A.M. Prime time, with its largest viewing audience, is the most expensive. Times are one hour earlier in Central and Mountain time zones.) Networks prefer advertisers who contract for year-round package plans, since this provides guaranteed income to the network long in advance of the spots' actually running. For this assurance, networks are willing to provide package discounts. Interestingly, the desire on the part of the networks for guaranteed income led to the development of the media-buying services in the 1960s and early 1970s. These specialized media-buying services buy large blocks of network time and resell it below the published rates. We'll review the advantages and disadvantages of media-buying services when we take a hard look at advertising agencies in Chapter 15.

Closing Dates

The *closing date* is the specific day on which all advertising tapes and films required by the networks have to be in their hands. It also refers to the last day an advertiser can cancel a buy without penalty. The purpose of a closing date is to allow the networks enough time to schedule commercials throughout all their affiliate stations with a minimum of face-offs between competitors. Another purpose is to give the network censor time to examine the commercials. Sometimes a commercial found offensive by one censor may be accepted at another network. Closing dates for a network may be set at one to two weeks before air time; for a local station only, the date may be as little as seventy-two hours before air time. In terms of all media—broadcast, newspapers, magazines—this is a short time indeed.

---

[13]Thornton B. Wierum, vice president and director of media services and administration, J.W. Thompson (New York), in a speech given in 1976.

[14]This does not include cable television systems, most of whom do not sell television time. Among the few systems that do, a thirty-second spot in a major market might cost as little as $200, compared to the conventional station spot cost of $4000. This situation may change rapidly as new "superstation" cable television systems are being erected in several major cities, with reaches that may rival those of some regional networks.

Measurement by Gross Rating Points

Sophisticated time buyers schedule television ads according to *gross rating points* or *GRPs*, a measurement of the viewing audience of specific programs. We generally express GRPs on a weekly basis, relying on ratings provided by either Arbitron and/or Nielsen. Thus, if a popular weekly situation comedy has an Arbitron rating of 20 among all audiences, we identify *that show* on *that day* and at *that time period* as being worth 20 GRPs. (To even out the chances of a single weekly rating's being distorted, GRPs for that show are determined by averaging ratings over a four-week period; see Figure 5-10.) Using our situation-comedy example, if two commercials are broadcast over station WNAC-TV during this show and 20 percent of the entire households in the area are tuned in, the GRP value is 40. (Reach × frequency equals GRPs, or 2 × 20 = 40.) Many national advertisers aim for 100 GRPs to a market or to a particular segment, such as women eighteen to forty-nine or men twenty-five to fifty-four. Experience has shown that combinations of reach ratings times frequency of messages that add up to 100 GRPs will usually satisfy most national advertisers. Thus, in our situation-comedy example, if we wanted to achieve 100 GRPs, we'd have to buy five commercials within that program, not two. However, if we didn't want to invest all our television dollars on that one show, we would have to look at other shows and other ratings. National advertisers look not only at the GRPs of regional markets but also at the average ratings of all the network stations coast to coast.

One confusing element of the GRP system is that it can be heavy on the reach or heavy on the frequency. For example, during a recent telecast of "Roots II," the show achieved a one-week rating of 50 GRPs. In other words, one single commercial broadcast at that time was equal to 50 GRPs of all households tuned in at that time period. Thus, only two messages would have given an advertiser 100 GRPs. The question to the advertiser must be: Are two spots to a larger audience worth ten spots to a smaller audience? Obviously, the answer depends on the advertising objectives of the advertiser.

GRPs are also used by time buyers to see how much their advertisers can afford to pay for a television spot. For example, if a national advertiser has allocated a budget of $1,500 a week to a group of regional markets and wants 50 GRPs in each market, it's apparent that the advertiser can afford spots of no more than $30 per rating point. Weekly budget divided by desired GRPs equals cost per rating point, or $1,500 ÷ 50 = $30). Thus, if "*Laverne and Shirley*" develops 16 GRPs and the cost for a thirty-second spot is $480, the advertisers stay within their $1,500 weekly budget if they buy spots on this show ($480 ÷ 16 = $30).

Sometimes advertisers are not as interested in GRPs as they are in the number of homes with sets tuned in at a particular time. If 15,000 households

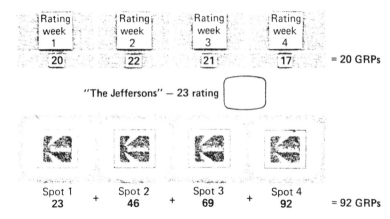

Rating week 1	Rating week 2	Rating week 3	Rating week 4
20	22	21	17	= 20 GRPs

"The Jeffersons" — 23 rating

Spot 1   +   Spot 2   +   Spot 3   +   Spot 4
  23   46   69   92   = 92 GRPs

FIGURE 5-10
Most national advertisers feel they are reaching enough people often enough with 100 GRPs per week. Prime-time television situation comedies like "The Jeffersons" attract both national and regional advertisers. In some regions, "The Jeffersons" share of television viewers is 50 percent. Probably the all-time ratings winner is the "I Love Lucy Show." One Nielsen rating in April 1953 gave the program a score of 67.3%. (Courtesy CBS Television Network.)

are tuned in at a specific 8:30 movie and the total number of households in that market is 60,000, the *sets-in-use figure* is 25 percent (60,000 ÷ 15,000). Advertisers are also vitally interested in the ages of the people who are watching any given show, because the total amount and type of demand for any product or service is closely related to age. For example, for Johnny Carson's "Tonight Show," a heavy majority of viewers during the 11:00–12:00 segment are women eighteen years of age and older. The age factor helps explain the number of advertisers promoting feminine hygiene products.

One last word about ratings. It's important for advertisers to look at the ratings of the shows that precede theirs. Do they regularly hold large audiences of the right sex and age group? What's taking place on the competing networks? Answers to these and other demographic questions concerning television audiences, both national and regional, help the advertisers arrive at a satisfactory television media buy (Tables 5-2 and 5-3.)

Make-Goods

How does the television advertiser or agent know whether commercials have run? With newspapers or magazines, there is a permanent record that is easy

TABLE 5-2

COST CONVERTER BY MARKET RANK GROUPINGS

Target audience	Daypart	ADI market group*	Avg. cost thirty sec. for every market group	Target audience (in 000)	Total audience (in 000)	Target audience cost per thousand (CPM)	Total audience cost per thousand (CPM)
Women	Daytime	Top 10	$1,817	398	1,037	$4.57	$1.75
18–49	(M-F)	Top 20	3,035	603	1,576	5.03	1.93
		Top 100	7,175	1,534	4,026	4.68	1.78
		Top 200	10,365	2,007	5,296	5.16	1.96
Adults	Nighttime	Top 10	19,223	2,701	4,421	7.12	4.35
18–49		Top 20	30,330	4,164	6,817	7.28	4.45
		Top 100	62,518	10,173	16,623	6.15	3.76
		Top 200	78,166	13,089	21,317	5.97	3.67
Men	Weekend	Top 10	4,386	679	1,991	6.46	4.09
18–49	daytime	Top 20	7,289	969	2,858	7.52	4.71
Children	Children's	Top 10	2,481	668	2,609	3.71	2.24
6–11	programs	Top 20	4,019	916	3,678	4.39	2.57
		Top 200	13,599	2,792	12,150	4.87	2.66

*Areas(markets) of dominant influence(ADI) are ranked from the top 10 through 200. Top 10 markets include New York(1), Los Angeles(2), Chicago(3), and Philadelphia(4). For example, the average cost of a thirty-second spot to reach woment eighteen to forty-nine in *all* of the top 10 cities(markets) during the day(weekdays) is $1,817. To obtain the ADI rating(a percentage), we tally the TV households reached by the average spot, and divide by the total TV households in the market group. This percentage(3.9) divided into the spot costs($1,817) gives us cost per rating point($466). Total audience and household figures found in TvB's *Ninth Annual Spot Television Planning Guide,* 1978–1979.

TABLE 5-3
COST PER RATING POINT FOR SPOT TV COVERAGE—* 30-SECONDS

Markets	Percent of United States	Weekdays	Prime Time	Late evening
Top ten	40	$290	$910	$595
Top twenty	52	420	1260	825
Top thirty	62	515	1535	1010
Top forty	69	570	1670	1110
Top fifty	75	635	1780	1190
Top sixty	81	680	1930	1280
Top seventy	85	720	2020	1335
Top eighty	89	770	2065	1395
Top ninety	92	805	2185	1450
Top one hundred	95	840	2210	1505

Source: Batten, Barton, Durstine & Osborn, 1976.
*Commercials placed through local market stations, not an overall network buy.

to file and review. Not so with the broadcast media. Traditionally, proof-of-airing has been a sworn statement from the station taken from information in the station's log. The sworn statement acts as an affidavit of performance. If commercials are not telecast because of a massive power blackout, for example, or if the audio or video portions of the commercial are faulty, a make-good will be scheduled. Advertisers want to be notified when there are make-goods so they can give their approval.

The Bartered Side of Television

Why would advertisers or ad agencies produce *and pay for* television programs that they offer *free* to the networks? That is the essence of one of the better-kept secrets of television—*barter*. Approximately 16 percent of all network prime-time half-hours are bartered.[15] Owners of the programs (advertisers or agencies) offer them to the networks in exchange for air time. This system permits the networks to sell the remaining commercial air time to other noncompeting advertisers without making an investment of its own in producing the show. Bartered shows are also called trade-out syndicated shows.

There is yet another form of barter involving the *barter house*. This company generally buys large blocks of the less popular air time from stations, which it then sells to advertisers in exchange for merchandise. Some advertisers like this arrangement because they are bartering their merchandise at much higher prices than it cost them to manufacture, thus getting more air time for their real investment. Often, the barter house simply acts as a selling agent for the stations and helps them sell merchandise such as cars, refrigerators, and the like to outside parties. Despite its old-fashioned connotation, barter shows no signs of dying.

[15]"Prime time half-hours," *Advertising Age*, February 1, 1977, p. 1.

The Clutter Problem

In Chapter 4 we pointed out that viewers' limited recall of brand names of products in categories seems to be a problem advertisers must face. This problem is exaggerated by the proliferation of commercials and station promotional announcements all during the broadcast day. The capacity of the mind to recall and the large volume of thirty-second commercials have led to what advertisers call "clutter." Clutter describes a state in which there are too many messages in too short a time, with the result that too few are remembered. An advertising industry report has this to say about clutter: "The average one hour of broadcasting . . . on three network-owned stations contained 30 separate visual elements . . . an average of one programming interruption every two minutes."[16]

Some advertising experts consider *selective perception* a defense against a barrage of messages. Selective perception is the process of screening out or tuning in certain objects and events so that messages are rejected or accepted or in some way altered to conform to our individual biases. If, for example, a television viewer believes that all foreign cars are expensive to repair, that viewer may filter out the sales message of a foreign car maker.

Television's clutter problems do not overshadow its ability to stimulate sales, however. When Gillette introduced its Trac II razor and blade in October 1971, it estimated that seven of ten homes saw its commercials at least once a week. In its first year, Gillette spent more than $10 million on advertising and promotion. By the end of the compaign's first month, the company had shipped more than 1.7 million razors and over 5 million dual-blade cartridges.[17] Likewise, when the musical *A Chorus Line* swept the Tony Awards on the ABC telecast, the citizens of Los Angeles lined up to buy a record $70,000 worth of tickets the first day after the Tony broadcast and $82,000 worth the next day.[18]

Advantages and Disadvantages of Television Advertising

A network commercial can entertain and sell at the same time. The sales message can be delivered well and dramatically, with the selling point clear and obvious. When sales messages are presented well, television offers advertisers several advantages:

1 National television delivers the broadest audience (reach) in the shortest period of time compared to other media. Over 95 percent of all households in the country tune in at some time during the week. Knowing this, some advertisers schedule

---

[16]Study by Association of National Advertisers with the Media Directors Council, reported by Philip Dougherty in *The New York Times*, December 1976.

[17]Presentation by William G. Salatich, vice chairman, the Gillette Company to masters of business administration from Boston University, November 12, 1971.

[18]Associated Press report, Los Angeles, May 1976.

commercials on all three networks to increase their chances of reaching as wide an audience as possible.

2 With television, viewers don't have to imagine things, because the products are right there on the screen, alive and real. It is a very direct and credible medium.

3 Television is excellent for realistic package and product identification.

4 Television's cost per impression is only pennies.[19] (*Cost per impression* refers to total number of households with sets watching an advertiser's commercial divided into the cost of the commercial. If 35 million households see a $35,000 spot, the cost per impression is $1/10$ cent.)

5 Dealers and distributors love television. They react enthusiastically when they know that it will be used to help move goods.

For some mass-produced and distributed products, television is ideal. The food industry spends $4 billion every year in the medium, with Coca-Cola alone spending $70 million. But strategists for other products need to examine demographics and wasted circulation (reach) before committing themselves to television. It is not a coverup for good marketing procedures. Some of the disadvantages of network television are:

1 The high costs virtually shut the door for any but the largest companies. The race for prime time, for example, inflates costs. (*Prime time* refers to the period from 7:30 to 11:00 P.M.)

2 Residuals, the payments to people who appear in long-running commercials (usually more than thirteen weeks), can become extremely expensive.

3 The clutter problem reduces advertising recall.

4 The short, short selling message can be a problem. How can an advertiser show and tell in thirty seconds? The thirty-second spot may require additional advertising in other longer-lived media. When the television commercial has left the screen, it is gone for good.

5 The problem of back-to-back competitive commercials invites a serious loss in advertising effectiveness. Many advertisers insist that commercials for competitive products be spaced at least fifteen minutes apart. This protection is exceedingly difficult for the networks to police.

6 Coordinating the times when commercials are aired on all the network's affiliate stations may pose a problem because of snarls in local scheduling. When affiliates do air programs and commercials, the time may not be favorable to an advertising strategy.

The Smaller Advertiser's Option

Network television is too expensive for most smaller advertisers. However, they can select target cities, buying commercial times the same way larger advertisers do. Advertisers may ask the television station or its national sales representative to help them select target cities as well as to provide them with

---

[19]Ted Bates, a New York-based advertising agency, claims that network television is $2.11 per 1000 delivered homes for the top 100 markets (thirty seconds.)

a list of current station "unsold" air time availabilities. Sales representatives usually handle many target market stations and thus can save the small advertiser hours of paperwork and production problems. Lists of station representatives appear in all broadcast reference books as well as in the Yellow Pages in major cities.

RADIO

Like television, national radio operates within a network system.[20] But its national audience appeal, which in turn affects its programming, has been seriously weakened by television. Advertisers can buy national coverage with a limited number of programs, usually news shows or some special event. Otherwise, radio has no national shows comparable to television. It wasn't always so.

From the 1920s to the late 1940s, national radio was as powerful and persuasive as television is today. It was an integral part of every large advertiser's budget, and national coverage was inconceivable without it. Radio performers such as Bing Crosby, Jack Benny, Fred Allen, Amos 'n Andy, Bob Hope, Arthur Godfrey, and Frank Sinatra delighted millions of consumers. They helped to make brand names like Pepsodent, Texaco, Kraft, and Jello household words. In 1941, two days after the Japanese bombed Pearl Harbor, the largest radio audience in history—estimated at 90 million—listened to President Franklin D. Roosevelt's plans for the future. Sponsorship of complete half-hour programs ran as high as $27,000 a week. For this, a half-hour sponsor received a ten- to fifteen-second introduction, three 1-minute spots and a ten-second closing announcement. The shows were expensive because stars often went on the air complete with cast of supporting players and large orchestra.

In 1948, the year of network radio's highest billings, B. B. Smith, in a clear look at both radio and television wrote:

> Even now, the AM radio set, pushed out of many a living room by the television receiver, is taking refuge in the bedroom . . . before finally being relegated to the store room.[21]

Segmented Audiences

The increasing popularity of television transferred the influence of radio to the local or regional level. Programming changed. Music, news, and sports were "tailored" to specific audiences: young singles, mature middle-of-the-roaders, rural people. To gain a share of market, each station began to build

---

[20]The American and National Broadcasting Companies and the Columbia and Mutual Broadcasting Systems. In addition, there are regional radio networks.
[21]B. B. Smith, "Television, there ought to be a law."

TABLE 5-4
RADIO COST PER THOUSAND (CPM)

	Spot radio—sixty seconds	
	6 A.M.–10 A.M. 3 P.M.– 7 P.M.	10 A.M.– 3 P.M.
Adults over 18	$1.20	$1.00
Women		
over 18	2.40	1.75
18–34	5.90	4.00
18–49	3.65	2.60
over 50	7.00	5.50
Working women over 18	6.40	5.90
Men		
over 18	2.80	2.30
18–34	6.40	5.10
18–49	4.10	3.30
over 50	9.00	7.60

Source: *Radio Facts,* (Radio Advertising Bureau, 1977), p. 14.

its own image, to concentrate on what it could do best. In so doing, all stations collectively segmented and decentralized the markets. Today these 6,000-plus stations* compete fiercely with each other and with all other media within their markets. Because of this extreme competition, shrewd advertisers believe some of the best media buys occur in segmented radio (Table 5-4.) National advertisers wishing to purchase network radio time find good availabilities more abundant than they do with network television.

According to *Advertising Age* (August 28, 1978), one-hundred leading advertisers account for the following percentages:

Network radio	Network television	Spot radio	Spot television
38.6%	79.3%	29.5%	64.6%

It's clear from these figures that smaller companies need not be frozen out of the national media picture of almost 73 million radio-owning households throughout the country. They may have to supplement network coverage, however, with strong spot radio support in key market areas because of the segmented audiences (Figure 5-11).

In larger cities, there are further audience divisions: Hispanic, black, ethnic, and religious stations. Each tries to carve out a segment of the total households in its market area, usually with the type of music it features (Table 5-5). It is necessary for advertisers to recognize that even though many radio stations may be located in large metropolitan cities, they may be far from

*4,537 AM and 2,448 FM stations.

FIGURE 5-11
The universal symbol of segmented radio is the glib, often well-read and locally admired disc jockey. He or she builds audiences on strength of personality and brand of music. If. the audiences are large, loyal and growing, the station becomes an important cog of the network, which sells its news shows to national as well as spot advertisers.

TABLE 5-5

MUSICAL FORMATS OF SEGMENTED RADIO

Format	Audience age	Characterized by
The good-music station (sometimes called middle-of-the-road)	25–49	Sounds of beautiful music; less dependent on the disc jockey than other formats; may cluster commercials for uninterrupted musical segments of ten minutes or more. Brief news provided on the hour.
The all news–All talk station	40–64	Frequent news bulletins in peak listening hours, weather and traffic information. Airs controversial programs. Better suited for metropolitan markets. Personality of talk host very important.
The classical station	25–64 limited audience	Classical music and intellectual talk programs, usually found on university or large metropolitan FM stations.
Country-western	25–64	Programs are primarily lower-income, blue-collar oriented with a wide geographical appeal.
Top forty tunes	25–34	Tuneful and inoffensive. Appeals mostly to the young and singles.
Heavy rock	18–24	Provides the latest in rock, personality of the disc jockey is important.
Black	18–49	Blues and soul, news and talk. Personality of disc jockey is important.
Progressive	18–30	Avant-garde, contemporary songs and music of little-known rock groups.
Ethnic	25–64	National music and news: German, Spanish, Greek, Polish, Italian, Hungarian, and so on.

equal in value. A clear 50,000-watt station in Chicago may carry 1,000 miles at night; a 5,000-watt carries only its neighborhood.

Advantages and Disadvantages of National and Regional Radio

There are over 425 million working-order radio sets in the United States informing and entertaining us.[22] An advertiser's sales message isn't received as easily as it is on television, because of the absence of a picture. This makes it even more important that the sales message be clear, and that the desired audience be listening to it. When these conditions are met, radio has a lot to offer advertisers:

1 National radio delivers more adults for less money than any other national medium.[23]
2 National radio can act as a substitute for network television if the latter can't be used because of cost or availabilities.
3 It is excellent support for a company's limited exposure on either national television or regional media.
4 Radio is a relatively inexpensive way to influence regional areas requiring special attention. For example, General Motors invests the bulk of its radio budget in support of its dealers in top metropolitan markets.
5 Regional radio permits an advertiser to adjust the budget to the relative importance of each market area.
6 Both national and regional radio have the flexibility to permit advertisers to identify their dealers in each market. This allows them to feature different products in various regions.
7 A short closing date encourages a flexible approach to special problems. For example, the dominant gasoline merchandiser in Ohio, SOHIO, frequently uses ten-second spots to promote its antifreeze. These spots are scheduled in flights to be broadcast whenever the temperature drops to freezing or below.
8 Regional radio commercials may be scheduled all through the day, night, and early morning because many stations never stop broadcasting.

Network and regional radio's disadvantages are:

1 As on television, all affiliated network stations may not be able to carry the same message at the same time.
2 Radio has an even greater clutter problem than television because it has only *one* receiving dimension, the ear, which makes the short selling message even less memorable than that on television.
3 During the most desirable radio commercial period (drive time), major target

---

[22]"A short course in broadcasting: 1978," *Broadcasting Yearbook*, 1978, p. A-2.
[23]Ted Bates.

audiences may not be relaxed or receptive to advertising messages due to traffic conditions.[24]

Rate Structures

Radio commercials may be ten, thirty, or sixty seconds long. As in other media, advertisers pay less per commercial as they purchase spots in larger volume. A $50 spot, for example, may become $40 if the advertiser buys ten or more per week. It may even drop to $20 if several hundred commercials are bought over a short period of time. Radio stations refer to volume purchases in several ways: six- and thirteen-week flights (in which the advertiser is represented consistently for six or thirteen weeks with a given number of commercials), package plans (in which stations put together an assortment of times from morning to night at a generally reduced rate), and scatter plans (in which advertisers are offered a collection of spots on drive time, daytime, evening time, and weekend time.) Scatter plans are generally more expensive than the package plans, which are considered to be the best buy offered by stations.

In addition to these discounted rates, advertisers may also buy radio spots as *fixed* (where there is positive assurance the ads will run as scheduled), *preemptible* (subject to possible bumping), and *run-of-schedule* (or ROS, where the station places the spots at its convenience and thus charges a lower rate). For the very large volume user, there are still other rates available, such as annual packages where the number of spots go beyond 1,000.

The many purchase plan possibilities offered by radio simply reflect the intense competition going on within this medium. Because of this competition, some buyers seldom pay published rates. They prefer to negotiate with the stations or their representatives.

Types of Stations

Radio stations are characterized by the type of signal they transmit. The most powerful signal is *amplitude modulated* (AM). This signal is a long, direct wave that travels along the earth's surface. AM signals can generally travel up to several hundred miles. Transmitter antennae on tall hills or buildings can extend their range even further.

Frequency modulated (FM) stations have limited reach because their signals do not follow the curvature of the earth. Like television signals, FM waves travel only as far as the horizon, about forty to fifty miles. FM signals, however, have noise-free reception, unhampered by atmospheric interference. FM stations have blossomed in small towns throughout the country and are essentially a medium for local advertisers (see Chapter 8). Because AM

---

[24]Fifty percent of radio listeners from 6:00 A.M. to 10:00 A.M. are driving. [Radio Facts (New York: Radio Advertising Bureau, 1978), p. 9.]

TABLE 5-6

TOTAL UNITED STATES RADIO AUDIENCE

	Percents		Teens	
Daypart	**Women**	**Men**	**Women**	**Men**
WEEKDAY				
6 A.M.–10 A.M.	23.0	19.0	13.0	11.0
10 A.M.–3 P.M.	16.5	9.5	5.0	4.0
3 P.M.–7 P.M.	14.0	13.0	24.0	16.0
7 P.M.–Midnight	6.5	6.5	20.0	17.0
Midnight–6 A.M.	.5	1.0	.5	1.0
6 A.M.–Midnight	14.5	11.5	15.0	12.0
WEEKEND				
6 A.M.–10 A.M.	13.5	10.5	7.5	6.5
10 A.M.–3 P.M.	15.5	13.0	18.0	10.5
3 P.M.–7 P.M.	10.0	8.5	16.0	9.5
7 P.M.–Midnight	3.5	3.5	10.5	10.5
Midnight–6 A.M.	.5	1.0	.5	1.0
6 A.M.–Midnight	10.5	9.0	13.0	9.5

Source: Batten, Barton, Durstine & Osborn estimates, 1976.

	Network Radio Costs—60 Seconds		
Network	**Number of markets**	**ROS**	**Fixed average cost**
ABC–Contemporary	290	$1400	$1700
ABC–FM	209	300	400
CBS	247	800	1200
MBS (Mutual)	550	800	1000
NBC	231	800	1150
Blair (Basic)	105	2300*	2580

*Based on commercial weight concentrated in Top 10 markets.
Source: Batten, Barton, Durstine & Osborn estimates, 1976.

stations generally reach more households, their rates are higher than those of
FM stations: a one-minute radio spot on Cleveland Ohio's WGAR, a strong
AM station, runs $102. WGAR's broadcast range includes multiple counties
with a population of over 2 million. The most powerful FM station in the
same market, WDBN, reaches a smaller geographical area. A one-minute
commercial on this station costs $35 (Table 5-6).

The Value of Saturation

As the buyers of commercials on radio and any medium see it, they have to
answer four gnawing questions:

1 Am I reaching the right people?
2 Am I reaching them at the right time?
3 Can I reach them in a more effective, more cost-efficient way?
4 How often must I reach them to make an impression?

The "right people," of course, refers to the demographics of those who are most likely to buy the product or service. The right people for a new slim wallet, for example, would be men twenty-five to forty-nine because they want to appear sleek and svelte without having bulgy pockets. The "right time" to tell fishers about a new lunker lure is in early spring and summer. The "right time of day" to tell young people about an herbal shampoo or any other product is between 3 P.M. and midnight.[25] Whether radio is the "right medium" can only be determined by an analysis of the listening habits of the advertisers' target audiences, and the cost to reach them compared to that of other available media. Having answered three of the four questions, media buyers go to the last: how often to advertise. What specifically does it take, they wonder, to make an impression with radio? The simplest answer is to buy a major share of all networks' commercial time. The target audience cannot escape. But that strategy is expensive and wasteful.[26] Advertisers should aim for *saturation* of the audience. The goal is to air enough messages for the product not to be forgotten. But how much is "enough," and what constitutes saturation? No one really seems to know. It depends on the product and the competition. From long experience, we'd offer this advice:

1 Radio, unlike television, depends on *one* sense, hearing. Therefore, radio usually takes more spots than television to make an impression.
2 A saturation schedule is approximately *fifty to one-hundred announcements a week for six to thirteen weeks*. A saturation schedule tends to give advertisers 40 percent or more of the total audience each broadcast day. The theory is that over a six- to thirteen-week period, most of the station's audience will be acutely aware of the product and the brand.
3 A minimum schedule is approximately five commercials a day, or between twenty-five and thirty a week for six weeks. Both the saturation and minimum schedules are based on the fact that radio, to many, has become a passive medium, one that can be switched on and enjoyed without anyone's paying attention to it. It has become part of the home environment. Since a passive listener is less apt to pick up each and every radio announcement, advertisers must resort to numerous messages. Sears, Roebuck sets an excellent example for its reliance on continuity. During a typical summer month, Sears, Roebuck ran national network spots for automotive products from the twelfth to the end of the month. Local Sears stores were urged to tie in with their own spots. The barrage of Sears' spots presenting specific buying opportunities developed the customer traffic the company wanted. Sears remains a heavy user of both network and spot radio year after year.

Nielsen, Arbitron, and Others

A radio market, as far as advertisers are concerned, consists of the total number of people twelve and older who live within signal range. The assumption is that youngsters under twelve do not listen to radio. Nielsen and

---

[25]The best time to reach teenagers by radio during weekdays is from 4 P.M. to midnight. Their fathers and mothers are best reached from 6 A.M. to 10 A.M. The second-best time to reach adults is during late commuting time from 3 to 7 P.M.

[26]The "falling rate of profit theory" holds that, after an optimal level of use is reached, each successive increment of added capital goods (advertising) yields a smaller return in investment. The practical problem for advertisers is to recognize when that level is reached.

its archcompetitor, Arbitron dominate the list of research services who measure radio markets. They regularly study audiences in selected cities and network markets. From their estimates, advertisers can compute cost per thousand listeners (CPM), a valuable measuring tool for comparing networks, stations, even competing media. Here's how it's done.

1 An appliance maker's network spot costs $1,100.
2 Audience rating for the spot translates into 750,000 listeners.
3 Divide the number of listeners into the spot cost ($1,100 ÷ 750,000 = $1.46 CPM).

If instead of one, the advertiser purchased ten spots on a rotating basis where the listener estimates for all spots still averaged out at 750,000, than we would multiply 750,000 by 10 to get *gross impressions*, or 7.5 million. We also multiply the single-spot cost by 10 to get total costs ($11,000). When we apply the same formula, our cost per 1,000 listeners is still $1.46. If by buying ten spots we reduce the costs, then the CPM will be lower.

If, however, time buyers are less interested in cost efficiencies (CPM) than they are in sheer numbers of listeners, they will use the radio GRP formula. According to Arbitron,[27] they need only two numbers to calculate GRPs: an average rating for a time period (quarter-hours in radio), and a number of spots to be run on a station in the period.

Day-Part	Number of spots		Station rating		GRPs
Monday–Friday 6 A.M.–10 A.M.	4	×	2.5	=	10.0
Monday–Friday 10 A.M.–3 P.M.	6	×	3.7	=	22.2
Monday–Friday 3 P.M.–7 P.M.	3	×	3.0	=	9.0
Saturday 10 A.M.–3 P.M.	1	×	3.8	=	3.8
Sunday 10 A.M.–3 P.M.	1	×	4.3	=	4.3

Ratings are calculated by dividing the population of the area by the number of listeners.
Source: Arbitron Radio.

There are other research companies who survey specific market areas on a regular basis as well as producing information for individual manufacturers. Essentially, their job is to help radio advertisers use their dollars in the most efficient manner. Once thought of as a luxury for large advertisers only, audience research is now seen as a necessity for companies, large and small, in all media.

[27]*Understanding and Using Radio Audience Estimates*, (New York: Arbitron Radio, 1977), p. 5.

IN SUMMARY

1   Television delivers a large audience to the national network advertiser. Although the initial investment is high, the cost per viewer is generally very low.

2   A difference of one rating point can mean hundreds of thousands of viewers.

3   When evaluating television—as well as other media—we must weigh three criteria: reach, frequency, continuity.

4   Today, 98 percent of all homes in the country are television homes; most owned sets are color sets.

5   Cable television appears to be the greatest competitor to free programming and the television networks. Some experts believe it could lead to a bidding war for talent and programs.

6   Most television programming comes from the networks. The primary role of the individual affiliate station is to deliver a clear signal to a large, loyal audience.

7   Individual affiliate stations are paid by networks according to audience ratings.

8   Costs for network commercials go up and down based on the demand from advertisers as well as on ratings of specific programs.

9   Gross rating points (GRPs) serve as a sophisticated media buyer's tool. The formula is reach (number of households) times frequency (number of commercials). The price of a rating point varies according to the density of viewership in each market area. Buyers like at least 100 GRPs per market.

10   Advertisers want to know the ages of people who are watching their commercials because age is closely related to product demand.

11   Advertisers who control programs may offer them free to the networks in exchange for air time. In the advertising business, this is known as barter.

12   The large volume of advertising messages has led to a problem of viewer recall known as clutter. Some advertising experts believe viewers use the process of selective perception to defend against advertising messages.

13   Television's advantages are: it delivers the broadest reach; it delivers it live for pennies per impression; it is excellent for product identification; dealers love it.

14   Television's disadvantages are: its costs are high for most advertisers; its costs go even higher due to residual payments; it suffers from clutter; a short selling message is often delivered back-to-back with that of a competitor; it may not be possible to get all network affiliates to run the same commercial at the same time.

15   Smaller advertisers may use spot commercials to concentrate on a region of the country instead of on the whole country.

16   Radio is a segmented medium. Generally, only its news and specials are national.

17   Radio's advantages are: nationally, it delivers more adults for less money than any other national medium; it can act as a substitute for network television or as an inexpensive way to influence regional areas; and it has a short closing date. Regionally, it permits advertisers to adjust budgets to fit specific market requirements, to identify dealers in specific markets, and to run all hours of the day on specific stations.

18   Radio's disadvantages are: all affiliates may not be able to run spots at same time; clutter is a problem; and distractions may interfere with listening.

19   Because of the intense competition within the radio industry, there is a tendency on the part of some buyers not to pay published rates but to negotiate on prices.

20   Because of their greater geographical coverage, AM stations charge more for their spots than FM stations.

STUDENT PROJECT

Imagine that you are about to be interviewed for a job in an advertising agency. The agency thinks you might work in its media-buying department, but it wants to get an idea of your media-buying I.Q. It decides that the best way to do this is to give you a fifteen-part quiz. Before you take it, review some of the key points in this chapter.

QUESTIONS ABOUT THE PROJECT

1   Why would a media buyer select three commercials during CBS network news instead of one announcement on a daytime quiz show? (See Table 5-1.)

2   If you had to plan media strategy for two years, would you prefer *continuity* or *reach* for a consumer product such as a chain saw? Why?

3   If you had a yearly advertising budget of $250,000 for promoting a gasoline additive, would you purchase three 30-second spot announcements on the 1980 Olympics at $75,000 each? Explain your answer. Would you give the same answer if the product were an orange soft drink facing reluctant retailer acceptance and distribution?

4   A lot has been said about America's free enterprise system and the pros and cons of media competition in the marketplace. Considering this, can you justify the coming of age of cable television if it seriously endangers the profitability of the local stations and the networks? Also, who will pay in the long run for the popularity of cable?

5   On any given evening, note the familiar advertisers on prime-time television. What accounts for the same companies' appearing night after night? Is it possible no other companies are interested in prime-time television? Explain.

6   Do you think it's fair for the smaller clients of this agency to be shut out of network television advertising because of the flexible rate schedules of the medium? Is there a fairer way? What can we do to get our smaller clients (with limited budgets) on television?

7   If your client's product is life insurance, do you think that as a media buyer you should pay as much attention to household GRPs as you do to the demographic breakdown of the audience? Justify your answer.

8   Which of these nationally advertised products would be more interested in high GRP scores, as opposed to lower GRPs, on programs appealing to specific demographic audiences?

toothpaste	feminine hygiene products
detergents	jeans
soft drinks	beer
fast-food restaurants	milk
chain saws	

9   Why should the advertiser be concerned about the scheduling of make-goods in radio and television?

10 Could the principle of *selective perception* affect the media buyer's use of GRPs? How?

11 Is it possible that television could become fragmented like radio? Explain.

12 If television did indeed become fragmented like radio, where a multitude of stations is available to advertisers at almost any time of day or night, what effect would this have on the following?

the television networks

the local television stations (network affiliates)

talent and musicians

cable stations

prices of commercials

GRPs

advertising agencies

small- and medium-sized national companies

13 Justify the use of advertising on FM radio stations in a market dominated by several AM stations.

14 Is there a relationship between the financial strength of magazines, billboards, and newspapers and the banning of cigarette advertising over television and radio? Explain.

15 What are closing dates all about and why must our agency be concerned with them?

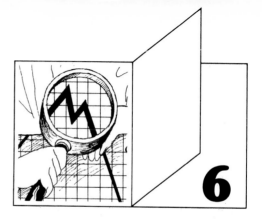

6

NATIONAL MAGAZINES
AND NEWSPAPERS

Update In the last chapter, we emphasized costs of the broadcast media. We will use the same procedure with magazines and newspapers, because in the advertising business, companies either have the money or they don't. Since many advertisers operate on restricted budgets, they learn to choose their medium or their combination of media carefully. And because all media are, in fact, competitors, there is most always a choice (Figure 6-1).

Advertising did not become an important national phenomenon in this country until the railroads and rivers tied the geographical sections of the country together so that mass production could logically lead to mass distribution. As goods flowed from the factories, rode the rails, and sailed the barges, advertisers were ready to accept a communications vehicle that would

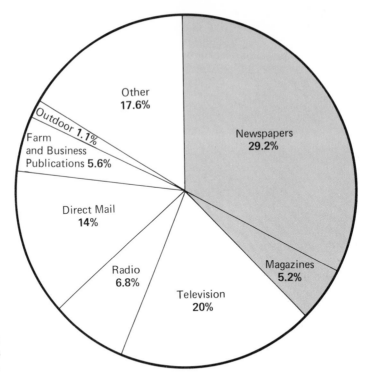

Other
17.6%

Outdoor 1.1%

Farm
and Business
Publications 5.6%

Newspapers
29.2%

Direct Mail
14%

Radio
6.8%

Television
20%

Magazines
5.2%

FIGURE 6-1
Share of ad dollars
in the major media.

carry their messages to a wider area than that normally covered by a city newspaper. They found their solution in the national magazine. While building national brand identification and consumer loyalty and broadening sales horizons through the ads they carried, national magazines also served to bring together a diverse, multicultural people. While the same can be said, to some extent, of all national media, magazines in particular have changed their character over the years. We have seen them evolve from a vehicle of general entertainment and information for all people into something else, a specialty periodical. We shall see what this means to advertisers.

MAGAZINES, THE SPECIALIZED MEDIUM

National magazines, like television, can reach broad audiences. But their *reach* is not the "majority of households" that television claims. Rather, magazines aim for specific groups of people with tastes and interests in common. It wasn't always this way. Before radio and television, national magazines partially succeeded at being most things to most people. There was no other continuous form of national entertainment. Since radio and television have changed the nation's leisure habits, magazines have tried to capture fragments of the national market. The result: hundreds of specialized *consumer magazines.* We define consumer magazines as periodicals written, edited, and produced for the benefit of the general public. Here are some recognizable types:

Family (women's)—*Ladies Home Journal, Better Homes and Gardens.*

Fashion—*Esquire, Glamour, Mademoiselle*

News—*Time, Newsweek, Jet*

General—*Cosmopolitan, Ebony, Ms., Reader's Digest*

Adventure—*Argosy, Male, Saga, Playboy*

Special interest—*Photoplay, Modern Screen, TV Guide*

Sports—*Sports Illustrated, Field and Stream, Golf Digest*

Youth—*Boys' Life, American Girl, Scholastic Magazine*

Gardening—*The Gardener, Horticulture, Family Food Garden*

Crafts and hobbies—*Ceramics Monthly, Coins, Model Railroader*

Outdoor recreation—*Camping Journal, Mobile Living, Snow Goer*

Business and finance—*Business Week, Fortune, Forbes*

Automotive—*Car Craft, Car and Driver, Pickup, Van & 4wd*

Antiques—*The Antiques Journal, Spinning Wheel*

Within these and other magazine classifications, there are many other magazines. Vital statistics about them can be found in individual magazine rate cards, or in the advertisers' "bible," Standard Rate & Data Service.[1] In Standard Rate & Data Service's *Consumer Magazine and Farm Publication rates and data,* we can find information about approximately 1,100 consumer and farm magazines published in the United States. The Standard Rate & Data Service (SRDS) is published as an all-inclusive working tool for buyers of magazine space. A profile of buyers of consumer magazine advertising (ad agencies and advertisers) revealed that SRDS is used by 87 percent of those who prepare the media plan.[2]

However, before these media buyers become involved, the advertisers have to make a basic decision: which medium shall we use? Earlier, we've discussed why national advertisers use television and radio. National magazines have advantages, too.

Advantages and Disadvantages of Magazines

Clearly, advertisers no longer look to most magazines in terms of a wide, general audience. This is abundantly clear since broadcast advertising has moved into popular favor. Yet if the advertisers do not select magazines for sheer numbers of people, why are magazines continuing to attract millions of

[1]SRDS information includes editorial purpose of the publication, frequency of issue, space rates and discounts, circulation, closing dates, and regional and demographic issues, if any.
[2]Source: Harvey Research Organization, April 1975.

FIGURE 6-2
The small boy in the magazine ad became nationally famous in the manufacturer's television ad. Using the same model provides the tie-in between the two media campaigns. (Courtesy Quaker Oats Company.)

dollars worth of advertising? The answers lie in the unique strengths of this flourishing medium. Advertisers choose magazines:

1 To reach an audience with special interests.
2 To reach an audience with above-average income and education.
3 When products and services require an explanation that thirty-second commercials cannot give.
4 When color reproduction is important.
5 To produce reader response or to insert coupons. Over 13 percent of manufacturers' coupons are distributed through magazines.[3] Some issues may contain over $50 worth.
6 When dealer promotions require ad reprint support.
7 To provide back-up support for television commercials. (The same can be said of other media. Figure 6-2).
8 When they need magazine ads for referral or passing along. *Pass-along readership* of consumer magazines is estimated to average over 3 readers per copy.

But like most media, magazines cannot be everything for everybody. There are some definite times when advertisers should not use magazines:

1 When they are short of time. *Closing dates* for magazine ads may be as much as three months before the date of issue. (Closing dates are the dates when the advertiser must deliver all reproducible materials to the printer.)

> *Closing dates for selected national consumer media*
> Magazines—one to three months before issue date
> Network television—fourteen days before airing
> Network radio—seventy-two hours before airing

2 When they need wide circulation among audiences of all ages, incomes, and education at a low cost per thousand (CPM). Exceptions are the *Reader's Digest* (18 million) and *TV Guide* (19 million), who still manage to retain their popularity across a wide spectrum of the national population.
3 When waste circulation—the wrong people, the wrong areas—is too great to justify cost.

Because so many magazines are available to advertisers, choosing the correct and most economical one is not easy. What factors besides circulation figures merit consideration? Let's look at *Better Homes and Gardens, Family Circle, Woman's Day*, and *Ladies Home Journal*. A small appliance manufacturer would be delighted if the company could buy all four and not have to worry about selecting the least productive. But like so many small companies, this manufacturer has a small budget. The persons responsible for making the

---

[3]Source: *Nielsen Researcher,* #1, A. C. Nielsen Co., 1976.

TABLE 6-1

CIRCULATION AND RATES FOR FOUR CONSUMER MAGAZINES*

	Circulation	One-time page rate/black & white	Cost per thousand (CPM)
Better Homes & Gardens	8.0 million	$38,375	$4.80
Family Circle	8.2 million	30,000	3.66
Woman's Day	8.0 million	29,370	3.67
Ladies Home Journal	7.0 million	27,540	3.93

*Standard Rate & Data Service/*Consumer Magazine and Farm Publication.* SRDS circulations and rates change frequently; thus, CPMs change also.

company's various media choices compiled the above information from SRDS (Table 6-1).

If our manufacturer goes strictly by the numbers, the choice would either be *Family Circle* or *Woman's Day* because their cost per thousand subscribers is considerably lower than their competitors'. But there are other considerations:

1 *Target audience for the product or service.* Who buys the product? How old are the buyers? Is average household income a factor? What other variables affect who buys the product? Does the magazine deliver enough of the kind of buyer we seek?
2 *Editorial content of the magazine.* This is probably the most important element of any publication's success. Is the magazine well read? Circulation cannot tell us this. An examination of the magazine, some readership surveys, a check of competitive (Audit Bureau of Circulations) statements (see page 222) will help (Table 6-2).
3 *Prestige of the magazine.* The content, honesty, and longevity of some magazines confer on them an aura of distinction. One such magazine was the weekly picture magazine, *Life,* whose advertisers frequently announced that they advertised in

TABLE 6-2

CIRCULATION OF LEADING SELECTED UNITED STATES MAGAZINES*

TV Guide	20,443,254	Time	4,273,962
Reader's Digest	18,371,000	Newsweek	2,947,406
National Geographic	9,756,312	Senior Scholastic	2,927,108
Family Circle	8,498,517	People	2,394,979
Woman's Day	8,404,618	Sports Illustrated	2,263,148
Better Homes & Gardens	8,056,355	Field & Stream	2,033,135
McCall's	6,512,186	Popular Science	1,828,600
Ladies Home Journal	6,004,334	True Story	1,797,127
National Enquirer	5,208,375	Outdoor Life	1,795,598
Good Housekeeping	5,170,007	Glamour	1,755,775
Playboy	4,970,753	Boys' Life	1,529,252
Redbook	4,613,908	Parents Magazine	1,511,065
Penthouse	4,606,134	Ebony	1,255,077

*Circulations and advertising rates are constantly changing for most magazines. Source: Audit Bureau of Circulations (ABC) FAS-FAX Report during six months prior to December 31, 1977.

Life on their packaging and point-of-purchase displays. Another such magazine is *Reader's Digest,* the most widely read magazine in the world.

4 *Pass-along readership.* Some magazines are kept for months or even years and are read by several family members or friends. Pass-along readership is not often reflected in normal CPM figures, although the rule of thumb is to multiply the circulation by 3.2 to find the total audience. Not all magazines can claim the distinction of being passed along although many try. Simmons' studies[4] of what it calls "Target Group Index" (TGI) indicate how the pass-along readership of our four family magazines compare:

	Circulation		Readers per copy		Total audience (readers)
Better Homes & Gardens	8.0 million	×	2.26	=	18,080,000
Family Circle	8.2 million	×	2.18	=	17,876,000
Woman's Day	8.0 million	×	2.25	=	18,000,000
Ladies Home Journal	7.0 million	×	2.26	=	15,820,000

Not all magazines do as well as these four in pass-along readership. On the other hand, some do much better. As an example, a more intellectual magazine like *Psychology Today* is estimated at 1.99 female and 1.77 male readers per copy, according to Simmons, while automotively oriented *Hot Rod* rolls along with a 4.29 male readers per copy. Pass-along readership figures are seldom static. They move up or down based on the magazines' popularity. Thus, advertisers who feel that pass-along figures are important in

[4]*Standard Magazine Audience Report,* W. R. Simmons & Associates Research, 1977–78, 1974–75.

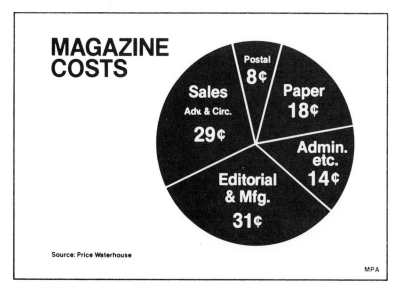

Source: Price Waterhouse

MPA

FIGURE 6-3
The cost of producing the average magazine. Only postal and paper costs have outpaced inflation by a wide margin. (Source: Price Waterhouse.)

their magazine selection should evaluate several years' increases and declines before making a positive media commitment.

The Selling of Magazine Space

Magazine advertising space is a product like shoes. It carries a cost. Instead of being made up of leather held together by nails and glue, it's made up of paper and ink and held together by staples, all of which cost money. Then there's labor to write and edit the magazine, print it, and mail it. Along the way, the publisher of the magazine will have to consider printing machinery and postage costs, the latter galloping ever upwards (Figure 6-3).

Most of these costs must be returned through the sale of advertising space, which is sold to advertisers in the following sizes (based on a standard 8½- by 11- inch format):

2-page ad (spread), 15 inches wide X 10 inches deep. Two-page ads are used for high impact. They grab immediate attention and are almost impossible to ignore (Figure 6-4).

1-page ad, 7 inches wide x 10 inches deep. A common size, but impressive. A small company looks just as big as a larger competitor if each has purchased a full-page ad (Figure 6-5).

⅔-page ad, 4-⅝ inches wide x 10 inches deep. This space takes up most of the page, allowing editorial material to abut it (Figure 6-6).

½-page ad (horizontal or vertical), 7 inches wide x 5 inches deep, 3½ inches wide x 10 inches deep. Either of these half-page sizes may permit another advertiser to share the same page and draw attention away from the original buyer's ad (Figures 6-7 and 6-8).

Island half-page ad, 4⅝ inches wide x 7 inches deep. A special position ad that is surrounded by editorial matter. No other ad can share the same page. The island half usually costs slightly more than the normal horizontal or vertical half page ad (Figure 6-9).

⅓-page ad, 2¼ inches wide x 10 inches deep (Figure 6-10).

¼-page ad, 4½ inches wide x 3⅔ inches deep (Figure 6-11).

⅙-page ad, 2¼ inches wide x 5 inches deep (Figure 6-12). These last three sizes are usually placed to the back of the publication. However, judicious use of color can help "pop" them out from the page.

Full-page ads that *bleed* to the edges of the paper are larger than nonbleed ads. A bleed can stretch a 7-x10-inch ad to the exact *trim size* of the magazine (8½x11 inches) (Figure 6-13).

Bleed ads generally cost about 15 percent more than others. Many advertisers consider them well worth the additional cost. There are other ways advertisers can improve the impact of their ads. A favorite is to purchase a *premium position* within the magazine. Premium positions usually deliver high readership. Magazines sell the three available cover pages as premium positions that, studies show, carry the highest readership ratings of all the ads within the magazine. Selected positions within the magazine that qualify as premium (next to the table of contents or editorial) cost 10 to 25 percent extra over the regular cost. Cover positions cost even more. Few consumer magazines ever sell advertising on their front covers; industrial magazines sometimes do.

Advertisers who wish to reduce the cost of their magazine advertising may purchase space as ROB (*run-of-book*). ROB ads are similar to ROS (*run-of-schedule*) in broadcasting and ROP (*run-of-paper*) in newspapers. Because they permit the media owners the most scheduling flexibility, they are generally the cheapest available spots (Figure 6-14). An advertiser should schedule four to six insertions per year in a given monthly magazine to make an impression on the reading public. Advertising investments go further when concentrated in one or two leading magazines than when scattered in a wide variety of magazines. And the investment can be substantial. Six black-and-white pages in any family magazine (Table 6-1) run at least $150,000. Six four-color ads run to over $200,000 in space alone. Basic space is priced as black and white; one can also buy one, two, or three additional colors for more money. (We'll discuss the cost of producing ads in Chapter 22.) These figures alone indicate that advertising in national consumer magazines is too expensive for the average company. However, smaller-budget advertisers have some alternatives.

1   They can forego full-page ads and substitute fractions of pages. It is estimated by the Magazine Publishers' Association that one of every five dollars invested in magazine advertising is for less than a full page (Figure 6-15).
2   They can buy the circulation of a geographic region or a specific demographic unit (for example, students, executives, doctors). Most consumer magazines with large circulations offer some of these options. *Time* magazine, for example, prices each region according to its circulation and adds a charge for the cost of making the necessary mechanical changes. (It is cheaper to print an ad through a full press run than to stop the presses, pull it off, insert another ad, and restart the presses. The extra press costs are charged to the regional advertiser.)
3   They can participate with other companies in a large ad and divide the costs. Generally, such participant ads have a common theme, and the participants are noncompetitive.

Discounts and the Short Rate

The dollar charges of magazine space to advertisers are fixed either *by number of insertions in any given year* or *by dollar volume in any given year*. Table 6-3 shows a typical rate structure based on number of insertions in a year for black and white ads. Note that the twelve-time buyer can buy each page for $2,255, whereas the three-time buyer must pay $2,410 per page. The more insertions per year, the greater the discount per insertion. What happens if an advertiser contracts for a page a month for twelve months but stops after six months? The advertiser then must pay the *short rate*: $2,365

FIGURE 6-4
A two-page spread.

We're looking for engineers who were born to lead.

Are you the kind of engineer who has what it takes to move into management someday? If you are, you already know it.

Now what you need to know is which companies can offer you the best opportunities. We think you'll find General Electric is one.

We're a high technology company. And that means we have to have managers who understand technology — women and men — to run the place.

Today, over 60% of the top managers at General Electric hold technical degrees. In fact, over 65% of the college graduates we hired last year held technical degrees.

Of course, just leadership ability and a technical degree won't get you into management. First, you're going to need solid engineering experience and a broad understanding of business.

And we have a lot of ways to help you get it.

One is our Manufacturing Management Program. A two-year program of rotating assignments that gives you broad experience with different products and manufacturing processes.

Another is our Engineering Program. For engineers with an interest in product and systems design and development. There's also a Field Engineering Program, a Technical Marketing Program, plus a number of programs sponsored by product operations.

And all with just one aim. To give you all the responsibility and all the perspective you need to move into management. As fast as you can manage it.

Of course, starting on a program isn't the only way to make it into management at GE. If you have a specific product interest, we have many direct-placement opportunities that can get your career started fast, too.

What kinds of product areas can you work in at GE?

Maybe nuclear power. Or more efficient turbine-generators. Or better mass-transit systems. Or medical equipment. Engineering plastics. Cleaner, quieter jet engines. Communications products. You name it.

Sound interesting? Why not send for our free careers booklet? Just write, General Electric, Educational Communications, W1D, Fairfield, Connecticut 06431.

Progress for People.

GENERAL ⊕ ELECTRIC
An Equal Opportunity Employer.

FIGURE 6-5
A full-page ad.

FIGURE 6-6
A two-thirds-page ad.

There Alone," November], I found your photographic accompaniment disappointing. It would have been refreshing if Psychology Today could have transcended the myth that stereotyped good looks are necessary prerequisites for good sex by including photographs of an average woman—over 30, with buck teeth and breasts that fail to fit the champagne-glass standard.

Susan Johnsen Ricker, Tucson, Ariz.

I suppose you think it's all right to feature exploitative photography because your name is Psychology Today instead of Playboy. It's a shame that a magazine that seems to be so advanced in some areas is still so backward in others. I hope that someday women will have themselves together enough to say "no" when a photographer wants to take an exploitative picture.

I.L. Turner, Venice, Calif.

Luck Is a Sign of Celestial Favor
Now, why should Kay Deaux ["Ahhh, She Was Just Lucky," December], find skill to be inherently more virtuous and positively valued than luck? In many cultures luck is the higher virtue, being a sign of celestial favor and harmonious passivity to the scheme of things, whereas skill implies a struggle to control and command events against their natural flow.

It strikes me as a shallow-minded and weak-kneed capitulation to macho ideals for women to seek equality in the vulgar traffic of commerce—to surrender their grace in luck for the effort at skill. There is no gratification in self-abnegation.

Larry Horstman, Trumansburg, N.Y.

I can draw a very definite parallel between the experiences of women and racial or ethnic minorities.

Generally when a minority person accomplishes a difficult task in an outstanding manner, his/her accomplishment is either ignored or credited to luck. But let that minority person fail to accomplish the task, then it's, "See, I told you; they can't do anything right." Whereas, if a nonminority person failed to accomplish the task, it is generally excused by "He/she had some tough breaks."

R.R. Luna, Rock Island, Ill.

Psychological Research or a Political Document
The most serious flaw in Teaching Styles and Pupil Progress by Neville Bennett et al. [reviewed by Sheila Schwartz, December], is that at no time was there ever any direct observation of teachers and classrooms. The researchers apparently came to their conclusions entirely on the basis of what I would call paper information, answers to the questionnaires, scores, etc.

Teachers were classified as either formal, in-formal, or mixed, solely on the basis of their own replies to a question. This is truly astonishing. Some of the most rigid, and I would say destructive, teachers that I have ever seen at work would, in answer to such a questionnaire, probably have classified themselves as informal.

To make judgments about children's ability or progress in the areas of reading, writing, or mathematical skill on the basis of achievement-test scores is misleading and ridiculous.

Your reviewer is, I am glad to say, critical of certain details of the report, but she does not get to the heart of it, nor expose its deepest weaknesses and errors. It is exasperating, though not at all surprising, given the temper of the times, that a report like this should have been written. It is even more exasperating that people who ought to know better are and will be taking it seriously as a piece of so-called "psychological research," instead of what it is, a political document.

John Holt, Boston, Mass.

Psychology Today welcomes letters from readers. All letters are necessarily subject to editing for length, style, and grammar. Except in extremely unusual circumstances, unsigned letters will not be published. The Letters department constitutes the readers' forum, and all shades of opinion are most welcome.

FIGURE 6-7
A horizontal half-page ad.

aesthetic has been limited to a relatively small intellectual elite, just as any of the great movements in art have been in the past. "The disillusionment with modern architecture," Brolin informs us on that same page, "came about because architects imposed their values on a public that did not share them," an assertion that skirts the issue of a public that did not even *know* of such values. In truth, the "majority of the public" has accepted some aspects of modern design without either indoctrination or comprehension. Did the "majority of the public" share the values of an Ictinus, a Borromini, a Wren? I think not. Need socially responsive architecture be based on some kind of popular consensus? Certainly not, though much of the great architecture throughout history has achieved that desirable result nonetheless.

The book proceeds with a vexing catalog of misrepresentations of which I will mention but two. Brolin informs us that in the early 20th Century "All traditional styles were declared null and void—to the point where putting ornament on a building was regarded as a criminal act." End of Brolin's discussion. He gives us no indication as to who declared what styles null and void, and no documentation as to who regarded putting ornament on a building as a criminal act. Brolin presumably refers to Adolf Loos's pamphlet *Ornament und Verbrechen* (Ornament and Crime), though from Brolin's distorted interpretation one could infer that such a notion was generally held, not merely by one architectural theorist and his followers. In another instance, the author takes on Ebenezer Howard and the Garden City Movement. Brolin attacks that idea as "a strange mixture of moralism, pragmatism, and optimism," and calls it "a classic example of the simplistic cause-and-effect relationship seen between behavior and environment that still dominates planning and architecture and that lulled modern architects into believing that they could change the way people live by modifying their physical surroundings." So much for the lost interest in social values that Brolin bewails from page one on. We are in the next breath treated to the news—slanderous to the memory of Howard and the great school of planners he inspired—that "apartment blocks surrounded by parks and abundant sunlight and air" (this above a photograph of a 27-story apartment complex surrounded by roads) derive from Howard's garden city idea. This is a gross misrepresentation, with the name of the man actually responsible for monolithic superblocks amidst vast parks nowhere in sight: for it was Le Corbusier who transmogrified Howard's idea into the vertical garden city.

Luckily, this form of architectural doublethink goes on for only 128 pages, 22 pages of which are devoted to Brolin's case studies of Chandigarh and of Sanaa in Yemen, which he hopes will prove the points he has been trying to make: arguments so far-fetched both geographically and intellectually that one's chances of making it all the way to the conclusion are happily reduced. Read it if you must, but for those who cannot wait for an authoritative reappraisal of the Modern Movement and its effect on contemporary architecture, all one can add is the urgent admonition: "Caveat lector." [Martin Filler]

FIGURE 6-8

A vertical half-page ad.

CAB to permit air shipper co-ops

A ruling by the Civil Aeronautics Board under the new cargo deregulation guidelines permits cooperative shippers' associations to consolidate airfreight shipments. In the past, the CAB had restricted the operation of co-ops to interstate surface transportation only.

"We've been approached by cooperative associations regarding the new rules," said Jerry Schorr, Eastern Airline's vice president for cargo sales. "Many manufacturers, especially those who have time-sensitive and price-sensitive products, are interested in the opportunity to consolidate their shipments, and now use air transportation."

Briefly...

A newly created subsidiary of CP Ships has leased a harbor site at Montreal for the operation of a **new multi-million dollar common user container terminal.** The terminal will serve as CP Ships' new North American base. The carrier formerly operated out of Quebec . . . **U.S. Lines** is reportedly negotiating with a S. Korean firm for construction of 12 large containerships. The same S. Korean firm was awarded a part of Sea-Land's recent contract for 12 new containerships . . . **McLean Trucking** has purchased the general commodity motor carrier **O.N.C. Freight Systems** from Rocor International. O.N.C. had revenues of $107 million in 1977. O.N.C. is a transcontinental carrier with route structures generally on the West Coast. McLean is the nation's fourth largest trucking company . . . **Arkansas-Best Freight** has acquired Navajo Freight Lines of Denver at a price in excess of $30 million. The merger moves ABF from 25th to 8th nationally in terms of combined carrier revenues . . .

Pan Am is prepared to begin service **between San Francisco and Peking,** pending CAB approval of its exemption application. In a separate application, Pan Am has asked for rights to fly to four cities in the Peoples' Republic of China from nine U.S. gateways . . . **Flying Tiger Line** has lowered its domestic air freight container rates as much as 15 percent, according to President Joseph Healy. More price/service options are expected to follow. ■

FIGURE 6-9
An island half-page ad.

en's rights and abortion and divorce—which caused Anna to disappear with the only pack of cards for thirty minutes. He talked about turning over another festival night to the village children, who would present a play or a dance of their own invention on the subject of the *compromesso storico*. He went on and on, and for a while the old-timers in the cell let him have his say, because, for a while, it was really rather pleasant to be addressed by someone who was *dottore*—even if he was only Mario and Anna Cecchi's boy. They listened to Alfredo's talk as if it were a kind of solemn, exhortatory entertainment, like a sermon, and did not bother much with what he said. When the big festival bulletins went up on stone walls and telephone poles and barn doors across the valley, the schedule ran pretty much as always, with dancing every night and a beauty contest for the local girls and nothing more egregiously Communist than a new movie from the Party secretary, called "Soil of Hungary." It was exactly the sort of L'Unità festival that brought the Party money, and brought the men and women who had worked so hard all year—and often for so little—the solace, and ideology, of nights when the wine flowed and the dancing never stopped and the pork turned, pungent and crisp and dripping, on oak spits over smoky open fires. Alfredo, in keeping with his position as *consigliere del comune*, was listed as referee for the Fifteenth Annual San Vincenzo Middleweight Championships—a boxing match, out behind the *spaccio*, that always involved one professional from Perugia going a round apiece with a lot of local boys while mothers shrieked and fathers preened and girls giggled and the Party made book.

THE Italian Communist Party is the biggest Communist Party in the West, and the most important. Nearly two million Italians belong to the Party. Twelve or thirteen million Italians always vote for the Party. And fifty-five million Italians can be said to have depended on it at one time or another for their government, since from 1974 until early this year it took a Communist parliamentary abstention to keep any of the various Christian Democratic governments going at all. No one in or out of Italy seems to agree about what, precisely, Italian Communism is, although there is quite a market in experts lately, and the American ambassador, for one, carries around a thick embassy scrapbook of clippings from the Party press which he likes to read out loud at meetings and diplomatic afternoons. It is usually what Americans mean when they talk about Eurocommunism—something not quite European, not quite Communist, something so incontestably and perhaps uncontrollably present that they needed to give it a new, friendly-sounding name before they could even begin to discuss it calmly. Americans say "Eurocommunism" the way primitives say "Grandfather" or "God" or "Great Big Bird" for the boom that fills the sky during summer storms and makes the children howl. The Italians themselves say that *their* Communism has very little in common with the Communism of the other two "independent" European Parties—French Communism being a Jacobin affair, vindictive and sour, and Spanish Communism being isolated in *its* country by strong memories of betrayal that date back to the Civil War. The Party in Italy is at the center of its country's politics. It takes the place that in the rest of Western Europe belongs, almost by definition, to Socialists, and, in fact, it owes that place to a kind of mass default by Italian Socialists, who in the sixties and early seventies had twelve years in a "center-left" government and in those twelve years showed no capacity at all for any activity but profiteering. The Communist Party grew to respectability on the back of Socialist scandals. Palmiro Togliatti's "giraffe"—which is what the old General Secretary used to call it, because the Italian Party seemed to him such a strange animal, with no reasonable explanation for existing—became the popular party of the Italian left, the party that cut through ideology and class to reach a third of the country's voters. By now, it is Italy's "other" party—a coalition of interest groups and attitudes which in breakdown looks less Italian, in a way, than American Democrat. People in Italy with real contempt for the Catholics and their party are voting Radical now, by way of protest, but if they want to take over a town or a province from the Christian Democrats they still usually vote Communist. The Communists are so respectable in Italy today that their main problem, with the voting age at eighteen for most elections, is persuading the young to vote for them. One reason the Party lost votes, for the first time in thirty years, in the parliamentary elections last June was that a million or so boys and girls—at the polls

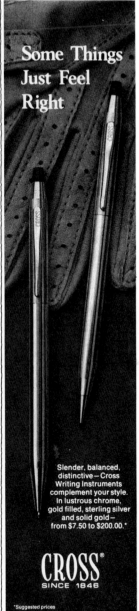
FIGURE 6-10
A one-third-page ad.

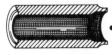
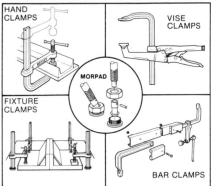
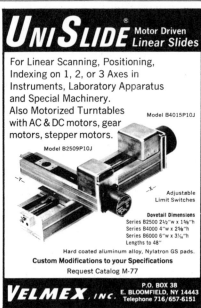
FIGURE 6-11
Quarter-page ads.

their neighbors' barns. Once, the village priest found them stealing wheat from a parish field. He denounced Anna and her friends in church that Sunday. He called Anna to the altar and told everyone to look hard into the eyes of an unrepentant sinner—and then, when she spat at him and ran home shrieking, he sent the police to arrest her. But the policeman who found Anna, under her grandmother's bed with the chickens, gave her candy and said it was the priests of Italy, not the children, who needed handcuffs. And though Anna has nothing good to say about the Communist Party, she often claims to vote Communist in honor of that policeman—who, she figures, was the first Communist she ever met. He and her grandmother are the only people from her childhood whom she wants to remember.

"If I have good memories, they are of the sea. Nothing else. No one else. For seven years, I went to the sea. It was because of a charity for orphans. Every summer, they came to collect the orphans, and then they took us to Perugia and from Perugia to the sea. Five or six hundred orphans and the sea. I do not know where. No one ever told us, but it was good—oh, very good. We were like *gran padroni* there. Every morning, the trucks arrived with fruits and vegetables and meats. There were women there just to comb our hair—to delouse it with petroleum and then to wash and comb it. We slept in tents, big tents for sixteen girls. And then there was a beautiful big house with a kitchen and machines for washing clothes. Every day, they came from the house and changed the sheets on our beds. Twice a day, they changed our clothes. Twice a day, we were showered and disinfected, and there were sprays in the showers, wonderful sprays like waterfalls, but if you shot your spray at the others you were punished. You had to peel potatoes. I had to peel potatoes often. I was wild then. I was not nice. I used to hit the others, and then there was no sea that day. I would have to go to the pine tree and sit under it without bread, without fruit, without my 'four-o'clock.' There was always bread and jam at four o'clock, just like the bread and jam rich countesses had. And there was water, good fresh water—never wine, like children who are poor have to drink at home. You see, they weighed us, they examined us, they gave us

medicine. We were healthy. We were fat and strong. And then one day the buses would come, and they would take away our wonderful clean white smocks and our hairbrushes, and dress us in our old clothes and send us home. What do you make of my childhood, eh? *Dica.* A month by the sea, a month in heaven every year, and then, for the rest of the year, sick and filthy.

"I was eight when I went to work at the tobacco farm. Every day, I worked from dawn until the sun went down and it was too dark to see anything. I carried tobacco from the farmers' carts to tables where the women sat and packed it into bundles, and the women would scream and hit me. You see, they were paid by the weight of what they packed. They needed to bundle a hundred pounds a day, at least, and so they wanted the dark leaves at their tables, because the dark leaves were heavy. But I was small and thin and so tired—I would choose the light leaves, because they weighed less, and then the women beat me and boxed my ears. Finally, I was *intossicata.* I was poisoned, breathing all that tobacco powder, and I turned green. *Vero.* I had to be purged with oil. That was my childhood. Green and poisoned all year long, and fat and brown and strong for a month in summer."

Anna says that she had no intention of marrying anyone—that by the time she met Mario at the *spaccio* she would rather have joined a nunnery, the way one of her sisters did, than wait on one more human being for her supper. Her family had been reunited, after a fashion. Gino, her brother, had found a good job on the railway, and then a wife, and he had added a room to his grandmother's cottage and was already acting like the family *capo.* Anna's second sister was at home, too, a disgrace to the family—pregnant by a blacksmith who was engaged to so many women at the same time that when Anna's sister finally delivered she had to share a room at the charity hospital with two girls who were also giving birth to the blacksmith's children. Anna was so sick of men by then, she says, that she told Mario he would be better off throwing his kisses to her pregnant sister. She did not know how bashful Mario was. The only shepherds she had ever talked to were the wild Sardo boys who grazed their sheep near the sea where she had gone in August—boys who would lure the old-

FIGURE 6-12
Two one-sixth-page ads.

Funny, you don't look like a Xerox machine.

Ask for a "Xerox machine," and you might get a surprise.

Like this Xerox display typing system. A Xerox Telecopier transceiver. Or even a Xerox computer printer.

You see, today Xerox makes a lot of different machines. So now, more than ever, you have to ask for the one you want by its full name.

Of course, we still make Xerox copiers. But, then, that should come as no surprise.

XEROX

FIGURE 6-13
A standard 7- by 10-inch ad that bleeds on all four sides.

203

NATIONAL
MAGAZINES AND
NEWSPAPERS

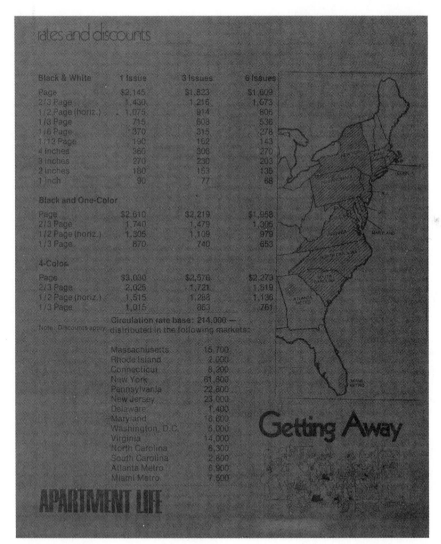

FIGURE 6-14
Some magazines offer special advertising rates for a particular promotion. *Apartment Life* initiated its travel advertising and editorial section in 1975 with a special deal for first-time advertisers: Buy two ads and get one free. (The "Getting Away" promotion began in the February-March 1975 issue.)

"That was really quite heroic, Grimsly... rushing the net against a Prince racket."

prince TENNIS RACKET.

For people who, given the choice, would rather win than lose.

For Men and Women

GOOSE DOWN SOX

Great to wear around home or as bed and sleeping bag sox. Take little space in luggage. Bauer Goose Down quilted in tough nylon taffeta. Machine washable. **Colors**, Men's: Taupe, Red, Winter Blue. **Sizes**, Men's: S(6½-8), M(8½-10), L(10½-11½), XL(12-13). **Colors**, Women's: Winter Blue, Powder Blue, Red. **Sizes**, Women's: S(5-6½), M(7-8½), L(9-10½). #0347 Men's or #0348 Women's Goose Down Sox $9.95 ppd.

Order Today! Money Back Guarantee!

Enclosed is my check or money order for $ _____ (Add sales tax where applicable.)

☐ #0347 Men's Goose Down Sox

Men's Size _____ Color_____

☐ #0348 Women's Goose Down Sox

Women's Size _____ Color_____

Name _____

Address _____

City _____

State _____ Zip _____

☐ Send me FREE your unique color catalog of quality outdoor apparel and equipment.

Eddie Bauer ®

Dept. QN3, Third & Virginia, Seattle, WA 98124

BALLOON RANCH
an outdoor adventure

After the thrill of flying, enjoy our many outdoor activities — tennis, swimming, horseback riding, rock climbing school and 4-wheel drive tours. Then top it off with sauna, hot tub and gourmet dining.

America's only ballooning resort
THE BALLOON RANCH
Del Norte, CO 81132 303/754-2533 or 3474

FIGURE 6-15
Fractional-page ads simply must be better than average for attracting readers. These examples do the job in a variety of ways.

TABLE 6-3
TYPICAL MAGAZINE RATE STRUCTURE

Size of ad	Once	Three times	Six times	Twelve times
1-page	$2,450	$2,410	$2,365	$2,255
⅔-page	2,150	2,120	2,085	1,995
½-page*	1,880	1,860	1,835	1,765
⅓-page	1,630	1,615	1,595	1,540
¼-page	1,475	1,465	1,450	1,415
⅙-page	1,370	1,345	1,335	1,305

*For an island half, add 15 percent.

per insertion (the six-time rate) instead of $2,255 (the twelve-time rate). The magazine will bill the advertiser for the difference at the end of the insertion year:

$$\$2,365 - \$2,255 = \$110 \times 6 = \$660.$$

To avoid the unpleasantness of short-rating an advertiser, many publishers have gone from the annual insertion rate discounts to the total yearly volume schedule. This simply means that advertisers earn a gradually increasing discount *based on the dollar volume of their business* (Figure 6-16).

State and Regional Magazines

Advertisers may prefer regional editions of national magazines, state magazines, or even city magazines to the total circulations of national publications. More often than not, smaller, restricted-circulation magazines provide advertisers with a more cost-efficient and reach-effective audience. Several reasons may account for the popularity of these magazines. A major one could be a limited geographical sales and distribution area of the advertiser's product. Others could be limited ad budgets and a desire to supplement national magazine advertising with heavy local support in much the same manner that companies use national spot radio and television. Usually the regional, state, and city magazines are general-interest publications with particular significance for the areas in which they are circulated. One of the better known is *Sunset Magazine* (circulation of over a million), a regional magazine whose readers are primarily found in California, Oregon, and Washington state.

Media buyers should be certain that a national magazine does not already provide better coverage at a lower cost per thousand readers than the regional or state publication. On the other hand, some advertisers prefer to use a combination of national, regional, and state publications without real concern over the cost per thousand. This practice is rather common among advertisers in the farm market where some of the best-read publications are

PICKUP, VAN & 4WD—Continued

5. BLACK/WHITE RATES

	1 iss	3 iss	6 iss	12 iss
1 page	2095.	2030.	1950.	1840.
2/3 page	1575.	1525.	1460.	1385.
1/2 page	1255.	1220.	1165.	1105.
1/3 page	935.	900.	870.	820.
1/4 page	735.	715.	685.	650.
1/6 page	525.	510.	490.	465.
1/12 page	275.	270.	255.	240.
1 col. inch	130.	125.	120.	110.

Frequency discounts earned on basis of total number of issues used within 12 months of 1st insertion. Space billed on contract basis; otherwise discounts given on an as earned basis. Minimum size space to maintain frequency 1/6 page.

VOLUME DISCOUNT

Payable over earned issue rate on 18 or more national pages (or its equivalent) within any 12 month period as follows:

Equivalent:	Discount
18 pages	4%
24 pages	6%
30 pages	8%
36 pages	10%

state farm papers such as *Wallace's Farmer* (Iowa), *Prairie Farmer* (Indiana, Illinois), and *Pennsylvania Farmer* (Pennsylvania and New Jersey).

Readership Profiles

Readership profiles are important in the media decision-making process. They paint a graphic picture of a magazine's target audience and are thus valuable to advertisers. Even without surveys of magazine readers, we could develop a general profile through simple reasoning. First, people who enjoy reading are likely to spend time with a magazine. Second, the ability to read and advancement in school have long been associated with higher-than-average income. Conclusion: Most magazine readers are better-educated, better-read, and better-paid than other members of the population.

Does this mean that magazine readers spend hours with their favorite publications? Hardly, Studies show that the average reader spends thirty minutes a day at most reading, a span that pales in comparison to time spent with television and radio. Yet the environments for learning and responding differ for these media. Reading a magazine's editorial matter and advertising takes active involvement. Readers don't consider the advertisements carried by magazines as intrusive as a series of television spots that interrupt programming every fifteen minutes. In a study by Opinion Research Corporation,[5] 59 percent of the men and 52 percent of the women said that advertising takes away from their interest in television; 21 percent of the men and 19 percent of the women felt that way about magazines.

[5] *A Study of the Climate for Learning from Media*, Opinion Research Corporation, Magazine Publishers Association, March/April 1975, p. 35.

Many magazines provide reader profiles to their advertisers to influence them to buy advertising space (Table 6-4). Frequently, the importance of the profile information for a specific advertiser may override another magazine's larger circulation. For example, if advertisers were interested in managerial and professional men (Table 6-4), they'd be more apt to select a magazine that attracted many such men than a competitive magazine with more male readers of *all* types.

Special Magazine Effects

Some companies will buy ten or more consecutive pages of advertising in order to create an impression. One of the most unforgettable impressions ever made on an audience was produced by Gulf & Western Industries' sixty-four-page special section in *Time* magazine.[6] This was the largest single insertion ever made by any corporation in any medium (Figure 6-17). Other companies looking to make a vivid impression try *gatefolds* (special-size ads

[6]*Time* magazine, February 5, 1979.

TABLE 6-4

DEMOGRAPHICS OF MALES WITH HOBBIES WHO PREFERRED MAGA-
ZINES OVER TELEVISION FOR INFORMATION ABOUT THEIR HOBBIES*

Education	Prefer magazines percent	Prefer television percent
Did not graduate from high school	54	12
Graduated from high school	70	9
Attended or graduated from college	76	9
Household income		
Under $5,000	55	12
$5,000-7,999	59	11
$8,000-9,999	66	7
$10,000-14,999	73	11
$15,000-24,999	71	9
$25,000 and over	78	7
Age		
18-24	70	14
25-34	79	6
35-44	70	7
45-54	61	11
55-64	56	11
65 and older	51	12
Occupation		
Professional	75	6
Managerial	79	6
Clerical sales	67	17
Craftsperson supervisor	64	8
Other employees	66	10

*Source: *Climate for Learning from Media,* Magazine Publishers Association. March/April, 1975, p. 21. Other answers adding to 100% of the respondents include radio, newspapers, and no opinion.

This week in TIME: a milestone in business communication.

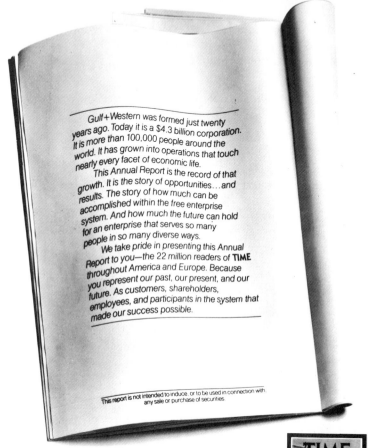

Gulf+Western was formed just twenty years ago. Today it is a $4.3 billion corporation. It is more than 100,000 people around the world. It has grown into operations that touch nearly every facet of economic life.

This Annual Report is the record of that growth. It is the story of opportunities...and results. The story of how much can be accomplished within the free enterprise system. And how much the future can hold for an enterprise that serves so many people in so many diverse ways.

We take pride in presenting this Annual Report to you—the 22 million readers of **TIME** throughout America and Europe. Because you represent our past, our present, and our future. As customers, shareholders, employees, and participants in the system that made our success possible.

This report is not intended to induce, or to be used in connection with, any sale or purchase of securities.

What you see above is an introduction to an extraordinary business communication: a 64-page special section in the February 5 issue of TIME Magazine reproducing the Annual Report of Gulf+Western Industries Inc.

It's a remarkable overview, financial as well as philosophical, of a company whose extraordinary growth is in itself a remarkable business achievement.

Gulf+Western is celebrating its twenty years of corporate innovation in characteristic style. No company has ever before made such a comprehensive statement on its activities and performance to so many people at one time. And no company has ever before conceived of communicating on such a grand scale: it's the largest single insertion ever made by any corporation in any medium.

TIME

FIGURE 6-17
Gulf & Western ran this history-making sixty-four-page insert in a single issue of *Time* magazine.

that open to three pages, usually found within the first few pages of the magazine), special inserts, or postage-paid cards. Some advertisers print their ads on foil, acetate, or heavy paper. A *heavyweight insert* makes it hard for a reader to miss the ad. It also makes it *easy* for a reader to pass over other advertisers' material. Readers' complaints have curtailed the use of heavyweight inserts, although their effectiveness has never been questioned. Some advertisers will negotiate for a small, thin sample of their product to be carried in the magazine. Some even create pop-up, three-dimensional miniatures of products. The limit to special-effect magazine ads depends on the willingness of the publisher to allow them. To the creative advertiser, such ads suggest new ways to attract the attention of prime prospects. In most cases, the use of special effects greatly increases the initial page rate of the advertising.

Split Runs

Many magazines and newspapers offer a *split-run* service to advertisers who are searching for the best way to present their sales messages. It works this way. An advertiser creates two separate headlines for the same ad and wishes to learn which will bring the greater response. The publication exposes half of its readers to each headline. If the ads carry a coupon, the returns are easily counted. A survey can also determine the pulling power of each headline. Some advertisers may wish to test several headlines or different photographs, even different copy. Some national publications permit national split runs by geographic areas, demographic editions, and state, regional, and large metropolitan markets. The charge for a split-run service may run 10 percent or more over the regular card rate. Some magazines even set up a special cost category on their rate cards for split-run rates. *Yankee Magazine*, published for New Englanders, offers split runs on a one-to-twelve-time basis with two ads in the same issue, each to reach half of *Yankee's* circulation. Many advertisers find the service well worth the effort and expense.

It cost Lillian Vernon, a direct-mail company, only $100 over the normal cost of the media to run the following test in *Yankee*. The object was to discover whether including a catalog request blurb in an ad would increase sales. The product was a wooden shadow box. *Yankee's* entire circulation saw the same photograph, the same layout, the same headline, and the same price. However, only half the readers saw the catalog blurb:

> Free for the asking—our exciting new 100-page color catalog. Just send your name, address, and zip!

Lillian Vernon's practice is to track its ads for six weeks, at the end of which time it expects the dollar sales to cover the media costs. At the end of nine months, the company determines whether the ad has been successful. It is considered successful if the ad brings in 2.25 times the media cost in dollar sales.

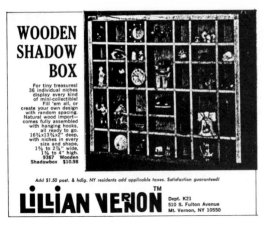

Here's the breakdown for the catalog blurb (Dept. K22) ad and for the straight product ad (Dept. K21)

Gross media cost	6 weeks' income		9 months' income	
	Dept. K21	Dept. K22	Dept. K21	Dept. K22
$1,120	$867	$592	$1,427	$1,197

However, the Dept. K22 also brought in 100 catalog requests; an estimated 10 percent of those requesting them actually ordered merchandise. The company decided not to mix product and catalog request ads.

Anyone making a split run should *test only one variable at a time.* Otherwise conclusions may be murky. Split runs can test the pulling power of photos over illustrations, male or female models, color or black and white, one headline or offer over another, and the like. Often advertisers use split runs on a restricted regional or metropolitan basis in order to decide on the best approach to use when the ad goes national (Figure 6-18).

Important Dates

Magazine advertisers are ruled by three dates. They are: the *cover date,* the *on-sale date,* and the *closing date.* We'll begin with the closing date because it determines the others. The closing date or "closing" is the last day a magazine will accept advertising materials (such as plates) for publication in a specific issue. Closing dates for magazines are the earliest of all national media, a decided disadvantage for the advertiser. Often the closing date is two or three months before the cover date, to allow the magazine's production staff enough time to plan the magazine's make-up. Ads scheduled for the issue can be canceled before closing, *but not after without a penalty,* if they can be canceled after closing at all. Large-circulation magazines such as *Reader's Digest* have staggered closings depending on the ad's printing complexity.

The cover date of an issue, as the term implies, appears on the cover.

The cover date differs from the date the issue goes on sale (the on-sale date.) Thus a magazine with a January cover date could go on sale December 15. The on-sale date is important because it tells when most issues reach the readers. Advertisers planning to introduce a new product precisely on January 1 would not want to advertise in the January issue (on sale December 15) unless their retail outlets had the product in stock.

The Future for Magazines

During the 1960s and early 1970s, *Life* and *Look* were among the most prominent magazines on the national advertiser's media schedule. *Life* at one time had a weekly circulation of over 15 million and had advertising revenues of nearly $100 million a year. But these magazines had to compete for advertising with the great growth of television. Too, postal increases and rising paper costs pushed the magazines' newsstand price to 75 cents. As readers' prices climbed, circulation dropped. Eventually, both magazines went out of business as weeklies.[7] Other publications know that they face similar problems. Between 1970 and 1976, for example, the cost of paper has increased by better than 55 percent; second-class postage—the service by which most magazines reach readers—will have tripled by 1980.

What are most magazines doing in the face of rising costs? Some are trimming the size of their pages. Between 1977 and 1979, *Better Homes and Gardens* went from $9\frac{1}{2} \times 12\frac{3}{8}$ inches to a new trim size of $8\frac{1}{8} \times 10\frac{3}{4}$ inches and saved approximately $225,000 a year on paper and $70,000 on postage and freight. Most magazines are also increasing newsstand prices to an average of 96 cents per copy, an increase of 52 percent since 1970. Mail subscribers are paying 49 percent more. The cost to the advertiser, however, has risen only 22 percent in the same period.[8] Readers will continue to pay for a greater share of the costs and, by 1980, they will share equally with advertisers. In 1966, the reader paid only 30 percent of the costs.

Strategies for magazine circulation are also changing. Although rising costs have reduced subscriptions, newsstand sales at higher prices have increased. In fact, newsstand sales may be where the future profitability of magazines lies. Many magazines are intent on securing distribution and sales at the checkout counters of supermarkets. They are, in fact, following the successful footsteps of *Reader's Digest, TV Guide, Woman's Day* and *Family Circle*, all of whom achieved widespread sales through supermarket distribution.

Battle for the Checkout Racks

"The supermarket has become the newsstand of America," says a consultant who works with magazine and supermarket officials.[9] Annual single-copy

---

[7] *Life* magazine returned on October 1, 1978 as a monthly.
[8] "Price Trends, Reader and Advertiser," *Advertising Age*, July 1977.
[9] R. E. Dallos, "Magazines slug it out at the markets," *Los Angeles Times*, May 23, 1977. According to Dallos, *People* magazine pays a supermarket chain $5 a checkout counter every 3 months if the magazine is displayed prominently.

sales were more than $1 billion by 1977, almost double what they were in 1970. Grocers make a higher profit on magazines than on food items, and there is never a loss; unsold copies are simply returned. Some publishers pay premiums to market owners to have their magazines prominently displayed at the checkout counters (Figure 6-19). These premiums are known in the trade as *retail display allowances*. As more publications begin to rely on single-copy supermarket sales for distribution, their designers will have to make them into more attractive packages, appealing from front cover to back cover. The impact of a dynamic front cover could well mean the difference in thousands of readers. When this happens, monthly and weekly fluctuations in single-copy sales will make it difficult to precisely describe the reach of certain magazines at the time the ad is contracted for.

In concluding our section on national magazines, it is only realistic that we recognize that they are often selected by advertisers to go along with other competitive media.

NEWSPAPERS

There are very few national newspapers. The exceptions are *The Christian Science Monitor* (circulation 215,000), which prints daily New England, Eastern, Midwestern, and Western editions; *The Wall Street Journal* (circulation 1.249 million), with four daily regional editions; and the weekly *National Enquirer* (circulation 4 million). *The New York Times* and *The Los Angeles Times* Sunday editions have spotty nationwide distribution. But, to compensate, national advertisers have a wide selection of local, regional, and even statewide newspapers, 1,794 daily and 634 Sunday newspapers. A one-page ad in every one (not counting the 10,000 weekly papers) would reach over 112 million people. It would also cost $750,000![10]

The newspaper kingdom presents a wide choice of advertising opportunities, either classified or display. Display, of the greatest concern to national advertisers, is characterized as having photographs, illustrations, large type matter, the "luxury" of white space, and color. Not all these elements will be found in each display ad, but at least one will. Like the spot television-and-radio buyer, the print buyer must pick and choose among newspapers according to marketing and advertising strategies. Top markets include our largest metropolitan areas. Many of the larger city newspapers actually cater to areas far beyond the territorial limits of the city.

Every day, about 63 million copies of newspapers are distributed in the country by mail, carrier, and newsstand. That is almost one paper for every United States household. Newspapers are available in Chinese, German, Italian, Polish, Greek, Russian, Spanish, Hungarian, and Yiddish. They represent every major and secondary marketing area in the country, and advertisers invest more in newspapers than in any other medium ($12 billion a year).

Advertising will normally fill up 50 to 60 percent of a newspaper's

---

[10]Based on line rates and circulations. Source: *Editor & Publisher Year Book*, 1976.

FIGURE 6-19
Will the proliferation of magazines sold at the supermarket checkout counters introduce the joys of reading to millions of new readers? Advertisers and publishers wonder about changes like this and also about the ethics of buying rack space in order to show off their magazines.

available space, and the majority of that advertising is local. Still, national advertisers often use newspapers that operate within the top markets. For them, newspapers have become an indispensable tactical medium.

Advantages and Disadvantages of Newspapers

When national advertisers evaluate newspaper buys, they are not as concerned at first with the papers' ability to cover certain market areas as much as they are in certain special qualities newspapers have. These qualities are:

1 Newspapers primarily reach adults who control most of the buying power in the country. Simmons reports that, nationwide, the highest rate of newspaper delivery went to readers with household incomes of $15,000 and over.[11]
2 The American public prefers advertising in newspapers to that found in any other medium.
3 Newspapers are a timely and economical vehicle for coupons.
4 Short closing dates of newspapers allow advertisers to make last-minute changes.
5 The average pass-along readership of two persons is not equal to magazines but is still an advantage.
6 Newspapers are an excellent outlet for cooperative ads between manufacturer and local dealers.

[11]Source: W. R. Simmons & Associates.

7 They offer market flexibility. Advertisers can select those markets where their distribution and acceptance are good, test various advertising themes, and tailor messages to the situation of the moment. But advertisers should be aware that newspaper readership varies by regions. In some areas, newspapers cover less than 45 percent of a market. In others, they reach over 80 percent. To determine the coverage of any given newspaper, advertisers can check audited circulation figures against the census of the region in which the paper operates.

8 Newspapers accept "hi-fi" ("spectacolor") preprint pages. These are newspaper-page-size ads printed in full color on white paper stock by an independent printer who ships to newspapers on the advertiser's schedule. The preprints become a regular part of the newspaper at black-and-white page costs because the color work is handled outside the newspaper plant.

9 Newspapers deliver advertising *inserts* at a low cost per thousand. Estimates for including and delivering a twelve-page tabloid-size insert ($11\frac{1}{4} \times 17$ inches) in top markets run to approximately $21.49 per thousand copies. That's a little over 2 cents per insert. Compare this to direct-mail postal delivery at 15 cents (first-class postage). Inserts also permit advertisers to control the quality of the color printing. (For some disadvantages of inserts, see below.)

Despite the attraction of newspapers for many national advertisers, the medium also presents some problems:

1 Newspapers have a relatively short life, generally a day or so.

2 Because of porous paper and high-speed printing, newspaper reproduction of photographs is mediocre compared to that of other print media. Some advertisers avoid photographs in favor of line drawings. (More about this subject in a later chapter).

3 An insert delivery date is hard to come by. Many newspapers accept inserts but run them at their pleasure during the week. Also, there is a growing concern among advertisers with what is being called "insert glut"—too many inserts in a single newspaper issue (Figure 6-20).

4 Young people in their twenties, the big spenders of the future, are below-average newspaper readers.

5 *Clutter* is a problem, particularly on the big supermarket advertising days: Wednesday, Thursday, and Friday. Other ads can easily get lost.

6 Local advertisers, the real bankrollers of newspapers, generally get the best spaces. National ads may fall in the back of the paper.

7 The *two-tiered rate structure system*, in which newspapers have traditionally charged both a national and a local rate *for the same size display ad*, is not entirely successful. The rationale, never happily accepted by national advertisers, is that local businesses offer goods to readers that are available immediately at a nearby store. Therefore, goes the argument, readers are more completely served by a local than by a national ad. This makes the newspaper more valuable to the reader; hence the reward and encouragement of lower ad rates given to local businesses. In addition, the claim continues, the multicounty coverage of the newspaper is of little value to the retailers tucked away in downtown streets. But they do serve the national advertiser well. National advertisers, in effect, receive more reach for their ads than individual retailers do for theirs. In addition, the argument says, newspapers charge a higher national rate because they have to pay a 15 percent commission to the advertising agency that places the out-of-town business. Local rates do not permit an agency commission. None of these

FIGURE 6-20

A typical example of what some critics are calling the "insert glut." The total number of inserts in this Midwestern Sunday paper was seven. The popularity of inserts comes from the low insertion and delivery rate charged by the newspapers. A twelve-page tabloid section can cost just a little more than $.02 per delivered household.

arguments blind national advertisers to the blunt fact that the same display ad costs them 50 to 75 percent more than it does the local retailer. Recently, a coordinated sales effort called NEWSPLAN, sponsored by the newspaper Advertising Bureau, was launched in an attempt to bring national newspaper rates more into line with retail. Over 800 newspapers have joined the plan that provides a discount to national advertisers who plan and schedule ads ahead.

Newspapers Within Newspapers

Newspapers within newspapers, or *magazine sections*, have long been part of most metropolitan Sunday papers. They are as close as an advertiser can come to national coverage. Magazine sections may be syndicated or printed by an individual newspaper. Some familiar syndicated magazine sections are *Family Weekly* (308 influential newspapers, more than 18 million readers), *Parade* (125 newspapers, more than 21 million readers), and *Sunday* (fifty newspapers, more than 22 million readers). As an example, *Sunday* syndicates and delivers a locally edited unit to fifty major cities. Its content differs from city to city and appears to be an essential part of the distributing newspaper. Supplements such as *Tuesday* and *Tuesday at Home* reach predominantly black communities in twenty-three metropolitan cities. The advertising for magazine sections must be arranged with the syndicate owners, not with the local newspapers. Rates depend on the number of newspapers delivered and the total circulation. By and large, the advertising revenue is kept by the syndicate to pay for the cost of producing the newspaper supplements. Individual Sunday papers pay a modest amount of money for supplements, which, they feel, help dress up the paper and add an important reader entertainment feature.

[12]Source: *Standard Rate & Data/Newspapers.*

FIGURE 6-21
This one-third-page, four-color ad distributed through the Metro Network will reach 20 million households. (Courtesy American Dairy Association.)

Comics

Comics might also be called "newspapers within newspapers" because they are distributed within Sunday papers. However, many are printed by the Sunday papers themselves, and a national advertiser who wishes to be a part of the comic pages will contact the sales department or representative of that paper. (The rights to print the comic strips themselves such as *Peanuts, Doonesbury,* or *Wizard of Id* are negotiated between the originator's agents and the newspapers. The comic illustrations are then sent to subscribing newspapers in reproducible form, ready for camera.) An alternative is to buy comic networks of newspapers such as syndicators Puck and Metro with about 150 newspapers between them. A one-third page, four-color ad within the comic pages of the Metro network will cost approximately $64,000 to reach 20 million households in sixty-eight selective markets east of the Rockies.[12] National advertisers have found that ads in comic pages attract adult readers as well as children (Figure 6-21).

The Weekly Newspaper

The 10,000 or so weekly hometown newspapers are an interesting development in American journalism. Local people don't expect news of the world. They want news of hometown activities considered insignificant by the large metro dailies: news of school board meetings, bake sales, scouting events, local sports, deaths, births, and marriages. Lest national advertisers dismiss these small-town weeklies out of hand, consider these average readership scores among all subscribers to two small-town Iowa papers:[13].

Item	Readership (%)
Hospital Notes	83
"Industry decided not to locate in Iowa Falls"	77
Town Talk	75
Letters to the Editor	64
Wedding in local family	56
Editorial	57

These figures as well as other signs of growth from weeklies, such as increased ad revenue and the development of small suburban newspaper chains, suggest that national advertisers might recognize these small circulation papers as a valuable link to millions of consumers.

Trends

The newspaper business is changing. Some observers even see newspapers delivered electronically into homes where a printing device produces long sheets of paper printed with news and pictures. While the technology for this vision is now at hand, the reality is further down the road. However, there are

[13]J. K. Hvistendahl, "Self-Administered Readership Surveys: Whole Copy vs. Clipping Method," *Journalism Quarterly*, Summer 1977, p. 354.

less dramatic but equally important trends of interest to users of national newspaper advertising.

Two-Color Printing

Surprisingly, national advertisers have been slow to use two-color printing (one color in addition to standard black). The value of color has long been recognized in consumer and industrial magazines. The charge for a second color is modest when set against the additional readership and attention it delivers. For an ROP (run of paper) 1,000 line ad, a second color costs about 35 percent extra. As the volume of newspaper inserts grows, manufacturers may soon turn to two-color ads.

Zoned Delivery

Some newspapers can break down their circulation into precise ZIP Codes. An advertiser for an expensive automobile, for example, who is interested in only certain affluent geographical sections of a city, could send inserts to the appropriate ZIP Codes only. *The Minneapolis Tribune*, among others, offers such a zoned plan much as a magazine would offer a particular geographic region.

New Technology

With computerized typesetting machines and high-speed offset presses, newspaper publishers can put out a better product with fewer high-priced employees. Newspapers that were operating profitably on the old labor-intensive base are now earning far beyond original estimates. This may explain why so many newspaper chains have been trying to acquire other papers. A chain of newspapers with a central printing plant can substantially reduce the cost of putting out all of its newspapers. A benefit for the national advertiser is the fact that one printing plate delivered to one of the chain's papers can serve all of its members. For example, the advertising department of Scripps-Howard Newspapers can deliver an ad into the homes of 2.3 million families through its fourteen newspapers.

The Mail Dilemma

With rising costs at the post office, many newspapers are concentrating on improving their carrier service. Some, in fact, have all but phased out mail in favor of private delivery. This trend eventually could lead to higher advertising rates as carriers demand more for papers grown increasingly burdensome with inserts. But higher postage rates have a brighter side, too, as more national advertisers place their coupons in newspapers instead of sending them through the mail.

There are other trends affecting newspapers that could suddenly become important to the national company: the rush to advertise by a small number of lawyers, doctors, and architects (which could, in turn, lead to their use as spokespersons in newspaper ads); an increase in the number of newspapers standardizing on the width of their columns (which will lead to a savings for advertisers in art and plate costs); and the growing experimentation by many newspapers with four-color printing. If the conventional daily newspaper manages to perfect its skill in four-color printing, what will the response of the magazine industry be?

Selling Newspaper Space

The advertising departments of most daily newspapers are divided into two parts: display (described earlier) and *classified.* Classified ads are generally all types of messages arranged into classifications of interest to readers, such as "houses for sale," "help wanted," and the like. Because display is the type of primary interest to national advertisers, we'll leave classifieds for our discussion of local advertising in Chapter 8.

Display ads come in almost any size and shape and are sold by the number of lines. Most standard-size newspapers follow a six-column format 22¼ inches deep with 1,869 lines per full page. Advertisers who wish to dominate the page should use at least half the lines. The smallest display ad is one column wide by one inch deep (written as *1 col. × 1″*). The largest can be several pages. There are fourteen lines to a column inch (Figure 6-22). Lines are simply a convenient unit of measure. They are not meant to be crammed with words. Lines should be considered a defined area in which the advertiser can "float" words or illustrations.

It is important to know how to convert column inches of display space to lines and lines to column inches. Space-buying directions are given either

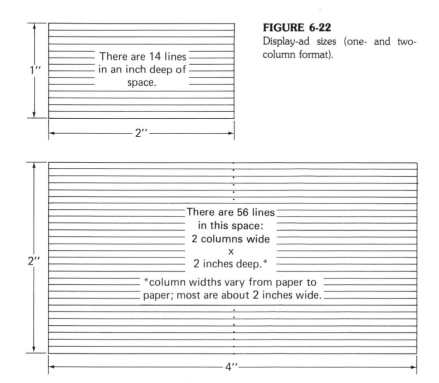

FIGURE 6-22
Display-ad sizes (one- and two-column format).

FIGURE 6-23
The open-line rate
for the *New York
Daily News* is
$10.75. Thus a
two-column, 5-inch
ad (140 lines) will
cost $1,505.00 for
just one insertion.
(Source: *SRDS/
Newspapers.*)

DAILYNEWS

(Manhattan Borough)
(Tabloid)
220 E. 42nd St., New York, N. Y. 10017.
Phone 212-949-1234.

ADVERTISING RATES
Effective February 1, 1978. (Card No. 60-G.)
Received February 13, 1978.

5. BLACK/WHITE RATES

Per agate line:	—Daily— Full Run	—Daily— City & Sub.	—Sunday— Full Run	—Sunday— City & Sub.
One time	10.75	9.63	14.32	12.22
52 insertions or 5,000 lines	10.37	9.25	13.84	11.74
10,000 lines	10.26	9.14	13.69	11.59
20,000 lines	10.10	8.98	13.63	11.53
30,000 lines	10.05	8.93	13.53	11.43
50,000 lines	10.00	8.88	13.42	11.32
75,000 lines	9.73	8.61	13.11	11.01
100,000 lines	9.57	8.45	12.90	10.80

way. To convert column inches to lines, remember that there are fourteen lines per column inch. Multiply the number of inches by fourteen to find the total number of lines an ad will take. If your ad is 2 inches deep, it will run twenty eight lines (2 × 14); if it is 5 inches deep, it will run seventy lines (5 × 14). If you want to find the number of inches, just divide the number of lines by 14. If an ad runs wider than one column, just multiply the number of lines by the total number of columns. Thus, if your ad is 2 inches deep and runs across two columns, it will measure twenty-eight lines (2×14) × 2 columns, or fifty-six lines. A three-column ad 1 inch deep would be forty-two lines (1 × 14 × 3).

Once you have figured the number of lines in an ad, it is a simple matter to find the cost of the entire ad. *Line rates* (also called *open line rates* and *agate line rates*) of newspapers are found in any of the following: the newspaper's own rate card, *Editor & Publisher Year Book*, and *Standard Rate & Data Service/Newspaper rates* (Figure 6-23).

Rates are set by the newspaper publisher. Although publishers know that rates must conform somewhat to circulation, line rates do vary from one newspaper to another, and advertisers should compare newspaper circulation and rates. They can use a tried and true formula called the *milline rate*. This formula does for newspapers what cost per thousand (CPM) does for magazines. A milline is the cost per line to reach a newspaper circulation of 1 million. (Even though few newspapers have a circulation that large, it works out to be a convenient formula.) The formula is developed by using three factors:

1 1,000,000.
2 the newspaper's line rate.
3 the newspaper's actual circulation.

For example, let's compare the line rates of two hypothetical newspapers:

	Circulation	Open line rate
The Journal	295,000	$1.20
The Gazette	58,000	0.46

If we multiply the line rate by 1 million and divide by the circulation figure, we get the milline rate. Here's the formula:

Journal: $\dfrac{1,000,000 \times \$1.20}{295,000} = \$4.06$

Gazette: $\dfrac{1,000,000 \times \$ .46}{58,000} = \$7.93$

What these figures say is this: *if* the *Journal* had 1 million readers, it would cost $4.06 per line to reach all of them (and $7.93 to reach *The Gazette's* 1 million readers). The *Gazette's* milline rate is almost double that of the *Journal*.

Those who dislike formulas can simply determine the ratio between the line rates. We see that the *Journal's* line rate is approximately three times the rate of the *Gazette* ($1.20:$0.46). Check to see whether we are getting *three times* the circulation (295,000:58,000). In this case, we are not. We are getting *five times* the circulation at less than *three times* the cost.

National Newspaper Representatives

There are over seventy national newspaper representative organizations in the United States, including the staffs of some of the nation's largest dailies. These reps call on advertisers and agencies on behalf of the newspapers they represent. Without them, many newspapers would lose valuable business because of their inability to make sales calls hundreds of miles away. One well-known firm, Matthews, Shannon & Cullen, provides advertisers immediate access to over 250 newspapers in thirty-one states. For selling national ad space for client newspapers, companies of newspaper representatives receive a 25 percent commission. This is a sales commission and has nothing to do with the standard advertising agency commission of 15 percent. (If a newspaper representative sells ad space from a client paper to an advertiser who uses the services of an ad agency, the newspaper pays the following commissions: 25 percent to the newspaper representative and 15 percent of the card rate to the ad agency.)

DUPLICATION OF READERSHIP

So far in discussing magazine and newspapers we have considered only circulation figures to decide which publications provide the greatest reach at the lowest cost. Now we should consider *duplication of readership*, the fact that some readers may receive more than one competitive newspaper or magazine. Some media buyers analyze all the candidates by a trial-and-error method called *iteration*. Iteration simply means repeating something over and over again. Applied to an analysis of media, iteration ranks the candidates by *reach* and *cost*. Iteration establishes a sort of "law of diminishing returns," with some publications' reach not justifying their cost to the advertiser. If, for example, the leading newspaper reaches four-fifths of a major market area and each additional paper delivers the remaining one-fifth as well as smatterings of the bulk of the market, the advertiser may not want to spend the money to secure the remaining one-fifth even if it could be done with one or two publications. Sometimes the combination of a strong daily and a suburban weekly may provide the greatest amount of reach with the smallest amount of duplication. The purpose of the exercise is to discover these facts so media buyers can make an economical buy. Marketing people recognize this application of iteration as the "falling rate of profit theory," which holds that after an optimum level of use is reached, each successive increment of capital goods (advertising) yields a smaller return on investment. Major media-buying agencies often use computers to determine when the law of diminishing returns takes effect.

A Matter of Discounts

Like everyone else, newspapers reward volume advertisers with lower prices per line. If advertisers use 5,000 lines or over during a period of one calendar year, they'll earn a lower base rate. Consistent advertisers can earn substantial reductions when they budget newspaper ads over the entire year, because they can take immediate advantage of the lowest rate for which they are eligible. Of course, if an advertiser is found eligible for a lower rate at the end of the year, the newspaper will give a rebate, a *short rate in reverse*.

Audits and Statements

Audit Bureau of Circulations (ABC) was organized in 1914 by advertisers, their agencies, and the publishers of newspapers and magazines. Its objective was and is to establish standard and acceptable methods of measuring circulations of member publications. Auditors employed by ABC regularly check circulation figures. (Publications pay modest membership rates based on their circulation.) ABC and similar auditing organizations[14] provide two benefits. One is that they have made ad rates of publications with comparable

---

[14]A.P.B. (Auditing Publications Bureau) for consumer magazines, B.P.A. (Business Publications Audit) and V.A.C. (Verified Audit Circulation Company) for business publications, and C.C.A.B. (Canadian Circulations Audit Board) for Canadian publications.

circulations more nearly equal. The other is that publications work to improve their product in order to maintain or exceed audited circulation figures. Many advertisers will only use audited publications, claiming that to do otherwise is like "buying a pig in a poke."

Not all publications belong to an auditing organization. They bear witness to their circulations in other ways. Most common is the *publisher's statement* supported by a sworn affidavit, or the *post office statement*, a newspaper's claimed circulation figures given once each year to the Post Office. If a publication stops using second-class mail, it no longer has to file a post office statement (Figure 6-24).

Professional audits have introduced a strong feeling of trust between advertisers and the publications they use and in so doing have helped make advertising the sound investment it is today.

IN SUMMARY

1 We use magazines to reach an audience with special interests and with above-average income and education. Magazine ads can tell a long story, present

FIGURE 6-24
When newspapers are not members of an official auditing organization like ABC, they convince advertisers of the validity of their circulation claims in other ways. One example is a statement verified by an official of the local post office who visits the publishing plant.

U.S. POSTAL SERVICE
REVIEW AND VERIFICATION OF CIRCULATION

NAME AND ADDRESS OF PUBLISHER: Iowa State Daily Publication Board Press Bldg. Iowa State University

| PUBLICATION TITLE | Iowa State Daily | PUBLICATION NO. 796870 |

| PUBLICATION FREQUENCY | See attached copy | ISSUE VERIFIED | Jan. 16, 1978* | PRINT ORDER OR PRESS RUN | 15,180 |

AUTHORIZING SECTION — ADVERTISING AUTHORIZED: ☒ YES ☐ NO

CONTRACT — NAME — PHONE NO. *(Include Area Code)* — DATE Jan. 16, 1978

Part A					Part B	
COPIES	VERIFICATION		MAILING STATEMENT COUNT			
	SUBSCRIBERS *(A)*	SAMPLES *(B)*	SUBSCRIBERS *(C)*	SAMPLES *(D)*	1. TOTAL NUMBER OF DIRECT SUBSCRIPTIONS *(Orders)*	344
					2. TOTAL NUMBER OF SUBSCRIPTIONS AS PART OF DUES	14,639
					3. TOTAL NUMBER OF SUBSCRIPTIONS THROUGH AGENTS, INCLUDING CARRIER DELIVERY	0
1. OUTSIDE COUNTY	164·				4. TOTAL NUMBER OF GIFT SUBSCRIPTIONS	64
2. WITHIN COUNTY	69				5. SINGLE COPIES SOLD OVER COUNTER, COIN MACHINES, STREET VENDORS	0
3. NON SUBSCRIBER	208				6. COPIES FURNISHED TO NEWS AGENTS AND DEALERS — WITH RETURN PRIVILEGE — TOTAL SOLD ▶	0
4. FOREIGN	0				6. WITHOUT RETURN PRIVILEGE — TOTAL SOLD ▶	0
5. TOTAL MAILED *(Sum of Lines 1 thru 4)*	441				7. COPIES PURCHASED IN BULK OTHER THAN NEWS AGENTS AND DEALERS	0
6a. MAILING AGENT'S COUNT	441				8. TOTAL PAID CIRCULATION *(Lines 1 thru 7)*	15,047
6b. GALLEY OR MACHINE COUNT	same				9. ADVERTISER PROOF COPIES	33
7. COMPLIMENTORY AND NOT REPORTED ON MAILING STATEMENT	0				10. EXCHANGE COPIES	0
8. FOREIGN ADDRESSED NOT SHOWN ON MAILING STATEMENT	0				11. OTHER CIRCULATION MAILABLE AT SECOND-CLASS POUND RATES NOT IDENTIFIED IN LINES 1-8 *(Specify)*	0
9. OTHER DISTRIBUTION *(Specify)* See attached copy	14,639				12. MAIL SAMPLES	
10.					CARRIER SAMPLES	
11.					COPIES PAID BY ADVERTISERS	·
					EXPIRED SUBSCRIPTIONS *(Over 6 months old)*	
12. DISTRIBUTION	TOTAL COL (A) 15,080	TOTAL COL (B)	TOTAL DISTRIBUTION		OTHER	
					TOTAL FREE OR NOMINAL RATE ▶	0
13. OFFICE COPIES, SPOILED, CHECKING COPIES, ETC.	100				13. TOTAL DISTRIBUTION *(Sum of Lines 8 thru 12)* ▶	15,080
14. TOTAL PRODUCTION *(Add Line 12 and 13)*	15,180				14. COPIES FURNISHED NEWS AGENT AND NOT SOLD ▶	
COMMENTS *(Continue on reverse side if more space is required)*					15. OFFICE COPIES, SPOILED CHECKING COPIES, ETC.	100
					16. TOTAL PRODUCTION *(Sum of Lines 13, 14 and 15)*	15,180
VERIFICATION PERFORMED BY					17. PERCENT PAID CIRCULATION *(Line 8 divided by line 13)*	100

PS Form 3548
May 1978

a cents-off coupon, reproduce products and packages in pictures as close to real-life color as possible, and support dealers and other media. A further advantage of magazines is pass-along readership estimated at over three persons per copy.

2   A major weakness in selecting magazines as an advertising medium is their long closing dates. This precludes last-minute strategy changes.

3   The most important elements of a publication's success are its editorial content and graphic presentation.

4   Magazine space is sold in several sizes, the most common of which is the full page size, 7×10 inches. To improve on the impact of their ads, advertisers may buy bleed pages and/or premium locations within magazines at higher prices. The lowest-priced ads are sold as ROB (run-of-book) ads.

5   Advertisers should schedule four to six insertions per year in any given magazine to make an impression on the reading public.

6   Smaller-budget advertisers who cannot afford a full, national run in a magazine may want to buy the circulation of a region or of a demographic unit (such as students or executives).

7   Magazine space is sold either by number of insertions per year or by dollar volume.

8   Reader profiles paint a picture of a magazine's target audience. Most magazine readers are better educated, better-read and more highly paid than other segments of the population.

9   The use of special magazine effects such as gatefolds, multipage ads, inserts, and postage-paid cards increases the initial page rates of the advertising space. Such effects also increase the ad's ability to attract attention.

10 Advertisers making a split run should test only one variable at a time; otherwise conclusions will be unclear. The charge for a split run may run 10 percent over the regular card rate or more.

11 The magazine advertiser's three important dates are: cover date, on-sale date, and closing date. The closing date is the last day the publication will accept ad plates and is often two to three months before the cover date.

12 Strategies for magazine circulation include distribution through supermarkets. Annual single-copy sales in supermarkets have almost doubled since 1970.

13 There are a few national newspapers: *The Christian Science Monitor, The Wall Street Journal, National Enquirer, The New York Times,* and *The Los Angeles Times.* Actually, these are not true national papers for their circulation is sporadic outside their own sphere of influence. Advertisers, however, have a wide selection of local, regional, and even statewide newspapers. Every day, about 63 million copies of newspapers are distributed by mail, carrier, and newsstand.

14 Newspapers' advantages are that they reach primarily adults, they are timely, they have short closing dates, they provide an excellent outlet for coop ads, they permit extreme market flexibility,and they accept high-fidelity color pages as well as inserts.

15 The disadvantages of newspapers are a relatively short life, poor photo reproduction, imprecise distribution dates for inserts, fewer young readers, clutter of ads on supermarket ad days, local advertisers getting the best locations for their ads in the paper, and the two-tiered rate structure system (which charges more for a national advertiser's ad than it does for the same size ad run by a local retailer).

16 Sunday supplements—newspapers within newspapers—and comics that are

syndicated into networks are the closest thing we have to national newspaper coverage available to a national advertiser.

17 There are 10,000 weekly hometown newspapers in the United States.

18 Two-color newspaper printing and zoned delivery are two of the growing list of options open to national advertisers.

19 Display ads are sold by the line, and there are fourteen lines to a column inch. Lines are simply a convenient unit of measure; they are not meant to be crammed with words. They are spaces where advertisers can "float" words and illustrations.

20 The milline rate formula helps media buyers compare the cost and the reach of competing newspapers.

21 Through a trial-and-error exercise called *iteration*, media buyers attempt to evaluate the readership duplication of publications.

22 The Audit Bureau of Circulations (ABC) and other auditing companies measure and report on the circulations of newspapers and magazines. These professional audits have introduced a strong feeling of trust between advertisers and publications.

CASE STUDY   Kabeelo Lodge, Evolution of a Magazine Ad by Kenneth J. Lohn, proprietor

At thirty-eight years of age, after having spent fifteen years in the advertising business, I approached my wife about a secret desire I had cherished for most of my life. "Let's chuck it all, go up to Canada, and start our own fishing camp." Thus began an odyssey that soon became the most fulfilling experience of our lives.

Our problems were many, but lack of money was the biggest. We started from scratch, buying the land, building our lodge and cabins, buying boats, motors, a generator for electric power, plus a million other things that you have to have to operate a fishing resort. We borrowed money from the Canadian government and from relatives and sold everything we had.

Our lodge operation was structured along the lines of many other Canadian fishing camps. We specialized in fly-out fishing. Something was needed that would set us apart and result in a large volume of business. We began with a three-phase plan of action: market research, development of a unique concept, and execution of a sales program based on our action plan.

Market research involved good old-fashioned footwork. I went from door to door visiting business offices, bait shops, taxidermists, sportsmen's clubs, neighbors, and acquaintances. I learned a lot: what people had found wrong on previous fishing trips, what they wanted for equipment and facilities, what they wanted to eat and to pay. Most important, I discovered they wanted a trip that lasted only three or four days. This was a revelation since most fishing camp literature offered one-week trips. Some of the market information was easy to obtain from the United States Fish and Wildlife Service. We discovered that 41 percent of all men and 18 percent of all women buy fishing licenses in the United States. Then we found a real gem that helped us in our planning: 68 percent of all fishing enthusiasts lived in metropolitan or suburban communities.

But we had a problem. Most fishermen and women associated good fishing with particular months. Since the best fishing in Minnesota was May or June, they also thought that it would be best in Northwestern Ontario at the same time. I knew this wasn't the case. Yet Canadian fishing camps are virtually abandoned during July and August. We had to educate our target audience that in Canada, July and August were best. Our initial research showed the following:

1 People preferred a trip lasting less than a week.
2 People wanted to know total cost of the trip before reserving space.
3 People wanted to enjoy the wilderness in solitude by themselves.
4 Many enthusiasts never entertained the idea of a Canadian fishing trip because they anticipated high costs—creating a huge untapped market.
5 Family relationships are important to a large part of the total fishing market which thus included a high percentage of women and children.

Armed with this information, we created a low-cost quality package that would appeal to a large number of people. The package filled seventy-two hours. We'd fly guests out the morning of their first day to some remote lake and bring them back the morning of their fourth day. To reduce flying costs of the pontoon-equipped planes, we scheduled all parties back-to-back so that no flights in or out would be empty. This three-day rotation schedule allowed us to offer the seventy-two-hour package for a total cost per guest of $179.50. It was revolutionary within the industry.

We now had to create an effective selling ad. But we had little money. We settled on a quarter-page ad in four small, outdoor-oriented publications that reached fishing audiences in and around Minnesota. We coded our box numbers so we could tell which small regional magazines gave us the best response. The 3-inch wide × 4-inch deep ad showed a floatplane with a banner across it saying "Just For You," a headline saying "Fly-out to Great Canadian Fishing," and a subhead that ran "Only $189.50 complete." We then crammed the rest of the small space with as much information as possible. The ads and our own sales efforts produced about $30,000 in gross sales that first year. Not enough to make a profit, but we came close to breaking even.

We discovered that one of the four regional publications, *Outdoor News*, produced quality inquiries for us, so we concentrated on it the following year. We increased our ad size to 8½ × 11 inches. We ran one insertion in January, February, and March. With more space, we retained the layout format of the first ad, but now we added details of the trip, day-by-day schedule, types of food provided, descriptions of boats, and so on. We added a headline (and proof) that "July and August are best." Our total ad program with *Outdoor News* cost less than $500.

As a result, sales increased 50 percent over the previous year and we handled 220 guests. An analysis of our coded ads showed that 30 percent of our new business came from *Outdoor News*. Our costs in obtaining these guests were less than $10 each and a lot of this business was for July and August.

In the next two years, we continued with our small ad program and built up our capital and facilities. Soon we bought our own plane, a brand new DCH-2 Beaver floatplane. And with that needed purchase went the set-aside profits for our ad budget! We now had a total of nine lakes licensed to us by the Ministry of Natural Resources—and thirteen outposts. To be able to maintain our package rates, we had to increase our business from a little over 600 guests in 1976 to 1,000 in 1977.

We knew that *Outdoor Life* magazine was the most widely read national publication directed at our clientele. But it was expensive. Even though it offered

FIGURE 6-25

This full-page ad evolved from a much smaller one that had proved that the advertiser's approach was sound. The magazine that carried this $6,000 ad helped propel Kabeelo to success. (Courtesy Kabeelo Lodge.)

regional rates (we could select certain states in which we wanted the ad to appear), the lowest cost for this limited exposure for a full-page, two-color ad was still about $6,000.

I went to my banker and showed him that I had a documented ad with proven results. He listened to my proposal, looked at the ad, studied the documented results, and gave me the needed money on a six-month note so it could be repaid in the summer when the receipts came in.

Since our *Outdoor Life* ad would reach readers as far away as Indiana and Kentucky, I had to estimate the declining value of the ad as a function of distance. My figuring indicated that we could expect 172 guests for the $6,000 investment. It was worth the risk.

A condition of buying regional advertising in *Outdoor Life* is that you must buy 500,000 names out of a total of almost 2 million readers. We drew the list to represent fourteen states and 509,000 persons. The full-page, two-color ad appeared in the March 1977 issue of *Outdoor Life*. It was rerun in the January and March issues in 1978 (Figure 6-25). The results were truly unbelievable, far exceeding our most optimistic projections:

Total inquiries	516
Letter inquiries	381 (74 percent)
Telephone inquiries	135 (26 percent)
Total guests reserved	386

Ad effectiveness: double what we had estimated. Gross income per guest exceeded our estimates also, dropping cost for obtaining each guest to below 7 percent. The following year 32 percent of these guests repeated, thus lowering our sales costs.

For the first time ever, our sales problems were over. We have had to put people on waiting lists. We now operate the largest fly-out resort in Northwestern Ontario. We have two De Havilland Beaver floatplanes, seventeen outpost lakes that are virtually always sold out, a new seven-unit staff building for employees, a new house-general office at the main lodge, and a new computer for all financial records, advertising, and media analysis as well as for responding to fifty to sixty inquiries a day with a personal letter.

QUESTIONS NEEDING ANSWERS

1 Some advertising experts might find fault with the appearance of the Kabeelo Lodge ad (Figure 6-25). Do you think a more esthetic approach would improve the ad's effectiveness? Explain.

2 Would it now make sense for Kabeelo Lodge to buy the entire national circulation of *Outdoor Life* magazine? Explain.

3 If you decided to place Kabeelo Lodge ads in other national magazines such as *Field & Stream* and *Sports Afield*, how would you be able to determine the duplication of readership among the magazines? Would it make sense to run an iteration exercise on all the magazines in your schedule? Explain.

4 Assume that two magazines boasting similar audiences are vying for your business. Their CPMs are fairly close. Unfortunately, you can afford to advertise in only one. Checking each of their ABC statements, you note that Publication A had a better

than 85 percent circulation renewal rate over the past few years; Publication B's rate ran approximately 65 percent. Yet Publication B seems to have a sprightlier editorial format. Which publication will you select? Why?

STUDENT PROJECT

Assume that you are a national representative selling either newspaper or magazine advertising space. The medium you choose represents the one you feel will do the best job for Hotel Good Times. The hotel has 100 rooms and is only five years old. It is located on an out-island of the Bahamas far away from the noise and hubbub of Nassau. The only way to reach the hotel (except by boat) is to fly from Miami. Round-trip fare is $100. Once you have decided which medium to represent, prepare a written or oral defense of your choice.

Here are some facts. A survey of patrons over the past five years reveals that the hotel is frequented by people mostly 35 years and older, mostly college-educated with average incomes of $20,000 a year and over. Over 80 percent of the patrons say they come to the hotel because it is quiet and peaceful. Hotel records show that the great majority of the patrons come from the eastern states, particularly around New York, Pennsylvania, and New England. The ad manager of the hotel tells you she has an annual budget of $100,000. To assist you in the decision, check Standard Rate & Data/ *Consumer Magazines* and *SRDS/Newspaper Rates and Data.*

QUESTIONS ABOUT THE PROJECT

1 Would a direct mailing restricted only to former patrons of the hotel be sufficient to keep the hotel's occupancy rate up? Explain.
2 What advantages, if any, can you see if you also advertised to travel agents?

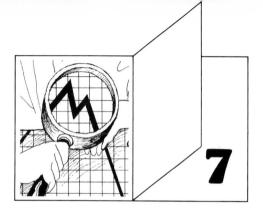

NATIONAL PRINT MEDIA: DIRECT MAIL, YELLOW PAGES, OUTDOOR, TRANSIT, AND SUPPLEMENTARY

Update No medium has a monopoly in this country. Consumers regularly use several sources of information for making purchases. Therefore more national advertisers are mixing their media as they attempt to cover the multitude of markets in the country. This chapter is concerned with the print media that account for more advertising dollars than national newspapers and magazines combined (Figure 7-1).

Few national advertisers concentrate their efforts on a solitary medium during any given budget year. Most, in fact, scatter their messages in diverse media in the knowledge that the combination of electronic and print advertising will achieve broad reach, frequency, and continuity at a reasonable cost. General Motors, for example, regularly budgets ad dollars for network television, radio, and magazines, but it also invests in direct mail, outdoor advertising, and display ads in the Yellow Pages. American Express, although familiar to consumers through the television tube, also reaches prospective subscribers for its credit card through direct mail; United Airlines uses reminder outdoor signs in addition to its other media investments. Is it emotion or good business sense that leads national advertisers to use the lesser-known media? Obviously advertisers would prefer a single medium if it could consistently reach their audiences at a low cost. There would be no need for a media mix. But few advertisers are that fortunate, because it is an accepted fact that individuals play favorites among the available media. Some are heavy television watchers. Others are readers. Still others neither watch nor read and must be reached in other ways. Our purpose in this chapter is to investigate those other ways.

DIRECT-MAIL AND COLLATERAL

Direct mail is advertising literature that is sent through the mails: brochures, sales sheets, stuffers, broadsides, and letters. If it is not sent through the mail but is used instead to support a company's sales effort, advertising is often called *collateral material*. Collateral material is not *commissionable* (as are television, radio, magazine, and newspaper advertising, in which ad agencies are paid a 15 percent commission). The material is bought outright by the advertiser—or through an ad agency—from the creator. When collateral is purchased by an ad agency, the agency will usually add on a commission for its services. Many times the ad agencies will create a large proportion of the collateral materials themselves and buy what they cannot create from the outside. (More on the services of an ad agency in Chapter 15.)

Direct mail, unlike a broadcast ad that mentions highlights or a brief print ad, can do a complete job of selling. It tells the whole story. Nobody really knows how much money is spent on direct mail at the national level. The best estimate suggests at least $5 billion, but the figure is probably much higher because many companies do not report what they spend. Direct mail is used more than any other form of advertising by most American businesses. A direct-mail piece can be solely informational or informational *and* designed to sell something. When its primary purpose is to sell something the piece is often called *mail-order* or *direct-response advertising*.

The largest users of direct mail are, of course, mail-order companies like Sears, Roebuck and Montgomery Ward. They are closely followed by other national companies—credit card and oil companies, for example. Insurance companies, national magazines, soap companies, food and tire companies—even Congresspeople send you direct mail. Direct mail brings the prospect to the advertiser. Of course, as with all other media, the performance of direct mail should be measured against its cost.

Advantages and Disadvantages of Direct Mail

Direct mail takes the rifle approach to advertising, as opposed to the shotgun approach. The rifle approach is a straight-line appeal from the manufacturer (advertiser) to a specific consumer. It differs from newspaper, magazine, and

233

NATIONAL PRINT
MEDIA: DIRECT
MAIL, YELLOW
PAGES, OUTDOOR,
TRANSIT, AND
SUPPLEMENTARY

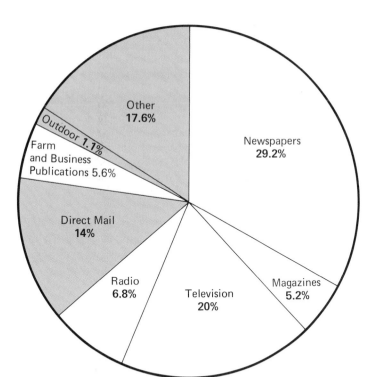

Share of ad dollars in the major media

FIGURE 7-1
Share of ad dollars
in the major media

broadcast advertising that employs the shotgun approach, in which messages are spread throughout media with no particular person in mind. It is hard to evaluate the effectiveness of direct mail because people don't always respond to it immediately. For example, Alberto Culver's own print shop produces millions of direct-mail pieces each month: sales bulletins, point-of-purchase posters, window banners, and company brochures. Yet it is difficult for the company's management to tally reader response to their direct-mail efforts. One reason may be that the direct-mail recipient may take a long time— months or years—to respond. Another reason may be that the recipient absorbs the message but makes no overt recorded response to the advertiser. Yet advertisers seek some fair and practical way to gauge the value of their direct-mail efforts. In an effort to be objective with their direct-mail programs, manufacturers may rate direct-mail responses as immediate, delayed, or making contact. For example, on a ten-point scale, an immediate response receives a rating of six points; a delayed response three points; and the making-contact response (merely the communication of the message) one point. An evaluation technique of this sort is much fairer than one that ignores any but immediate responses. Regardless of how any direct-mail operation is measured, however, there are certain built-in advantages to this most personal of advertising media:

1 Direct-mail prospects are specially selected; they are not just the general population.

2 Advertisers can send out sales messages whenever it suits their purposes.
3 Advertisers can easily test variations of their messages to find the most effective one. For example, they may want to see whether a change of copy will improve the returns from an earlier mailing. They may want to change prices and offers, or the length of time the offer is available. Most direct-mail experts recommend a test mailing of at least 10 percent of the entire list, and advertisers should make only one change at a time so they know what does or does not succeed.
4 Direct mail can be tailored to fit any budget.
5 Direct mail emphasizes and complements other media.
6 Direct mail is excellent for samples and coupon distribution.
7 Direct mail is a low-cost, effective means for conducting consumer research, welcoming new customers, and acknowledging payments and orders.

We can only offer a partial list here because novel ways of using direct mail are constantly cropping up. But direct mail, like all other media, has some drawbacks. Some advertisers may find these serious enough to use the medium only sometimes or not at all. These disadvantages are:

1 Direct mail lacks the prestige of magazines, newspapers, television, and radio. For example, *Time* magazine confers its authority on an unfamiliar product advertised in its pages. The same product advertised in literature that arrives at someone's home is a suspicious stranger.
2 Postage rates keep climbing. Postage has become one of the major costs of sending direct-mail advertising to large groups of people. Once it was considered poor business practice to send direct mail any way except first class. Now much of it goes third-class bulk rate because advertisers can save almost 50 percent of the cost this way.
3 Production costs are high. For example, a *Newsweek* advertisement may cost $1800 for engraving, art, and type. But once these costs have been paid, the ad can be reproduced 850,000 times and distributed to a like number of households. To send a direct mailing to the same homes would require: (1) printing 850,000 pieces; (b) purchasing and printing 850,000 envelopes; (c) folding and inserting the pieces; (d) buying postage for 850,000 units; and (e) delivering the 850,000 units to the post office.
4 Many people, perhaps unfairly, consider direct mail "junk mail" and dump it unceremoniously.

Major Types of Direct Mail

Different products and different audiences encourage different direct-mail solutions. Yet despite the wide variety of sizes and shapes available to advertisers, there are certain recognizable types.

Letters are the most widely used kind of direct mail. Letters are easy to reproduce in quantity and can be accompanied by reply cards, enclosures, and other advertising collateral.

Circulars, folders, brochures, booklets, stuffers (so named because they are "stuffed" into envelopes without requiring a fold), and *broadsides* are other types of direct mail. Definitions vary from user to user, but most are printed on sheets of paper that permit the most printing and the least waste. In all direct mail, the quality of paper is important. An expensive product can be cheapened by poor-quality paper that is dull or thin. Advertisers may send special mailings in unusual shapes or odd sizes, but these cost more to process. Broadsides, for example, usually open up to 17 × 22 inches, a multiple of the popular 8½-11-inch size (Figure 7-2).

Catalogs may be specialized or general but are always an important form of direct mail. Their appearance may differ from company to company, but their purpose is the same: to provide customers and prospects with an itemized and illustrated inventory of merchandise. Many companies publish catalogs, from Sears, Roebuck to Ace Hardware, from the Wayside Gardens to Radio Shack. Most catalogs are designed for year-round use, although a growing number of specialty houses publish Christmas catalogs each year. Catalogs also play an important marketing role in industrial advertising, as we will discover when we investigate that market in later chapters.

House organs are a form of direct mail that act as an advertiser's own specialized newspaper or magazine. Advertisers send them to customers and prospects because they often contain news about the advertiser's industry or provide reading entertainment. House organs can be as uninvolved as a single 8½-× 11-inch sheet of paper or as elaborate as a sixty-four-page magazine (Figure 7-3).

Self-mailers and postal cards are less imposing types of direct mail. *A self-mailer* does not hide in an envelope and saves the cost of buying, printing, and stuffing the envelope. An advertiser can design any direct-mail piece, broadside, letter, circular, or booklet as a self-mailer. The major disadvantage of this method is that without an envelope exterior, the piece betrays itself immediately as a direct-mail advertisement. It is not always as easy to identify direct mail as such if it arrives inside an envelope. Self-mailers have to allow space for both the recipient's name and address and the sender's return address. Postal regulations require at least a 2¾-×3½-inch area for the recipient information.

Postal cards are available to advertisers through the post office, private companies, or the advertisers' own publishing efforts. Advertisers wishing immediate response may buy them or print them on a *double*, with one section to be used as an easy return. Contrary to popular belief, a postal card need not be 5½ × 3½ inches. It can be larger. Outsized post cards, however, are subject to mutilation, spindling, and bending. Before designing an outsize card, advertisers should check with the post office for clearance (Figure 7-4).

Lists and Brokers

Names, names, names. The heart of any direct-mail operation is the mailing list. The cleverest, most appealing mailing packet will flop if the names or addresses are wrong or outdated. The disposable diaper or baby food manufacturer who mails a "$1 off" coupon to new mothers can't expect much retail action if the list of mothers is three years old!

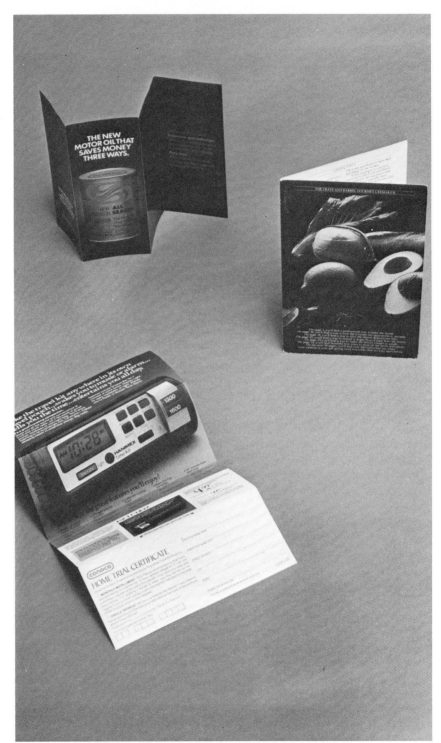

FIGURE 7-2
The sizes, shapes, and appeals of direct-mail pieces appear to have no limit. The two Conoco stuffers fit very nicely into a conventional envelope when they are folded. The digest-size (5½ × 8½ inches) catalog was mailed as is without a covering envelope; the area for the address and the return information is on the back.

Personalized advertising messages expand receipt/statement communications

The purpose of a receipt/ statement is to tell a customer at a glance everything he needs to know about his account. Now, however, each receipt/statement from DCSC's subscribers has an additional function as part of a new advertising program — carrying personalized advertising messages.

Advertising messages have been available through DCSC for some time, but under the old program, the same one-line message was printed on each receipt/statement, and each message was used for one month. Once each year, subscribers submitted their 12 messages to DCSC who programmed them into the computer. Then, the appropriate messages were automatically printed on the receipt/statements each month.

Under the new advertising program, messages of up to five lines can be printed on the receipt/ statements by the computer. Messages can be designated for specific groups of accounts, and several messages can be used simultaneously. The greatest difference in the new program, however, lies in the fact that the messages can be personalized to refer to the customer by name and to refer to specific facts about the individual's account.

The home office of each subscriber has complete control over the messages included in its receipt/ statements and is responsible for the security and timing of the messages. The messages, which are transmitted to the DCSC computer through the home office terminals, can be initiated once a year, once a month, or whenever the subscriber chooses, and messages can be delet-

ed or added at any time. Messages can also be coded to begin and end on pre-determined dates, so several messages can be transmitted at one time, with each stored in the computer until the date on which it is to be used.

Preparing The Message

Under the new advertising program, customer accounts can be divided by such characteristics as state, age, home ownership, account balance, loan limit, type of account, and many more. The divisions are limited only by the amount of information from the applications, legal and state requirements, and account activity that is stored in the computer. By dividing, and even subdividing, the groupings, the advertising messages can be personalized so that they correspond to the characteristics of each account.

In addition, messages can be modified to include the customer's name (full name or just first name), the dollar amount of credit available, state maximums, amount due this statement, or the name of the branch manager.

For example: A subscriber decides to print an advertising message on the receipt/statements of homeowners whose account balances are at least $3,000 below the state loan maximums. The message is to be modified to include the customer's name, the dollar amount of the state loan maximum, and the name of the branch manager.

With proper coding, the computer selects the appropriate

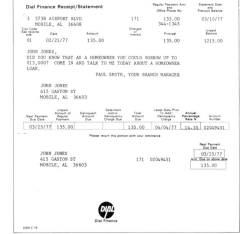

accounts and prints the following message, inserting the personalized information for each account.

"John Jones, did you know that as a homeowner you could borrow up to $15,000? Come in and talk to me today about a homeowner loan. Paul Smith, your branch manager."

At the same time, the subscriber also runs a message directed to another audience — delinquent accounts. This message includes the customer's name, the exact contractual amount due (including late

charges and delinquent amounts), and the branch manager's name.

"John Jones, your account is now delinquent. A payment of $75.32 will bring your account up to date. If you are having money problems, come in and let's talk about it. Paul Smith, your branch manager."

The advertising messages can also be divided in another way: those that are continuing, and those that are periodic. Continuing messages include standard messages that would always be sent to new

continued on page two

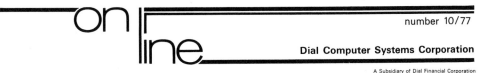

number 10/77

Dial Computer Systems Corporation

A Subsidiary of Dial Financial Corporation

FIGURE 7-3

Keeping company managers aware of Dial Computer Systems is the purpose of this direct-mail house organ, a vital instrument of communications for the advertiser. Companies often reprint magazine, newspaper, or television ads in their house organs to squeeze out the last drop of value.

FIGURE 7-4
Color postcards
attract attention, and
advertisers may use
them to promote
their products. This
card was used to
promote an African
violet plant food.

How do advertisers go about securing a good mailing list? They need to define *what* and *who* they are after. When advertisers know who their target audiences are and where they are, they are ready to secure a list of appropriate names. They can either build, buy, or rent a list. They may also swap lists among themselves. Let's look at all the options.

Building the List   Although building a list is the most difficult of the three methods in terms of time and effort, it provides the owner with an exclusive property. It lets advertisers make contact with customers at any time, and that can prove to be a real competitive advantage. Advertisers can compile a partial list of customers through retail outlets, credit applications, warranty cards, and/or responses to advertisements and offers. Companies or institutions can supplement their lists with names from city directories; phone books; local, state, and national organizations; licenses; and voting records. Building a mailing list is usually a long-term operation.

239

NATIONAL PRINT
MEDIA: DIRECT
MAIL, YELLOW
PAGES, OUTDOOR,
TRANSIT, AND
SUPPLEMENTARY

Buying the List   Some consumer magazines may sell—or even build—a special list to an advertiser's order. These lists are generally made up of readers of the publications. Commercial list houses will also sell or compile names. They may have some of the names you want already in stock. However, if a list has been previously accumulated at great cost and difficulty, generally it is *not* for sale. Advertisers need to be aware that some list owners may mix various lists into one in order to provide more names and thus get more money for the purchase. Some names on the list may be closely related to the products sold by the advertisers; others may not be so closely related. Some names on the list may even include customers who resent direct-mail advertising.

To avoid purchasing a mediocre list, it might be wise for the advertiser to determine how the list owner developed the list in the first place. Advertisers who suspect that a list may not be made up of "good" names may want to buy only a portion of the main list and test that portion first before buying the entire list. For example, buying a subscriber list of names from a magazine may include expired names that may not be as valuable as the names of those currently reading the publication.

Renting the List   By far the most common practice among advertisers is to rent a list from a mailing list broker who acts as an agent between the owner of the list and the renter. Brokers publish catalogs describing available lists and mail them free to advertisers and their ad agencies. It would be hard to come up with a group of names, job functions, or professions not already catalogued by the list rental brokers. Most of the categories can be rented by city, state, or entire country. Here is a typical sampling:

1   Owners of recreational vehicles
2   African-violet growers
3   Republicans who donated over $100 in the last election
4   Mobile-home park managers
5   Owners of aircraft
6   High school principals
7   Department store buyers
8   Home owners
9   Elvis Presley record and tape buyers

Names, addresses, and phone numbers of list brokers appear in the phone book under *Mailing lists* or in *SRDS/Direct Mail List* (Consumer and

Business); this source also includes information about 52,000 list selections.

Costs for renting a list vary. They range from $20 to $75 per thousand names. Lists come in several physical forms: labels affixed by a special machine, labels put on by heat transfer or pressure, 3 × 5 inch cards, and tape for computer runs. Advertisers should remember that all rented lists are the property of someone else. List brokers protect themselves and their list owners by including a number of "dummy" mailing addresses so they know about each mailing when it goes out. Considering the mobility of the average American, it is always wise for advertisers to insist on a written warranty of deliverability before they rent lists. Advertisers who want to use the same list for several mailings might be able to negotiate special terms or buy the list outright (Figures 7-5, 7-6, 7-7, 7-8).

Rule of 2 Percent

Over the years, some direct-response advertisers determined that 2 percent is a reasonable return for a successful, conventional mailing. Of course, a superior mailing with an excellent offer and value may bring as high as a 10 percent return. (Publication surveys are among the notable exceptions to the rule of 2 percent, with some returns exceeding 60 percent. A major reason is that respondents are not being asked to make a purchase. A second is that recipients may feel an obligation to the publication.) If we recognize that a typical direct-mail response may bring a 2 percent return, we can easily compare costs with anticipated earnings and decide whether the mailing has a chance of paying off.

Response alone, however, is not often an advertiser's primary objective. Introducing people to the product may really be the primary objective. Each advertiser has to decide what degree of response will make the mailing a success. Only a naive advertiser enters into a direct mailing program without first considering the probable returns. (For a more precise anticipated response using test mailings, see Table 19-1, Chapter 19.)

Production and Budget Planning

The time from the conception of an idea to the finishing of a direct-mail piece may be several days or several months, depending upon the complexity of the project. Advertisers should include writer, artist, printer, and typographer in the planning conferences, to permit an exchange of ideas and information about the job as well as the budget. At the conference, the ad manager should give the experts all the facts and any background information that may be helpful. To withhold information in the belief that this would stifle creativity is a mistake. Actually, a full disclosure will prevent false starts, just as a firm budget will effectively eliminate wasted time and motion and expensive experimentation. Everyone involved on the project should also have a due date when his or her part of the job is needed in order to make the deadline.

The artist and the writer must consider the purpose of the mailer, its

FIGURE 7-5

For advertisers looking for names of consumer and/or business groups, SRDS has the perfect reference: 1,200 pages and 50,000 lists.

This Is What JAMI Can Do For You!

- **LIST BROKERAGE**
- **LIST MANAGEMENT**
  Promotion
  Maintenance
  Trafficking
  Control
- **PACKAGE INSERT PROGRAMS**
  Brokerage
  Management
- **CO-OP PROGRAMS**
  Brokerage
  Management
- **DIRECT RESPONSE COUNSEL**
- **CREATIVE GUIDANCE**

WAREHOUSE SOUND COMPANY: 300,000 1978 MAIL ORDER BUYERS $35.00/M HOTLINE, $40 Per M. Warehouse Sound Company, a unique and thriving high fidelity equipment company offers a complete line of stereo components, professional recording equipment, video tape machines and accessories, all, via direct mail. Purchasers (average unit of sale: $300) have responded to space ads in major national magazines for the 63 page catalog. Buyers have purchased directly from this catalog. Featured name brand suppliers include Pioneer, Marantz, Kenwood, Teac, Harmon Kardon, and Sony. Projections indicate that this list will grow to over 500,000 before year end. WSC, won the Gold Mail Box Award for their catalog at the 1978 DMMA Convention.

FIGURE 7-6
A list manager advertises to companies who own their own lists. JAMI asks these list owners to allow them to totally manage their lists to include, among other services, marketing, planning, processing, billing, and bookkeeping. Warehouse Sound Company is one of their many current clients. List managers promote clients' mailing lists and share in the rental income.

**JAMI Direct Marketing
Direct Media Specialists**
616 Palisade Avenue
Englewood Cliffs, N.J. 07632
Phone: (201) 569-1764

THE FUTURE IS FINALLY HERE.

You now have the ability to reach potential consumers, each of which has been identified as having **known** demographic and psychographic traits.

THE LIFESTYLE SELECTOR master file contains
• Demographics • Interest Areas • Lifestyle Patterns for each buyer name.

All names **less than 12 months old.**

Growing to **11 million new names** each year.

All **direct** buyer information—**no** census overlays, averages, assumptions, or clustering.

You can choose any combination of the following **known** characteristics to tailor a list to exactly fit your direct marketing needs:

HOBBIES/ INTERESTS
☐ Tennis
☐ Golf
☐ Snow Skiing
☐ Running/Jogging
☐ Camping/Hiking
☐ Hunting/Shooting
☐ Fishing
☐ Bicycling
☐ Racquetball
☐ Sailing/Boating
☐ Bowling
☐ Motorbiking/Motorcycling
☐ Physical Fitness/Exercise
☐ Stamp/Coin Collecting
☐ Home Video Games
☐ Home Video Recording
☐ Recreational Vehicle/ 4-Wheel Drive
☐ Flying
☐ Photography
☐ C.B. Radio
☐ Home Workshop/ Do-It-Yourself
☐ Gardening/Plants

☐ Electronics
☐ Automotive Work
☐ Sewing/Needlework
☐ Pottery/Ceramics
☐ Crafts
☐ Collectibles/Collections
☐ Art & Antiques
☐ Stereo Music Equipment
☐ Foreign Travel
☐ Attending Cultural/ Arts Events
☐ Gourmet Foods/Cooking
☐ Health/Natural Foods
☐ Wines
☐ Fashion Clothing
☐ Home Furnishings/Decorating
☐ Records & Tapes
☐ Avid Book Reading
☐ Science Fiction
☐ Astrology/Occult
☐ Self-Improvement Programs
☐ Community/Civic Activities
☐ Raising Dogs

SEX ☐ Male   ☐ Female (Mrs., Ms., or Miss available)

AGE
☐ Under 12
☐ 12-17
☐ 18-24
☐ 25-34
☐ 35-44
☐ 45-54
☐ 55-64
☐ 65 and over

INCOME
☐ Under $5,000
☐ $5,000-$9,999
☐ $10,000-$14,999
☐ $15,000-$24,999
☐ $25,000-$49,999
☐ $50,000 and over

MARITAL STATUS
☐ Married   ☐ Unmarried

HOME
☐ Own Their Home   ☐ Rent Their Home

PROFESSION
☐ Professional/Technical
☐ Upper Mgt./Administrator
☐ Sales/Service/Middle Mgt.
☐ Clerical/White Collar
☐ Craftsman/Blue Collar
☐ Student
☐ Housewife
☐ Retired

AGES OF CHILDREN LIVING HOME
☐ Under age 2
☐ Age 2-4
☐ Age 5-7
☐ Age 8-10
☐ Age 11-12
☐ Age 13-15
☐ Age 16-18

TYPES OF CREDIT CARDS USED
☐ Travel/Entertainment
☐ Bank
☐ Gas, Department Store, Etc.

LOCATION ☐ Zip or SCF Selection

LIFESTYLE* PATTERNS
☐ Working Women
☐ Working Wives
☐ Homeowners
☐ Renters
☐ Young Marrieds
☐ Outdoorsmen
☐ Investors

☐ Affluent Culture Consumers
☐ Active Middle Americans
☐ Professional People
☐ White Collar Workers
☐ Blue Collar Workers
☐ Students
☐ Opinion Leaders

*Additional Lifestyle Patterns Also Available.

Note: All names on THE LIFESTYLE SELECTOR master list have passed a negative check-off question.

In addition to tailored lists, THE LIFESTYLE SELECTOR also offers a **unique Response Analysis** which enables you, as list user, to learn more about your market from analyzing buyer response. THE LIFESTYLE SELECTOR's Response Analysis provides a statistical comparison of the characteristics of respondents to your mailing to those of the entire list. That way, you know which consumer segments represent your best prospects, and future mailings can be directed more on target. You may even discover a new buying segment which was never apparent in the past.

THE LIFESTYLE SELECTOR
1624 Market Street
Denver, Colorado 80202
(800) 525-3533, (303) 534-5231
A division of
National Demographics Ltd.

the lifestyle selector

List brokers:
Our list manager is
List House E/W
130 Lyons Plain Road
Weston, Connecticut 06883
(203) 227-6027

FIGURE 7-7

Tailoring its lists to known demographic and psychographic traits, this list management firm encourages the direct-mail advertiser to select target audiences according to life style patterns and hobbies.

FIGURE 7-8
Thousands of people on a mailing list found this handsome International Harvester (IH) self-mailer in their mail boxes. The object of the mailing was to get the recipients to visit their local IH dealer. To accomplish this, the implement manufacturer used a premium, a free pair of red garden gloves.

theme, and its major selling idea. The artist should choose a paper stock on which the art (photographs or illustrations) will reproduce well. The typographer complies with the artist's request for a specific style of type, or the typographer may suggest certain styles in keeping with the nature of the product or service. When the preparatory artwork and typography is completed, the printer moves into action. In essence, it is the printer's job to turn out a professional-looking mailer that shows a precise fidelity to the artist's original artwork. Unless it does, the beautiful (and expensive) artwork and typography are wasted.

When advertisers operate on a limited budget, they are usually able to reduce costs by substituting type set by a small printer or small newspaper. While the type choices are usually limited compared to those offered by a professional type house, the final appearance is still better than if the message appeared in simple typewriter type. Limited-budget advertisers will also scout around for lower-priced printers or large printers who may want the job at a minimum profit just to keep the shop's presses operating.

Rights of the Public

Millions of people who find their names on mailing lists did not ask for them to be put there. But in our complex society, mailing lists are compiled from many sources. For example, when people buy auto licenses or vote, they become names on a list. When they apply for credit cards, passports, or admission to a college, they are placed on a list. They are almost sure to find themselves on a list if they have ever responded to a premium offer, because their actions are proof that they are good direct-mail prospects. Some companies (credit card companies, for example) rent their lists to almost anyone who can pay their price. Until recently, people could do little to prevent their names from appearing on a mailing list. But the direct-mail industry lately has been advertising to the public that there are ways to be taken off lists. (Write to the Direct Mail/Marketing Association, 1730 K St. N.W., Washington, D.C. 20006.) The industry claims that fewer than 0.5 percent of the target audience asks to be removed. Perhaps people do appreciate the fact that direct mail introduces new products, special deals, and information that would be otherwise unavailable to them (Figure 7-9).

THE YELLOW PAGES

Most people know that the Yellow Pages of the phone book are an effective medium for local advertisers, but they don't know how valuable they can be to national companies. Advertising agencies do, however, because growing numbers are setting up special task forces that work exclusively on their clients' Yellow Page advertising. Their major interest, as well as their advertisers', is to promote their clients' trademarks. A *trademark* is a legal device that points to and identifies a specific company. It can be a word, a symbol, or an exclusive design. The purpose of the Yellow Pages is to help consumers find local businesses, and the trademark serves as a pointing device, a brand identification. For example, a manufacturer of water softeners may run its trademark listing in the Yellow Pages of the top 100 markets. Dealers within these markets then list their stores under the trademark. Often *dealer listings* (as these are called), as well as display ads in phone books, are eligible for a manufacturer's coop funds. Barring such an agreement, manufacturers pay for their trademark listing; dealers pay for their individual listings.

Yellow Page ads are billed by the month. Charges depend on the circulation of the phone books. When advertising agencies handle the Yellow Page advertising of their clients—an extremely detailed and time-consuming operation—phone companies will allow those agencies their traditional 15 percent commission (Figure 7-10).

BILLBOARDS (OUTDOOR)

Of all major media in the United States, billboards are the oldest and, in their way, the most visible. Virtually everyone who leaves the house for work or play is exposed to these giant ads. With shorter work weeks and longer

Did you know there's a way to STOP advertising mail you don't want?

You can now get your name off – or on – advertising mailing lists by writing the Mail Preference Service of the Direct Mail/Marketing Association

By CELIA WALLACE

Whether you realize it or not, you are exposed to over *300* advertising messages per day while you watch TV, read newspapers and magazines and ride the highways. And there is no easy way to "turn off" these messages.

But if you don't want to receive advertising mail, there's a simple, effective way to stop most of it. Just contact the Direct Mail/Marketing Association (DMMA), a group of businesses that use mail to advertise their products and services, and they'll send you a *name-removal* form.

Think you want to be taken off mailing lists?

According to Robert F. DeLay, President of the DMMA, once you've returned the name-removal form you should notice a substantial decrease in the amount of mail advertising you receive. "But," he added, "very often people take steps to get their names removed from mailing lists, objecting to what they consider 'junk mail.' But then later decide maybe it isn't so bad after all when they consider some of the good offers that come through unsolicited third class mail. Such as catalogs, new product samples, chances at sweepstakes, introductory offers from magazines, and coupons that knock a dime or so off prices at the supermarket or drugstore."

However, for those who decide they *still* don't want to be bothered by advertising mail, Mr. DeLay assures that their names will be removed from the lists of many DMMA member companies who conduct most large-scale mail adver-

tising campaigns. "It's just too expensive to waste on people who don't want it," he says.

MPS also enables you to be added to lists.

If, on the other hand, you feel you don't get your fair share of mail offers, the DMMA offers another service to get your name *on lists* that will make you a candidate to receive more offers in special interest areas such as arts and crafts, books, investments, clothing, sports, travel and gardening.

Both services are offered to the public by the DMMA in an effort to make shopping by mail more enjoyable.

If you want to take advantage of either of these services offered by the DMMA, simply send the coupon below for a free application or write the association at 6 East 43rd Street, New York, New York 10017.

MAIL TO:
MAIL PREFERENCE SERVICE
DMMA
1730 K. St. N.W.
Washington, D.C. 20006

☐ **STOP IT!** I don't want to be on anyone's "list." Please send me a *Name-Removal Form.*

☐ **SEND ME MORE!** I'd like more mail on my favorite interests and hobbies. Send me an *"Add On" Form.*

PRINT NAME_____

ADDRESS_____

CITY_____

STATE_____ZIP_____

AL-3

FIGURE 7-9

Magazine and television ads produced under the direction of the Direct Mail/Marketing Association are designed to improve public acceptance of the medium.

FIGURE 7-10
National trademark listings help the local consumer find the products of national concerns.

vacations, more Americans are riding the roads. As they travel, in city or country, the billboard is there urging a buying decision for a fast-food restaurant, a cigarette, liquor, a soft drink, or an automobile. Not surprisingly, the billboard is also the advertising vehicle most criticized by the public for desecration of the natural beauty of the countryside. In fact, federal subsidies for interstate highway construction include a provision prohibiting billboards within easy viewing distance of the roadway (Highway Beautification Act of 1965).

How do we reconcile the medium's selling ability with its appearance? The industry itself has policed the size and shape of its boards, claiming that nonregulated boards cause "eye pollution." Nonregulated boards are on-premises signs that identify a place of business, or any outdoor signs or posters that do not conform to two uniform types: the *poster panel* and the *bulletin* (Figures 7-11 and 7-12).

The regulation outdoor *poster panel* measures 12 feet 3 inches high by 24 feet 6 inches long including the frame. Once it took twenty-four sheets of printed paper to cover this area, but modern printing presses can now do the job with ten to fifteen sheets. However, the term "twenty-four-sheet poster" lingers on. (There is actually space on the standard poster panel for three poster sizes: the twenty-four-sheet [8 feet 8 inches × 19 feet 6 inches], the thirty-sheet [9 feet 7 inches × 21 feet 7 inches], and the bleed [10 feet 5 inches × 22 feet 8 inches]. The bleed extends message area by reducing the margin.) Outdoor advertisers prefer to locate their posters near retail outlets, if possible. Posters are rented for thirty-day periods.

The regulation outdoor *bulletin* measures 14 feet high by 48 feet long and is thus almost twice as long as the poster panel. Bulletins are usually rented for longer than thirty-day periods because artists handpaint ads right

FIGURE 7-11

This standardized-structure, regulated outdoor advertising space is available to advertisers in most major and minor markets across the country. Most structures are in commercial and business areas.

Poster Panel

FIGURE 7-12

Properly billed as the largest full-page ads in the world, painted bulletins (unlike posters) are produced one at a time by skilled artists from designs supplied by the advertisers.

Painted Bulletin

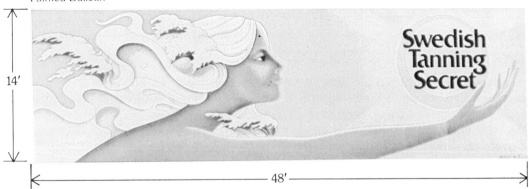

on the bulletin's surface. (They used to be called "painted bulletins.") Most bulletins are illuminated. The painting on the bulletin often is moved from one high-density location to another (although it is easier to move poster panels because of their size and method of reproduction). Some bulletins have rotating elements to tell a more complete story.

How Outdoor Advertising Is Sold

Taking a cue from its rival, television, outdoor advertising is now sold by the month in packages of gross rating points (GRP). A 50-GRP package delivers a daily exposure to half the population of an area. A 100-GRP package delivers 100 percent of the population; a 25-GRP buy exposes one-fourth of the population. Panels used to be sold in packages called "showings" (a #100 showing delivered 100 percent of the market with each person expected to see at least one billboard during the thirty days), but the industry changed to the GRP system in 1973 in order to standardize the unit of sale from market to market. Like television ratings, a GRP in one city is the same as in another; the cost will differ based on the population, but the relative importance remains the same. How many panels make up a 100-GRP package? There is a different answer in each market because, as the industry uses the term, a 100-GRP package is the number of panel posters and bulletins considered necessary to reach 100 percent of the auto and pedestrian traffic in a marketing area within one month. Axiom Market Research Bureau, a noted research organization, sees outdoor in a slightly different perspective: a 100 showing reaches 86.7 percent of the adults in a market by the end of a normal thirty-day posting period and, at the end of a sixty-day posting period, 90.3 percent.[1] In the Des Moines market area, with a population of 389,400, advertisers can buy a 100-GRP package for $6,460 a month. For this price, their message will appear on twenty-six poster panels and thirty-four illuminated bulletins, a total of sixty units. Poster panels are

[1]*Target Group Index Spring 1978*, Axiom Market Research Bureau, Inc., New York, Spring 1978, p. 1.

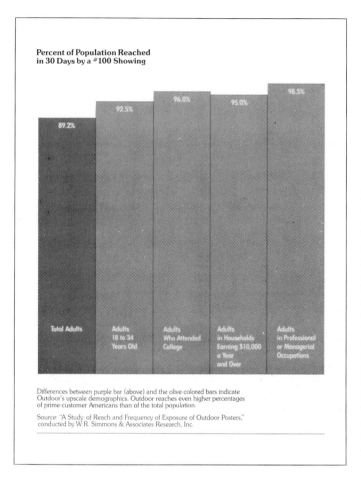

Percent of Population Reached in 30 Days by a #100 Showing

89.2% — Total Adults
92.5% — Adults 18 to 34 Years Old
96.0% — Adults Who Attended College
95.0% — Adults in Households Earning $10,000 a Year and Over
98.5% — Adults in Professional or Managerial Occupations

Differences between purple bar (above) and the olive-colored bars indicate Outdoor's upscale demographics. Outdoor reaches even higher percentages of prime-customer Americans than of the total population.

Source: "A Study of Reach and Frequency of Exposure of Outdoor Posters," conducted by W. R. Simmons & Associates Research, Inc.

FIGURE 7-13
A major reason for outdoor's popularity with national advertisers is the rapidity with which adults can be reached. Most recent figures (1978) conform very closely to the conclusions shown in this bar chart. Source: "A Study of Reach and Frequency of Exposure of Outdoor Posters," conducted by W. R. Simmons & Associates Research, Inc.

FIGURE 7-14
Some of outdoor's best posters reveal a leaning toward brevity and cleverness.

available in all major marketing areas of the country, and national advertisers pay over $400,000 a month for 100-GRP packages in the top ten markets, over $1,200,000 a month for the same reach and frequency in the top 100 markets[2] (Figures 7-13 and 7-14).

251

NATIONAL PRINT
MEDIA: DIRECT
MAIL, YELLOW
PAGES, OUTDOOR,
TRANSIT, AND
SUPPLEMENTARY

TRANSIT ADVERTISING

Because most transit advertising is inside buses, subway cars, and streetcars, it has the advantage of giving people a relatively long time to look at it. Advertisers can tell a more complete story than with a billboard. But not all markets have mass transit facilities to justify transit advertising; only the larger metropolitan areas do. Interior car cards—11 × 28 inches—are generally sold as full, half, or quarter runs for thirty days or more. In a full run within the top ten markets, every one of approximately 41,000 vehicles carries the advertiser's message at a monthly cost of $60,000. Transit advertising also refers to cards carried in special positions on the exterior sides, fronts, and backs of buses traveling on major roads and highways serving a marketing area. These traveling displays are sold on a unit basis in any individual market or in any combination of markets. Rates are generally quoted for monthly showings with discounts granted for three-, six-, or twelve-month contracts. Exterior traveling displays are usually located on the sides of the bus, as well as the front and the back. Within the top ten markets, the advertiser will need to supply 2,820 vehicles with posters at a monthly cost of over $140,000. At this price, the typical advertiser can hope to reach 85 percent of the population an average of fifteen times in a thirty-day period[3] (Figures 7-15 and 7-16). Taxis also carry small advertising cards on the outside.

Station posters are another form of transit advertising. These are scaled-down billboards for bus, railroad, subway, and air terminals. Often they are handled by the same companies that place interior car cards. An interesting restriction established by numerous outdoor plants throughout the country is the requirement that political advertising must be paid for in advance.

ADVANTAGES AND DISADVANTAGES OF BILLBOARDS AND TRANSIT

"For announcements and introductions and just plain timely messages . . . you can't beat outdoor's fast reach to spread the word," says Budweiser's ad manager.[4] Plough, Inc., makers of Coppertone (suntan preparation) and Solarcaine (sunburn relief remedy) echoes this sentiment and adds, "Out-

[2]Source: National Outdoor Advertising Bureau (NOAB)
[3]*Out-of-Home Media Facts*, compiled by Batten, Barton, Durstine & Osborn, 1974, p. 40.
[4]Source: Institute of Outdoor Advertising brochure, January 1977.

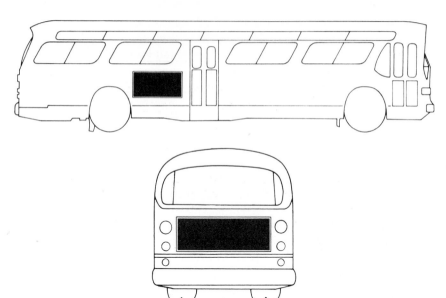

FIGURE 7-15
Passersby and motorists see exterior posters carried by transit vehicles, making these ads favorite buys of national advertisers. To cover all the vehicles in the top ten markets for one month costs an advertiser over $140,000.

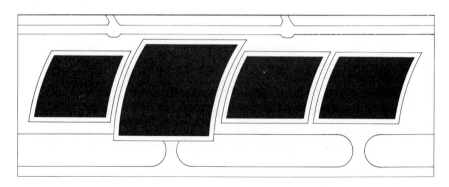

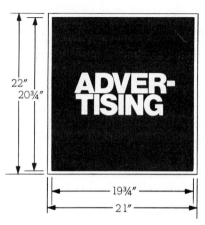

FIGURE 7-16
A typical arrangement of interior car cards within a bus. The interior cards are considerably less costly than those riding on the outside of the bus.

door has indeed been very instrumental in building our business. . . . we've more than tripled our outdoor advertising budget over the past five years."[5] These and other national advertisers are enthusiastic about billboards (and transit) for the following reasons:

Billboards

1 Reasonably priced, billboards provide excellent reach. Cost per billboard in a major metropolitan area is about $100 a month. The reach is 86.7 percent of adults in the area.
2 Billboards are generally located in the neighborhood where the product can be purchased.
3 Billboards can be extremely dramatic and spectacular: they are the largest ads available. An automobile can be shown full size.
4 Illuminated billboards are valuable for increasing after-dark shopping and for selling twenty-four hours a day.
5 Most drivers who see billboards are eighteen to forty-nine, within the age bracket most advertisers wish to influence.
6 Through selective posting of its billboard messages, an advertiser can zero in on its best customers in any market.
7 Billboards provide many impressions in a short period of time.

Transit

1 The cost of transit advertising on the outside of buses averages about $50 per vehicle per month for the top ten markets. Interior car cards are considerably less. (In the Dallas-Fort Worth area, they range from $1.50 to $3 per vehicle per month.) For outside posters, the cost per thousand averages less than 7 cents.
2 Transit advertising delivers repeat exposures because a transit rider averages twenty-four rides per month, sixty-one minutes a day.[6].
3 The mobility of buses takes them many places during the same day, creating multiple exposures among people on sidewalks, in shopping centers, and at intersections and on drivers following or passing the transit vehicles.
4 Transit advertising often delivers the advertiser's message close to the point of sale.
5 Transit advertising techniques are flexible and provide an assortment of new attractions: backlighted displays, king-size posters, three-dimensional plastic molds, curved metal frames with a special protective sheet, and optical effects made possible through the use of polarized plastics. Always available are the "take-ones," a technique in which brochures are attached to inside displays to make special offers to transit riders. In essence, this enables the national advertiser to tie direct mail in with the advertising message on the car cards.
6 Transit ads inside vehicles can tell a complete story because riders have time to read.
7 Both transit and billboards are excellent as reminder advertising used in conjunction with other media.

---

[5]Source: Institute of Outdoor Advertising brochure, September 1974.
[6]*SRDS Transit Advertising*, Transit Advertising Association, August 3, 1973.

Not all companies can use billboards and transit cards, however, despite their attraction as a potent advertising medium. National coverage using either billboards or transit cards is far beyond the financial capabilities of all but the largest companies ($350,000 per month for a full transit run, $1,200,000 per month for a 100-GRP package). There are other disadvantages:

Billboards

1 Statements on billboards must be short since the audience is in motion and at a distance. An involved or lengthy sales message must be communicated by some other medium.
2 Nonregulated signs, trees, or structures may shield the view of the billboard from some approaches.
3 Too many billboards in an area (plus traffic lights and store signs) lead to clutter and confuse people.
4 Some potential customers may object to large billboards as an ecological nuisance.
5 Some billboard advertisements may be placed next to others that are controversial such as liquor, beer, or cigarettes. This, advertisers fear, wll damage their own image.
6 Strategically placed billboard structures may be destroyed by high winds. Second-best locations may not be good enough.

Transit

1 Exterior transit card messages must be short and cannot tell a complete story.
2 If there are too many interior car cards, some of them may be overlooked or ignored.
3 Crowded transit cars make car card reading difficult for seated passengers.
4 There are limited places on vehicles for exterior display cards. Thus, the big-budget advertiser enjoys an advantage.
5 Transit cards are subject to graffiti and destruction by riders and passersby.

POINT-OF-PURCHASE ADVERTISING

Printed advertising found in the retail store is at the point where the actual sale or purchase is made. Hence the name *point of purchase* (P.O.P.). The intent of P.O.P. is to remind customers about a product while they are in a position to buy it. Because so many people buy on impulse, point-of-purchase advertising is important in national marketing plans. In fact, impulse buying accounts for approximately 50 percent of all supermarket purchases by men, according to The Supermarket Institute.[7]

Point-of-purchase advertising includes cardboard, wire, and plastic floor and window displays, signs, display cards, and counter, wall, and shelf racks.

[7]Source: Supermarket Institute, Chicago.

It includes banners, mobiles, decals, reprints of magazine and newspaper ads, television storyboards, and sales literature. (Conceivably, the term could also apply to product packaging.) How important is point-of-purchase advertising to manufacturers? Here's what Jel Sert, a Chicago-based manufacturer of soft-drink powders and freezer bars, has to say:

> Jel Sert's experience has been that once distribution has been obtained, the massive power of its network-television campaign plus mass displays will produce high-volume sales and high store profits. Every effort has been made to create packaging that attracts and sells customers in the store. Fla-Vor-Aid, Fla-Vor-Ice and Pop-Ice displays have proven highly effective in generating impulse sales.[8]

This company, like many other consumer goods manufacturers, regularly sends its dealer organization sales sheets featuring its shipper displays illustrated as attractively as possible (Figures 7-17, 7-18, 7-19).

SUPPLEMENTARY PRINT MEDIA

The variety of print materials available to the national advertiser seems limitless. Advertisers can buy advertising specialties such as book matches, lapel buttons, rulers, a wide variety of timely calendars, ballpoint pens, pencils, and so on. Advertisers can also use couponing, sales promotional literature, and premiums. Sometimes advertising specialties are called novelty items. They almost always carry the imprint of the advertiser. The addition of an advertising specialty to an ad campaign can usually improve results. A large national advertiser's credit union mailed a two-color brochure, an application form, and a return card to its 10,000 members. It drew 182 applications, good for $179,000. Six months later, an identical mailing was sent to the same group, except that a ballpoint pen was enclosed with the imprint "This pen is worth $2,500—just use it to fill out your enclosed SLS application." The second mailing—with the ad specialty—drew 354 applications for $461,000, an increase in response of 200 percent.[9] To find companies that sell advertising specialties, look in the Yellow Pages under "Advertising Specialties." Specialty advertising works because the article of merchandise—a pen, a calendar, a ruler—is useful. The recipient keeps it and uses it constantly. Experts in the field estimate that there are 15,000 items available as advertising specialties.

Couponing

Selective couponing is the distribution, usually by mail, of cents-off coupons to a particular group of recipients. A coupon is usually a promise on paper by

[8]*Fifty Years of Progress*, The Jel Sert Company, Chicago, 1975, p. 21.
[9]*Specialty Advertising versus Direct Mail*, Specialty Advertising Information Bureau, March 1975, p. 2.

FIGURE 7-17
These are part of
the American Dairy
Association's dealer
promotions, which
inform the trade of
some of the
point-of-purchase
materials available to
them. The colorful
collateral materials
perk up the interior
of supermarkets.
(Courtesy American
Dairy Association.)

a manufacturer to allow a cents-off discount on a specific brand at the time of purchase. Retailers receive several cents for handling each coupon. Coupon recipients share characteristics that make them attractive to an advertiser: hobbies, age, home ownership, and so forth. Selective couponing aims either to introduce a new product or to bolster the sales of an existing product. For couponing to be effective, the coupons must get to the right people at the right time. For example, when Purina entered the competitive pet food market with its Whisker Lickins food for cats, it determined that it should send coupons and samples to only the 22 percent of United States households that owned cats. Without this prior knowledge and selective couponing, the waste

257

NATIONAL PRINT
MEDIA: DIRECT
MAIL, YELLOW
PAGES, OUTDOOR,
TRANSIT, AND
SUPPLEMENTARY

FIGURE 7-18
Simple wall posters
for Ralston Purina
dealers tell farmers
of the new program
that will help them
sell half again as
many pounds of
beef.

in postage, printing, time, and effort would have been excessive (Figure 7-20.) With zoned distribution available both through some newspapers and magazines, it is now also practical to employ selective couponing in these media.

Premiums

The difference between an advertising specialty, a novelty, and a premium is cost. Ad specialties are low-cost giveaways. Premiums are items of value given free or at a reduced retail price with the purchase of a product or

FIGURE 7-19
So strongly does Chicago-based Jel Sert believe in the selling power of P.O.P. that each sales sheet to the trade includes a four-color replica of the displays it is promoting. Some point-of-purchase displays are very elegant and expensive; others are even motor-operated to attract attention.

PRODUCT SAMPLING

There is only one medium that can simultaneously communicate a product message, carry a product sample and offer a purchase incentive to an audience prone to high trial and initial purchase: Carol Wright.

FIGURE 7-20
It has been estimated that the total number of coupons available through the mail, magazines, and newspapers exceeds 35 billion a year. A single Carol Wright mailing reaches 18 million households. (Courtesy Donnelley Marketing.)

service. Caps, T-shirts, silverware, and glassware are all eligible to be premiums; their purpose: to stimulate sales. A secondary purpose of premiums is to excite retailers about an advertising campaign.

The trick in providing premiums is to make sure they all relate closely to the products they are supposed to sell. Norwich (Necta Sweet saccharine tablets) offered a handy tablet dispenser for 40 cents and one proof-of-purchase label. Sergeant's, the pet care company, offered a free rawhide dog bone to customers who proved they had purchased a Sergeant's product. To find a valuable premium to offer, advertisers need only ask themselves what associated product their customers would appreciate.

Premiums that require the customer to send money as well as a proof of purchase are called *self-liquidators*. The customer's money usually covers (liquidates) the cost of the item to the manufacturer. But the success of a self-liquidating premium depends on its reduced cost's being immediately apparent to the consumer. On occasion, manufacturers will offer premiums at a price below their own cost in the hope of presenting the consumer with an even greater bargain.

Premiums, whether free or paid for by the customer, have long been popular with national advertisers. Dry-cereal companies have used their packages to encourage generations of boys and girls to send box tops and 25 cents for magic rings, dog whistles, and an assortment of toys. Raleigh

FIGURE 7-21
Smart Tickle premium promotion sells the product (deodorant) and then continues to sell it as a walking signboard. (Courtesy Bristol-Meyers Company.)

cigarettes used premium coupons to build the brand into one of the big successes of the tobacco industry. Recently, one of the more common premiums, a ballpoint pen, turned out to be the instrument that increased chapel attendance at Lowry Air Force Base. Attendance at the chapel had been averaging forty to forty-five people. In an attempt to encourage more people to attend services, a newcomers' orientation was held for newly assigned students. These students received ballpoints in assorted colors with the message, "Let God straighten out your life," and a suggestion to attend services each Sunday. Average attendance rose to 300 people each Sunday as a result. The chapel's success prompted the chief of Air Force chaplains to publicize the promotion in his worldwide newsletter, urging other chaplains to follow suit (Figures 7-21 and 7-22).

Advantages and Disadvantages of Premiums   The introduction of premiums into a national advertiser's campaign does not automatically ensure success. Like most other media, premiums have their strengths and weaknesses. Here are their major advantages:

1 Premiums induce customers to buy the product.
2 They are a constant reminder to the customer of the brand name of the product if the name is imprinted. Some premiums "sell" for years.
3 They encourage distributor and dealer participation.
4 Premiums encourage continued purchases of the advertisers' products if they have been designed for that purpose. For example, a carafe premium will help to sell a brand of coffee or a coffee-cream substitute; a cookie cutter premium will help encourage repeated purchases of cookie mixes.

In the final analysis, a premium's weaknesses rest more with improper use than with an inherent lack of advertising drama. However, when disadvantages surface, they usually include the following:

1 Advertisers who commit themselves to a premium program usually must buy many of the items for a substantial sum of money.
2 The premium may fail to excite the target audience.
3 It is difficult to get off the premium "merry-go-round" once the manufacturer has begun. (Customers may decide not to buy unless a premium is involved, as has been occurring within the savings and loan industry.)
4 Advertising premium notices take up needed selling space in ads, and they often clutter up package designs.
5 Premiums have a strange way of lingering within a manufacturer's retail outlets and often introduce customer confusion when succeeding campaigns and promotions begin.

Conclusion

As we have seen in this chapter, national manufacturers have a variety of print advertising options. Since these permit them a certain scheduling

FIGURE 7-22
An excellent example of selecting a premium that complements an advertiser's product line. Note in both the Tickle and Remington ads how the emphasis is on the premium.

flexibility, they also allow advertisers to compete even if the companies never meet head-to-head in the same medium. For example, Procter & Gamble's Prell shampoo may be mailed with cents-off coupons to young women under thirty-five—an expensive promotion. Smaller Wella Balsam Company may avoid a couponing showdown but still aggressively promote its shampoo through point-of-purchase displays in drug and mass merchandising stores. Eventually, smaller companies hope that their astute use of secondary ad media will result in their finally being able to challenge the leaders in any medium.

IN SUMMARY

1 Of all forms of advertising, direct mail is probably the one form used most often. It can be informational or designed to sell something. When its primary purpose is to sell, it is called either mail-order or direct-response advertising.

2 Direct mail takes the rifle versus shotgun approach to advertising because it can aim at selected individuals. It can be tailored to any budget, it complements other media, and it is an excellent way to distribute coupons and samples.

263

NATIONAL PRINT
MEDIA: DIRECT
MAIL, YELLOW
PAGES, OUTDOOR,
TRANSIT, AND
SUPPLEMENTARY

3 A major drawback of the medium is that it lacks the prestige of other major media.

4 Advertisers can build, buy, or rent mailing lists. Renting is the most common practice.

5 A successful, conventional direct-response mailing produces about a 2 percent return. This anticipated return helps advertisers compare their costs with probable earnings before a mailing.

6 Advertisers should plan conferences with the key people involved in the creation and production of their direct mail pieces. These meetings help everyone keep to a budget.

7 People who do not want to be on many mailing lists may ask the Direct Mail Marketing Association to remove their names.

8 Yellow Pages of phone books are valuable as an advertising medium for national advertisers, primarily for promoting a company's trademark and identifying its local sales outlets.

9 The outdoor industry has two uniform types of billboards, the poster panel and the bulletin. The bulletin is almost twice as long as the poster panel and is usually rented for longer than the conventional thirty-day period.

10 Outdoor advertising is sold to advertisers in gross-rating-point packages. A 100-GRP package delivers 100 percent of the population. Some outdoor plants and advertisers still refer to billboard coverage as "showings," a term abandoned by the industry in 1973.

11 Research studies reveal that a 100 showing or GRP reaches 86.7 percent of the adults in a market by the end of a normal thirty-day posting period.

12 Poster panels are available in all major marketing areas of the country; national advertisers pay over $400,000 a month for 100-GRP packages in the top ten markets.

13 Billboard reach is excellent. Billboards are generally located in the neighborhood where the product advertised can be purchased. Most drivers who see billboards are eighteen to forty-nine, the age bracket most advertisers wish to influence. Billboards can also provide frequency for the national advertiser.

14 A major disadvantage of the billboard medium is that messages must be very short.

15 Sometimes structures and trees hide billboards from the viewing public. Some people may dislike billboards as an unsightly nuisance.

16 Transit advertising includes both interior and exterior car cards for buses, subways, streetcars, and taxis.

17 Interior car cards are sold as full, half, or quarter runs for thirty days or more. Exterior traveling cards are sold on a unit basis with monthly rates.

18 Transit posters on the outside of vehicles deliver a cost-per-thousand average of less than 7 cents. The mobility of the medium creates multiple exposures.

19 Transit cards, particularly those on the outside of vehicles, also suffer from a short-message problem. The limited space available for exterior cards gives the big-budget advertiser an advantage over the small advertiser. Transit cards are subject to destruction by passersby and riders.

20 Point-of-purchase (P.O.P.) items are important to national advertisers because they are final reminders to consumers entering and leaving stores.

21 P.O.P. takes advantage of the fact that so many items in stores are purchased on impulse.

22 Advertising specialties used as an advertising medium are often called novelties.

Novelties almost always carry the imprint of the advertisers and keep reminding recipients of them. A wide variety of advertising specialties is available to advertisers.

23 Selective couponing is the distribution of cents-off coupons to recipients who share common characteristics of interest to advertisers. The purpose of this medium is to bolster sales of an existing product or to introduce a new one.

24 The prime difference between an ad specialty and a premium is one of cost; premiums are generally items of some value and are used to stimulate sales.

25 The best premiums are those that relate to the products they have been selected to promote.

26 Premiums that ask the customer to send money as well as proof of purchase are called self-liquidators.

CASE STUDY The Sound of Fast Relief: Alka-Seltzer, An Outdoor Advertising Success Story[10]

For years, Alka-Seltzer has been America's favorite headache and upset stomach remedy. However, strong competition was giving it brand awareness and sales problems, particularly in its top ten major metropolitan sales markets (combined population of over 47.5 million people.) None of these markets had received any local media support in the previous five years.

Alka-Seltzer wanted quick turnaround in these key markets, and outdoor advertising was put to the test in a 50-daily-GRP showing in April and May of 1977. Sixty days later, Alka-Seltzer dollar volume in food and drug outlets shot up in all ten markets!

Additionally, as Nielsen Consumer Sales reported, "the highest sales gains during the most recent bi-monthly period (July/August 1977) were achieved within the three major loss districts" (plus 27 percent, 23 percent and 16 percent, respectively). No wonder that Alka-Seltzer's 1978 outdoor advertising expanded into 101 markets with an ad investment in excess of $2 million.

Why is outdoor a successful medium for Alka-Seltzer? Mitchell Streicker, Miles Laboratories vice president of marketing services, puts it this way, "It gives us a lot of impressions in a short period of time, with heavy frequency in the hard-to-reach eighteen to forty-nine group. It has a far lower CPM than spot television and newspapers. It also provides a tremendous boost for our sales force, our management, and our retailers."

Mr. Streicker summed it up with, "There's nothing like Alka-Seltzer and outdoor. They're there when they're needed" (Figure 7-23).

QUESTIONS NEEDING ANSWERS

1 Do you think this outdoor industry-prepared case study would persuade an advertiser to redirect advertising dollars from another medium?

[10]"*We're Spending $2,000,000 in Outdoor Because It Brings Quick Results,*" Institute of Outdoor Advertising brochure, 1978, pp. 2-3.

The sound of fast relief.
Plop plop, fizz fizz.

Alka-Seltzer
SPEEDY RELIEF

For upset stomach with headache.
Read the label. Use only as directed.

Copyright. 1978 Miles Laboratories. Inc.

FIGURE 7-23
Sammy Davis, Jr.,
spokesperson for
Alka-Seltzer in all
media, is larger than
life on a billboard,
the world's largest
one-page ad.

2 Would you substitute outdoor for newspapers? For television? For radio? For magazines? Explain.
3 If you were the director of marketing of competitive Anacin, how would you react to the news of Alka-Seltzer's excursion into outdoor?
4 Would it make economic sense to boost the 50-GRP package in the top ten markets to 100 GRPs? Explain.

STUDENT PROJECT

Assume that you are the marketing services director of a new headache remedy, All's Well. Your budget is under $1 million. Your research staff informs you that 17 percent of American adults do not use headache remedies, for varying reasons. Further research points out that your most likely target audience is the eighteen to forty-nine age groups. Your job is to make media recommendations and to authorize the media recommendations of your advertising agency.

QUESTIONS ABOUT THE PROJECT

1 With your limited advertising budget of under $1 million, why would it be unwise to concentrate on the 17 percent of current nonusers? Explain.
2 Can you justify sending a direct-mail program to your target audience? Explain. Could you use advertising specialties? What kind?
3 Your ad agency recommends investing 35 percent of your first year's ad budget promoting All's Well to doctors. What is your response?

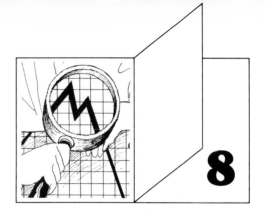

8

THE RETAILER'S MEDIA CHOICES

Update We've approached the print media from the point of view of the national advertiser. Now it's the turn of the retailer who needs less expensive, narrower media for a restricted sphere of influence. The secret for retailers is not how many dollars they spend, but how effectively they spend them. This chapter confronts that problem.

Retailers need to draw the public's attention to their store's existence. They have several options available. Retailers can simply identify their place of business with a sign and hope enough people will stop in and buy something. They can send solicitors door to door, a slow, costly process; or they can phone each household in the area—again, a slow way to reach a large audience. A more efficient and cost-effective way is to advertise in

FIGURE 8-1

A tale of two auto ads in the same weekly newspaper. The Ford ad has the earmarks of a professional creator. Logically it should attract high readership. But the hometown ad prepared by nonprofessionals attracts the readers. The Ford ad readership was men 10.3 percent, women 2.6 percent. The S&H ad readership was men 15.4 percent, women 6.4 percent. Source: Elizabeth Hansen, "Readership Study of Laurens *Sun* Subscribers," 1976 masters thesis, Journalism Department, Iowa State University, Ames, Iowa.

media seen, heard, or read simultaneously by most of the retailers' customers and prospects. Whether their advertising features products and asks people to visit a store and buy or sells an idea (institutional advertising), the point of it all is to keep the public conscious of the retailer. The question for most retailers is not "Shall we advertise?" but "Where shall we advertise?" There always seems to be a choice.

DAILY AND WEEKLY NEWSPAPERS

The very same large metropolitan newspaper carrying the advertisement of the national advertiser also carries the sales message of the local retailer. In fact, the great majority of the $12 billion spent on all newspaper advertising comes from local businesses. Do the newspapers know this? Yes. Most cater to the needs of locals before national advertisers. But local retailers often have the problem of waste circulation when they use either daily or weekly newspapers. For example, if they have only one retail outlet, they profit less from their ad than a merchant with two or three separate locations. Thus selecting media hinges on several points:

1 What is the cost of primary coverage and the medium's effective reach? For example, will heavy suburban coverage help the dress shop in the city? Can a retailer buy only a zoned portion of the circulation (by ZIP Codes)?
2 On which day(s) should the ad(s) appear for the greatest impact? For example, on the "food days" (Wednesday, Thursday, Friday), papers are crammed with eye-catching sales messages.
3 Should large metropolitan retailers pay more attention to nearby weekly newspapers?
4 Should the retailer place ads in special tab sections? "Tab" is a shortened form for tabloid pages, magazine-sized newspaper sections usually measuring 11 inches wide × 17 inches deep.) Some weekly papers publish a tab for every special event: high school graduation, Halloween, vacation and travel time, and so on. Are tab ads as well read as those in the regular pages of the newspaper?
5 Should ads be run on a regular basis or when there are sales?
6 Should the retailer use the medium that also provides "free" publicity plugs?
7 How effective are cooperative ads in both metropolitan and weekly papers? Evidence suggests that slick, manufacturer-prepared co-op ads draw less readership in weekly newspapers than in larger metros because their professional appearance tells the local reader that the ad was not locally inspired (Figure 8-1).
8 Will the retailer invest more in advertising than the 2 percent of sales average, a figure generally considered too low to satisfy most advertising goals?

All these questions, and their answers, help retailers decide on the media mix best for them. The last question, that of an adequate advertising budget, determines how consistent a retailer's promotion will be (continuity). To encourage retailers to advertise consistently, most newspapers provide a schedule of discount rewards. These discounts become significant when the retailer uses at least 2,000 lines during a year. The Bloomington (Illinois) *Pantagraph* offers the schedule of costs per line shown in Table 8-1.

TABLE 8-1
PANTAGRAPH SCHEDULE OF COSTS

Unit of measurement	Cost	Unit of measurement	Cost
Up to 1,050 lines	$0.57	10,500 lines	$0.524
2,100 lines	0.56	26,250 lines	0.52
3,150 lines	0.55	46,900 lines	0.515
5,250 lines	0.54	78,750 lines	0.51
7,700 lines	0.53	105,000 lines	0.505

Five thousand lines translate into 357 column inches, or six large ads of four columns 15 inches deep, or twenty-four ads of two columns 7½ inches deep. (Courtesy Bloomington *Pantagraph*.)

Classified Advertising

At one time, when we spoke of classified advertising, we meant the factual, local information that appeared in small print in the back of the newspaper or in the Yellow Pages of a phone directory. These ads were generally arranged in categories, such as "Used Autos For Sale," "Homes for Sale," "Help Wanted." But now we must include in our definition the "shopper," a phenomenon of the 1960s and 1970s. A shopper generally appears in tabloid form without news of any kind. It is simply a vehicle for one citizen's messages to another about the sale of household items. Because of its high readership, local retailers find the shopper effective as an advertising medium. In some communities, the shopper has become the major competitor of local newspapers for the retailers' ad dollars. Shoppers, unlike newspapers, cost the readers nothing. They are delivered both by carriers and by mail. (Critics claim that because shoppers are free, a high percentage of their recipients are in the lower-income brackets and cannot afford high-priced merchandise.)

As a rule, many people read classified ads appearing in newspapers and shoppers. (Our earliest newspapers carried classifieds on the front page.) Because retailers recognize the popularity of classifieds, they invest considerable sums in these pages, the ads of which are sold by the number of *words* rather than by the number of lines (Table 8-2).

Occasionally, local retailers will use small-space classified ads in the newspapers when they lack the money to meet their competition head-to-head in the larger display ads. In the classifieds, their ads look as large and as important as all the others. Some retailers, notably car dealers and realtors, find that their best business comes from the classified pages.

Recently, the classified pages have begun to feature professionals who never advertised before. This is a result of a Supreme Court ruling that lawyers may not be denied their rights of free speech, and that they may advertise. In addition to lawyers, some doctors and dentists are also taking to the classifieds to inform the public of their services. Traditionally bar, medical, and dental associations have put pressure on their members not to advertise in any way. Those that do, still a minority within their profession, merely indicate their specialties.

Of all the newspaper linage printed all over the country in the past few

TABLE 8-2
TYPICAL CLASSIFIED ADS

CHAIN SAWS, HOMELIGHT GRABER'S BOAT SALES 6125 Merle Hay Rd. 278-1250	TRAVEL TRAILERS – CAMPERS IMPERIAL 545 COACHMEN '78 MODEL INTRODUCTION REGISTER FOR DOOR PRIZES NOW THRU OCT. 29th FREE HOT DOGS
BUILDING MATERIALS 420 PANELING–70 kinds in Stock Paneling from $3.99 PLYWOOD MART 333 S.W. 6th 283-1969	Also see Airstream, Argosy, Royals International and many used units. **IMPERIAL R-V CENTER** Hrs. 9–6 Monday through Sat. Ankeny, Iowa 515-964-1424

years, classified linage continues at a record pace, with double the volume of national newspaper advertising. (Only retail linage exceeds it.) Of that classified linage, 32 percent belonged to real estate advertising.[1]

The Advertising Sales Rep

As soon as a newspaper receives a display advertising contract from a local retailer, it assigns a member of its sales staff to the account. The importance of this salesperson cannot be overstated. He or she is to the retailer what the ad agency account executive is to a large client. Newspaper ad salespeople can be a source of information, inspiration, and creativity. Properly used, they are a free advertising bonus to retailers. In effect, these salespeople have two bosses. They are paid by the publisher and owe primary allegiance there, but they are also "employed" by the accounts they serve. Their effectiveness in selling advertising space may depend entirely on how well they help retailers create and prepare successful advertising.

Effective advertising representatives—"reps"—design campaigns and image-building promotions for their accounts in conjunction with the newspaper's art department. (Retailers who don't depend on newspaper sales and art staff are chain food stores, department stores, and fast-food franchise restaurants. They usually employ their own advertising personnel, artists, and writers.) In addition to their own art staff, the newspaper sales representatives borrow heavily from the files of syndicated idea and art services such as Metro Associated Services, the MacDonald Space Builder, Multi-Ad Services, and Stamps Conhaim Advertising Services. These companies have been providing newspapers and shoppers throughout the country with photographic reproductions and illustrations for many years. The material, ready for reproduction, saves time and money for both newspaper and retailers. It provides on a monthly basis a large reservoir of professional-looking material: illustrations of goods and services, a variety of banner headlines and type styles, even photographs of models. Rates for the services are modest and are generally based on a newspaper's circulation and frequency of publication (Figure 8-2).

Syndicated Campaigns

Local retailers can buy the creative advertising services of several syndicates. These carry art and copy, generally structured as comic strips, in stock. The materials can be adapted easily to almost any retail business or service. The idea of the syndicated service is to provide retailers with complete advertising campaigns designed to run for an entire year. Retailers' costs for the campaign are based on the circulation of the newspaper in which it is run. Campaigns may range from $200 to $500 for a fifty-two-week campaign series.[2] What retailers buy is reproducible art. The newspaper advertising

---

[1] "Newspaper Advertising Expenditures," a report, Newspaper Advertising Bureau, August 1978.
[2] Local Trademarks, Inc., of New York City, has been selling its cartoon-type promotions since 1911.

FIGURE 8-2

Syndicated art services make ideas and illustrations such as these available to newspaper ad departments. They are typical of the large variety of retail ad components that many daily and weekly newspapers buy monthly.

space to accommodate this art and copy is extra. It is not unusual for the same campaign series to be sold to widely separated retailers within the same state, with each having exclusive rights to the series in his or her own newspaper (Figure 8-3).

City Magazines

City magazines, sometimes called metropolitan magazines, are of particular interest to some local businesses. Typical city magazines are published in New York, Baltimore, Boston, Chicago, Cleveland, Houston, Louisville, Los Angeles, Nashville, Honolulu, and many other cities. City magazines are attractive buys for retailers who serve a higher-income population. And readers seem to develop a certain community loyalty that spills over to the magazines' advertisers. Page rates average about $770 but are primarily based on circulation. Although cost per thousand readers (CPM) may be relatively high—$31.45 for *San Francisco Magazine*—there may also be no practical alternative for some retailers such as eating and drinking places. They could advertise in *Time's* San Francisco edition (185,000 persons) at a

FIGURE 8-3
A complete year's
campaign in
comic-strip style may
not be very
sophisticated, but
many retailers use
such strips. Their
use saves the
newspaper
salesperson a lot of
time; it provides the
retailer with a
consistent
identifiable ad
program. Note that
some retailers
incorporate coop
elements to
construct a larger
ad. (Courtesy Local
Trademarks, Inc.)

CPM of $13.29 or in any one of twenty major magazines circulated in the area that may offer a city edition. But these are national magazines, and the hometown flavor is missing. So, despite a high cost per thousand for most city magazines, retailers may still feel their best buy is the hometown product devoted to urban concerns, consumer service, ideas for leisure, and stories of local personalities and the arts. An excellent data base for retailers looking for the most effective media buys is *Test Market Profiles* published every year by A.C. Nielsen Company. Major cities in the country are charted according to effective buying income, television viewing habits, selected demographics, magazines and newspapers circulated in the metropolitan area, retail sales in certain categories, and the names and numbers of major supermarkets and drug stores.

DIRECT MAIL

Next to local newspapers, perhaps retailers' most popular method of reaching customers is by direct mail. It usually costs little, and despite rising postal costs, direct mail thrives because it is effective in a restricted market area. National advertisers may think in terms of millions, but local retailers think in thousands or even hundreds.

Much of a retailer's direct mail is prepared by suppliers (manufacturers). But no matter who prepares a mailing piece, even a simple letter, the most important element is the offer. Is it compelling and powerful? Will it bring people to the store? Most retailers would be wise to visit nearby printers who are associated with commercial artists. Printers without artists can often recommend freelance artists and copywriters who can produce a rough layout and sales message that can then be sent to several printers for bids.

Retailers who make frequent mailings should consider investing in an automatic labeling/addressing machine. The investment will soon pay for itself. Smaller businesses may find it practical to make frequent mailings to their entire list of customers and prospects. Large businesses, like major department stores, generally make few mailings to their entire list. Their mailings are frequent and go to various segments of their list. Postage, of course, is the problem, although third-class bulk rate offers a partial solution: it averages 8.5 cents per ounce as opposed to 15 cents for first class. Bulk rates apply when advertisers plan to mail at least 200 pieces. Any business can arrange for bulk mailing privileges. Here are the steps:

1 Get a third-class postal permit from the local post office. This permit costs approximately $30 a year and entitles the business to a specific identification number. The number must be printed on each mailing envelope or unit of sales literature if it is designed as a self-mailer.
2 Pass the identification number on to the printing companies that will be producing the bulk third-class mailings.
3 When the literature is ready to be delivered to the post office, arrange by ZIP Codes as postal authorities require.

Tips For Successful Retail Direct Mail

If the retail advertisers can afford them, they'll hire competent direct-mail counsel or an advertising agency. Often advertisers learn of these specialists from friends, other companies (particularly manufacturers), the Yellow Pages (under Commercial Art Studios), and sometimes the classified ads in the newspapers. Occasionally artists working for ad agencies may take on direct-mail projects on a freelance basis. If retailers can afford none of these courses of action, they should clip attractive ads from newspapers and magazines and use them as guides in the development of their own direct mail. Borrowing ideas is a common practice in the advertising business. Ads owned by retailers already run in newspapers and magazines can be reproduced for direct mail. This helps to lower the cost of the production. Retailers who know beforehand that they will use an ad in a mailing can order extra reprints at a modest cost when the newspaper or magazine is printed. They can even request better paper for reprints.

Retailers who can't get necessary photographs for modest fees from local photographers should see what is available through a stock photo company. (Editor & Publisher International Year Book's "News and Picture Services" lists names and addresses of stock photo houses), or ask a photographer on the local paper for help. A stock photo company's business is photographing models at conventional pastimes, working and playing. These photographs, usually of excellent quality, are then sold at very modest prices to advertisers (Figure 8-4).

Retailers who are serious about perfecting their direct-mail techniques are wise to get themselves on as many direct-mail lists as possible. In this way, they can analyze what other direct-mail experts have done and learn from them. In particular, each direct-mail project should have a specific objective. In this way, retailers won't expect too little or too much.

Considering the rising costs of distributing retail literature by mail, retailers should consider using Boy Scouts and Girl Scouts or other civic groups for the job. It could save money. Other money savers are to solicit advertising literature from suppliers and to take advantage of coop funds. Lastly, for best results, local advertisers should plan a consistent mailing program. Few products and services are sold on a solitary sales call.

CATALOGS

Department stores are the largest users of locally created and distributed catalogs. The most common catalog is published for the Christmas season, often in glorious color. Upwards of 25 percent of a store's yearly business takes place around the holiday season. Aside from soliciting business, catalogs also provide a basic inventory of a store's merchandise. Once the exclusive province of Sears, Roebuck and other large mail-order houses, the catalog has become a major source of business for other retail merchants. In recent years, local discount department stores have taken to inserting their

FIGURE 8-4
Retailers can find excellent photographs in stock photo company catalogs. Photographs are usually sold on a one-time-only basis at modest cost. (Courtesy H. Armstrong Roberts.)

holiday catalog in Sunday newspapers. Hardware stores, also associated with central buying groups, publish and distribute catalogs two to three times a year. It is interesting to note that co-op help is provided for dealer-produced circulars and catalogs by manufacturers of hardware goods, but only 28 percent of retailers take advantage of these funds for this purpose[3] (Figure 8-5).

THROWAWAYS

Simple, inexpensive sheets of paper with a sales message of immediate interest are referred to as throwaways or circulars. They can range from plain, handwritten messages to illustrated pieces. Throwaways are found tucked under car windshields, folded inside newspaper and milk delivery boxes, distributed in crowded foot-traffic areas, and tossed into shopping bags along with purchases. Almost any business can afford throwaways. As a candid retailer said, "Throwaways are a quick and thrifty way to announce a sale. For $20, I can run off 1,000 sheets and spread them around the community." A survey of hardware retailers indicated that their prime advertising medium was circulars.[4] But other retailers like circulars also. Gemmel Drug, a ten-store chain based in Ontario, California, is a good example. It sends out a more sophisticated, eight-page circular, every month, the main purpose of which is to bring people into its stores. According to the advertising manager for the chain, the circular program is "the most effective advertising we've done in our twenty-five-year history. . . . Our stores' volume increased . . . and we've got to give most of the credit to our circulars."[5]

Often groups of retailers will join in a voluntary association to produce a circular of eight to twelve pages. Within these pages, they'll feature seventy-five to 125 items. When the individual retailers receive their bulk circulars, they will usually distribute them through direct-mail (the costliest way), through insertion in a local newspaper, or door to door. The typical cost for an eight-page circular is about 4 cents a copy divided between printing and distribution costs.

Some circulars feature the best buys on the front page; others disperse the best buys throughout the circular in order to encourage the readers to look at all the pages. While there is no general agreement on where the best buys belong, there is agreement that the throwaway circular, be it one or twelve pages, can be one of the retailer's most effective advertising tools (Figures 8-6 and 8-7).

LOCAL RADIO

In most markets, many AM and FM radio stations compete fiercely. Lower prices are a direct result of this competition, and they make radio advertise-

[3]"The Bad and Beautiful of Co-op Usage," *Hardware Retailing*, December 1976, p. 49.
[4]"A Do-It-Yourself Ad Program," *Chain Store Age* (Drug Edition), March 1974, p. 56.
[5]Ibid.

FIGURE 8-5
Over 300,000 catalogs were mailed in 1978 by Higbees to its charge account customers in the Cleveland metropolitan area. Co-op funds from manufacturers pay for approximately a third to half the cost of most Higbee catalogs; its Christmas catalog was delivered as an insert through newspapers—some 670,000 copies. (Courtesy Higbee Company.)

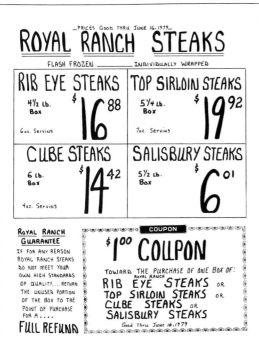

FIGURE 8-6
The common throwaway message has many variations. The chief advantages of this form of local advertising are the speed with which it can be printed, its immediacy, and its low cost.

FIGURE 8-7
This variety department store uses inexpensive circulars and succeeds in making itself a part of community activities.

ments affordable to most retailers. A study by the Marshalltown (Iowa) chamber of commerce[6] asked 779 persons which radio stations they listened to en route to shopping. No fewer than twenty-eight separate stations were mentioned! Although a few commanded a major share of the audience, all twenty-eight sought retailers' dollars, and costs ranged from as little as $1 to $35 per commercial. Of course, in major metropolitan centers, spot radio costs are proportionately higher.

Retailers contemplating radio ads should know:

1 who listens to each station under consideration.
2 how many people listen.
3 when they listen.
4 how often they listen.

Without this knowledge, retailers can only guess and buy out of ignorance. Fortunately, there is research help. Best known is Arbitron with 1,250 radio broadcaster clients, which gathers its information about radio listenership through a weekly diary given to a sample of the population. But other listenership rating services, such as Pulse, Inc. and Hooper, compile data on listeners' ages and sex. Usually, information is recorded by each quarter-hour time period. Most radio salespeople can provide these rating reports. Although they're important, listenership reports are not infallible, because each report is history. That is, ratings always reflect the past, and audience composition often changes.

Where two or more stations provide the specific audiences a retailer seeks, a good plan is to compute the cost per thousand listeners (CPM) based on their spot rates. The simple formula is *price per spot divided by listening audience* (expressed in thousands). For example, a rating of 10 percent of a total of 25,000 sets tuned in at a certain quarter hour equals 2,500 households (25,000 ÷10=2,500). Expressed in thousands according to our formula, these 2,500 households with radios are equal to 2.5 (2,500÷1,000=2.5). If the cost per one-minute spot for Station A is $20, then the CPM is $8 ($20÷2.5=$8). Computations are better than decisions based on emotions or the attractiveness of the radio station's salespeople! But remember that CPM evaluations are inexact, because no two radio stations are exactly alike and because audience commitment is difficult to measure.

But what does the retailer do when only a small percentage of all sets in an area are tuned in at a particular time? In New York City, a given rating may have to be divided (not equally) among some fifty AM signals. When that happens (individual stations rate a tiny portion of the total listenership), retailers must face the fact that they will need to advertise on more than one station to do an adequate job. Understanding this is as important as understanding that a solitary commercial is also inadequate (Table 8-3).

[6]Marshalltown (Iowa) Shopping Center Survey, November 2–8, 1976.

TABLE 8-3

AVERAGE PERSONS LISTENING (IN HUNDREDS), MON.-FRI. 6 A.M. TO 10 A.M.—SELECTED RADIO STATIONS, CLEVELAND, OHIO

Station format	Total persons over 12	Men				Teens	Women		
		18–24	25–34	35–54	55–64	12–17	25–34	35–54	55–64
WCLV/classics	99	20	8	10	1	5	1	40	6
WERE/talk	343	2	8	43	49	3	9	45	54
WGAR/good music	500	23	112	79	4	28	120	53	4

Source: Arbitron Radio, January-February 1979.

When To Use Radio

Radio is an excellent medium for backing up and reinforcing television, newspapers, and magazines. It is particularly useful in creating an air of excitement over a sale or local event. Radio is also useful when retailers wish to reach an audience they normally don't contact. In a week or two, they can saturate any given station. Millet's Kitchens of Salt Lake City, a thirty-year-old kitchen cabinet store, uses radio spots on broadcast performances of the Utah Symphony Orchestra to secure sales leads for Millet in a very competitive market. According to the owner, "We offer free a $2 booklet that St. Charles (a cabinet manufacturer) puts out. All the listener has to do is walk into the store. We run spots because we cater to the carriage trade. People who buy custom kitchens are the ones most likely to be tuning into the symphony."[7] Stan's Cabinets of Lynden, Washington, runs radio spots every Tuesday morning during drive time. Periodically, Stan runs a saturation campaign of twenty to thirty spots over a few days.[8]

The American Dairy Association promotes milk consumption by supporting local retail dairies and supermarkets with spot radio ads. The target: young people six to eighteen. Normally, this age group is difficult to reach at almost any time except weekends, which explains why the association's media experts insist on running all their milk spots on two-day weekends, and only on youth-oriented stations. The American Dairy Association *knows* its target audiences. Retailers, likewise, should know whom they are trying to reach. As we mentioned in an earlier chapter, if the audience information is not readily available, the retailer needs to discover it through interviews and surveys.

The Canned Co-op Spot

Manufacturers often give their retailers previously taped radio spots, often called "canned" spots. Most of these radio ads require "doctoring" to make them sound local. To do this, retailers may simply retain an identifying

[7]*Kitchen Business*, March 1977, p.32
[8]Ibid.

musical jingle and replace the remainder of the canned commercial with material of a local flavor delivered by a local announcer. These doctored spots now sound as if they belong to the local retailer. A variation of the canned spot is the typed copy sheet that may accompany the co-op ad material manufacturers send to retailers. Such sheets provide local announcers with a script for the radio spots. For the retailer, the problem with copy sheets is that they concentrate on the manufacturer's brand to the exclusion of the local firm and its strengths. Here is a typical prepared thirty-second radio commercial from AMF, Lawn & Garden Division:

> You can enjoy the snow this winter with an AMF Snowthrower. That's right, AMF can make it easy to clear your walks and driveways in less time. An AMF Snowthrower will gobble up the largest drifts in minutes and send the snow on its way through an adjustable high capacity chute. They're built rugged with you in mind, and AMF extras like single lever shifting, and rear mounted controls let you clear a 26-inch width effortlessly. Special Tecumseh winter engines mean quick and easy starts to get you going, and get you done with a minimum of effort. See the complete line at (dealer identification).

Advantages And Disadvantages Of AM and FM Radio

Although AM radio reaches more people than FM radio, it is more expensive for the advertiser. But there are additional comparisons that retailers must make:

1 AM radio has a greater carrying distance than FM radio; thus, if the advertiser requires a mass reach, the best selection would be an AM station.
2 Because of the greater advertiser appeal of AM stations, AM is able to provide listeners with more station personalities and thus build larger and loyal audiences. FM stations are often underfinanced, are often run by automatic apparatus, and usually have skeletal staffs.
3 AM stations may get shaky if their audience ratings drop and quickly switch from one musical format to another (for example, from rock to country-western music). In this situation, advertisers may find they cannot depend on the station's traditional audiences because they will be moving somewhere else on the radio dial. AM stations are more susceptible to rating pressures than FM stations.
4 Besides being considerably less expensive to the retailer, FM radio remains attractive to listeners who dislike all the commercial breaks typical of AM radio.
5 For retailers interested in people who like classical music, FM radio is usually the better choice, for there is generally at least one station in each large metropolitan area dedicated to this kind of music. Often listeners are members of better-educated and affluent households.
6 Although the best times for using AM radio are during commuting hours, the increased installations of FM radios in new cars might make some FM stations more attractive to retailers.
7 AM radio with its stronger signal assumes an even greater importance for retailers in such sparsely settled areas as Wyoming and Kansas. It is not at all uncommon

for listeners to rely on AM radio in order to learn about grocery sales—including prices—at regional stores. No newspapers can satisfy this consumer need at a reasonable cost.

Does Radio Pay Off for Retailers?

Media buyers say that farm radio can deliver a defined, limited audience. That's because farmers use radio as a major source of news and commodity price information. What holds true for farmers also holds for other radio-listening consumers. Radio, with its talk shows, music, DJ personalities, news, and public affairs programs attracts segmented groups of men and women of all ages. They, in turn, attract the advertising of automobile dealers, banks, realtors, insurance agents, shopping malls, supermarkets, restaurants, department stores—even competitive media like newspapers and city magazines. All these advertisers need to advertise frequently, especially if they do not use other supporting media. In specific terms of frequency, retailers, by and large, should think of placing twenty-five to thirty spots per week. The content of the commercials is equally important. Retailers who sell products (not services) generally get best results when they quote exact prices. When they forget they are retailers and advertise like manufacturers without mentioning price and terms, store hours, and payment plans, they reduce their effectiveness.

Banks, too, are retailers—retailers of money and financial services. They also fare better in the marketplace when their advertising is specific and unique. Although banks and savings and loans tend to look and sound alike in their advertising, the more aggressive of these institutions try to be different by promoting specific and memorable programs. The First Women's Bank of New York, described at the end of Chapter 2, adopted an aggressive advertising philosophy. So did this savings and loan association:

> Wouldn't it be great if someone came up with a way to make saving money easier? Like one statement that came to you every month. Not a different statement for each account. But a summary statement. One that listed all your savings accounts. And the accounts would be listed by names you gave them. Not just numbers. A statement that told you how you were doing with your savings in plain, simple English. Sound good? It is. And only Des Moines Savings has it. We call it "The Bookkeeper" and it makes saving money a lot easier. Just decide what it is you'd like to save for. Name the account with a name that means something to you, and that's just the way you'll see it on your statement. And that goes for all the things you want to save for. And they all come to you, every month on one statement, when you have account activity. The Bookkeeper, a very special summary statement from the savings place. The Bookkeeper, another *now* service, only at Des Moines Savings.

Does radio pay off for retailers? Evidently hardware retailers believe it does: over 54 percent of a group of 270 surveyed schedule local radio ads in cooperation with their manufacturer-suppliers.[9] So does Dodd's, Cleveland's most eminent retail store for photographers and artists:

> For the month of October 1978, we did an extensive amount of advertising on WGAR. This was the first time that Dodd used WGAR Radio. I am very happy to say that sales for that month were the highest in the history of the Dodd Company.[10]

TELEVISION

Retailers are attracted to the glamor of television. But television, like radio, requires frequent and consistent advertising for best results. Used often and consistently, local television can be an excellent way to establish identity. It happened this way for a group of local McDonald's restaurants. The narrator is Roy Kroc, founder of the McDonald's hamburger chain.

> In midsummer of 1963, Nick Karos came to me with a proposal for a television advertising campaign. The projected cost was $180,000 and he wanted to pay for it by raising the price of hamburgers in our company-owned stores a penny, from fifteen to sixteen cents. "Nick, this is a terrific plan," I said, "but we're not gonna raise the price. . . . The logic of his one page memo was irrefutable. It demonstrated precisely how an ad campaign would repay its cost many times over, while failing to spend the money would cost us much more in the long run. . . . The advertising campaign we put together was a smash hit. It turned Californians into our parking lots as though blindfolds had been removed from their eyes, and suddenly they could see the golden arches. That was a big lesson for me in the effectiveness of television.[11]

Car dealers throughout the country have discovered that appearing often on television in a Superman outfit or a clown suit fixes their dealership in the minds of the public (although negatively for some viewers). Supermarkets have learned that presenting price specials in novel ways reaches a widespread audience and ties in well with their newspaper ads on food days. Add to these retailers, department stores and financial institutions, and that pretty much covers the "regulars" on local television.

Yet television has great potential for other retailers as well. For example, any local service business in a medium or small city, such as a photography studio, a department store, or a jewelry or gift store could sponsor a series of thirty-second commercials featuring a local bride-to-be. The appeal of television is such that all family members, relatives, and friends of the bride will be glued to the set awaiting her appearance. Other brides-to-be would soon be beating a path to the retailer in hopes of also getting on television.

[9]"The Bad and Beautiful of Co-op Usage," *Hardware Retailing*, December 1976, p. 49.
[10]Letter to WGAR Radio by Dodd's promotion manager, November 17, 1978.
[11]Ray Kroc, *Grinding It Out: The Making of McDonald's* (Chicago: Henry Regnery Company, 1977), p. 131–132.

The goodwill generated by the creative use of the medium can be quickly evaluated in increased people-traffic and sales. In larger cities, television is a medium most small retailers cannot afford, but it is affordable if groups of noncompetitive or geographically separated merchants join forces and divide commercial costs. For larger retailers who can afford the cost of television, the medium provides advertisers a chance to tell their story without local competitors cluttering the airwaves immediately before or after their announcements. Also, the prestige of a television commercial, even locally produced, is still strong among the general public.

Local commercials are usually produced cheaply, for no more than $100 to $300. Contrast that with $10,000 to $100,000 for some of the artistic network spots! Many local television stations create local spots in their own studios. Production budgets are usually so low that they tax the ingenuity of the creator—even that of the local ad agency. The least expensive commercial productions are usually live presentations recorded on videotape or series of slides backed by an unseen voice. Retailers often can convince smaller manufacturers who can't afford national television themselves to permit their co-op monies to be used for local, lower-priced spots.

Costs and Coverage

Not all television markets are too expensive for a small or medium-sized retailer. In some of the more sparsely populated areas of the country, television can be most attractive. For example, there are approximately 109,000 children ages two to eleven in the overall Huntsville (Alabama), metropolitan area who are of interest to local retailers of sporting goods.[12] Buying a thirty-second spot on a preemptible basis on a daily children's show (A.M.) costs as little as $25 on the local CBS affiliate. Obviously, retailers need to know how many youngsters are watching that show at that particular time, but $25 is an attractive price. In Spokane, Washington, the sporting goods retailer can run announcements on Saturday children's shows for as little as $75, with a target audience of 138,000.[13] How do retailers decide whether their television buy is worth the money? Unfortunately, there is no easy answer. At best we can only apply the same analysis media buyers use: How many of our target group are watching, and what does it cost to reach them?

Using the example of our hypothetical sporting goods retailers, let's see how they might analyze a buy on a typical television station. The market: Providence, Rhode Island. The target audience: youngsters two to eleven. As the retailers scan a recent Arbitron television study of the Providence area, they discover that on a particular Saturday at 10 A.M., the most popular show reaches approximately 41,000 children two to eleven.[14] They also learn through station rate cards that a thirty-second spot at that time costs $280, if any are available. If they apply the CPM formula (price per spot divided by

---

[12]*Test Market Profiles*, Nielsen Station Index, 1974, p. 177.
[13]*SRDS/Spot TV*, January 15, 1978, p. 31.
[14]*Arbitron Television Audience Estimates in the Arbitron Market of Providence*, November 1976, p. 44.

THERE WAS A TIME YOU DIDN'T HAVE THE SUPER STATION TO TURN TO.

WTCG. It's got a lot going for you. Sensational, round-the-clock, 24 hour programming. Over 200 live sports events each year, including professional baseball, basketball, and hockey.

Great family entertainment—show after show every member of the family can laugh and cry over.

Movies galore. Your all-time, Holly-

wood favorites from our incredible library of nearly 3000 films. This and much, much more awaits you on WTCG. So subscribe to Cable today. You'll discover what millions of people all over the country have already found out for themselves. WTCG is the Super Station. And it's all yours through Cable TV.

NOW YOU CAN ON CABLE TV WITH WTCG - ATLANTA.

FIGURE 8-8

In addition to reaching viewers in its home town of Atlanta, Super Station WTCG, cable channel 17, claims it has penetrated areas in Alabama, Mississippi, Louisiana, Florida, Texas, and even as far away as Zanesville, Ohio. A recent WTCG ad headline states: "Audience. That's the growing word for channel 17 in more than 2.6 million homes nationwide." (Courtesy WTCG.)

viewing audience, expressed in thousands), the retailers will find that the cost to reach a thousand youngsters is about $6.82. This seems reasonable, a little over 0.5 cents to reach *each* youngster. In addition, television has the advantage over other media of offering a commercial that has both picture and sound.

Individual store owners are at a disadvantage when buying television spots, however, compared to local chains, drugstores, and supermarkets. Multistore outlets have more money and can scatter spots throughout the time schedule, thus reducing their CPM. One way an individual retailer can achieve a lower CPM is to schedule spots around the late, late show. These are usually a fraction of the price of spots at the more desirable time periods. Remember that Alpo dog food got started toward national prominence by buying low-cost spots around the old-time movies on the late show.

Local Cable Television

For retailers who cannot afford the spot costs of conventional television, local cable fills a need. With 18 percent of all television households now enjoying cable services (subscribers pay for a wire or cable hookup that permits them to receive a greater variety of signals), some cable companies are selling low-cost cable time spots. In fact, the ad staffs of some city newspapers sell both their own display space and cable time to the same retailers. Usually, they sell cable's news programs, the material of which is supplied by their newspaper (Viewers see a reproduction of the printed news on their television screens.) For the cable station and the newspaper, this is a marriage of convenience. The cable station saves an investment in a news-gathering, editing, and delivery staff; the newspaper promotes its product (news) over cable television and shares in the advertising revenue it sells for cable. As far as retailers are concerned, they must keep in mind that the 18 percent of the nation's population hooked to cable is an average over the country. In Huntsville, the cable coverage is over 30 percent; in Providence, it is less than 5 percent; in Spokane, it's 23 percent.[15]

If retailers plan to use cable television, they should keep in mind that cable further fragments the viewing audience because it offers more than the three conventional channels to choose from. Despite this, retailers may find cable, with its lower cost, a practical medium. And for the larger retailer, able to justify the cost of a wider geographical reach, new and more powerful cable television stations are emerging, some with as many as 3 million subscriber tie-ins (Figure 8-8).

OUTDOOR ADVERTISING

Outdoor posters and painted bulletins are usually sold for periods of thirty days. They rent for as little as $100 a month in some markets and are found

---

[15]*Test Market Profiles,* Nielsen Station Index, 1974, pp. 176, 300, 352.

FIGURE 8-9
Cherry & Webb, a prominent Rhode Island department store, runs billboards all year long. They share the cost with their suppliers, but so successful is their program, that there's a waiting list of suppliers hoping to participate. (Courtesy Cherry & Webb).

on heavily traveled streets near retail shopping areas. Retailers often prescribe where a board should be placed in order to cover major roads leading to their stores. Experts recommend that retailers select boards near their outlets for best results. Outdoor is effective with younger customers and families with children because these groups are very mobile.

Retailers who have used outdoor over the years select these giant ads to tell people about:

1 specific merchandise
2 a department within the store
3 new merchandise
4 new stores
5 special events
6 seasonal sales
7 price and item sales
8 holiday promotions

Once retailers have decided to use outdoor, they should contact the outdoor company for help. Its artist can usually come up with a satisfactory design. Occasionally retailers get co-op assistance and artwork from their manufacturer-suppliers. Perhaps the most effective billboard approach for retailers is price and item selling. Even if prices change frequently, new prices can be posted over the old without redoing the rest of the board (Figure 8-9).

Retailers, as we have seen, have their own specific reasons for advertising. A major one is that they expect almost immediate sales reaction, be it from newspapers, city magazines, direct mail, catalogs, throwaways, radio, television, or outdoor. This expectation is not unrealistic because retailers, by and large, need store traffic to survive. In fact, they look upon store traffic as the best way to tell whether their advertising is working and worth the investment.

Of course, not all the media choices we've discussed are applicable to each retailer. Some work better than others, often for unplanned reasons. Sometimes retailers must experiment with different media, keep records, and repeat successes. Experience in media, as in everything else, is an excellent teacher.

IN SUMMARY

1 Retailers as a group invest more dollars in newspapers than in any other medium. Many advertise only in newspapers.

2 The selection of media for the retailer hinges on several points: the cost of the primary coverage for the medium's reach, the best day (for newspapers) for ads to appear, the availability of nearby weekly papers, the readership value of special tab sections, the relative worth of regular or irregular ad insertions, the readership quality of co-op ads, and the ratio of advertising to sales invested in advertising.

3 A shopper generally is in tabloid form without news. In recent years, the shopper, almost totally made up of classified ads, has begun to attract retailers' advertising dollars.

4 Classified advertising linage continues to be the percentage pacesetter of all newspaper advertising. Its volume is double that of national newspaper advertising.

5 Retailers' best advertising counsel usually comes from the sales representatives from their local newspapers. The reps' expertise can mean the difference between success and failure.

6 Newspaper advertising syndicates provide retailers with complete advertising campaigns at modest prices. These prices are usually based on the circulation of the newspaper in which the campaign is run.

7 City magazines, of which there are a growing number, are attractive buys for retailers serving a higher-income, better-educated population; their CPMs are generally higher than those delivered by nationally circulated magazines.

8 Nielsen's *Test Market Profiles* is an excellent data base for retailers looking for effective media buys in their areas.

9 Next to local newspapers, direct mail may be the retailers' most popular method of reaching customers. The most important element of the direct-mail piece itself is the offer.

10 Retailers with continuing direct-mail programs should look into third-class bulk mailing privileges.

11 Retailers needing help with their direct-mail programs can hire it from outside

agencies who work in the field. Some retailers learn about direct-mail techniques by getting themselves on as many direct-mail lists as possible. For best results, retailers should plan on consistent mailings, not a single venture.

12   The catalog has become an important source of business for many retail merchants, either through the mail or as an insert in newspapers.

13   Throwaways are simple, inexpensive pieces of paper with sales messages, generally of immediate interest. In a more sophisticated form, they become circulars and are preferred by some advertisers over all other forms of advertising.

14   As a result of the fierce competition between local radio stations, retailers can usually buy time spots at a low price.

15   Retailers intending to buy radio spots need to know who listens to what station, how many people listen, and when and how often they listen. Arbitron and other research companies provide this information.

16   To choose among stations—and even among competing media—retailers should compare their costs per thousand. The CPM formula is: price per spot divided by listening audience (expressed in thousands).

17   Radio is an excellent way to back up and reinforce television, newspapers, and magazines.

18   Canned radio spots and typed copy sheets primarily advertise the manufacturers' brands to the exclusion of the local retailer. When the retailer's name is given, it is usually at the end of the commercial.

19   AM radio reaches more people, provides more station personalities, and builds larger audiences than FM radio. But AM radio is more susceptible to rating pressures than FM radio.

20   FM radio is less expensive for the retailer than AM radio, and it retains the loyalty of those listeners who dislike the many commercial breaks typical of AM radio.

21   Retailers who advertise on radio should think in terms of buying twenty-five to thirty spots per week and should mention the price of their products, terms, store hours, and payment plans if applicable.

22   The prestige of a television commercial is strong among the general public, although in larger cities television is a medium most small retailers cannot afford.

23   Local commercials are produced locally for as little as $100 to $300, although they tax the ingenuity of their creators.

24   In some of the less-populous areas of the country, television can be both attractive and affordable for small and medium-size retailers.

25   Multistore outlets have more money for television than do individual store owners and thus can scatter more spots throughout the time schedule. This serves to lower their costs per thousand viewers.

26   For retailers who cannot afford conventional television spots, spots are available on some cable television systems. These are generally far below the cost of conventional television. Retailers must keep in mind that cable coverage varies widely between communities.

27   Outdoor posters and painted bulletins are usually sold for thirty-day periods and may rent for as little as $100 a month per board. Retailers can use these boards to tell people about specific merchandise, new stores, special events, seasonal sales, and holiday promotions. Perhaps the most effective way for a retailer to use outdoor advertising is to promote specific items and prices.

CASE STUDY *The Philadelphia Inquirer* promotes drama and discovers newspaper-television synergy.

The dictionary defines *synergy* as "the combined action of two different groups so the total effect is greater than the sum of the two effects taken independently." That's what happened when the crusading *Philadelphia Inquirer* decided to promote the dramatic teleplay, "Eleanor and Franklin" to its readers and the total community. In a way, it's another "Philadelphia Story" with a happy ending for all participants.

But first, some background. It's no secret that newspaper executives are concerned about declining interest of the young in reading newspapers. To them, this disinterest poses a serious problem for the survival of newspapers in this country. Their concerns are shared by educators dismayed by evidence of declining reading abilities in the schools. This much is not new. Each city newspaper and school system in the nation is beset with the same problem. What *is* new is what the Philadelphia superintendent of schools[16] and *The Philadelphia Inquirer* decided to do about it, with the cooperation of the city's school board, the American Broadcasting Company (TV), and the financial assistance of International Business Machines Corporation (IBM).

What was different was this: On Friday, January 9, 1976, *The Philadelphia Inquirer* ran a sixteen-page insert consisting of the full text of the teleplay, "Eleanor and Franklin," which was presented on the ABC Television Network the following Sunday and Monday nights. (Figure 8-10). The insert was part of the television reading program of the school superintendent and his board. Its objectives were to improve the reading skills of the students through greater student and community involvement in quality literature, and to improve the image of the board. IBM, the sponsor of the network teleplay, picked up the cost of printing the sixteen-page *Inquirer* insert, which went into the paper's full circulation run of 415,000. Another 126,000 inserts went into a like number of *Inquirer* copies hand-delivered to all the secondary school children in the school district. These extra newspapers (not just the inserts) were bought by the students.

The *Inquirer* allowed its public service advertising rate to the school board, and the entire section was considered paid advertising. (IBM supplied a grant to the board.) When it became apparent that the newspaper would get a big circulation boost for the Friday's insert issue, the *Inquirer's* management went beyond the customary house ad support (Figure 8-11) and bought television and radio spots to promote the program. The paper also printed a full page of school enrichment materials on the back page of the paper carrying the insert (Figure 8-12).

The results: About 5,100 letters of commendation were received.

Ratings were 48 percent of the viewing public on Sunday; 51 percent on Monday. (The same teleplay in New York without comparable promotion rated a little more than half as high.)

Eighty-four percent of students and their families viewed the program both evenings.

---

[16]Dr. Michael P. Marcase, who introduced Philadelphia to a television reading program using tapes and scripts of quality television programs. (Information from a School District of Philadelphia letter, Board of Education, April 29, 1976.)

The
ABC THEATRE:
Television Presentation
of
ELEANOR & FRANKLIN

Written For Television by
JAMES COSTIGAN

Based Upon The Pulitzer Prize Winning Book
ELEANOR & FRANKLIN
by
JOSEPH P. LASH

The ABC Theatre Television Special Presented by IBM

Part I	Part II
Sunday January 11, 1976	Monday January 12, 1976
9:00–11:00PM	9:00–11:00PM

This script of ELEANOR AND FRANKLIN is from the ABC THEATRE Television presentation and is a dramatization based on fact. The reproduction of the script in its entirety has been arranged by The Philadelphia School System, IBM and the ABC Television Network as an aid to education. Distributed to Students throughout the Philadelphia Schools as well as to homes through the cooperation of the Philadelphia Inquirer, the script will be used as a very important aid in helping students to improve their reading skills.

On behalf of the Philadelphia Board of Education, I welcome this opportunity for every reader of The Inquirer to share with our students an extraordinary educational experience.

One of my priorities as Superintendent of Philadelphia Schools has been to evaluate the use of commercial television as an important aid to education. I believe that this use of the script of "Eleanor and Franklin" is a major step in that direction. IBM and ABC-TV have given their full support to the success of this concept.

Our thoughts are that this enrichment exercise will help influence our students to become more discriminate in their television viewing while at the same time motivating them to improve their English and Social Study skills.

I trust that this concept will become a most entertaining and educational experience at home as well. I invite your comments.

Dr. Michael P. Marcase
Superintendent, Philadelphia Public Schools

FIGURE 8-10
Part of the full script of "Eleanor and Franklin," printed in the *Inquirer.*

FIGURE 8-11
Philadelphia *Inquirer* advertisement for "Eleanor and Franklin."

FIGURE 8-12
The *Inquirer* also printed materials to enrich the script.

A Public Service Feature: School Enrichment Materials

This support material was prepared by the following staff members of the Philadelphia Board of Education: Naomi Hamilton, Irene Reiter, Joseph Phillips, William Brown, Jerome Ruderman and William Ruderman.

They were under the direction of Dr. Marjorie Farmer, executive director of English and Dr. George French, director of social studies.

Introduction

For adults over 40, the dominant political figure in their school years was FDR. To the present generation, Eleanor and Franklin Roosevelt are remote figures. Through the magic of television the lives of these two great people are relived. For the older generation, the script and telecast will be a bit of nostalgia.

To the younger generation, an introduction to the history of the 20th century. To both, an opportunity to view the accomplishments of a great American lady in spite of overwhelming personal tragedy.

Although the play is Eleanor's story, it is difficult to view her alone for her life was inextricably interwoven with Franklin's. It is doubtful if either would have achieved such greatness alone. Together, they helped change the course of history.

The play opens on April 12, 1945 with the death of Franklin. Eleanor is in Washington, D.C., and rushes to Warm Springs, Georgia, to make final funeral arrangements. While in the death room and later on the funeral train bringing the body back to Washington, Eleanor's mind drifts back to her earliest years and the events that led up to her marriage to Franklin.

Through a series of flashbacks we see the young, awkward Eleanor

Note to Parents, Teachers

This page of enrichment exercises has been printed as a public service by The Philadelphia Inquirer's Educational Services Department. Use of these curriculum materials, in conjunction with the 16-page tabloid section containing the script of the upcoming "Eleanor and Franklin" TV special, appearing elsewhere in this edition, will allow parents and teachers to guide their students' learning experience as they participate together in this unique educational experiment.

Those wishing further information on The Inquirer's Newspaper-in-the-Classroom Program should write to: James Leonard, Educational Services Department, Philadelphia Inquirer, 400 N. Broad St., Phila., Pa. 19101.

TV as Art Form

This four-hour biographical drama is primarily the work of the dramatists' hand. It is primarily an artifice, made from the amorphous mind of human experience. Therefore, biographical drama like this must be witnessed with a critical eye. If it is truthful, it is truthful in its fashion. It captures something of the reality that was. It cannot pretend to tell all. What is omitted, is omitted without apology in the interest of a unified final creation.

To unify his work, the dramatist

School libraries reported a 43 percent increase in borrowings.

Over 1,800 telephone calls were taken, virtually all expressing approval.

About 3,500 inquiries from other school systems were received.

The *Inquirer* has continued with its reading program tabloids, which have included "Roots" and Shakespeare's "A Mid-Summer's Night Dream."

One teacher's comment: "I wasn't prepared for such a high level of motivation on the part of the kids."

QUESTIONS NEEDING ANSWERS

1 What types of retailers would want to associate themselves through advertising with this television reading program experiment? Explain.
2 Would the Philadelphia ratings for "Eleanor and Franklin" suggest that the best ad campaign is that in which television and newspapers work together? Explain.
3 Instead of using television and radio spots as it did, wouldn't The *Inquirer* have been better served by thirty outdoor boards around the city? Explain, and be sure to consider costs.
4 Do you think the sale of 126,000 extra newspapers to high school students for one day only would also serve to sell these same students a long-term subscription? Explain.

STUDENT PROJECT

Assume that you have taken over the operation of a new health club in Philadelphia. The club features tennis, racketball, handball, running, and weight lifting. Your job is to attract patrons from the greater Philadelphia metropolitan area.

QUESTIONS ABOUT THE PROJECT

1 What groups and ages would you be interested in? Explain.
2 What media would you use to reach them if you had a yearly budget of no more than $35,000?
3 What is the cost of an 800-line ad in the *Inquirer* and the Philadelphia *Bulletin*? (See *SRDS/Newspaper Rates.*) How do the milline rates of these two popular newspapers compare? (See Chapter 6.)
4 Would you recommend that a four-page insert about your new health club be placed in a zoned circulation area of one or both of the major Philadelphia newspapers? Explain the pros and cons.

Unit

2

INDUSTRIAL ADVERTISING

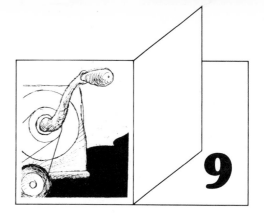

INDUSTRIAL
ADVERTISING

Update In earlier chapters, we talked about consumer products such as washing machines, food products, deodorants, and clothing, to name a few. These are the fruits of an affluent society, which produces anything from the necessary to the trivial and has it waiting for us at retail stores within 5 miles of our homes. But who buys the parts and materials that go into the making of consumer products? Who does the selling? Is it a retailer or a special kind of wholesaler?

When the washing machine we buy for our home boasts a "no stall" motor and switches that cut off automatically in the event of trouble, where do these features come from? What does it mean, for example, that the automotive industry's retooling bill in the next few years will reach $6 billion?

Who gets that $6 billion? The answer is industry—the hundreds of companies that manufacture and sell motors and switches to the Maytags, the Whirlpools, the Hotpoints, or the firms that make tools and dies, steel and plastic and aluminum, tires, and the like.

Why should we be concerned with the industrial marketplace? We need to know about a vitally important segment of our economy. What industries do concerns us all. The United States is an industrialized nation, with all that that implies: a high standard of living, powerful corporations, massive worker organizations, and massive ecological problems. Major groups of industrial companies accounted for 18,753,000 employees with a payroll of over $233 billion.[1] When plants employing these workers finished operations, they had shipped goods and materials worth nearly $2 trillion to the economy.[2] To grasp the scope of this figure, consider that consumer retail sales in the relatively same period (1977) came to $708 billion.[3]

IMPORTANCE OF INDUSTRIAL ADVERTISING

Because many people think of consumer advertising whenever we say "advertising," we need a definition for industrial advertising. *Industrial advertising is a way to create awareness of and preference for nonretail goods and services among "special" buyers who work in manufacturing, process, construction, and service industries.*

We don't buy industrial products in the conventional hardware or retail store. We buy them through an agent called an industrial distributor or directly from the manufacturer. For example, the South Carolina manufacturer of an air conditioning compressor finds it difficult to visit customers headquartered in many different states. Therefore, local distributors act as the company's sales agents because they are readily available. These distributors are independent business firms that send salespeople to call on industrial plants. They buy, take title to, and stock the goods they sell.

For their part, manufacturers of air conditioners (such as Carrier) require current information about all the components that they buy and assemble into a finished product. They can get this information in many ways: through the specialized medium of business publications, magazines devoted to reporting information of value to industrial buyers and specifiers; through product literature sent by the manufacturers of component parts such as air compressors; and through advertising literature and samples delivered in person by an industrial distributor.

When industrial customers receive the information they need, they inevitably respond by purchasing a variety of things: machinery, nuts and

---

[1]"General Statistics for Major Industry Industry Groups," Bureau of the Census, *The World Almanac & Book of Facts* (New York, 1977), p. 138.
[2]"General Manufacturing Statistics for States," Census of Manufacturers 1973 General Summary, *The World Almanac & Book of Facts* (New York, 1977), p. 139.
[3]"Retail Store Sales," Department of Commerce, *World Almanac* (New York, 1977), p. 142.

bolts, electronic devices, and the like. In many cases, industrial advertising is a cross-pollinator among technologies. An advance in chemistry reported in the business press may end up as a Teflon part in a jet engine. An innovation in ceramics may result in a digital wrist watch!

However, the advertising strategist for a company selling to industry must recognize that there is a vast difference between the technical industrial buyer of industry and the buyer in an average household. Industrial manufacturers range from those whose sales are no more than $100,000 a year to those whose sales are $35 billion. One major difference is that the industrial buyer works for a company whose customers number in hundreds or thousands, but never in millions. This restricted market is easier and more economical to reach than the vast consumer market because of its smaller numbers and specialized publications.

Industrial manufacturers produce a staggering array of goods. Some buy components, add to their value in some way, and then resell them. An example of such resold components are bicycle tires. Tire manufacturers make and sell them to a company like Schwinn, which in effect resells them when it ships Schwinn bicycles to retail outlets. Other companies, largely unknown to the general public, buy and sell raw materials and product components only. They may have no direct concern for the retail market, as the bicycle manufacturer does. Yet their contributions are necessary to the proper functioning of many retail products.

THE INDUSTRIAL SALES TARGET

Companies who sell and advertise to industry are often important sales and advertising targets themselves. An example is the Container Corporation of America, a leading boxboard manufacturer. Through sales calls and industrial ads, the corporation systematically tries to sell containers to companies in the food industry such as Kellogg and Nabisco, to companies in the soap industry such as Procter & Gamble, and to other consumer product companies. At the same time, Container Corporation's own plants in turn are the target of sales calls and ads of companies selling logs, chipping machines, motors, controls, maintenance equipment, and other products necessary to produce containers. In fact, most companies, regardless of size, present important sales potential for industrial products and services. A manufacturer of the common steel bolt is just as anxious to sell to smaller customers as to the giants because of the constant pressure of competition. Also, smaller manufacturers may grow into giants and reward past service with increased business.

BUYING, SELLING, AND DISTRIBUTING

Industrial products, by and large, are warehoused and sold by industrial distributors. They handle such items as abrasives, drills and bits, hand tools, nuts and bolts, valves, pumps, power transmission equipment, industrial rubber goods, material-handling equipment, and more. Distributors are important in the cast of characters who make up the buyers and sellers of the industrial market. All in all, there are four major groups who are most directly concerned with the sale and purchase of industrial goods:

1 The industrial manufacturer's *sales force*, generally headed by a sales manager or vice president in charge of sales.
2 The *industrial distributor*, who buys and warehouses the manufacturer's products and makes them available to factories within a specified territory.
3 The *manufacturer's representative*, who acts as an agent for the manufacturer's own limited or nonexistent sales staff. Manufacturer's representatives do not stock or buy from their manufacturer. They perform a sales function only.
4 The *industrial buyers* spread throughout the country.

The Industrial Manufacturer's Sales Force

To understand why industrial companies need to advertise, we must begin with the manufacturer's sales force. Unlike the manufacturers of consumer products, the makers of component parts usually have no showcase, no convenient retail outlet, easily available to customers. This means they must rely on traveling salespersons to display and sell merchandise. Companies may sell direct by using their own salaried sales force or elect to sell through distributors and manufacturers' agents or representatives. The choice of distribution method depends on the type of product, its popularity, price, and profitability. Some industrial products are in greater demand than others; such as screws, bearings, bolts, and paint, among others. Therefore, in any trading area, it is easier to locate salespersons who sell these popular items. The fewer salespersons who sell heavy, expensive machinery are less accessible and usually cover wide geographical areas. This is why advertising plays such an important role for industrial manufacturers. It enables them to reach customers and prospects where their selling force calls infrequently or not at all.

The Industrial Distributor

Manufacturers select and contract with local distributors according to specialized knowledge, reputation within the territory, number of inside and outside salespersons, and financial strength. In most cases, a distributor handles a group or line of allied products. For example, if the major sales line is antifriction bearings (Figure 9-1), the distributor is likely also to handle pillow blocks and O-rings—all replaceable components for moving parts of machinery. These distributors of bearings will generally have the exclusive rights to sell in a specified geographical area set aside by the bearing manufacturer. In return, the manufacturer expects an exclusive distributor to work the territory effectively and profitably. Generally, manufacturers permit only one distributor per trading area. In the event a distributor fails to measure

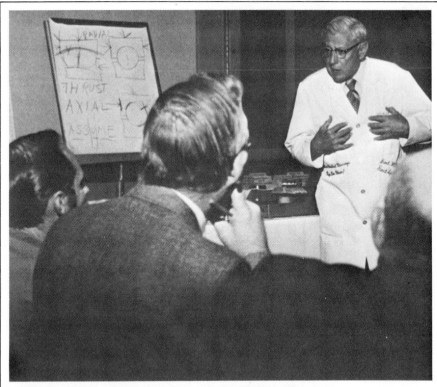

Walt Sinclair helped 2,374 plants reduce bearing costs last year.

A bearing and power transmission seminar helps you reduce downtime and squeeze more value from your bearing and PT dollar. Available to our customers, it covers bearing and PT selection, installation, adjustment, lubrication and safety. We don't sell in a seminar but we do tell you a lot about the 85 top lines we represent. Over the past 20 years, customers have asked Walt, our Director of Product Use, to conduct 1,300 seminars for 26,000 plant maintenance and engineering managers. If he's booked we have at least one "Walt Sinclair" at each of our 150 branches. Free brochure tells how to arrange for one. Call our local branch or send coupon.

This free brochure explains a bearing and PT seminar and how to arrange for one.

FIGURE 9-1
This advertisement for replacement bearings appeared in industrial publications read coast-to-coast by plant owners, engineers, and purchasing agents. Bearings, Inc., once a small, local distributor in northern Ohio, uses effective advertising that helped it open over 175 branch offices in industrial centers. Note how the ad stresses service in contrast to specific bearings.

up to expectations, the manufacturer can cancel the contract at its termination date.

Some specialized distributors act as engineers in addition to their usual stocking, transporting, selling, and invoicing responsibilities. A distributor of automatic lubricating equipment, for example, may have one of its engineers design a complete lubricating system for a customer's new machinery. Another distributor selling an overhead conveyor system may design a complete installation for an entire plant. Selling the conveyor components alone without the necessary engineering might result in making no sale at all.

The Manufacturer's Rep

Manufacturer's representatives, or "reps," exist because some manufacturers cannot afford salaried salespeople. But the major distinction between manufacturer's representatives and distributors is that the reps don't stock merchandise or take title to it. They cover great chunks of territory for their principals, perhaps several noncompeting manufacturers whose products are not in such demand that they require a nearby stocking distributor. The rep prefers to sell related lines of products. For example, a rep might handle welding equipment, electrodes, welding helmets, a line of welding fluxes, and safety gloves, glasses and shoes. Thus, reps will have several items to sell on a single sales call, an effective use of time. Reps appreciate manufacturers who advertise extensively because advertisements make the rep's sales job easier. Reps usually insist on an exclusive contract with manufacturers. They work hard if there is a demand for the products they represent. If not, they may concentrate on other, more popular items. In short, the rep prefers the manufacturer who makes a product that is in demand; the manufacturer, in turn, admires the rep who gets the selling job done consistently.

The Industrial Buyers

The industrial customer at a plant is a person or buying committee responsible for buying specific products. It is important to understand that different people buy according to the role they play at the plant, because this is a unique aspect of industrial marketing. For example, some advertisers mistakenly lump all engineers together. Engineering is a field of specialists with widely differing backgrounds and abilities. On the whole, engineers restrict their purchasing and specifying responsibilities to the components relating to their specialties.

People often wonder, "How many separate buying influences does industry have?" We can only guess. But it may be as many as 4.7 million.[4]

---

[4]To arrive at the total number of buying influences, we subtracted total number of production workers from total number of employees in manufacturing industries. Then, we took off another 1¼ million clerical workers. Construction, oil production, and nonmanufacturing industries are not included.

The average purchase per buyer comes to approximately $150,000 a year.[5] Compare that to the $15,925 the average household spends each year.[6] No wonder salespeople travel hundreds of miles to call on just one industrial customer.

Although there are many descriptive job titles within industrial plants, we can categorize our buyers and specifiers by the jobs they perform.

The Purchasing Agent   Most plants with more than twenty employees generally appoint a purchasing agent (P.A.). In a large factory, the agent's title may be director or even vice president of purchasing, and he or she may have several purchasing assistants. As the name implies, the P.A. has the primary responsibility for buying merchandise for the factory and offices. Purchasing agents rely upon industrial catalogs for information. These may include *Thomas Register of Manufacturers, MacRae's Blue Book,* and *Fraser's Canadian Directory* and contain basic information and advertising from thousands of industrial manufacturers: their products, their locations, their phone numbers, even the names of their chief executive officers. In addition, the purchasing agent relies upon smaller catalogs published by individual manufacturers and distributors. And the P.A. usually reads the editorials and advertisements in a few industrial, trade, and business publications of interest. *Purchasing,* a magazine devoted to the function of purchasing, is one such publication. From these publications, the P.A. receives a continuing education on subjects relating to the field.

The Design Engineer   The design engineer makes sure that the products the company makes look and perform properly. Design engineers are also responsible for updating current product models and for introducing new ones. They are concerned with the availability of necessary materials and components, and with making the components they specify for purchase perform correctly nearly all the time.

Design engineers are idea people. They avidly read industrial publications, which provide information about new materials as well as new products. Although the design engineer may not sign the purchase order for a given component, he or she is often the power behind the scenes. A purchasing agent generally carries out a design engineer's wishes on buying technical materials.

How important are the approximately 125,000 persons in industry performing a design function? In 1977, eight of ten chief design engineers reported that they had an average of 3.6 completely new products in some stage of development. And nearly as many plan to start new product development in the future.[7] The same number said they had also redesigned

[5]Bureau of Economic Analysis, U.S. Department of Commerce, 1977.
[6]"Survey of Buying Power," *Sales and Marketing Management Magazine,* July 1978.

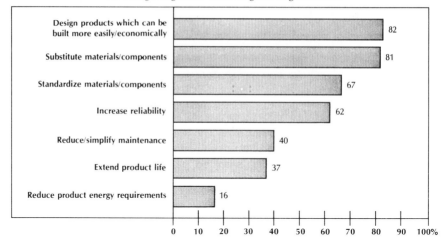

How Design Engineers Solve Engineering Problems

existing products. Unless industrial suppliers, both manufacturers and distributors, keep design engineers aware of their products, they may lose business to competitors. The business controlled by one design engineer employed by a large plant, for example, may total thousands, perhaps millions of components.

Design engineers spend much of their time adapting the latest technologies to existing products. A recent study shows how they view their major job problems (Figure 9-2). Their answers provide sales opportunities for manufacturers and also serve as a reservoir of ideas for industrial advertising copywriters.

The Plant/Project/Production/Research/Maintenance Engineer Depending on its size, a company may have plant, project, production, research, and maintenance engineers, or one person may perform all the functions. All these engineers read several technical publications each month that are geared to their specific interests. What are these interests?

A plant engineer is interested in products for the physical structure of the plant and its functioning. These products include roofing materials, concrete work stations, overhead lighting, conveyors, and the like. A project engineer is interested in all the materials and components needed for a specific work project. For example, if a plant is manufacturing a new lightweight typewriter, every component part and every process involved in its manufacture may be

---

[7]"New Design and Redesign Activity in the O.E.M.," *Machine Design* magazine (Cleveland, Ohio, 1978) Annual Survey, pp. 6-7.

under the temporary supervision of a project engineer until all the "bugs" are eliminated. At that point, the project is released to the production engineer. Production engineers are primarily concerned with getting the manufactured product out the door and are therefore concerned with the machinery and the systems needed to do this. Maintenance engineers are usually involved with the upkeep of both the physical plant and the production facilities. Research engineers are involved in defining and solving company problems, theoretical and practical.

Frequently, titles do not indicate exactly what work is being done by whom. In a series of interviews, chemical, food, textile, and metalworking publication readers revealed that the 5,147 persons (in 2,444 plants) who influenced the purchase of oil and grease carried 584 different job titles.[8] In a later series of interviews over a three-year period, subscribers to a chemical publication revealed that readers' buying a product depends on whether the reader's company uses the advertised product and whether the reader has any influence on the purchase of the product. The job titles varied, including company executives, works managers, supervisors, engineers, technical directors, and chemists.[9]

The Administrators

Administrators include owners, presidents, vice presidents, comptrollers, and office managers. They, too, play a vital role in the selection, specification, and purchase of industrial goods. They read publications written for their own industries as well as broader business magazines such as *Industry Week, Business Week, Forbes, U.S. News & World Report, The Wall Street Journal,* and *New York Journal of Commerce.* It is not unusual for administrators to be part of a buying committee made up of the plant, production, maintenance, design, and purchasing functions whenever large equipment purchases are under consideration.

ADVERTISING VERSUS SALES CALLS

Few people will argue that industrial ads are more economical than personal sales calls, despite the fact that their individual costs are at opposite ends of the pole. For example, the cost per reader impression for an industrial ad is measured in pennies. Even an ad printed in full color costs pennies when divided by the magazine's circulation. A typical example: If the average circulation of an industrial publication is 40,000 and a full-color ad costs $1,800, the price per reader impression is only 4.5 cents. Yet this low cost is

---

[8]*Laboratory of Advertising Performance,* (New York: McGraw-Hill, 1955), p. 1045
[9]"Buying influences vary by type of product," research report, *Laboratory of Advertising Performance* (New York: McGraw-Hill, 1975) #1027.1.

understated. That's because not every single recipient of a magazine will read your ad. Some may never see it. Others may skip over it. Still others may simply be too busy to read the issue that month. However, even if we assume 80 percent readership per publication issue and further reduce that figure by half, we still end up with a reader impression cost of under 20 cents. On the other hand, the cost of a personal sales call to industry has been going up steadily. The average price is now over $100.

Advantages of a sales call	Advantages of an advertisement
1. Knowledgeable salespeople can display merchandise in person and also counter negative impressions.	1. Properly placed advertising messages can reach all or most of a company's prospects and customers quickly. Compare this to a full nine-hour sales day in which the industrial salesperson spends only three hours fifty-two minutes in actually selling (Figure 9-3).
2. Salespeople can interpret product and service features.	2. Advertising calls reduce information-distribution costs to pennies.
3. Salespeople can persuade and motivate prospects to buy now or in the future.	3. Advertisers control the message, so it is consistent.
4. Salespeople can adapt sales presentations to the needs of individual plants.	4. An ad provides information not covered by a personal sales call.
5. Salespeople physically get the order.	5. Ad messages lower selling time spent in a personal sales visit by predisposing prospect toward the product.
6. Salespeople ensure additional orders by acting as an on-the-spot source of service.	6. Printed messages build the reputation of the advertiser.
	7. Ads remind potential buyers of the product during the incubation period between arousal of interest and actual sale, estimated at up to two years.

This does not imply that salespeople are being overpaid. But salaries and commissions are related to what actually takes place during a full work day. It is here that we must make a distinction between "the oral and the printed word." The pie chart in Figure 9-3 sheds more light on the way an industrial salesperson spends a selling day. Note that industrial salespeople spend almost as much time in traveling from plant to plant and waiting as they do in face-to-face selling. Faced with this major limitation on personal selling, salespeople hope their companies will place advertising in appropriate industrial media. They know that advertising will reach most of their buyers within a week.

INDUSTRIAL ADVERTISING OBJECTIVES

If the industrial product has value, works consistently, and is priced properly, advertising helps to create and develop demand. Advertising works:

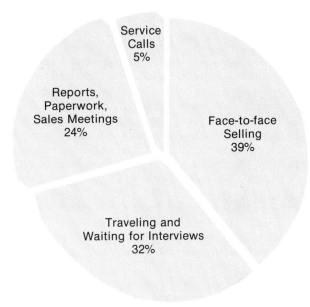

Figure 9-3
The average industrial salesperson is able to spend only about three hours and fifty-two minutes in face-to-face selling, less than 50 percent of the working day. This severely limits ability to contact all customers and prospects quickly. (Courtesy *Laboratory of Advertising Performance,* McGraw-Hill)

1   *To help sell a product or service.* This objective for an industrial ad, brochure, sales specification sheet, or catalog is self-evident.
2   *To help the sales force sell.* Industrial advertising paves the way for the sales follow-up. It creates a favorable image for the product and the company.
3   *To reach hidden buyers.* Industrial salespeople do not call on all the persons involved in buying their products because of time and other limitations. In a documented study of United States Steel's sales calls to one of its larger customers, there were many influential buyer decision makers who were not called on. Time simply would not permit it. Yet these people read magazines containing United States Steel ads.[10]
4   *To improve market position.* A competitor may increase or withdraw advertising for a variety of reasons. A company may increase its own ad budget in order to take advantage of a competitor's aggressiveness or lack of it. The competitor that stops advertising may lose *market share* to a consistent advertiser.
5   *To achieve recognition.* For advertising to achieve recognition takes time. Recognition usually results from an integrated program of ads and sales literature that promotes a brand, trade name, or trademark.
6   *To provide information.* Industrial publication readers eagerly seek information. Often their very business lives depend upon it. Ads that provide new information achieve good readership.
7   *To create a decided preference.* Informative ads and brochures presell and postsell sales calls. They create a decided preference. There is strong evidence that familiarity does breed business. (See Westinghouse Study, p. 310.)
8   *To produce inquiries.* Many companies advertise to solicit inquiries. Inquiries give them some idea of the attractiveness of their offers and tell whether anyone is reading their ads. Soliciting inquiries has the advantage of beginning the long,

[10]*An Evaluation of 1100 Research Studies on the Effectiveness of Industrial Advertising,* Arthur D. Little, Inc., American Business Press, Inc. (New York, 1971).

drawn-out sales process. Product development time from design to completion, for example, is a year and a half for over one-third of new products.

9 *To interest investors in the company's common stock.* Customers and prospects inevitably notice a company that advertises consistently. They begin to wonder about its future prospects, its sales, and its earnings, and whether they should buy its stock. It is quite possible that advertising designed to sell equipment could also recruit a new investing public.

10 *To recruit personnel.* Technically oriented people feel at ease with companies they know. In many cases, their only contact with a prospective employer will have been through that company's industrial advertising.

11 *To aid distributors, wholesalers, jobbers, and dealers.* These agents appreciate the manufacturer's advertising, which supports them in face-to-face meetings with buyers and helps them in locating prospects.

12 *To create a good image.* Not all companies rely on product advertising. Some use advertising as a means to improve the image of and build favor for the advertiser. We call this institutional advertising. Companies use it to register a corporate name or to influence top executives of other companies who may not be exposed to many trade papers.

Companies that have specific objectives for their advertising, as we've outlined, usually are able to concentrate on reaching these goals. Setting objectives keeps advertising specific and on target!

EFFECTIVENESS OF INDUSTRIAL ADVERTISING

To begin a meaningful discussion of advertising payoff—and that's what we mean by effectiveness—we need to know what advertisers expect. Some expect their advertising to return sufficient volume in sales to repay the cost of the product and the advertising many times over. Others are content with increased recognition of a brand or company name. Still others believe industrial advertising is effective if all it does is to take the edge off competition. No matter what the objectives are, one thing is clear. Those who believe in the effectiveness of industrial advertising back this belief with a supportive ad budget.

Yet, some powerful managers don't really believe in advertising. They have both implied and specific objections. In smaller companies, sales managers may consider advertising a threat to their job security. They feel that successful advertising will render them superfluous, although this fear is never voiced. Managers who feel this way seldom support the call for an aggressive ad budget. On the other hand, there are managers who do have specific reasons for cutting an ad budget. They may feel that the company needs to show greater profits and will "save" an entire quarter's ad budget. They may need operating capital, and it is easier to reallocate money than to borrow from a bank at extremely high interest rates. Management may argue that the money is needed elsewhere for a more important project such as new product development. And, finally, they may argue that the economic "fortune tellers" are gloomy. With no sales prospects out there, why advertise?

All but the final arguments above reflect management's doubts about advertising's ability to perform. What are the facts and counterarguments?

The Little Report

In a report to the American Business Press, an organization of business paper publishers, the Arthur D. Little Company evaluated 1,100 research studies on the effectiveness of industrial advertising and found that there is research evidence of the effectiveness of industrial advertising. Here are some pertinent conclusions.[11]

> (1) There is evidence that in certain situations industrial advertising acting as a partner to the personal sales call can generate sales more economically than the salesman himself. . . . This conclusion is based primarily on the following references: (a) Readership studies done by several American Business Press members, notably Chilton and Cahners, have repeatedly shown the growth in number of buying influences. (b) The U.S. Steel-Harnischfeger study showed the unsuspected number of latent buying influences in a particular situation. (c) The *Production* magazine study shows still further how difficult it is for the salesman first to *find*, second to *cover* all buying influences.

> (2) There is evidence that the cost per sales dollar can be reduced by proper allocation of funds between direct sales effort and industrial advertising.

> (3) There is evidence that companies which maintain their advertising in recession years have better sales and profits in those and later years.

> (4) Certain types of findings are 'ageless'. . . . Several of the studies quoted were done some years ago and subsequently updated (e.g., U.S. Steel-Harnischfeger and Buchen studies). The repetitions simply confirm the original findings.

> Thus, we come to the final conclusion that there is no overall formula that top executives can apply to determine when to increase and when not to increase the advertising budget. Nor is there a formula which can predict the return they can reasonably expect on a given advertising investment.

The U.S. Steel-Harnischfeger Study

In 1962, U.S. Steel approached the Harnischfeger Corporation in Milwaukee, Wisconsin. (Harnischfeger manufactures hoists and materials-handling equipment.) U.S. Steel wanted to study how well its industrial advertising was working with the steel buyers within Harnischfeger.

U.S. Steel identified all employees who influenced purchases of steel. Although salespeople from the steel company regularly called on fifteen

[11]Ibid.

members of Harnischfeger's management, the study uncovered an additional 150 people who directly or indirectly exerted buying authority. When U.S. Steel reviewed the circulation lists of seventeen industrial magazines in which its ads appeared, it learned that it was reaching every Harnischfeger official with buying influence. Furthermore, on the basis of the percentage of readers who fully read a specific ad, the total cost per publication sales call was 15 cents.

An update of this study in 1969 revealed that 181 persons were regularly reached by the steel company's advertising. Again, most of them had no contact with U.S. Steel's sales force. The cost per completed advertising sales impression was almost identical to that of the earlier study: 14.2 cents. U.S. Steel's conclusion: the business press is an extremely economical way of presenting its messages to those many who influenced buying but were not covered by the sales force.

The Westinghouse Study

Over the years, other studies have attempted to prove advertising's effectiveness. One of the best known was conducted by Westinghouse.[12] It arrived at these important conclusions:

1 Advertising directly influences how many people buy a particular brand of industrial equipment.
2 In the case of every product studied, and where there was a significant amount of advertising, the sales per dollar of advertising ran from a high of $154 to a low of $9.
3 There is a direct relationship between industrial buyers' attitudes toward a supplier and how many buyers select that supplier's products.
4 Buyer attitudes can be directly influenced by the industrial salesperson as well as by industrial advertising.
5 Industrial advertising is a profitable business investment.

INDUSTRIAL ADVERTISING BUDGETS

A company's philosophy will determine the amount of money set aside for the industrial advertising budget. Several methods exist for determining the size and apportionment of the budget. The newer methods include model simulation on a computer that "plays out" a series of situations based on past records, controlled advertising experiments, and variables such as competition, sales and profit patterns, and so on.

Another new method is field experimentation, an actual trial-and-error approach. Sets of objectives and varying budgets are set up for different states

---

[12]"How Advertising Helps Sell Industrial Products—A Westinghouse Measurement," (New York: American Business Press, 1975).

or regions. A uniform objective for each state is supported by a variety of budgets. The advertiser uses regional or statewide media only and monitors the results. A major problem in analyzing this method of budgeting is the difficulty of finding a comparable starting point for all the individual markets involved in the study. This poses real problems with the interpretation of the data.

Two more conventional budgeting techniques, the fixed or guideline method and the task method, are currently popular for both industrial and consumer-oriented products.

Fixed or Guideline Budgeting

The fixed or guideline budgeting technique comes in four familiar variations: fixed, guideline, percentage of sales, and per unit allocation. All are based on history. The simplest and least effective is a fixed budget, which remains the same year in, year out. The guideline method relies on past experience. For instance, a company will let its own experience dictate what percentage of gross sales to apply to advertising. This can fluctuate between 1 and 10 percent. Or, a company may use a guideline percentage developed by its industry. An accepted rule-of-thumb figure for many industries is 3 percent. In

TABLE 9-1

SUMMARY OF INDUSTRIAL ADVERTISING

(Percent of sales spent on advertising by product classification, average of reported cases, 342 companies, 1977).

Industry	Percent of sales
Lumber and wood products	0.1
Furniture	2.0
Paper	0.14
Printing and publishing	0.79
Chemicals and allied products	0.91
Petroleum	0.35
Rubber and plastic products	1.14
Stone, clay, and glass products	1.24
Primary metals industry	0.333
Fabricated metal products	1.35
Heating apparatus/plumbing	3.1
Fabricated structural metal products	1.24
Construction, mining, and materials handling	1.59
Metalworking and general industrial machinery	1.19
Office, computing, and accounting machines	1.26
Electrical machinery	1.2
Transportation equipment	0.6
Optical and measuring instruments	1.25
Electronic components	0.97

Source: "Percent of Sales Invested in Industrial Advertising Varies From Industry to Industry," *Laboratory of Advertising Performance*, McGraw-Hill Research, 1977, #8008.7.

TABLE 9-2

PERCENT OF SALES SPENT ON ADVERTISING
BY AMOUNT OF SALES

Amount of sales in millions of dollars	Median percent
Under 5	1.5
5 to 10	1.2
10 to 25	1.4
25 to 50	1.0
50 to 100	0.8
Over 100	0.5

Source: *Survey of 1976–1977 Advertising Expenditures and Budgets,* McGraw-Hill Research, 1978, p. 3.

this instance, no matter what happens to sales, the fixed 3 percent figure applies. If sales go up, then the number of advertising dollars go up proportionately. If sales drop, the ad budget drops. Either way, a company can overspend in boom times and underspend at a time when greater advertising impact is needed. Some companies use a per unit basis for setting their ad budgets, since this seems to indicate specific ad support for unit sales.[13] However, even though this method may please distributors and dealers, it is still based on past sales performance history. Compare the conservative industrial ad budgets in Table 9-1 to consumer budgets in Table 1-3.

Notice that primary metals, the steel industry, spends one of the smallest percentages of all groups listed. Does this mean steel producers are ignoring the marketplace? Not at all. They are among the most visible in the entire field of industrial advertising. U.S. Steel, for example, has sales of almost $9 billion. It's closely followed by Bethlehem Steel with nearly $5 billion.[14] Yet they spend less than 0.4 percent on advertising. On the other hand, giant consumer advertiser Procter & Gamble invests from 5 to 7 percent of its more than $6 billion in sales in advertising. The primary reason for the vast difference, of course, rests in the fact that P & G has many more competitors; it must reach everybody, whereas steel companies have a restricted marketplace. (See Table 9-2).

The Task Method of Budgeting

A slightly less popular conventional budgeting technique is task budgeting, by which a company allocates specific amounts to achieve specific objectives. If

[13]Example: company allocates 25 cents for every barrel of grease it sold the previous year. Anticipated sales are ¼ million barrels. Ad budget is $62,500.
[14]"50 U.S. Companies with large annual sales or revenue," New York Stock Exchange Research Department, *World Almanac & Book of Facts,* (New York: Newspaper Enterprise Association, 1977), p. 123.

the objective is to make 30,000 county engineers aware of a new waste disposal system, the advertiser estimates how much it will cost. The task method seems very reasonable, but advertising is not a science. The marketplace contains too many variables: new competition, material shortages, distributor changes, government regulations. Despite these, some companies feel this method is more responsive to the conditions of the marketplace.

Apportioning the Advertising Budget Each industrial company must, of course, look to its own operation to determine how to spend its budget. But a pattern has emerged among regular advertisers. For example, most companies that advertise regularly invest approximately 40 percent of their total ad budget in publication space. Catalogs, the next largest single item, account for 15 percent. Direct mail and trade shows both run at 8 to 9 percent each. The next largest sum, except for the cost of supporting the company advertising department itself, is the cost of producing all the advertising materials—6 percent. Companies who find there are no magazines or trade shows to reach their audiences will more than likely apportion the majority of their ad budget to catalogs and direct mail.

WHAT TO EXPECT FROM YOUR ADVERTISING DOLLAR

There are many benefits you can expect from your advertising dollars. Expect a heightened awareness of your company and its brands, of course. Expect a certain stature in the eyes of your competitors as well as of your own sales force. Expect that the overall sales costs will be reduced because good advertising helps the sales force sell more effectively. Also, companies that advertise seem to attract good personnel, good dealers, and good distributors. There is a further bonus. Advertisers enjoy a sense of loyalty among all the people financially supported by the company's promotional activities. These people—agency groups, media persons, and suppliers of engravings, typography, photography, and art—are all anxious for the advertiser's campaigns to succeed. To that end, they contribute what they can: their talents, their knowledge, and their information about the marketplace.

IN SUMMARY

1 Industrial advertising helps stimulate sales through its own specialized media.
2 The major intermediary between the manufacturer and the plant is the industrial distributor, who handles a related family of products within a given territory.
3 Some specialized distributors perform an engineering function for their customers.
4 Manufacturers who can't afford a salaried sales force may hire manufacturer's

representatives (reps) to call on customers. Reps work on a commission basis in specified territories.

5 Industrial buyers buy components and equipment according to the type of work they do in the plant: management, engineering, and purchasing. Engineering is fragmented into many job categories, each having its own basic interests.

6 There is a decided and dramatic difference between an industrial sales call costing over $100 and an advertising "sales call," which may cost no more than pennies per impression.

7 Industrial salespeople spend less than 50 percent of their working day in actual face-to-face selling. Most of their time is taken up with traveling, compiling reports, and attending meetings.

8 Unlike consumer advertising, which generally has a quick payoff, industrial advertising takes longer—up to two years in some cases.

9 Industrial advertising objectives are: to help sell a product, to help salespeople sell, to reach hidden buying influences, to improve market position, to achieve recognition, to provide information, to create preferences, to generate inquiries, to interest investors, to help recruit employees, to aid distribution, and to create a good image.

10 Westinghouse, among others, concluded that: (a) advertising directly influences the number of people who buy a particular brand of industrial equipment, (b) sales per dollar of advertising ran from a low of $9 to a high of $154, and (c) industrial advertising is a profitable business investment.

11 Industrial advertising budgets are generally set up on the basis of a percentage of gross sales or sales of a total number of units; approximately 40 percent of the industrial ad budget goes for publication space.

CASE STUDY   The Metal Disintegrator

What do you do if the drill you're using on an engine block production line snaps off and remains stuck in the hole? The answer to that question launched Fred Cammann into the business of making metal disintegrators. In essence, his machine literally "erases" the broken metal drill in the hole so it can be flushed, saving the expensive engine block. Although Cammann Manufacturing Company of Bay Village, Ohio, is a small business, its customers are mainly large manufacturers: makers of automobiles, construction machinery, and appliances. During the early years, the company depended mainly on manufacturer's representatives for its sales, in addition to its own factory sales force. Later, recognizing that salespeople can only see a few prospects a day, Cammann decided to invest in a consistent advertising program in order to increase the number of sales leads.

In 1970, the company allocated $20,000, the largest appropriation until that time, for advertising. The ad program had two major objectives: to increase company recognition among potential customers and to help its factory-based sales force sell machines.

According to vice president Mary Jane Cammann, "We had assumed that most production engineers in industry understood the function of our metal disintegrator and its value on a production line. When we discovered that this wasn't necessarily so because of frequent personnel changes, we switched from a product-oriented

When you buy a Cammann Metal Disintegrator, guess who else you buy?

Fred's our best customers' man. Always on-the-go.
His notebooks are filled with practical sketches and ways
to make Cammann Metal Disintegrators do *more* than you had
expected. While *you* were thinking of a dependable
Cammann to quickly remove broken taps, drills and reamers,
Fred was concerned with integrating it into your line.
To reduce parts handling. To maximize your profits.
Write about one of Fred's machines today and see what we mean.

CAMMANN MANUFACTURING COMPANY, INC.

27016 Knickerbocker Rd., Bay Village, Ohio 44140, U.S.A. (216) 871-9450

Fred Cammann
President

VISIT US AT THE IMTS '78 SHOW, CHICAGO, IL, SEPT. 6-15, BOOTH 2837

Cammann
METAL DISINTEGRATOR

FIGURE 9-4

Surprisingly, the president of this company *does* make service calls. In fact, it's that personal service that he wishes to stress in his ads. This small company's advertising program begins with basic sales literature before any publication space ads are run. (Courtesy Cammann Manufacturing Company.)

approach to one dramatizing the service we provide to back up each one of our machines. Many of the largest and most prestigious companies in the United States and the world have Cammann metal disintegrators on their lines."

The company's ad program begins with its basic literature: brochures and sales sheets designed for production engineers and distributed in the mail and at trade shows. The basic literature is necessary because engineers want to study features and specifications and to compare them with machines found in competitive literature. Without literature, industrial companies have no way (short of a personal sales call) to thoroughly inform prospects. With the literature program completed and available for inquirers, the company next schedules its publication space advertising. Through the years, favored magazines have been *Tooling and Production, Metlfax, Machine Tool Blue Book, Modern Machine Shop*, and *American Machinist*. These publications bring inquiries that the company follows up religiously, either by mail or in person. Publication space advertising is one of Cammann's major sales efforts. The second is appearances at all the important national machinery and tool shows. Thousands of potential customers attend the shows. Cammann takes this opportunity to display its disintegrator machines and to pass out publication ads and literature. Since nothing is static in industry, Cammann is constantly fine-tuning its media mix in order to arrive at the best and most effective combinations (Figure 9-4).

QUESTIONS NEEDING ANSWERS

1   What is the logic of preparing sales literature *before* the industrial ad program is launched in magazines?
2   Why is Cammann depending on its own factory sales staff instead of relying on manufacturer's reps? What are the advantages? What are the disadvantages?
3   Is it demeaning for the president of a company to be photographed on the top of a wooden packing crate (Figure 9-4)? Is this good advertising?

STUDENT PROJECT

Select any ad from any of the industrial publications used by Cammann. Bring a copy of it to class and be prepared to identify its target audience: purchasing, design engineering, production engineering, administrative. Is it possible that one ad may be directed at more than one target buying influence group?

QUESTION ABOUT THE PROJECT

In a recent issue of *Standard Rate and Data Service/Business Publications Rates and Data,* find the one-time cost of the ad you selected. What will you save if you purchase the same ad on a twelve-time basis?

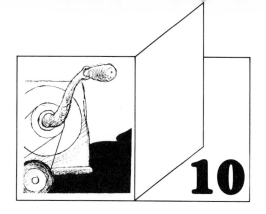

PROFILING
THE INDUSTRIAL
BUYERS

Update The average industrial purchase, whether made by the purchasing agent, engineer, or president, is worth at least $150,000 to the manufacturer. How do the industrial buyer's motivations compare to the household consumer's? And do the industrial buyer's psychological needs change between job and home?

Different industrial jobs require certain abilities, traits, and personalities. Engineers who design products, for example, work with new and substitute materials. Since their products face constant, daily competition in the marketplace, a major goal of the design engineer is to cut manufacturing costs without harming the product. Advertisers who want to attract design engineers might appeal either to their curiosity about how things work or to their practicality. To do this, they can effectively adopt the design engineer's own workday graphic techniques: photographs, sketches, drawings, and diagrams. The production engineer, on the other hand, oversees the transformation of assorted parts and raw materials into finished goods. These specialized engineers are less inclined to respond to creative or theoretical ideas. They are more apt to appreciate the practical.

Just these two examples should be sufficient to alert advertisers to the necessity of looking behind industrial titles. We know the psychological needs of industrial buyers vary depending on the roles they play in their plants. To communicate effectively with the many different industrial buyers, the advertiser should learn everything possible about their characteristics.

TYPES OF INDUSTRIAL BUYERS

Buyers in the Manufacturing Industries

Engineers who work for manufacturing companies also buy for them, directly or indirectly. Although their names may not appear on company purchase orders, they influence and help select materials and equipment. Some people refer to these "indirect purchasers" as buying influences. Others feel that when it comes to technical buying decisions, the engineers alone are the real motivators. For this reason, advertisers should be anxious to recognize the important differences among engineers.

Design Engineers We know that engineers who design goods share several characteristics. New and unusual machines and materials attract them. They are interested in cost- and time-saving ideas that they can include in their designs. They insist on reliability in components that they can substitute for other components to extend product life and reduce energy requirements. They are practical dreamers with one foot advancing into the future while the other is moored to the past.

Research Engineers Research engineers, in contrast, work more on theoretical problems, although they are also concerned with practical problems. The nature of their work requires imagination and curiosity. They read more than the popular industrial and business publications and are aware of the more advanced theories in their fields. Business needs these visionary engineers to introduce new products and applications. If the design engineer looks one year into the future, the research engineer looks five to ten years ahead.

Production Engineers The production engineer, on the other hand, oversees the transformation of assorted parts into finished products and their delivery to customer. Lost production or "downtime" are dirty words to a production engineer, whose job is to keep personnel and machinery operating efficiently. Production engineers like to read about equipment designed to cut costs and increase production, and they like complete information. Most produciton engineers recognize the seriousness of recommending a $100,000 machine for purchase. Production engineers have to be cautious. They can't make snap judgments.

Plant Engineers Plant engineers are likely to be among the older employees at a plant, because they are responsible for the physical soundness of the manufacturing facility. (Young engineers don't usually have the requisite years of experience). A plant engineer has many problems. Is the lighting adequate for efficient production? Does the roof leak? Are there slippery, dangerous floors? Are there other safety hazards? How can the company improve the environment of the plant and thus increase efficiency? If the plant has a buying committee to decide about purchases of costly equipment, the plant engineer is likely to belong. These all-around engineers respond well to ad copy like this from Robertshaw Controls:

> Energy savings in the first five months more than repaid the cost of two Robertshaw H 100 selector units for LaSalle Plaza. Added to the office tower's existing air conditioning system, the H 100s significantly cut the energy used by the air chillers.[1]

Project Engineers "Project engineer" can be a permanent or temporary title, and to further confuse matters, the job functions it describes may vary from one plant to the next. Project engineers work on one project—say the establishment or improvement of a manufacturing production line—and then go on to another. They supervise everything necessary to build and start the line, supervise its performance, and assume some of the responsibilities of both plant and production engineers until the line goes into full production. Then they go to another project. The job calls for diversified knowledge. Advertisers can best appeal to the project engineer by describing entire systems of economical interrelated equipment or by selling the end results.

[1]Ad: Robertshaw Controls Company, *Business Week*, November 14, 1977, p. 220.

Maintenance Engineers   The maintenance engineers are responsible for the upkeep and proper operation of existing machinery and equipment. They lubricate machinery, replace necessary suppliess, and in general keep equipment running properly. Often maintenance engineers move into their positions because they are both knowledgeable and skilled mechanics capable of assembling most of the machinery in the plant. Advertisements for this audience often describe proven, authenticated, efficient maintenance techniques that save money.

Most large industrial purchases are the result of committee buying decisions, and trying to determine the buying influence of each member is important for advertisers. Many companies, sad to say, never bother. An exception, Industrial Controls of Talley Industries, Inc., did it with some originality and skill.

> First, the advertising staff defined their markets by using current company sales records, field experience, and current market studies sponsored by a few business publications. This information helped to eliminate most of the major SIC groups except the three of the greatest importance. By concentrating on only three SIC groups, the ad staff eliminated over 82,000 manufacturing plants. However, that still left over 40,000 plants, far too many for the small sales staff to handle effectively. Enlisting the sales staff's help, the ad staff made further eliminations. These were based on choosing only the types of companies that presently account for over 90 percent of Industrial Control's sales. Noting, too, that the great majority of present key sales accounts employ over 100 people, the ad department followed suit by eliminating all companies hiring under 100 people. Now the company had something it could control. These remaining companies became the potential key account group, and the sales force went to work discovering and recording key buying influences and their titles. The names serve the ad department both as a direct mail list and as a check against subscriber lists of prospective advertising media. From start to finish, the cost of determining these key buying influences was extremely modest.

Decision Makers in Distribution

Manufacturers who depend on industrial distributors look to the owners of these companies as the primary decision makers. The distributor's employees are usually of secondary importance, although this may not be true in large organizations. Owners usually decide whether to handle a product line and how much effort they will make to sell it. These owners are usually keen, financially wise businesspeople. Many are engineers themselves who have decided to substitute selling for the drawing board. They are primarily concerned with the profits they can earn from the reliability of a manufacturer's products. They are less concerned with the manufacturer's commitment to advertising.

Within the distributorship, buyers are charged with choosing and buying lines of related products such as nails, screws, bolts, hinges, doorknobs, and the like. These buyers choose products they believe their sales force can sell.

They are knowledgeable in their fields and are generally open to new products with good sales potential. Because distributors can't sell products they don't have, buyers are concerned with a manufacturer's ability to deliver consistently.

Another important group for the industrial manufacturer is the distributorship's sales force. Many are graduate engineers. They serve as technical and engineering consultants to their customers about the products they sell. They must be convinced of the value of a product or they won't sell it successfully. They look to the manufacturer for reasonable prices, informative sales literature, consistent advertising schedules, and occasional technical assistance. Like buyers, they expect goods to be shipped on time.

Decision Makers in Service Industries

Buyers of industrial equipment are also active in service industries. Service industries include companies made up of specialists who aid and assist manufacturers and processors. For example, oil companies do not generally do their own drilling; they hire professionals employed by service companies. Many factories and commercial buildings do not repair their own roofs; they hire professional roofers. Within service industries, we find a wide variety of professionals: food caterers, security personnel, truckers and railroaders and airline personnel, bankers, insurance and credit experts, construction and painting contractors, and many others. Market research companies and advertising agencies are also included within the definition. All these specialists exist for the service they provide. Those charged with buying or specifying are keenly interested in any equipment, system, or technique that improves service or makes it more profitable: a new rotary rig that drills a water well deeper and faster, truck headlamps that extend a beam of light an extra 25 percent along the road, an improved cafeteria service for the factory and office workers.

Like manufacturers, service industry companies are also concerned with liability claims when things go wrong: for example, a railroad delivering coal and chemicals derails in a populated community, a painting contractor fails to halt wholesale peeling of paint on a job, an oil tanker company contaminates beaches and harbors, and so on. Protection against accidents and product failures has become a major business expense for many service industries. Knowledge of this problem can help advertising strategists to plan their appeals to buyers.

PSYCHOLOGICAL MAKEUP OF THE INDUSTRIAL BUYER

The people who provide stability to industry can be classified in three categories: those mainly concerned with services and products, those concerned with research and analysis, and those concerned with the management of personnel. For all of them, company prosperity is *their* prosperity; company failure is *their* failure. When employees buy products that improve the efficiency, profitability, or safety of a plant, they earn praise from both their peers and management. Many companies, in fact, pay executives according to how well their departments meet profitability objectives. Thus, buyers are concerned with achieving departmental objectives and company goals.

Buyers also gain a sense of satisfaction in providing for consumer needs. When raw materials and component parts emerge at the end of a production line as refrigerators, stereos, and automobiles, the buyers as well as the assembly line workers feel a sense of importance. Maytag regularly capitalizes on this feeling in its consumer ads that feature Ol' Lonely, the Maytag repairman who never has any repairs to make.

The pharmaceutical industry has 24,000 scientists and support personnel who require more than $1 billion a year for their research and developmental activities. The industry invests that sum because it expects to earn a profit. But the employees are motivated by the personal satisfaction of doing something for others. Sometimes the desire to serve may actually outweigh all other reasons for operating a business.

Engineers are similarly motivated. Often they work on projects that require the active assistance of other engineers. They become interdependent; a team spirit prevails. Yet, surprisingly, pay is *not* the principal reason engineers work hard. Engineers work to accomplish a shared, meaningful objective with other employees. In a conference report, "Maintaining Professional and Technical Competence of the Older Engineer—Engineering and Psychological Aspects," it was reported that the psychological work needs of experienced engineers revolve around the following: (1) desire for personal achievement, (2) desire to contribute to the performance of the company, (3) a personal concern for excellence and technical competence (keeping up to date is a symptom), (4) desire for problem-solving tasks and challenging work assignments, and (5) desire for responsibility that is recognized by others.[2]

The conference report stresses that these opportunities for personal growth are actually *internal* rewards. There are also external ones: pay increases, promotions, favorable evaluations, bonuses, and trips. From this information, an advertiser could conclude that both internal and external rewards motivate engineers and color their buying habits. The advertiser's challenge is how to use this knowledge to sell goods and equipment.

VARIATIONS IN PRODUCT INTEREST

Some items enjoy greater demand and heavier use among industrial buyers than others. Although this situation is not unique to industry, it does definitely

---

[2]*Maintaining Professional and Technical Competence of the Older Engineer—Engineering and Psychological Aspects,* Conference Report, American Society For Engineering Education, So. Berwick, Maine, July 1973.

TABLE 10-1
PRODUCT INTEREST ANALYSIS OF READER INQUIRIES

Major product category	Editorial Average inquiry per item	Advertising Average inquiry per item
Materials	218.25	186.02
Shapes and forms	195.31	150.19
Finishes and coatings	199.13	270.09
Hardware	195.48	195.15
Electrical and electrical components	131.59	119.83
Hydraulic and pneumatic components	78.70	89.40
Mechanical components	141.35	113.40
Research and development equipment	165.26	111.62
Methods, processes, and services	618.07	144.50

(Courtesy *Product Design & Development Product Scrapbook*, #18, 1972, p. 25.)
Product Design & Development is a design engineering publication. Note the wide variance in reader interest between ads and editorials, as well as among major product groups.

limit the numbers of industrial buyers who show interest in any one product. Flow meters or hydraulic filters, for example, have less appeal to design engineers than do power transmission components. Lubrication devices generate far less excitement among all industry buyers—even maintenance engineers—than do bearings and motors. Advertisers need to pay attention to these variations in product interest, because numbers of ad inquiries as well as ad readership scores depend upon the reader's interest level. The number of business publication readers primarily interested in lubrication, for example, is usually quite low—perhaps no more than 25 percent. Since product interest usually goes along with the job functions of readers, advertising can often select the business publications best for their products by analyzing inquiry responses to their ads (Table 10-1). Many publications regularly provide advertisers with inquiry counts resulting from their ads and publicity. Magazine readership research firms also provide advertisers with interest level information.

COPING WITH THE INDUSTRIAL ECONOMY

So far, we've looked at some of the people who buy for manufacturing, distribution, and the service industries. We've considered their motivations and their product interest levels. At this point, it might be worthwhile to examine how these people react as buyers to the ups and downs of the business cycle.

When you decide not to buy a car because of unemployment or inflation or for whatever reason, the industrial sector of the economy suffers. When car sales drag, Ford's and General Motors' professional buyers cut back on their purchases. (Ford and General Motors also cut back on their labor force.) In quick reaction, the thousands of companies that sell industrial parts to Ford and General Motors also cut back on their purchases.

Another example: When farmers are hit by falling commodity prices and don't earn enough to pay for production of various crops, they stop buying farm machinery. The reaction is immediate. Farm implement manufacturers cut back on purchases of steel, tires, and batteries and often lay off workers who, in turn, don't buy consumer goods. The ties between the consumer and the industrial sectors of our economy are close.

What can advertising do to revive these lagging industries? Some manufacturers argue that it is foolish not to cut the advertising budget when people aren't buying. On the other hand, some argue that industrial companies should not cut their ad budgets during economic slowdowns. They reason that many companies suspend advertising during recessions, allowing advertisers who remain in the magazines even greater exposure and less competition.

National Acme, a prominent machine tool builder, decided to keep advertising up during a recession. Instead of cutting the ad budget, it increased it 30 percent, a daring maneuver in the face of general pessimism within the industry. While its competition reduced ad budgets, National Acme kept in contact with influential production engineers throughout the country. Its inquiry response in the first nine months over a like period of the previous year increased 93 percent. Many of these inquiries led to orders. Would National Acme do it again? Read what Dorsey H. Rowe, manager of advertising and sales promotion, machine tools, has to say: "By all means, yes, if I had the authority to do so. . . .You have to beat the bushes all the time for sales if you want to remain known when things get a little tougher . . . there is no other way to stay alive."

Yet logic dictates that companies must ultimately limit their advertising during a general slowdown with no end in sight. The problem is where to fix that budget limit. Smaller companies may cut advertising completely and allow larger competitors to gain an advantage.

There is no cut-and-dried rule on how to advertise when industry experiences an economic slowdown. But planners must always consider that the primary role of industrial advertising is to help salespeople sell. Even during the worst recessions, industries continue to purchase goods from someone. There is also evidence that buyers regularly notice advertising before they are aware of being in the market for a product. Newman and Staelin report that this habit of reading ads can substantially limit buyers' information searches when they are once again in the market.[3] Consistent advertising during recessionary times obviously benefits in these situations.

Here are some guidelines for advertising during an industrial recession:

1 Reduce or eliminate ads aimed at minor markets with weak, short-term sales potentials. In better times, you can try to make up lost ground with heftier budgets.

[3]Joseph W. Newman and Richard Staelin, "Multivariate Analysis of Differences in Buyer Decision Time," *Journal of Marketing Research*, May 8, 1971, pp. 192-198.

2 Maintain (or increase) concentrated advertising on major markets, your "bread and butter." One proven way is to weed out fringe-benefit publications and concentrate on the leaders. This provides impact where you need it most—among your best customers and prospects.

3 Repeat good ads previously run. This saves ad preparation money.

4 Explore the possibility of supplier companies' featuring your products in their ads.

5 Redouble publicity efforts at minimum costs to you.

6 Consider sharing ad space and costs with a related but noncompetitive product.

7 Analyze your media mix of publication space, direct mail, and sales literature in order to effect economies.

ADVERTISING IN A PERIOD OF SHORTAGES

Some marketing analysts believe that we are entering a period of recurring shortages brought on by the scarcity of various forms of energy as well as of raw materials. Companies dependent upon fuel oil, gas, or coal lose production time whenever they have to move from one form of energy to another. Costs for electric power increase whenever utilities convert from coal to oil or from oil to nuclear fuel. When higher costs result in restricted production, we experience shortages. In addition, whenever chrome and copper, among others, are in short supply, we see fewer products incorporating these materials. Under these conditions, the problem is: How can a seller turn down the order of a loyal customer because of shortages, while continuing to advertise the product? Won't those same buyers who have supported the product in the past be the first to turn away and seek another supplier? Advertising during a period of shortages, some marketers contend, merely rubs salt in the wound.

There are no easy answers to these problems. They are particularly galling because so many shortages are temporary. Often advertisers are unable to cancel their ads in time when they become aware of critical shortages that affect their products. At other times, when they do cancel their ads in time, the shortages go away.

Continuing studies have demonstrated that recognition of a manufacturer drops when advertising stops.[4] A purchasing agent for a manufacturer of maintenance chemicals said it bluntly: "I buy from someone who advertises . . . it spells quality to me. It's like going to the grocery store; you'll buy a brand of coffee because it is highly advertised, so you know the name, and you would not buy some off-brand you never saw advertised. I buy with confidence from people who advertise and I read their ads to see what they have to say."[5]

When advertising in a time of shortages, some advertisers openly discuss the problems in their ads and ask for customer understanding. Others switch

---

[4]"Recognition Increased with Advertising—Dropped when Advertising Stopped," *Laboratory of Advertising Performance* (New York: McGraw-Hill Research, March 1961), #1198.
[5]"Good Advertising Builds a Corporate Image," (New York: McGraw-Hill Research, November 1964), p. 4.

from product to institutional or image-building advertising in the belief it is better to be seen in the marketplace than to be absent. The image-building messages generally promote goodwill for the company without promoting specific products. For those who do stop advertising as they wait for shortages to end, the major concern is knowing when to resume.

WHERE BUYERS WILL BE IN THE 1980s

The first industries in the United States spread from the Northeast southward along the coast. A sales manager of the 1800s would have had a simple time describing where to find customers. During the late 1800s and early 1900s, the job became somewhat more complex, although mass production facilities were still concentrated in the northern states. Industrial sellers of the 1970s and 1980s have a very tough job. Target plants are dispersing throughout the country. Furniture making, once the exclusive province of the New England states, is no longer so concentrated. More plants are located in the South today than remain in the North. Some locate in the unlikeliest places. When the average industrial sales call costs over $100[6] and will more than likely continue to increase, sellers have to know where the industrial buyers are. Advertising planners must also know where the buyers are because their job is to support the personal sales effort, before and after the sales call.

The Bureau of the Census offers help; it tells where the top industrial markets are and where they will be. This information allows advertisers to concentrate on areas where most industrial purchasing takes place. The Census Bureau estimates that over 80 percent of industrial purchasing takes place in the top 100 industrial markets. Thus it makes sense for companies to mount their major marketing efforts there. Companies with a small sales force can further concentrate on the top twenty-five or fifty markets, reducing travel time and expense and maximizing sales.

A quick look around the country helps us to identify some of the changes that have taken place during the past ten to twenty years. Chicago continues to be the nation's largest industrial market, followed closely by New York and Los Angeles. However, new geographical contenders are cropping up: Louisville, Albuquerque, Phoenix, Dallas-Fort Worth, Atlanta, Spartanburg, South Carolina, and Springfield, Missouri. In some cases, industry follows people as they move from region to region and from state to state. In other cases, industries blaze the trail and are followed by former employees or joined by new recruits living in the region. Industry is spreading to the southwest and western states, to the South, and to the sparsely settled midwestern states. In fact, at no time in history have industries been so courted by states and chambers of commerce. The inducements are a plentiful labor supply, ample water, transportation, and—equally important—a liberal taxation philosophy.

[6]McGraw-Hill Research, 1978.

Transient Policy Makers

At the present, standard operating procedure is to locate the geographical headquarters of the buyers and reach them there with sales calls and advertising. But nothing remains static in industry, and a new group of buyers is developing. For want of a better name, we can call them "project teams" or "task force managers." They seem to have no permanent home base. They get together to solve specific short-term problems. Then they disband and assemble with others at another plant. These "transient policy makers" develop new organizational structures with their own relationships and their own loyalties. The challenge for advertising strategists is reaching these influential nomads on a timely and regular basis.

Companies with sensitive market research systems will more than likely be among the first to locate and profile these transient buying influentials of the 1980s. Computerized systems will maintain buyer profiles of important customers and prospects and keep a running update on *all* their perceived buying actions such as request for literature, prices, and other information. A computerized system will also keep track of transient addresses so no important groups of buyers on the job will remain out of reach of the seller.

The business media, too, will have a vital stake in reaching the important policy makers. Even more than that of industrial sellers, the media's very existence depends on ability to deliver editorial and sales messages into the right hands—of both fixed and mobile buyers. Media's job is made easier by computers. It may not be too long before business media provide special news updates—even on a daily basis—to sophisticated buyers by means of special computer terminals that produce "hard copy," computer-printed sheets. Advertising messages eventually will go along with this information. Some visionary sellers will begin to store a supply of ads and sales literature "on call" through media computer banks. Others are already investigating the possibility of special industrial cable television systems that can process, store, and circulate technical advertising information. It's a safe assumption that as long as buyers maintain their ties to advertisers with computer hook-ups, they'll never be too remote for periodic advertising sales calls!

IN SUMMARY

1 Design engineers are interested in cost- and time-saving ideas to include in their designs. They are attracted by new products and materials.
2 Production engineers are responsible for getting the finished product out the door. They are attracted to ads that promise production increases or savings.
3 The integrity of the entire physical structure of the plant and of all items apart from the actual production lines and machinery is the concern of the plant engineer.
4 Project engineers assume some of the responsibilities of both plant and production engineers during the time they are responsible for manufacturing a

new or revised product. Once this item has been successfully launched, they may go on to a new project.

5 Research engineers deal in matters of theory and practice. They work in the practical world of today and the theoretical world of tomorrow.

6 The prime responsibility of maintenance engineers is to keep machines and equipment running efficiently. Ads directed at them do best when they describe ways to make their jobs easier and more effective.

7 Industrial buyers carry a wide assortment of job titles that may not accurately describe all their true job functions.

8 The buying influentials within industrial distributorships are usually owners of the business. In larger distributorships, buyers may segregate themselves according to types of products they buy.

9 Companies and individuals within service industries exist to provide assistance to industry.

10 Advertisers recognize that the psychological needs of engineers on the job include a desire for personal achievement, excellence, and responsibility, plus a need to be challenged by work assignments. In addition to these internal needs, there are some major external ones: pay increases, promotions, favorable evaluations, and extra benefits.

11 Advertising planners should be aware that not all industrial products carry the same level of interest for industrial buyers.

12 Industrial and consumer sales activity are interdependent; slowdowns in one affect the other.

13 Readership studies show that when advertising stops, recognition of the manufacturer's name drops.

14 Industries in the past ten years have been expanding and moving to the South and Southwest. Over 80 percent of all industrial purchases are made by plants within the top 100 markets. Chicago remains industry's top market.

15 A fast-growing, fast-moving group of new buying influentials called "project teams" or "task force managers" may play a vital part in the industry of the 1980s.

CASE STUDY Locating the Market for Plastics Machinery (Cincinnati Milacron)

The Plastics Machinery Division of Cincinnati Milacron makes machines that process plastics from raw resins to finished parts and products. From the toothbrush to the toaster to the telephone, from plastic pipe and siding to moldings in industries such as transportation, communication, recreation, toy manufacture, packaging, construction, and furniture making, there are machines that work amazing transformations in plastic. Just about everyone who processes plastics knows Milacron. Yet its fame didn't come about by chance. It all began with machine tools back in 1884. From that time to this, the company has been among the leaders in the machine tool industry. Its knowledge in precision machine design and control gave it a real advantage when the company moved into plastics machinery production in 1968. In just ten short years, Milacron

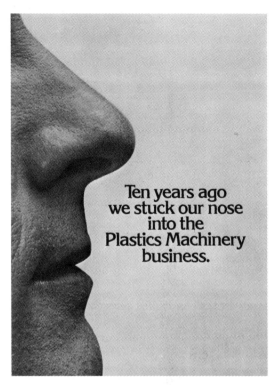

Ten years ago
we stuck our nose
into the
Plastics Machinery
business.

FIGURE 10-1
Plastics processing machinery is bought by a wide variety of companies in automotive, appliance, electronics, packaging, household goods, and recreational markets. Ads and literature must appeal to managers as well as to engineers.

Today we know the   sweet smell of success.

And we couldn't have done it without you.
It seems like only yesterday we put our nose into the plastics machinery business. And, in many ways, it was. Because, thanks to the support of our fine customers, in just ten short years we've become the industry leader. And the same kind of encouragement that got us where we are today will take us even further tomorrow.

You've helped make us #1 in Plastics Machinery.
You see, it takes a lot of good people from both sides for a company to achieve the kind of growth we've experienced.
And it's only the beginning.
Because we intend to continue to search for new and better ways to serve you. To anticipate your needs. And to provide the kind of leadership that'll keep the sweet smell of success around for both of us in the future.

Thanks.
The way we see it, we're pretty fortunate. We've got hard-working, dedicated employees. We've got supportive customers like you. And that's what it takes to be #1. **CINCINNATI MILACRON**

4165 Halfacre Road, Batavia, Ohio 45103. Tel. (513) 724-7001

became the number-one company in the field, selling more than $100 million worth of machines worldwide each year. How did the company go about finding the buyers of plastics machinery? John Ligon, Supervisor, Marketing Communications, tells us.[7]

> We do not attempt to develop any profiles or stereotypes to describe potential buyers. Plastics processing machinery is bought by companies in every imaginable SIC [Standard Industrial Classification], with predictable concentrations in automotive, appliance, electronics, packaging, household goods, and recreational markets. Regarding geographical breakdown, our markets follow the trends of light- to medium-duty manufacturing, which means the established manufacturing belt from Massachusetts to Illinois, a separate market following the entire West Coast, some growth in the Sun Belt, plus the surprising Corn Belt market in the Iowa-Nebraska-Kansas area.
>
> Regarding psychological needs, we want to assure our customers that we won't ever let them down. Many managers don't know the nuts-and-bolts end of the business and are more afraid of being caught in a mistake than of missing an opportunity.
>
> During recessions, we do curtail our advertising exposure to a maintenance level. With money short, few companies will be buying, which means a slim return on investment on the ad dollar. Also, the various company functions must each build a case for their share of a shrinking budget dollar, and in a showdown between production and advertising, guess who wins?

During normal times, Milacron seeks out and supports its widely separated geographical markets with consistent advertising in the following business publications: *Modern Plastics, Plastics Machinery & Equipment, Plastics Technology, Plastics World, Ward's Auto World.* See Figure 10-1

To promote its new specialized line of machines for making plastic soft drink bottles, Milacron advertises in *Beverage Industry, Beverage World, Food & Drug Packaging,* and *Packaging Digest.*

QUESTIONS NEEDING ANSWERS

1 Why do you think it took a short ten years for Milacron to become the leading company in the plastics field? Explain.
2 What Standard Industrial Classification (SIC) numbers are assigned to automotive, appliance, electronic, and packaging manufacturers?
3 What are machine tools, and what kinds of industries are interested in them?

STUDENT PROJECT

In a recent issue of either *American Machinist* magazine or *Iron Age* magazine, select several ads that reflect the writers' knowledge of the needs of

[7]Letter: John Ligon, Supervisor Marketing Communications, Cincinnati Milacron, November 22, 1978.

the production engineer as well as those of the maintenance engineer. Could any of the ads have some interest for the purchasing agent? Explain.

QUESTIONS ABOUT THE PROJECT

1 Does it make sense for a company to advertise maintenance equipment in a magazine read by production experts?
2 What can you learn about the buying influentials who read *Iron Age* when you look over the circulation breakdown listed in *Standard Rate & Data Service/ Business Publications*? Compare its circulation breakdown to that of *American Machinist*.

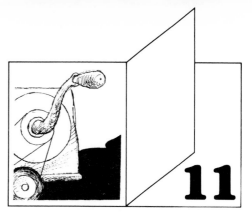

BUSINESS MEDIA SELECTION

Update In the last chapter on business advertising, we examined the job functions and interests of individual buyers. Industrial advertising strategists must learn how to reach these buyers. In this chapter, we will discuss how best to choose business publications, a large class of industrial publications. Professional and trade publications will be discussed in other chapters.

By *business media* we mean magazines, a few specialized newspapers, company house organs, and directory-references. These are the communication vehicles that carry the ideas and sales messages of business and industry to buyers. They serve to draw buyers and sellers together because of their special appeal to business persons. Without their editorial material, many business people would lose valuable insights into their areas of specialization as well as vital information for improving individual job performances. The major cost of publishing business media (with the exception of the company house organ) is borne by advertisers, who select each publication according to the type of business reader it attracts.

Not all industrial companies use all the available business media, but most do use some. In addition to magazines, some companies also consider direct mail, sales literature, and even films and slide shows as business media. But these are created exclusively for the advertiser and generally lack the element of objectivity found in bona fide media.

However, there *is* a direct relationship between the effectiveness of of the business media for advertisers and the availability of industrial sales literature. The relationship follows a practical sequence of industrial advertising commitments: sales literature first, directory references second, and publication advertising third.

Since the sales force does the selling, it should start calling on plants right away. As sales support, salespeople need: (1) sales literature such as product descriptions and specification sheets; (2) illustrative brochures that present features, benefits, and important product details; and (3) company catalogs that describe groups of related products for sale.

Manufacturers should prepare sales literature before they run any publication advertising. Then they can respond to requests for information from people who have seen the ads. Without ready literature, manufacturers have only unsatisfactory alternatives. The sales force won't make widespread contact for weeks. Individual letters are time-consuming and often a poor substitute for literature. Advertisers can apologize to inquiring readers and promise to send literature. But none of these responses builds sales or develops customer confidence.

Directories and reference books are the advertiser's next media commitment. These books include *Thomas Register of Manufacturers* and *MacCrae's Blue Book*, among others. Such annual directories, indexed lists of industrial suppliers, are usually kept in the purchasing agents' offices. Manufacturers advertise in them because purchasing agents all over the country refer to them repeatedly. Most ads are merely itemized lists of equipment. There is nothing fancy or psychologically moving about them. Small advertisers particularly like to advertise in annual buyers' guides because they reach a wide, diversified audience at a modest price and remain available for at least a year. (Figure 11-1). Many larger companies first learned about the power of advertising through inquiries from these specialized annuals that cover diverse fields such as machine tools and electrical goods and job functions like purchasing and engineering.

Once represented by sales literature and listed in the advertising pages of specialized annuals, the manufacturer can make the next logical media commitment—to the weekly and/or monthly business publications, themselves a veritable smorgasbord of special interests. These business publications do more than merely list equipment; they expand and dramatize an

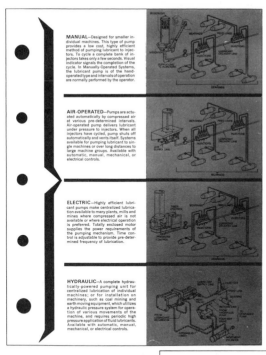

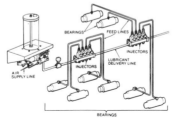

FIGURE 11-1

Industrial advertisers follow a logical advertising sequence. Sales literature is first as represented by this lubricating systems sales sheet. Then comes the scheduling of directory and publication ads. When print ads appear, the literature will be available to inquirers.

advertiser's offerings using all the professional techniques of printed logic and persuasion.

TYPES OF BUSINESS PUBLICATIONS

Business publications include business, trade, and technical magazines. This chapter will consider only those magazines devoted to business, industry, and construction. (We'll discuss trade and technical magazines in later chapters.)

A business publication is one dealing with management, manufacturing, sales, or operation of industries or some specific industry, occupation, or profession and is published to interest and assist persons actively engaged in the field it covers.[1]

The business press serves many functions. It alerts readers to the availability of new machinery, markets, processes, and inventions. It interprets the significance of new technologies. It presents theories and pros and cons and serves as a platform for readers to express opinions. The business press serves as an unofficial voice of an industry. The physical appearance of publications within the business press is strikingly different from that of consumer publications. Covers show heavy pieces of equipment, operators at the controls of bulky machinery, and often diagrams and flow charts. Static and uninspiring as these covers may appear to the general public, they do serve to attract industry's specialized readers.

Not everyone who works in industry, construction, or business receives a business magazine, because the various circulation departments exercise controls over recipients. For example, there are over 500,000 machinists and machine tool job setters employed by American industry.[2] Yet *American Machinist* and *Tooling and Production*, two major industrial magazines of interest to these workers, carry no more than 70,000 subscribers. These magazines do so because their publishers need to demonstrate to advertisers that their respective subscribers exert a buying influence in their places of employment (Figure 11-2). They justify this action because advertising rates are based on circulation. Companies would not advertise if readers were not in a position to buy or recommend the purchase of advertised products.

Business people read the business press for information about a specific industry or job. They receive business magazines weekly or monthly, and many think of them as continuing educational programs. The magazines provide news about the industry; about other companies' products, processes, ideas, and equipment; editorial reflections on current problems; and of course, an outpouring of advertising, often as popular as the editorial material.

[1]Audit Bureau of Circulations *Bylaws and Rules*, Edition AH, January 1968, p. 51.
[2]Employment and Training Report of the President, U.S. Department of Labor, 1976, p. 161.

83B. MANUFACTURING/INDUSTRIES, EQUIPMENT, PRODUCTS & SYSTEMS

(Also see Plant—Engineering & Plant Operations.)

New Equipment Digest

Where Industry Comes To Shop

A Penton/IPC Publication

AUDITED

Industrial Bulletin
Industrial Equipment News
New Equipment Digest

NON-AUDITED

American Industry
Business & Industry
Delaware Valley Business Magazine
Equipment Reporter
Industry's Products & News National
  Engineering & Maintenance Show Daily
  Plant
Michigan Plant & Equipment
Smaller Manufacturer, The
Wisconsin Industrial Product News

84. MARITIME, Marine, Shipbuilding, Repair & Operating

AUDITED

Marine Engineering/Log
Maritime Reporter and Engineering News
Motor Ship, The*
Ocean Industry
Offshore*
Waterways Journal
Work Boat, The

NON-AUDITED

Great Lakes Red Book
Inland River Record
Marine Catalog Buyers Guide
May Day Pictorial News
Seaway Maritime Directory
Seaway Review
Wold Dredging & Marine Construction

85A. MATERIALS HANDLING & Distribution

(Also see Industrial Distribution, Motor Trucks & Accessories, Physical Distribution, Transportation, Traffic, Shipping & Shipping Room Supplies.)

AUDITED

Handling & Shipping Management*
Industrial Engineering*
Material Handling Engineering
Modern Materials Handling
Traffic Management*

NON-AUDITED

Material Handling Engineering Directory
  & Handbook
Material Handling Product News
Western Material Handling/Packaging/
  Shipping

EDITORIAL STAFF
Jane Young Wallace, Editor-in-Chief
Betsy Raskin, Executive Editor
Steven M. Weiss, Food and Beverage Editor
Madelin Schneider, West Coast Editor
Judith K. Wiley, Senior Editor
Jacqueline Rance, Production Editor
Hilary Green, Feature Editor
William Marks, Feature Editor
Sylvia Riggs, Feature Editor
Elisa Tinsley, Products Editor
Robyn Wisher, Feature Editor
Liz Adams, Editorial Assistant
Nila Giles, Editorial Assistant
Peter Rigney, Field Editor

Julie R. Woodman, Editorial Analyst
Russ Carpenter, Consulting Editor
Eulalia C. Blair, Consulting Editor (NYC)
Alta B. Atkinson, R.D., Contributing Dietitian
Elizabeth B. See, Ph.D., Consulting Editor
Gwyneth Lackey, Newsletter Editor

GRAPHIC SERVICES
Antonios Pronoitis, Director of Art Department
Karen Carlson/Hansen, Art Director
Rosalie Wax, Staff Artist
Paul Nelson, Staff Artist

SERVICE STAFF
Ed Christ, Circulation Director
Ronald Walinder, Director of Advertising/
  Production
Susan Waxler, Production Manager
Karen Hallberg, Awards Program Manager
Liz Adams, Awards Program Assistant Director

MARKETING AND RESEARCH
Ed Karlins, Marketing Research Director
Michael Engdall, Marketing Director
Karen Hallberg, Marketing Services

SERVICE WORLD INTERNATIONAL
205 E. 42nd St., Suite 1501, New York, N.Y. 10017
Phone: 212/949-4377
Fergus McKeever, Publisher
Julie R. Woodman, Editor

FOODSERVICE EQUIPMENT SPECIALIST
Paul Considine, Publisher
Russ Carpenter, Editor
Barbara Behof, Managing Editor
Larry Natta, Assistant Editor

FOODSERVICE DISTRIBUTOR SALESMAN
Audrey Garvey, Editor
Ronald Fink, News Editor
Bruce Srachta, Feature Editor

William M. Woods, Administrative Vice President
Paul Considine, Associate Publisher (NYC)
David Sisk Wexler, Publisher

EDITORIAL OFFICES: Chicago—5 S. Wabash Av., 60603. Phone: 312/372-6880. New York—Suite 1815, 205 E. 42nd St., 10017. Phone 212/949-4373. West Coast—5915 Corbin Ave., Tarzana, Calif. 91356. Phone: 213/345-0300.

FIGURE 11-2

Some of the over 3000 magazines listed in the advertisers' bible, *Standard Rate and Data Services/Business Publications*. The numbers refer to "market service classifications," which divide and categorize the large, soft-cover volume. Advertisers who know their general target market can select specific magazines from these classifications.

FIGURE 11-3

An organizational description of a business publication that serves readers employed by restaurants, hotels, motor hotel chains and franchise headquarters, and school and college restaurants. Among its many services to advertisers and readers, it provides editorial reprints at reasonable prices.

Vertical and Horizontal Publications

Industrially oriented magazines are divided into two main categories: verticals and horizontals. *Vertical magazines* cater to a single major industry. For example, *Textile World* is a vertical magazine. It reaches the maintenance engineer within a textile mill, the supervisor of a spinning room,[3] the president of the mill, and many others in the textile market. Thousands of different job functions within the industry are tied together by the communications and graphic skills of the publication's editors. *Oil and Gas Journal* is another vertical publication. It covers the industry from exploration and drilling to transporting gas and oil through pipelines. Typical advertised products may interest all or only a segment of readers. Yet, advertisers find this and other vertical publications the most effective way to generate new business.

A *horizontal publication* crosses over into many industries but defines itself by appealing to people with a certain job. For example, *Tool Engineering* primarily appeals to people who supervise drilling, cutting, and shaping materials such as aluminum and steel. Tool engineers for an automobile manufacturer read it as avidly as tool engineers for an appliance manufacturer. Naturally, advertising in *Tool Engineering* and other horizontal publications reflects the interests of the magazines' readers. Typical advertisers in *Tool Engineering* are companies who manufacture drills, bits, and holding tools as well as auxiliary equipment.

Many manufacturers study the editorial content of several possible magazines to advertise in. This is a good approach. The advertiser can study several issues of a magazine to spot trends and gauge reader interest. The advertiser should also ask questions. Do competitors use the magazine? How many advertisers are there in all? Who are they? Does the magazine look artistically and editorially professional? These are important questions because the prestige of a magazine and that of its advertisers are often interrelated and mutually beneficial. By and large, horizontal and vertical publications make up the most prestigious members of the business press.

Regional Publications

Regional publications are very specialized, smaller-circulation business magazines and papers. They may be horizontal or vertical, but they appeal to a limited geographical audience. These publications are the industrial counterparts of the regional consumer publications or city magazines, although they have smaller circulations than consumer magazines. For example, *The Detroit Purchaser* is a horizontal publication for purchasing agents around Detroit; *Arizona-New Mexico Contractor and Engineer*, a vertical publication, is for people in road construction in those two states. Because of their small circulations, regionals generally charge low advertising

---

[3]In a spinning room, fibers are given required twist, firmness, and strength on automatic machines.

rates. Lower rates permit even the smallest companies and distributors to advertise.

ORGANIZATION OF A BUSINESS PUBLICATION

Most business publications start with a base of four departments: editorial, circulation, production, and sales. Individual magazines may have other departments according to the publisher's interests and ambitions.

The *editorial* department includes everyone from a field editor, who tracks down stories, to the editor-in-chief, responsible for the textual and graphic totality of the magazine (excluding the advertising). The editorial staff write the magazine. Some editors have technical or professional training. From the advertiser's viewpoint, the magazine's editorial content is the most important consideration. It makes or breaks the magazine (Figure 11-3).

The *circulation* department builds and maintains a list of readers, a difficult undertaking in this age of worker mobility and stiff competition from similarly oriented publications. Some readers will read only one or two publications, and so the weakest magazine in a field of three or more has difficulty keeping an active, loyal circulation list. Many publications have computerized their circulation lists to keep pace with rapid changes within industry: one of five persons changes some aspect of job function each year. The purchasing agent retires, the production engineer moves up to vice president, the president becomes chairperson of the board, the design engineer leaves to take another job, and so on. Circulation must be aware of all of these changes in order to keep the mailing list current. Since business publications are not sold at newsstands, circulation also has the job of promoting the value of the magazine to its readers. The department does this primarily through direct mailings.

The magazine *production* staff oversees the actual physical preparation and manufacturing of the publication and its delivery on time to all readers. Often, when advertisers need special effects such as inserted postcards or samples, the production staff works closely with them.

The responsibility of the *sales* staff is to bring in the advertising dollars that support the magazine. These salespersons, called "space representatives" or simply "reps," are reservoirs of industry information. Many advertisers discover that space reps supply them with new business insights and marketing data not readily accessible. They provide information about copy testing, mailing lists, and mailing services provided by the publisher. They pass along valuable advertising successes of other manufacturers, circulation demographics, and cost per thousand reader analyses. In short, space reps are the business contacts between the magazine and its advertisers. In many instances, their contributions actually improve the caliber of a manufacturer's advertising.

BUSINESS AND INDUSTRY	TOTAL QUALIFIED COPIES	PERCENT OF TOTAL	CLASSIFICATION BY TITLE			
			General Management: Presidents, Vice-Presidents, Secretaries, Treasurers, General Managers, Owners, Partners, Proprietors and other Officials	Supervisory: Managers, Superintendents, Supervisors, Foremen and other Supervisory titles	Engineering: Power Engineers, Chief Engineers, Mechanical Engineers, Electrical Engineers, Resident Engineers, Maintenance Engineers, Master Mechanics, Chief Electricians and Other Engineering and Maintenance Executives and Engineers	Other titles
Investor Owned Utilities	12,729	27.0%	531	5,042	6,061	1,095
Government Utilities	2,157	4.6	33	784	1,179	161
Municipal Utilities	1,593	3.4	108	939	464	82
Rural Electric Cooperatives	478	1.0	59	264	121	34
Sub-Total Utilities	16,957	36.0%	731	7,029	7,825	1,372

FIGURE 11-4
Two competitive magazines aimed at the electric power industry. Publishers provide the answers to the listed items. An independent auditing firm—in this case BPA (Business Publications Audit)—checks the accuracy of the information. Compare job function classifications.

BUSINESS AND INDUSTRY	TOTAL QUALIFIED COPIES (*Full Run)	PERCENT OF TOTAL	+Energy Generation (See Note 1)	Multiple Energy/ Generation & Transmission Distribution (See Note 1)	+Transmission/ Distribution (See Note 1)	CLASSIFICATION BY PRIMARY JOB FUNCTION					
						General & Corporate Management (A)	Engineering; Systems, Planning & Design (B)	Operations, Including Construction & Maintenance (C)	Purchasing & Stores (D)	Commercial (E)	Other Qualified Functions (See Note 1)
1. Electric Utilities											
a. Investor-Owned Electric Utilities ...:........	28,477	67.7%	6,999	7,612	13,866	3,596	12,038	9,747	1,112	443	1,541
b. Municipal Electric Utilities	3,471	8.3	458	988	2,025	757	1,114	1,252	176	40	132
c. Rural Electric and Other Electric Cooperatives	2,326	5.5	92	265	1,969	805	562	668	187	24	80
d. Federal Power Agencies, Systems and Projects	1,883	4.5	853	577	453	119	1,151	483	49	5	76
e. Other Publicly Owned Electric-Utilities including State Agencies and Districts	968	2.3	212	315	441	158	392	303	46	11	58
Total to Electric Utilities	37,125	88.3%	8,614	9,757	18,754	5,435	15,257	12,453	1,570	523	1,887

The typical business publication also provides additional services to advertisers: market research of the industry and readers, reprints of articles available for direct mailing, analyses of inquiry and sales leads. It is also an accepted fact in the business community today that business publications provide some of the best research data available from any source, private or public.

Analysis of Circulation

When manufacturers buy advertising space in business publications, they hope they're reaching large, interested audiences capable of buying what they have to sell. It helps to know whether the publications are audited or nonaudited. *Audited* magazines depend on independent, outside agencies to verify their circulations. These agencies are like those who audit consumer publications. (Several, in fact, audit both consumer and industrial publications.) *Nonaudited* magazines rely on other means of providing the advertiser with proof of circulation. These may take the form of sworn publishers' statements or declarations from private accounting firms unrelated to publishing. Because advertising rates depend directly on how many readers receive the publications, some advertisers will only schedule ads in publications audited by any of the following: Audit Bureau of Circulations (ABC), Business Publications Audit (BPA), Office of Certified Circulation (OCC), Verified Audit Circulation Corporation (VAC), and Canadian Circulations Audit Board (CCAB). Each year these auditing groups examine and verify the circulation statements of their member magazines.

An audit details the composition of the circulation: job titles, specific industries served, renewal rates of readers, and so on. With this information, an advertiser can compare competitive publications. (Unfortunately, not all audited information is directly comparable among competitors. Discrepancies in preparing the audit exists and have not been resolved). (Figure 11-4).

Media Comparability Council (MCC) Media Data Form

Because of discrepancies among the various auditing forms, industrial advertisers had earlier developed one of their own. It differed from all others in that it allowed a media buyer to evaluate and compare competitive magazines on an equal basis. This form (once called the AIA[4] Form) has evolved into *The Media Comparability Council (MCC)* made up of buyers and sellers of business and professional publication advertising. Its form provides required information in a standard, concise, and convenient format. The forms are filled out by the publishers and sent to the MCC where they are validated and filed. Validation is not in any way an audit. The only policing or verification comes from the publisher's competition, who reads the forms. If publishers disagree with the data submitted, they can register their complaints with the MCC, who will react. (Figure 11-5).

Item 12 of the MCC form is typical. It asks about the place to which the magazine is delivered: home, business establishment, or other. It also asks for the numbers of copies delivered to each of these places. Some media buyers may want a magazine that is delivered to the buyer's home where there are no disturbances or interruptions. Other media buyers may prefer delivery at a plant where the magazine can be passed around to several readers. Regardless of how media buyers interpret the data in Item 12, or any other item, the point is that the MCC form clearly presents a mosaic of information in a standardized and comparable arrangement.

---

[4]The Association of Industrial Advertisers (AIA) is now the Business/Professional Advertising Association.

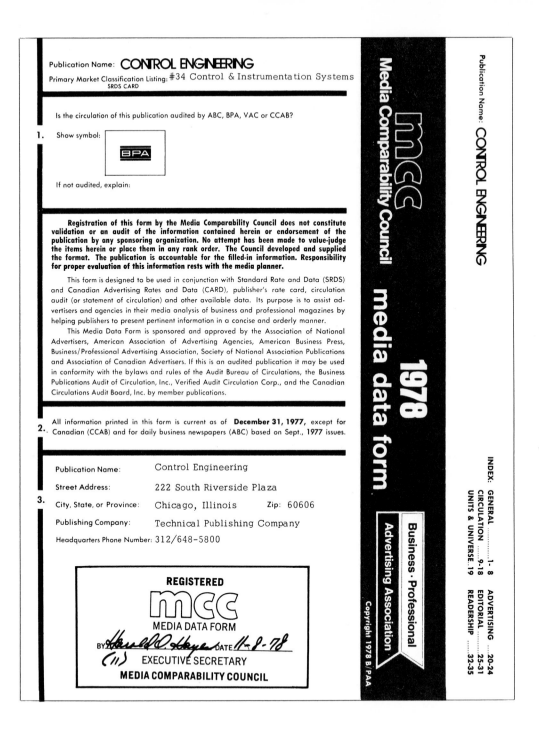

FIGURE 11-5

The MCC Media Data Form asks about editors' experience, advertising rates for the past five years, inquiry-producing capabilities, and reader enthusiasm for editorial reprints among its major 35 questions. The form is accepted by advertisers because it allows for accurate comparisons among publications.

Paid Versus Controlled Circulation

Once most readers paid for their industrial magazines, and that system provided good feedback about how valuable readers found the magazine. When newcomers began to offer their magazines free, the established publications began to experience renewal problems. Even though there are still "paid" magazines, a new kind of circulation has evolved. The new circulation system is *controlled circulation*. Under this arrangement, publishers send magazines free to *selected* recipients. To remain on the circulation list, recipients must be buying influences. Value in the form of interested buyers is what the publishers promise the advertisers. Value is what the advertisers pay for.

Business publications have greatly increased in number since advertisers accepted the controlled circulation philosophy. Now it is not unusual for individual plants to receive ten to twenty separate publications aimed at different job functions: *Iron age, Tool Engineering, Welding Engineer*, and the like. Because no individual can read them all and still do a job, many readers restrict themselves to one or two publications. The trick for the advertiser is to discover which are the favorites, not which are paid or controlled.

Inquiry Publications

Seizing on the fact that new products are very interesting to industrial readers, publishers have developed a tabloid-size ($11\frac{3}{4} \times 14\frac{3}{4}$ inches) "inquiry book." From front to back, its editorial material and advertising concern new equipment and new products, usually arranged in one-ninth-page units. The outstanding characteristic of these tabloids is the number of inquiries they develop, hence the name "inquiry book." Readers flip through rapidly for headlines and photos that touch upon their specialties. *New Equipment Digest*, an inquiry book sent to over 62,000 diversified plants throughout the country, can return several hundred inquiries from a single one-ninth-page ad costing approximately $750. The same ad in a standard-sized publication might generate only thirty-five inquiries. Typical inquiry tabloids are:

New Equipment Digest—general industry

Mining & Quarrying—coal and metallic mining

Product Design & Development—design engineers

Industrial Machinery News—machinery for metalworking

American Metal Market—steel, metals, metalworking

Fleet Management News—motor trucking industry

School Product News—school equipment and materials

Water & Wastes Digest—water and sewer works

Soliciting inquiries is not necessarily the primary objective of every industrial ad. Yet inquiries tell advertisers whether their message is getting

FIGURE 11-6

One of the most popular and best-read inquiry publications in the country, *PD&D* is "must" reading for design engineers. Advertisers have discovered that the best way to get results in an inquiry book is simply to state what they have to sell. Some small-space ads return several hundred responses in a month.

across. To make it easy for readers to inquire, publishers of both conventional and tabloid magazines insert a "bingo" card into the back of the publications. This is nothing more than an oversized post card addressed to the publication. By simply circling a number identifying a specific news or ad item, the reader signifies interest. When the postage-paid card arrives at the publisher, it is processed through a computer, and the actual inquiry forms are sent on to the individual advertisers. (Figure 11-6).

STANDARD INDUSTRIAL CLASSIFICATION CODE

Media buyers often evaluate industrial publications by means of the government's *Standard Industrial Classification* Code (SIC). This code identifies each manufacturing plant in the nation according to what it makes. For example, SIC Group 22 consists of plants that make textile mill products. Group 38 identifies manufacturers of instruments and related products. Knowing the code can help advertisers narrow the field of possible magazine contenders for their ad dollars. For example, if advertisers are primarily interested in companies that manufacture instruments, they can request publications to provide exact subscriber totals of that specific SIC. But within each group SIC number, there are also additional numerical breakdowns to further qualify manufacturers. If advertisers want only aircraft flight instrument makers (SIC 381111), they will be asking publications for totals of those subscribers who are specifically listed under that six-digit identification number. The refined SIC six-digit code permits advertisers to fine-tune their selection of industrial publications to match their precise target audiences (Figure 11-7).

Industrial advertisers can use SICs in other ways. SICs can be useful for developing:

1 checklists to evaluate business publications according to reader job functions.
2 lists for periodic mailings.
3 sources of sales leads for the sales force.
4 customer profiles to assist distributors.

The first three items above are self-explanatory. But the last, using the SIC code as a sales tool to aid distributors, does require an explanation. Here's how it works. A manufacturer of heavy greases recognizes that its California distributor is a weak link. The sales or ad manager requests of the distributor a random sample listing, by name, of current customers. The sales manager requests the identical information from a strong distributor in another state. When both lists arrive, the manufacturer assigns an employee, armed with a descriptive SIC code book, to codify each company with an SIC number. Some industrial publishers provide this codifying service for a small fee to advertisers. Then the manufacturer only has to compare both distributors'

STANDARD INDUSTRIAL CODE	Titles of Industry Groups	TOTAL PLANTS employing 20 or more	TOTAL EMPLOYMENT in plants employing 20 or more	NUMBER OF PLANTS by employment size			OTHER PLANTS MAKING THIS PRODUCT	TOTAL PLANTS PRIMARY AND OTHER
				20 to 99	100 to 499	500 or more		
370292	R&D-TRAVEL TRAILERS AND CAMPERS	1	–	–	–	–	3	4
370295	R&D-TANKS AND TANK COMPONENTS	2	1,500	–	–	1	–	2
370299	R&D-TRANSPORTATION EQUIPMENT NEC	–	–	–	–	–	–	–
3711	MOTOR VEHICLES AND CAR BODIES	168	363,799	35	31	102	24	192
371111	PASSENGER CAR MANUFACTURERS	19	56,384	6	5	8	2	21
371112	PASSENGER CAR ASSEMBLY	47	175,766	–	3	44	2	49
371116	PASSENGER CAR BODIES	18	43,433	3	2	13	4	22
371121	TRUCK TRACTOR & TRUCK MANUFACTURERS	33	59,434	2	6	25	12	45
371122	TRUCK TRACTOR & TRUCK ASSEMBLY	8	18,450	–	2	6	5	13
371131	BUS COACH & FIRE DEPT VEHICLE MANUFACTURERS	36	5,971	22	11	3	10	46
371141	MILITARY VEHICLES EXCEPT COMBAT	7	4,361	2	2	3	7	14
3713	TRUCK AND BUS BODIES	319	40,302	231	73	15	116	435
371301	TRUCK BODIES	295	30,940	224	63	8	112	407
371305	COACH BUS AMBULANCE & HEARSE BODIES	24	9,362	7	10	7	20	44
3714	MOTOR VEHICLE PARTS AND ACCESSORIES	855	387,182	382	305	168	308	1,163
371413	AUTOMOTIVE RADIATORS & PARTS	30	15,678	15	10	5	6	36
371414	TRANSMISSIONS INC AUTOMATIC FOR CARS TRUCKS & BUSES	34	49,638	6	9	19	8	42
371415	UNIVERSAL JOINTS (AUTOMOTIVE)	15	7,086	1	9	5	6	21
371416	SHOCK ABSORBERS (AUTOMOTIVE)	12	14,795	3	3	6	4	16
371417	FUEL PUMPS WATER PUMPS (AUTOMOTIVE) EXC REBUILT	16	5,187	5	8	3	26	42
371418	CLUTCH DISC & FACING ASSEMBLIES (AUTOMOTIVE)	14	2,080	9	4	1	5	19
371419	BRAKE CYLINDERS BOTH WHEEL & MASTER (AUTOMOTIVE)	27	14,591	8	12	7	19	46
371421	NEW GASOLINE ENGINES (AUTOMOTIVE)	21	47,592	5	1	15	4	25
371422	EXHAUST SYSTEMS INC MUFFLERS & PIPES (AUTOMOTIVE)	73	16,938	31	31	11	18	91
371423	PASSENGER CAR TRUCK & TRAILER WHEELS	24	13,797	7	11	6	11	35
371424	CONVERTIBLE TOPS (AUTOMOTIVE)	1	100	–	1	–	1	2
371425	OIL FILTER ELEMENTS (AUTOMOTIVE)	34	10,549	11	16	7	13	47
371426	HUB & DRUM ASSEMBLIES (AUTOMOTIVE)	20	4,304	8	8	4	15	35
371429	OTHER PARTS & ASSEMBLIES FOR CARS TRUCKS & BUSES NEC	451	173,554	214	162	75	271	722
371432	REBUILT FUEL & WATER PUMPS (AUTOMOTIVE)	7	2,236	6	–	1	9	16
371433	REBUILT GASOLINE ENGINES (AUTOMOTIVE)	31	3,379	20	10	1	6	37
371434	REBUILT AUTOMATIC TRANSMISSIONS (AUTOMOTIVE)	1	21	1	–	–	3	4
371435	REBUILT CLUTCH DISCS & PRESSURE PLATES (AUTOMOTIVE)	10	2,100	7	2	1	10	20
371439	REBUILT PARTS FOR CARS TRUCKS & BUSES NEC	34	3,557	25	8	1	19	53
3715	TRUCK TRAILERS	171	33,281	93	61	17	102	273
371501	COMPLETE TRUCK TRAILERS	165	32,691	90	58	17	99	264
371505	TRUCK TRAILER CHASSIS	6	590	3	3	–	5	11
3721	AIRCRAFT	117	230,550	27	35	55	10	127
372111	COMPLETE MILITARY AIRCRAFT	15	79,723	1	2	12	2	17
372121	COMPLETE PERSONAL & UTILITY TYPE AIRCRAFT	25	23,304	8	8	9	2	27
372125	HELICOPTERS	10	31,220	–	3	7	3	13
372131	COMPLETE COMMERCIAL TRANSPORT TYPE AIRCRAFT	12	44,490	1	4	7	3	15
372140	AIRCRAFT MODIFICATIONS CONVERSIONS REPAIR OVERHAULING	55	51,813	17	18	20	9	64
3724	AIRCRAFT ENGINES AND ENGINE PARTS	106	82,116	47	35	24	55	161

FIGURE 11-7

Iron Age Metalworking Data Bank sells analyses of eight major SIC groups to advertisers and marketers. Information in the forty-page booklet provides a statistical analysis of the United States metalworking market. *Iron Age* also sells a multivolume computer printout of its eight metalworking classifications broken down by company name, address, major and secondary SICs, and number of employees. Reprinted from the *Iron Age* market guide.

lists to see whether the "weak link" has been missing good sales opportunities by not calling on certain SICs (Table 11-1).

UNDERSTANDING STANDARD RATE & DATA

"Change," reports Standard Rate & Data Service (SRDS), "is part of the basic nature of all media."[5] That's why SRDS, Skokie-based national authority serving the media buyers of the nation, constantly updates its information. Its business is compiling and cataloging current information about media: ad space costs, discounts, circulations, and makeup of readers by geography as well as job function. It sends this information out in printed form to 31,000 subscribers in advertising agencies, advertiser companies, and media companies. Of the twelve specialized editions of SRDS, two are of particular interest to business publication advertisers: *Business Publications Rates and Data*, issued monthly, and *Print Media Production Data*, issued quarterly.

    Business Publications provides current data on more than 3,000 business, trade, and technical publications in the United States. These are

[5]"Three factors made SRDS a necessity for buyers of media," *SRDS Consumer Magazine and Farm Publication Rates and Data*, August 27, 1976, p. 496.

TABLE 11-1

MAJOR INDUSTRIAL GROUPS BY STANDARD INDUSTRIAL CLASSIFICATION (SIC)

Group	Description
Group 19	Ordnance and accessories (Remington, Daisy)
Group 20	Food and kindred products (Libby, Hershey)
Group 21	Tobacco manufactures (Marlboro, Dutch Masters)
Group 22	Textile mill products (L'eggs hosiery, Lee carpets)
Group 23	Apparel and other finished products (Haggar slacks, Act III dresses)
Group 24	Lumber and wood products (Georgia-Pacific)
Group 25	Furniture and fixtures (Bassett, Kroehler sofas)
Group 26	Paper and allied products (Hallmark, St. Regis)
Group 27	Printing, publishing and allied industries (McGraw-Hill, Christian Science Monitor)
Group 28	Chemicals and allied products (Chanel, Treflan [herbicide])
Group 29	Petroleum refining and related industries (Quaker State oil)
Group 30	Rubber and miscellaneous products (Converse, Kelly [tires])
Group 31	Leather and leather products (Hush Puppies, Buxton wallets)
Group 32	Stone, clay, glass and concrete (Ball)
Group 33	Primary metals industries (U.S. Steel, Bethlehem Steel)
Group 34	Fabricated metals industries (American Can, Black & Decker)
Group 35	Machinery, except electrical (Rapistan [conveyors], Harris [printing presses])
Group 36	Electrical machinery (Reliance, General Electric)
Group 37	Transportation (AMC Pacers, Beech, Harley-Davidson)
Group 38	Professional, scientific and controlling instruments (Polaroid)
Group 39	Miscellaneous manufacturers (Wilson [sporting goods])
Group 73	Miscellaneous business services (J. Walter Thompson, Arthur Andersen Accountants)

subdivided into 173 "Market Service" classifications. All include publishers' statements of the editorial purpose, advertising rates, contract and copy regulations, mechanical requirements (size of ads and the nature of acceptable reproduction materials), issuance and closing dates, and circulation breakdown into paid and nonpaid, geographical regions, and job titles. The cost for this invaluable reference to subscribers is extremely modest.

Print Media Production Data is a supplement. It serves the needs of business publications as well as consumer magazines and daily newspapers. Each publication's listing contains general shipping instructions for advertising materials, method of printing used, production personnel, ad dimensions, and other necessary information.

Media buyers in both advertising departments and advertising agencies are keenly interested in SRDS data. Working from it, media buyers can analyze circulations by numbers, by region, by costs per thousand (CPM), or by job titles and functions. They use it to develop media budgets, a much simpler job than keeping over 3,000 individual magazine rate cards up to date. In fact, this single reference book serves the entire advertising community.

However, SRDS has some limitations. Its information is furnished exclusively by publishers who make every effort to appear to their best advantage. Because two-thirds of all business publications are not audited, SRDS may contain exaggerations or misstatements. Also, sometimes the latest cost information does not make it into print in time. And finally, in instances where SRDS "flags"[6] a publication for not answering its request for information, the flag may not necessarily prove weakness in coverage. The publication might be undergoing revisions, or the publisher might not want numerical comparisons for some reason.

Analyzing circulations of publications by means of audited forms, inquiry response, SIC readership, and SRDS data go a long way in helping media buyers perform their jobs. But there are other variables as well: what readers think of the magazines they receive, the quality of ad and editorial reproduction, the presence or absence of competitive manufacturers. Not all these variables can be reduced to numbers, which is one reason why selecting business media is not a science.

IN SUMMARY

1 An unwritten rule for effectiveness in industrial advertising is: sales literature first, directory reference ads second, and publication advertising last.
2 Business-publication advertising links the makers of goods and the providers of services with their target audiences.
3 Business publications alert readers to new machinery, processes, and technologies; present theories and case histories; serve as the voice and news of an industry; and deliver news of the business world.

---

[6]Typical "flagging" by SRDS occurs at the end of the individual listing with this statement: "After three requests, publisher has failed to file circulation statement on SRDS form."

4   Industrial magazines are divided into verticals and horizontals. Vertical publications report on news and technology affecting all job functions within one industry. Horizontal publications cover many industries but concentrate on a specific job function (such as purchasing).

5   Editorial staffs of business publications are usually specialists in their fields and often have technical training and experience.

6   Advertising space reps are indispensable links between publication and advertiser. Their knowledge of business and their marketing suggestions often serve to improve advertising.

7   Auditing groups attest to the credibility of business-paper circulation claims.

8   The comprehensive MCC media form, presents a logical way to compare publications without bias.

9   The majority of magazines in the industrial field are "controlled circulation" types whose audiences are restricted to certain industries and jobs.

10 "Inquiry" publications, usually in tabloid form, deliver greater immediate response than most other business magazines. They are devoted to introducing new products and processes, thus accounting for their greater reader interest.

11 Standard Industrial Classification (SIC) numbers permit precise identification of what companies manufacture. The coding system was devised by the United States government to aid marketers.

12 SICs can aid advertising strategists in the following ways: to evaluate specific business magazines, to develop a mailing list of prospects, to develop sales leads for the sales force, and to draw up customer profiles for industrial distributors.

13 Standard Rate and Data *Business Publications Rates and Data* provides current information about more than 3,000 business, trade, and technical publications. This single-volume reference is the primary media selection tool of media buyers in advertising departments and advertising agencies.

CASE STUDY   How Clayton Manufacturing Company (El Monte, California) Tracks Industrial Inquiries.

"At Clayton Manufacturing Company, we view the incoming inquiry very simply as a sale in the making. We have developed and maintain an inquiry processing, tracking, and follow-up system that makes use of the latest in computer techniques and inquiry management theories. As a result, we can and do track inquiries through and including conversion to sale and can, in the end result, fairly well relate our advertising expenditures on the basis of inquiry to conversion-to-sale statistics.

"During the next twelve months, we expect to process approximately 8,000 inquiries from prospects and customers in the United States and Canada alone. These inquiries come through business press advertising, directories, Yellow Pages advertising, trade shows and conventions, sales seminars, direct mail, and publicity/public relations efforts.

"We had found after a review of our department and others that inquiries were being given cursory treatment, usually limited to counting them, screening out the obvious duds and frauds, and then sending them to a field sales representative for contact, with little or no follow-up from the factory. We then worked out a comprehensive inquiry-handling system that is accomplished outside the factory by Inquiry Handling Service (IHS), North Hollywood, California. Benefits for "farming out" the inquiries included a reduction in overall expense, the release of advertising department personnel for more productive tasks, and reduction in the need to store and stock large quantities of catalog literature on our premises, freeing space in our literature stockroom.

"We then redesigned our inquiry fulfillment package. As a consequence, we now have a specially imprinted outer transmittal envelope; a customized sales letter; a small business card carrying the name, address and telephone number of the inquirer's local Clayton field sales representative; and a "bounceback" card that asks the inquirer to respond to ten questions (Figure 11-8). This card enables us to determine whether the information forwarded was adequate; what additional information the prospect needs; whether or not the prospect intends to purchase the type of equipment about which he or she has inquired; whether he or she has been contacted by our salesperson; the application for our equipment the prospect has in mind; when he or she will buy; and whether or not a formal presentation and price quotation are required.

"At the time Inquiry Handling Service fulfills the incoming inquiry with the package described, it creates, by means of computer, a field salesperson's sales lead evaluation form. The inquiry is fulfilled within twenty-four hours. The salespersons' lead forms are batched and mailed to them weekly. Forms ask them to rate the *quality* of the inquiry for us and give us an indication of when they think the prospect will purchase. The computerized form gives our salespeople the telephone number, address, and title of the prospect; the source of the inquiry; the date the inquiry was processed; the product line involved; and the SIC code of the firm involved.

"If the inquirer returns the original bounceback card to us, we advise the salesperson involved. If not, Inquiry Handling Service mails a similar card within thirty days of receipt of the lead. If inquirer fails to respond, IHS mails another bounceback card in sixty days. At 180 days, a carefully constructed marketing survey is mailed to the prospect that fully determines the status of the prospect's purchasing intentions.

FIGURE 11-8
Clayton's inquiry package includes a customized sales letter, the business card of the local sales representative, and a "bounce-back" card asking the inquirer for specific information. When the local sales representatives have had a chance to study the inquiries, they are asked to rate them according to quality.

PLEASE RETURN THIS CARD TO CLAYTON MANUFACTURING COMPANY

1. Is the information you received adequate? ☐ Yes ☐ No
2. What additional information do you need? _____
_____
3. Do you plan to purchase this type of product? ☐ Yes ☐ No
4. Have you been contacted by a Clayton salesman? ☐ Yes ☐ No
5. What is your application? _____
_____

6. Is your requirement: ☐ Immediate
   ☐ 1-3 Months ☐ 3-6 Months
   ☐ 6-12 Months ☐ Longer
7. Do you wish to be on our permanent mailing list? ☐ Yes ☐ No
8. Your product interest is:
   ☐ Steam Generators ☐ Steam Cleaners
   ☐ Dynamometers
   ☐ Electronic Engine Analyzers
9. Is your name, title, company name and address correct? ☐ Yes ☐ No
   Correction: _____
10. Do you want us to quote prices? ☐ Yes ☐ No
    Clayton Product: _____
    Phone: _____

Clayton

You inquired regarding Clayton products two months ago. Won't you please take a moment to complete and return this card? It will help us help you. C-2326.1-60/5M/4-74/CP

Bounceback cards and sales lead evaluation reports are encoded in computer language and furnished to IHS for computer storage for our use later in finding out the status of our system at any given point in time. A national summary of all inquiries for all product lines for the current year and the total average overall cost per inquiry runs slightly in excess of $13. Clayton also receives, on a monthly basis, a complete printout of each current inquiry standing in our data bank. When the prospect does purchase our equipment, we can assign a dollar value of the sale to the inquiry involved. The master inquiry report allows us to finally track the inquiry through conversion to sale. We can then report our results to management in the most specific of terms. An analysis of data derived from sales evaluation reports received from our own sales representatives indicates that 55 percent of the prospects contacted fall into the "excellent," "good," or "fair" categories, and that 47 percent plan to purchase within one year. Clayton Manufacturing makes steam generators, steam cleaners, dynamometers, electronic analyzers and compounds."

(Study based on an article in *Industrial Marketing*, September 1974).

QUESTIONS NEEDING ANSWERS

1   Why do you think advertising managers feel that inquiries are the most tangible results of advertising that they can offer to management as proof of effectiveness? Explain.
2   Why does Clayton go to so much trouble to qualify inquiries? What would happen if Clayton simply responded to inquiries by sending literature and following up by a visit from a sales representative?
3   If you were the advertising manager for Clayton, would you concentrate all your advertising on only those publications that provided you with heavy inquiry response? Explain.

STUDENT PROJECT

Assume that you are a media buyer representing a manufacturer of air-powered impact wrenches used extensively to tighten and loosen bolts on motor vehicles. The manufacturer has allocated you a budget of $60,000 to reach its primary buyers. Using a recent edition of SRDS, draw up a proposed media space budget and justify it. Begin by identifying the company's target audience of buyers.

QUESTIONS ABOUT THE PROJECT

1   How many different market classifications can you find in SRDS of interest to an air-powered impact wrench manufacturer?
2   Are there any tabloid inquiry-producing magazines designed for the company's primary audience? Name them.
3   Are industrial magazines the most effective way to reach the company's primary audience? How about direct mail or an appropriate annual buyers' guide?

Unit

3

PROFESSIONAL AND TRADE ADVERTISING

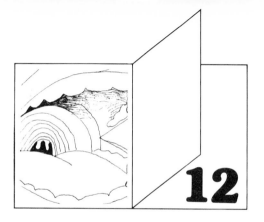

THE PROFESSIONS
AND THEIR MEDIA

Update Effective advertisers select their target audiences and tailor their messages to them. We have seen that the consumer's needs and the industrial buyer's needs differ. The consumer seeks personal gratification; the industrial customer, career advancement, financial rewards, and job satisfaction. Now we will examine whether professionals share the industrial buyer's needs or whether they are unique sales targets.

Who are the people we loosely call "professionals?" We can list them as follows: doctors, dentists, pharmacists, veterinarians, architects, consulting engineers, interior designers, educators, ministers, lawyers, and accountants. All carry a license to practice their professions or a certificate of professional competency. They are among the highest money makers in the total population, with doctors on top.

We mention the professionals' earning power because it affects the way they view life and their work. It tells advertisers, for example, that professionals, like many upper-income people, are more interested in long-lasting, high-quality products. Their earning power also suggests that advertisers can explain the benefits of their products in terms of tax credits and depreciation and be understood. In fact, the tax advantages of a purchase may often play a major role in influencing a professional to buy. For example, dentists who purchase the most expensive operatory equipment may do so because they are able to offset the higher costs against their income. Without favorable tax credits, they might choose the least expensive equipment.

PURCHASE INVOLVEMENT OF THE PROFESSIONALS

People who sign purchase orders for many products and services may have very little to do with influencing the buying decisions. The people who really specify what to buy may never sign an order. For example, when building contractors order a specific type of paneling for office buildings, lumberyards consider them the real buyers when, in fact, architects specified the product down to the very brand name. Again, mobile-home park owners may buy portable waste disposal systems, but the real specifiers (those who select and approve products) were consulting engineers. Even when a customer buys a prescription from a pharmacist, the real specifier was the doctor, not the customer. And manufacturers must recognize that their major advertising efforts should be directed at the specifier, the originator of the order.

Manufacturers of many products recognize the power of the professional specifiers and devote a substantial portion of their advertising to them. Professionals specified products and materials for an estimated $154 billion of construction projects in 1979.[1] *Architectural Record,* a professional publication, sells manufacturers over $5 million of space a year to reach these specifiers.[2] And the same manufacturers also support many other trade publications.

Many professionals play a dual role in involvement with products. They buy for themselves and they specify purchases for others. Doctors, for example, buy medical and office equipment for themselves *and* specify the medication their patients will buy. What else should advertising strategists know about the professional?

The advertiser can assume that professionals have at least a four-year college degree and probably more. Doctors spend four years in medical school and several more in hospital residencies after four years in undergraduate college.

[1]*1979 National Estimates of Dodge Construction Potentials,* Sweet's Division, McGraw-Hill Information Systems Co., February 1979.
[2]*Architectural Record* Magazine, 1977 sales.

Educators with doctorates spend six to eight years in preparation for their careers. Architects spend anywhere from five to six years in school, then complete three years of apprenticeship in an office doing drafting and specifications work before taking their state examination for registration. The other professions require comparable preparations. Because of the additional schooling and training facing professionals, it is not surprising that they are a fairly mature target audience.

DOCTORS, DENTISTS, PHARMACISTS, AND VETERINARIANS

There are 345,000 practicing doctors of medicine, but basically they can be divided into four categories: the general practitioner, the specialist, the institutional practitioner (a hospital administrator, for example), and the researcher. By far the greatest number are engaged in private practice, in either offices, clinics, or hospitals, and their interests are so diverse that it takes well over a hundred different medical magazines to serve their need for information.

Yet, advertisers share some conclusions about doctors, dentists, pharmacists, and veterinarians. About doctors, they recognize that these professionals enter the field to relieve human suffering and to help sick people get well. In their quest for these goals, doctors respond well to advertisements that describe:

1 improved treatments.
2 new surgical techniques.
3 new drugs.
4 ways to improve the effectiveness of their practice in terms of dollars, time, and benefits to patients.

For the 121,000 practicing dentists in the country,[3] advertisers list these common desires:

1 to help people.
2 to enjoy the same prestige as medical doctors.
3 to treat more patients in a normal workday through the use of new equipment and more efficient operatory procedures.
4 to reduce both the physical and mental tensions that accompany the practice of dentistry.
5 to own modern equipment that functions without breakdowns.

Like medical doctors, some dentists also specialize in other branches of dentistry such as oral surgery or treatment of irregular teeth (orthodontia).

[3]American Dental Association.

Advertisers need to recognize these specialties because they often require separate publications and different sales appeals.

When advertisers analyze the country's 155,000 pharmacists, they see a combination of a professional and a retail businessperson. Although not all pharmacists own or operate drugstores—some work for government institutions and hospitals—most do. Pharmacists respond well to advertising appeals that:

1 treat them as knowledgeable professionals.
2 keep them up to date on new drugs and treatments so they can build a rapport with doctors of the community.
3 help them run their retail stores more efficiently and profitably.
4 help retain old customers and secure new ones.

In the future, in the United States, if druggists are permitted (as they are in some countries) to substitute general, unbranded (generic) drugs for those specified by doctors, advertisers may increase their promotions to pharmacists. The pharmacist would then become as important as the doctor to the pharmaceutical manufacturer (Figure 12-1).

Of the 26,000 veterinarians practicing today, the majority work with small, domesticated animals, mainly dogs and cats. Those who prefer the larger animals (horses, cattle, pigs, sheep, and goats) are generally from a rural background. Advertisers see all veterinarians as interested in appeals to their:

1 professionalism as doctors of veterinary medicine.
2 desire to prevent epidemics of animal diseases.
3 concern for controlling diseases transmittable from animals to humans.
4 desire to keep up with the current state of veterinary science.

Most veterinarians are graduates of a small number of excellent veterinary colleges whose standards for admission are, in some cases, more restrictive than those of medical schools. Manufacturers of pet foods, drugs, and animal pharmaceuticals are anxious for the vets' approval of their products. These advertisers have learned that the most effective approach to these professionals is one based on scientific proof and performance. In this respect pharmacists and doctors of medicine, dentistry, and veterinary medicine all agree (Figure 12-2).

ARCHITECTS, INTERIOR DESIGNERS, AND CONSULTING ENGINEERS

Architectural Record magazine estimates there are 45,610 architects practicing in the country.[4] As for their common professional skills, they have an

[4]Ad for *Architectural Record* in *Standard Rate & Data Service/Business,* January 24, 1978, pp. 98–99.

Save your life: $20.

This startling headline is sure to grab the attention of anyone who is at all health conscious. Many people who can't pronounce "sphygmomanometer" nonetheless realize its importance as a device for measuring arterial blood pressure at home. The ad makes a dramatic point.

Diabetics: One stop shopping

Everything a diabetic needs—including such diverse items as sugarless candy, identification necklace, and cotton swabs—is included in this layout. Why should supermarkets be the only ones to benefit from the "one-stop shopping" concept?

"PRESCRIPTION PRICE advertising." These are fighting words.

The Federal Trade Commission is all for the idea.

Most independent drug store operators dislike it.

Consumer groups favor it, because it is supposed to promote competition between pharmacies.

Chains are wary. Those which have tried it have had mixed results.

The Newspaper Advertising Bureau believes that if Rx advertising is to be directed at consumers, it should be carried out with flair, expertise, and professionalism.

Hank Simons, vice president and creative director of NAB, has accordingly come up with some original approaches to the subject, as depicted on these pages. They are presented by AMERICAN DRUGGIST not in the spirit of advocacy, but rather to stimulate thinking about a matter that is likely to influence the way Rx business is conducted in the future.

Background: The issue achieved national prominence in 1976, when the Supreme Court overturned as unconstitutional a Virginia statute which declared that a pharmacist was guilty of unprofessional conduct if he advertised the prices of Rx drugs. The Court's decision rendered unconstitutional similar laws or
(Continued)

FIGURE 12-1

This is what a pharmaceutical ad for consumers might look like if druggists' promotions were more aggressive. In turn, pharmaceutical manufacturers would intensify their advertising to pharmacists. (Courtesy Newspaper Advertising Bureau; reprinted by permission of *American Druggist*, copyright Hearst Magazines.)

FIGURE 12-2
Veterinarians are interested in animals. This advertiser believes in big, appealing animal photographs to attract the attention of its selected audiences. In a publication filled with technical data and illustrations, simple photographs stand out!

aptitude for organization, drawing, and engineering. Architects' fees usually run from 6 to 10 percent of the total cost of a building project. For that fee, they plan a structure for a site and supervise its construction. They must evaluate and choose among competitive products before they write building specifications, which means they must know the intricacies of many structural components: roofs, floors, lighting, insulation, heating, and cooling, to mention just a few. Architects authorize the spending of 90 percent of all apartment building construction dollars spent in the United States, 95 percent of all school construction, 89 percent of all commercial construction, and 95 percent of all hospital construction.[5] At one time, architects restricted their practice to the building itself and left finishing of the interiors to interior designers (decorators). Today, more architects consider interior work an adjunct to their structural work and design. Thus they have also become a prime advertising target for manufacturers of interior finishing products.

Interior designers work either for themselves, for engineering-architectural firms, for large department stores, for home furnishings manufacturers, or for hotel chains. Their art is the planning of room furnishings such as drapes, floor and wall coverings, pictures, and furniture to complete the room in keeping with the physical structure of the building and the esthetic needs of the occupants (Figure 12-3). They need to know how people will use a room and know about styles and products so they can create habitable space from a group of mostly inanimate objects. The interior designer is of primary interest to manufacturers of furniture, decorative tiles, photographic art, wall coverings, draperies, carpeting, and lighting.

"Consulting engineer" is a term that covers a multitude of engineering titles and activities. Engineers must select, evaluate, and specify machinery, materials, and systems for their clients or their employers. They must be informed about many fields because of the interdependence of engineering activities. For example, a heating and ventilating engineer needs to unify a building's heating, ventilating, and air conditioning with the electrical, lighting, and power systems in order to achieve the greatest efficiency and the minimum operating cost. The same engineer must also be knowledgeable about fire, smoke control, and high-rise elevator regulations, even though the basic planning and design work of these components may be done by some other engineering specialist. Typical advertisers who seek to influence consulting engineers are manufacturers of insulation, elevators, solar panels, roofing materials, water heaters, couplings, pipe, pumps, structural steel, sprinkler systems, sewer pipe, and automatic surveying equipment.

The more widely known consulting engineering titles and their activities are: *civil* (planning roads, airfields, and bridges), *structural* (designing large, multistory buildings, and factories), *sanitary* (designing sewage disposal systems and water systems), *electrical* (projecting power requirements in buildings and selecting appropriate electrical machinery such as motors and manufacturing equipment), *mechanical* (evaluating and choosing operating

[5]*Architectural Record* Magazine, 1977 review.

FIGURE 12-3
Classic, simple, dramatic—all describe Herman Miller's graphic advertising appeal to interior designers. The Michigan manufacturer is a favorite of both interior designers and architects.

machinery—other than electrical—in plants), *heating and ventilating* (planning and designing systems for keeping buildings warm or cool and ventilated), and *chemical* (planning plants and production lines making fertilizers, plastics, foods, and so on. There are others, too: *agricultural, marine, automotive, aeronautical, nuclear, solar.*

Modern engineering has made life easier. The engineers' expertise is crucial to our affluent society. In their capacity as specialists, these professionals must also select, evaluate, and specify machinery, materials, and systems for their clients or employers.

EDUCATORS, MINISTERS, LAWYERS, AND ACCOUNTANTS

Educators are more likely than ministers, lawyers, or accountants to influence the purchase of materials on a regular basis. Although ministers, lawyers, and accountants may on occasion recommend a product or service, they do not regularly perform this function. Even lawyers who are involved in large-scale purchasing do so as an official agent of management: president or treasurer or the like. But college professors, school system superintendents, principals, librarians, classroom teachers, curriculum coordinators, and athletic coaches are all in a position to recommend purchases of a variety of goods and services (Figure 12-4).

363

THE PROFESSIONS
AND THEIR MEDIA

INFORMATIONAL NEEDS OF THE PROFESSIONALS

Modern technology has solved some problems and made some problems worse. For example, sophisticated computer analyses are much faster than older methods, but they require a greater amount of knowledge from the professional about how to program and interpret results. Professionals are faced with a knowledge revolution. Each year there is a deluge of new information for them to digest, and the information raises even more questions in its wake. Architects and engineers wonder whether solar roof panels will withstand the velocities of the wind in the Plains states and whether we can trade reductions in fireproof standards for complete sprinkler systems. Doctors and lawyers ask controversial questions like, "When does life really begin and end?"

Professionals require new answers to keep pace with progress in their fields, and they turn to their professional journals for help. Not long ago, professionals only had to keep pace with professional developments in their own country, but this is no longer enough. United States engineers reading about a revolutionary modular crane used in low-cost construction in Sweden demand its equivalent. Medical consumers pressured the United States medical community to adapt South African cardiologist Dr. Christiaan Barnard's radical procedures for treating heart disease.[6] Much of the technical debate was carried by the professional journals.

But journals provide other information besides the latest developments in the fields. They tell professionals how to run their businesses, too. They help them with tax forms, with office design, with patient flow charts, with billing procedures, with information about what other members of the profession are earning each year—even with the proliferation of malpractice suits aimed at doctors, engineers, architects, and even educators! The professional media accumulate, screen, edit, and publish this mass of information month after month.

THE PROFESSIONAL MEDIA

Medicine has the most clearly defined specialties of any of the professions. It supports over 100 medical publications in twenty-six standard classifications, ranging from the *Journal of the American Medical Association* to more

[6]His methods were developed in Capetown, South Africa, in 1967.

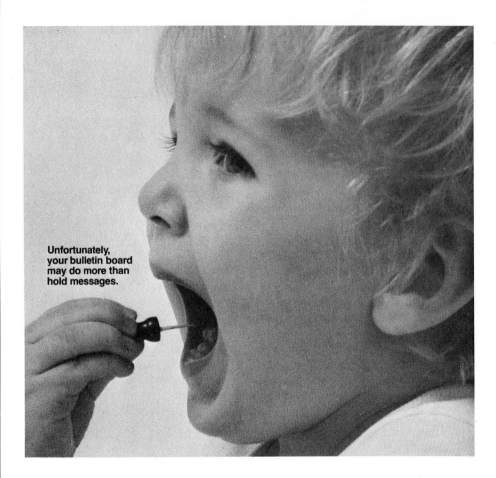

Unfortunately, your bulletin board may do more than hold messages.

Although we staged this photo with a harmless push pin, the problem is real.

While your bulletin board may look innocent enough, if it uses pins and tacks, there's a very real possibility that they'll fall into the wrong hands.

That's why 3M designed Post-it® products.

Post-it is a strange and wonderful adhesive that holds messages without pins or tacks. You can stick messages to it and remove them at will.

What's more, the backing adheres to most any surface. So you can put Post-it bulletin board products all over the hospital. In the halls, patient rooms—any place you want to post messages, schedules or instructions.

You can get Post-it in bulletin boards, tiles and 1" wide rolls from your office supply dealer. Or circle our reader service number for more information and a free sample tile.

"Post-it" holds messages without pins or tacks.

"Post-it" is a registered trademark of 3M

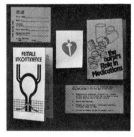

3M

FIGURE 12-4
What can be more appealing to an educator than a child? Advertisers rely on the personal appeal of children to sell anything from 3M Company's "Scotch" Brand Color tape to bleacher seats. (Courtesy 3M Company.)

specialized magazines concerned with allergies or podiatry. There are national, regional and even city medical journals. It is virtually impossible to find a medical specialty without its own professional journal. This variety, of course, forces advertisers to pick and choose among the journals.

In evaluating professional media, advertisers should depend on audited media wherever possible. They should also request from publishers a specific breakdown of their circulations. With doctors, advertisers need to know numbers, specialties, and even geographical distribution. With architects, they need to know if the subscriptions are sent to architectural firms or to individuals, and to how many of each. Advertisers need to know how many architects are draftspeople and specifiers, how many restrict their practice to schools or commercial or residential buildings, With consulting engineers, advertisers need to know how many are mechanical, structural, electrical, and so on. With interior designers, it's also important to establish specialties: commercial, residential, church, school.

In short, advertisers need to define and analyze each group. When the sales departments of publications send audit forms like those of Business Publications Audit (BPA), Audit Bureau of Circulations (ABC), or others, advertisers should make their own comparisons among magazines to establish a frame of reference. As a further aid in comparing one publication with another, advertisers can request publishers to provide several readership studies of their circulation. One study is never sufficient to establish an average or a trend because of the possibility of an error in sampling or some other occurrence (Figure 12-5).

Measuring Media Effectiveness

As we learned earlier, the performance of a publication can be measured in several ways. First, we can divide the total number of subscribers into the cost per page and arrive at a cost per thousand readers (CPM). For example, a publication with a circulation of 50,000 and a per page cost of $2800 gives us a CPM of $56. This is the customary way to measure circulation costs per magazine. Second, we can adjust these costs by adding total annual numbers of inquiries and requests for editorial reprints. These are specific examples of reader response and indicate reader involvement. Here's how this simple comparison technique works (Table 12-1).

This technique, of course, says nothing about the relative popularity of the magazines. Media buyers look to readership studies to help in this

TABLE 12-1
ANNUAL MEDIA CHECK (BLACK-AND-WHITE PAGE)

	Circulation	Costs	CPM	Requests for reprints	Inquiries	Adjusted CPM
Publication A	50,000	$2800	$56	75,000	400,000	$5.33
Publication B	50,000	2800	56	60,000	240,000	8.00

in 269 out of 288 independently sponsored studies
architects and engineers have voted Architectural Record "preferred"

Year	Sponsor	Group Surveyed	Number Surveyed	Replies	Architectural Record	Architectural Forum	Progressive Architecture
1937	Hart Manufacturing Co. Hartford, Conn.	Architects in Hartford (active in first five months of 1937)	29	100%	20	16	14
1937	Addison Vars, Inc. Buffalo, New York	Architects in Buffalo (active in first half of 1937)	45	100%	36	26	23
1937	Batten, Barton, Durstine & Osborn, Inc. Minneapolis, Minn.	Architects in Minneapolis and St. Paul (active in first seven months of 1937)	76	100%	61	55	41
1939	A. M. Byers Company Pittsburgh, Pa.	Architects of known importance to manufacturer.	†	†	1st		
1940	A. M. Byers Company Pittsburgh, Pa.	Architects of known importance to manufacturer.	†	†		1st	
1941	American Seating Company Grand Rapids, Mich.	Architects who had specified products of this manufacturer.	78	37%	39	44	21
1941	Minneapolis-Honeywell Regulator Company Minneapolis, Minn.	Architects who had specified products of this manufacturer.	100	40%	33	28	21
1941	A. M. Byers Company Pittsburgh, Pa.	Architects of known importance to manufacturer.	†	†	1st		
1941	Jenkins Brothers New York, N.Y.	Specification writers named in distribution list for Sweet's Architectural file.	974	17%	110	102	
1942	A. M. Byers Company Pittsburgh, Pa.	Architects of known importance to manufacturer.				34	13
1942			1,000	15.0%	29	6	11	5
		Architects On Market List for Sweet's Architectural Catalog File.	2,000	9.9%	58	14	27	11
1972	Overhead Door Corp. Dallas, Tex.	Architects on Market List for Sweet's Architectural Catalog File.	3,000	18.2%	224	97	76	44
1972	Anemostat Scranton, Pa.	Architects on Market List for Sweet's Architectural Catalog File.	1,000	5.1%	18	7	6	13
1972	Rixson, Franklin Pk., Ill.	Client's own list.	1,000	20.0%	75	42	52	19
1972	Crouse-Hinds Syracuse, N.Y.	Architects on Market List for Sweet's Architectural Catalog File.	1,000	16.2%	41	17	27	11
1972	AVM Jamestown, N.Y.	Architects on Market List for Sweet's Architectural Catalog File.	1,000	21.7%	73	31	40	19
1972	All-Steel Equipment, Aurora, Ill.	Client's own list.	1,000	27.3%	177	139	165	74
1972	H. B. Fuller St. Paul, Minn.	Architects on Market List for Sweet's Architectural Catalog File and Industrial Construction list.	1,000	13.7%	27	17	18	10
1972	Welded Tube Philadelphia, Pa.	List of American Institute of Steel Construction, Inc.		52.0%	97	78	77	59
1972	Eaton Lock & Hardware, N.C.	Client's own list.	4,000	n.a.	100	74	77	73
1972	Spaulding, Cincinnati, Oh.	Client's own list.	3,350	25.0%	184	98	123	—
1973	Modine Racine, Wis.	Architects on Market List for Sweet's Architectural Catalog File.	50	100%	43	39	39	18
1973	Thiokol Chemical Trenton, N.J.	Architects on Market List for Sweet's Architectural Catalog File.	1,000	14.9%	80	46	72	22
1973	National Gypsum, Buffalo, N.Y.	Client's own list.	1,200	17.3%	53	12	29	20
1973	Tyler Pipe Tyler, Tex.	Architects on Market List for Sweet's Architectural Catalog File.	1,000	17.0%	60	11	23	8
1973	B. F. Goodrich Akron, Oh.	Architects on Market List for Sweet's Architectural Catalog File.	1,000	22.2%	63	19	36	17
1973	Levolor-Lorentzen Hoboken, N.J.	Architects on Market List for Sweet's Architectural Catalog File.	1,000	11.5%	48	13	21	3
1973	American Sterilizer, Erie, Pa.	Client's own list.	900	20.2%	49	9	22	16
1973	Concrete Reinforcing Steel Institute, Chicago, Ill.	Architects on Market List for Sweet's Architectural Catalog File.	1,000	18.4%	59	8	29	17
1973	Modine Racine, Wis.	Architects on Market List for Sweet's Architectural Catalog File.	1,000	23.0%	70	24	22	21
1974	Eberhard Faber Wilkesbarre, Pa.	Architects on Market List for Sweet's Architectural Catalog File.	1,000	15.1%	28	5	11	20
1974	Jamison Cold Storage Door Co. Hagerstown, Md.	Client's own list.	698	34.8%	66	1	27	40
1974	Hillyard Chemical Co. St. Joseph, Mo.	Architects on Market List for Sweet's Architectural Catalog File.	1,000	9.2%	31	3	10	12
1974	Inland-Ryerson, Milwaukee, Wis.	Client's own list.	1,687	38.0%	125	—	47	72
1974	Sweet's/Engineering News-Record, N.Y.C.	Architects on Market List for Sweet's Architectural Catalog File.	9,562	31.0%	743	149	283	82
1974	Eberhard Faber Wilkesbarre, Pa.	Architects on Market List for Sweet's Architectural Catalog File.	1,000	18.0%	41	2	16	20
1975	American Plywood Assn. Tacoma, Wa.	Architects on Market List for Sweet's Architectural Catalog File.	1,000	29.4%	AR 80	BD&C* 4	PA 32	AIA 27

FIGURE 12-5

A portion of 288 individual readership studies conducted by advertising agencies or building product manufacturers indicates a significant preference for an architectural magazine by architects and engineers. The independent studies go back to 1937. (Courtesy *Architectural Record* Magazine.)

evaluation, although they often have some misgivings about such studies because many are commissioned and paid for by the publications. Occasionally advertisers conduct their own studies, which observers claim are more objective, but often they refuse to make the conclusions public. Their explanation is that the studies reveal reader attitudes and buying tendencies that they can use to secure a competitive advantage over other companies. Therefore, they prefer not to reveal the information. Publications that conduct frequent readership studies would probably prefer advertisers to conduct their own and relieve them of the burden. But many advertisers still look to the media for basic readership research.

Some advertisers make the mistake of not taking into account all a professional's interests. Engineers, for example, spend as much time with specific-industry publications as they do with their own. Architects employed by a fast-food restaurant franchise may spend as much time with *Institutions* as they do with *Architectural Record*. They may also find *Building Construction & Design* extremely informative, since its editorial material is aimed at building contractors and consulting engineers as well as architects. Experienced media planners buy space in several appropriate publications, professional and industrial, although individual circulations may, in fact, overlap and reach the same professionals within the same market.

The media buyer's job is to determine which of the magazines deliver the greatest number of qualified professionals. Sometimes a publication with a larger circulation and a lower cost per thousand is not as effective as one with fewer recipients and therefore a higher cost. That's because significant numbers of professionals reached through the larger circulation publication are not prospects for the advertised product. This is "waste" circulation. It can be "waste by job function," as when an advertisement meant for surgeons also reaches general practitioners. It can be "waste by geography," as when advertisements for a product that is only available in certain sections of the country appear in a national magazine. It can be "waste by size of specifier," as when small businesses receive the publication in which your product, appropriate only for large businesses, is advertised. Media buyers may still elect to buy space in magazines with substantial waste circulations simply because there are no practical alternatives. The important thing in such cases is for manufacturers to tailor their ad message directly to the readership they want. In this respect, even if the cost per thousand readers is high, the advertiser will at least be sending the right message to the right audience (Table 12-2).

REFERENCE ANNUALS

Manufacturers of professionally specified products are also fortunate to have buying guide reference publications available to them for advertising. Most prominent as far as architects are concerned is the multivolume annual, *Sweets System for the General Building Market*. With sixteen volumes—each

TABLE 12-2
TYPICAL PROFESSIONAL MAGAZINES

Publication	Circulation	Cost per black-and-white page
Architectural Record	54,539	$3220
AIA Journal (architects)	26,903	1805
Construction Specifier	10,610	995
Progressive Architecture	65,255	2800
Journal of Accountancy	212,184	2200
CPA Journal (accountants)	31,720	575
Consulting Engineer	25,811	1525
Interiors	27,665	1400
Interior Design	40,256	1403
Journal of the AMA (medical doctors)	248,256	3180
American Family Physician	120,215	2250
Medical Economics	164,037	2950
Annals of Internal Medicine	81,901	1260
Journal of the ADA (dentists)	122,329	1900
Dental Products Report (tabloid)	123,911	3470
Dental Management	99,666	2035
Dental Survey	100,618	1850
Drug Topics	71,147	2475
American Druggist	66,717	2430
DVM (veterinarians)	25,612	630
Journal of American Veterinary Medical Association	33,890	880
Veterinary Medicine/Small Animal Clinician	17,636	870
Today's Education	1,666,689	8850
American School and University	45,208	1840
Instructor	232,331	2850
National Elementary Principal	25,925	525
American Bar Association Journal	230,797	3600
The Practical Lawyer	20,865	535
Your Church (Protestant and Jewish Pastors)	189,101	3230

Source: *Standard Rate & Data/Business Publications,* 1978.

the size of the largest metropolitan phone book—*Sweets* provides an organized product literature service to approximately 23,000 architectural, engineering, and contracting offices. Each volume covers the sales literature of an allied line of products. For example, Volume 8 concerns itself with doors and windows. Volume 14 includes "conveying systems" such as elevators and moving stairs and walks. The sales literature in each volume comes from advertisers who buy four-page space units (or multiples thereof). These space units are printed by the advertiser in quantities of 23,000 and made available to the publisher. The publisher, Sweets, binds all the sales literature according to category and mails the sixteen-volume sets to its selected list. Within these volumes, architects and other specifiers have at their fingertips most of the pertinent product literature they will need for their building designs (Figure 12-6). Many advertisers with limited budgets advertise only in *Sweets*, which serves the architect the way the *Thomas Register* serves the industrial purchasing agent.

Sweets distributes other valuable reference volumes: *Industrial Construction & Renovation, Light Residential Construction, Sweets System for the Engineering Market,* and *Sweets System for Interiors.* These are sent to architects, engineers, and interior designers. Other professions depend on their own buying guides for help in specifying. There are annual reference buyers' guides for doctors, dentists, pharmacies, and educators. These professionals use their single-volume references to compare types of equipment side by side, and for referral throughout the year. Some of the better-known annual reference publications are listed in Table 12-3).

DIRECT MAIL

As we have already stated, most companies who advertise use direct mail. Direct mail is particularly effective because advertisers can target it to specific interests. It extends the reach and frequency of publication advertising and lets advertisers mail current information without having to wait for publication dates. Advertisers can justify the cost of mailings to professionals because even a limited response to a high-priced item may include enough profit to more than pay for the entire cost of the mailing program.

FIGURE 12-6
Nearly 2,000 manufacturers annually distribute their product literature through the Sweet's System to key specifying and buying offices in the construction industry. (Courtesy Sweet's Division, McGraw-Hill Company.)

TABLE 12-3
ANNUAL BUYERS' GUIDES (SELECTED)

	Circulation	Cost
The Official Catholic Directory (educators)	11,290	$1870/page
American Druggist Blue Book	64,955	1890/page
Drug Topics Red Book	70,000	1785/page
Interior Decorators Handbook	19,593	700/page
Interior Design Buyers Guide	26,526	1403/page
Sweets System for Interiors	7,000	2451/4 pages
Sweets System for The General Building Market	23,000	3867/4 pages
Sweets System for the Engineering Market	11,000	3867/4 pages
Construction Equipment Buyer's Guide	74,030	2265/4 pages

Advertisers also use direct mail for the dramatic device called "the teaser." When Tremco (see the case study at the end of the chapter) wanted to interest New York-based architects in a waterproof sealant, it developed a teaser campaign, aptly called "The perfectly dry Manhattan." Tremco set the stage with a series of mailings. First, it mailed its selected group of architects a cocktail glass—for Manhattans, naturally. It then sent tickets for two free Manhattans at a well-known city bistro. Finally, Tremco sent sales literature and specifications on the waterproof sealant. Teasers are advertising clues that disclose minimal information. They tease the recipient to solve the mystery.

The advantage of direct mail is that it allows companies to maximize their advertising efforts by reducing waste circulation. Yet sometimes professional office procedures interfere. Receptionists and assistants may screen mail. Devising ways to overcome the screening barrier still taxes the imagination of many manufacturers. Some purposely direct mail to the office assistants and ask them to pass it along. Others reward the office staff with premiums and inducements.

One of the attractions of direct mailings for manufacturers is the easy availability of names. For example, *Progressive Architecture* allows its advertisers to mail (through the publication) to names on its circulation lists at approximately $40 per thousand names. *Drug Topics* rents the use of its names to advertisers at $20 per thousand, a somewhat below average cost for most industrial and professional magazines. Many advertisers know that the names on publication circulation lists are probably the most up-to-date ones available from any source (Figure 12-7).

THE ADVERTISING APPEAL

The best way to attract professionals to your ads is to analyze their job functions. If your own research hasn't provided you with the data you need,

DENTISTS

OFFICAL ADA MASTER LIST

141,500 Licensed dentists, including members and non-members of the ADA

List Owner: American Dental Association

List Maintenance: Daily by the ADA Service Bureau

Update Frequency: Monthly from magnetic tapes provided Business Mailers by the ADA

DESCRIPTION

The only mailing list covering every licensed dentist in the U.S. and Possessions. The dentist is well above the average American in income and education and is highly responsive to quality offers for professional, business and personal products and services.

SELECTIONS

By general or specialty practice, dental teaching, age, geographic location, dental school and year of graduation, ADA membership.

Selected Dental Counts	APPROX. TOTALS
General practice	109,915
Oral surgery	3,609
Endodontists	939
Orthodontists	6,220
Pedodontists	1,818
Periodontists	1,932
Prosthodontists	738
Oral pathologists	75
Private practice under 65	106,829

RENTAL CHARGES

Over 100,000	$ 14.00/m
50,001-100,000	17.00/m
30,001-50,000	20.00/m
20,001-30,000	24.00/m
10,001-20,000	26.00/m
5,001-10,000	30.00/m
Minimum order	125.00
Plus ADA Royalty Fee	4.00/m

DENTAL STUDENTS

18,000 1st, 2nd, 3rd, and 4th year students (List available October thru May only)

List Owner: American Dental Association

List Maintenance: Daily by the ADA

Update Frequency: Monthly from magnetic tape provided Business Mailers by the ADA

DESCRIPTION

Important group to pre-sell dental products and equipment, recruitment, for insurance, office furniture and personal products.

SELECTION

By dental school, geographic area, anticipated year of graduation, age.

RENTAL CHARGES

	$20.00/m
Minimum order	75.00
Plus ADA Royalty Fee	4.00/m

FIGURE 12-7

Sample of a mailing list breakdown of dentists that specifies type of practice and the rental charges for use of the names. Professional magazines offer their readers' names to advertisers for direct mailing purposes. (Courtesy Business Mailers, Inc.)

professional publications can answer these questions:

1 How much time do their readers spend with their magazines?
2 What type of editorial matter is of interest?
3 Why do readers prefer one magazine over another?
4 What kind of advertising do readers like and why?

Armed with this information, your creative people can begin to formulate a meaningful advertising approach. Table 12-4 lists some suggestions.

A word about language. Make certain that your advertising language does not betray you as an amateur. Nothing turns off a professional faster than ads that are simplistic, incorrect, or open to serious debate.

TABLE 12-4
SELECTED COPY APPEALS TO PROFESSIONALS

Job functions	Appeals
Architects	Use colorful, innovative designs to attract attention; provide informative details and specifications; use architectural designs as art; avoid brag-and-boast copy. Architects are designers at heart and want to be remembered for their buildings. They also want to avoid product failures and unhappy clients. In the final analysis, they are more concerned with esthetics and reliability than with costs.
Consulting engineers	Use specific data that has meaning to these electrical, mechanical, structural, chemical, and other specialists. They need facts. They are interested in function before beauty. They don't appreciate manufacturers who advertise "free engineering services" because they see these offers as reducing their income.
Doctors, dentists, veterinarians	Use headlines that promise benefits relating to their practices; provide proof in lieu of claims; communicate your message quickly.
Pharmacists	Use two distinctly different appeals. One concerns information about the product and what it does for the patients; the other, relating to profits, includes advertising support from the manufacturer such as point-of-purchase displays and coop deals.
Interior designers	Use good design, the more dramatic the better; don't be afraid of a relevant emotional appeal. Interior designers work with furnishings and fabrics that convey a wide range of emotions. Use a businesslike profit approach. Like pharmacists, interior designers are sensitive to the financial success of their operations.
Educators	Use case histories and educator testimonials about successful installations of your products. Most educators are progressive in outlook as a result of working with young people; they will accept the new provided there is evidence it will work or has worked.

THE ROLE OF THE PROFESSIONAL SOCIETY

Iron and steel engineers have the IASE (Association of Iron and Steel Engineers); architects have the AIA (American Institute of Architects); doctors and dentists have the AMA (American Medical Association) and the ADA (American Dental Association). These are some of the professional societies to which professional people belong as a matter of competence and pride. Members of professional societies unite in common cause to promote the advancement of their professions and to spread knowledge about and appreciation of their work.

What do professional societies have to do with advertising? Actually their influence is more on the side of "thou shalt not" than "thou shalt". For example, most professional societies look with disfavor on members who actively advertise their own services despite a professional's legal right to do so. This feeling carries over to attempts by manufacturers to enlist the help of professionals in promoting their products. A sure-fire way to turn off professionals, for example, is to show several doctors saying that "XYZ high blood pressure pills" resulted in unqualified success for their practices. This attitude may eventually change as a result of the 1976 Supreme Court decision[7] but it will take time before advertising by doctors and lawyers is condoned by the majority of their peers. Interestingly enough, the federal government (through the Federal Trade Commission) is anxious to encourage advertising by professionals. Its argument, disputed by the professional societies, is that advertising fosters competition (Figure 12-8).

Professional societies often establish standards of product excellence that manufacturers must meet. The approval of most professional societies is thus available to any manufacturer who can meet designated standards. For example, heating and piping work must meet ASHRAE (American Society of Heating, Refrigerating, and Air-Conditioning Engineers) standards. Mechanical, structural, and other products must conform to standards set by other societies such as the American Society of Mechanical Engineers (ASME), the American Institute of Electrical Engineers (AIEE), and the American Society of Civil Engineers (ASCE) (Figure 12-9). The inclusion of professional approvals in ads and literature reassures many specifiers. Even though these approvals are relegated to small type and usually appear at the bottom of the page, they do provide the same kind of assurance to the specifier as the Good Housekeeping Seal of Approval does for the homemaker.

THE FUTURE FOR PROFESSIONAL MEDIA

Because of their need for comprehensive information in a fast-changing world, professionals will continue to depend heavily on outside communications sources. But the information may not come to them in the customary

[7]*Virginia State Board of Pharmacy v. Virginia Citizens Consumer Council*, 425 U.S.748 (1976).

Dentists (Cont'd)

Allegretti Anthony J Inc
 General Dentistry
 Santa Teresa Professional Center
 Suite B
 6128 Camino Verde Dr 226 3870
Allen Donald E Dr
 Practice Limited To Endodontics
 1680 Westwood Dr 264 0600
Allen John W Dr 2075 Lincoln Av ... 265 2011
Almaden Valley Dental Group
 Practice Of General Dentistry
 Country Club Medical-Dental
 Professional Bldg-Suite 8
 6529 Crown Bl 997 1272
Alvarez A D DDS
 7176 Santa Teresa Bl. 226 7760
Alwyn David J DDS
 2034 Forest Av 293 3280
 If No Answer Call 248 2700
Anderson Bruce K DDS
 Practice Limited To
 Dentistry For Children
 Almaden-Country Club
 Medical-Dental Building
 6529 Crown Bl 268 5511
 If No Answer Call 246 6053
Anderson Bruce K DDS
 Practice Limited To
 Dentistry For Children
 Santa Clara Medical-Dental
 Building
 1080 Scott Bl SClara 241 6870
 If No Answer Call 246 6053
Anderson Kenneth J
 Foothill Medical Dental Center
 877 W Fremont Av Sunyvl 739 1130
Anderson Kimball M Dr
 235 E Santa Clara. 295 0215
Anderson Ronald L 2011 Forest Av . 286 3421
Andolina Nicholas R
 General Dentistry
 Medical Center-Suite 33
 Day Or Night Call
 100 O'Connor Dr 287 5704
Angelo A Orphan
 Practice Limited To
 Dentistry For Children
 266 N Jackson Av 272 2720

Araldi Donald P DDS Inc
 Practice Limited To Orthodontics
 10353 Torre Av Cprtno 252 7827
Armstrong Bill F DDS
 Altos Medical Center Suite B-1
 881 Fremont Av LosAltos 941 8250
Asatani Robt M DDS Inc
 Practice Limited To Orthodontics
 1888 Saratoga Av 379 8323
August A M
 19000 Cox Av Saratoga. 255 9060
Baet Francisco DDS
 General Dentistry
 2451 S King Rd. 274 3646
Baker Norman A DDS
 General Dentistry
 Evenings & Saturdays By Appt
 545 Saratoga Av SClara 246 9922
Baldwin Jay K DDS
 Downer Square
 420 Blossom Hill Rd. 227 0910
Barnes Donald H Dr Inc
 1610 Westwood Dr. 264 6160
Barr R E DDS
 Family Practice
 Day Or Night Call
 3031 Tisch Wy 247 9626
Barr Ronald H DDS
 205 Union Sq Mall UnionCity 489 4660
 Cor Alvarado-Niles & Decoto Rds
Barrett Darwin S Dr
 Practice Limited To Periodontics
 West Valley Professional Center
 5150 Graves Av 257 4558
Basta Thos F
 20445 Pacifica Dr Cprtno. 252 4570
Baughman Gary R DDS
 Practice Limited To Orthodontics
 West Valley Professional Center
 5150 Graves Av 253 4880
Beck Braden W
 General Dentistry
 843 Altos Oaks Dr LosAltos 941 8330
Beck Josiah D DDS
 2500 The Villages Pkwy. 274 9554
Befu George S DDS Inc
 Practice Limited To Orthodontics
 Torre Professional Center Suite D
 10353 Torre Av Cprtno 257 0723
 (Continued Next Page)

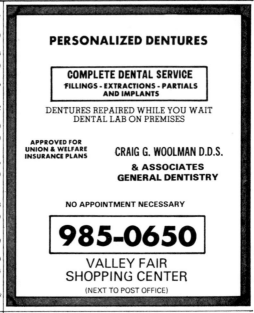
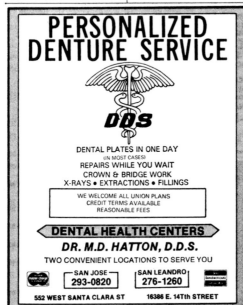

FIGURE 12-8
A page from a California phone book introduces dentists who advertise. Most dental societies still frown on such advertising as lacking professionalism.

TINTED GLASS

Ford Heat-Absorbing Float Glass (Sun-X)

Through its chemical composition, Sun-X—Ford's heat-absorbing float glass—absorbs and re-radiates a high percentage of the sun's heat energy, thus reducing total solar transmission. In addition, Sun-X has a higher light transmission than gray or bronze glass for bright, cheerful interiors. Produced in an attractive blue-green tint, Ford heat-absorbing float glass not only helps reduce solar heat gain and energy consumption, but also adds a decorative appeal for many commercial structures, such as hospitals, institutions and schools. All Ford heat-absorbing float glass is of glazing quality and can be obtained in thicknesses from ⅛" to ¼". Sun-X float glass is an attractive alternative that can be used to minimize "life cycle costs."

Specifications—Heat Absorbing Glass

All Heat Absorbing glass shall be Sun-X glass as manufactured by Ford Glass Division. The glass shall be of glazing quality,_____thick and shall meet Federal Specification DD-G-451c.

SOLAR CONTROL TINTED GLASS

Product	Nominal Thickness mm.	Nominal Thickness in.	Type or Quality	Available Size (1)(2) in.	Approx. Weight lb./sq. ft.	Transmittance Visible %	Transmittance Total Solar %	U-Value Btu/hr.- sq. ft/F°	Shading Coefficient	Relative Heat Gain (3) Btu/hr.- sq. ft.
Bronze	3.0	1/8	Glazing	72 x 110	1.65	69	66	1.0	0.84	184
	5.0	3/16	Glazing	128 x 168	2.47	59	55	1.0	0.76	168
	6.0	1/4	Glazing	128 x 168	3.29	52	48	1.0	0.70	156
	10.0	3/8	Glazing	128 x 168	4.94	37	33	1.0	0.58	130
	12.0	1/2	Glazing	128 x 168	6.58	28	24	1.0	0.50	115
Gray	3.0	1/8	Glazing	72 x 110	1.65	62	65	1.0	0.84	184
	5.0	3/16	Glazing	128 x 168	2.47	50	53	1.0	0.74	165
	6.0	1/4	Glazing	128 x 168	3.29	41	46	1.0	0.67	150
	10.0	3/8	Glazing	128 x 168	4.94	28	33	1.0	0.58	130
	12.0	1/2	Glazing	128 x 168	6.58	19	24	1.0	0.50	115
Sun-X	3.0	1/8	Glazing	80 x 120	1.65	83	65	1.0	0.82	184
	5.0	3/16	Glazing	120 x 180	2.47	78	53	1.0	0.74	165
	6.0	1/4	Glazing	130 x 180	3.29	74	46	1.0	0.71	150

(1) Sizes listed are maximum available sizes, and may exceed recommended windload requirements. Refer to Page 8 for windload charts.
(2) Contact Ford Glass Division General Office for sizes exceeding those shown above.
(3) When Solar Heat Gain Factor from ASHRAE is 200 Btu/hr.-sq. ft. and outdoor temperature is 15°F. higher than indoors temperature with no indoor shading.

FIGURE 12-9

Creators of this specification literature made certain that the reference to ASHRAE was included. Advertisers include references to society standards because they build confidence among professionals. (Courtesy Ford Glass Division, Ford Motor Company.)

magazine, reference book, or direct-mail format. It may arrive as a microscopic film (microfiche) for subsequent enlargement and reproduction. The microfiche approach has been tried in the past and will undoubtedly grow more popular as businesses purchase more electronic and computerized equipment.

But michofiche may seem rather primitive compared to the communication capabilities of the "optical fiber," an extremely thin glass strand that carries laser-beam messages simultaneously in both directions. With the growing popularity of cable television and the adaptability of computers, cassettes, and facsimile transmission equipment, the likelihood of two-way optical-fiber communication between the professional and the media source (and even the advertiser) become probable. Professionals with new-generation video playback equipment can store visual and audio messages for replay. By pushing the right buttons, they'll get a hard-copy printout. Incorporating the telephone into facsimile transmission systems, professionals will in turn converse with the advertiser, review a case study stored in a memory bank, or conduct a conference-call buying review among experts separated by hundreds of miles but linked by wall-sized telescreens. Contributing to the new communications revolution is the fact that optical glass fibers are made from low-cost, plentiful silicon. Inevitably, as this optical fiber revolution develops, professional media sources, now heavily print-oriented, will expand their activities to include direct telecommunication channels to their audiences of specialized professionals. Can advertisers do anything but follow?

IN SUMMARY

1 Because of their long training period, practicing professionals are fairly mature.
2 Advertisers need to recognize that the primary reason people enter professional fields is their desire to serve others.
3 Professionals' informational needs are increasing; they look to their specialized media for help.
4 Media buyers searching for appropriate professional magazines should begin with audited magazines and request publishers to provide a circulation breakdown.
5 Readership studies directed and paid for by advertisers are less likely to be accused of bias than studies subsidized by involved publications.
6 It is not unusual for several magazines to claim the same readers because professionals often read more than one journal.
7 The *Sweets System for the General Building Market* is a sixteen-volume annual compilation of advertising literature prepared by associated manufacturers. Professionals of other specialties also read annual buying guides.
8 One of the hazards of direct mail to professionals is the tendency for office staff to screen the mail for their employers.
9 Advertisers frequently refer to professional standards to establish credibility in their ads and literature.

CASE STUDY   Tremco

For over fifty years, Tremco of Cleveland, Ohio, has been supplying its customers with maintenance and construction products. Tremco has its fair share of competitors, but its approach to advertising to professionals is unique. Tremco tries to:

1 develop the finest products to solve problems.
2 train and educate field representatives to explain, recommend, and sell these products.
3 assume responsibility for their performance.

The soundness of the Tremco business philosophy is reflected in its excellent sales history: the company has grown at an annual average rate of 15 percent over the past five years.

Tremco is divided into three marketing divisions: building maintenance, industrial-construction, and consumer products. The industrial-construction market receives most of Tremco's media advertising dollars. Tremco serves this market with a national (United States and Canada) sales force of field representatives who call on architects, construction specifiers, and contractors. These field reps are supported by advertising in the following business publications: *Architectural Record, Progressive Architecture, Building Design and Construction, Construction Specifier, Canadian Architect*, and *Specification Associates* (Canada).

In late 1968, Tremco and its advertising agency, Carr Liggett Advertising, conducted a creative review of Tremco and its advertising competitors. A group of architects and a group of contractors discussed their problems and evaluated Tremco's response to these problems. Tremco and the agency learned that:

1 Architects liked good taste and straightforward claims.
2 Product-oriented ads were not receiving high readership among architects because of competition and the increasing use of multipage and four-color ads.
3 Contractors liked ads showing practical solutions to problems they faced.
4 Contractors disbelieved overstatement.

In late 1971, Tremco initiated a new architectural series of prototype ads with a panel of specifiers from major New York firms. Tremco and its ad agency saw to it that:

1 Proposed ads provided interesting, informative material to architects.
2 Readers recognized the difference between Tremco and its competitors.
3 All promotional material displayed Tremco's technical leadership.

After the approved ads appeared in Tremco's media list, an evaluation of their performance based on this new creative approach showed that:

1 The new ads outperformed all others in their category except those that were multipage, four-color inserts or those that were announcing new products.
2 The new ads outperformed any competitor by at least 7 percentage points.[8]
3 A new ad in *Architectural Record* outscored all previous Tremco ads in that publication with the exception of one four-color ad (Figure 12-10).

[8]With *Architectural Record's* circulation of 54,539, this amounts to 3,817 additional readers per ad.

FIGURE 12-10

Stylized illustrations and bold headlines feature in Tremco's approach aimed at architects. The Starch ad-as-a-whole rating: noted 32 percent, associated 31 percent, read most 8 percent. These percentages reveal that 32 percent of the entire publication's readership "noted" the ad and that approximately that same percentage associated the two-page ad with Tremco. Starch studies are accepted, among others, as reliable indicators of magazine readership. (The second page of the ad discussed details of the system.)

Follow-up studies of panel members indicate that Tremco's new approach is still preferred, although the company continues to watch readership studies carefully. Tremco achieved its position of eminence through research and experimentation; the company sees no reason to switch its philosophy now.[9]

QUESTIONS NEEDING ANSWERS

1 What are the advantages of setting up a panel of architects to review prospective ads? Are there any disadvantages to this arrangement?
2 What are the advantages or disadvantages of large amounts of explanatory copy in industrial ads?
3 Can you think of another creative approach for Tremco that would perform as well or better?

STUDENT PROJECT

Select an ad from any of the professional publications listed in Table 12-2. Cut out or photocopy the ad and bring it to class. Be prepared to analyze the effectiveness of the advertiser's communication message.

QUESTION RELATING TO THE PROJECT

Find the cost of the ad (on a one-time basis) you selected in *Standard Rate & Data/Business Publications.* Based on whom you consider the specific target audience, would direct mail or publication space have been cheaper? (Check the circulation breakdown in SRDS to help you with your analysis).

[9]Information provided by Anthony Paglia, Jr., former advertising manager of Tremco.

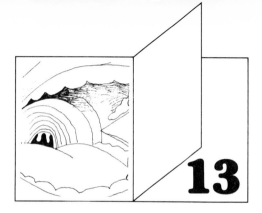

CONVENTIONS, TRADE SHOWS, AND DEALER PROMOTIONS

Update We've emphasized publication space advertising in the last two chapters because it is the manufacturer's principal way of communicating with professional and industrial buyers. But publication advertising has its limitations. It can only make contact, arouse interest, and create preferences. It cannot physically introduce the product or make personal sales contact. Advertisers use another promotional medium for these purposes— the annual convention and/or trade show. To some manufacturers, these also represent an important commitment to advertising.

Long ago, advertisers discovered that an exhibit of their products at a large gathering of their customers and prospects could reduce the cost of making a personal sales call followed by a sales proposal. Professional people call their gatherings conventions or conferences; industrial buyers and retailers call them trade shows. All these groups attend annual events for somewhat similar reasons: to talk to others in their field about mutual problems, to exchange ideas, and to see whether the products displayed are worth buying. Perhaps the most unique aspect of conventions and trade shows is that show attendees are buyers in search of sellers, a complete reversal of the usual buyer-seller relationship. Let's examine the reasons for this turnaround.

THE NATIONAL CONVENTION

A national convention is a large, temporary show restricted to members of the group sponsoring it and to the advertisers that support it. Advertisers display current and new products of special interest to the professionals attending the convention. Attending national conventions is very important to many companies who sell to and through professionals. Abbott Laboratories, for example, manufacturers of medicines and life-support pharmaceuticals, invests some of its large promotional budget in annual exhibits at medical conventions. So do Affiliated Hospital Products of St. Louis and I.T. Baker Chemical Company of Bridgeport, Connecticut, manufacturers of medical instruments. I.T. Baker is a small company that invests over 36 percent of its total promotional budget in displays at conventions. The importance of and attendance at national conventions show no sign of slackening over the years (Table 13-1).

What magnet draws advertisers to expensive professional conventions year after year? Advertisers display at conventions because:

1 They are good places to develop sales leads among professionals from all over the country.
2 Advertisers can show and demonstrate even the most complicated equipment.
3 Advertisers can make their own engineering and technical people available to prospects to solve problems.
4 Conventions provide immediate professional response to new products.

Like advertisers, professionals have compelling reasons for attending conventions. The professional societies and associations, for example, have certain common needs: for membership, for regular meetings, for media contact, and for funds. Conventions help these groups meet their needs in the following ways:

1 Conventions foster a sense of pride among members and help justify the cost of belonging to the society.
2 Conventions permit members to gather in one place to exchange ideas, to socialize, and to receive national publicity.
3 Exhibitors pay for most of the convention's cost and even return money to the society's treasury.

TABLE 13-1

TYPICAL SHOWS, CONVENTIONS. AND CONFERENCES*

Ranking Number 77 76	SHOW	77 SF	76 SF	SPACE RATE	77 No. Exhibs	76 No. Exhibs	77 Attend	76 Attend	DATE	PLACE
1 1	RVIA National Show	500,450	530,329	$1.75 Mfr. $3.50 (Supp)	324	312	9,846	23,155*	Nov 28-Dec 1	Kentucky Fair & Expo Center, Louisville, KY
2 2 (75)	Forest Products Machy & Equip. Exposition +	500,000	600,000	$.20-$5.00	245	220	12,000*	15,000*	June 10-12	Texas State Fairgrounds, Dallas, TX
3 3	National Hardware Show	462,571	439,026	$5.25	2,170	1,934	75,039*	65,677*	Aug 22-25	McCormick Place, Chicago, IL
4 4	International Marine Trade Exhibit & Conference	450,000	432,000	$4.25 (bulk) $5.50 (booths)	940	816	37,000*	37,000*	Sep 22-25	McCormick Place, Chicago, IL
5 5	NHMA National Housewares Exposition +	421,003	408,988	$2.50	1,502	1,431	15,243*	14,064*	Jul 11-14	McCormick Place, Chicago, IL
6 6	NHMA National Housewares Exposition +	420,000	407,000	$2.50	1,572	1,457	19,352*	19,111*	Jan 17-20	McCormick Place, Chicago, IL
7 10	National Manufactured Housing Show	400,000	374,000	$2.50-$3.00	260	230	11,000*	10,000*	Jan 11-16	Kentucky Exposition Center, Louisville, KY
8 7	Offshore Technology Conference	394,283	383,000	$7.00	1,700	1,600	65,511*	60,000*	May 2-5	Astrodomain, Houston, TX
9 12	Summer Consumer Electronics Show	392,000	350,000	$4.50	711	650	50,000*	45,000*	June 5-8	McCormick Place/ McCormick Inn, Chicago, IL
55 66	14th National Fashion & Boutique Show	120,000	110,000	$7.50-$9.50	850	850	30,000	30,000	Jan 6-9	The Coliseum, New York, NY
56 62	New York Stationery Show	119,000	113,058	$3.75-$4.25	534	617	12,037	10,906	May 15-18	The Coliseum, New York, NY
57 64	National Merchandise Show New York	115,900	111,000	NA	957	812	28,879	27,411	Sep 17-20	The Coliseum, New York, NY
58 91	International Trucking Show +	114,000	79,011	$4.00-$4.50	294	239	22,700*	21,251*	Mar 30-Apr 1	Anaheim Convention Center, Anaheim, California
59 63	Dallas Gift, Jewelry & Housewares Show	111,800	111,800	NA	576	576	15,162	15,162	Jul 2-8	Dallas Market Center, Dallas, TX
60 77	Design Engineering Conference & Show	111,000	93,044	$9.00	423	343	24,691*	23,021*	May 9-12	McCormick Place, Chicago, IL
61 73	SEMICON/West	110,000	98,400	$6.00	350	300	20,000	14,000	May 24-26	San Mateo Fairground San Mateo, CA
62 57	Atlanta National Gift Show	105,770	120,000	$3.50	420	330	15,000	11,000	Jul 24-28	Georgia World Congress Center, Atlanta, GA
63 80	International Tool & Manufacturing Exposition & Engineering Conference	105,471	90,000	$8.00	336	262	24,325*	19,663*	May 9-12	Cobo Hall, Detroit, MI

*Courtesy Tradeshow Week, Inc., 1978.

For some professional societies, the annual convention is the biggest money maker of the year. Promotion of the show may fall to members of the society's staff or it may be passed along to a professional show producer such as Clapp & Poliak, the nation's largest such producer. Regardless of who does the work, it boils down to contacting the appropriate advertisers, alerting members to the upcoming convention, assisting with program events, negotiating with convention bureaus and hotels to ensure adequate lodging at reasonable prices, and informing the press.

The national convention is an organized advertising meeting place for keeping professionals up to date about new ideas and materials. It also serves to introduce buyers to new vendors and new sources of materials. These are some of the reasons 500 advertising exhibitors show their wares at a school administrators' convention, for example, where approximately 100,000 educators rub shoulders each year.

The Advertiser Prepares for a Convention

Manufacturers often budget their usually substantial convention expenses directly from the total advertising budget. It is a truism that the smaller the company, the larger the percentage of the ad budget that goes for convention expenses. It is crucial that the advertiser receive the most from such an investment. Regular exhibitors have learned through experience that certain steps help make the convention successful.

They try to introduce a new product or the revised version of an existing product at each convention. This action will justify the professionals' annual pilgrimage to an exhibition booth. They try to include something animated or moving in their product exhibit to attract attention. They might keep a technical expert at their booth every day so professionals can assess the company's technological philosophy and competence.

They design the most attractive display possible so it can be used for several years. It's best to avoid the homemade look that will compare poorly to the professionally built displays at the convention. Most major cities have display builders who can advise you and provide cost estimates. A minimal cost estimate for a well-built, 10-foot display is about $5,000 (Figure 13-1). They early on must decide what size booth they will require, and then *reserve* that space with the promoters of the convention. The basic unit of exhibit space is the 10×10-foot module, that is, 100 square feet of floor space. The average square-foot cost falls into the $5 to $8 range. Thus, the basic 100-square-foot unit of space you can rent will cost approximately $500 to $800 for the duration of the convention—in most cases, three to five days. Rental costs are generally a small part of all convention costs.

Other tips for exhibitors:

Design all electrical and mechanical devices and mount them right into the display. Hiring electricians and other high-priced labor at the show can be very costly, and often frustrating. Get to know the union regulations at each convention site where you expect to exhibit. Your display builder will know

FIGURE 13-1
Typical convention display is designed to permit easy access. Courtesy Oscar & Associates, commercial photographers.

most of the problems and can advise you. Reserve your exhibit space early, and prepare the booth display and other supporting materials in plenty of time before the show. Some veteran exhibitors ship displays three to four weeks before opening day. A heavy, rugged, wooden crate is almost a necessity to enable small items to withstand repeated shippings and handling. Ship heavy machinery and equipment uncrated if possible. It saves handling costs.

Contact both company and distributor personnel to find out what they would like to be shown at the convention. Plan to automate attendance record keeping with imprinting devices for recording names and addresses of convention-goers. Convention promoters often distribute plastic name and address cards for this purpose. The imprinting machine is similar to those used in hotels and service stations. You can use these names and addresses to compile a mailing as well as a sales call list.

Plan a few questions to ask conventioneers about their publication readership habits and their reactions to your ads. You can learn about your advertising's effectiveness. Leave press kits and photos in the press room for the business editors who attend the show. Keep an ample supply of literature and sales sheets at the booth to satisfy prospects. Make it a point to meet any business editors who may be attending. They could be good public relations contacts later.

Run a brief notice in your publication ads that you will be at the show, to alert readers who will be interested in visiting your booth. Schedule plant tours if the convention is held nearby; they are a good way to show off your facilities.

Some companies enter national conventions without recognizing the demands of this commitment, or some of the drawbacks. They may fail to realize the expense of bringing salespeople from all parts of the country to the convention and disrupting other normal sales activity. The company may not have sufficient personnel to arrange for transporting exhibits, nor for staffing the booth for several days. Also, by underestimating the true costs of the convention, the company may be forced to shelve or curtail other critical promotional projects. Few advertisers care to rely solely on one convention per year as their total communications effort.

INDUSTRIAL TRADE SHOWS

An industrial trade show is usually a major "show and tell" for buyers and sellers of industrial products and services. It may be produced on behalf of an association (such as the Association of Iron and Steel Engineers [AISE]) or an industry (such as the textile industry).

Advertisers who don't know when and where trade shows relating to their industries are being held can check with the editors of appropriate publications or with *Industrial Marketing Magazine* or *Advertising Age*. These magazines include calendars of trade shows and conventions. Sometimes show promoters or the staff of the industrial association can provide information. The prospective exhibitor needs to know the following:

1 Who attends the shows? What are their job functions, company names, SIC numbers (Figure 13-2)?
2 Where do attendees come from? Are they from within a 500-mile radius or beyond? Studies reveal that shows held in New York, Philadelphia, and West Coast cities draw people only within 500 miles. Chicago, on the other hand, attracts people from all over the country.
3 What has been the show's total attendance in the previous two or three years?
4 Who are the current and past exhibiting firms? Determine whether your competitors are active on the show circuit.

The modern trade show is generally a smoothly run pageant produced by an experienced organization whose job it is to serve the needs of the attendees. Buyers want to find solutions to their problems; and exhibitors want to find buyers for their products. Some trade shows occur every year, others less often. Generally these shows are held in interesting cities such as Chicago, New York, and Las Vegas, where the show's meeting facilities and hotel accommodations are ample and pleasant.

Budgeting for Trade Shows and Conventions

Because a trade show or convention can eat up large amounts of money, it's wise to prepare a complete budget for the event. The convention kit sent by

Product Categories	Percent of Engineers	Estimated Audience at Show
Metals	54	10,800
Plastics	48	9,600
Mechanical Components	73	14,600
Fluid Power Components	42	8,400
Electrical Components	40	8,000
Electronic Components	39	7,800
Power Transmission Components	40	8,000
Finishes, Coatings	37	7,400
Fasteners, Adhesives	55	11,000
Shapes, Forms	26	5,200
Engineering Services & Equipment	36	7,200

Analysis By Job Function

	Visitors	Percent
Design Engineering	6,417	31.3
Marketing Management	3,619	17.7
Production/Manufacturing	1,798	8.8
Company Officer	1,754	8.6
President/Owner	1,694	8.3
Industrial Engineering	1,535	7.5
Research/Development	1,440	7.0
Purchasing	472	2.3
Other	1,748	8.5
Total registered attendance	20,477	100%

Analysis By Industry

	Visitors	Percent
Metal Products	3,941	19.3
Electrical Machinery	2,792	13.6
Instruments/Controls	2,029	9.9
Machinery/Non-Electric	1,964	9.6
Engineering Services	1,443	7.0
Rubber/Plastics	1,311	6.4
Industrial Distributor	1,202	5.9
Chemical/Petroleum	766	3.7
Transportation Equipment	628	3.1
Food/Beverages	604	2.9
Construction	535	2.6
Paper/Printing	526	2.6
Government/Military	376	1.8
Primary Metals	330	1.6
Transportation	258	1.3
Textiles/Apparel	245	1.2
Stone/Clay/Glass	215	1.1
Not Classified	851	4.2
Miscellaneous Manufacturing	461	2.2
Total	20,477	100%

FIGURE 13-2

The anatomy of a show reveals itself through attendance figures. Advertisers can analyze attendees by industry, job function, and product. For over twenty-five years, the Design Engineering Show has brought buyers and sellers together in a market estimated at $190 billion. (Courtesy Clapp & Poliak, Inc.)

the promoters will explain most costs. Budget items should include:

1 Cost of convention rental space (number of square feet × cost per square foot).
2 Cost of building or updating a display.
3 Cost of labor to set up and dismantle an exhibit at the site.
4 Cost of building a shipping crate.
5 Cost of shipping the display to the convention city, and of storage and return.
6 Cost of any necessary electrical, phone, or water connections.
7 Cost of furniture and floor-covering rentals.
8 Cost of the cleaning porter.

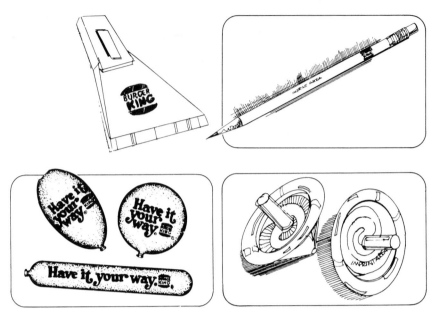

FIGURE 13-3
A small assortment of the hundreds of premium items available to advertisers for handouts at shows and conventions. Sometimes a unique premium will attract large crowds to an exhibition booth. Most convention handouts cost a few pennies each. (Courtesy Rogers Merchandising, Inc.)

9 Cost of any special project for the show: film, slide show, newspaper, magazine, give-away premiums. (Figure 13-3).
10 Cost of sales literature and of the time of booth participants or models.
11 Contingency funds for emergencies.

Some advertisers on limited budgets invest their whole budget in trade shows. To them, as well as to others, it's important to gauge all the costs, not merely the most visible ones. Only by recording all trade show costs can an advertiser in the final analysis determine the value of the show.

Trade Show Values for the Advertiser

If an advertiser can learn in one place and at one time everything that competitors intend to unfurl during the following year, that time and place is an annual trade show. Within the space of one or two hours, advertisers can evaluate new products and their general acceptance. They can accomplish this by simply walking up and down the aisles, observing and questioning conventioneers. What they learn will most certainly affect their marketing strategies. Attending shows permits technical experts of both selling and buying companies to confer and to see their products in action. This interaction can often resolve problems impossible to settle by long-distance communication.

For smaller companies, attending and exhibiting at trade shows confer a certain prestige. Many small companies provide their manufactured components free of charge to larger exhibiting companies who need them. The components bear an identifying tag that small companies consider good public relations. Trade shows offer advertisers other opportunities. For example, advertising staffs can easily accumulate sales literature from exhibitors and competitors. They can visit with business publication editors. They can take advantage of the presence of thousands of their customers and prospects by running surveys on a variety of subjects. Occasionally, competitors will discuss mutual problems and may even exchange sales literature. The net result of a successful show is a keener awareness of what is going on in the marketplace. No wonder companies look forward to the annual event (Figure 13-4)!

FIGURE 13-4
Convention and trade show exhibits begin as proposed artists' sketches made by professional display builders. Everything is shown to scale. If a sketch is approved by the advertiser, the builder submits a cost estimate. (Courtesy Rappaport Exhibits.)

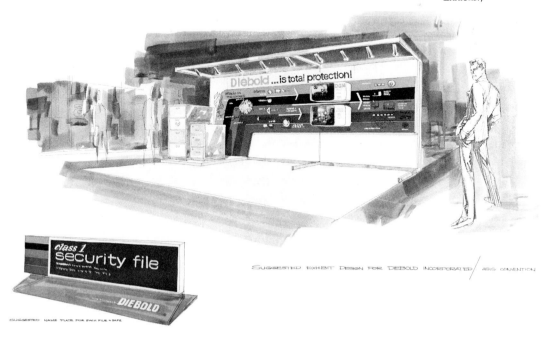

Generally, trade show exhibits are a bit more flamboyant than those at professional conventions. This difference stems from the professionals' traditional conservatism. At trade shows, though, a panorama of selling techniques is employed. These techniques harken back to old exhibitions and fairs in which exhibitors tried to outdo each other in noise and visual delights. Although most advertisers have outgrown this type of exhibitionism, some companies still treat the show as a carnival.

Trade Show Values for Dealers

We've been concentrating our discussion on professional and industrial buyers. We know why they attend conventions and trade shows. Retail dealers attend *their* trade shows for somewhat similar reasons: to talk to other dealers about mutual problems, to exchange ideas, and to see whether the products displayed are worth buying and reselling.

Retailers attend with the intention of writing out orders on the convention floor, and many do so. (Many industrial trade show attendees also visit exhibitors with the intention of ordering equipment.)

The dealer trade show is geared toward selling. Manufacturers want retailers to buy and sell their products. Manufacturers use the trade show as an integral part of their promotional strategy. (Most industrial exhibitors consider the trade show an important but isolated event.) To see how the dealer show fits into the manufacturer's strategy, we need to review how advertisers go about wooing and winning retailers.

DEALER PROMOTIONAL PROGRAMS

Consumer goods manufacturers appeal to the public through the consumer media: television, radio, magazines, and newspapers. But they appeal to dealers through a segment of the business press known as trade books, listed in *Standard Rate and Data Service/Business Publications*. The major purpose of the wide range of trade books—magazines edited for the buying and selling activities of specialized retailers—is to help dealers operate more efficiently and profitably. Advertisers use them to reach dealers. Almost every industry that sells through retailers and/or distributors has its own or several trade magazines. *Implement and Tractor* serves the farm implement dealer; *Dental Industry News* the managers of dental depots; *Hardware Age* and *Hardware Retailer* the retail hardware store and lumber dealer; *Super Service Station* for the gasoline station operator. Manufacturers promote new and existing products in the pages of appropriate trade magazines. They use their ads to illustrate many of the promotional materials available to their dealers: store banners, window signs, floor displays. They also trumpet the news of their consumer advertising efforts on behalf of the dealer.

Here's how the manufacturers of the Snapper riding mower tell their dealer story in a full color ad in *Home & Garden Supply Merchandiser:*

With the new Snapper "high vacuum" rider, I can really mow down the competition.

. . . Snapper has always supplied me with the best in lawn and garden equipment. And they do everything they can to help me sell it. Take advertising, for instance. Sure, they do a lot of national advertising and they come up with special promotions to help me sell Snapper. But best of all, they have the most liberal co-op advertising program in the industry. Another thing. I know that none of my competitors is selling Snapper under another name. Because Snapper is sold only through authorized dealers like me. And we all make a good profit.[1]

It is common practice for manufacturers to develop new dealer programs each year. They hope to inject a continuing sense of excitement into their programs for dealers to convey to the ultimate consumer.

Why Manufacturers Help their Dealers

Manufacturers advertise for dealers and support them with promotional programs for several reasons. One manufacturer's dealers could become another's. Therefore, manufacturer-advertisers invest in dealer programs because if they don't promote to the dealers' customers, dealers will lose sales to retailers that *are* backed by manufacturer advertising. If one manufacturer provides coop funds, dealers often pressure other manufacturers to do likewise. If a manufacturer employs dealer sales incentives such as premiums and free vacation trips, can competitive manufacturers ignore these tactics? Many feel they cannot, and that is why their annual campaign strategies include complete dealer programs advertised to dealers in trade books and through direct mail. Manufacturers often use their industry's annual trade show to physically present the year's promotional materials to dealers (Figure 13-5).

Manufacturers plan complete dealer programs with certain objectives in mind. We'll discuss each of these objectives in turn; they are:

1 To establish dealer program objectives.
2 To establish the program's budget.
3 To formulate the specifics of the program (publication advertising, direct mail, sales calls, deferred billing).
4 To implement the program.
5 To evaluate the dealer program and make recommendations for the succeeding year.

Meeting these five general objectives satisfies most manufacturers. Many withhold the dealer program until the annual trade show and present it there with great fanfare.

[1]Snapper ad, *Home and Garden Supply Merchandiser*, October 1977, p. 13.

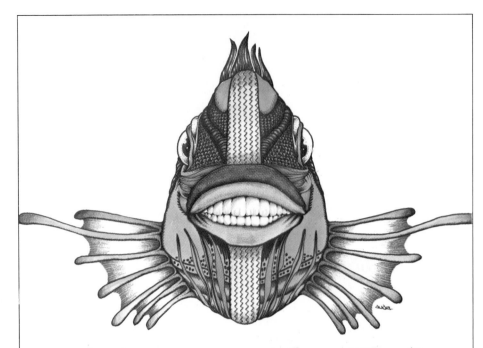

You're a Big Fish with Hercules

Supplying independent tire dealers has been our most important business for over twenty four years. Hercules pioneered the independent brand concept of TBA marketing in 1952. Since the beginning, we've treated all our dealers as "big fish" in the tire business. We learned that sales and company growth go much further than merely handing dealers a line.

This means you can rely on Hercules for a lot more than a quality line of passenger, truck, farm, special-purpose tires and tread rubber. And you get service and delivery when you want it, not just when it suits us. We'll also get you off the hook of having to compete with "own-supplier" competition.

It's a fact: The fish stories you've been hearing about us are true. If you want to be a "big fish" in the tire business — write or call Craig Anderson, V.P. Marketing, Hercules Tire & Rubber Co., 1300 Morrical Blvd., Findlay, OH 45840; telephone (419) 423-7202.

HERCULES TIRES

Visit us in Houston
Booth 1201-1202
NTDRA Convention
September 18-21, 1976

FIGURE 13-5

Taking dead aim at the independent tire dealers, Hercules tells its "big fish" story through the trade publications. The ad tells readers to visit the company's booth. (Courtesy Hercules Tire & Rubber Company.)

Establishing Dealer Objectives To be successful, manufacturers' dealer programs must reach a goal, be it higher unit sales, more knowledgeable dealers, more trade show business, or more retailers involved in the display program. If the goal is unit sales, the manufacturer needs to motivate dealers to put more effort into their sales presentations to consumers. One method manufacturers use is the "loading" principle. Manufacturers "load" dealers with their products by offering special deals and inducements, even delayed billing. When dealers' shelves are filled with products, they become more responsive to investing their own money in co-op advertising. They also direct their store personnel to push the product. Result: more sales and profits for the dealers and reorders for the manufacturer!

If the manufacturer's goal is more knowledgeable dealers, the manufacturer educates retailers about available products and services. Manufacturers know that informed retailers can respond authoritatively to customers' questions and objections.

Attracting as many dealers as possible to the national trade show and to the manufacturer's booth are other measurable goals. Manufacturers take advantage of dealer attendance at trade show booths to present their promotional packages as well as their new pricing and profit schedules.

Some manufacturers establish as a major goal a specific increase over the previous year in the number of point-of-sale displays put up in retailers' stores. They know only too well that many displays never leave the warehouses of either distributors or dealers, where they produce no sales. Some manufacturers react by offering small bonuses to distributor salespeople who physically set up retail displays. Other manufacturers sponsor contests for retail displays of their products.

Establishing the Budget When they've outlined their goals, manufacturers can decide how much to spend to attain them. This decision can raise controversy because various forms of communications cost varying amounts. Also, manufacturers must weigh the relative influence of the dealer upon prospective customers. In some products such as television sets, the dealer has considerable influence. Obviously, in this situation, it is to the manufacturer's advantage to encourage dealer cooperation in promotional programs. Manufacturers would be more inclined to invest more in dealer promotions than if their product were a low-cost, infrequently purchased item such as salt. Some companies regularly ask their dealers what types of promotional materials they prefer as an aid to selling customers. When all the research is in and has been analyzed, the budget determines the media mix.

Formulating the Program Always aware of the budget, the advertising and marketing staff evaluates the relative merits of dealer publications, direct mail, and dealer incentives. One popular incentive for dealers is "dating," an extension of credit to the dealers. Manufacturers ship merchandise with the proviso that the distributor or dealer does not pay until ninety days have elapsed, rather than the usual thirty or sixty days. Dating lets the dealer extend working capital at the expense of the manufacturer. Here's how Jacobsen mowers put it to the trade in a dealer ad:

> Make money on no money . . . with Jacobsen's new dealer floor plan. . . . How long can you go without putting up any money when you're a Jacobsen dealer? Not thirty days. Not sixty days. But all the way to July 1, 1978. . . . This generous "no money-down" floor plan is a great way to free up your working capital while you stock and sell the hot-selling Jacobsen mowers and tractors.[2]

Implementing the Program   As they develop the dealer program, manufacturers must ask themselves a series of leading questions. Here are some typical ones: "If it's to be a direct-mail program, do we use odd-shaped cards, oversized banners, house organs, a series of teaser letters to the dealer and spouse, football tickets to a game held at the site of the annual trade show (Figure 13-6)? If it's to be publication advertising, do we use four-color, multipage ads; do we use multiples of small space ads in one or two colors, or special dollars-off coupons? How about showing the company's entire line in a twenty-four page catalog bound right into the publication so no dealer who receives the trade publication can possibly miss the catalog? If we intend to print new literature, should we send rough layouts to selected dealers to gauge and learn from their reactions?" The promotional choices are restricted only by imagination and the budget.

Evaluating the Program   Some advertising departments dislike finding out how effective dealer programs have been. They consider the time and money spent in evaluation an added burden on a restricted budget. Yet, without meaningful evaluations, departments will repeat errors year after year. In addition, evaluations help support staff recommendations for succeeding years when they present their program to management. Here's how one company, Republic Builders Products, went about evaluating its distributor program when it first presented its campaign budget requirements to management.

The product: a standard, hollow, metal door with a unique seamless edge, called the McKenzie Edge, that costs no more than other popular-priced doors.

The distributors: wholesalers of commercial contract hardware, builders' supplies, concrete blocks, glass, sash and door parts, wholesale lumber, paint, hardware, and hollow metal. Metal fabricators are also part of the target audience.

[2]Jacobsen ad, *Home and Garden Supply Merchandiser*, October 1977, p. 79.

FIGURE 13-6
Maytag dealers were urged to collect "remembrance of things past" in a special energy issue of the company's twenty-four-page house organ, *Maytag Merchandiser*. The direct-mail order form, stapled into the center of the publication, folds into a colorful envelope ready for mailing.

Company's objectives for present and potential distributors: increase or establish:

1 awareness of the name Republic Builders Products Corporation (RBPC).
2 awareness of the relationship between the name RBPC and desirable price, quality, and service.
3 RBPC's reputation as a long-term, distributor-committed manufacturer of hollow metal doors and frames.
4 awareness of the fact that RBPC is a division of Republic Steel Corporation.
5 awareness of the RBPC product offering and the distributors' willingness to serve.
6 awareness of RBPC-distributor relationships within applicable geographical trading areas.
7 a maximum number of qualified prospective distributor and product sales leads.

Through its advertising agency, Meldrum & Fewsmith, RBPC scheduled recruiting and reassurance messages in *Doors and Hardware*, the magazine read most by prospective and present distributors. It followed these ads with a series of direct-mail kits aimed at "hot" distributor prospects (as designated by company sales representatives). To further support present distributors and aid in recruiting new ones, RBPC made envelope stuffers available to them on a cost basis. The stuffers were designed to sell the distributors' customers, the local dealers. They included an imprint space for the distributors' signatures. Finally, the company initiated a magazine schedule to help distributors sell to architects, building owners, specifiers, and manufacturers of metal buildings. These ads appeared in *Metal Building Review, Construction Specifier, Progressive Architecture*, and *Buildings* magazines (Figure 13-7 and 13-8).

Evaluation: A brand preference study[3] indicated that Republic Doors had moved from fifteenth place to the top three in brand awareness. The total advertising space budget for the introductory year was $56,434, with distributor space advertising in *Doors and Hardware* alone at $8,954. RBPC advertising was awarded a first prize by the Fifth District American Advertising Federation. (More on the accountability of advertising in Chapter 21).

Dealer Incentives

In their attempt to influence dealers, manufacturers go beyond the conventional banners, point-of-purchase displays and coop programs that, in the final analysis, are designed for the ultimate consumer. Dealer incentives are prizes and items given for the express use of dealers and their families. The concept is growing in popularity. For example, nearly one in four feed manufacturers will give away hats and caps to dealers. Nearly one in five will offer dealers and salespeople incentive trips if they meet quota.[4] The Ford Parts Division merchandising department manager states, "Our wholesale

FIGURE 13-7
Basic sales literature compares Republic's new McKenzie Edge Door with seven competitive doors. As one of its services, the advertiser supplied quantities of this four-page brochure to its distributors.

[3]"Benchmark 1977 Building Team Brand Preference Study", *Building Design and Construction* magazine, Chicago 1977, p. 30.
[4]"Feedstuffs Survey," *The New Agriculture* magazine, Winter 1977, p. 23.

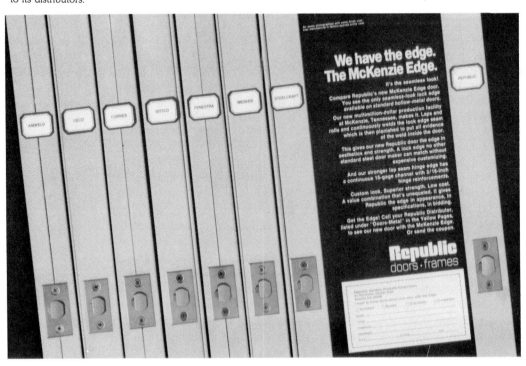

FIGURE 13-8
The advertiser used quarter-page and full-page ads with color to attract distributors and customers. Recapping its entire year's program, billed as the "McKenzie Advertising Edge," Republic informed distributors of its promotional support through a 34- × 22-inch broadside. This quarter-page ad was included among others in the distributor broadside featuring "the quality edge," "the winning edge," "the price edge," and "the service edge."

distributors find that premiums open doors to their customers." Ford generally has one concentrated dealer program in the spring and another in the fall.

So important do company managers consider incentive programs that they often turn them over to specialists in the field called sales promotion companies, because, as a Chicago-based concern points out, "The sales promotion agency is a professional partner and on an equal basis with the advertising agency. It's a relatively new development and came about mostly because advertising agencies do badly what we do well. We are involved with the client in all major decisions and see to it that both promotion and advertising are going in the same direction."[5] Robert Sandelman, another specialist, defines sales promotion as "a selling message *in media the client owns,* while advertising is a selling message in media the client rents, such as television."[6]

Typical sales promotion agencies such as Maritz of St. Louis, Rogers Merchandising of Chicago, and Robert Brian Associates of New York take over the entire planning and implementation phases of manufacturers' dealer/distributor programs. Often they prepare colorful brochures that offer expensive gifts dealers can win by fulfilling specific sales quotas (Figure 13-9). Sales promotion specialists often target dealers' spouses for direct-mail letters, although this tactic has its critics as well as supporters. Supporters feel that the whole family stands to benefit from vacation trips and other gifts. Critics contend that this aspect of the incentive program is degrading to dealers and salespeople and that it is resented by them. Despite the strong feelings on either side for bringing the salesperson's family into the incentive program, both sides are in general agreement that incentive programs work. But there are other ways to build loyalty among dealerships. These have to do with helping dealers become more efficient by providing them with the buying trend statistics of their industry and with forecasts of consumer buying intentions. A logical extension of this statistical assistance to dealers is the customized profit system.

Customized Profit Systems

An innovation among manufacturers for recruiting and keeping dealers is the customized profit system, a scientific method of appraising a retailer's space allocations and profits from various product lines. The service is offered free to the manufacturers' dealers. It is, in effect, a management service. It often begins with a comprehensive four-to eight-week survey that compares the ratio of product sales to shelf space. It includes an analysis of retailers' inventories and deliveries. All this information is fed into a computer and compared to predetermined successful models. After the survey period, retailers learn which items are their best and their slowest sellers, which provide the greatest profit potentials, which should go, and which new ones should be stocked (Figure 13-10).

Some manufacturers feel that dealer-manufacturer relationships are really games of one-upmanship. With so many companies providing sales promotion materials to dealers, manufacturers feel that the chances of doing something unique and startling in this area are diminishing. Soon, they feel, the banners, the point-of-purchase displays, the window signs all begin to

[5]Letter from Henry Bird, Rogers Merchandising, Chicago.
[6]"How to pick a sales promotion agency," Robert Brian Associates' ad, *Advertising Age,* May 26, 1975, p. 42.

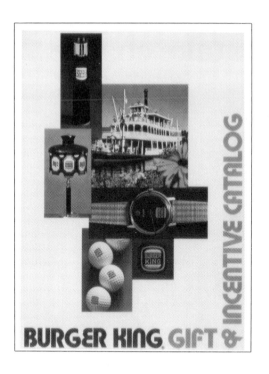

Gift Incentive Catalog
ORDER FORM

ROGERS MERCHANDISING, INC.
PREMIUM & INCENTIVE DEPT.
20 North Wacker Dr., Suite 1600
Chicago, Illinois 60606
(312) 781-9719

FIGURE 13-9
A variation of the typical dealer incentive program was designed for Burger King dealers. This twelve-page catalog offers franchise owners and their families a choice of costume jewelry, watches, lighters, jackets, belt buckles, Tiffany lamps, suede portfolios, sports equipment—even a trip to Disney World. (Courtesy Rogers Merchandising.)

ORDERED BY

NAME

ADDRESS

CITY

STATE   ZIP

SHIP TO

NAME

ADDRESS

CITY

STATE   ZIP

QUANTITY	ITEM NO.	DESCRIPTION	SIZE	COLOR	UNIT COST	TOTAL

FIGURE 13-10

Ace Hardware woos dealers with its offer of a computerized management aid for inventory, cost, and profit control. This service, a recent innovation in the advertisers' arsenal of dealer-programming ideas, is very attractive to retailers.

look alike. But they see in their customized profit system service a new way to win and influence dealers. The chief executive officer of Nabisco puts it this way: "It is my own strong conviction that it is in the areas of marketing, distribution, and merchandising that we can make the most significant contribution to the success of our retail customers."[7]

IN SUMMARY

1 A national convention is a gathering of professional society members and the advertisers who support them. It is often the highlight of the year for societies, members, and advertisers.

2 Advertisers exhibit at conventions because, among other advantages, they can demonstrate equipment and develop sales leads.

3 Hints for improving convention exhibits include introduction of new products, use of animated displays, availability of company technical people for consultation, and an exhibit design that partially or totally lends itself to reuse.

4 Manufacturers can learn about upcoming conventions and trade shows from publications such as *Advertising Age* and *Industrial Marketing*.

5 Advertisers can learn demographic information about attendees from show producers and the organizations sponsoring the show.

6 Budgeting for either a trade show or a convention requires planning and attention to the following: renting exhibit floor space, constructing the display, shipping it to its destination and returning it, and budgeting for costs of site utilities, installation labor, booth personnel, and literature.

7 Trade shows are more flamboyant than conventions; they cater to buyers and sellers of industrial as well as consumer products.

8 Participating in a convention or show lets an exhibitor check on competitors' booths and literature.

9 Manufacturers often integrate trade shows with their complete dealer program. Dealer programs are designed to maintain the loyalty of dealers and, through them, the loyalty of the ultimate consumer.

10 Typical dealer programs include objectives and budgets as well as the formulating, implementing, and evaluating of specific programs.

11 The popularity of dealer incentives has led manufacturers to hire incentive-oriented sales promotion agencies to handle details of the programs.

12 One working definition of sales promotion is "a selling message in media owned by the client".

CASE STUDY Lennox Dealer Program Lennox

Industries, Incorporated, a major force in residential and commercial air-conditioning systems, believes almost religiously in supporting its 5,500 dealers throughout the United States. This support takes the visible form of annual dealer campaign themes

[7]"Achieving rapport with retailers," Lee S. Bickmore, *The Chief Executive*, vol. 1, no. 2, (November 1970), p. 138.

backed by a host of sales promotion items. Lennox makes it easy for dealers to order any of these promotion items by listing or illustrating them on printed order forms. There are forms for banners, sales literature, television commercials, and billboard ads. In addition, there are examples of direct-mail letters the dealers can copy on their own stationery. As Dave Lennox tells it (Figure 13-11), "To help you take advantage of this national campaign, Lennox has assembled this promotion package. Enclosed are details of the niftiest TV campaign ever available to Lennox dealers. New newspaper ads. Radio spots. Billboards. Banners. Materials that promote you as the quality dealer talked about on national television."

Lennox has been organizing and promoting dealer packages similar to this one since 1949. According to Robert D. Hayes, manager of sales promotions, the company invests approximately 10 percent of its total advertising budget in dealer promotions. In addition, dealers earn up to 2 percent of their Lennox purchases for

FIGURE 13-11
Dealers use a company order form for a thirty-second Lennox "customized" television commercial.

Dave Lennox "Customized" TV Commercial Order Form

Lennox Division
☐ Eastern _____
☐ Southeast _____
☐ Southwest _____
☐ Pacific _____
☐ Midwest _____
☐ Northwest _____
☐ Canada _____

(Please fill in, sign and return to your TM or Lennox Sales Office. Retain bottom copy for your records.)

Mr. Dealer: This is your application for use of one or more of the Lennox "Customized" Dealer Television Commercials. The commercials are listed below. If you have any problems or questions, see your Territory Manager or call your Lennox Sales Office.

1. Please purchase TV time in following city or cities: _____
2. Maximum dealer budget for TV time $ _____ .*
3. Dates: Start week of _____; End week of _____ .

Additional requests or comments on above: _____

*Note: This tie-in program is available only through your Lennox Sales Office. Please contact the Sales Office for average TV costs in your city. The Lennox corporate advertising agency will handle **ALL** buys for you. Time of showing and stations used will depend on current availabilities and the best judgement of the advertising agency in coordinating national and local TV schedules. Agency-bought schedules are more effective for reaching your best prospects.

DAVE LENNOX 30 SEC. VIDEO TAPE TV COMMERCIALS

PLEASE DO NOT WRITE IN THIS SPACE
Dealer Code

COMPLETE SCRIPTS ARE PRINTED ON BACK OF YOUR COPY. CHECK BOX FOR DESIRED COMMERCIAL(S).* COST FOR EACH ORIGINAL COMMERCIAL PRINT WILL BE $185.00. DUPLICATE PRINTS COST $25.00 EACH. YOU WILL BE BILLED LATER.

ADD-ON AIR CONDITIONING   To run in spring ☐   fall ☐

☐ General

☐ Special Offer: Fill in your offer here: _____
(See script on back for sample alternate copy)

TOTAL COMFORT SYSTEM   To run in spring ☐   fall ☐

☐ General

☐ Special Offer: Fill in your offer here: _____
(See script on back for sample alternate copy)

SERVICE

☐ General

☐ Special Planned Service (PS)

Note: If more than one commercial is ordered for a season, all commercials will alternate equally unless specified otherwise.

LENNOX Outdoor Advertising

BILLBOARDS-24 SHEET POSTERS-236"x104"
JUNIOR PANELS-125"x54"
Use Billboard Order Form OA-73

BILLBOARD - BD-732
JUNIOR PANEL - JP-732
All Season Sale

BILLBOARD - BB-712
JUNIOR PANEL - JP-712
Heating

BILLBOARD - BB-731
NO JUNIOR PANEL AVAILABLE
Humidifier

BILLBOARD - BB-721
JUNIOR PANEL - JP-721
FOR PLANNED SERVICE DEALERS ONLY

BILLBOARD - BB-723
JUNIOR PANEL - JP-723
Air Conditioning Sale

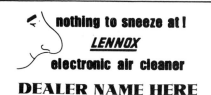

BILLBOARD - BB-702
JUNIOR PANEL - JP-702
Electronic Air Cleaner

BILLBOARD - BB-722
JUNIOR PANEL - JP-722
All Season Comfort

BILLBOARD - BB-681
JUNIOR PANEL - JP-681
Electronic Air Cleaner

BILLBOARD - BB-711
JUNIOR PANEL - JP-711
Central Air Conditioning

FIGURE 13-12
Increasingly, manufacturers are providing billboard posters as part of their dealer programs. The twenty-four-sheet posters (billboards) are 19½ feet long and approximately 9 feet high.

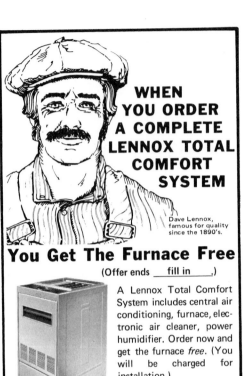

WHEN
YOU ORDER
A COMPLETE
LENNOX TOTAL
COMFORT
SYSTEM

Dave Lennox,
famous for quality
since the 1890's.

You Get The Furnace Free

(Offer ends ___fill in___.)

A Lennox Total Comfort System includes central air conditioning, furnace, electronic air cleaner, power humidifier. Order now and get the furnace *free*. (You will be charged for installation.)

This system is designed to give you the right temperature the year 'round. Clean, filtered air is held to the proper humidity level. Get your free furnace now during Lennox Nifty Weather Days. Call for a free estimate.

Dealer Name
Address and Phone

2 Col. x 7-3/4'' (216 lines)

NOTE ''fill in''

If your newspaper is printed by letterpress, order ads by number from your sales office. If your newspaper is printed by offset, these ads are camera ready. Just add your name, address and phone.

FIGURE 13-13
The typical Lennox dealer ad changes each year along with the company's advertising theme. Lennox offers its dealers numerous ads in various sizes.

1. (Music under) DAVE LENNOX: Take it from Dave Lennox.

2. (VO) A Lennox cooling/heating system...

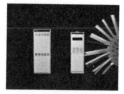

3. ...has over 80 years experience...

4. ...behind it. We've earned...

5. ...a reputation...

6. ...for good, dependable equipment.

7. A Lennox system keeps you in total...

8. ...comfort and is a solid investment...

9. ...that increases the value of your home.

10. *Paitson Brothers is an authorized Lennox dealer.

11. They'll design a...

12. ...Lennox system for your home and...

13. ...make sure you get the most...

14. ...for your money.

PAITSON BROS.
12th and Wabash
Terre Haute
phone: 232-2347

15. Call 232-2347 for a free estimate.

* YOUR SPECIAL OFFER MAY BE INSERTED AT THIS POINT. PLEASE SEE YOUR ORDER FORM FOR SAMPLE ALTERNATE COPY.

FIGURE 13-14

Here's how the Lennox advertising agency tailored one of the company's commercials to a local dealership. This more personalized commercial has given way to a tag slide of the dealer's name at a cost of approximately $25. The real cost of the commercial far exceeds this modest dealer charge.

coop advertising; the company reaches dealers through the following trade publications: *Air Conditioning, Heating & Refrigeration News, Air Conditioning & Refrigeration Business, Heating, Piping & Air Conditioning Contractor*. The company also uses its own house organ, *Lennox News*.

At the company's annual dealer meetings held at ten locations in the United States, 4,000 Lennox dealer personnel showed up to see and hear the company's future promotion and sales plans.

Robert Hayes says this about how Lennox views dealer programs, "Essential. Our success relies on our dealers' success" (Figures 13-12, 13-13, and 13-14).

QUESTIONS NEEDING ANSWERS

1 Why do manufacturers such as Lennox and Republic Builders Products (see discussion on page 394) charge their dealers for sales literature that essentially promotes the manufacturer's product? Do you think dealers resent this? Can you think of a more equitable way to assign costs? Explain.
2 Some manufacturers exhibit at conventions and trade shows simply because competitors do. Is this a valid reason for participation? Explain.
3 Is it good for a professional society to organize its convention so that few members have the time to visit advertisers' exhibits? What are the implications of this policy for future advertiser support?
4 Does it make sense for Lennox to personalize television spots for dealers? At $185 for each personalized dealer television commercial, what kind of interest should Lennox expect from its 5,500 dealers?
5 If you were the manufacturer of an industrial paint, would you dress your trade show sales force in "armor" to dramatize your paints' "armor-plate protection"?

STUDENT PROJECT

Contact local manufacturers and ask about the percentage of their advertising budget that has gone into trade shows or conventions in the last three years. Inquire into their feelings about the worth of attending and exhibiting at these shows.

QUESTIONS ABOUT THE PROJECT

1 Is show attendance by the manufacturers you have contacted increasing or declining? Why?
2 Have manufacturers found a more effective way to contact their dealers or buying influentials than conventions and trade shows? Do you believe them?
3 Is there a possibility that a company's advertising department and sales department might reach different conclusions regarding the relative merits of investing heavily at trade shows? Explain.

Unit

4

THE ADMINISTRATION OF ADVERTISING

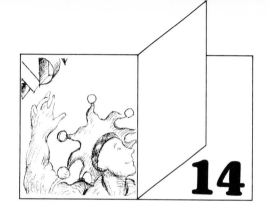

THE COMPANY ADVERTISING DEPARTMENT

Update We've examined what advertising is all about; who does it; whom it is aimed for in consumer, industrial, and professional markets; and what media are available and appropriate. Now we will examine how companies administer all the various inputs that go into an advertising program. The formal company structure responsible for this administrative work is the advertising department. The other formal structure is the advertising agency, which we will take up in the next chapter.

An advertising department can be a one-person operation within a small industrial company or the nearly fifty employees of Pepsi-Cola's Creative Services Department. Large or small, all advertising departments have similar responsibilities: the formulation and supervision of an overall advertising program. Within these boundaries, advertising departments for manufacturers, distributors, and retailers plan and perhaps even prepare their advertising. They may operate on a national, regional, or local level or all three. They administer the advertising budget and evaluate the results even if haphazardly.

As we've said before, most companies do not give advertising top priority. They have been traditionally more concerned with other areas of company operation such as labor, materials, taxes, and so on. This concern is reflected in the size of the advertising budget. Advertising departments not only receive a small part of the total corporate budget; they must also face second-guessing from those outside their departments about the best way to spend their money. Sometimes this interference involves redirection of budget dollar spending. Management can take all the money budgeted for advertising and restrict it to samples, coupons, rebates, and trade shows. They can increase or slash the budget at any time and thus realign media commitments. All these management options serve to unsettle advertising departments. Despite these uncertainties, the staffs of thousands of ad departments labor hard, long, and effectively.

WHO DOES WHAT IN THE AD DEPARTMENT?

Most ad departments with fewer than ten employees operate with a fixed but simple chain of command. Everyone reports to one individual who supervises the entire output. This individual usually carries the title "advertising manager." In larger companies, the organization is appropriate to the size of the operation and the nature of the work. The advertising department of the general office of Beatrice Foods, for example, operates as a functional service organization to the Dairy Division in that it provides the corporation's dairies with television and radio commercials, newspaper and dealer ads, and the like. The other decentralized companies within the Beatrice Foods corporation are responsible for their own advertising activity. In other large companies, brand managers are responsible for the success of specific products. For advertising help they look to staff specialists who perform the advertising function. These specialists are assigned by the manager. Often, the ad manager will confer with brand and product managers as well as distribution managers as they initiate and develop programs. There is a division of authority between the ad manager and the product managers. In most companies, the product manager is the higher authority.

In large companies (like Black & Decker) that decentralize their marketing operations by product or division, a tightly knit advertising staff is often an integral part of the division. This staff, headed by an ad manager, works solely for its own division within the corporation.

TABLE 14-1

AGRICULTURAL AD MANAGERS ANSWER: WHICH FUNCTIONS ARE PART OF YOUR RESPONSIBILITY?

Functions	Percent of responses
Advertising	100
Public relations	63
Development of product literature	91
Market planning	42
Market research	40
Sales training programs and meetings	50
Media placement	75
Other	31

Source: "Ad Managers Look at Themselves," *Agri-Marketing,* April 1978, p. 27.

Regardless of a company's organizational structure, the advertising manager's duties usually include the following:

1 Planning and formulating the advertising program.
2 Implementing the program.
3 Controlling the program (Table 14-1).

Planning and Formulating the Advertising Program

Managements ordinarily hold advertising managers responsible for everything classified under the labels "advertising" and "sales promotion," whether designed by an advertising department or by a hired advertising agency. Advertising managers are responsible for translating management *marketing* goals into *advertising* goals. They take stated company advertising goals and plan how to achieve them. In planning, ad managers develop budgets and plans describing why they have selected certain courses of action. These plans provide explanations to management reviewing officials. If management accepts the plan and budget—usually for a year's duration—the ad manager has a blueprint to follow. (Figure 14-1).

Implementing the Program

Simply stated, one of the jobs of the ad manager is to see that approved plans are acted on. Managers of small staffs usually involve themselves with all aspects of the development of the advertising. Managers in larger corporations turn over many details to subordinates. Few company matters do not involve the ad manager or the staff. Even a manufacturing problem can mean changes in advertising claims, such as when durable, heavy-duty motors replaced lightweight ones in a line of electric power drills. The additional weight of the motor made it necessary to discard all advertising claims that the drill was easy to maneuver. The ad department had to find other features to promote.

FIGURE 14-1
Designed to influence children, this page from Jel-Sert's yearly ad program spells out the broad strategy.

In implementing programs, ad managers often need to hire permanent as well as temporary skilled personnel: copywriters, artists, production specialists, publicity writers, photographers. During any one day, they or their staff may see printers, typographers, audiovisual salespeople, artists, and media representatives. For reasons of efficiency and economy, some large corporations have a production manager who is in charge of all printed materials. Printers and typographers see the production manager instead of the advertising manager.

A major responsibility of ad managers is the hiring and supervising of advertising agencies. Unless ad managers and ad agencies can get along and complement each other, friction results. Advertising managers should determine whether they respect their ad agencies, whether the agencies know anything of the manager's business, what the agencies' present clients think of them, and whether the agencies pay their bills.[1] The last consideration is very important, because an agency's bills are a company's bills. If the agency

---

[1] "How to work with an advertising agency," *Advertising Age*, April 9, 1973, pp. 51–2, 54.

doesn't pay its suppliers, the client looks bad. Generally, ad agencies earn the equivalent of a 15 percent commission, and all the other monies they receive from a company are for suppliers.

The advertising manager and the ad agency usually work as a team and schedule regular meetings to keep abreast of company advertising affairs. Some advertising managers make written reports on these meetings. The reports help clarify to company management the activities of its administrators of advertising.

Controlling the Program

Once an advertising plan has been implemented, the manager must control it. Projects must be scheduled and deadlines met. If an annual report is due at the bank for distribution by September 1, it had better be there. If a slide show is the first step of a distributor campaign, it must be ready on time. Control demands a sense of purpose and discipline from ad managers, even at the risk of offending staff members and suppliers.

Ad managers administer the budget of the department and that portion entrusted to the ad agency. There is nothing quite so distasteful to top company officials as a mismanaged budget. Ad managers who overspend are soon moved to other jobs or out of the company entirely. To prevent having a runaway budget, ad managers resort to various control systems. One of the simplest is the *monthly declining balance*, with each major area of expenditure defined in terms of specific dollar values (Figure 14-2). This system, plus a monthly reckoning from the advertising agency, helps keep the ad manager on target. Some ad managers run a declining balance system with a monthly comparison between current and previous years. This procedure helps alert them to trends in expenditures that they may have forgotten.

Presenting The Budget

Advertising departments need to make an "event" of their presentation of the budget to management, especially when the budget reflects objectives that remain the same, year after year. In typical cases, the ad manager is content to send several copies of the typewritten budget to key people and await their approval or rejection.

Instead, advertising departments should marshal their forces to satisfy top management's doubts about whether their advertising goals are reasonable and attainable, whether there's a better way to accomplish these goals, and whether they've budgeted enough to reach their goals according to the advertising plan. By recognizing that top management's concern is the achievement rather than the means of achievement, the ad manager will take a giant step toward presenting a meaningful budget. How do managers to this? Here are some ways: They begin the presentation to management with a colorful review of some of the television, radio, print ads, and sales literature produced in the past year. They follow these with clear evidence of results,

SHEET NO.						ACCOUNT NO.		

TERMS NAME *Jenel Division*
RATING ADDRESS *Ad Budget*
CREDIT LIMIT $103,933
MCM No. 92 FORM D

DATE 19 80	ITEMS	FOL.	DEBITS	CREDITS	DR. OR CR.	BALANCE
1/1			*Cost*		$	103933 00
1/10	Doors & Hardware Mag.		1019 00			102914 00
1/15	Construction Specifier Mag.		1595 00			101319 00
1/23	Quick Type		49 50			101269 50
2/3	Engravo, Inc.		1299 27			101140 23
2/10	Progressive Architecture Mag.		3260 00			97880 23
2/15	Four Seasons Print Co.		12635 00			85245 23

FIGURE 14-2
A simple guide for the ad manager is this declining balance ledger sheet. As each invoice from either media or supplier arrives, it is subtracted from the total budget.

such as number of letters and inquiries produced by advertising; audience viewership and readership studies proving high quality; and written testimonials from members of the company's sales department, distributors, dealers, and customers. All this serves to remind management that the ad department has been busy and effective. Once the ad department has shown its worth, it will introduce the current marketing goals, followed by the advertising goals and the budget. Experienced ad managers note in their presentations the work done by the company's ad agency. Otherwise, management may think that the company's ad department is doing all the work.

Since the acceptance and authorization of the budget actually reflects management's confidence in its advertising manager, nothing should be allowed to detract from the logical and persuasive presentation of the budget. Treating the budget as a mass of boring statistics instead of as an open door to greater company profits is a mistake, one that will often encourage management to make drastic reductions.

Relationships with Suppliers

Because the people in an advertising department often create sales literature, catalogs, pamphlets, price lists, house organs, employee newsletters, and publicity, they are in constant contact with outside specialists who either assist or physically produce the work. Experienced advertising managers employ a universal bid policy when dealing with suppliers. This policy requires that suppliers of services submit bids for the work they are expected to do. Generally, the ad manager or someone else in authority on the staff awards the job on the basis of the lowest bid consistent with expected quality. (Suppliers welcome a company bid policy as long as all bidders make estimates according to identical criteria). Advertising departments that neglect to ask for bids may be unpleasantly surprised at costs after it is too late to do anything about them (Figure 14-3).

JENEL
INDUSTRIES

P. O. BOX 52   CHAGRIN FALLS, OHIO 44022

October 26, 1979

Mr. S. Horwitt
Horwitt Auto Parts Inc.

Dear Sandy,

We take pleasure in submitting this quotation based on
the following specifications:

Description	Auto Parts Co. brochure and envelope
No. of Pages	6 pages
Quantity	1,000 and add'l 500's
Finished Size	25 3/8 x 11 9 x 12-EPS
Paper	100 lb. White Vintage Enamel
	28 lb. White Kraft Envelopes
Copy	Camera ready art
Proofs	Brownprint
Presswork	Offset
Binding	Folded to $8\frac{1}{2}$ x 11
Price	1,000= $1,097.00 add'l 500's=$125.00
	1,000 EPS= $220.00 add'l 500's=$75.00
Delivery	To be arranged
Terms	Net 30 days

Very truly yours,

J. J. Jenel

J.J. Jenel

FIGURE 14-3

Typical bid form for suppliers of ad services. Companies who use the bid procedure often avoid unpleasant and
unexpected price increases from suppliers.

Ad managers who treat their suppliers as professionals and listen to their suggestions and recommendations discover that they have enlisted allies in the cause of effective advertising. Generally, specialists are aware of the latest in their respective fields and are happy to pass ideas along. A disadvantage in dealing with suppliers is the time it takes to see them. Yet, by establishing an appointment procedure, ad managers can make the most out of these meetings.

Establishing Internal Communications

Many ad departments develop and supervise internal communications from top company officials to employees or from one department to another. These communications vary in complexity and cost. An *internal house organ* is a newsletter of sorts that reports on the activities of employees and passes along management policies (Figure 14-4). In-plant and office banners dramatize company slogans. Some companies communicate with employees through intercoms and closed-circuit television. Still others use weekly bulletin board notices.

Of all these techniques, none is more effective than the internal house organ published and distributed on a regular schedule. Its effectiveness relies on the number and activity of company "correspondents." The more active the correspondents, the newsier the house organ. Advertising managers often provide correspondents with hints on writing news stories, taking photographs, and getting story leads. Some ad managers reward correspondents by printing their bylines or small photographs, or even by giving prizes for the best story of the month.

Less complex but preferred and respected by many ad managers are simple wall posters. Subjects vary widely: from J.C. Penney's "clean up your act" campaign for keeping air-conditioning vents clear and discouraging eating in offices or smoking in elevators, to the Zale Corporation's posters on appearance, employee courtesy, and selling techniques. Poster messages should be simple, like, "Use safety glasses," "Wear protective clothing," or "Watch moving vehicles" (Figure 14-5).

Good internal communications require effort and planning. That's why experienced ad managers often assign their most competent people to the job. Some even hire professional editors and photojournalists to handle all the company's internal communications: house organs, posters, and publicizing of work rules and policies. The department head is thereby free to do other things.

Setting Professional Standards

Ad managers, even those with the exalted titles of director or vice president, are responsible for setting and maintaining professional standards for their departments. These standards are generally expressed as ethical business practices supported by commercial custom and the law. The great Leo Burnett, founder of one of the nation's top advertising agencies, placed his

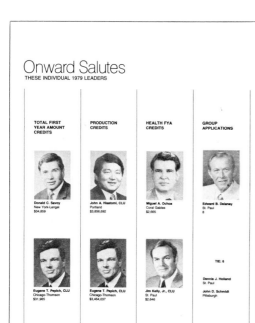

FIGURE 14-4

Internal house organs are common to companies with widespread employee networks such as insurance and stock brokerage firms. This page from Bankers Life's "Onward" serves a dual function, praise and stimulation. The Black & Decker house organ keeps employees aware of company activities.

National Safety Council   Printed in U.S.A.   5988-A

FIGURE 14-5

Ed Brown, Group Brand Manager, Texize:

"Henderson helped us make Spray'n Wash #1. And it didn't cost us the shirt off our back."

"Remember this Incredible Shirt Guarantee? 'If Spray 'n Wash doesn't remove the stain, we'll replace the shirt.' Henderson created it for us three years ago. It helped create a new, multimillion dollar category for us—overnight. The aerosol laundry soil and stain remover category is still growing rapidly and is highly competitive. But, again this past year, Henderson has helped us maintain our #1 sales position."

Thanks, Ed. Not just for the kind words, but for letting us get so deeply involved that we were able to learn *everything* about your product and your market. That's how we knew, when we created the Incredible Shirt Guarantee, that Spray 'n Wash would live up to it. That customers would respond to it. And that you wouldn't lose your shirt on it.

It's a perfect example of the Henderson kind of total involvement that leads to our Creativity That Sells. And it really *does* sell. It has helped five of our other national products to #1 positions in their respective categories, along with three of our seven regional brands.

Could Creativity That Sells help your present brand or a new product?

Talk to Jim Henderson at Henderson Advertising.

Henderson sells.

Henderson Advertising, Inc.
55 South Pleasantburg Drive
P.O. Box 5308
Greenville, South Carolina 29606
(803) 242-5230

FIGURE 14-6

Texize group brand manager takes time out to praise its Greenville, South Carolina, ad agency. An ad in which a client goes on record praising its ad agency is a rare occurrence.

professional imprint on these standards when he rearranged them as "ten commandments" for advertisers. Some experts feel his list could serve as a model for operating a professional advertising department.

1 Thou shalt not close thy mind to the different, the fresh, the unexpected.
2 Thou shalt not follow where thou can lead.
3 Thou shalt not advertise to thyself.
4 Thou shalt honour thy public's intelligence.
5 Thou shalt not belittle thy competitor.
6 Thou shalt not adulter the truth.
7 Thou shalt not rob the words of their warmth.
8 Thou shalt not deprive the pictures of their magic or the music of its lilt.
9 Thou shalt not worship thy sacred cows.
10 Thou shalt not covet thy competitor's advertising.[2]

If ad managers are to act professionally, they need the authority, too. They need, in fact, full responsibility for the total ad program. This means that they should report directly to top management without having to go through intermediaries. Too often, their initial plans are returned to them with major revisions and with no opportunity for questions. Company officials tell ad departments what they can spend without regard to the specialized knowledge of the ad staff. These practices undermine ad managers, encourage them to avoid risks, perpetuate the status quo, and discourage professionalism. Many ad managers become purchasing agents of advertising rather than creators and developers. Weakened ad managers creep into the niches carved for them by top management and end up deserving their minimal salaries!

Selecting an Advertising Agency

No independent consulting organization works as closely with the advertising manager as the advertising agency that selects the media and creates much of the advertising for the company. When ad managers go about selecting an agency, they might follow these basic steps:

1 Define what you want in an agency. Write down the major points and circulate them to key people in your company who may be working with the agency in the future. You'll avoid problems later on if you get their approval at the beginning.
2 Call your present agency, and tell them that you'll be seeking new counsel. Then send them a formal letter. If you're not sure whether to change agencies, ask your present agency to make a presentation demonstrating their capabilities. (Often the present agency ends up looking better than any of the other candidates).
3 Tell the news media, such as *Advertising Age, Industrial Marketing,* and *Sales and Marketing Management,* as well as local business editors that you are changing agencies. They will spread the news. Tell media sales representatives and your

[2]Leo Burnett, *Communications of an advertising man* (Chicago: Leo Burnett Company Inc., 1961), p. 95.

suppliers. When agencies inquire, you can respond with a short letter plus a list of criteria agreed to by your key management people.

4　Screen the agencies that meet your criteria. Ask them for an informal presentation that demonstrates their ability to handle your account. Be prepared to spend enough time on these presentation sessions to evaluate them properly.

5　Narrow the field to five or fewer agencies. Present them with information about your company, and let them see how you attack problems.

6　Tell each of the finalists what you want in their final presentation. Set a time for each presentation, and go to each with an open mind. If you have misgivings about any of the agencies, don't invite them to make presentations; they're costly and time-consuming. (The ad managers' common complaints about agencies are lack of creativity, mediocre account people, lack of knowledge and experience in the field, apathy, size of agency, and lack of marketing ability). If you want them to develop themes and a media plan, pay agencies for their time. Some ad managers have a policy against agencies making "creative" presentations. They feel that the agencies still know little about the company and should not be asked to come up with special material. Instead, these ad managers ask to see what the agencies have done for others.

7　At this point, if not before, reply to each agency that has responded and that has been rejected. Explain why you eliminated them.

8　Choose your new agency, but be sure you know how they intend to staff your account and to charge for their services.

9　Once you choose the ad agency, be fair to it. Praise as promptly as you criticize (Figure 14-6).

　　If your selection process is good, you and your agency will be spending many stimulating years together. The Green Giant Company has been with the Leo Burnett agency for forty-three years, Pillsbury for thirty-three. It's no wonder that some people compare choosing an agency to getting married.

The In-House Ad Agency

Ad agencies hate in-house agencies. But they refuse to die and go away. The in-house advertising agency looks and acts like independent agencies, except that it usually handles only the account of its employer-advertiser. The company ad manager usually heads it. The number of in-house ad agencies has grown since an important 1956 Justice Department decision voided the restraints on media permitting "house agencies" to collect media commissions previously paid only to independent agencies. (See Chapter 15 for more on this topic). Until the decision, companies could and did operate their own agencies, but media did not have to recognize them and thus pay commissions.

　　Why do independent ad agencies dislike them? The obvious reason is that the company-controlled ad agency deprives an independent of commissions. Some in-house agencies even solicit outside business and thus become "subsidized" competitors of the independent ad agencies.

　　Advertising managers must evaluate in-house agencies according to standards different from those they apply to independents. They must above all determine whether the in-house agency equals or surpasses an independent agency. Independent-agency supporters claim in-house agencies are too subjective. In-house supporters argue that subjectivity is the fault of a timid advertising manager.

Strictly defined, the in-house agency plays a double role—that of advertising department and that of agency. Its advantage to the company is essentially financial. (For example, ABC Company spends $5 million a year advertising on television, in magazines, and over the radio. By placing the media orders themselves—and not through an independent ad agency—they receive $750,000 in commissions, the traditional 15 percent. Although the company does not save all this money, because of the necessity of adding some advertising personnel, the company's total ad bill is not $5,000,000 but somewhere between $4,250,000 and $4,500,000). When advertising budgets swell, company comptrollers often look longingly at the commissions paid to their independent ad agencies and wonder out loud about the advantages of an in-house operation. Increasingly, top management has been listening.

Social Responsibilities of Advertising Managers

Aleksandr Solzhenitsyn, the exiled Russian writer, said it quite clearly: "An oil company is legally blameless when it purchases an invention of a new type of energy in order to prevent its use. A food product manufacturer is legally blameless when he poisons his produce to make it last longer; after all, people are free not to buy it. . . . A society with no other scale but the legal one is not quite worthy of man either."[3]

What are the social responsibilities of advertising managers of companies? Can they reasonably expect their companies to underwrite programs that cost money but earn none? Should a steel company install expensive antipollution devices when there is no profit payback? Should companies advertise sugary cereals to children despite evidence that sugar is a potential health hazard? How should advertisers communicate with children? Can they continue to pressure susceptible young minds to buy any product, even one of dubious value? Should women be portrayed solely as floor-waxing, ever-washing housewives who go into ecstasies over a "shinier shine" or a "whiter wash"? What do advertisements say about members of minority groups: Are they all unskilled, low-paid workers subordinate to whites?

These and others like them are not idle questions. They are questions that ad managers, as the voices of industry, must grapple with. Some adopt the "See no evil, hear no evil, speak no evil" approach. Others try to temper management policies by relaying the opinions of the community and its leaders. In this age of consumerism, modern companies *are* concerned with what are loosely called "social responsibilities." Some try to find out exactly what the public expects of them. In the early 1970s, for example, Coca-Cola

---

[3]Commencement address at Harvard University, June 8, 1978.

and some other large firms hired researchers to draw up a checklist that lets them evaluate their activities against social expectations.[4]

The matter of ethical and moral conduct can cause advertising people considerable anguish. How do they tell their president when their company's advertising deliberately misleads? It's a question not of taste or vulgarity but of pure, simple deception. Is the standard, "If we don't do it, others will" sufficient as an answer? Critics of advertising contend that ad managers' social responsibilities should outweigh corporate responsibility when the two conflict. They argue that the corporate injunction to the ad manager, "Do it our way or else" is outdated. Ad managers, these critics say, need to muster the strength to speak out against deceptive practices and to suggest ethical alternatives to their managements. Peter Drucker claims that the consumer movement marks the failure of the marketing concept. "Consumerism means that the consumer looks upon the manufacturer as somebody who is interested, but who really doesn't know what the consumer realities are."[5]

Yet who in a company, other than the ad manager, knows the public pulse so well? A growing number of companies, among them Xerox and Greyhound, appear to recognize, along with their ad managers, that concern for the public goodwill is good, long-term business practice. This is no better said than by a Greyhound board chairperson: "On the one hand, our program represents an investment, and we have an obligation to our owners to realize a return on that investment. On the other hand, we have an obligation to our social environment in which we function."[6]

The challenge of the 1980s will be for company ad managers to reconcile these conflicting obligations with minimum damage to each side.

IN SUMMARY

1 Advertising departments may be any size.
2 The person who usually heads the advertising department is called the advertising manager and has these responsibilities: planning and formulating the ad program, and implementing and controlling it.
3 Usually ad managers prepare an advertising plan for a full year.
4 The advertising manager is responsible for all the elements that go into the advertising and sales promotion programs, whether they are created in house or by outside consultants.
5 An essential characteristic of effective ad managers is to be able to control programs and particularly budget expenditures.
6 When presenting the department's budget to top management, the ad manager keeps in mind three top management doubts: are the ad goals reasonable and attainable; is there a better way to achieve these goals; and will the money

[4]"The great what-is-it: The 'social audit,' " John J. Corson, *Nation's-Business*, July 1972, pp. 54-56.
[5]"Consumerism: The shame of marketing," Peter F. Drucker, "The Chief Executive," *Marketing Communications*, March 1970, p. 82.
[6]"A sensitive approach to black relations," Gerald H. Trautman, "The Chief Executive," *Marketing Communications*, November 1970, p. 106.

accomplish the goals if invested according to plan?

7   One important way for ad managers to control costs is to insist on bids for all outside work.

8   To achieve professionalism, ad managers need to enjoy full authority and responsibility for the total ad program.

9   In selecting an advertising agency, ad managers might follow these guidelines: define what they expect of an agency, notify their present agencies of dissatisfaction, inform the news media, screen all applicant agencies until there are a small number of quality candidates, present the necessary marketing information about their companies to the screened contenders, and request that they make presentations.

10   The in-house agency is set up by the company and is controlled by it. It acts as both advertising department and ad agency. Critics maintain that the in-house agency's major weakness is its lack of objectivity.

11   There is a growing feeling that advertising managers (and their companies) have certain social responsibilities.

CASE STUDY   Avis, A Company Made By Advertising

In 1963, Avis had a negligible share of the auto rental market. Annual sales were $35 million. Then, the car rental market was dominated by its major competitor. Operating from a relatively small budget, Avis directed its ad agency—new at the time—to make Americans highly aware of the company. Although this directive is not unique, the results were. In essence, Avis is a company that was made by advertising. We'll see how after we take a look at the makeup of the Avis Advertising Department.

The four major management officials directly connected to the company's advertising are vice president, advertising; director of advertising; sales promotion manager; and advertising coordinator. The workload handled by the department includes national advertising, local advertising, outdoor advertising, sales promotion, travel industry sales and commercial sales, and direct mail. Avis' various advertising agencies handle the creative work under guidelines established by the department. The company's public relations department produces an in-house newsletter that is heavily illustrated with pictures of people throughout the Avis System.

The Avis advertising campaign begun in 1963 has continued to this day because it successfully sold two major points to the American public: high awareness (widespread consumer recognition) and a good image. Indeed, it is difficult to find anyone today, from business to the traveling public, who has not heard of Avis.

The company adopted the Horagio-Alger theme: "We're only number two, so we try harder." Few companies had ever admitted that they were *not* the leader in sales before. Aside from this admission, the ads did tell the traveling public that Avis was bent on providing better service. They also put Avis employees on notice: "Try harder." The results of the campaign were

There is no Avis office in Moscow. But we're working on it.

A likely location.

We found a nice spot right in the heart of downtown Moscow, between St. Basil's and The Tomb. Now we just need a "Da" from the Commissar of Transport.

And about time. We're almost everywhere else.

If we ever get the right papers, we'll gladly rent you a new Plymouth. Or a Zil, Volga or Moskvich.

With empty ashtrays. A full gas tank. And a comradely smile from one of our girls. (Just like Avis U.S.A.)

A call to any Avis office would arrange it all. As it does now for rentals in Europe, the Caribbean, North Africa and the Far East.

We've been doing this sort of thing for years.

Though the Russians will probably say they invented it.

AVIS RENT A CAR
(address and phone number)

Avis is only No.2 in rent a cars. We have to work on Labor Day.

We try harder

There's no rest for No. 2.
We have to keep our Plymouths in top shape.
With wipers that wipe. Lights that light. And no cigarette butts in the ashtrays.
So if you need a car for the Labor Day weekend, call Avis.
The workers of the world should stick together.

AVIS RENT A CAR
(address and phone number)

Newspapers—200 lines-Local Advertising
This advertisement prepared by DOYLE DANE BERNBACH Inc., for
AVIS—Job No. ALO-614

We cannot tell a lie. Avis is only No.2 in rent a cars.

Being No. 2 is a truth we could live without. But it's a very good reason to come to Avis.
We have to try harder. When we say you'll get a spotless Plymouth you get a spotless Plymouth.
Give us a try on Washington's

Honesty paid off for him. Birthday.

If we're not everything we say we are, give us the axe.

AVIS RENT A CAR
(address and phone number)

Newspapers—200 lines-Local Advertising
This advertisement prepared by DOYLE DANE BERNBACH Inc., for
AVIS—Job No. ALO-617

The writer of this ad rented an Avis car recently. Here's what I found:

Cigarette butts. A whole ashtray full.

I write Avis ads for a living. But that doesn't make me a paid liar.

When I promise that the least you'll get from Avis is a clean Plymouth with everything in perfect order, I expect Avis to back me up.

I don't expect full ashtrays; it's not like them.

I know for a fact that everybody in that company, from the president down, tries harder.

"We try harder" was their idea; not mine.

And now they're stuck with it; not me.

So if I'm going to continue writing these ads, Avis had better live up to them. Or they can get themselves a new boy.

They'll probably never run this ad.

AVIS RENT A CAR
(address and phone number)

This advertisement prepared by DOYLE DANE BERNBACH Inc., for
Local Advertising-Newspaper-560 Lines
AVIS RENT A CAR-Job No. ALO-606

FIGURE 14-7

quick in coming. The company began to grow. Sales increased from $35 million in 1963 to $393 million by 1977. Typical ads like this created by Doyle Dane Bernbach appeared in newspapers and magazines throughout the country:

> Avis is only No.2 in rent a cars. We have to work on Labor Day . . . There's no rest for No.2. We have to keep our Plymouths in top shape. With wipers that wipe. Lights that light. And no cigarette butts in the ashtrays. So if you need a car for the Labor Day weekend, call Avis. The workers of the world should stick together.

Or this excerpt from a 560-line newspaper ad run during the heat of the Cold War:

> There is no Avis office in Moscow. But we're working on it. [An illustration showed an X placed between Lenin's Tomb and St. Basil's.] We found a nice spot right in the heart of downtown Moscow, between St. Basil's and The Tomb. Now we just need a "Da" from the Commissar of Transport. And about time. We're almost everywhere else. If we ever get the right papers, we'll gladly rent you a new Plymouth. Or a Zil, Volga or Moskvich. With empty ashtrays. A full gas tank. And a comradely smile from one of our girls. (Just like Avis USA).

An interesting sidelight to Avis advertising is that it, too, has worked harder. Its major competitor outspends Avis almost two to one. Yet research surveys conducted on upper-income men and women who travel frequently on business show that Avis is equal to or better than its major competitor[7] (Figure 14-7).

QUESTIONS NEEDING ANSWERS

1 Do you think an ad in *The Wall Street Journal* would be more effective for Avis than a television spot adjacent to Monday night football? Explain.
2 Does it make sense for a company to admit that it is only number two? Explain.
3 What kind of an advertising manager does it take to accept an offbeat theme such as "We're only number two so we try harder"? How many managements would accept the proposition?

STUDENT PROJECT

Between advertising managers and ad agencies, there have been frequent discussions of the relative merits of large and small agencies. Contact one large advertising agency ($20 million worth of sales billing and up) and one

---

[7]"Avis is a company that was made by advertising," *Wall Street Journal* ad in *Advertising Age*, December 1, 1975.

small (under $1 million in sales billing) in your area. Ask them for their opinions on the subject of large versus small agencies. (*Standard Directory of Advertising Agencies* frequently reveals sales billings of agencies in the United States. Another way to determine agency size is by the number of accounts handled).

QUESTIONS ABOUT THE PROJECT

1 If you were a relatively small car rental agency, what size advertising agency would you hire? Explain.
2 What would your reaction be if you were told that henceforth you would act as the ad agency for the company as well as the head of its ad department? Your reward for the additional responsibilities: a $1,000 bonus for the year. (The company's media expenditures equal $1 million a year).

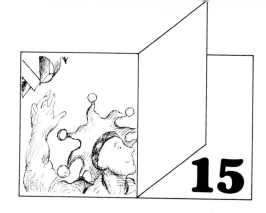

15

ALL ABOUT THE
ADVERTISING AGENCY

Update The corporate advertising department, which we discussed in the previous chapter, is one of two formalized administrative structures responsible for advertising. The other is the advertising agency. Experienced consumer marketers claim that the ad agency is crucial to the welfare of a company. Perhaps this consideration explains the elaborate care with which ad managers select their agencies.

THE AGENCY'S ROLE
IN THE BUSINESS WORLD

An advertising agency is usually defined as an independent organization hired by a company to conduct its advertising affairs. (Agencies call such companies

FIGURE 15-1
Instead of using a traditional gift catalog (18½ × 11 inches), the agency for Chicago-based retailer Crate & Barrel created a miniature shopping bag full of cardboard gifts representing knives, cups, baking pans, and the like. Descriptive copy is on the back of each gift item.

"clients" or "accounts"). There are approximately 7,000 agencies in the United States. Some ad agencies control all aspects of their clients' advertising programs; others do much less. In any event, the details of the ad agency business can be separated into four traditional agency functions:

Creating the advertising
Producing the advertising
Selecting the media
Placing the advertising

Creating the Advertising

On a blank sheet of paper, a writer types a headline and words describing a product. An artist takes the creative work of the writer and translates it into a sketch. The blank sheet of paper is now a selling message, the foundation for a written or spoken advertisement. This transformation from blank sheet of paper to ad is one example of what people call ad agency creativity. In fact, of all the agency functions, clients consider creativity the most important. Ad agencies also create sales literature, slide shows, public relations events, direct mail, and billboard messages. In all these cases, someone has to originate something that urges people to buy or take action. David Ogilvy considers a good, creative advertisement to be one "which sells the product without drawing attention to itself."[1] But whatever the definition of creativity, clients expect their agencies to have it in abundance and to produce examples of it consistently on their behalf (Figure 15-1).

Producing the Advertising

Once the ad has been composed of copy, colorful photographs, and illustrations, the ad agency transforms it into *reproducible form*. The agency does not do this work itself; instead, it hires specialists in typography, engraving, printing, and other graphic arts. Recently, many agencies have been contacting independent television and radio production studios for help in producing broadcast commercials. The production aspect of an ad agency is important, if for no other function than to guarantee that the agency's creative ideas look their best when they finally reach the consumer.

Selecting the Media

Agencies plan and select appropriate advertising media after careful study and evaluation. A media buyer handles this function in a small agency; a media director in larger agencies. Some agencies develop a "media plans book and strategy," which provides background information about buying influentials, their attitudes and buying habits, and the media they are most

[1]David Ogilvy, *Confessions of an Advertising Man*, (New York: Dell, 1963), p. 112.

likely to see and hear. When the advertiser-client approves its plan, the media department issues the media contract. The contract informs each selected medium of the general conditions of the agency's "buy." It indicates agency and client name, how many times the ads will run and in which weeks or months, the total cost of the "buy," and any special instructions. A media buyer or director usually signs the contract. When it returns from the medium with an acceptance stamp, it is a legal contract between the agency and the medium (Figure 15-2).

Placing the Advertising

A further responsibility of the ad agency is to see that the advertising arrives at the media's production departments at the proper time. Agency people refer to this function as traffic control or simply traffic. Essentially, it is a clerical job in that traffic personnel alert the media that the ads are coming. The formal document they use is called the "insertion order" (Figure 15-3). An insertion order identifies the agency and the client, describes the print ad or commercial, and lists when the ad is to run, its cost, and who will be sending the reproducible material. The last item is important in the event that the material fails to arrive or there are identification problems.

At one time, agencies performed only the functions of creating, producing, and placing ads in selected media. Now advertisers expect more. The Association of National Advertisers, a group of the nation's larger companies, expect additional services such as marketing direction and market research studies.[2] These expectations disturb some ad agencies. They contend that marketing is better done by clients themselves because they are closer to the sources of information. They further argue that agencies who do extract and distill marketing data often find their clients reluctant to pay for the added services. On the other hand, agencies that do provide these extras claim they charge for them. Competition for accounts may also force agencies to provide extra marketing services.

One major benefit for agencies that offer more than the four basic services is that they can call themselves "full-service agencies." Advertisers generally take this to mean that such agencies will do all the work associated with the term *advertising*: marketing, sales promotion, broadcast production, public relations, and the like *from within their own organization*.

COMPENSATION

Advertising agencies earn their money through media commissions, production "add-ons," and fees. Best known is the media commission, usually 15 percent,[3] which media owners pay to an advertising agency which has sought

---

[2]"Consideration in Adopting a Formalized Procedure for The Evaluation of Advertising Agency Performance," Association of National Advertisers Management Committee, April 1970, p. 3.
[3]Companies providing billboard advertising space give agencies $16\frac{2}{3}$ percent of gross billings.

BROADCAST CONFIRMATION

FAULKNER & ASSOCIATES INC.

1601 Broadway/P.O. Box 1028
Little Rock, Arkansas 72203/501-375-6923
ADVERTISING/MARKETING
PUBLIC RELATIONS

Member American Association of Advertising Agencies

Date _____

Advertiser	**DILLARD'S**
Product	
Contract Year	
Cancellation Notice Required	
Station/Market	
Salesman/Office	
Contract ☒ Contract No. **DIL -**	
Modification ☐ Modification No.	

Schedule Dates	Billing Week SUN. - SAT.	Billing Method As Earned ☒ Blanket ☐	Starting Rate Card	Future Rate Card No. Effective

SCHEDULE

Day*	Time From	Time To	Type	Effective Dates	Class Sec.	Spots per Week	Earned Rate/Spot	Total Spots	Total

4-5-4 ACCOUNTING CALENDAR

Jan.	April	July	Oct.
Feb.	May	Aug.	Nov.
March	June	Sept.	Dec.

*Times listed represent programming and/or adjacencies as declared at time of sale. **BILL ON COMPLETION OF SCHEDULE.**

Accepted For Agency, Date _____

(signed)

Accepted For Station, Date _____

(signed)

FIGURE 15-2

This contract is typical of ad agency contracts with the broadcast media. When it returns from the station with an approval, the document becomes a legal contract. Most agency contracts include contractual conditions set up by the American Association of Advertising Agencies. These conditions are often found on the reverse side of each page of the contract.

Order Blank For Publications   (MEMBER OF A.A.A.A.)

FAULKNER & ASSOCIATES INC.
P.O. BOX 1028
LITTLE ROCK, ARKANSAS 72201
TELEPHONE (501) 375-6923
MEMBER AAAA

☐ If checked here this is a SPACE RESERVATION

☐ If checked here this is a FIRM SPACE ORDER and
   BINDING unless cancelled before closing date*

☐ If checked here this is CANCELLATION
   or change of: _____

To the publisher of:

ORDER NO. _____

Date _____

Advertiser _____

Product _____

Contract Year _____

Discount Level _____

Edition: (specify) National _____

              Regional _____

*Subject to conditions stated above and on back hereof

ISSUE DATE	SPACE	COLOR/BLEED	FREQUENCY	RATE

Position

Additional Instructions:

Copy instructions & material ☐ to follow   ☐ herewith

Address all other correspondence to:

_____

Less agency commission   on gross

Cash discount   on net

Mail all invoices to:

FAULKNER & ASSOCIATES, INC.

_____
(Authorized Signature)

FIGURE 15-3

This insertion order is the agency document that alerts media that an ad will be arriving shortly. Copies also go to the client, the engraver (for print), the production house (for broadcast), and the agency's accounting department.

recognition from the media and has been accredited. Media owners pay agencies for their "saleswork" in convincing their clients to appear in specific broadcast and print media. Another justification for the commission is that agency ads contribute to the professional appearance of the media. The 15 percent agency commission is an eighty-year-old tradition that, in the opinion of many in the business, has worked well.

Prior to 1956, groups of media owners, organized as associations, could require an ad agency seeking recognition not to rebate any or all its commissions to the advertiser. In a landmark decision for the industry, the Department of Justice in 1956 held that for an association to do this constituted price fixing. The media associations as well as the American Association of Advertising Agencies (AAAA) signed consent decrees on this matter. (The AAAA once included a no-rebate stipulation as part of its requirements for membership). Today, each medium decides for itself what it takes for an agency to be accredited with it. By and large, media owners accredit agencies that show financial strength and stability.

There are other unique arrangements between agencies and media. The present agency-medium relationship, for example, can pose a disadvantage for the agency, because the agency rather than the client must pay the medium for the advertising. Even though agencies are called agents of the advertisers, they are actually independent contractors and therefore liable for the total media bill (minus their 15 percent commissions). If a client does not pay an agency, there is no particular hardship for the television station, for example, because its contract is with the agency itself. Some agencies have gone bankrupt when clients have failed to pay, and so they are very wary about companies with poor credit records.

Agencies can also earn money through production add-ons. When agencies subcontract for services for their clients, they charge their clients for the service plus a markup of 15 to 20 percent, with 17.65 percent being the norm. This mark-up is the agency's attempt to earn the equivalent of its traditional media commission on noncommissionable purchases of photography, typography, engraving, printing, and so on. The agency justifies add-ons because its personnel supervise and handle the myriad of details involved with most production projects. These details include selecting and briefing skilled specialists from among a list of qualified companies, implementing a bid procedure, and supervising the quality and accuracy of the work plus all the clerical details that accompany the job.

The third agency money maker is the retainer fee or straight project fee. The amount of the fee is generally negotiated and usually depends on how many work hours the agency puts in. Larger agencies charge $50 to $75 an hour for work performed by artists and copywriters, and a lower rate for production and traffic people. Most agencies keep accurate records of all the people involved in any phase of the work. They later bill the client for each person's time plus a markup for agency overhead and profit.

There are agencies that establish a set fee they expect to earn from each client. If their earned media commissions exceed that fee, they return the

TABLE 15-1
TOP ADVERTISING AGENCIES BY BILLINGS, 1973 AND 1978

Agency	1973 Billing	1973 Standing	1978 Billing	1978 Standing
J. Walter Thompson	$845,000,000	1	$1,476,500,000	1
McCann-Erickson	680,989,000	2	1,404,500,000	2
Young & Rubicam	650,000,000	3	1,359,500,000	3
Leo Burnett Co.	512,443,000	4	865,100,000	7
Ted Bates & Co.	484,282,500	5	890,000,000	5
SSC&B Inc.	483,494,000	6	840,500,000	8
Ogilvy & Mather	432,000,000	7	1,003,700,000	4
BBD&O	428,585,000	8	890,000,000	6
D'Arcy-McManus	396,000,000	9	698,800,000	10
Grey Advertising	352,000,000	10		
Foote, Cone & Belding			743,300,000	9

Reprinted with permission from the February 25, 1974 and March 14, 1979 issues of *Advertising Age.* Copyright © 1974, 1979 by Crain Communications, Inc.

difference to the client. If the earned agency commissions fail to reach that goal, the client makes up the difference.

There are variations on all these methods, because each company has its own needs. Albert Molinaro, Jr., president of Klemtner Advertising, Inc., reports on the basic compensation plans that are employed by agencies in the health care field. One is a flat or fixed fee based on the agency's anticipating what its personnel requirements to serve the account will be. The client pays this, usually in monthly increments. The other is a "cost plus" fee plan. Agencies keep accurate records of staff time spent serving their clients. This time is billed to the client using a factor to cover time, direct costs, and profit. Factors range between 2.5 and 3.0. This arrangement provides the agency with an operating profit of between 15 and 20 percent of gross income. The plan is usually periodically reviewed to make sure that the fee is fair to client and agency.

Advertising agencies handle vast amounts of money during the course of a year. J. Walter Thompson, for example, one of the world's largest agencies, is responsible for over $2 billion in total sales or, as agency people call them, "billings." Yet the agencies are really only custodians of this money. The huge sums may make them lose sight of the need for making adequate profits *after* they've paid all the bills. Agencies are pleased when their net profits equal 5 percent. Most, however, don't reach that goal!

AGENCY JOB DESCRIPTIONS

Of the over 7,000 ad agencies in the country, the majority bill less than $10 million a year. Only 60 or 70 bill over $25 million[4] (Table 15-1). No one really knows what many of the smaller agencies bill, because many don't respond to financial questionnaires. We consider size of billings here because they

[4]"66 agencies billing over $25,000,000," *Advertising Age*, February 25, 1974, p. 30.

have everything to do with how many people an ad agency employs. A good rule of thumb assigns one agency employee for each $100,000 in billings in the smaller agencies and as few as one person per $250,000 in the largest. Thus, a smaller agency billing $1 million will employ approximately ten persons. These ten people will be distributed among the following jobs: copywriter, artist, account executive, media buyer, production buyer, traffic coordinator, accountant, and administrator. For purposes of this discussion, we will leave out the usual clerical help found in any business. (As agencies grow in billings, they add copy chiefs, art directors, media group supervisors, market researchers, sales promotion specialists, public relations people, and television- and radio-production specialists). Returning to our hypothetical ten-person agency, we find that the basic division of labor is as follows.

Copywriters

Considered by many to have the most exciting and rewarding of all agency jobs, copywriters produce the concepts that become written words and visual images of advertisements. Copywriters may work alone or with an artist. Hanley Norins, veteran copywriter and author, paraphrasing Charles Dickens, claims that "the copywriter is the best of writers, the worst of writers, a practical businessperson, a temperamental artist, the bearer of benefits, the apostle of greed, an inspired craftsman, a frustrated hack." [5]

Copywriters dig for facts. They read voraciously. They borrow ideas. They talk to customers, suppliers, *anybody* who can possibly give them a clue about how to attract the reading and viewing public (Figure 15-4).

Artists

Artists are the other indispensable part of the creative team. Although their major function is to translate copywriters' ideas into dramatic visuals called "layouts," (see Chapter 17), they often originate the basic communications concept. Ad agency artists develop print layouts, package designs, television layouts (called "storyboards"), corporate logotypes, trademarks, and symbols. They specify style and size of typography, paste the type in place, and arrange all other details of the ad so it can be reproduced by engravers and printers. Most agency artists don't go beyond layouts, leaving the "finishing" operation to freelance art studios. In many cases, a particularly perceptive art director or copy chief becomes the creative director of a group of artists and copywriters, or of the entire ad agency. Creative directors oversee all the advertising developed by the agency. Within the organizational structure, they rank near the top of the agency ladder.

[5]Hanley Norins, *The Compleat Copywriter* (New York: McGraw-Hill, 1966), p. 3.

FIGURE 15-4
Bob Rosser, a copy
chief at Meldrum &
Fewsmith, points out
a major copy feature
of a client's door
sold to the
construction market.
Like most good
copywriters, he
immerses himself in
the client's ad
campaign. Rosser's
first rule of
copywriting is
"Remember that
you are an
advertising person
first, and a writer
second."

Account Executives

Among the highest-paid employees of the ad agency are the account executives, the liaison between client and agency. Their industry reputation has them hobnobbing with glamorous movie stars and athletes; flitting between New York, Hollywood, and the Riviera; making monumental decisions that spell success or failure for major brands. Some account executives do all this, but their major responsibility is to know marketing and all its components. They explain client plans and objectives to their creative teams and supervise the development of the total advertising plan for their accounts. Portions of the advertising plan may be their own work. Above all else, however, account executives work to keep the client happy with the agency! Because "account work" is essentially a job of personal relationships, account executives are usually personable, diplomatic, and unusually bright people.

Some agencies rotate account executives regularly among their clients. One reason for this is that change is stimulating for creative or marketing people. The second reason is to show clients the breadth of agency capability in case the client is unhappy with a particular account executive. The third reason is actually a defensive move on the part of the agency against account "piracy." It permits a top administrative official of the agency to establish contact with some of the client's highest officials and to maintain that contact regardless of what is taking place at the ad manager and brand manager levels. This precaution, the agency hopes, will reduce the possibility of their account executives' breaking away and starting agencies of their own. Although there is nothing immoral about employees' going out on their own, agencies don't want accounts to follow favorite account executives who become agency competitors.

Media Buyers

In the final analysis, a media buyer's job is simply to make the best buys for agency clients. But since representatives of the media flock to the buyer's office whenever word gets out that a buy is under consideration, the job gets quite difficult. During a long working day, buyers host a procession of media representatives who come armed with statistics to prove that *their* numbers are better than the competitors', *their* costs per thousand are less than those of any other medium short of a free public service announcement, and *their* medium delivers more ripe, ready-to-buy audiences than any others. Evaluating these claims is time-consuming and painstaking. It demands a wide knowledge of many marketing facts. Media buyers also bargain with the broadcast media for best rates and make deals with the print media for good positions for their accounts.

Some critics of media buyers claim that they are merely "order clerks" juggling Standard Rate & Data records and slavishly following computer printouts. But today's agencies consider their media buyers another creative arm of the agency whose investigative approach can reveal ideas to copywriters and artists.

Media directors consult reference books, media rate cards, research studies and special media and industry reports. In growing numbers, agencies are developing computer programs, which they update regularly. Young & Rubicam, a pioneer in this technique, uses a computer program to set the stage for media buys. Aside from saving the buyer from checking reference books like SRDS, the computer also guarantees that no medium among hundreds will be overlooked. However, computers thrive on repetition and sameness. They cannot adapt to changing conditions without being repro-grammed. Critics of computer media selection call it "formula" buying. They contend that all the information it provides is already available through SRDS and other sources (Figure 15-5).

Media buyers believe good planning and selection cannot be overesti-mated. They claim it is far better to reach an audience of one million potential buyers with a mediocre message than an audience of a quarter million with a brilliant advertising story. Few disagree.

Production Buyers

Production department buyers see to it that the creative work of the agency—the words and pictures—is properly transformed into reproducible

```
SYSTEM: SM1977 ON 06/20/79 AT 11:31:25

BASE:   MEN.


DEMO:   MEN AND(A18T34 OR A35T39 OR A40T44) AND
        UP15 AND COL AND LIFEINSURANCE.



SORT:   CPM




                                               AVERAGE
        MEDIUM              UNIT        COST    AUDIENCE   CPM
                                                 (000)

        PB                  PAGE2C   36955.00    12378    2.99

        PENT                PAGE4C   31085.00     9506    3.27

        SCIAM               PAGE4C   12925.00     1710    7.56

        PSYCHT              PAGE2C   18435.00     2388    7.72
```

FIGURE 15-5
Computer printouts save media buyers time when selecting specific media vehicles. The computer's memory bank houses thousands of vital pieces of information that are integrated with target audience objectives. Magazines listed are: *Playboy, Penthouse, Scientific American,* and *Psychology Today.*

ads. They may be the only agency personnel who truly understand how newspapers and magazines are printed, how printers change photographs into a series of dots on a film, how different artistic techniques reproduce on various kinds of paper and newsprint, and so on. Because they understand these mechanical processes, they logically operate as the link between creative departments and outside mechanical suppliers. They accept and reject bids and maintain daily contact with their suppliers.

One of their jobs is to expedite the flow of advertising through the agency from one department to the next and at last into finished form. Another is to insist that suppliers meet agency standards of excellence. A third, and often overlooked responsibility, is to advise the creators of the advertising whenever their concepts will be practical, economical, or prohibitively expensive to reproduce *before* the work gets into full swing.

Traffic Coordinators

Through official agency correspondence (insertion orders), traffic coordinators oversee the shipment of the agency's advertising to media. Traffic coordinators send copies of each insertion order to the media, mechanical suppliers, clients, and the agency accounting department. In particular, insertion orders inform clients that the agency has things in hand, while they tell suppliers to which media to ship the materials they have developed, like engravings or printing. In some agencies, the volume of traffic paperwork in a single year may run as high as 700,000 separate insertion orders sent to newspapers, magazines, and radio and television stations. Facing this paperwork avalanche, traffic coordinators must be precise, accurate, and prompt. To facilitate delivery of insertion orders, some coordinators rely on computers to print out commonly used names and addresses of media. More rely on card files for each client's media list. Although everyone in the agency involved in creating ads works against deadlines, the traffic coordinator is the last person in the chain of command responsible for producing the ad on time (See Figure 15-6).

Large agencies generally assign a traffic coordinator to a small group of accounts. This system lets the individual become thoroughly familiar with all the media. When one coordinator is responsible for too many clients, agencies fear the job becomes too methodical, leaving no room for personalized service and improvement.

Accountants

After the traffic department has notified one medium that a specific ad will run at a certain date or in a certain issue, the department passes the information to the accounting department. The goal is to have the agency bill the client in time to be paid *before* it is billed by the medium. To further encourage prompt payment by clients, some agencies pass along a 2 percent cash discount if their invoices are paid within ten days. (This discount is what agencies receive from media if they pay within an allocated time period). Agencies that are slow to bill their clients often end up having to dig into surplus working capital or borrow short-term money from banks at high interest rates. One of the key contributions agency accountants make to smooth financial operation of their agencies is in the areas of cash flow and profitability. Also, they often question unprofitable agency practices.

Administrators

Agency administrators generally carry the title of president or executive vice president. Their job is to see that the agency makes money and grows. Consequently, they must be aware of agency-client problems before they end in divorce. They need to watch the ratio of agency billings to agency personnel in order to keep overhead costs down. Approximately 70 percent of a typical agency's cost of doing business is labor. Administrators need to

FIGURE 15-6
Traffic coordinators
at work in a large ad
agency. Their major
responsibility is to
make certain that
the media receive
the agency's
advertising materials
in time. (Courtesy
D'Arcy-MacManus,
J. Masius, Inc.)

keep abreast of any developments that affect any of their clients' businesses and of any new developments in technology that might contribute to better agency operations and lower costs.

Administrators often spend time with top executives among their client companies and leave the agency account people to make contact with ad, sales, and brand managers. Administrators are often called upon to operate under stress, to solve problems, and to compete.

Agency administrators also solicit new business. With the duration of the average agency-client relationship estimated at about six years, most agencies regularly need new business. Many chief agency administrators head up a team of "new business" executives whose principal job is to secure new clients. Agencies have been known to invest up to $50,000 in soliciting just one large multimillion dollar account. In one recent seven-month surge, Young & Rubicam's New York office added $77 million in billing, the largest annual gain in the agency's history. The president of the agency explained the reasons for his agency's success as essentially creative. "What we have been successful in doing is giving clients confidence that we will fulfill what we feel is their greatest need." Other top agency officials attribute success to the diversification of the agency and its ability to offer a wide variety of services.[6]

[6]"$77 million in 7 months—Y & R credits creative," *Advertising Age*, November 21, 1977, p. 2.

PROBLEMS OF CLIENT SATISFACTION

Keeping clients happy is the number-one problem of ad agencies. Even the largest agencies worry about competitors wooing a choice account. It happens all the time (Figure 15-7). A typical weekly issue of *Advertising Age* contains items like these: "Keds assigned to McCann as Uniroyal scrubs DDB," "Harold Cabot & Co., a Carling agency for many years, is losing all of its Carling business," "Oneida Ltd. Silversmiths has severed relationships with Conklin, Labs & Bebee," "Marathon Oil Company and Campbell-Ewald, Detroit, have mutually agreed to terminate their relationship," "Institutional Investors Trust, New York, to Newmark, Posner, & Mitchell succeeding Doremus & Co.," "Air Florida Airlines to Ted Carlon, Inc., previous agency was Peter Evans, Inc."[7]

In an ad designed for the eyes of "unhappy" advertisers, Adolf Wirz Advertising Agency claimed no less than twenty-one new accounts in a given year. Estimates vary on the amount of agency business that changes hands each year. It is substantial, perhaps as much as $1 billion. When the Datsun automobile account left a West Coast agency for an East Coast replacement, over $20 million in billings changed hands. Fifteen percent of that figure is $3 million, a disastrous loss for one agency, a bonanza to another.

How does an agency keep a client happy? Here are ten principles:

1 **Competent specialists** Administrators should make certain that competent people are assigned to the account.
2 **Intelligent money management** People responsible for spending the client's money should make certain that the client knows that they are doing it wisely.
3 **Obvious interest in client's welfare** Advertisers want to know that their advertising agency personnel are totally committed to the company's business interests. However, this does not mean that agency people must pander to client weakness.
4 **Demonstration of personal interest** Agency representatives need to remember that they are dealing with people. They need to consider the personal advancement of the brand manager or the ad or sales managers. These people want to move upward on the corporate ladder. It makes sense to counsel with them if such help does not interfere with an agency's primary loyalty to its client.
5 **Honest billing** Ad agencies need to establish a mutually acceptable basis for their charges and stick with them. Clients dislike agencies that appear to charge whatever the traffic will bear or that surprise them with unexpected invoices. Clients will not hesitate to fire an agency they suspect of cheating or overcharging.
6 **Reliance on knowledge and experience** Responsible advertising agencies attempt only those projects within their capabilities. In an area where they lack expertise, they will usually subcontract the work after consultation with the client.
7 **Bold assurance** If an agency's regional client has been building nationwide distribution, the agency owes it to the advertiser to suggest national programs and

[7]*Advertising Age*, March 25, 1974.

Hoefer gets Foremost bread; new Timex line goes to Grey

SAN FRANCISCO, June 10—Foremost Foods Co., operating unit of Foremost McKesson Inc., has named Hoefer, Dieterich & Brown agency for Simple 'N Delicious packaged homemade bread mix which is going national (AA, Dec. 9). McCann Erickson had handled the product, marketed by Foremost's grocery products division.

■ Timex Corp., Greenwich, Conn., has assigned its quartz analog and solid-state digital watches to Grey Advertising, a new assignment. Warwick, Welsh & Miller continues as agency for all other Timex watches. A "multi-million-dollar" campaign for the quartz product is scheduled for the fall.

Other changes:

Hebrew National Kosher Foods, New York, division of Riviana Foods, to **Scali, McCabe, Sloves** from Walpert Co., Cherry Hill, N.J. Hebrew National, the largest marketer of Kosher meat products in the U.S., expects to spend about $1,000,000 to promote its products in most major U.S. markets.

Wausau Homes Inc., Wausau, Wis., moved its $1,200,000 account from Kinzie & Green to **Cramer-Krasselt Co.,** Milwaukee. Also to Cramer, **Burdick Corp.,** Milton, Wis., from Towell Inc., Madison; consumer products division, **Packerland Packing Co.,** Green Bay, no previous

agency, and **Gay Lea Foods** of Pennsylvania, Philadelphia, subsidiary of Gay Lea Foods Cooperative Ltd., Toronto, no previous shop. Gay Lea is entering test market with new dairy products, Packerland with frozen and canned beef products. Combined billings for the latter three accounts: About $1,000,000.

British Ford, London, moved its $2,300,000 account, resigned by Collett, Dickenson, Pearce, to **Ogilvy, Benson & Mather.**

El Chico Corp., Dallas, restaurant division, from McCrary-Powell Advertising to **Glenn, Bozell & Jacobs,** its agency for prepared foods.

Welch Foods, foodservice products, Westfield, N.Y., from Bozell & Jacobs, Chicago, to **Campbell-Mithun,** Chicago.

Estee Candy Corp., Parsippany, N.J., manufacturer of dietetic candies, gums, mints, wafers and cookies, to **Weissberg Associates,** New York. No recent agency of record.

Kevin H. White, Mayor of Boston, to **Hill, Holliday, Connors, Cosmopulos,** to develop an ad program for his reelection campaign. Hill, Holliday was the mayor's agency when he won election in 1971.

Hoechst-Roussel Pharmaceuticals, Somerville, N.J., assigned special projects advertising to **Warren, Muller, Dolobowsky,**

FIGURE 15-7

Bad news for one agency is good news for another. The winning and losing of accounts is openly proclaimed in the ad agency business, a practice unique to the industry.

Ford may pick two agencies after biggest-ever shift

Chrysler moves to Kenyon & Eckhardt

By JOHN J. O'CONNOR

NEW YORK—Now that the advertising world has had time to digest the fact that Kenyon & Eckhardt has swallowed up the largest account in history—$120,000,000 to $150,000,000 in Chrysler Corp. billings—the big unanswered question revolves around K&E's successor on the $80,000,000 Lincoln-Mercury assignment.

Parent Ford Motor Co. late last week reportedly was tilting toward selecting two new agencies—one for Lincoln-Mercury and another for other K&E business, including corporate and parts and services advertising.

■ An

K&E resigned to work for Chrysler. Y&R is one of three agencies fired by Chrysler in the shift.

Mr. Iacocca, who joined Chrysler last November after being fired as

president of Ford Motor, pink-slipped Y&R, BBDO and Ross Roy Inc. about three hours before he went to the Chrysler board for approval of the precedent-setting account move.

Ford chairman Henry Ford II, the man who ousted Mr. Iacocca from the Ford empire last year, is irate over the Chrysler coup, according to a source. "While it be logical for F___ ecs to c___

strong feeling in many quarters that Ford will tap Ogilvy & Mather instead. Rumors have been circulating for weeks that O&M, which handles Ford in the United Kingdom, would be getting some U.S. Ford business and w___ scouting for D___ De___

count of the phone call, Robert Owens, general mana___ advertising and Mercedes-Be___ poste___

Chrysler switch stuns Detroit

By RALPH GRAY

DETROIT—The fog that swirled outside the 27th floor offices of Lincoln-Mercury division in the Detroit Renaissance Center was just as thick inside last Thursday when an ADVERTISING AGE reporter broke the news.

Robert Rewey, general marketing manager, hadn't heard that Lincoln-Mercury's agency was going to Chrysler. K&E didn't tell Mr. Rewey that it was talking with Chrysler. "I would think they would have out of ethics," he said.

The notification came hour later in a hand ter from K___ Bour___

ations through separate contracts. Mr. Clark said he'd sever relations with his dealer group clients if BBDO landed another car company. Otherwise, "we'll continue to service them as long as they want us."

K&E is the latest Chrysler pro___ has ___

will have a five-year contract. The agency will be operating on an incentive compensation plan that involves a full 15% commission. He was unable to say whether the incentive compensation plan would be based on Chrysler's sal___ earnings.

The fact that workin___

who have been work have all l job under diffi "This only much t___

national media. If the agency doesn't make these suggestions, another agency might and go on to glory.

8 **Praise for agency creativity**   Advertising agencies must remember that their major stock in trade is creativity, and, therefore, the agency must be forceful in promoting what their creative people have developed. If very little of what the agency has contributed is being used in client campaigns, there is really little to hold the account to the agency.

9 **Communication of agency capabilities**   Generally, clients are satisfied when their advertising programs are unique and successful. Under those circumstances, most accounts fear to replace a capable, proven agency with a question mark. However, experienced ad agencies never let their clients forget how capable they are! They tell them through ads, through publicity, through awards, and through the mouths of satisfied clients, media representatives, and graphic arts suppliers.

10 **Elimination of dissatisfaction**   If an advertising agency senses that there is client dissatisfaction, it won't be allowed to smolder. The agency must act on the dissatisfaction by making necessary changes. If the changes are meaningful, they usually put an end to the trouble. On the other hand, some clients may not know what they want and will use their ad agencies as scapegoats.

Sometimes these ten principles won't work because the advertiser has other grievances: the agency is too small or too large, there are personality clashes or poor service. Sometimes advertisers fire agencies when they consistently miss deadlines, make major errors in ad claims, or fail to extend the continuity of an advertising program through an appropriate sales promotion program. Lastly, advertisers may discard an agency when they see a lack of attention paid to the account by top agency officials.

CONFLICTS OF INTEREST

To belong to the American Association of Advertising Agencies (AAAA), members must not own or control a printing company, a typography or engraving shop, or any other graphics arts business supplying agencies with services. There is good reason for this regulation. The AAAA feels that if agencies own print shops, for example, they might place a larger-than-normal share of clients' printing with the agency's "captive" print shop, regardless of costs. The AAAA contends that this situation not only costs clients money but also represents a conflict of interest. The ideal situation, they feel, is for the agency to evaluate the need for each service, then send the work out for bids. This procedure helps assure clients that their agency is spending their money wisely and efficiently.

Most advertising agencies do not own other businesses that would compromise their selection of suppliers. Those who do argue that agencies who control several allied businesses can provide better quality control and faster turnaround time in printing, typography, and engraving.

One agency action is almost universally condemned: taking on competitive accounts. Clients don't like it. They reason that the agency-client relationship is one of mutual trust, mutual exchange of information—much of it confidential. Within this relationship, they feel free to pass on trade secrets. But when a competitor enters the same agency, they feel uneasy.

Some agencies handle several banks, for example, but they are separated geographically. When Grey Advertising took on the Taco Bell fast-food account in one of its two West Coast offices, its Minneapolis branch lost the regional McDonald's business because McDonald's viewed this move as a definite conflict of interest. Yet the likelihood of the creative people in the two offices confiding in each other seems remote.

The third case of agency conflict of interest concerns the hallowed 15 percent commission system. Some advertisers think the system causes agencies to choose the most expensive media rather than the most effective. The president of Wilson & Co. (meat products) of Oklahoma City said: "There's nothing in the commission system that is really in the best interest of the client that I can see. It's archaic." The Zale Corporation president: "The fee system* sure clears the air. As soon as you go to it, you know nobody has an axe to grind. As long as we were on a commission basis, we always felt as though there was an ulterior motive for the recommendation."[8]

In the final analysis, the individual advertiser must decide whether the commission system encourages agency self-interest. Experienced agency executives admit that growing client concern over the fee system reflects client self-interest. They point out that the perpetual "buyers' market" in the advertising business always forces agencies to think of their clients first or risk losing them.

AGENCY NETWORKS AND THE AAAA

An advertising agency network is an organization of noncompeting agencies—in various cities in the country—who band together to improve services to clients. Usually these are small and medium-sized agencies that exchange local market and media information and local promotional plans. In essence, members of the group act as local branch offices for another distantly removed member. Usually they limit their cooperation to individual projects. Members of agency networks use their affiliation as a selling advantage when calling on new prospects or servicing existing accounts. There are six leading advertising agency networks: The National Advertising Agency Network, Affiliated Advertising Agencies International, Advertising & Marketing International Network, Mutual Advertising Agency Network, National Federation of Advertising Agencies, and Transworld Advertising Agency Network.

The American Association of Advertising Agencies is not a network of cooperating agencies. Members are, in fact, direct competitors, often within

---

*A system where agencies charge clients a set monthly amount instead of relying on the 15 percent commission paid to them by the media.
[8] "Management views future, sees tougher customers, more research, agency fees," *Advertising Age*, December 29, 1975, p. 19.

the same city. Their common bond through the AAAA is a code of conduct and standards. Originally, this set of standards helped media judge an agency's professional responsibility and financial soundness. Over the years, however, the AAAA has become recognized as the principal voice of the ethical advertising agency—member or not—in the United States. Most large advertising agencies are members of the AAAA. All have to meet these basic requirements:

1 The agency must be free of control by an advertiser, in order that it may not be prejudiced or restricted in its service to all clients and free of control from a medium owner, in order to give unbiased advice to advertisers in the selection of media.
2 The agency must be able to furnish evidence of its business and advertising ability on behalf of clients.
3 The agency must possess adequate personnel with experience and ability to serve general advertisers.
4 The agency must have the financial capacity to meet the obligations to media owners it incurs.

MEDIA-BUYING SERVICES

Another avenue open to discontented clients or those looking for more effective ways to reduce their advertising costs is to hire a media-buying service. This service, a relative newcomer to agency operations, is a miniagency in that it concentrates on one function only, the buying of media. Thus it feels it can coexist with a client's conventional agency, which will handle all the other functions. Some media-buying services operate as the early admen did: by buying large blocs of broadcast time at wholesale and selling them at special prices below what conventional agencies can buy. Other more sophisticated services, like SFM Media Service Corporation, offer media planning, buying, and postevaluation services on an *à la carte* basis. The major inducement to the advertiser is a service's ability to negotiate with broadcast media owners, to respond quickly to sudden changes in market conditions, and to prepare more efficient media plans better tuned to objectives. Some media services are paid a negotiated fee; others split the savings they realize with the advertiser.

Conventional ad agencies keep hoping that media buying services will go away. Some are attempting to go the "wholesale buying" route themselves. It is still too soon to tell whether media-buying services are here to stay or whether they're a temporary expedient for cost-conscious advertisers.

BOUTIQUE AGENCIES

Ad agencies that promote themselves as full-service agencies notify advertisers that they offer the four basic services: creative services, media selection and placement, production, and traffic, plus marketing, public relations, research, television and radio production, and even distribution assistance.

The advertiser assumes that the agency handles all these services within its own organization. Only by hiring the agency can any advertiser determine how proficient an agency is in any of these areas.

A *boutique agency*, however, tells advertisers that it is a specialty shop, that it deals in a few services, not all. Most boutiques concentrate on the creative functions of the agency business: art and copy. They rely on the advertiser's ad and sales departments for marketing data. Thus their overhead is lower than that of the larger, full-service agencies, so their fees may be lower, or they may divide media commissions with a client. Owners of boutiques claim that they are restoring the basic purpose of the ad agency: to create ads. All other services, even media selection, they claim, are clerical and should be handled by others.

The choice of a boutique or a full-service agency depends on how clients analyze their own needs. If clients expect each of their products to have its own account group, they will want a full-service agency. Those who feel their own marketing departments can take care of marketing strategies may want the boutique to provide intensive care in a special area.

TWO AGENCY MONOLOGUES

Ad agencies have particular images according to where they are located. The Madison Avenue (Manhattan) agency, long the topic of praise, derision, and envy, brings to mind enormous sums of money, intense pressures, and rapid turnover of both personnel and clients. The Midwestern or Southern agency comes across as less flamboyant, more businesslike, and less profitable. The Western agency hasn't yet been stereotyped, although it seems philosophically to resemble the East Coast brand of advertising. How do representatives of some of these agency types view themselves? Studs Terkel[9] interviewed a copy chief at a New York advertising agency:

I am what is called a creative supervisor. Creative is a pretentious word. I have a group of about six people who work for me. They create radio commercials, print ads, billboards that go up on the highways, television commercials, too. Your purpose is to move goods off the shelf (laughs): your detergents, your soaps, your foods, your beers, cigarettes. . . . It's an odd business. It's serious but it isn't. (Laughs) Life in an advertising agency is like being at a dull party, interrupted by more serious moments. There's generally a kind of convivial attitude. Nobody's particularly uptight. Creativity of this kind flourishes better.

My day is so amorphous. Part of it is guiding other people. I throw ideas out and let them throw ideas back, shoot down ideas immediately. In some ways, it's like teaching. You're trying to guide them and they're also guiding you. I may sit with a writer and an art director who are going to create a commercial—to sell garbage bags, okay? A number of ideas are thrown out. What do you think of this? What do you think of that? . . . It's very hard to know if you know something in this business. There are very few genuine experts. It's a very fragile

[9]Studs Terkel, *Working* (New York: Pantheon Books, 1972), pp. 73–77.

thing. To tell somebody they should spend ten million dollars on this tiger that's gonna represent their gasoline, that's quite a thing to sell somebody on doing.

Gee, why should it be a tiger? Why shouldn't it be a llama? . . . Advertising is full of very confident people. (Laughs) Whether it's also full of competent people is another question. Coming into a meeting is a little like swimming in a river full of piranha fish. If you start to bleed, they're gonna catch you. You have to build yourself up before you're gonna sell something. You have to have an attitude that it's terrific.

I say to myself, isn't it terrific? It could be worse—that's another thing I say. And I whistle and skip around and generally try to get my juices moving. Have a cup of coffee. I have great faith in coffee. (Laughs) There's an element of theater in advertising. When I'm presenting the stuff, I will give the impression of really loving it a lot. . . . When an older writer gets fired, he doesn't just get another job. I think there's a farm out in the Middle West or something where they're tethered. I don't know what happens to them.

A somewhat different version of an advertising agency specialist is this monologue from a Midwestern agency president.

People get the wrong idea of ad agency people from the daydreams coming out of New York. The ad agency business is hard work. You work during normal working hours and then you keep at it until late at night. People who say it's easy are either geniuses or liars. Most agencies never deal with movie stars or TV personalities. We're trying to get people excited about banks, potato chips, motors, chemicals, steel products—you name it. These companies need the advertising as much as the largest companies, like General Motors and Procter & Gamble. You can afford to make some mistakes with a large company. You can choose the wrong media. You can use TV when you should have put the money in print. But smaller companies can't afford that kind of mistake. Most agency people I know consider it a business, not a game. We can't afford to play musical chairs with clients because our investment in time is too great considering the amount of profit we make. . . . It's a good life. We're well paid. Perhaps our greatest thrill is to help a small or medium-sized company grow large and profitable because of our direction. Don't ever forget that a good agency is an idea factory. All too often we never get really reimbursed for the value of our ideas. I doubt if that will ever change.

IN SUMMARY

1 An advertising agency is an independent organization hired by a company to conduct its advertising affairs.
2 Traditional advertising agencies create, produce, and place (traffic) the advertising in media they select. Of these functions, clients (advertisers) consider creativity the most important.
3 Agencies don't physically produce the ideas they create into reproducible forms such as television commercials and engravings; they hire outsiders to do this work.
4 The media contract is a legal contract between the ad agency and the media. An

insertion order is traffic control's method of alerting media that ads are coming.

5 Full-service ad agencies do all the work associated with advertising: creation, media selection and placement, marketing, sales promotion, broadcast production, and public relations from within their own organizations.

6 Ad agencies earn their money through media commissions (15 percent), production add-ons, and fees.

7 When an agency purchases media advertising time and space, the agency and not the client is financially responsible to the media.

8 When agencies purchase other services such as typography, art, or photography, they add a specified percentage (17.65 percent) to the cost. This reimburses the agency for the time its personnel put into handling and supervising each job.

9 Agencies may also charge clients according to an agreed-to retainer fee or some variation based on time and talent. The "cost plus" fee plan reimburses the agency for its time, direct costs, and profit.

10 Agencies need to remember that the bulk of the money they handle belongs to others: media, suppliers, and the like. In general, agencies are mere custodians of most of the money clients pay them.

11 Of the over 7,000 ad agencies in the country, most bill less than $10 million a year.

12 Agency people fit into general job categories of copywriters, artists, account executives, media buyers, production buyers, traffic coordinators, accountants, and administrators.

13 Account executives are among the highest-paid employees in an ad agency, primarily because they are responsible for keeping clients happy and "wedded" to the agency.

14 There are a number of ways to keep clients happy. Some of the more important are: showing accounts they are important, proving to them that agencies are spending their money wisely, showing deep interest in clients' problems and business, maintaining a fair billing system, and creating unique and successful advertising.

15 Ad agencies can have conflicts of interest if they own a graphic arts supplier company, handle competitive accounts, or select media solely on the basis of how much revenue the agency will receive.

16 A media buying service specializes in selecting and buying media, and in its ability to negotiate with broadcast media owners.

17 A boutique agency is a specialty shop generally restricting itself to copywriting and art. Boutiques contend that clients can better perform other agency functions.

CASE STUDY The Recycling of an Ad Man

In twenty years Louis Schneider moved successfully from copywriter to account executive to account supervisor, ending up as vice president and treasurer in one of the largest advertising agencies in Louisville, Kentucky. Then, in January 1974, he went into the agency business on his own. What makes Louis Schneider unique among new ad agencies is that he decided to see whether an advertising agency itself could be built on *advertising*. In January 1974 Schneider began business with six accounts. At that time, he instituted a campaign in Louisville's daily newspapers, *The Courier-Journal* and *The*

Louisville Times. A year later, he had a total of fourteen regular clients.

"Of the eight new accounts gained, I give my newspaper ads credit for seven. Of course, no one picked up the phone and said, 'Come over and pick up our account.' What they did say was, 'We think we'd like to talk to you.' And of course, I followed up the desired leads aggressively."[10]

What made Louis Schneider leave a secure position in one agency to try his hand at something new is a story in itself. In his old job, he started writing copy and moved up the ladder. Then, as happens even in the best of agencies, office politics led to his leaving to open his own shop. (It is a story familiar to a nation founded on the free enterprise system.) Perhaps Louis Schneider is thriving because the owner puts his business philosophy on the line for everyone to see, as he did in a *Courier-Journal* ad headlined, "Shrewd as he was, old P.T. Barnum didn't quite tell it all."

> Barnum lived before the days of mass communications, but many of today's marketers appear to employ tactics aimed at the one sucker at the risk of turning off the other five people. But there are hopeful signs: increasing skepticism of absurd, overdrawn or meaningless claims: less and less tolerance of shoddy goods: more impatience with inferior services—in short, the whole consumerist movement. It's one of the best things going on in America now.
>
> This new, small ad agency intends to limit its association to advertisers who offer a worthwhile product or service; who emphasize value rather than price and terms; who are not exploiting human weaknesses—but who aim to go to market in the most effective manner consistent with truth and taste. . . .

As Louis Schneider sees his business now, "After almost five years, I'm having more fun than ever in my working life. I take only clients I like and approve of. No tobacco [processor], brewer, distiller, or politician; no schlock, nobody that sells on price. No garbage like 'Lose 20 pounds and eight inches in 3 days.' In five years, I've had only about four months which were in the red. It's hell to be little and selective sometimes, but virtue brings its own rewards. The agency recently got the account of the second largest savings and loan in Kentucky. Incidentally, I've run a quarter-page ad in both Louisville dailies every month since the agency opened." (Figure 15-8.)

QUESTIONS NEEDING ANSWERS

1 What advantages and disadvantages are there for a mature business person in switching from the role of an employee to advertising agency founder?
2 Was Louis Schneider wise in making the move in Louisville? Wouldn't he have been better off to have moved to another geographical area? Explain.
3 Obviously the majority of readers of the *Courier-Journal* and the *Louisville Times* are not owners of businesses or sales and ad managers. Wouldn't it have been more effective to conduct a direct-mail campaign?

[10]*Business Building Bulletin*, Newspaper Advertising Bureau, November 1975, No. 569.

Put us in the running to improve your advertising...

We get into everything from TV to T-shirts, from farm magazines to fortune cookies.

We advertise ourselves. We believe in it. (Never go to a restaurant if the owner doesn't eat there.)

Recently we got into a retail business. Putting your advertising theory into selling practice can be quite instructive.

If you like our attitude and approach, but don't like your own advertising, please call.

Louis Schneider, Advertising
Incorporated
100 North Sixth
Louisville, Kentucky 40202
(502) 585-5253

...while we put in our ad to improve your running.

Our almost totally unrelated (but much beloved) affiliate, Jogger-Runner-Racer, carries everything the budding jogger, improving runner, or seasoned racer, is likely to need.

Bob Kinny, manager of this great little store, points out that cross-country season is fast approaching. Jogger-Runner-Racer offers a 10% discount on all regularly priced shoes (flats and spikes, men's and women's) to all high school, college, and club team members.

The Puma 9190 is an excellent jogging and leisure shoe. Unfortunately, it hasn't sold. So, we're reducing the price from $21.99 to $17.99. (No team-member discount on this one.)

Congratulations to all AAU Junior Olympics qualifiers, and good luck in Detroit.

We're going to hold our first clinic soon. Watch for it.

Jogger⟩ Runner⟩ Racer⟩
116 Bauer Avenue
St. Matthews, Kentucky 40207
(502) 896-4064
Bob Kinny, Manager

FIGURE 15-8
There is a great undocumented complaint by agency clients that agencies who have the greatest stake in advertising don't use advertising themselves on a regular basis. Perhaps that explains the success of the Louis Schneider agency in Louisville. Right from its inception, it put its money in the service it knew best. Just as important, it advertised its individualistic philosophy.

4 In his ad aimed at advertisers, Schneider admitted that his was a new, small agency. Was this politically wise? Explain.
5 Do you think the agency could have succeeded in acquiring new clients without follow-up sales calls?
6 Why wouldn't a large half-page ad in the Yellow Pages of the Louisville phone book have been as effective as, if not more effective than, Schneider's newspaper campaign? Explain.

STUDENT PROJECT

Artists and copywriters complain that the work they do for clients, and for which the agency is paid but once, often lives on even after a new agency has taken over. They feel this situation is unfair and that they deserve "residuals" much like television personalities who star in commercials. Check appropriate reference books to determine how television residuals are set up. Note the specific amounts of money "on camera" people can expect for the first thirteen weeks and for subsequent periods.

QUESTIONS ABOUT THE PROJECT

1 What justification do you think there is for agencies to negotiate a residual contract for their creative work that outlasts their tenure with the advertiser? Explain.
2 What about such a contract for a freelance art studio that sells its creativity for a one-time charge, or for the production studio that creates a radio or television commercial?
3 If you were going to create such a contract, what steps would you take to enforce it? Do you feel advertisers would accept such a contract from their ad agency? Explain.

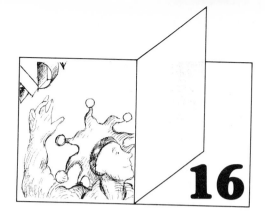

THE LEGAL YARDSTICK

Update Advertisers spend considerable time and money investigating us, the consumers. When they feel they have us identified and stratified, they design messages for us. But suppose the messages are false? What recourse do consumers have? Formerly, advertisers could make outrageous claims without fear of interference. But today society applies a legal yardstick to advertisers. We'll investigate who applies it and whether it encroaches on the freedom of private industry.

The commercial laws governing business activities in the United States protect the buyer with an implied warranty. In other words, when we buy something, we have the right to expect it to work. The opposite condition is described by the Latin expression *caveat emptor*, "let the buyer beware." In that case, we buy at our own risk.

Manufacturers know that few products are failsafe under all conditions. The automobile industry presents an example of a dilemma that faces all advertisers: how to reveal complete information about products and still sell them. Can Plymouth claim Horizon's front-wheel drive "gives Horizon great stability and gives you a great feeling of confidence,"[1] when it knows *not all* its cars can do it? It is common knowledge that auto companies regularly recall cars because of defects. Should this prevent a manufacturer from putting its best foot forward? Witness, as an example, this Ford Company ad:

Headline: It's tough to get to be a Ford, Mercury or Lincoln engine.

Copy: All Ford Motor Company engines are the result of one tough test after another. Here are just a few. This is a Camshaft Feeler feeling a camshaft . . . 'cause a flaw in a camshaft could mean a rough running engine. That's 'cause the camshaft makes the valves open and close . . . *exactly* when they're supposed to . . . [2]

The same copy discusses how to discover flaws down to .000050 of an inch and goes on to describe ten other tough tests. Ford's and all other car maker's problem is that despite many tests, some cars simply do not function well. Should Ford or any other advertiser write ads to cover every contingency? Suppose Ford ran the following headline instead of the original.

It's tough to get to be a Ford, Mercury or Lincoln engine *under most circumstances.* (Human nature and wear and tear on machines and testing equipment may permit a minimal number of subpar engines to pass. We'll protect you if that unlikely situation occurs.)

And where should this explanation appear in the ad—in the headline? in the body copy? In what size type? The Ford advertising people would certainly complain that ads hedged with qualifications not only slow readership but also discourage sales. Should a company refrain from advertising its achievements until it's solved every product problem?

The problem facing business today is less one of outright lies than one of credibility. Consumers differ on what they consider a credible claim because everyone has different expectations. For example, if an air-conditioning system is advertised as able to keep you "comfortable," who defines what "comfort" is?

DECEPTION IN ADVERTISING

Let's first make a distinction between falsity and deception: "Falsity and deception may seem the same. But they are not; what is deceptive is what is

---

[1]Plymouth ad, "America takes to the horizon," *National Geographic,* , July 1978.
[2]Ad, "It's tough to be a Ford, Mercury or Lincoln engine," *Outdoor Life*, September 1977, p. 145.

injurious to the consumer."[3] Falsity is an untruthful claim that may not harm the purchaser.

What steps can consumers take to protect themselves against deceptive ads? Their first step should be to contact the manufacturer and complain. Then they can contact either media, business, or governmental agencies. Local agencies include the Better Business Bureau, advertising clubs, and even small claims court. On the national level, there is the Federal Trade Commission (FTC), a governmental regulatory agency, and the National Advertising Division of the Council of Better Business Bureaus. These groups can persuade advertisers to stop making deceptive claims; their methods are of vital interest to advertisers, lawyers, and the public. We begin with the most formidable of all, the Federal Trade Commission (FTC).

The Federal Trade Commission

The FTC was organized in 1914 to enforce laws against unfair business practices. Since then it has issued thousands of decisions. Although its most publicized actions are suits involving false or misleading advertising and rules about what ads can and should say about product warranties,[4] most of the FTC's decisions do not concern deceptive advertising; they concern unfair trade practices.

As an example of the FTC's power, consider this example: after seventy-five copywriters have worried a new Sears, Roebuck catalog into shape, and after some thirty-five photographic advertising studios have been called in to take the required photographs, and after artists have rendered words into layouts, and hundreds of thousands of words have been set into type, "the pages go to the editorial department, which looks after the major headings. Even more importantly, it checks to make sure that all the advertising meets Federal Trade Commission requirements and the dictates of other regulatory bodies."[5] This state of affairs at Sears is instructive because, years before there was an FTC, founder Sears, a successful writer of direct-mail literature, churned out extravagant claims.[6]

Some advertisers think the FTC is an ogre, out to destroy them or run them out of business. Most, however, recognize that the agency has the unhappy task of walking a tightrope between the manufacturer's freedom to describe products and the consumer's need for protection against fraud and deception. The FTC has historically gone from decisiveness to weakness depending on the nature of its commissioner. In the last several federal administrations, the heads of the FTC have been strong, determined administrators who have expanded the commission's role of public protector

[3]Ivan Preston, *The Great American Blow-Up* (Madison, Wisc.: University of Wisconsin Press, 1975), p. 6–7.

[4]The Magnuson-Moss Warranty Act of 1976 directs the FTC to issue discretionary regulations concerning the promises made in warranties.

[5]Gordon L. Weil, *Sears, Roebuck U.S.A.* (New York: Stein & Day, 1977), p. 33.

[6]Ibid., p. 16.

in regard to advertising. Yet, far from wanting to do away with advertising, the FTC has indicated support of it by demanding that noncompetitive groups such as morticians, opticians, and pharmacists be allowed to advertise their prices. The commission's argument is that advertising encourages competition and results in lower prices for the public. The Supreme Court has supported the FTC's position at least three times in striking down state regulations prohibiting advertising.[7]

One major problem between advertisers and the FTC is what goes unsaid. Recent television commercials by a stock brokerage firm, for example, imply that its customers make money every time they hear from the firm.[8] While the rewards are never stated in the commercials, the "unsaid" gains could develop friction between the FTC and the advertiser. Zenith claimed in a television commercial that "every color TV Zenith makes is built right here in the United States by Americans like these" (the video screen showed Zenith employees at work). Subsequent investigations placed foreign-made components at approximately 14 percent of total component parts. Was it fair to ignore those components in making the claim? Was there misrepresentation?

> There is little doubt about the contents of the literal statement. . . .But there is considerable doubt about the implied statements. Implications are a function of each citizen's mind, and it is difficult to determine what is in those minds. It is also difficult to determine whether a statement implied to 5 percent or 20 percent or 50 percent of those minds should be deemed to be implied sufficiently to affect the public generally.[9]

Manufacturers contend they have no idea what the FTC considers "an implication." They claim that the legislative wording of the responsibilities of the FTC is vague, leaving precise definition to the FTC itself, or to the courts. Understandably, this vagueness makes business people uneasy. Both the FTC and responsible business people agree, however, that deliberate misrepresentations are not vague and should be prosecuted. Such was the case when the FTC moved against the STP Corporation for advertising that adding a can of STP Oil Treatment to a car's engine would save 20 percent on oil consumption. When this claim could not be substantiated, STP was fined $700,000 and forced to recant (Figure 16-1).

Listerine, a long-time advertiser, has also felt the power of the FTC: "Kills germs by the millions on contact," said the familiar Listerine copy. The idea that one could cure colds or sore throats by gargling with Listerine had

---

[7]Kent R. Middleton, "A case against First Amendment protections for commercial advertising," paper presented at Association of Education in Journalism (Madison, Wisconsin), July 1977, pp. 1–2.

[8]Stock brokerage firm of Dean Witter.

[9]Ivan Preston, "The FTC's handling of puffery and other selling claims made by implication," paper presented at Association for Education in Journalism (Madison, Wisconsin) July 1977, p. 1.

FTC NOTICE

As a result of an investigation by the
Federal Trade Commission into certain allegedly
inaccurate past advertisements
for STP's oil additive, STP Corporation
has agreed to a $700,000 settlement.
With regard to that settlement,
STP is making the following statement:

It is the policy of STP to support its advertising with objective information and test data. In 1974 and 1975 an independent laboratory ran tests of the company's oil additive which led to claims of reduced oil consumption. However, these tests cannot be relied on to support the oil consumption reduction claim made by STP.

The FTC has taken the position that, in making that claim, the company violated the terms of a consent order. When STP learned that the test data did not support the claim, it stopped advertising containing that claim. New tests have been undertaken to determine the extent to which the oil additive affects oil consumption. Agreement to this settlement does not constitute an admission by STP that the law has been violated. Rather, STP has agreed to resolve the dispute with the FTC to avoid protracted and prohibitively expensive litigation.

February 13, 1978

FIGURE 16-1
Admitting to the world that lab tests did not support its oil consumption reduction claims, STP ran this ad to resolve its dispute with the FTC. Part of the agreement with FTC included a $700,000 settlement.

long been that company's claim to fame and fortune. The FTC said that Listerine's advertising was misleading, and the courts agreed.[10] Bayer agreed to withdraw advertisements in which a man wearing a trenchcoat and standing before the Washington Monument delivers "the news from the Federal Drug Administration"— that rival Tylenol is no safer than Bayer.

The intent of the FTC is the protection of the consumer. Some advertisers contend, however, that the agency oversteps its powers and interferes with the conduct of business. Observers who can see both sides of the problem point out that private companies have the *right* to contest an FTC ruling and suggest this be done. On the other hand, they applaud the FTC's vigilance in guarding consumers against false and misleading advertising.

FTC Guidelines   When the FTC uncovers what it considers to be a deceptive ad, it serves a complaint upon the advertiser. If the advertiser contests the finding, there is a trial before an FTC "administrative law judge." If guilty, the advertiser must "cease and desist." Each subsequent violation costs $5,000.

Here are the major deceptive advertising practices under surveillance by the FTC:

1   unsubstantiated claims
2   vague, ambiguous language
3   fraudulent testimonials
4   puffery and exaggerated sales talk
5   deceptive pricing
6   deceptive television demonstrations
7   libeling, slandering, or defaming competition in comparative advertising
8   contests that are in actuality lotteries (lotteries are illegal)
9   misuse of the word "free"
10   "bait" advertising (offering to sell a product that the advertiser doesn't want to sell)

Corrective Advertising

The FTC has the relatively new power to demand corrective advertising from a company. The reason is that the agency is concerned that residual effects of years of advertising cannot be eliminated by simply stopping questionable or misleading claims. The advertiser, according to the FTC, must take positive steps to erase the false impressions advertising has created.

---

[10]*Warner-Lambert Company v. FTC* F. 2nd 749, (C.A.D.C. 1977). The Supreme Court made final an FTC order by refusing to review the Second Federal Circuit Court's order. In effect, this was the first court test of FTC's "corrective advertising" ruling which required the makers of Listerine to declare in its next $10 million worth of ads, "Listerine will not help prevent colds or sore throats or lessen their severity."

Listerine, a product of Warner-Lambert Company, is one of a number of products that has had to provide corrective advertising. To undo fifty years of what the FTC termed "misleading advertising," Warner-Lambert was ordered to accompany $10 million worth of its advertising with this statement: "Listerine will not prevent colds or sore throats or lessen their severity."

In 1971 the makers of Profile Bread were ordered to invest 25 percent of a year's media budget to correct their false promise that eating the bread would cause significant weight loss. The Sugar Association was ordered to run corrective advertising from December 1972 to April 1973 in seven national magazines because its ads had suggested that eating sugar before meals would dull the appetite. The FTC indicated the size of the ads and their placement in the magazines. The makers of Domino sugar spent 25 percent of one year's budget informing people that Domino was not more nutritive than other sugars, nor was it a unique source of energy.

The FTC policies affect retailers, too. Wasem's retail drug store in Clarkston, Washington, consented to run a week of corrective sixty-second spots on the same television stations and at about the same time that their previous ads had run. The correction stated that most people don't need to take vitamins and that neither the FTC nor the Food and Drug Administration had ever endorsed the Wasem's brand of Super B Vitamins.

Corporation lawyers describe "corrective advertising" as violating the First Amendment, adding that it is overbroad and punitive. They claim that this new assumption of powers by the FTC propels it into an arena better left to private regulatory boards, the competition of the market place, and local consumer groups. One private regulating board they point to with some pride is the National Advertising Division of the Council of Better Business Bureaus (CBBB).

The Council of Better Business Bureaus

The original Better Business Bureau movement began over sixty-five years ago because legitimate businesses were being hurt by false and misleading advertising. Local Better Business Bureaus pioneered in exposing misleading ads and, around World War I, originated the "truth in advertising" slogan.

More recently, the growth of the advertising industry and consumerism gave rise to possible restrictions that, it was felt, would hamper advertising's freedom to communicate as well as its traditional role as a vital part of marketing. To meet the very real challenge of such restrictions, the Council of Better Business Bureaus sponsored a new self-regulatory organization called the *National Advertising Review Board* (NARB). This organization has been promoted by the leaders of the American Advertising Federation, the Association of National Advertisers, and the American Association of Advertising Agencies. The National Advertising Review Board acts as a court of appeals for advertisers cited for misleading ads. It consists of "the chairman, thirty members representing advertisers, ten from the agency business, and ten public members who have no direct connection with advertising or industry. . . . NARB members are chosen for their stature and experience in their respective fields'' .(Figure 16-2).[11]

Public members include professors, executive directors of educational and cultural institutes, editors, and consumer affairs advocates. The avowed purpose of the NARB is to sustain high standards of truth and accuracy in national advertising.

If the NARB is a court of appeals, who initiates the action that brings an advertiser to it? That function belongs to the Council of Better Business Bureaus.

The National Advertising Division

The National Advertising Division (NAD) of the CBBB reviews all challenges to the truth of national advertising. As the investigative arm of the CBBB, the NAD is a voluntary, self-regulatory operation of private industry. It evaluates advertisers' substantiation of claims and arrives at fair decisions. The NAD also helps advertisers with questions of truth and accuracy so they can avoid problems in the future. To date, there appears to be a willingness on the part of advertisers to negotiate with the NAD and abide by its decisions rather than to take their cases before the NARB (Table 16-1).

When a complainant contacts the CBBB, the Council channels the problem to the NAD where it is checked and evaluated. Complainants can be consumers, associations, or even competitors. If the NAD finds that the ad violates good advertising practices, the division tries to convince the advertiser to change or alter the offending advertisement. If the advertiser refuses to change, the NAD (or the advertiser) appeals the case to the NARB.

Although the actions of the NAD and the NARB do not have the force of law, they appear to deter most advertisers from repeating questionable claims. From 1971 to 1978, during the first seven years of the NAD's operation, four product categories (automotive, cosmetics, food, and household products) accounted for more NAD case reviews than any other. Yet of the 1,380 complaints, few got as far as an NARB appeal because they were settled or dismissed by the NAD.[12]

Here are some typical examples of the NAD at work from one of its reports.

> *American Consumer Company:* The advertising claims questioned by NAD were: "Three famous fat melters, kelp, lecithin, Vitamin B6, plus B complex—all in one tiny, dynamite tablet. You can lose twelve pounds in two weeks without a single hunger pang." In the print ad, diet was mentioned as part of the program, but the NAD felt its role was far overshadowed by those of the other "fat melters." When NAD requested substantiation of American Consumer Company's claim, it was told that the ads had ended.

---

[11]"A review and perspective on advertising industry self-regulation," National Advertising Review Board, May 1978, p. 10.
[12]Ibid., p. 6.

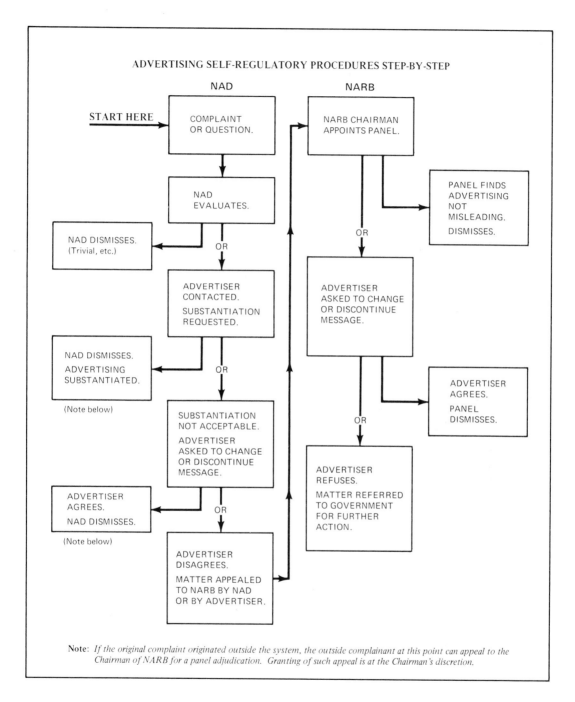

FIGURE 16-2

A step-by-step procedure for the self-regulation of advertising. It all begins with the National Advertising Division (NAD) of the Council of Better Business Bureaus. Note that the NAD requests advertisers to supply substantiation of their claims. (Courtesy NAD.)

TABLE 16-1

NAD STATISTICAL CASE RECORD
As of April 30, 1978

	Cumulative (June 1971 to Present)
TOTAL COMPLAINTS	1380

Includes 93 investigations of advertising directed to children.

DISPOSITION
Dismissed –

Adequate Substantiation	530

Dismissed –

Advertiser Modified or discontinued	474
Administratively closed	298
Referred to NARB by NAD	13*
Pending	65

*Other cases appealed to NARB by outside complainants or advertisers.

SOURCES OF COMPLAINTS

Consumers	197
Consumer organizations	179
Competitors	201
Local Better Business Bureaus	268
NAD monitoring	486
Other	49

Since 1971, the record of the National Advertising Division's actions reveals that few cases ever reached the National Advertising Review Board, the ad industry's court of appeals. Notice that most complaints come out of NAD's own monitoring. (Courtesy NAD).

General Mills: Print ads claimed that Crisp n' Tender coating mix was preferred by a substantial margin of consumers over Shake n' Bake in a comparative taste test. "We guarantee you'll like it better than the leading brand," and Crisp n' Tender makes chicken "that is superior to the leading brand," the advertiser said. When asked to support these claims, the advertiser discontinued them.

Johnson & Johnson: Television and print ads for Johnson & Johnson disposable diapers compared absorbency to other diaper products. NAD questioned whether demonstrations reflected actual use conditions. Johnson & Johnson supplied adequate data and substantiation for the claim that its diapers were the "driest" of all disposable diapers.

Owens-Corning Fiberglas: Advertiser claimed that its insulation would save consumers on cooling and heating bills and was able to adequately substantiate the claim: "Insulate your attic yourself with Fiberglas six inches thick. You'll save a total of (figure varied according to the market) a year on air conditioning and heating."

As we review the recurring voluntary codes, standards, and slogans by which advertisers have attempted to police themselves over the years, it is evident that most were attempts to deter federal regulation of advertising. Regardless of motive, however, the result has been more, rather than less, protection for the consumer.

Critics of the NAD, the industry's latest attempt at self-regulation, point out that all NAD actions take place after misrepresentation has appeared. They argue that business has not evolved a system that either prevents or punishes fraudulent or misleading advertising. Business, in turn, has a four-part reply: (1) for the first time, the National Advertising Review Board now includes a public representative. (2) For the Board to mete out punishment could lead to charges of monopoly and self-interest. (3) Public disclosure of misleading ads and cooperation with the FTC helps to discourage unsubstantiated claims. (4) NAD notice to the advertising media of misleading advertisers puts the media on notice and permits them to take justifiable preventive measures (for example, to refuse to accept the misleading ads) (Figure 16-3).

BROADCASTING REGULATIONS

In the early days of television, broadcasters and government officials feared that fewer than ten advertisers would dominate independent stations because of their sheer economic strength. At that time, these few companies controlled about 50 percent of the total broadcast advertising for the independents. Fortunately, competitors soon began advertising, and the federal government did not have to act to interfere.

Recognizing that the government is ready to act in order to protect the people's airwaves, the National Association of Broadcasters adopted a Radio and TV Code that set standards of conduct and acceptable advertising. Some of the early standards were: no whiskey advertising, no promotion of intimate products, and no doctors advertising drug products. (Recently, we have seen repeated promotion of intimate products. Does this signify the end of other prohibitions?) In addition, the Federal Communications Commission (FCC) and the FTC evaluate the truth of broadcast advertising. The FCC can, with Congressional help, prevent objectionable ads from being aired. But precisely defining what is objectionable is very difficult, and so it is not uncommon for one major network to refuse to run an ad while the other two networks accept it readily.

Broadcast stations are particularly sensitive to ads that might cause consumer unhappiness because they are licensed by the federal government and fear they might lose their franchise to broadcast over the people's

NA RB NATIONAL ADVERTISING REVIEW BOARD

Established for the self regulation of national advertising ▪ Sponsored by The National Advertising Review Council, Inc.
845 Third Avenue, New York, N.Y. 10022

For further information:

Ralph H. Alexander, Jr.   For Release on and after December 1, 1975
212-832-1320

DRACKETT DISAGREES WITH NARB DECISION,

BUT AGREES TO DROP "BEHOLD" COMMERCIAL HELD TO HAVE "CAPACITY TO DECEIVE"

———————————————

Panel rules in favor of "Behold" in price advantage claim

———————————————

New York, December 1,1975--In a precedent setting decision, a
National Advertising Review Board panel found a recent Drackett Company
television commercial comparing its furniture polish, "Behold," with
S.C. Johnson's "Lemon Pledge" had the capacity to deceive viewers into
the belief the demonstrated comparison established overall superiority
of its product.

The Panel ruled that although Drackett was able to establish "Behold's"
superiority in one area (i.e. removal of an oil-based stain), it did not
establish the product's overall superiority. They recommended that the
advertising be discontinued.

While recognizing that comparative advertising can be of value to
the consumer, if done properly, the NARB panel also stated that an
advertiser utilizing this technique takes on an extra burden of conclusive
substantiation.

This is especially important, the panel believes, when the advertising
concerns a product with multiple qualities and characteristics which are
significant to the consumer. "It is insufficient," they held, "to establish
proof of one characteristic in such a way that the consumer can be led
to conclude overall superiority."

--more

FIGURE 16-3

The press receives all National Advertising Review Board reports on individual cases after the board takes action. Note that the self-regulatory system resulted in a change in the television commercial for Behold furniture polish.

airwaves. That's why ad agencies submit commercials to networks with ample time for the censor's review. And that's why ad agencies supply the networks with affidavits from people who can attest that a demonstration is real.

The Fairness Doctrine

Another government regulation that can unsettle broadcast advertisers is the Fairness Doctrine, requiring a station (or network) to allow proponents of

NA
RB

NATIONAL ADVERTISING REVIEW BOARD
Established for the self regulation of national advertising ▪ Sponsored by The National Advertising Review Council, Inc.
845 Third Avenue, New York, N.Y. 10022

For further information:

Ralph H. Alexander, Jr.   For Immediate Release
212-832-1320

NARB PANEL FINDS NEW DRACKETT COMMERCIAL

IN COMPLIANCE WITH PREVIOUS DECISION

New York, April 6, 1976-- A new television commercial by The
Drackett Company comparing its furniture polish, "Behold," with
S.C. Johnson's "Pledge" has been upheld in a supplementary opinion by the National Advertising Review Board panel. The panel
has held that an earlier "Behold" commercial had the capacity to
deceive by implying overall superiority while substantiating
only superiority in certain criteria.

The new "Behold" commercial, prepared and released by
Drackett after the December 1 decision, had been challenged by
the Johnson company which alleged that the new commercial continued
to be "misleading" and "deceptive."

After careful consideration of the questioned commercial,
which compares "Behold" against "Pledge" on the basis of price and
ability to clean grease or wax marks, the NARB panel concluded that
Drackett had met the test laid out by the panel and that the new
"Behold" advertising is "not inconsistent" with the previous opinion.

In a statement issued by The Drackett Company, Mr. Nicholas
M. Evans, President, said that "this is an important decision, because it recognizes the significant role and responsibility of comparative advertising in helping consumers to make informed buying
choices."

both sides of a controversial issue of public importance to present their views. When Chevron Oil Company radio ads claimed that their gasoline additive reduced exhaust emissions from automobile engines, petitioners who felt this was a controversial public issue tried to gain access for a radio counterattack under the Fairness Doctrine. The station involved and the FCC refused access and were supported by the U.S. Circuit Court of Appeals, which saw no controversy. To date, the FCC has shown restraint in applying the Fairness Doctrine to commercial advertisements, although this attitude could change.

AVOIDING LEGAL PITFALLS IN ADS

Advertising managers and ad agency account executives need to establish clear lines of communication with their legal departments. Communication is essential if the company has had disputes with a federal or industry watchdog agency. Together, lawyer and ad manager need to set up procedures for all personnel to follow *before* they approve broadcast and print ads for final reproduction.

The ad manager can designate someone in the ad department to screen all copy and artwork for possible legal implications. If an ad passes the first test, it should be sent to the legal department with an explanatory note. Some companies insist that all advertising be scrutinized by their lawyers. Other companies distribute a list of "thou shalt nots" to their ad departments so most legal difficulties are nipped in the bud. Here is a suggested list of practices to avoid:

1 It is unlawful to use a false description or misrepresentation of goods shipped through interstate commerce.
2 Don't attach a warranty to a product if you are not prepared to honor it for the entire warranty period. In case of qualifications, provide a limited warranty, which may mean:

   a giving a pro-rata refund or credit that is less the longer a customer has the product,
   b covering the cost of the parts, but not the labor involved in assembling and disassembling,
   c requiring the customer to get the product to the factory or the store,
   d covering only the original purchaser of the item.
3 Don't use a slogan, trademark, or symbol without clearance from the owners.
4 Don't use a trademark without putting proper registry notice at least once in the ad: ®, or, for example, "Coca-Cola is a registered trademark of the Coca-Cola Bottling Company."
5 Don't use photographs in ads of identifiable persons without their written consent as witnessed by a third party. Be sure that quotes used in ads are accurate.
6 Don't use any quote or advertising copy that libels other persons, products, or companies existing now or in the past.
7 If you compare your products to another, be certain the comparison is just, because truth is the most effective defense against libel.

Companies that adhere to these rules of good business in their advertising will usually avoid the expense, time, and embarrassment of legal challenges.

Trademark Problems

A *trademark* is a name, symbol, word(s), or mark used by a company to identify a product and distinguish it from all others. Protecting it is serious business. Companies either protect their trademarks, which are registered

"But Mr. Carruthers, you said you needed forty Xeroxes."

Mr. Carruthers used our name incorrectly. That's why he got 40 Xerox copiers, when what he really wanted was 40 copies made on his Xerox copier.

He didn't know that Xerox, as a trademark of Xerox Corporation, should be followed by the descriptive word for the particular product, such as "Xerox duplicator" or "Xerox copier."

And should only be used as a noun when referring to the corporation itself.

If Mr. Carruthers had asked for 40 copies or 40 photocopies made on his Xerox copier, he would have gotten exactly what he wanted.

And if you use Xerox properly, you'll get exactly what you want, too.

P.S. You're welcome to make 40 copies or 40 photocopies of this ad. Preferably on your Xerox copier.

XEROX

FIGURE 16-4

Xerox, leader in the copying industry, is eternally vigilant in protecting its trademarked name. The intent of the ad is to discourage the use of the name as a synonym for any copying operation. (Courtesy Xerox Corporation.)

with an agency of the government, or risk losing them. Xerox spends thousands of dollars explaining what its name means and repeating that it is not a synonym for the process of making paper copies (Figure 16-4). Coca-Cola retains several lawyers to protect the trademark "Coke." The problem is that the advertising success of a trademark can turn it into a generic word. "Frigidaire" is a classic example of a trademark that became so firmly entrenched in the language that it literally came to identify *all* refrigerators, regardless of brand. When Frigidaire failed to use registry marks in ads and literature to inform the public that "Frigidaire" was an exclusive name, it lost the right to use the name exclusively. Thus, any competitive model could advertise itself as the ABC frigidaire, or the XYZ frigidaire.

When the National Broadcasting System (NBC) introduced its new NBC logo, it inadvertently adopted a mark that had been created for the Nebraska Educational Network. NBC recognized that the Nebraska station had prior rights, and the two networks settled out of court, agreeing on television equipment and a modest cash amount for the Nebraska network and the exclusive right to continue to use the logo for NBC (Figure 16-5).

In addition to distinguishing their names, symbols, and words with trademarks, some companies also copyright all of their advertisements. The Copyright Law provides protection for a copyright owner against infringement. Sunkist, for example, requires anyone reprinting their ads to include the copyright notice (Figure 16-6).

Tampering with or infringing upon a protected trademark or copyright is a serious breach of business conduct and is punishable by law.

IN SUMMARY

1 Most advertisers have more problems with misleading claims than with outright lies.

2 Consumers combating deceptive ads can complain to any or all of the following: the seller, the media, the Better Business Bureau, a local ad club, the Federal Trade Commission.

3 The FTC has supported advertising to foster competition among funeral directors, prescription druggists, and opticians.

4 The FTC was formed to enforce laws against unfair business practices, including misleading ads.

5 The FTC considers the following as misleading advertising: unsubstantiated claims; vague, ambiguous language; fraudulent testimonials; puffery; deceptive pricing; deceptive television demonstrations; libel; slander or defamation of competition; lotteries; misuse of the word "free"; "bait" claims.

6 The FTC uses the power of "corrective advertising" to make good deceptively advertised claims. The FTC concern is that the residual effects of years of advertising cannot be eliminated simply by stopping questionable ads.

7 The National Advertising Review Board (NARB) acts as a court of appeals for cases of alleged advertising misrepresentation. It is a creation of several

**NEBRASKA
ETV
NETWORK**

FIGURE 16-5
This logo created by
William Korbus for
his Nebraska ETV
Network appeared
soon afterwards as
the symbol of the
NBC Network. NBC
settled out of court
for the exclusive
rights. Logo and
symbol design are
big business in the
United States.

sponsoring organizations: the Council of Better Business Bureaus, the American
Association of Advertising Agencies, the American Advertising Federation, and
the Association of National Advertisers. The NARB is made up of a chairperson
and panel members from industry, the ad agencies, and the public.

8 The National Advertising Division (NAD) of the Council of Better Business
Bureaus (CBBB) acts as the investigative arm of the CBBB. So far, it—and not
the NARB—has settled the vast majority of cases involved with misleading
advertising.

9 Critics of the NAD and NARB say they don't prevent misrepresentation.
Proponents say they do indirectly because they can notify media and the FTC of
deceptive advertisers.

10 The FCC, as well as the FTC, evaluates truthfulness in broadcast ads.

11 Major points guiding the advertising of any company are: don't use a false
description of goods shipped in interstate commerce; don't attach a warranty to a
product unless you are prepared to honor it; don't use a disputed slogan or

FIGURE 16-6

To qualify for copyright protection, advertisements must include a copyright notice and be deposited with the Copyright Office in Washington, D.C. The procedure is simple and the filing fee extremely modest. When the author of this textbook requested the use of this Sunkist ad, permission was graciously given with this proviso: "All Sunkist advertising is copyrighted and should be so indicated. Please include the following two lines in conjunction with the ad; 'Sunkist is a trademark of Sunkist Growers, Inc. © 1976. Reprinted with permission of Sunkist Growers, Inc.' "

trademark; don't forget to use proper registry notices in all promotional material; don't use photographs of identifiable persons in ads without their written consent; be sure that quotes used in ads are accurate; don't use ad copy that libels persons, products, or companies; and be certain, in comparison-type ads, that your words speak the truth.

CASE STUDY   NARB *vs* Alpo

In February 1976, the investigative arm of the Council of Better Business Bureaus, the National Advertising Division (NAD), received complaints that two Alpo dog food commercials featuring Ed McMahon and Lorne Greene were misleading. The ads implied that Alpo was all meat and nutritionally superior to other dog foods, particularly those containing cereals. Neither of the two commercials mentioned that Alpo contained soy flour.

Comprehension testing among consumers showed that among 134 users of canned dog food, 58 percent believed Alpo was an all-meat product; 21 percent believed Alpo was more nutritious than other dog foods. The technique used in the survey was "unaided recall." A second "aided recall" survey produced these results: 89 percent believed Alpo was an all-meat product, 75 percent believed it was more nutritious than other dog foods.

The NARB panel found the Lorne Greene commercial misleading. It drew attention to the sentence: "I feed my dog Alpo Beef Chunks Dinner because it's meat by-products, beef, and balanced nutrition." The panel found that "balanced nutrition" does not adequately inform the consumer that Alpo is not an all-meat product. As expert testimony established, despite Alpo's high meat content, it is no better in maintaining a healthy dog than other dog foods.

The panel recommended the discontinuance and the avoidance of advertising that states or implies that Alpo is an all-meat product and that meat is essential to a complete and balanced maintenance diet.

The advertiser disagreed, saying that it did voluntarily disclose the fact that Alpo had a small amount of soy flour and had advertised that fact for two years. "While we question the necessity of continuing to make this previously oft-repeated disclosure in the short 30 seconds allotted to our commercial, nevertheless, in our desire to cooperate fully with the NARB, we will undertake as soon as practicable to modify the commercial. . . ." (Figure 16-7).

QUESTIONS NEEDING ANSWERS

1   In your opinion, was Alpo guilty of deception? Explain.
2   If Alpo decided to switch to a new copy approach abandoning its "all-meat" sales pitch and never reran the altered commercial, would the NARB action be sufficient to protect the public?

LORNE GREENE: You want to see something? Watch this.

C'mon. ALPO Time! ALPO Time!

Look at 'em. Every natural instinct tells 'em they should eat meat. And you know something? Their instincts are absolutely *right*.

Meat is good for dogs. Full of protein, energy, nourishment. I feed my dogs ALPO Beef Chunks Dinner because it's meat by-products, beef and balanced nutrition.

ALPO's all a dog ever needs to eat.

There's no better dog food in the world.

FIGURE 16-7
Alpo spokesperson Lorne Greene emphasizes the value of an all-meat diet for dogs. NARB recommended that the commercial be changed because Alpo contained soy flour.

3 Most ads contested by the NAD are either canceled or altered. Does this indicate adequate self-regulation of the industry? Explain.

4 Should Alpo be pleased with an "unaided recall" score of 58 percent? Explain.

STUDENT PROJECT

Check your nearest local Better Business Bureau and get examples of several misleading ads run within the past five years. Ask the BBB whether there is a local Advertising Review Board.

QUESTIONS ABOUT THE PROJECT

1 Are the ads you located local or national?

2 If there is a local Advertising Review Board, what is it doing to combat misleading local advertising? If there isn't one, who polices local ads?

3 How do you think that local advertisers who mislead the public should be treated?

4 How do local business people feel about self-regulation of their advertising? Explain.

Unit

5

THE CREATIVE CONNECTION

CREATIVITY IN PRINT MEDIA ADVERTISING

Part 1: Layout

Update All advertising agencies lay claim to creativity. But what is creativity? Is it digesting all the marketing data about a product, isolating the most important data, and dramatizing them? Or is it elevating a common product or service to a position of uniqueness through a made-up, attention-getting device? No matter how creativity is defined—and we won't try it except by analogies and examples—the plain facts are that creative ads can change a good, common product into a good, uncommon one. Translated into profits, creative ads are worth their weight in gold.

THE STRATEGY PLATFORM

Advertisers use white knights, hands in toilet bowls, talking tunas, cowboys, and other devices as part of the serious game of breaking the "boredom

```
          Copywriter's Strategy Platform

                         Date_____


    1. Specify your target audience_____

       _____

       _____

       _____


    2. Most important idea of the ad (campaign, literature,etc.)

       _____

       _____

       _____


    3. Most important selling feature_____

       _____

       _____


    4. Other important sales features in order of importance____

       _____

       _____

       _____


    5. Reader/viewer action desired_____

       _____

       _____
```

FIGURE 17-1
Copywriters originate their strategies on copy platform sheets that can be used for individual ads or complete
campaigns. The platform saves the copywriter many false starts.

barrier."[1] These devices are the inventions of copywriters. The drama all begins with them.

Contrary to popular opinion, copywriters do not simply sit in front of typewriters and dream up green giants and talking cats. They usually work from a copy *strategy platform* (Figure 17-1), a creative road map that outlines the direction their ads are to take. The platform is intended to prevent copywriters from straying from the objective of the ad as they engage in the creative process. Assuming that the product itself is good—advertising will kill a poor product faster than any other marketing tool—copywriters develop the platform with the following facts:

1 the specific target audience (such as working men and women eighteen to fifty-four).
2 the most important selling idea (for example, U.S. Savings Bonds help you plan for the future).
3 any other important features (U.S. Savings Bonds are safe; millions of Americans buy them).
4 the type of action ad is designed to evoke (buy U.S. Savings Bonds) (Figure 17-2).

The copy platform is simple. It can be added to, and copywriters can use it as a step-by-step formula. Let's see how a copywriter would use our simple copy platform.

Let's assume we are writing an ad for a magazine. The product is a small resort hotel in the Caribbean. The hotel research and sales department tell us that our primary target audience consists of men and women between thirty-five and sixty who have above-average income, are college educated, and prefer a quiet vacation spot. Quietness, in fact, is the hotel's most important selling idea.

This information gives us the answers to two of our copy platform questions: who is our target audience? and what is the most important selling idea? The manager of the hotel tells us that we are to encourage people to write or call for brochures or reservations. (That gives us the information for 4 above.) To learn about additional features, we speak to management, read previous brochures, and study the hotel and its location. Now we can begin to integrate copy and layout ideas.

INTEGRATION OF LAYOUT AND COPY

Print ads are made up of two major parts: copy and layout. *Copy* refers to all the words that appear in the ad, including headlines. *Layout* refers to the way all the elements of the ad, photographs or illustrations and type, are esthetically arranged. Both copywriter and layout artist must fuse verbal and visual elements into an easily understood message.

Even though copywriters usually do not devise layouts, they need to consider the appearance of the finished ad. Copywriters may describe their

[1]An expression coined by Batten, Barton, Durstine, & Osborn, a New York-headquartered ad agency.

How to tie the knot without getting in a bind.

Some folks get all hung up about getting married.

Maybe 'cause they think they'll be paying for it the rest of their lives.

Starting a family. A home. College for the kids. Even retirement.

So do what 9½ million other Americans do. Buy U.S. Savings Bonds through the Payroll Savings Plan.

Savings Bonds are the safe, dependable way to look out for the wonderful future you're planning.

And at the same time, they look out for America's future, too.

So buy United States Savings Bonds.

That way if you're about to tie the knot, they'll give you plenty of rope.

E Bonds pay 6% interest when held to maturity of 5 years (4½% the first year). Interest is not subject to state or local income taxes, and federal tax may be deferred until redemption.

Take stock in America.

 A public service of this publication and The Advertising Council.

SP-1650

ideas to layout artists, or they may even "rough out" a layout. Most often, copywriters and artists meet and brainstorm (throw ideas back and forth) until they arrive at a mutually acceptable solution. Layout artists are important even when ads contain no illustration (Figure 17-3). The way words are placed on the page, the type style, and "white space" all determine the effect of an ad. Experienced copywriters and artists like ads whose headlines and art reinforce one another; they are easier to read and to recall. Daniel Starch and staff, a research company specializing in readership of magazine ads, have attested to this fact for many years (Figures 17-4 and 17-5). The joining of layout and copy early in the creativity process saves time and money and prevents false starts.

In this chapter, we are going to investigate layouts; we'll handle copy in the next chapter. We divide these topics reluctantly, and only because when they are combined, they make a formidable chapter. However, in the minds of creative advertising people, layout and copy are an integral unit.

PRAGMATIC RULES OF LAYOUT

The purpose of a layout (the arrangement of photos, illustrations, headlines, body copy, and other visual elements) is to convey the copywriter's message in a logical and pleasing manner. The artist strives for balance, line, and color. But first let's consider what kinds of layouts attract readers. They're not always the same as what artists and copywriters consider good layouts!

The Focal Point of an Ad

When readers first look at an ad, their eyes habitually fix at about 10 o'clock, regardless of the photos or type in the ad. More than likely, this focusing tendency reflects our training to read from left to right. From the 10 o'clock position, the eye then moves up and to the right (clockwise). Once the eye has made this first pass, the skill of the layout artist takes over in directing the reader's gaze[2] (Figures 17-6 and 17-7).

Studies have yielded several important considerations for advertisers. The 10 o'clock position is a good place to put headlines, subheadlines and art. ("Art" here is a general term for photographs and illustrations in ads.) Placing headlines at the top of the page or immediately beneath large photographs will attract good readership. Interested readers automatically look for identifying logotypes (logos) at the bottom of the page, where they are accustomed to seeing them.

Artists and copywriters who want to develop a pragmatic approach to layout should study the conclusions reached by Dr. Herman Brandt and corroborated by Daniel Starch and Staff, Readex, Inc., and other reports. These studies have suggested at least ten layouts that have proved to be highly succcessful in attracting readers. Other layouts may be just as successful, but we *know* these work!

[2]Herman F. Brandt, *The Psychology of Seeing* (New York: Philosophical Library, Inc., 1945) p. 31.

WHY WE'RE INTRODUCING AUTOMATIC SAFETY BELTS NOW

WILL YOU LIKE THEM? WILL YOU CHOOSE THEM? WE NEED TO KNOW.

In May we will make automatic safety belts available as an option on the Chevrolet Chevette. We're doing this now because we need to know how well you like them and whether you'll choose them.

Not enough people use the safety belts that are now standard equipment in every car. So the government has directed that some form of passive restraint, such as air cushions or automatic safety belts, be built into every car by 1984.

The automatic safety belt is very easy to use. When the door is opened, the safety belt automatically moves out of the way so that the passenger has room to sit down. As the door is closed, the safety belt automatically fits around the passenger. Knee bolsters are built into the instrument panel to help limit forward movement during an accident. In addition, regular lap belts can be fastened to supplement the automatic safety belts.

We also have plans to offer air cushions in some of our future cars, because they have advantages in convenience and appearance. And we are working hard to improve them.

On the other hand, automatic safety belts have these advantages: they are lighter, which helps gas mileage; their cost is relatively low, and they would be easy to replace.

We'd like you to try the new automatic belts and judge them for yourself. How many people order automatic safety belts, and what they think of them, will help us plan our cars for the 1980's.

That's why we're offering the option of automatic safety belts now, so you can tell us how to design these cars the way you want them.

This advertisement is part of our continuing effort to give customers useful information about their cars and trucks and the company that builds them.

General Motors
People building transportation to serve people

FIGURE 17-3
A bold headline, heavy horizontal rules, and a balanced, symmetrical layout are the artist's contributions to this all-type ad. (Courtesy General Motors.)

FIGURE 17-4
When headlines and photograph reinforce each other, the result is excellent readership.

FIGURE 17-5
Headline and art say the same thing. Result: high readership. This ad received a Starch-noted score of 65 percent among women. (Courtesy STARCH INRA Hooper, Inc., and Procter & Gamble.)

FIGURE 17-6

A perfectly placed headline (at 10 o'clock) gets the reader into the ad quickly. As the eye begins its descent, it sees the follow-up copy. (Courtesy American Railroads.)

FIGURE 17-7
Recognizing the tendency for readers to scan the top of an ad page—as described by Dr. Brandt—artists increasingly place headlines there. (Courtesy Elanco Products Company)

Ten Attention-Getting Layouts

Figure 17-8

The important message at 10 o'clock assures advertisers that readers will see the headline as soon as they spot the ad. Whether they continue reading depends on the *promise* of the headline.

Figure 17-9

A popular layout arrangement, often called the "big picture-headline approach." Notice how many contemporary ads use this arrangement or variations of it. Photographs like this are called "square halftones." (*Square* because the rectangular photograph looks like it has four equal sides; *halftone* because the photograph is transformed into a halftone screen to be reproduced in varying tones.)

Figure 17-10

Here the artist places the headline to correspond to the path of normal *eye movement* (from the 10 o'clock position up and to the right.) In cases where backgrounds are dark, the artist can *reverse the headline* and run white type on black ground. Where backgrounds are light, it is safer to stick with fairly large, black type.

Figure 17-11

A split ad, half copy and half illustration, has proved to be an *eye-catcher*.

Figure 17-12

The same layout as before, except that the copy and the art have been "flopped" or reversed.

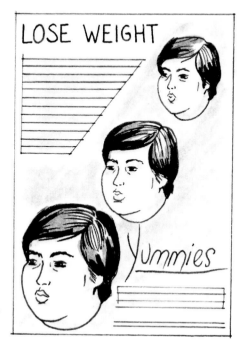

Figure 17-13

Repetitive elements that increase or decrease in size do well in enticing readers.

Figure 17-14

A photograph enclosed in an interesting shape often attracts greater attention than if it appeared as a square halftone.

Figure 17-15

Artists achieve visual excitement by breaking out of the traditional square-halftone format. Breaking from the square-halftone tradition is a favorite technique among retail layout artists.

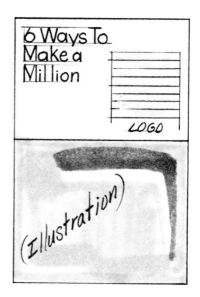

Figure 17-16

Reversing the big-picture format, the artist emphasizes headline and copy before the reader reaches the photograph.

Figure 17-17

A "checkerboard" variation of the familiar big-picture format attracts attention because of its individuality.

NOTE:

In all ten layout formats, copy blocks are generally no wider than 3½ inches (21 picas. A pica is a printer's linear measurement, with six picas to an inch). "Research has revealed that excessively short lines (four to five words) and excessively long lines (twenty to twenty-five words) are both read much more slowly than lines of moderate length—of eight to ten words."[3]

[3]Ibid., p. 49.

THE ESTHETIC APPROACH TO LAYOUT

Good design has balance, movement, and unity. Artists achieve unity by juggling many components into a unified whole. But unity of design can be elusive. For example, industrial ad layouts must combine many elements. Figure 17-18 is a typical example. The copywriter included a large photograph of a new motor, several sketches, a specification chart of technical details, a bold logo, and detailed explanatory copy. With all the clutter, the artist had trouble attracting reader attention in the 7×10 inch space allocated for the ad. The problem required a compromise solution. Cluttered ads with no dominant visual element attract few readers. Figure 17-19 illustrates one solution to the problem. There are others, of course. The important point is that copywriters do a disservice to their clients—and their colleagues in the art department—when they insist on cramming too many elements into a restricted space.

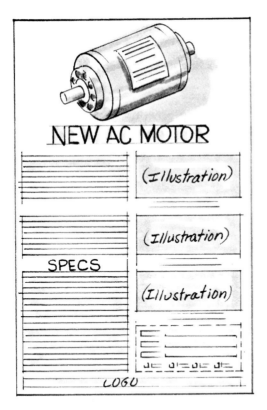

FIGURE 17-18
Even the best artistic intentions lose out when copywriters insist on jamming too many visual elements into one ad. Originally the artist had planned for the motor to occupy 50 percent of the ad space; it had to be reduced.

FIGURE 17-19
A larger photograph and more pronounced headline plus better use of white space present industrial readers with a more interesting layout. Various studies point to poorer industrial readership when less than one-third of the page is illustration.

Artists face the same problem of too much material and too little space with some retail ads. To create an effective ad, they must eliminate words and pictures. But retailers balk at the thought of removing a single element. This attitude explains why so many retail ads sink into obscurity on a newspaper page or look like jungles of headlines and illustrations. Yet food stores often run busy newspaper ads with screaming headlines and border-to-border prices. Despite the congestion of words, borders, boxes, illustrations, and photographs, the food stores find busy ads to be effective.

Would the supermarkets' ads be more effective if the layouts were better? No one really knows for certain. Some stores, like Heinen's in northern Ohio, abandoned price advertising and substituted store-image and goodwill copy, only to reinstitute price advertising under the guns of competition. We know that people read food store ads to check prices and to clip coupons. Although the store image may carry some weight, it is less important than the appeal of economy. Layout artists may have to accept clutter as an enduring feature of food store layouts.

However, when price is less important than decor, mood, and atmosphere, the skill of the layout artist can make a big difference in a retailer's ads. Compare Figures 17-20 and 17-21. Which do you think would attract more attention? Which conveys an image of quality and prestige?

Balance

Layout artists consider balance extremely important in achieving harmony or a layout that is pleasing to the eye.

A layout can by symmetrical (evenly balanced) and formal, or it can be asymmetrical (unevenly balanced) and informal. In a symmetrical layout, the artist draws an imaginary center line through the space to be filled and places equally "weighted" graphic elements the same distance from the line. If a large graphic element falls on the imaginary center line, it becomes formally balanced if equal parts fall on either side of the line (Figure 17-22.) The formal layout is pleasing and dignified. Although all graphic elements on each side of the line need not be identical for good balance, they should be equal in shape or size.

Uneven asymmetrical balance or asymmetry is more interesting to the eye. Artists create it by moving unequally weighted visual elements closer to or farther from the imaginary center line. They manipulate elements so that important ones balance unimportant ones (Figure 17-23.) Informally balanced layouts seem to have movement, drama, and excitement, all the requirements for good readership.

The Role of White Space   No matter how artists balance their layouts—formally or informally—they all use white space, a weighty graphic element in itself. As the name implies, white space is the unprinted area of an ad. It serves the artist best when it is used in a planned, concentrated block rather

FIGURE 17-20
Eaton's in a formally balanced layout says one thing . . .

TURN ON THE HOLIDAY LIGHTS
What a sparkling stroke of sweater dressing . . . royal navy knit, roped with rhinestones. A study in dramatic contrast: covered arms, covered throat, deliciously bare in back and banded with brilliants. Isn't this a dazzling way to dress for the holidays? By Knit Bazaar, 8 to 14, 118.00. Misses' Dresses, Fourth, "F" Street, and all suburban stores.

Garfinckel's

FIGURE 17-21
Garfinckel's in an informal, dramatic arrangement says something else!

FIGURE 17-22

A formally designed layout with equally "weighted" graphic elements on both sides of the imaginary center line. This unusual ad appeared in *Seventeen* magazine.

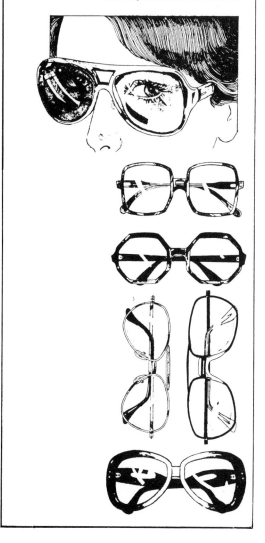

foleys

**famous maker
sunglasses with
sun-sensitive lenses
now tagged
especially low**

9.95

At our low price, protection for your eyes is easy.
You'll buy several styles for all the ways you spend your
time when the sun's out. Glass lenses are optical quality,
gradually darken with exposure to light. This sunny collection
includes metal frames in gold or silvertone and black.
Plus, plastic frames in lots of fashion colors and shapes.
Come in to Sunglasses, Downtown, first floor and all Branches.

FIGURE 17-23
The effect of this
small retail ad is
enhanced by an
asymmetrical layout
in which the store's
unusual logo offsets
the major
illustration.
(Courtesy
Newspaper
Advertising Bureau.)

In our family business
there's three things you don't mind
spending your money on. Copper tub-
ing. Fast cars. And a fine pair of warm,
dry boots. And that third one is just as
important as the first two. When you're
crouching down in some gully with your
feet in ice-cold ditch water, never moving a muscle for hours, whilst them
damn Treasury agents snoop around
with their dogs barking and sniffing,
well, that's the time you're glad
you didn't cut corners on your boots.
These boots we bought are fine boots,
well made, need no breaking in. But
to us, that don't mean so much compared to the way they're waterproof
and warm.

Timberland ®
A whole line of fine leather boots
that cost plenty, and should.

FIGURE 17-24
The artist surrounds the logo with a concentrated field of white space so there is no mistaking who makes
these boots. The ad's entire concept shows creativity at its best.

than in patchwork fashion (Figure 17-24). White space points up any element near or within it. A full-page ad becomes intensely interesting if it contains nothing but white space and a single line of copy, for example. No matter what size the copy, a full page of white space points to the message just as effectively as if the page were filled with arrows! A full page of advertising space divided vertically in half with a long message on only one side is less exciting than the same message accompanied by a single word placed within the blank half of the page. The surrounding white space acts as an arrow. Layout artists particularly like to use white space above and below headlines, a most important visual considering the prominence of headlines in advertising.

Color

Some time ago, color meant a single color, because most ads were either black ink on white paper or black plus one color (a two-color ad). Common sense tells us that a two-color ad among black-and-white ads will attract attention. One rule of thumb is that the increase in readership is 15 percent. In general, the different ad, the black-and-white or four-color ad among many two-color ads, for example, attracts extra readers. Just how many is difficult to determine. Nonfunctional or wasteful use of color may not increase readership at all. But color used for a reason usually does increase readership. Here are some functional ways color can be used in ads:

1 To identify a trade name or trademark. Coca-Cola, for example, specifies a certain kind of red for its internationally known trademark.
2 To identify the ad by using a special company color (matched) as a background in all campaigns.
3 To dramatize key words and phrases.
4 To create realism, especially in four-color ads.
5 To direct attention to illustrations or product features.
6 To focus on key charts and graphs.
7 To key headline to specific body copy or illustrations.
8 To direct the reader's eyes from one point to the next.

Color also delivers an emotional impact (red for warmth, blue for coolness, for example). Along with its value as a functional device for the artist, it can often turn a "so-so" ad into a widely read winner.

Photography and Illustrations

Some advertisers prefer photographs to illustrations, and for good reason. Photographs are representational and realistic. Photography is so advanced that photographs can contribute drama, human interest, and beauty. Few food advertisers, for example, will hire an illustrator, no matter how talented, to render a delicious sandwich when a four-color photograph will do it better. The human face is likewise more dramatic and interesting in photographs than in illustrations. Industrial advertising relies heavily on photography. Customers want to see the machine *as it is*, not as a designer visualizes it. Not only are photographic prints faster to come by than illustrations, but they also permit the artist to choose from many and thus deliver the best, most realistic impression. They also encourage photographers to experiment with unusual angles, close-ups, and long shots that the artist can review for final layout.

Illustrations, on the other hand, are widely used in the advertising of apparel and beauty aids. They let the artist exaggerate aspects of the human body, something photography seems unable to do without ugly distortion. In the apparel and beauty aids markets, illustrations are quite acceptable because products are sold on the basis of illusions; the buyer seeks a mood that illustrations can bring. Not all good layout artists are good illustrators. The skills for each task do not go hand in hand. Consequently, layout artists often call on freelance illustrators. Recently there has been a gradual increase in the number of illustrative ads in both magazines and newspapers. Illustration skills also help artists in the rendering of television storyboard layouts that are used in the production of television commercials. Although photographs remain dominant in print ads, illustrations help create distinctive looks and, advertisers hope, increase readership (Figures 17-25 and 17-26).

The Retail Layout

When we speak of retail layouts, we mean those that appear in newspapers, although retail layouts also appear in local throwaways, direct mail, and Yellow Pages of phone books. Many are small ads surrounded by editorial material and other ads. Small ads—less than 300 lines—can get lost in a black-and-white sea. The medium of the newspaper presents artists with other problems—coarseness of paper, absorption of ink—so artists must use a variety of devices to attract attention and to move readers' eyes from one part of the ad to another. One device is to have the model in the ad look at, face, or point to something. Readers will automatically follow the gaze or pointing finger of a model. Another device is to use unique borders, printers' rules (generally lines of a specified thickness set around the perimeter of an ad), and arrows. These serve to separate ads on a page from all others. Other commonly used retail ad devices are *screens* and *reverses*.

Screens refer to a tonal gradation of a color. For example, the artist may wish to fill the ad space with a gray tint that is actually a *screen of black*. (A one-hundred percent screen is solid black. A ten percent screen is a barely perceptible gray tone.) Screens tie graphic elements together into a cohesive whole.

Reverses generally describe the artist's use of a strong background color on which the copy is reversed so it prints white on the dark background (Figures 17-27 and 17-28). Artists use reverses to get attention, although some newspaper managers claim they don't do as well in attracting readers as the conventional black-and-white ads. Reverses that appear in magazines generally show up better than in newspapers because of the higher-quality paper and the minimal ink absorption.

FOUR-COLOR PHOTOS
(starting next page)

Contemporary advertising is as much a triumph for photography and camera techniques as it is for the industry's information-gathering instrument, market research. These full-color advertisements help to dramatize the impact of the camera lens on the printed sales message.

Great sauces... by Hellmann's!

PIQUANT HERB SAUCE
(A Bearnaise-like sauce for red meats or fish.)

1/2 cup dry white wine	1/4 tsp dried chervil
1/2 cup parsley sprigs	leaves, crushed
1/4 cup white vinegar	1/8 tsp pepper
1 small onion, quartered	1 cup HELLMANN'S®
2 large cloves garlic	Real Mayonnaise
2 1/2 tsp dried tarragon	
leaves, crushed	

Place first 8 ingredients in blender container; cover. Blend on high speed until uniform. In small saucepan stir over medium heat until reduced to 1/3 cup. Strain; return liquid to saucepan. Stir in Real Mayonnaise. Stir over medium heat just until warm. Garnish with chopped parsley. Makes 1 1/4 cups.

CONTINENTAL LEMON SAUCE
(A quick sauce with the taste of Hollandaise.)

1 cup HELLMANN'S®	3 Tbsp lemon juice
Real Mayonnaise	1/2 tsp salt
2 eggs	1/2 tsp dry mustard

In small saucepan with wire whisk stir together all ingredients until smooth. Stir over medium-low heat until thick (do not boil). Serve over vegetables, seafood or poached eggs. Sprinkle with paprika. Makes 1 2/3 cups.

HELLMANN'S REAL MAYONNAISE

Bring out the Hellmann's and bring out the Best!

© 1978 Best Foods, a Division of CPC International Inc. CPC

Food manufacturers in particular prefer photography over illustration in their ads. The realism brought out by photography can start salivary juices flowing in a way no illustration can.

Those FTD Florists... Really Get Around... For You.

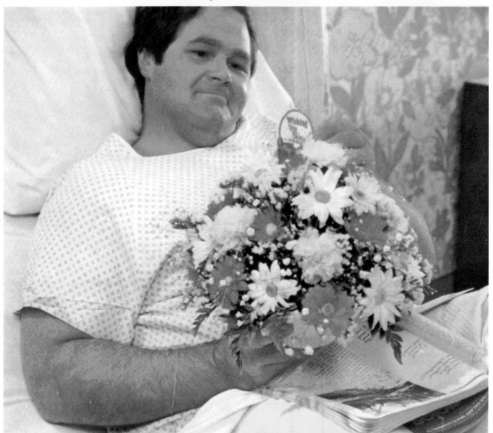

FLOWERTHERAPY!

The new FTD Wish 'N Well™ Bouquet...with a penny for luck.
It's so easy to send. Spreads cheer on sight. Makes people feel good all over in seconds. And you don't need a prescription. Just call or visit your FTD Florist (most accept major credit cards). He'll send this cheerful Wish 'N Well Bouquet almost anywhere, the FTD way.

©1979 Florists' Transworld Delivery

Say FTD, and be sure...worldwide.

People are interested in people, real people, and the photograph brings them to us complete with wrinkles, freckles, and skin blemishes.

Tradition,
like you've never seen it before.

Tropical weight dress slacks are a staple of any wardrobe. And nobody's got them in more fabrics, colors and styles than we have. Ranging from the very traditional to tradition with a twist.

Tropicals by Thomson Slacks.
Division of Salant Corp.
The Thomson Co., 1290 Avenue of the Americas, New York, New York 10019

The secret of good "people photography" is the photographer's knowledge of lighting and the mood it can create.

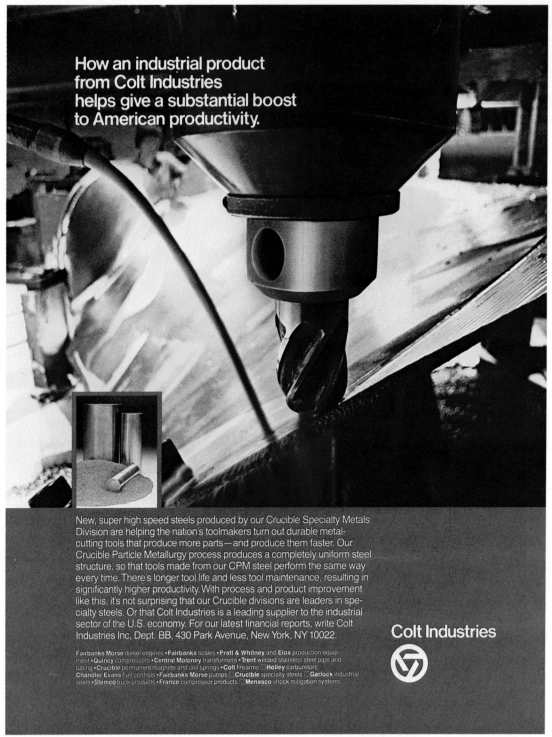

Courtesy of Marsteller Inc.

As important as photography is in consumer advertising, it is more so for the industrial
market. Photography informs the reader that the product actually exists and is not a
theoretical design.

You've got sunset hands. Red and sinking fast.

Try **Palmolive®** Dishwashing Liquid for those red hands. It's got a breakthrough **Proticare™** formula. More than just mild. Independent tests show it truly helps improve red, chapped dishwashing hands. Don't get caught red-handed.

Madge

softens hands while you do dishes

PALMOLIVE
DISHWASHING LIQUID

HAND IMPROVEMENT INDEX

60% OF PALMOLIVE USERS' HANDS IMPROVED

AFTER 3 WEEKS

AFTER 2 WEEKS

DAYS 5 10 15 20 25 30 35

Palmolive's Proticare Formula Is a Mildness Breakthrough. This chart displays the results of independent tests in which users of Palmolive with Proticare showed a high degree of chapped hand improvement.

Palmolive helps improve red, chapped dishwashing hands while you do dishes.

A good photograph can be the layout artist's best friend. Sometimes a variety of photographic perspectives can suggest an improvement on what the artist originally had in mind. This is one reason that photographers usually shoot a variety of poses and angles on each job.

Catch a legend, if you can.

Only a few of these "legends" exist. Because only a few artists in the entire world are capable of creating it. It takes the most skillful of glass blowers to mouth-blow the full-lead crystal. It takes a master artist to hand-shape its subtle curves, to hand-engrave its delicate design. It takes Kosta Boda...we've been creating legendary crystal since 1742. "Jonah in the Whale," 14 inches long, $520.00. Kosta Boda Swedish crystal, from $7.50 to $2900...at fine stores everywhere. For brochures, send 25¢ to Kosta Boda, Dept. J, 225 Fifth Avenue, New York, N.Y. 10010

Kosta Boda

Where there's Kosta Boda, there's a new idea in crystal.

Through the magic of the camera, the photographer can produce "instant" compositions and effects—psychological, scientific, subtle, or obvious. An illustrator might take days to accomplish what the camera can do in a few hours, and still fail to arouse readers.

"13 YEARS AGO I BOUGHT THIS VOLVO BECAUSE IT WAS ADVERTISED AS THE 11 YEAR CAR."

— William Stiles, Bronx, New York

13 years ago, William Stiles, an expert in American Indian history and artifacts, discovered the treasure you see here: a 1966 Volvo.

He bought it because ads of the time said Volvos were so durable they lasted an average of 11 years in Sweden.

As Mr. Stiles recalls: "One ad said that a Volvo was so tough, you could 'Drive it like you hate it.' I did exactly that. In my field work I've driven this car 295,000 hard miles, much of it through former Indian territory. It's held up even better than promised. Driving it like I hated it made me love it."

Expressions of love are not uncommon among Volvo owners. In fact, 9 out of 10 people who have bought new Volvos are happy.

So if you're unhappy with your current car, do what Mr. Stiles once did after reading one of our ads. Buy one of our cars.

VOLVO
A car you can believe in.

Courtesy of Scali, McCabe, Sloves, Inc.

Nothing brings home the reality of a testimonial or a case study as does a photograph of a person or a business installation.

"crystal clear"

Sand River

For all the clean green wilderness your heart desires – come north. Fish the streams,
fly by float plane to an outpost camp or enjoy the big-hearted hospitality of our lakeside lodges.
For all you need to plan your vacation, call us COLLECT (416) 965-4008, or write:
Ontario Travel, Dept. C.C., Queen's Park, Toronto, M7A 2E5.

Ontario Canada
We treat you royally

Photography permits the advertiser to set models and machines in specific locations
throughout the world in order to achieve an unmistakable air of authenticity. For these
and other reasons the majority of national advertising in the past twenty years has
featured photographs over illustrations.

FIGURE 17-25
Lifelike illustrations are quite suitable for personal-care products. This distinctive layout, like the stated purpose of the ad, is not intended for everybody. (Courtesy Yves Saint Laurent Parfums Corp.)

Let the Tiger flex his muscle.

USS TIGER BRAND Interlocked Armor Cable is flexible. It goes where you need it without conduit, it has its own flexible metallic covering, is easier to work with than jacketed cable in conduit and can be installed in about half the time. So you can cut your installation and labor costs.

USS TIGER BRAND Interlocked Armor Cable has a higher ampacity in many applications than three single-conductor jacketed cables pulled into conduit, takes up much less space and is always visible and accessible.

We frequently supply this cable with a color coded plastic jacket—for use in corrosive atmospheres, or where the cable is exposed to moisture.

For more information, write to Don Vickers, USS Electrical Cable Division, Ballard Street, Worcester, Mass. 01607.

USS Tiger Brand Interlocked Armor Cable
USS and Tiger Brand are registered trademarks.

Tiger Brand
Electrical Cable

July, 1976   Circle 155 on Card

FIGURE 17-26
A naturalistic tiger glares at electrical contractor readers in a recent issue of *Electrical Contractor* magazine. The interest created by the photographic likeness of the tiger was somewhat diminished by the overly wide lines of copy. "Tiger Brand" currently identifies Tiger Brand Wire Rope. (Courtesy United States Steel.)

FIGURE 17-29
To operate this
projection machine,
the artist or
copywriter places
the borrowed art in
the top copyboard
area, tapes a piece
of tracing paper on
the working surface,
adjusts the art to the
desired size, and
traces the projected
image. (Courtesy
M. P. Goodkin
Company.)

A major esthetic problem for retail layout artists is the lack of imaginative typography in newspapers. Proprietors of small businesses generally rely on the newspaper's narrow type selection. Even when layout artists provide the newspaper with competent direction, the restricted range of typefaces falls short of conveying the artist's intent. Thus we see one or two typefaces used in ad after ad, regardless of the advertiser or its target audience.

But there is a more significant esthetic problem than the newspaper's restricted selection of typefaces. This is the universal habit of setting newspaper headlines by dividing the space by the number of lines. Thus, if there are four lines of headline copy to be placed in a four-inch space, the lines are placed approximately one inch apart, making it extremely hard for the eye to read in one easy, sweeping glance. Arranging advertising headlines in this way also detracts from the professional appearance of the ad.

By and large, retailers need all the help they can get in attracting customers to their ads. Layout artists, whether employed by retailers or by newspapers, can help by recognizing that layouts, artwork, and typography should be distinctive, eye-catching, and easy to understand and act upon.

THE LAYOUT TOOL: THE PROJECTION MACHINE

Good layout artists depend mightily on their ability to draw recognizable figures, products, and objects, an ability that many copywriters lack. Copywriters with easy access to artists have no serious problem. But problems arise when a copywriter's amateurish attempts at illustration go directly to advertisers for review. Poorly rendered illustrations kill good advertising ideas.

Short of taking a protracted course in art, how can nonartists illustrate their ads? One answer is the projection machine, a compact wall- or floor-mounted device that projects and illuminates an image upon a

FIGURE 17-30
An amateur's rough layout, made with the projection machine and a borrowed piece of art. Look left for the same art reduced to one-column newspaper size. The time to devise each layout was approximately five minutes.

transparent working surface. It can enlarge or reduce existing images: photographs, ads, illustrations, lettering—even layouts. The copywriter (or other nonartist) just finds a reasonable approximation of the art intended for the ad and puts it on the machine. Sometimes nonartists who own Polaroid cameras can create their own "instant" art.

Most art studios and advertising agencies have projection machines (Figure 17-29). Professional artists like the projection machine because it saves them time. Amateur artists like it because it lets them produce a reasonably professional looking layout. The machines also lets people experiment with various layout arrangements (Figure 17-30).

Projection machine users should remember that existing art can be borrowed only for layout purposes and not for the final reproduction. To use art in the actual ad, one must first get the written permission of the original creator and/or models (Figure 17-31).

FIGURE 17-31
A typical written release form provides legal protection to an advertiser who employs models in advertising.

IN SUMMARY

1 Copywriters usually work from a copy strategy platform, a creative road map that helps them keep to the purpose of the ad.

2 A strategy platform asks for the following information: the specific target

DE139

Print or Type Name_____

                                           Last Name   Middle Initial   First Name

Date_____

For value received and without further consideration, I hereby irrevocably consent that the photographs taken of me by (_____),
                                     (Name of person who took picture)

(at_____on_____19__) or any reproduction of the same, may be used by Dix & Eaton, Incorporated, or by others with the consent of Dix & Eaton, Incorporated, for the purpose of illustration, advertising or publication in any manner.

I hereby certify and represent that I am over twenty-one years of age.

Job No.		(Signature of subject)—Also see above
User		(Address)
Client		(Signature of witness)
		(Address)

audience, the most important selling idea, any other important features, and the type of reader action desired.

3 Copywriters and artists need to integrate copy and layout into an easy-to-grasp sales message.

4 Because people tend to focus on an ad at about 10 o'clock, that is a good spot for a headline or an important photograph.

5 Research has shown that excessively long or short lines of copy make reading difficult. A good width for a copy block is about 3½ inches (21 picas).

6 Cramming too many visual elements into one ad does a disservice to advertisers and readers. Good layout design has balance and movement.

7 Achieving balance is one of a layout artist's most important goals. A layout can be symmetrical (formal) or asymmetrical (informal). Asymmetrical design is more interesting to the eye.

8 "White space" is the unprinted area of an ad (or any other piece of advertising literature), which serves to emphasize any element it is near or surrounds.

9 Color in an ad should be functional. Properly used, color can, among other things, identify trademarks, dramatize key words, direct attention to product features, and direct readers' eyes from one point to the next.

10 Photographic art is more commonly used in advertising than illustrative art because it is naturalistic.

CASE STUDY Designing for the "With It" Customer: Bonwit Teller

Whenever the management of Bonwit Teller decides that the image of its retail stores needs to keep pace with a changing world, it moves to change its style of advertising. To a store whose beginnings stretch back to 1898, this has been a regular occurrence over the years. The latest in a long line of advertising changes reflects a store that aims at the younger, contemporary, "with it" customer without forgetting those who remain loyal to the traditional classics.

Overall, Bonwit Teller's newest format of its advertising is designed to be clean, modern, and direct. Creating consumer awareness of the ads falls to the art, which can be illustration or photography. A recent series of ads relied on the illustrator's use of big figures and impressive white space, centered in a symmetrical format (Figure 17-32). Often the illustrator draws faces as if they were lit from below in order to impart drama to the ads. There is a sense of the photographic in each ad, and since newspapers are a primary advertising medium for Bonwit Teller stores, it is important that the advertising illustrations reproduce well on newsprint.

Generally, the company will change its current advertising layout format three times a year in keeping with the fashion seasons: fall, holiday, and spring. To develop an ad, the creative people start with an idea that lends itself to a strong visual concept. In one recent series of ads, the copy is set to read in staccato fashion to heighten the mood of action (Figures 17-33 and 17-34):

Red made easy in
Lloyd Williams'
breezy, gentle crepes.

B O N W I T · T E L L E R

The Missoni Face.
Glorious color in concert
with our springlike Missonis.
And what color!
Iced Opal. Rosegleam.
Golddipped Plum. Bluebell.
A spring-struck radiance
of tint, shadow and shine
celebrating your cheek, mouth, eye.
Perfected by Estée Lauder
stylists here this week and next.
At the Estée Lauder bar,
in the Missoni Boutique.

The Missoni collection.
A wondrous harmony
of color, shape and weave
as in the bubble blouson
underscored by pared down
dolman and soft drape pants.
A rich yield of Missoni
for face, body, soul
all on One. Fifth Avenue.

MISSONI   **ESTEE LAUDER**

SUNDAYS, SHOP BONWIT TELLER MANHASSET AND SCARSDALE. 12:00 TO 5:00

FIGURE 17-32

B O N W I T · T E L L E R

Red made easy in
Lloyd Williams;
breezy, gentle crepes.
Left: T-sleeved
slipover, 38.00.
Right: shoulders
pleated, capped, 34.00.
Above for P-S-M.
Leggy dirndl repeated.
6-14, 33.00.
All in polyester.

Lloyd Williams.
Here Monday the 19th.
Bright prospects,
soft textures.
Can spring be far behind?
Collection modeled
from 12:00 to 4:00.
Blouses on One.

CARDINAL BRIGHTS

SHOP BONWIT TELLER FIFTH AVENUE EVERY THURSDAY 10:00 TO 8:00. MANHASSET AND SCARSDALE TILL 9:00. SHORT HILLS TILL 9:30.

FIGURE 17-33

B O N W I T · T E L L E R

Fragrance: creation,
uses, wear.
Seminars
Monday-Saturday,
the 12th to 17th at
11:30, 12:30, 1:30, 2:30.
Perfumes on One,
Fifth Avenue.

Masterpiece: Norell.
Each time is the first time.
Perfume, ¼ oz. 27.50.
½ oz. 47.50, 1 oz. 87.50.
A gift awaits with purchase.

NORELL PERFUMER'S ART

FIGURE 17-34

SUNDAYS, SHOP BONWIT TELLER MANHASSET AND SCARSDALE, 12:00 TO 5:00
FIFTH AVENUE AT 56TH STREET. CALL (212) EL5-6800. MANHASSET SCARSDALE SHORT HILLS

or

Fragrance: creation,
uses, wear.
Seminars
Monday-Saturday (etc.)

Masterpiece: Norell.
Each time is the first time.
Perfume, ¼ oz. 27.50,
½ oz. 47.50, 1 oz. 87.50.
A gift awaits with purchase.

Despite the artist's preoccupation with the dramatic as a device to create awareness, Bonwit Teller ads never forget that the merchandise is the most important element in each ad. The illustrations of the figures, the dresses, and the accessories provide sufficient detail to satisfy customers yet retain an aura of casualness and suggest *action*.

A substantial portion of most ads is a cooperative arrangement with a vendor, but unlike so many retail ads, these manage to retain the unique Bonwit Teller image. The cooperative financial effort extends the budget and permits the company to continue its campaign of photographic likenesses.

The response to Bonwit Teller's series of near-photographic illustrations has won applause from customers, store managers, buyers, and even other retailers. From Bonwit Teller comes a word of advice for not-so-large retailers with limited ad budgets: Spend money on good artwork and focus on the proper merchandise!

(*Note:* Bonwit Teller currently operates several branch stores. The Manhattan store is expected to reopen in late 1980.)

QUESTIONS NEEDING ANSWERS

1. Can a retail store whose ads include both a photography series and a series devoted to illustrations build a unified store image? Explain.
2. What should a retail store do if its principal artist is hired by a competitor and the competitive ads begin to look similar to its own?
3. If you were the manager of Bonwit Teller could you justify the continued use of large figures and dramatic white space even though many other apparel stores are adopting that layout technique?
4. What lessons in cooperative advertising are there in these examples of Bonwit Teller layouts?

STUDENT PROJECT

Package Delivery Service, Universal Xpress.

Market research indicates that the average wait for a package sent through the post office to any place in the country varies from three to ten days. This information led to the creation of Universal Xpress, which advertises that it can deliver a package from one place to another *overnight*. The minimum charge for a package weighing about 10 pounds and measuring 14 × 20 inches is $12.50 to anywhere in the country, door-to-door. Universal intends to concentrate its sales efforts on business and industry and on packages weighing under 50 pounds. The system operates in the following way. The company picks up packages by truck and delivers them to one of its aircraft, which flies to specific cities. At the destination, company trucks deliver the packages to the consignee.

Assuming that the copywriter gave you, the layout artist, the following headline, develop a complete layout for a 7×10 inch ad in *Business Week:* "How IBM saved a bundle by spending $12.50!"

QUESTIONS ABOUT THE PROJECT

1 Would another headline have permitted you greater latitude in your layout design? Explain.
2 Explain your layout according to the principles of attracting high readership through a knowledge of eye movement.

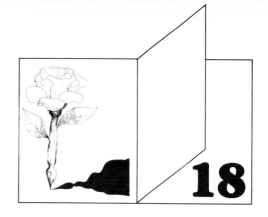

CREATIVITY IN PRINT MEDIA ADVERTISING

Part 2: Copy

Update As we have seen, good layouts turn ideas into clear visual statements. However, good ad layouts do not automatically ensure high readership, because the heart of most ads is the precise message they carry to their target audiences. This chapter explores what this message, or copy, is all about.

THE EXCITEMENT OF COPY

Copy is the printed words in an advertisement. Copy is made up of two main components: headlines and body copy. Together, they sell, inform, or move someone to action. Copywriters, no two of whom seem to work the same way, are responsible for writing copy. An ad is not ordinarily read for its intrinsically beautiful language or its philosophical insights. It is more often than not an intrusion.

Copy is composed of words, and the best copy is composed of the best words. Words that stop you in your tracks, excite you about a proposition, convince you to buy Brand X tomorrow! Maybe today! What are selling words? Most copywriters agree they are specific. Learning about "obesity in animals" doesn't excite people quite so much as learning "how to tell whether your dog is overweight." People prefer to hear "$12 to $42 below nationally advertised prices" rather than "at reduced prices."

Selling words create a point of view and reflect the interests of the target audience. Copywriters must have a sense of empathy, an ability to put themselves into another's shoes. But they also need to know the following: Who are the buyers? What do the buyers buy? What are their motives for buying? Where do they buy? When do they buy—daily, weekly, monthly? How do they buy—in pairs, dozens, single units? We've discussed how to answer these questions in previous chapters. Now we're concerned with the application of the facts into a powerful selling message. Here are some examples:

> Elizabeth Dass was admitted to Nazareth Home a few days after we received this report and she is doing better now. Her legs are stronger . . . she can walk and sometimes even run with the other children. She is beginning to read and can already write her name. Every day desperate reports like the one above reach our overseas field offices. Then we must make the heartbreaking decision—which child can we help? Could you turn away a child like Elizabeth and still sleep at night?

> American Dreams. Move into yours for only $999! It's true. You can afford your own Pulte home. With VA financing, only $999 moves you and your family into a beautiful 3-bedroom Pulte home in woodsy St. Charles.

Adopting the audience's point of view has evolved into what copywriters call the "you" approach in advertising. The ad speaks directly to "you:" "The XYZ boltmaker doubles your plant's capacity—produces up to 100 steel bolts a minute in the same space you're now using for your old machine." A copywriter for the Florida Division of Tourism put it this way:

> There's really no need to make long range plans to vacation in Florida. Just pack the family and come. . . . Florida has great hotels and motels that love families and offer attractive rates to prove it. And if you come by camper, you'll find excellent facilities at Florida's campgrounds.

Modern copywriters also use words that have *style*. Sometimes their words walk, sometimes they gallop. They develop a rhythm, a lilt. Copywriters avoid stilted and monotonous words. Monotony in the written language is just as deadly as it is in speech! Copywriters encourage readers to begin reading an ad and to stay with it until the bitter end. They vary their sentence structure and choice of words to keep the prose lively. Copywriters also adjust sentence length to heighten interest, using two or three long sentences followed by a short one or even a single word. Occasionally, copywriters coin or deliberately misuse a word. Properly selected words kindle images: *sizzle* instead of *burn* or *howl* instead of *shout*. The right words can enliven a drab ad. Compare these descriptions of an automobile feature:

> When you wish to allow passengers easy access to the back seat, simply move forward and the seat follows.

> Whoosh . . . a remarkable little mechanism automatically scoots the passenger-side front seat forward—allowing easy walk-in access to the back seat.

Compare these words and decide which would make you reach for your checkbook:

> Erlinda Cosay needs help! She is a 5-year-old Apache Indian child who lives with her mother in a small two-room house. They have no running water or heat or electricity. Erlinda hasn't seen her father since she was three. . . .

> You can help save Erlinda Cosay for $15 a month. Or you can turn the page. An Apache Indian child. A family of six in a tiny two-room house. No water. No heat. No electricity. In the center of this desolation, Erlinda Cosay. A child of five. A child who hasn't seen her father since she was three. A child whose last dress was a castoff. Erlinda needs your help so she can help herself. . . .

The Anatomy of an Ad

Copywriters consider an ad a complete sales presentation. It must gain attention, must be easy to understand. Its claims should be provable. And it should ask the reader to do something: stop in at a store, call a phone number, send a coupon. Generations of copywriters have used the acronym AIDA as a guide to writing the complete ad:

Attention

Interest

Desire

Action

Attention—The Headline

The headline is the most important part of the ad, by some estimates 75 to 80 percent of its value. It isn't difficult to discover the reason. People read a newspaper or magazine by scanning the headlines. They pick and choose. If the headline interests them, they read the story or the ad. If the headline doesn't grab them, the advertiser has lost a reader and perhaps a customer. Copywriters spend a great amount of time working on headlines. They write and rewrite, developing fifteen to twenty good headlines for just one ad. Then they rework those until there is only one left, the best. Over the years, copywriters have evolved three basic types of headlines: *benefit, news,* and *curiosity.* The benefit headline is the most effective.

Benefit Headlines   Benefit headlines take readers' points of view and tell them how they will benefit if they continue to read the ad. Benefit headlines make promises and appeal to basic psychological needs. They are used as "grabbers," attention-getters. Finally, good benefit headlines are simple, because the more complex they are, the more readers they lose to other headlines. (A rule of thumb accepted by some ad people is that a good ad may command fifteen seconds or so of a reader's time.) Here are some good benefit headlines:

"Get a college degree in one easy lesson!"

"I gambled 15 cents and won $25,000!"

"Earn money in your spare time."

"Datsun saves about a gallon of gasoline a day."

"Dance your way to romance."

"Print No. 10 envelopes at 60,000 per hour."

"With a Merry Tiller you can cultivate more ground in five minutes than you can spade up by hand in an hour."

"The 60-second breakfast from Dole."

"Introducing New Sure Roll-On with the most effective anti-perspirant formula you can buy. Nothing will keep you drier."

Good benefit headlines are specific. The target audience is clear, the reason for the headline's wording apparent. When a good benefit headline is coupled with a supporting photograph, readers absorb the message faster (Figure 18-1).

Poor benefit headlines say very little because they either are too general or rely on clichés. Here are some typical examples: "We've been serving you for over 50 years." "Your great-grandmother ate here." "You can rely on big-hearted Joe for a good used car." "Our products *really* do the job." "We sell quality." Name someone who doesn't. What does *quality* mean? Is the quality proclaimed by Product A as high as that of Product B? If you must sell quality, dig into the product more and find out what it is that makes quality. Fabergé Organic Shampoo could have headlined its ad, "It gives my hair a top-quality look." Instead, a lovely model says, "It gives my hair super shine, super body, and leaves it smelling fresh as a meadow."

Poor headlines that talk about "quality" and "reputation" in general terms do not specifically tell readers what benefits they will enjoy if they continue reading the ads. Experienced advertisers call these headlines examples of the "brag and boast" school of headline writing. Such headlines

Little One Stays Down!

Still $2625[*]

©Volkswagen of America 1974.

[*]Sedan 111-1 P.O.E. Suggested Retail Price, Local Taxes and Other Dealer Delivery Charges Additional.

Dealer Name
33-11-49520

AUTHORIZED
DEALER

FIGURE 18-1
Headline and photo reinforce each other. When these two major ad elements convey the ad's central idea, the benefit headline is memorable. (Courtesy Volkswagen of America.)

are primarily designed to make the advertiser feel good; seldom are they effective selling instruments.

News Headlines   News headlines inform. They reveal something of topical interest to readers and can intrigue them to continue reading the rest of the ad. "What fuel," asks a headline by the Edison Electric Institute, "could supply America's electricity for about 250 years?" The reader learns the answer is coal. Gillette informs teenage girls: "Now, freshly made curls anytime, anywhere with the first carry-around cordless curler." ITT informs journalists who read *Columbia Journalism Review:* "About fifteen companies in the U. S. pay yearly dividends of a quarter of a billion dollars or more. This year we'll be one."

Industrial ad copywriters find that news headlines pay off with increased inquiries because industrial readers are looking for help with a wide variety of problems. News headlines that touched on "OSHA, Noise and Troubleshooting[1]" did extremely well for advertisers in *Plant Engineering Magazine.*[2]

Retail ads that carry necessary price information about a product and where to buy it use news headlines. In fact, carrying the news about sales is one of the primary functions of retail ads. "An American favorite. The Hitchcock Fantop Chair at a very special price—$49." "Plan to attend Riverside's Big Grand Opening Celebration." As a rule, news ads "piggyback" on the events of the day (Figure 18-2).

Curiosity Headlines   Curiosity headlines are fun to write but are the weakest of the three general headline types in producing readership. They depend on a reader's sense of mystery. If readers aren't curious, the ad fails. While news headlines have the advantage of being topical, curiosity headlines depend entirely on their own uniqueness.

"What makes the beans in the jar different from the beans in the can?" asks a Presto ad. People who garden or buy fruits and vegetables for canning might be encouraged to continue reading the ad. "Look what you can do with one can of Spam," says the colorful Hormel ad. Some people simply might not care to find out.

On the other hand, some advertisers use curiosity headlines very successfully. Volkswagen, for example, has used the excellent headlines "Think small" and the Department of Transportation the more recent "I was in love with a girl named Cathy." (Figure 18-3).

Even industrial copywriters find the curiosity headline irresistible. "NCR is out to put the world of business on a new computer," proclaims the headline of a three-dimensional piece of sales literature that "pops" up into a mockup of a computer. "La Pietà and Lime have a common heritage," says a

---

[1]OSHA (Occupational Safety and Health Agency) was a formidable threat to businesses in the mid-1970s, and manufacturers, in particular, were extremely interested in anything that would help them pass OSHA inspections.

[2]"Use of Color in High-Pull Advertising," Vern Kempf, unpublished internal report for *Plant Engineering Magazine,* 1972.

FIGURE 18-2
A news headline that also carries a benefit. The copywriter wisely played up the nation's preoccupation with energy prices in the headline. (Courtesy Nissan Motor Corp.)

I WAS IN LOVE WITH A GIRL NAMED CATHY.

I KILLED HER.

"It was last summer, and I was 18. Cathy was 18 too. It was the happiest summer of my life. I had never been that happy before. I haven't been that happy since. And I know I'll never be that happy again. It was warm and beautiful and so we bought a few bottles of wine and drove to the country to celebrate the night. We drank the wine and looked at the stars and held each other and laughed. It must have been the stars and the wine and the warm wind. Nobody else was on the road. The top was down, and we were singing and I didn't even see the tree until I hit it."

Every year 8,000 American people between the ages of 15 and 25 are killed in alcohol related crashes. That's more than combat. More than drugs. More than suicide. More than cancer.

The people on this page are not real. But what happened to them is very real.

The automobile crash is the number one cause of death of people your age. And the ironic thing is that the drunk drivers responsible for killing young people are most often other young people.

DRUNK DRIVER, DEPT. Y*
BOX 1969
WASHINGTON, D.C. 20013

I don't want to get killed and I don't want to kill anyone. Tell me how I can help.* Youths Highway Safety Advisory Committee.

My name is_____
Address_____
City_____State_____Zip_____

STOP DRIVING DRUNK. STOP KILLING EACH OTHER.

U.S. DEPARTMENT OF TRANSPORTATION • NATIONAL HIGHWAY TRAFFIC SAFETY ADMINISTRATION

FIGURE 18-3
The curiosity headline and appealing photo are designed to make the reader continue beyond the headline.

National Lime Association ad aimed at chemical engineers. "This message comes to you from 5,000,000 miles away," is Firestone's intriguing headline for a steel-belted radial tire.

Some copywriters supplement the information contained in a curiosity headline with a caption or subcaption that *does* provide some inkling of what the ad is all about: "Baldness and the cue ball" is a curiosity headline, but a subheading, "News about a hair-growing hormone" explains what the ad is all about.

Interest—The Follow-up

The headline gets readers' attention. Copywriters try to follow up the promise of the headline with information that kindles further interest. If they fail, readers will stop reading. Suzuki doesn't make that mistake. Here's an example:

> Headline: Suzuki conquers boredom.
>
> Opening sentences: Life has always been what you make it. Excitement or just routine. And the line between freedom and feeling trapped can be as simple as two wheels. Something like getting on a Suzuki and breaking away.

Here's the headline and the follow-up on a retail shoe ad:

> Headline: Strappy, sexy, sensationally you!
>
> Opening sentences: It's Socialites' tall, strappy sandal shimmering in patent and trimmed in goldtones on a super poly bottom. Perfect for all your social occasions, day or evening . . . $33.

Each of the opening sentences of these ads follows up the promise of their headlines. In so doing, they play fair with their readers. Here is the work of some other smart copywriters:

> Headline: Save an endangered species. Buy one.
>
> Opening sentences: The convertible, alas, is fast becoming extinct. Since 1970 alone, 54 foreign and domestic makes have disappeared. Even the Corvette and Eldorado fell victim. (Ad for Triumph Spitfire 1500 convertible.)
>
> Headline: San Francisco, 75 cents or less.
>
> Opening sentences: Did you know that for just 75 cents or less you can have a three-minute visit with friends in San Francisco, or for that matter, any other city out of your state . . . (Northwestern Bell Telephone ad.)
>
> Headline: Dul-Lite Plastic Lenses are lighter, thinner, safer.
>
> Opening sentences: It's easy to see why plastic lenses are gaining in popularity. They're much lighter than glass. Thinner than glass. And more impact-resistant. (Duling Optical retail ad.)

Headline: The Party's Over.

Opening Sentences: All too often, when the party ends, the trouble begins. People who shouldn't be doing anything more active than going to sleep are driving a car. Speeding and weaving their way to death. (National Highway Traffic Safety Administration ad)

Then there are the copywriters who create hard-hitting headlines but somehow fail to get on with their story until much later on in the ad.

Headline: Buried Treasure.

Opening sentences: PEP is the Dickey name for Plain End Pipe. There are no bells. This means you get all the advantages of Dickey clay pipe, the strongest and most durable sewer pipe available, plus the cost-saving factors of our new flexible coupling. (Later on in the ad, we begin to get a faint glimmer that PEP will save us money, that is, treasure.)

Headline: Plain talk from Armco on finding a job.

Opening sentences: How would you like to be forced to get permission from 379 separate government agencies before you could work? That's what Armco has to do. We think you could hear a similar story from nearly any large company in America—if the regulatory paperwork leaves them any time to talk to you. Excessive regulation threatens your chance of getting a job. (Armco finally gets around to following up its headline promise over 150 words later (Figure 18-4).

The argument over the virtues of brief or lengthy copy continues. Some copywriters believe in allowing the photograph and headline to tell most of their story. They use body copy sparingly. Others feel that consumers want all the information they can get. So far, no one seems to have proved that length of copy is a determining factor in sales. Yet we do know that Daniel Starch and Staff and other readership survey companies indicate that more people may "note and recall" ads that have minimal copy. Perhaps the solution to the argument over copy length is for the copywriter to include everything that will move the reader into action.

Desire—The Convincers

Whether desire for a product or a service is created depends on how well the copywriters weave their spell of words, promises, and features to make their product stand out. Here's creative head Reva Korda's formula:[3]

> In print you've got to get hold of the strongest selling point about your product. You've got to write a compelling, interesting, involving headline. You've got to craft each sentence, each caption, each crosshead so they all work together to deliver that promise. In print you can never substitute cute techniques for thinking. . . . I try to write an ad as if I'm talking to somebody—talking to one person. A friend. An intelligent friend. Telling her what I want her to know about

[3]Ad, "Korda's keys," *The Wall Street Journal,* December 16, 1977.

PLAIN TALK FROM ARMCO ON FINDING A JOB:

How the energy crisis chills your chances

So you're getting your degree and looking for that perfect job. More power to you. Literally. You'll need it. America will have to find the energy it takes to make you a job.

Expressed as heat, this nation spends at least 71 *quads* of energy a year. That's 71 quadrillion BTUs. A 71 followed by 15 zeroes. Since one BTU will heat a pound of water one degree Fahrenheit, we're talking about bringing 219 trillion pounds of ice to a boil. That's a glacier thirteen miles long, two miles wide and a mile thick. Every year.

Each working man and woman's share of our 71 *quads* comes to 800,000,000 BTUs. Of course all that energy isn't spent on the job. Nor do all jobs take the same amount, although most spend more than we think. But when you look at our available energy and the 89,000,000 people at work, then 800,000,000 BTUs is each job's share.

Now think about the 18,000,000 *more* U.S. men and women experts say will be looking for jobs over the next ten years. At 800,000,000 BTUs apiece, we'll have to come up with an extra 14.4 *quads* of energy to create new jobs for them.

At Armco, we face the energy problem every day because it takes about 29,000,000 BTUs to make each ton of steel. Our energy bill last year came to over $300,000,000. The cost keeps climbing every year. No wonder companies conserve energy. We have to, even though most of Armco's energy comes from coal which we mine ourselves. When companies can't get energy, people lose their jobs. We all learned that during the winter. The energy crisis is here. And it's huge.

Plain talk about ENERGY

We Americans already know how to solve the energy crisis. We have the technology to reach solutions. Yet each solution comes with its own set of political problems. Natural gas mustn't cost too much. Offshore oil mustn't spoil our beaches. Coal mustn't rape the land or poison the air. The atom mustn't threaten to destroy us. Energy conservation mustn't interfere with spending BTUs for worthy reasons.

Fair enough. But so far, we're paying more attention to the problems than we are to the energy itself. We've got to stop making every social goal an ideological crusade. We need to think things through and make rational trade-offs if we're ever going to get those 18,000,000 additional jobs.

Next time some zealot crusades for anything, test the crusade against this question: *Does it produce at least one BTU's worth of energy?* If not, it won't do a thing to help you get a job.

Free—Armco's plain talk on how to get a job

We've got a free booklet to help you get a job. Use it to set yourself apart, above the crowd. We answer 50 key questions you'll need to know. Like why you should bone up on companies you like. What to do *after* the first interview. Hints to make you a more aggressive, attractive job candidate. All prepared for Armco by a consulting firm specializing in business recruiting, with help from the placement staff of a leading university.

Send for your free copy of *How to Get a Job*. Write Armco Steel Corporation, Educational Relations Dept., General Offices, U-2, Middletown, Ohio 45043. Our supply is limited, so write now.

Armco wants *your* plain talk about energy and jobs

Does our message make sense? We'd like to know what *you* think. Your personal experiences. Facts you've found to prove or disprove our point. Drop us a line. We'll send you a more detailed report on energy and jobs. Our offer of *How to Get a Job*, above, tells you how to write us. Let us hear from you. We've got a stake in more American jobs.

ARMCO

FIGURE 18-4

College students interested in learning how to find a job will have to wade through a full column of exposition before they find out how . Copywriters should follow up the headline's promise immediately.

the product. I try to be very specific, very informative—and *very* interesting. Because I know you can't bore people into a store.

Creating desire means convincing readers, giving them an excuse to buy. Killington Ski Resort (Vermont) does it this way in their ads:

Every winter, something extraordinary happens at Killington Ski School. Many beginners—who confess that they've had lessons before, but couldn't seem to learn—make an important discovery. "Hey," they shout ecstatically, "I can ski." Obviously, something happens at Killington that doesn't happen anywhere else. That something is called the Accelerated Ski Method. And it's more than just a teaching system. It's a total learn-to-ski environment.

The ad briefly summarized seven sales points, from instructional films to instructors to the learning slope. Each sales point is presented in plain talk, reasonably. Each point reinforces the one before until, at the conclusion, you're ready to sign up. As the final convincer, Killington includes this bold guarantee:

No one can teach you to ski if you don't want to learn. But if you do, our five-day program will teach you. If it fails after five days, the full cost of your lessons is on us. No strings.

Guarantees and warranties are great convincers. Testimonials (independent, third-party statements testifying to benefits received) can also build credibility if the spokesperson is appropriate to the product. Mickey Mantle, for example, is a natural to say good things about a foot powder that eases athlete's foot. Properly used, testimonials add to readers' desire for products and services. For years, they have been among the most powerful selling tools in the copywriter's arsenal.

Action—The Closer

In door-to-door selling, the people who can get prospects to sign contracts or make down payments are called "closers." They are esteemed beyond all others in the business of direct selling. Copywriters must also learn the "closing" function. Their words must motivate readers to *act*. They should, in fact, be asking for the order! In most cases, that is the whole purpose behind any advertisement. The manufacturer wants the reader to drop everything and go out and buy the product. Copywriters must never assume that readers know automatically that they are expected to do something after reading the ad. Their job is to suggest or tell people outright what to do. Here's how Avon gets readers to join its door-to-door, direct selling sales force: "Find out how you can become an Avon Representative. Call 800-325-6400."

Here are other clear and forceful action closings:

So come visit the Ritz Carlton Chicago soon. Discover a hotel that's the sensible choice for those whose affairs require a serene environment. For reservations, see your travel agent. Or write the Ritz Carlton . . .

If you'd like to know more about instant 8×10, contact a Polaroid Professional Products Dealer, or call us toll free: 800-225-1618 . . .

For complete information contact your Fairchild representative or distributor; he's a pneumatic specialist. Or write for Bulletin 100.

Copywriters use other guides besides the AIDA acronym. Some ad agencies insist that writers learn about their prospects and their prospects' problems before they go to work on a product. Other advertisers recommend guidelines of their own.

1 Write to gain attention instantly.
2 Hold attention and create reader involvement with the message.
3 Tell the major idea of the ad quickly and repeat it several times.
4 Be specific.
5 Be believable.
6 Identify the brand name *before* presenting its benefits.
7 Repeat the brand name several times.
8 Ask for the order.

TRANSFORMING FEATURES INTO BENEFITS

One of the most difficult copywriting chores is explaining product features. For example, we hear about the automotive feature "rack and pinion steering." But what does it mean to the average car buyer? (Copywriters must assume we all know its meaning, because few explain it.) When copywriters claim that a garden tractor has "all-gear transmission," they should explain it, as manufacturer Gravely does: "And because it is all-gear, *it completely eliminates bothersome belts which have always been prone to break, slip or wear out.*"

Features do not mean much unless the reader understands them and their benefits. Consider the following sentence from a Hathaway shirt ad (Figure 18-5): "The careful formula for Hathaway English Poplin requires sixty percent of the fabric to be cotton." Had the copywriter stopped there, readers might have assumed the shirts were tough or lightweight (both characteristics of cotton). But the copywriter prevented misinterpretation by continuing: "This allows the shirt to breathe, to keep cool air circulating next to your body."

Admittedly, translating features into benefits takes up space in a print ad. If every feature required an explanation, ads might be nothing but solid type. Copywriters get around this dilemma by explaining the most important

Hathaway divulges an insider's secret: English Poplin.

The Man in the Hathaway shirt is wearing Hathaway's English Poplin. A fabric that was no lucky accident. Hathaway's fabric experts regard it as one of their most triumphant blends.

The careful formula for Hathaway English Poplin requires sixty percent of the fabric to be cotton. This allows the shirt to breathe, to keep cool air circulating next to your body. Forty percent polyester is the level our experts have determined for easy laundering.

Hathaway English Poplin: a cool tip for pure comfort, and ridiculously easy care.

FIGURE 18-5

Hathaway's man-in-the-eye-patch ads have always been an example of a unique creative twist coupled with good, specific, persuasive copy.

features of the product and listing those whose benefits are generally well known.

There is a further advantage to the advertiser when copywriters get into the habit of explaining features. The practice forces the copywriter to get answers from engineers, chemists, dealers—even consumers themselves. From this personal research, copywriters often come up with an aspect of a product that really is unique.

THE COPYWRITER'S CHECKLIST

Writing copy for advertising follows the same logical steps as selling. It *is* selling, in fact, through the medium of print and broadcast. Because some writers forget to include key sales points in their presentations, it has become commonplace for copywriters to work from a checklist such as this.

1 Be sure that the idea is clear.
2 Tell your story simply, with pictures, if possible.
3 Avoid cleverness for its own sake. (It's acceptable in outdoor advertising because of severe space restrictions.)
4 Address a particular person or group.
5 Promote your product in a fresh way.
6 Use good taste. Don't give offense.
7 Avoid political, religious, or racial bias.
8 Don't use female models as "sex objects" in order to attract attention. It's an admission on your part that you don't really have much to sell. It's also becoming increasingly socially unacceptable.
9 Remember that people buy "satisfactions" rather than things.
10 Mention brand names, sizes, colors, materials, styles, and *prices* in retail ads. Be specific.
11 *Sale* is a magic word to readers. So are words like *now, new, free, amazing, at last, revolutionary.* Use them where appropriate.
12 Remember that people accept truth. They hate liars.
13 Industrial copywriters need to stress greater productivity, less maintenance, greater safety, more profits, greater efficiency, less pollution, lower labor costs, and trouble-free operation.
14 Make your ads easy for the reader to respond to. Include a coupon, a mailback postcard, a toll-free phone number.

IN SUMMARY

1 Copy is the printed words that appear in an ad, brochure, sales sheet, or the like. Copy is made up of two components: headlines and body copy. The purpose of copy is to sell, inform, or move someone to action.
2 Selling words are specific words. They have a point of view and reflect the interests of the target audience.
3 To adopt the point of view of an audience, copywriters need a sense of empathy.

4   Good copywriters have a style. They avoid stilted and monotonous words; they keep their prose lively, with words that kindle images.

5   A good guide for developing the complete ad is the acronym AIDA (Attention, Interest, Desire, and Action).

6   The most important element of an ad is the headline, which some advertising experts believe is worth up to 80 percent of the ad.

7   Of the three major types of headlines—benefit, news, and curiosity—the benefit headline is most effective. Curiosity headlines are the most fun to create.

8   After the headline has caught the reader's attention, the follow-up sentences must create interest, desire, and, finally action. Guarantees, warranties, and testimonials are good creative devices for producing action.

9   Copywriters must never assume that readers will act without being told or encouraged to do so.

10 A product *feature* doesn't mean much unless the readers understand its benefits.

11 A copywriter's checklist might include the following points:

(a) be sure that the idea is clear;
(b) tell the story simply, and with pictures, if possible;
(c) avoid cleverness used for its own sake;
(d) write to a particular person;
(e) promote products in a fresh way;
(f) use good taste;
(g) avoid political, religious, and racial bias;
(h) don't use female models as sex objects;
(i) remember that people buy "satisfactions";
(j) be specific in retail ads and mention prices, sizes, brands;
(k) use words like sale, new, free;
(l) stick to the truth;

FIGURE 18-6
Al Hampel.

(m) emphasize productivity, maintenance savings, safety, lower labor costs, greater profits, and the like in industrial advertising copy;

(n) use coupons and toll-free numbers—in short, make ads easy to respond to.

CASE STUDY Reasons I Like Print by Al Hampel, executive vice president and director of Creative Services, Benton & Bowles, Inc.[4]

I sometimes wonder what would have happened if print had followed TV as an advertising medium. Think of print as a *brand-new* medium and the possibilities become astounding. Imagine a new form of advertising that lets you stretch out and sell your product in ways that no 30- or 60-second time span could possibly handle. For example, if you sell toothpaste for cavity prevention on TV, in print you can reveal ten ways you can get children to brush with your toothpaste—a story too long to be squeezed into a TV commercial.

Even in less than single-page units you can often say more than you can in a TV commercial. Grab your prospect with a provocative headline and an interesting visual, write bright informative copy, make it easy to read, and smaller space becomes no obstacle to good print advertising (Figure 18-6).

GREAT RECIPE FOR SELLING

It may look like just another ad to you, but to the woman of the house it's tonight's dessert—or Saturday night's dinner. Any food or beverage advertiser who doesn't consider print for recipes or serving suggestions does so at his own risk.

And in print the recipes aren't limited to food or drink. Learn how to select a mattress or a fine vintage wine. Get a crash course in make-up or how to insulate a house. Cut along the dotted line and file an airline schedule in your wallet. Find a new color for a rug and take it to the store when you shop. No TV set can convey color as accurately as four-color print. There are as many variations of hues on TV as there are sets in use.

And only in print: The information in an ad is yours to keep and refer to as long as the paper lasts. . . .

MAIN IDEA AND SECONDARY IDEAS

In print you can highlight a main selling idea in your headline. Your secondary selling idea can go into a subheadline. Other key points can be emphasized with crossheads. And, of course, you can get down to details in the body copy.

This is not as easily done in TV where every word carries as much weight as every other word and it's difficult to communicate more than one major selling idea. . . .

[4]Ad, "It would take eighteen 30-second TV commercials to tell you what's on this page . . . and other reasons why I like print," *Advertising Age,* November 18, 1974

OVERNIGHT RESPONSE

If you have a son or daughter who wants to be a copywriter, encourage him or her to get a job in a department store. It's the best training they could get. When you write retail print copy, you can expect response to your ad at the point of sale the day after it runs. The buyer of ladies' ready-to-wear will tell you within days how good a copywriter you are. You won't need research to tell . . .

My advertising philosophy is very simple: "It's not creative unless it sells!"

QUESTIONS NEEDING ANSWERS

1 What kind of visual would it take to interest a consumer in using your brand of pears for a Saturday night dessert? How would you handle the problem in a quarter-page ad?
2 How would you go about developing a headline for a vintage wine? For insulating a house?
3 What changes would you make in your insulating-a-house headline if it were a department store ad?
4 Do you agree with Mr. Hampel's advertising philosophy that "it's not creative unless it sells?" Explain.

STUDENT PROJECT

Your job as a copywriter is to convince your school district to vote for a new $3 million bond issue to build an addition to the Pleasant Valley High School. You'll be concentrating your advertising in the newspapers, with each ad running to 800 lines. Facts: The school is overcrowded. Built to hold 1,000 students, now holds 1,400. Juniors and seniors do not take gym because of overcrowding. The library is pre-World War 1 and holds only 1,000 volumes. The school's additional volumes are farmed out to several classrooms on other floors. State requirements indicate that a school with Pleasant Valley's population requires at least 15,000 volumes. The cost to the average homeowner for a new addition is $12 per year if the bond issue passes. The $3 million will build fifteen new classrooms, a new gym, and a central library. Write a hard-hitting ad: Headlines, copy, and a visual suggestion.

QUESTIONS ABOUT THE PROJECT

1 Explain why you selected the headline you did. Who is your target audience?
2 Do you think that a curiosity-type headline would work in this situation? Why?
3 Describe the specific words you used to kindle the imagination of the district's homeowners.
4 Do you think it is wise to include the cost of the bond issue to each taxpayer in your ad? Explain.

ACTION IN DIRECT MAIL

Update From the previous chapters, we learned about the business of direct mail: the advantages and disadvantages, the building and the renting of lists. In this chapter, we'll learn how to make all these preparations pay off. Our principal players, as in the print media, are the copywriter and the layout artist.

Many businesses use direct mail to get closer to prospective customers. They want to call them by name, to talk to them directly and personally. Direct mail doesn't push them to get their message across in thirty seconds. It doesn't corset them within a 7×10 inch space. Direct mail may be the least inhibiting medium. The creative staff can let its imagination soar, restricted only by the budget and a few postal regulations.

Designing a successful direct-mail piece means first considering its physical appearance or *format*. The format serves as an attention-getting device as well as a mood setter. It communicates to recipients even before they read a word of copy.

CREATING THE FORMAT

Many copywriters fill out a copy strategy platform before they begin creating a direct-mail piece. (See Chapter 17 for a fuller discussion of copy strategy platforms.) Among other things, the platform will ask for the main idea of the direct-mail piece. Once the objective has been firmly established, it is time to investigate the format possibilities.

The simple exterior envelope is one format. There are two conventional sizes: $7\frac{1}{2} \times 4$ inches (#6) and $9\frac{1}{2} \times 4$ inches (#10). What can we do with envelopes? We can print them in colors and design them. We can emboss them (that is, impress an image on the envelope so it stands in relief above the surface). We can print photographs on them that cover everything except the address area. We can cover them with reflecting materials such as Mylar. We can print, write, or stencil "teaser messages" on them.

Inside the covering envelope can be a conventional black-and-white letter, or one in color. The letter can be illustrated and printed on heavy, coated, or tissue-thin paper or even a specialty paper. (Some papers are made to disappear when mixed with water—ideal for a "trick" mailing for a company selling supplies to magicians!)

The important question for the copywriter is this: Does the physical format do justice to and complement the product or service? Quality department stores don't send invitations to a bridal show on mimeographed postcards, any more than machine shops solicit subcontracting work with embossed invitations.

There are many format variations open to advertisers who restrict themselves to conventional letterheads and envelopes. But some businesses come up with new formats. The Russo Corporation of Albuquerque, for example, introduced a laminating service for restaurants by preparing a small menulike mailing piece. Inside, the copy read:

> Our chef recommends a new development in menu lamination, Russo-Lamination, [which] now makes possible the permanent bonding of lamination to any menu stock, providing a complete seal-front. It increases strength and menu life TENFOLD, cuts 60–75% from menu costs. Completely eliminates cracking and tearing and retains character of the textured stock.[1]

Business Week magazine sent foot-long foam manikin heads to selected advertisers and agency personnel to dramatize its circulation theme, "thinking executives." *Better Homes and Gardens* sent "slogan-mobiles" to groups of

[1]*Direct Mail Techniques*, E. S. Advertising Services (Cleveland), December 1970, #30.

media buyers. Many retail businesses and service companies religiously send "doodle pads" and calendars to customers and prospects, year after year. A manufacturer of a paint additive for contractors gets excellent response from its biannual mailings of aluminum watchband calendars. A boxboard company sends mailings on corrugated paper. A manufacturer of foam products and novelties sends business solicitations in its unique, reusable foam mailing envelopes.

These are some of the "costumes" direct-mail messengers wear as they enter the business office or the home. They are designed to attract favorable attention. Then it's up to the message to sustain reader interest.

THE BIG IDEA

Congratulations! You've accomplished quite a bit. The recipient has opened your mail presentation and hasn't discarded it, *yet*. This is a critical moment. Success or failure hangs on the content of your next few sentences. If you're experienced, you've learned not to waste time and space on nonessentials.

Good direct mail copywriters try to imagine themselves standing inside their prospect's front door or office and saying: "We've got an important message to give you—and here it is." They then make meaningful statements, an important way to reach their target audiences. Here are some examples:

Statement	Product or service
Good news for thin men!	Diet enrichment food
As a manufacturer, you face some difficult problems today.	Minicomputer system
If we had sealed this envelope with the enclosed material, you'd never get it open!	Roof repair material
Here's your copy of *The World Trader*.	Customhouse brokerage service
For our Bicentennial Year, National Geographic invites you to . . .	Historical volume

Another good way to gain attention in a letter is to begin with an intriguing question that can't be answered with a single "yes" or "no." Some examples:

Question	Product or service
What's the best replacement for an old gas water heater?	Gas water heater
How many unusual offers like this have you seen?	Shoe catalog
Where else can you learn advertising from professionals who make their living at it?	Advertising club school
Can you name any other thrill equal to flying the winds?	Hot-air balloons

A third, and perhaps the most fascinating way to sustain interest, is through the "big idea." The "big idea" evolves from almost anything. It might come from a chapter in history or it can be as current as this morning's newspaper. Generally, the "big idea" is a copywriter's response to something unique and timely about the product, the advertiser, or the audience. Here are some examples.

The situation	The big idea
A company wanted to convince young boys that its product, a clutch, could propel small minibikes up hills without destroying clutch bearings.	The advertiser ran a small 4-horsepower minibike (with its clutch) up Pike's Peak. The bike was the smallest vehicle to make the 14,110-foot climb under its own power. Direct mail to dealers trumpeted the news (Figure 19-1)!
A national news magazine wanted to stress its coverage of elections to an audience of media buyers.	The magazine's promotion department direct-mailed to media buyers election posters filled with historical campaign slogans. Each campaign slogan contained the name of the recipient, for example: "Tippecanoe and Engel, too." The personalization was done by a computer tape.
An industrial company wanted to reach top management officials only.	The ad department designed a series of personal letters from its president to other presidents.
An insurance company with a widely scattered sales force wanted to tie top producers closer to the company.	The ad department introduced "President's Week." Salespersons who sold more than three contracts that week phoned the company president personally and reported the sales. "President's Week" initiated a sales contest the company had introduced through a series of direct-mail letters.
A trade publication wanted to draw attention to an upcoming article on pollution in factories.	The publication mailed a plastic record to industry leaders and agencies. Appropriately titled "Polluted Airs," the record opened with a variety of choking coughs.
An appliance manufacturer wanted to create an image of long life and reliability for its products.	The company's ad agency created a trade character, "Ol' Lonely, the repairman," for direct mail to dealers as well as for use in other media. Real-life, fictional, and even cartoon characters—Morris the cat or the Jolly Green Giant—serve as attention-getters.

Direct mail places few restrictions on the number of big ideas advertisers can use. They can mail posters, catalogs, clothing, books, food. Letters postmarked and stamped with an overseas address usually capture attention. Contests and samples work well. Some advertisers like games. They'll mail

See Page 4 for exciting news of 1972 Promotion & Dealer Prizes!

MERCURY CLUTCH TIMES

To our MERCURY DEALERS:

This 8-page newspaper is the very first news to the trade of an unusual event. Read on and you will see why we believe you are about to experience a real breakthrough in clutch sales for 1972 . . .

Mercury Clutch!

BULLETIN:

MERCURY CLUTCH "HILLCLIMBER" conquers Pikes Peak FAMOUS 14,110' mountain

COLORADO SPRINGS, COLORADO: On Wednesday, September 22, 1971, Roger Falasco, a teenager from Chagrin Falls (Ohio), ran a distance of 20 miles to the top of Pikes Peak on a mini-bike. It was the first mini-bike that had ever made it to the top of America's most famous mountain. The most amazing part of the endurance test conducted by a Canton (Ohio) Company was the fact that the ucccess of the venture depended on a compact, 4-inch diameter centrifugal clutch called appropriately, The Hillclimber. Experts in the field have always considered difficult hills as an impossibility for all centrifugal clutches preferring the costlier torque converters. The "Hillclimber" has rather dramatically shown these experts that it is no ordinary clutch.

Snow a Hazard

The 20-mile mountain course is famous for its annual Auto Race and its hairpin turns, switchbacks, 35° grades and unbelievable beautiful scenery. Despite the fact it was still September, snow decorated part of the trail and created somewhat of a hazard for the young rider who was accompanied to the Peak by two men representing Mercury Clutch. The station wagon they brought along, at one point, konked out at 11,000 ft., 3,110 feet below the Peak. Some snowmobiles have found climbing to and operating at this altitude an impossibility. During the run to 14,110' which was authorized

as a special endurance project by officials in Colorado Springs, the rider experienced sleet, snow, rain, fog, sun and mud.

People surprised

Visitors who reached the Peak by the Cog Railway at first refused to believe that the small vehicle had made it to the top under its own power, a standard 4 h.p. engine and The Hillclimber Clutch. Others asked permission to have themselves photographed with it as a memorable keepsake. A professional photographer recorded many action shots of the event from start-to-finish.

Dealers to win BIG Prizes

Be sure to check page 4 of this issue. It tells you how to win one of 19 exciting dealer prizes including a fabulous weekend expense paid extravaganza to LAS VEGAS or New Orleans or Hiltonhead (S.C.)* for you and your wife! Nothing to write, nothing to clip. It's all part of Mercury Clutch's National Sweepstakes honoring the Hillclimber conquering Pikes Peak.

FIGURE 19-1

Using a newspaper format as direct mail, this minibike clutch manufacturer explained how its clutch took a 4-horsepower bike up the steep Pike Peak's trail to the top. Approximately 5,000 dealers received news of the feat through the direct-mail program. (Courtesy Mercury Products.)

playing cards one at a time with the best poker hands at the end of the contest period to win prizes. Of course, each playing card will carry a message about a company product. At the end of the poker game, every recipient knows the important features of the company's products.

A small fast-food franchise introduces its new stores by mass mailing its menu to all apartments and homes within a 5-mile radius. Among local retailers, big ideas often take the form of unique calendars, special sales, and premiums. One United States Congressman sent his constituents a small consumer information booklet published by the federal government on the subject of making life a little easier on the pocketbook. He's betting constituents will remember his concern come Election Day.

Brainstorming for the Big Idea

The easiest way to begin to look for that one great idea that stops people in their tracks is to begin with the product. If it's a consumer product, copywriters ask themselves; What's so different about it? Is the difference meaningful? Then they wonder how they can dramatize the difference.

If the advertiser is a retail store, the big idea can come from the character of the store itself, or the type of merchandise it buys and stocks. The local retailer has a vast inventory of ideas to work with—the ideas passed down through the years from one store to the next or publicized by media promotion departments. For starters, retailers have the traditional annual holidays and seasonal promotions. A hardware store, for example, can begin with the coming of spring in the search for the big idea.

Copywriters, in a running dialogue with themselves, might ask: "What do most people think of when spring arrives?"

They answer: "Vacations, picnics—and *do-it-yourself home repair.*

"What makes spring so special for do-it-yourselfers? Well, spring brings the best weather for those outdoor jobs like repairing the fence, fixing the garage door, painting the lawn furniture, and even—for the really ambitious—fixing the roof.

"Yes, that's it. Spring home repairs you can do yourself.

"How about 'Tools for your spring projects, 1980'?

"Or 'Tools 'n' things for the fix-it person around the house'?

"Or we can send our direct-mail list a large envelope with an empty tool box on one side and a proud homeowner holding a filled tool box on the other.

"How about a special tool sale? We'll stay open later and have special store hours. Maybe we can call it the "Side-Door Sale," with all tools marked 15 percent off for that day only.

"Maybe we can include a reduced-rate coupon good for a month on any tool in the store. We could send it to all the homeowners in the area. Maybe this could be the beginning of a "Tool of the Month" mailing? It could start on the first day of spring and go on throughout the year. Mailings could consist of individual die-cut replicas of the actual tools.

"Suppose the store gives a free tool kit to anyone who signs up for all twelve of the year's tools. Maybe we can include a large colorful wall poster—great for the family workshop—of commonly used tools and instructions for maintaining them. Perhaps *this* should be the first mailing piece of the series, along with a special offer?"

One big idea for R. H. Donnelley, a direct-mail marketing company, was a "$50,000 All-Cash Sweepstakes" promotion in red, white, and blue with fourteen redeemable coupons for everything from Heinz 57 Sauce to a genuine Heiress Ambassador Purse Organizer (Figure 19-2).

The big idea for Lloyd McKee Motors, a Chrysler-Plymouth dealer in New Mexico, was an attention-getting $100 coupon. The coupon simulated paper currency but was plainly marked "not legal tender." The mailing went to 15,000 owners of three- and four-year-old cars in the dealer's trading area and produced excellent results.

For Henderson Realty of Phoenix, the big idea was the creation of the "Hener-Sell Man," a caricature with a bulbous nose, large head, and tiny body. Company officials believe that the cartoon character was responsible for 10 to 15 percent of their yearly sales.

Since many creative big ideas are variations on existing promotions, many advertisers maintain a file of previous campaigns. If nothing else, these files serve to get the creative juices flowing. The industrywide habit of collecting good ideas is not illegal. No one can copyright an idea, which may explain why companies sometimes use similar ideas at about the same time.

Copy Style

Direct mail copywriters must learn to write simple sentences. They should direct their messages to the individual. In *The Art of Readable Writing*, Rudolph Flesch maintains that writers can improve reading ease by keeping to 17 words per sentence and 147 syllables per 100 words.[2] Longer sentences may contain too many large words. They become too involved, too confusing. Examples of the syllable formula are:

See Brand X immediately. (eight syllables)
See Brand X at once. (five syllables)

Flesch rates sentences of eight words or less as a "very easy style." Writers should also let their personality come through their words. They should use present tense, active voice, and strong action words:

No: "Hard, durable floors are provided when you use Enamel PLUS."
Yes: "Get hard, durable floors with Enamel PLUS."
No: "Inferior air-filter products are being sold by dealers because of chronic distributor-inventory shortages with a profit loss to you, Mr. Distributor."

[2]Rudolph Flesch, *The Art of Readable Writing* (New York: Harper & Bros., 1949).

FIGURE 19-2

The sweepstakes promise has long been a major attention getter for many direct-mail ventures. (Courtesy R. H. Donnelley.)

Yes: "When you don't stock factory-approved air filters, your dealers sell cheapies. You lose cash!"

When choosing words, writers should keep in mind that words kindle images. Are the images clear? Are the words "insider's language," known only to a small group? *Everyone* who receives a direct-mail piece should understand it. Writers must be sure their thoughts are logical, that one thought flows into the other. They must be careful of extravagant qualifiers: *fantastic, best in the world, lowest price, spectacular, super.* Would you buy from a company that advertises:

> Sensationally modern boots, incomparably low-priced at far below wholesale . . . a fantastic bargain never seen before in this country. You'll never believe it until you see it. Now, for a limited time only at XYZ Stores. The price is so low, we simply can't reveal it in print. Come, run, rush, fly on your broom, but get here anyway you can. Our lease has expired! It's SUPERDUPER BARGAIN-BOOT TIME. NEVER BEFORE AND NEVER AGAIN SUCH BARGAINS!!!!

The problem with extravagant language is that once you are on that merry-go-round, it's hard to get off. Witness the last ten years of automotive advertising, in which one superlative has exceeded the other. The result of all this frantic exaggeration is that if an automotive company were to use calm, restrained language, dealers and customers would think there was really nothing particularly good about the cars.

Some copywriters have the mistaken notion that their job is to entertain. They confuse advertising copy with fiction. Very few people can successfully sell and entertain at the same time. Too many "entertainers" fail in their primary job: *selling.* Unfortunately, entertaining copywriters infect one another and confuse people.

Copywriters should beware of the tongue-in-cheek approach. When a Chicago advertising agency introduced a series of tongue-in-cheek tough-guy television commercials for Schlitz, the commercials insulted many viewers. In the four commercials, husky men were asked by a timid announcer to buy another brand of beer.

"What," snarled the men, "you want to take away my gusto?" Then their actions indicated that they might beat up the announcer. It was all in fun, the agency thought. Complaints poured into Schlitz headquarters, and the series was dropped after ten weeks. Subsequently, the agency lost the account. A bitter lesson, indeed.

One of the better methods of learning to write direct-mail copy is to take cues from the strong and informative style of mail-order catalog writers. Their space is limited. They have just so many words in which to sell a piece of merchandise. But they say everything that a customer needs to know. Their use of the language is concise, correct, and consistent with the product they are selling. Catalog copywriters are not trying to win awards for lyrical language. They're just trying to sell.

Finally, copywriters should learn to work hard at the job: write, rewrite, then rewrite again. Eventually, they'll develop a style of their own, and the sincerity will shine through. David Ogilvy, internationally known creative president of Ogilvy & Mather advertising agency, claims the best ad he ever wrote went through seventeen drafts.[3]

The Action Offer

Some companies survive entirely on the business they get through the mails. These, the direct-response advertisers, develop good headlines to attract attention. They follow up by telling respondents in the first paragraph how the product will make them richer, wiser, better looking, healthier, more comfortable, and the like. Direct-response copywriters must get a certain percentage of readers to digest the *entire* ad. If they don't, the advertiser soon goes out of business.

The technique the copywriter uses to hold and reward readers is the *offer*. Some direct-mail experts contend that, next to a good mailing list, the offer is the heart of direct-response advertising. What is a good offer? It could be an excellent price. It could be easy credit terms. It could be a premium—an article of clothing or a tool box. It could be almost anything that people want and can get without too much trouble or expense. The job of the direct-response copywriter is to make sure that readers recognize the offer as exceptional.

Here's how the Postal Commemorative Society of Norwalk, Connecticut does it as they announce "the stamp collection of a lifetime!"

> Do you wish someone had left you a collection such as this? Do you wish you owned historic U.S. postage stamps going back 10, 20, 30, 40, and 50 years—in mint condition, as originally issued by the Post Office?
>
> Yes?
>
> Then let me tell you the good news . . . . And now, for a limited time only, you can become a first Edition subscriber to this collection . . . . The entire collection of 200 covers will be housed in a magnificient, custom-crafted album—a truly appropriate showcase for so extraordinary a collection. The historical information contained in this fact-filled volume will be an educational experience for your entire family; there is a wealth of detail on both stamps and the subjects they commemorate . . . .

McDonald's direct-mail birthday party promotion for children is one big, hard-to-refuse offer:

> Your local McDonald's has organized a complete birthday party plan to make your child's special day one to remember. And there's almost no work for you!

[3]David Ogilvy, *Confessions of an Advertising Man* (New York: Dell Publishing Company, 1963). p. 123.

FIGURE 19-3
This complete direct-mail packet addressed to birthday children presents an offer no one can refuse—especially parents! (Courtesy McDonald's.)

You can hold a McDonald's "Happy Birthday Party" at McDonald's or in your own home. If your party's at McDonald's, a special "McDonald's Helper" will stay with it the whole time and see that everyone has a good time and handle the clean-up chores. If your party's at home, a "McDonald's Helper" will supervise your food order and make sure that everything is ready for your pick-up . . . . They'll eat their favorite McDonald's foods, have fun with their friends—and get McDonald's party favors. . . ." (Figure 19-3).

Everyone likes an offer, even sales managers of companies that themselves use special offers in direct mailings. The Research Institute of America introduced its regular biweekly *Marketing for Sales Executives* with this offer:

> This 36-page special report covers virtually every key area where a sales executive can step in, take the initiative, and bring about a significant boost in sales and profits for the company.
>
> To get your first press-copy of the RIA special report, "Sales Logic that works," by return mail, simply complete and mail the enclosed postage-free request card.
>
> We are making this special report available, *without cost*, to those sales executives who agree to receive the Research Institute's regular biweekly report, *Marketing for Sales Executives.*[4]

Not all direct-mail advertisers expect an immediate response. Some design advertising pieces solely to provide information. They recognize that their payoff will come later. For example, when Okonite wanted to remind 3,300 important telephone company buyers that it was a major supplier of three types of telephone cable, it sent a series of monthly pieces with special envelope designs. Not a direct-response advertiser by any means, the company nevertheless later showed a sharp increase in the sale of the newer cable constructions.[5]

When full-service banks throughout the country wanted to promote their sponsorship of a national CBS-TV special, they mailed envelope stuffers to all their customers informing them of the show. In addition, the banks had their own message:

> We, too, can help you—to solve your money problems. Your full-service banker is a *professional*, aware not only of the financial world, but also money management. Let us select the proper checking account for you, design a savings plan to make your money work harder, or lend you money for any worthwhile purpose.
>
> Come in and let us help you solve any money problem because . . . no other

---

[4]*Sales Logic That Works*, a direct-mail letter, Research Institute of America, 1974.
[5]*Programmed Reminder Series Benefits Sales*, Mini-Studies in Mail Marketing, Association of Industrial Advertisers, September 1972 (#505).

financial institution can help you and your community more than a *full-service bank*.[6]

Advertisers with a sales force may feel no urgency to instigate action in their mailings. But they do like their readers to do something. Calls to action vary, of course, with the advertiser. Some imply action. Others barely suggest it. Most, however, like this garden tiller manufacturer, like to tell the reader quite positively what to do.

Simply drop this card into your nearest mailbox right away and I'll rush, by return first-class mail, all the details you'll need to know whether a Troy-Bilt *horse* or *pony* model best suits *your* gardening needs. . . . I'll also enclose a good bit of gardening information which I know you'll find useful as you prepare for and plan this coming year's garden.

Art & American Antiques Magazine emphasizes its no-risk action offer:

As you see, this is a *no-risk* invitation. You don't even invest a postage stamp or a single penny until you're convinced that *American Art & Antiques* is for you . . . with nothing to lose . . . and a world of new beauty and information to gain—take a moment *today* to mail the accompanying postage-free card (Figure 19-4).

DEPENDABLE GIMMICKRY

Copywriters attract readers in a number of ways. Some use effective and inexpensive gimmicks:

The Personal Memo   When personal memos are added to brochures and stuffers, they contribute a personal touch. They also contribute a suggestion of urgency. Some copywriters prefer them to personal letters.

The Underline   Copywriters simply emphasize phrases, sentences, and paragraphs by underlining them in black or another color.

The Postscript   The postscript gives copywriters another chance to remind prospects of what they're selling. It's a popular device.

---

[6]*The Human Body: The Miracle Months*, envelope stuffer, Full Service Banks, August 27, 1978.

FIGURE 19-4
Direct-mail
reproduction of the
cover of *American
Art & Antiques*
magazine is
designed to whet the
reader's appetite for
the real thing. The
new magazine
publisher used a
reflective "mirror" of
Mylar on the outside
of the mailing
envelope to highlight
a no-risk offer.
(Courtesy *American
Art & Antiques.*)

The Fill-in   Computer tapes now make it easy to insert an individual's name several times during the course of a letter. A recent tire manufacturer's fill-in program included the prospect's name repeated several times, the type of automobile owned, specific tire sizes required by that type of vehicle, and the price of the tires at a local dealership.

The Booklet Offer   Any offer of a booklet, catalog, record, or cassette develops excellent response from both consumer and industrial audiences.

The Free Trial Offer   Once prospects get the trial offer in their hands, chances for a sale are greatly increased. Industrial buyers, in particular, respond well to the offer of a demonstration.

Special Paper Stock   Copywriters and artists can select from many types of paper. There are parchments for the appearance of antiquity, wallpaper, graph paper, foil for dramatic impact, and so on. Ad people can also choose from double-coated papers, white on one side and colored on the other.

Special Typography   Creative people can have a field day with the many varieties of type now available. Estimates indicate that there are over 1,000 recognizable type styles. A note of caution: Too many type faces in the same direct-mail piece can be confusing.

Special Shapes   Giant or miniature letters, computer-type tab cards, circular letters, die-cut letters, and unusually shaped cards are some of the many variations from the conventional that will get attention. If you're selling eggs, try an egg-shaped card.

Unusual Layouts   Handwritten letters, simulated telegrams, stock certificates, cardboard shipping tags, insurance policies, savings books, maps, passports, and the like are tested and proven ways to stimulate interest in mail recipients.

Unusual Art   When everything else seems to fail to spark copywriters, they often fall back on stick figures, children's drawings, surrealistic or enlarged sections of photographs, combined art and photography, doodles, architect's or designer's sketches, and realistic illustrations.

There simply is no end to the library of gimmicks open to copywriters and advertisers. When they are appropriate to the product or service, they usually help increase audience attentiveness and response.

DIRECT-MAIL CONTINUITY

Because direct mail is such a personal medium—and more costly per thousand than all the others—some advertisers tend to underuse it. Whereas they may run six to twelve insertions a year in a publication, they run only one or two direct-mail pieces. Yet, if direct mail is indeed the rifle approach (the next best thing to a personal sales call), it may make sense to plan a series of mailings. Some experienced sales executives believe that:

Two percent of sales are made on the first sales call.
Three percent of sales are made on second sales calls.
Three-and-one-half percent of sales are made on third sales calls.
Ten percent of sales are made on fourth sales calls.
Eighty-one percent of sales are made on subsequent sales calls.

A direct-mail piece is part of a long-term investment. If the mailing proves successful, why not repeat it? It is customary to repeat good publication ads and television commercials because there is little or no loss in reader or viewer interest. Why not repeat successful direct mailings?

COPY TESTING

Copy testing is probably most important to direct-response advertisers. Copy testing is a simple technique whereby advertisers evaluate the effectiveness of their copy by mailing two versions of the written message on an every-other-name basis. Whereas publication, outdoor, and broadcast ads direct people to a store, direct-response advertisers have no similar advantage. Copywriters can only depend on the selling they can do within the confines of an envelope. This limitation is a major reason why copywriters test before, during, and/or after a direct mailing. To them, copy testing is an insurance policy. It helps to prevent disasters.

Advertisers can test variations in the format, the big idea, the headline, the opening sentences, the body copy, the offer, and the call to action—even the price and the terms of payment. However, testing takes time. If advertisers tested every single variable, they might never get a single mailing piece to their total mailing audience! For this reason, copywriters are content to limit their testing to the headline and action offer. They mail variations of these elements to a small percentage of the entire list. The rules are the same as for any other survey. In particular, however, copywriters need to discipline

TABLE 19-1
EVALUATING TEST MAILING RESULTS

Percent of response	Limits of error in percents				
	0.16	0.18	0.20	0.25	0.30
0.1	1,499	1,184	958	614	426
0.2	2,994	2,336	1,917	1,226	852
0.3	4,467	3,546	2,872	1,838	1,276
0.4	5,977	4,723	3,826	2,448	1,700
0.5	7,464	5,897	4,777	3,057	2,123
0.6	8,948	7,070	5,727	3,665	2,545
0.7	10,429	8,240	6,675	4,272	2,966
0.8	11,907	9,408	7,621	4,877	3,387
0.9	13,382	10,573	8,564	5,481	3,806
1.0	14,854	11,736	9,506	6,084	4,225
1.1	16,322	12,897	10,446	6,686	4,643
1.2	17,788	14,055	11,385	7,286	5,060

This chart provides direct-mail advertisers with a statistical basis for using the response to one test mailing to project what they might expect from a larger mailing chart based on the law of probability that there are 95 chances in 100 that the returns will fall within given percentages. To use the table, assume a mailing of 6,084 has given a 1 percent return. We can be assured that the identical mailing made to a much larger group, say 30,000, will deliver almost identical results plus or minus $\frac{1}{4}$ of 1 percent. Follow the percent of response column down to 1.0%, move across to the size of the test mailing of 6,084, and learn how close we'll be, with a limit of error of 0.25 percent. This means that if a test mailing pulls a 1 percent response, an identical larger mailing will produce results falling between .75 percent and 1.25 percent—95 of 100 times. (Courtesy Direct Mail/Marketing Association.)

themselves not to make major changes based on minor results. In other words, major decisions should be based on "statistically significant" results. Table 19-1 illustrates the point for large direct response advertisers.

The advertisers' purpose in testing, of course, is to discover the sales approach that will bring the greatest response and orders. Unless there is a proper response, the company will not remain in business. Direct mailers usually operate on one of these two economic formulas for evaluating their operations: percent of response, and cost per order.

The percent-of-response formula is simply a method of reporting and comparing one mailing to another; it does not mean that the advertiser made money.

$$\text{Percent of response} = \frac{\text{Number of orders or inquiries} \times 100}{\text{Total number of pieces mailed}}$$

If we mailed 100,000 pieces and received 2,000 responses, our percent of response would be 2 percent.

The cost-per-order formula provides insight into how economically effective the advertisers' mailings have been.

$$\text{Cost per order} = \frac{\text{Total cost of mailing}}{\text{Number of orders received}}$$

If the advertiser has sent out 100,000 pieces at $85 per thousand ($85/M), the total cost of the mailing is $8,500. Assuming that the advertiser received 2,000 orders, the cost per order is $4.25. To determine whether the advertiser has made or lost money on the transaction, the cost of goods, labor, and overhead must be added to the mailing costs. The example below is a typical cost-evaluation technique:

Volume mailed	Total mailing cost	Number of orders
10,000	$1000	250

Percent response	Cost per order	Income at $15	Actual product cost
2½	$4	$3750	$1250

Total cost/mailing and product	Gross profit
$2250	$1500

FINALLY—THE POST OFFICE

In the last few years, postal rates and regulations have been changing. For example, 1978 standards for mailing postcards prohibited those that are less than 3½ inches high or 5 inches long. Pieces of mail that measure more than 6⅛ inches high or 11½ inches long cost more to mail. The safest action for advertisers preparing a mailing is to check with the postal service *before* developing a unique layout or format. Otherwise, they may have to alter their plans radically later on. Advertisers should keep in mind that the postal service is an extension of their creative mailing operations. Last-minute changes are costly!

IN SUMMARY

1　The first step in designing a direct-mail piece is to develop its format or physical appearance.
2　Within the two conventional envelope sizes, many formats are possible.
3　"Big ideas" are good attention getters. They generally develop from something unique and timely about the product, the advertiser, or the audience.
4　Copywriters should use short sentences and words of few syllables. They should try to let their personalities come through. They should use the present tense, the active voice, and strong words.
5　Some copywriters confuse entertainment with selling. They would be better advised to learn from the mail-order catalog copywriters, who write informatively as well as persuasively.
6　Some direct-mail experts believe that the offer is the heart of direct-response advertising. It's the job of the copywriter to make sure that mail recipients recognize the offer as exceptional.
7　A variety of dependable gimmicks help copywriters attract reader response: the

personal memo, the underline, the postscript, the fill-in, the offer of booklets, free trials, and special paper, typefaces, shapes, layouts, and art.

8 Some experienced sales executives believe that the more times a salesperson calls on a prospect, the better chance there is for a sale. Their findings support the need for advertisers to run a series of mailings in order to develop the equivalent of continuous sales calls.

9 When copywriters test elements of their copy on a small, representative sample of their audience, they need to learn not to make major changes based on minor results. Major decisions should be based on statistically significant results.

10 The safest way for a creative staff to prepare for a mailing is to check with the postal service before developing a unique format. Last-minute changes are costly.

CASE STUDY Radio Stations Go Direct Mail

How do radio stations advertise? On the radio? This would seem to be the most logical medium to reach radio listeners. But how does radio go about trying to influence its advertisers and advertising prospects? Certainly not in the evening, when advertisers and their advertising agency personnel are relaxing and perhaps not listening to radio. So how do many of America's radio stations tell their advertising story? By direct mail. For example, instead of sending out the usual announcement that Radio Station KVOD in Albuquerque was now KDAZ, station management sent a series of five folders offering various time spots at bargain prices. These were mailed to a list of 400 local advertisers considered by station management to be likely prospects. The results were excellent for the seven-week campaign. In fact, on one Friday the station sold out all commercial time available, something unheard of in its entire history.[7]

Station KTTS in Springfield (Missouri) uses direct mail on occasion to alert advertisers to ratings of the station and other station promotions. One brochure claimed, "KTTS AM-FM #1 in Springfield Metro and Area" (Figure 19-5). One of the station's more powerful sales messages was a four-page advertising piece prepared by the national Radio Advertising Bureau (RAB) and mailed by the Springfield station (Figure 19-6).

Station WGAR in Cleveland regularly mails sales messages to advertisers and prospects. These mailings describe awards earned by station personalities, audience ratings, testimonials of pleased advertisers, and commendations given to the station by community leaders.

At the very least, most radio stations mail station rate cards to their advertisers, prospects, and the prospects' advertising agencies. Some send specialty items like engraved matchbooks and calendars on a regular basis to prime customers. Inevitably, whenever the audience rating companies issue their reports, the station-rating winners throughout the country send out a barrage of direct-mail letters trumpeting the good news: WSB in Atlanta, KYNO in Fresno, WGIL for farm listeners in and around Galesburg (Illinois), WBEN in Buffalo, and WRV in Central Virginia, among others.

---

[7]*Direct Mail Techniques,* E. S. Advertising Services (Cleveland), December 1970, #30.

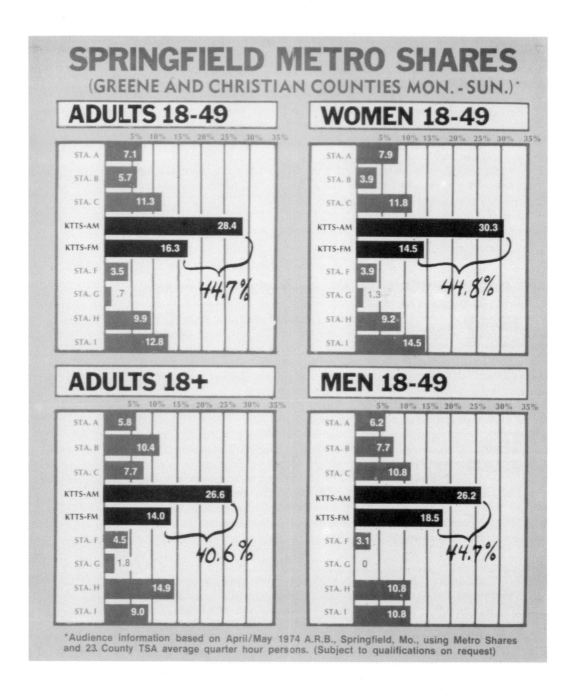

FIGURE 19-5

Obviously delighted because KTTS AM-FM dominates the listening habits of Missourians living in the Ozarks, the station management produced this direct mail piece proclaiming KTTS was number one in the region. The piece was sent to advertisers and their ad agencies and reflects the latest Arbitron (ARB) audience information. (Courtesy KTTS AM-FM)

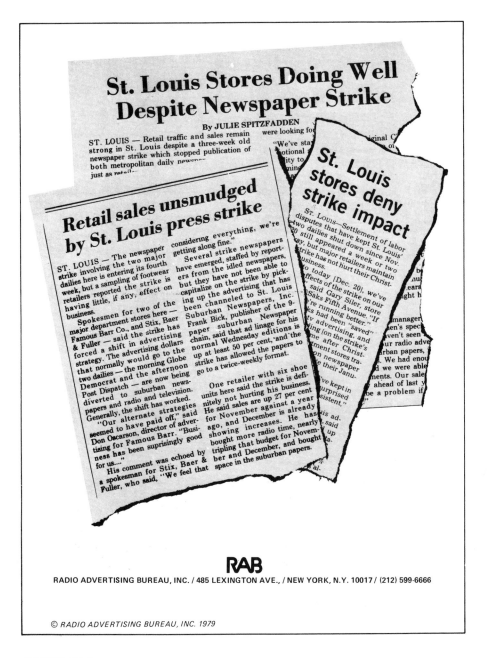

FIGURE 19-6

Always alert to promotional possibilities, the Radio Advertising Bureau produced a slick four-page "mailer" available to radio stations throughout the country. Its purpose was to prove that retail sales continue to be strong when newspapers are on strike and radio carries the advertising. The newspaper strike took place in St. Louis on November 20, 1978 and was settled on January 10, 1979, leaving retailers without major newspapers during Christmas. KTTS included this mailing piece as part of its direct mail campaign to advertisers. (Courtesy Radio Advertising Bureau)

While many radio station managements find it difficult to determine the exact payoff delivered by direct mail unless they offer specific bargain-priced commercials (like KDAZ, the small Albuquerque station), most find direct mail improves the effectiveness of the sales department. On occasion, radio stations will conduct a direct campaign to retail outlets of some radio advertisers with a view toward securing distribution of a product. This is an added service the stations perform for the advertiser. Sometimes campaigns aimed at improving distribution of advertisers' products include personal store appearances of the station's best-known air personalities.

While radio stations do not restrict their promotional activities solely to direct mail—they use newspapers and outdoor posters as well—the medium does lend itself to telling a complete story and permits stations to contact their advertisers *at any time* without concern for closing dates.

QUESTIONS NEEDING ANSWERS

1 Do you think that low advertising rates provide an effective way to gain new advertisers for a small radio station? Explain.
2 Can you think of another advantage that might do as well? Explain.
3 Do you feel that it's a radio station's job to help an advertiser with its distribution problems? Why? If you were managing the radio station, would you set up a policy to determine when to offer this added service, using criteria like the size of an advertiser's radio budget with your station, the type of product, or the like?
4 Other than from direct mail and personal sales calls by station representatives, how can a radio time buyer learn about a radio station, its rates, and its coverage?

STUDENT PROJECT

On page 544, there is a very generalized, direct-mail message from full-service banks. Critics of this message might say it lacks specific, individualized reasons for encouraging customer response. How would you tailor it to fit a local bank in your hometown? Consider these additional facts about your hometown bank: (a) the bank has helped finance a new shopping center; (b) it has begun paying interest on checking accounts with a minimum balance of $100; and (c) it has devised a computerized program that permits it to clearly estimate any family's earnings and expenditures for the next ten years.

QUESTIONS ABOUT THE PROJECT

1 Do you think it is necessary to rewrite the bank's direct-mail copy? Explain.
2 If you made any radical changes in the copy, explain your reason for doing so.
3 Can you think of other interesting formats for the bank's simple envelope stuffer? Explain.

THE BROADCAST COMMERCIAL

Update Although good ad writers should feel at home in any medium, there are important differences between print advertising and broadcast advertising. In fact, some advertising people claim that creating television and radio commercials is entirely unlike newspaper, magazine, and direct-mail selling. Let's see for ourselves.

TELEVISION ADS— MORE THAN ENTERTAINMENT

During the six and one-half hours a day an average American family spends watching television, 117 commercials will be shown, most of which are thirty seconds long.[1] Many of these commercials simply flit by, hardly noticed. Ad agencies, ad managers, and production houses who make their living from creating, approving, and producing commercials might argue that the $50,000 it costs to run the average network prime-time thirty-second commercial[2] and the production expenses of $10,000 to $100,000 should ensure good viewership. But do they?

San Diego Surveys[3] conducted 471 interviews on the day after Super Bowl XII in 1978. Their sample was nearly equally divided between males and females. They found that 62 percent of San Diegans were tuned in at kickoff. But when the teams walked off the field, only 24 percent were still watching (Figure 20-1). Worse still, the average aided recall of brand names and companies came to a mere 6 percent![4] How can these expensive commercials fail to impress a simple brand name on a captive audience?

The content of the ad message can explain some viewers' lack of interest. Many of the Super Bowl viewers weren't interested in a utility storage wall (1 percent were interested), or a felt-tip writing pen (3 percent were interested). Part of the problem, however, arises when copywriters and layout artists see themselves as entertainers rather than as salespeople. They often put on a better show in their thirty-second segments than the program itself does. We see singers in razzle-dazzle production numbers, marching bands, sequined chorus lines, and so on. When the thirty-second "entertainment" has left the screen, the audience hardly remembers the name of the advertiser. That's because the creators of the commercials, basking in the glow of "show biz," have forgotten to involve the viewer with the product and with the people on the screen. Without involvement, there can be little awareness of the message or the product.

COPY AND STORYBOARDS

In 1961, Rosser Reeves, then president of the Ted Bates Advertising Agency and a heavy user of television, listed these items as what ought to be included in every ad:

1 Information about the product and its unique advantage.
2 A clear statement of the information.
3 A unique presentation.[5]

[1]Non-prime time can run 50 percent more ads per hour than prime time. Prime time advertising averages about eight minutes per hour.
[2]"A short course in broadcasting: 1978," Broadcasting Yearbook, 1978, p. A-2.
[3]An independent interviewing service hired by The Marketing Services Department of the Union-Tribune Publishing Company; 471 interviews were conducted on January 16, 1978 in San Diego County, California.
[4]Highest scores were turned in by an auto rental company (28 percent) and a tomato cocktail juice (22 percent). Local company spots did quite poorly. Another consideration: the spots that ran early in the game reached a larger audience than those at the end. This may have been caused by the obvious dominance of one team over the other, which led many viewers to turn the game off early.
[5]Rosser Reeves, Reality in Advertising (New York: Knopf, 1961), p.22.

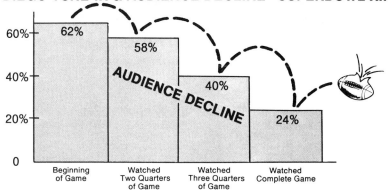

FIGURE 20-1
Descriptive chart prepared by members of the media information staff of the *San Diego Union & Evening Tribune*. The chart is based on the 471 interviews conducted the day after Superbowl XII.

Since that's a lot to get into thirty-seconds (the length of the most commonly purchased television commercial), it helps to start with a theme or an idea. In addition, the layout artist and the copywriter need to agree that their best television commercial will communicate *a single idea through sight, sound, and movement*. Once they've reached this understanding, they can begin the creative process.

To start, they can adopt the typical scenario format: a single sheet of paper equally divided into two vertical columns (Figure 20-2). On the left side, they place the heading *Video*, on the right side, *Audio*. The copywriter then gets to work.

Suppose the intent of the commercial is to sell the concept of a child-proof prescription container. The copywriter sees the situation as a family scene where a mother is about to take a pill. She does so and returns the pill bottle to a table. Later, while occupied with other things, she fails to see her small son reach over and try to open the pill container. He cannot open it, however. That's all there is to this basic concept.

Here's how the scenario develops. Note that sometimes copywriters number each "change" on the scenario script so that the video corresponds to what the viewer hears. See Table 20-1 for the meanings of the abbreviated terms.

Video	Audio
1 LS of pleasant living room in a neat, middle-class home. Mother in her thirties sewing before a highly visible grandfather clock. Three- to four-year old boy near her playing with toys on a rug.	**1** (SFX: clock ticking)
2 DOLLY IN toward mother	**2** (SFX: clock ticking)
3 CU of mother opening prescription bottle and taking a tablet. Replaces cap on bottle on small chairside table.	**3** (SFX: clock chimes) Announcer: The child-resistant prescription container . . . .

TV COMMERCIAL

D/628 – DIEHARD BATTERY – 30 SECONDS

"SAVE $7"

Order Number: V7-776-2830
Usage Limitation: 7/4/76 - 10/2/76

VIDEO	AUDIO
OPEN ON CU OF HEADLIGHTS.	ANNCR (VO): The battery that proved itself...
PULL BACK TO REVEAL CARS LINED UP IN SNOW. ("FROSTY ACRES")	in the freezing cold of Colorado.
CUT TO CU OF HEADLIGHTS.	And in the...
PULL BACK TO REVEAL CARS LINED UP IN DESERT. ("DEATH VALLEY")	scorching heat of Death Valley
CUT TO BATTERY IN LIMBO. SUPER: SAVE $0.	is now on sale nationwide. Save $0 on the DieHard.
ADD SUPER: NOW $00.00. WITH TRADE-IN.	Now only $00.00.
CUT TO START SCENE FROM "FROSTY ACRES".	Get the battery that has extra power...
	SFX: CAR STARTING
CUT TO START SCENE FROM "DEATH VALLEY". SUPER: CERTIFIED BY UNITED STATE AUTO CLUB. TEST DATA AVAILABLE.	to start your car when most batteries won't.
	SFX: CAR STARTING
CUT TO BATTERY IN LIMBO. SUPER: SAVE $0. SIMILAR SAVINGS IN CATALOG.	Get the DieHard. And save $0.
CUT TO LOGO.	Only at Sears.

FIGURE 20-2

Typical television scenario commercial format with video instructions on the left and audio on the right. (Courtesy Sears, Roebuck.)

TABLE 20-1
TELEVISION LINGO

559

THE BROADCAST
COMMERCIAL

CU (close-up)
Camera moves in for a tight shot.

ECU (extreme close-up)
Camera comes in even closer.

MS (medium shot)
Camera pulls away from subject. We see
    subject from waist up.

LS (long shot)
Camera lens places subjects at some
    distance so audience can relate them
    to surroundings.

PAN	Camera eye moves slowly horizontally or vertically.
DOLLY IN/DOLLY BACK	Camera rolls smoothly backward or forward.
CUT	Camera scene jumps abruptly from one thing to another. A dramatic device.
DISSOLVE	Camera scene gradually changes. One scene slowly replaces another.
ZOOM	Camera scene quickly and smoothly shifts from an extreme close-up to an extreme long shot or vice versa.
WIPE	An electronic control that cleans the screen and either leaves it blank or fills it with something else.
SFX (sound effects)	An audio command. Example: crowd noises.
SUPER (superimposition)	Placing the image from one camera over the image on another.

4 CUT to medium shot of child looking up.	4 (SFX: clock ticking)
5 MS of mother bending over from her chair to pick up something, child reaching for prescription bottle.	5 It may take a few more seconds to open . . .
6 ECU of child trying to open the bottle.	6 (SFX: container cap clicks) but it might save a child's life.
7 CU of woman's face. She shouts a warning.	7 Woman: Michael, no!
8 MS shows child with a mischievous smile holding out bottle to mother.	8 Announcer: That's why your pharmacist uses it to fill your prescriptions.
9 ECU of woman's hand returning bottle to table. SUPER copy: *Presented on television as a Public Service Message.*	9 (SFX: clock ticking)
10 CU of four prescription bottles of varying sizes, all with child-proof container caps. One bottle on side. Logo: Prescription Containers from Owens-Illinois.	10 (SFX: clock ticking)

This commercial meets Rosser Reeves' three criteria in the following ways:

1 The *uniqueness* of the presentation is the dominant ticking of the grandfather clock. Not only does it create suspense, but it also alludes to the common practice of taking pills by the clock.
2 The product's *unique advantage*, safety, is demonstrated when the child cannot remove the cap.
3 The clear, *informative statement* is apparent from beginning to end (Figure 20-3).

The *storyboard* is a sort of comic-strip layout divided into frames. Each frame represents a miniature television screen. The layout artist develops the storyboard after consultation with the copywriter. As a rule, six to seven frames will run thirty seconds, twelve to fifteen frames one minute. Most of these frames will consist of close-ups and medium shots since these are of greater interest to viewers. In addition, both copywriter and layout artist try to have video and audio say the same thing at the same time. This technique reinforces the message. The theory is to *see*, then almost immediately *hear*.

Coordinating sight and sound is one storyboard achievement. Another is the proper use of *typography*. In each commercial there is usually some message, theme, slogan or price that appears in type on a frame. The artist should try to keep type styles as legible as possible. Too-heavy letters, too-fine strokes, overlapping letters, or script typefaces make reading difficult. (More about typefaces in Chapter 22.)

Color also acts as a means of communication, particularly because the great majority of American families own color sets. For example, color conveys emotions: red suggests passion; blue, coolness and tranquility;

It may take a few more seconds to open our Clic-Loc® and Screw-Loc® child resistant prescription containers

Prescription Containers from Owens-Illinois

But it might save a child's life.

Child Resistant Containers can be effective in reducing the rate of accidental poisonings.

(CLOCK TICKING IN BACKGROUND)

(CLOCK CHIMES.)
The child resistant prescription container...

(CLOCK TICKING.)

It may take a few more seconds to open...

(CONTAINER CAP CLICK ALARM.)
...but it might save a child's life.

Michael, no!

That's why your pharmacist uses it to fill your prescriptions.

Presented on television as a Public Service Message.

FIGURE 20-3
Owens-Illinois uses one of its television commercials to create a print ad aimed at druggists. It also uses the same commercial as part of a drugstore counter display. The company sent television stations two public service announcements promoting child-resistant containers.

green, growth or springtime; yellow, warmth. But color also affects legibility. Warm colors like orange, red, and yellow appear closer to the viewer than the cool ones, green, violet and blue. The most legible typography combinations are black type on yellow background, yellow on blue, and blue on white (or the reverse of any of these). The least legible of eighteen full-color combinations is yellow or gold on maroon.[6]

Layout artists, copywriters, and production directors should also consider that, as on a magazine page, the 4×3 proportion of the television screen causes the eye to glance first at the 10 o'clock position before it follows the movement of people or camera. How many creative people plan their set and camera instructions so the action follows natural eye movements? How many important copy slogans and telephone numbers appear at 10 o'clock or at the top of the picture screen?

At one time, any ad seen on television attracted attention because the medium was new. But television is now saturated with advertisers, and the copywriter and layout artist need to adopt a strategy to combat clutter. The use of a simple, clear statement, unique presentation, dramatic camera angles, color selection, and placement of type matter on each frame may go a long way toward developing more effective, selling commercials.

FAMILIAR SCENARIO STRUCTURES

If the average family, which watches thirty-five to forty-five hours of television a week, were to analyze the commercials, it would recognize certain recurring scenario structures. The advertising industry has named these as a means of distinguishing among them. These familiar ones are seen every day.

The seven structures described here are the most easily recognized scenario structures used by copywriters. Copywriters may begin with one structure and end with another, or they may combine scenarios. Scenario structures help copywriters to streamline messages that can last only thirty seconds.

On-Camera Spokesperson

The on-camera spokesperson is the man or woman, sometimes a celebrity, who speaks for the advertiser. Spokespersons may be hired on a one-time or a long-term basis to explain why they like Oxydol or Wisk or Pledge. The spokesperson structure includes testimonial givers.

Once it was thought that a star was all an advertiser needed to sell the product. The star's presence alone, it was thought, would set the cash registers jingling. But too many failures made advertisers cautious about using stars as spokespersons, not only because of the initial cost, but also because

[6]*Comparative Visibility of Full Color Combinations,* (New York: Institute of Outdoor Advertising, 1975), p. 5.

of talent reuse payments. Some copywriters contend that few viewers identify with stars but do get emotionally involved when an ordinary person tells his or her credible story.

Demonstration

The purpose of the demonstration structure is to show how a product works and to prove its claims. In some respects, a demonstration is more persuasive than a personal sales call. The advertiser can animate it and can show, for example, what goes on inside a product or under a user's skin. The demonstration commercial can compare what one product does to what a competitor does not do. The strength of the demonstration commercial is that it is usually credible.

Slice of Life

In the slice-of-life technique, the copywriter develops a story line about what could take place in Anytown, U.S.A. The family gathers for a funtime vacation in the back yard. Everybody is there, and so are good ol' Hyland Potato Chips. Or you hear a woman calling "Anthony," and you see a young Italian boy running toward home, past the loaded pushcarts, past the bocce players, up the narrow alleys until he finally arrives home in time for Prince's spaghetti. The logic of slice-of-life commercials is for viewers to recognize that what happens on screen could happen to them. Soft-drink companies have heightened interest in this scenario structure by introducing appealing music and a kaleidoscope of young people enjoying themselves.

An occasional industry problem with the technique has been unfortunate casting. We see men who look and act like slobs and empty-headed women who act as if their only joy in life is to shine the furniture or wax the floors. Slice of life is effective when the characters look and act like credible human beings.

Problem Solution

Some advertisers call the problem solution structure the "Procter & Gamble structure" because so many of P&G's commercials follow it. As the name suggests, the person on the screen has a problem. Suddenly, a second person arrives with the solution and proceeds to give viewers a sales pitch (Figure 20-4). Generally the problems are quite simple: Daughter falls into a mud puddle and dirties her dress. How to get it clean for the party that evening? Or the child tells the world that Daddy has "a ring around the collar." Mother responds that Wisk will take care of that and redeems her honor.

Humor

Most copywriters would love to create humorous commercials. They're fun to do, and if they get talked about in the industry, the copywriter can earn a lot

1. WOMAN: Well, Christopher Michael Junior's about ready for his christening.

2. GRANDMOTHER: Want me t'finish dressing him, dear? WOMAN: Could ya, Mom?

3. Hold'n up, Dad? MAN: Barely. Did some last minute shoppin' for the party. Picked up a few bargains.

4. WOMAN: Bargains??? MAN: Even did the dishes. WOMAN: Bargains??? MAN: You're not the only one who knows how t'shop.

5. That's funny.

6. MAN: Look at the difference. The glasses you washed yesterday came out nice and clear. The ones I did came out spotty.

7. WOMAN: My Cascade did that? MAN: We were outa Cascade, so I bought a cheaper brand.

8. WOMAN: Y'saved a few cents. But now we've got spots. See how much better Cascade can do?

9. ANNCR: (VO) For virtually spotless dishes, you can see why Cascade's the better buy.

10. Most bargain brands can leave drops that spot. But Cascade's sheeting action.

11. leaves glasses virtually spotless.

12. GRANDMOTHER: Everything's beautiful, kids. MAN: 'Specially this little guy. S'got his old dad's nose, ears, chin.

13. WOMAN: Let's hope he has his mom's eye...for a bargain.

14. ANNCR: (VO) For virtually spotless dishes,

15. you can see why Cascade's the better buy.

FIGURE 20-4

Often called the Procter & Gamble scenario-structure because so many of P&G's television commercials follow this storyline, the problem-solution quickly involves the viewer. (Courtesy Procter & Gamble.)

of money. Unfortunately, unless humor commands attention and sells, it is an expensive experiment for the advertiser. Through the years, the Xerox commercials have proved to be both funny and effective selling instruments. (Figure 20-5). Three in particular stand out. One shows Brother Dominic, who has just laboriously completed copying a manuscript by hand only to have his Father Superior ask for 500 copies just like it; another presents the monkey armed with a letter swinging through an office and jumping from desk to desk on the way to the Xerox machine where it copies the letter in seconds with no muss or fuss; the last features the benchwarmer on the professional football team who gets his chance to star, but not in the game. His contribution is to race into the locker room to the Xerox machine where he duplicates a "trick" play eleven times and passes it out to the players, who go on to win the game. Wendy's recurring "fun musical motif" never sounds better than when we see a policeman biting into a "hot n' juicy" hamburger that sprays his uniform and discreetly moving his badge over to hide the stain. Alka-Seltzer also uses humor very effectively in its "First Home-Cooked Meal" commercial. A new bride is recalling her cooking triumphs in front of her husband while he nods agreement, all the while slipping himself two Alka-Seltzers on the sly.

Usually, advertisers are wise to pretest humorous commercials to make certain that the copywriter's sense of humor is shared by others. The modest testing costs—compared to the cost of the air time—are well worth the effort.

Animation

We see little of animation—except adjacent to children's shows—in television commercials because it is so expensive. Yet the techniques that brought us Mickey Mouse and Donald Duck have great potential to sell. Hamm's Beer uses a combination of animal cartoons and real-life photography. AMF (American Machine & Foundry), a conglomerate selling sporting goods among other things, tells its story about "making weekends" for overworked people through surrealistic animation. AID Association for Lutherans, a life and health insurance company, reaches farmers through television with animated farmers driving huge, animated tractors. Most animated commercials advertise products and games aimed at children.

Special Effects

Special effects are unusual sights and sounds created by manipulating machines and devices—mechanical, photographic, electrical, and electronic. By and large, they are underused in television commercials. "Trick" photography is an example of special effects. So is a hollow voice seeming to come from the inside of an automobile's gasoline tank. Sometimes special effects can be created by using animals and disguised humans. Mercury has long used a mountain lion perched atop a Mercury dealer's sign as its logo.

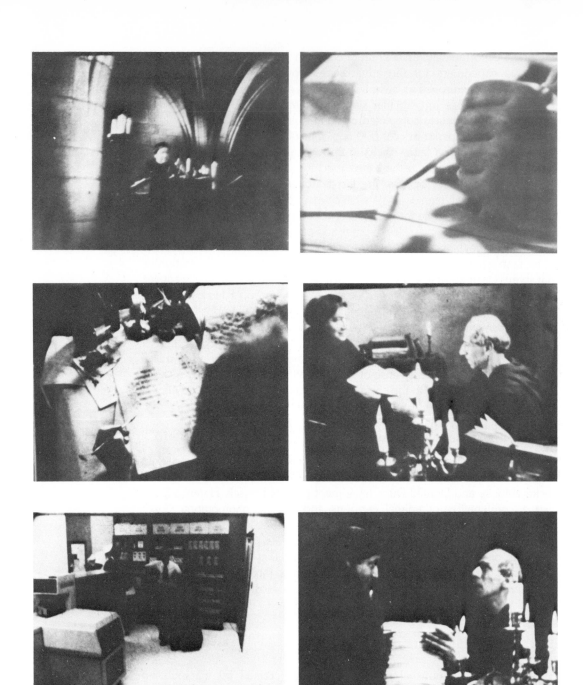

FIGURE 20-5
Surely Brother Dominic makes one of the funniest, yet relevant, commercials on television. Xerox has consistently been able to produce tastefully humorous commercials *that sell*. (Courtesy Xerox Corporation.)

Maybe you've already seen it. It features these three crazy monkeys. When we produced it, we thought it was good. Our client, Blue Cross & Blue Shield in Northeast Ohio, thought it was good. And, needless to say, to have it named the Best in the World in the 17th annual International Broadcasting Awards made us all very happy.

This year's I.B.A. competition attracted 3,500 television and radio en-tries from 47 nations. Twelve trophy winners were first selected, including ours in the "Local—one market" category. Then from these 12, ours was selected as the sweepstakes winner. It was the first time a local spot had been named the Best Commercial in the World.

We've always thought a lot of good things came out of Cleveland, and, as we see it, our award is just further proof of it.

The World's Best Television Commercial was created right here in Cleveland, Ohio by Carr Liggett Advertising.

This is our I.B.A. award. If you'd like to see it in person, just stop by our offices on the fifth floor of the Superior Building, 815 Superior Avenue.

FIGURE 20-6
What could be more special than three monkeys who satirize American life styles? The International Broadcasting Awards named this Carr Liggett commercial the best in the world. (Courtesy Blue Cross and Blue Shield in Northeast Ohio.)

One of the more recent comic uses of special effects is Blue Cross & Blue Shield of Northeast Ohio's employment of a trio of monkeys to expose the gluttony of humans (Figure 20-6).

DEVELOPING THE SCENARIO

After advertisers and copywriters have decided on the scenario structure, listed important sales points, and pinpointed the objective of the commercial, someone has to write the commercial. Returning to the sheet of paper divided into *Video* and *Audio* sections, the copywriter describes on the video side, how the commercial opens. With each change of character or scenery, the copywriter describes what the audience will be hearing in that same frame.

Here's an example. The copywriter's assignment: sell local residents on the advantages of keeping streets and sidewalks free of litter. That's the entire message. The slogan is, "Litterbugs are ugly Americans." As copywriters begin the creative work on this assignment, they must keep in mind that television is a show-and-tell medium, and that they must go easy on the copy and heavy on the pictures and movement.

Video	Audio
1 LS of trick car, gaudily custom-painted, bouncing up and down the street. DOLLY IN to show teenagers laughing, waving, drinking pop from cans.	**1** (SFX: loud rock music UP and UNDER)
2 MS of one boy. He finishes pop and tosses can into the street. Camera follows its flight.	**2** (SFX: can clanking down the street.)
3 CUT to side of moving panel truck. CU of hand dropping a half-used cigar.	**3** (SFX: loud country-western music.)
4 CUT to expensive sedan. Hand discards newspaper from side window.	**4** (SFX: loud top-forty tune.)
5 Quick CUTS in succession to: newspaper blowing down sidewalk and tin cans careening down a street with a tire's-eye-view of a car trying to avoid hitting the cans.	**5** (SFX: sound of wind, tin cans, tires squealing.)
6 MS of newspaper coming to rest against a pair of feet. PAN UP to shot of town's mayor.	**6** Hello. I'm Mayor———
7 He picks up paper and two cans. Looks into camera.	**7** You've just seen some ugly Americans at work.
8 PAN with mayor as he walks to a trash receptacle and drops paper and cans into it.	**8** Use the trash cans, *please.* (SFX: cans hitting bottom.)
9 CU of poster on side of container: "Litterbugs are ugly Americans!"	**9** (SFX: cans rolling down the street.)

This version would represent a first draft of a thirty-second spot. It will need cutting. It takes at least five to seven seconds just to establish a change of scenes in the eyes and minds of viewers. Chances are the copywriter would eliminate the cigar episode and alter the rest of the copy. There are only seventeen spoken words in this first draft. The pictures tell the story. Notice how the copywriter also changes the style of the music to introduce new characters.

But some copywriters might not like this approach. They might want to open on the mayor in his office, giving his best sales pitch staring right into the camera. To keep things moving, he rises on cue from his chair and strolls to the window. He points to his glorious city. Then he uncovers a flip chart that diagrams the tons of litter infesting the city. He moves to still another chart that shows how much littering is costing each taxpayer. All this is quite typical of mayoral pronouncements. Technically, it's very simple. It demands very little camera versatility. It's also very boring. Worse, it doesn't make an impression on viewers.

A better scenario is "Trashball," a sixty-second musical spot highlighted by special camera effects and created by ad agency Vansant Dugdale for the city of Baltimore. The creative people at the agency decided that preaching to people to pick up litter was an exercize in futility. So they enlisted the help of the city's professional basketball team, the Baltimore Bullets, and various citizens. The result was a memorable message that had the whole town playing "trashball" (Figure 20-7).

The Low-Cost Spot

When advertisers use celebrities in commercials, there is sure to be big money involved. When bands come strutting down the street, or people hang-glide or pop into jeeps, or Bob Hope talks to us from an oil rig deep in the Gulf of Mexico, the advertisers are paying a considerable amount of money to arrange these events and to pay for the difficult camera work required. Does that mean that creating a good, hard-selling commercial is beyond the means of small-budget advertisers? Not at all. The big production number may be beyond the financial capability of many advertisers, but money does not ensure a good *selling* commercial. Again, we go back to the commercials shown San Diegans during Super Bowl XII[7] (Figure 20-9). The automobile commercial with a mere 2.5 percent average recall cost between $60,000 and $120,000 to produce. The padlock commercial with 19 percent average recall cost $16,000.

Actually, if a company merely wants to register its name in the minds of the public, it has many low-cost ways of proceeding. It can try using puppets and marionettes, for example. Almost any city with more than 20,000 people will contain someone skilled in the art of handling either of these props. The effect is very interesting and the cost low.

[7]San Diego Surveys for the Marketing Services Department of the Union-Tribune Publishing Company. The study holds true for San Diego only. It may not hold true elsewhere.

FIGURE 20-7
Using upbeat music, professional basketball players, and a host of ordinary people—and starring the mayor of Baltimore—copywriters at the Vansant Dugdale ad agency put together a winning commercial that actually makes a game of picking up litter. (Courtesy Vansant Dugdale.)

1.) On December 5, 1973 at a rifle range outside Los Angeles

2.) A high-powered 30 caliber rifle . . .

3.) was fired at a distance of 40 yards . . .

4.) to try and open this Master padlock.

5.) The Master Lock Model No. 15 sustained considerable damage . . .

6.) but did not open.

7.) Repeat: did not open.

8.) Whatever your protection needs, there's a Master Lock ready to do the job.

FIGURE 20-8
A demonstration at its dramatic best. Who can doubt the claims of the company when you see the truth with your own eyes? (Courtesy Master Lock.)

Then there's the even simpler device of running the name of the company in many different type styles up and down the screen, growing larger and smaller, zooming in and out, scrambling letters, mixing colors, all to the beat of appropriate music. Advertisers may also want to use this same technique in flashing still photographs on the screen, first from the left, then the right, the bottom, and the top, and then simultaneously from top and bottom.

Occasionally, the proprietors of retail stores stand in their premises to make a simple heart-to-heart commercial. If they restrict their rhetoric to one single idea and allow the camera to help make the sales pitch, the overall effect can be good. Some retailers break the boredom barrier by including their young children, a technique that is effective if handled with modesty and discretion. (If the children cannot speak distinctly, though, they should not be used.)

Copywriters need to remember that television requires moving images. Movement catches attention and helps develop interest. Generally speaking, "fixed" slides fail. Audiences have long been bored with the standardized slide show. A slide of a quart of milk and a package of wieners comes on the screen. The announcers tells the viewers about the food while the milk and wieners remain embalmed. Slide presentations can be exciting if a television film processor and editor are called in, which does cost a little money. The camera might move in very tight on the product—an extreme close-up (ECU)—and move back slowly. This technique produces an air of mystery until the product is revealed for what it is. Alternatively, the camera can start out at a great distance and move in.

There are other little tricks. The station engineer, through electronic controls, can "cube," "square," "triangle," and "divide" scenes. The same electronics technique can blow up one element and offset it somewhere on the screen with a miniaturized version of the same thing. A retail advertiser could have a model displaying a jacket on the full-sized screen dissolve into the following frame with the entire outfit, jacket *and* skirt. These are but a few of the variations accomplished through the magic of the engineer's electronic console.

Small-budget advertisers can also use the seven common storyboard scenario structures to good advantage.

Problem-Solution for Ralph's Men's Store.

Locale: A men's store.

Characters: a salesman, a reluctant middle-aged male customer, and his wife.

CUSTOMER: I'm not gonna say it again, Martha, I don't *need* a pair of pants.

WIFE: (to salesman) He wears size 38.

CUSTOMER: I've got twenty pairs at home.

WIFE: Yeah, and not one fits. (to salesman). Let me see the blue pair.

CUSTOMER: They just don't make them the way they used to.

SALESMAN: You'll like *these*, Mr. ----. They're expandable and cut high.

CUSTOMER AND WIFE: Expandable? Cut High?

Salesman then goes on in the tradition of "problem-solution" to explain the unique advantages of Ralph's select stock of men's trousers designed for mature, well-built men. Note the suggestion of conflict between husband and wife in the very first sentence. Conflict is an excellent dramatic technique.

Here's how a retail furniture store can use a *demonstration* scenario to describe why they handle specific brands. The presenter can be anybody from the boss to a customer of the store.

PRESENTER: You've heard people say that Span Furniture is the only place that sells Regal Upholstered Chairs. Here's why.

Two chairs. One is Regal, the other Brand X. Here's the amount of material you get with Brand X. Kinda skimpy. So, the manufacturer stretches it. Materials wear out faster.

Now, Regal. Almost 25 percent more material. No one stretches it. Corners are neat. No wonder careful furniture shoppers buy at Span. Span—we're looking *out* for *you!*

For advertisers who want something a little more professional than a local station can accomplish, there are production houses all over the country that charge modest fees. They'll produce a professional-appearing commercial for $900 to $5,000. Some local stations videotape thirty-second spots for as little as $300.

Marvin & Leonard advertising agency in Boston produced a series of modestly priced television spots for the "pure one, the natural-tasting chicken." The objective of the commercials and the newspaper ads was to secure supermarket distribution. The campaign depicted three shoppers descending on a store's meat manager.

SHOPPER #1: Do you have any Pure 1?

MANAGER: We're temporarily out of stock.

MANAGER TO ASSISTANT: What's Pure 1?

ASSISTANT: I don't know.

MANAGER: Well, find out!

SHOPPER #2: How soon is Pure 1 coming in?

MANAGER: We're working on it.

ASSISTANT: It's a new kind of chicken.

MANAGER: Well, get some.

ASSISTANT: We can't get much.

MANAGER: How much?

ASSISTANT: Two.

MANAGER: Well, get them!

SHOPPER #3: Do you carry that delicious Pure 1 chicken?

MANAGER: We're expecting a shipment tomorrow (Figure 20-10).

The commercial has no big stars. There is nothing more involved than a typical supermarket setting and five people (who could be local playhouse or agency talent). This modest commercial cost approximately $20,000 to produce. Six months after its initial introduction, the Pure 1 name had achieved a 90 percent recall in the Boston area. Could a $100,000 production have improved on that?

The Buck Stops Here

Copywriters lean heavily on other people to bring their ideas to a successful conclusion. The television experts from the ad agency are the account

1. We are behind the meat counter with the meat manager. Two ladies in rapid succession ask him how soon the Pure 1 chicken is coming in.

    Meat Manager: We're temporarily out of stock.

2. Meat
    Manager: (Turns to his flunky behind him, loud whisper)

        "What's Pure 1?"

    Flunky: I don't know.

5. Man: Where's the Pure 1 chicken?

    Meat
    Manager: It's on order, Sir.

6. Flunky: We can't get much!

    Meat
    Manager: How much?

    Flunky: Two!

    Meat
    Manager: Well, get them!

FIGURE 20-10

A creative commercial need not be expensive. The total cost for this production featuring five people and a supermarket as a backdrop was approximately $20,000. (Courtesy Marvin & Leonard Advertising Company.)

3. Lady #3: How soon is Pure 1 coming in?

    Meat
    Manager: We're working on it.

4. Flunky: It's a new kind of chicken.

    Meat
    Manager: Well, get some!

7. Lady #4: Do you carry that terrific Pure 1 chicken?

    Meat
    Manager: We're expecting a shipment tomorrow.

8. Anncr: Pure 1 chicken. You'll find it delicious . . .

    if you can find it.

executive and the television producer. From the production house come director, assistant director, camera crew, sound crew, electrician, set designer, makeup crew, and hair stylist. If it's a food product, add a home economist. Yet copywriters must never forget that *they* are the architects of the commercial. They, better than anyone, know exactly what went into the commercial and why, and therefore they cannot reassign responsibility. Sometimes directors and camera crews deviate from the primary intent of the creators. When this happens, copywriters must insist on the original. The client accepted and approved the original, and that is what the client should get.

THE RADIO COMMERCIAL

Radio poses special writing problems. It depends on the human voice. It has no pictures to attract attention. Also, there are often many radio stations per market, in contrast to the two to three television stations per market. Thus, radio stations individually have smaller audiences than individual television stations.

But radio has advantages. The major one is that copywriters can set the location of the commercial anywhere in the world without once leaving the recording studio or causing elaborate sets to be built. The stage can be under the ocean, at the Taj Mahal, even on the moon. Another advantage is that copywriters can suggest probable or even improbable situations to prove a sales point. In short, radio copywriters often rely on their ability to stimulate the imagination of their listening audiences.

How do they do it? One method is to describe common, everyday experiences. For example, copywriters can assume that most people dislike traffic jams, that many men and women are interested in keeping fit. There are other shared experiences that copywriters have in common with the rest of the population. The copywriters' job is to find some experience that somehow relates to the product or service they are selling.

Copywriters also gain attention through humor and music. As on television, humor needs to be used judiciously. Does the humor add to or subtract from the message? Is it appropriate? Music, of course, is what radio is all about. There is always the opportunity to tailor the "sound" to a specific listening audience. In fact, one Helene Curtis' Everynight Shampoo commercial set the same jingle to fourteen different musical styles in order to satisfy a wide variety of musical tastes. National advertisers will quite often go after radio's fragmented audiences by adapting their musical commercials to each station's musical format: rock, country-western, middle-of-the-road, and so on.

A third attention-getting technique for radio copywriters is simply to make a statement that benefits listeners. Here's a hypothetical example: "Home owners who visit the Yes Bank this week can get a free place setting of silverware."

Of course, radio ads depend heavily on the sincerity of the announcer and on repetition of message and key points. The most effective presenters have voices that inspire confidence within the fifteen, thirty, or sixty seconds available.

To heighten listener recall, copywriters should simplify commercials by repeating the product or store name several times, repeating the major point of the copy platform, and avoiding too many details.

Here's how a local Sears commercial did it for its Kenmore microwave oven:

> Save time . . . energy . . . and $70 with a microwave oven from Sears. A Kenmore microwave oven . . . regular $549.95 is now on sale for only $479.95. Choose any power setting from 60 to 600 watts. Use low levels for delicate foods or increase the power for fast cooking. Sale ends September 29. Ask about Sears credit plans. That's Sears, Roebuck and Co., Ft. Dodge.

One trademark of a Sears commercial at the local level is the headline, which usually includes news of a sale, news of a price reduction, and the name of the store. Although it may seem like formula copywriting, these elements do give Sears' commercials an up-to-the-minute flavor.

Writing headlines for radio is very similar to writing them for the print media. The same three headline types occur: benefit, news, and curiosity. However, in radio, copywriters make certain that headlines sound like actual speech. Here are some hypothetical examples:

> "Hi, I'm your friendly Handi-Sweep Man. We're just about to visit the Handi-Sweep factory to find out about our annual broom sale. . . ."

> "Check the paint on your house. Is it peeling? Peeling paint can be pretty costly, as you know. Well, here at . . ."

People don't usually speak in polished sentences. They use fragments and phrases as well as contractions. They make noises expressing pleasure—"great," "terrific"—or disappointment—"doggone" or even a clicking of the tongue. People also generally use simple, easy-to-pronounce words. These are important lessons for copywriters to learn and absorb as they write advertising meant for the ear alone.

"Twelve Full Ounces, That's a Lot"

Ever since the musical jingle "Pepsi-Cola hits the spot, twelve full ounces, that's a lot" came winging over the airwaves well over thirty years ago, the rush has been on for advertisers to develop their own jingles,. Now seemingly every financial institution, insurance company, and grocery store boasts a musical identification. Most are simply bad—bad music, bad instrumentation, bad lyrics. But the bad ones make the good ones all that more outstanding. If bouquets were passed out for the best, one would have to go to Ajax.

GROUP: Use Ajax,

BASS VOICE: Bum-bum . . .

GROUP: the foaming cleanser,

BASS VOICE: Ba-ba-ba-ba-ba-ba-bum . . .

GROUP: wipes off stains just like a whiz,

BASS VOICE: Ba-ba-ba-ba-ba-ba-bum . . .

GROUP: no hard rubbing—just relax, there's a white, bright bleach in Ajax!
So use Ajax,

BASS VOICE: Bum-bum . . .

GROUP: the foaming cleanser,

BASS VOICE: Ba-ba-ba-ba-ba-bum-bum . . .

GROUP: floats grease and stains right down the drain.

BASS VOICE: Ba-ba-ba-ba-ba-ba-bum![8]

Along with memorable music and lyrics, copywriters can use sound effects in radio commercials. Copywriters should feel free to use effects to establish a locale, strengthen a mood, interpret some type of action, heighten tension, and even bridge time gaps. Sound effects can reduce the number of words needed in a commercial, and words consume time. (There are approximately 130 words in a sixty-second commercial.) Sounds are often more effective than words at developing an emotional response, because we associate sounds with past experiences.

Here are a few ways sounds interpret action for an audience listening to some hypothetical radio commercials:

Message	Sound effects
Here we are in deepest Africa testing SIMPLO WATCHES	DRUMS, ANIMAL SCREAMS
Wienerschnitzel Wine began life in seven-teenth-century Bavaria	STRAINS OF A MINUET
Parents! When your child spends the night coughing . . .	HACKING COUGH
Listen! The Tornado is back in town.	SQUEAK AND CLACKING OF ROLLER COASTER, PEOPLE SCREAMING

Producing the Radio Commercial

Like television, radio has a scripting format of its own: a single sheet of paper on which writers type their sales messages double spaced and in capital letters. They indicate music and sound "cues" in parenthetical descriptions. In essence, this is the instrument advertisers see unless the creator presents a rough tape production of the script. Once the script has been approved by the

[8] ©1950 Colgate-Palmolive Company. Words and music by Joe Rines. ASCAP.

Iowa Sports & Vacation Show

FACT SHEET

TITLE: 37th Annual IOWA SPORTS, BOAT & VACATION SHOW

DATES: March 20 thru 25, 1979 (six days, Tuesday thru Sunday)

LOCATION: Veterans Memorial Auditorium, Des Moines, Iowa

PRODUCER: United Sports & Vacation Shows, Saint Paul, Minnesota

OPEN
TO THE PUBLIC: Tue., Wed., Thur.: 4pm-10:30pm, Stage Show at 8:30pm
(Exhibits/   Fri.: 1pm-10:30pm, Stage Shows at 3:30 and 8:30pm
Stage Shows)   Sat.: 11am-10:30pm, Stage Shows at 1:00, 4:30 and
                       8:30pm
                 Sun.: 11am-6pm, Stage Shows at 2:30 and 5:00pm

TICKETS: Adults, $2.50; children under 12, 75¢.
                Tickets on sale at Auditorium box offices
                (both levels) during hours of show.

EXHIBITS: Everything needed for a family vacation in 1979!

                Dozens of displays for the travel-minded all manned
                by experts eager to supply advice and money-saving
                tips.

                • resorts
                • fly-in fishing lodges
                • summer camps
                • campsites and attractions from the continent's
                  most inviting recreational areas -- from
                  Arkansas, Illinois, Iowa, Kentucky, Louisiana,
                  Manitoba, Michigan, Minnesota, Missouri,
                  Northwest Territories, Oklahoma, Ontario, South
                  Dakota, Texas and Wisconsin

                Dazzling fleets including:

                • sailboats
                • cruisers
                • runabouts
                • canoes
                • houseboats
                • fishing boats
                • new models of outboard motors

The finest 1979 recreational vehicles:

• motor homes
• mini-homes
• 5th wheel trailers
• camping trailers
• ATVs
• mopeds

And more:

• sporting goods
• fishing tackle
• camping equipment
• guns
• taxidermy
• and many new products

THE
ENTERTAINMENT: A fast-moving, 60-minute package of aerialists,
                music, animals, acrobats and pure fun featuring:

                • THE FLYING LANES, the most exciting trapeze
                  act performing today
                • LIFE, ten talented, dynamic, young people in
                  a whirlwind of musical harmony
                • TED DEVLIN, Iowa's favorite fisherman
                • THE ROLLING DIAMONDS, show-stopping skaters
                • RAY SOMMERS' SPORTING DOGS, magnificent
                  pointers and retrievers working on land and
                  in the water
                • MISS DIAI , an amazing demonstration of
                  foot-juggling
                • the rowdy, riotous NORTHWOODS CANOE TILTERS
                • BILL BROWN, "The Voice of the Sports Show"
                • and KARL KILLINGER and his fine orchestra

FOR
FURTHER
INFORMATION: Contact Joan or Martin Kelly, United Sports &
                Vacation Shows, First National Bank Building,
                Saint Paul, Minnesota 55101, 612/222-8695.

                Or March 19 thru 25, contact Bill Brown, Sports
                Show Office, Veterans Auditorium, Des Moines,
                Iowa 50309, 515/280-3027.

                Or Louie Laurent/Steve DeGrasse, Wesley Day Advertising,
                Suite 606, 717 Mulberry, Des Moines, Iowa 50309,
                515/243-4135.

FIGURE 20-11
Occasionally, informational fact sheets are sent to radio stations in lieu of finished commercial scripts. The fact sheet permits the presenter to create a more personalized, impromptu commercial.

client, it goes back to the ad agency. At that point, the agency decides either to produce it in-house or send it out to a package house. In either case, the commercials end up as tapes, records, or cassettes ready for shipment to all the radio stations on the "buy" schedule.

There is also a third possibility. The agency may want to hire certain radio station personalities to present their client's message live. The advantage here is that the presenter injects his or her mannerisms into the commercial. Arthur Godfrey was a superb salesman for almost every product he presented live over the airwaves because of his reputation for honesty and candor. If the agency decides on live commercials, it will send scripts to all the appropriate stations. There is one danger in pursuing this course, however. Generally, during the course of local programming, radio personalities are extremely busy. They may be operating turntables, reading aloud, reading ahead to their next commentary, or coordinating upcoming commercials with the station's engineers. Under these circumstances, it is not at all unusual for them to read a commercial in a flat, hurried, insincere voice. To counter this possibility, some ad agencies send a fact sheet of product features to radio stations instead of a script. The fact sheet allows the local talent to pick and choose among the facts and in effect, to create an impromptu, highly credible commercial (Figure 20-11).

No matter how audiences hear commercials—live or canned—*they* are the self-appointed critics of the content. If they are slow to get the message or uninterested in what copywriters have to say, they have the ultimate weapon. They can turn the dial and tune commercials out!

IN SUMMARY

1 Often the entertainment aspects of a television commercial overshadow the real message and produce poor audience recall of the advertiser. Copywriters should involve the viewer with the product in some way.

2 Before a copywriter and layout artist begin to work on a television commercial, they should agree to communicate a single idea through sight, sound, and movement.

3 The typical scenario format used by the copywriter is a single sheet of paper divided into vertical columns headed *Video* and *Audio*.

4 The storyboard created by the layout artist is a sort of comic-strip arrangement divided into frames. As a rule, the artist uses six to seven frames for a thirty-second commercial, twelve to fifteen for a sixty-second commercial. The copywriter and layout artist try to have video and audio say the same thing at the same time.

5 For printed screen messages, layout artists should keep to legible type styles.

6 With a great majority of families owning color television sets, color becomes another aspect of audience involvement. Color affects legibility.

7 Artists, copywriters, and production directors should think of the television screen as being similar to a page in a magazine. The eye glances first at the 10 o'clock position.

8 The most familiar scenario structures—creative techniques for telling a story—are these seven: on-camera spokesperson, demonstration, slice of life, problem-solution, humor, animation, and special effects.

9 In developing a scenario, the copywriter allows approximately five to seven seconds just to establish a change of scenes in the eyes and minds of viewers.

10 There are various ways to produce low-cost commercials. These include use of marionettes and puppets, trick photography and still photographs, and electronic changes in the size, shape, and position of people and products.

11 The major advantage radio copywriters have over writers for other media is that they can set the location anywhere in the world without actually having to build an expensive set or transport camera equipment and actors. Their ability to set the stage in the minds of their audiences allows them to stimulate listeners. One way they do this is to describe or relate to shared experiences common to writer and audience.

12 Radio copywriters gain attention through humor and music as well as through statements that suggest benefits.

13 Radio ads depend heavily on the sincerity of the announcer and on the repetition of the message and key points.

14 People don't normally speak in polished sentences but rather in fragments and phrases.

15 Outstanding musical jingles stand out against many of poorer quality and content. Jingle music needs to be memorable. Lyrics should emphasize the major selling point in good rhyme.

16 One way to reduce the number of descriptive words in a minute-long commercial (130 words) is to use sound effects.

CASE STUDY   Shooting Television Spots in Europe by Fred Siegfriedt, president, Fessel, Siegfriedt, & Moeller Advertising, Louisville

L.A. Frey & Sons, a New Orleans meat packer whose founder emigrated from Alsace to start a sausage and meat shop in New Orleans' French Quarter 110 years ago, agreed to a plan to send a television crew to four different countries for eight days of filming. The plan, which we proposed as Frey's agency, was to take Frey frankfurters back to Frankfurt, Germany; bologna to Bologna, Italy; wieners to Vienna, and ham to Copenhagen—for candid interviews with natives as they taste the American products and compare them with their own. . . .

The client and I made the preliminary trip to choose locations and test consumer response to the product. Our first obstacle was to bypass the regulations of Germany and Denmark, which prohibit the importation of United States meat. Many calls later, it was the agricultural attachés at the U.S. Embassy in each country who saved the project. They arranged for special permits, volunteered to receive and hold the meat, and provided the names of ad agencies or individuals who would be the local contacts. . . .

Five weeks and another set of meat samples later, I was back in Europe with an American announcer and film crew. My first contact, a German friend from World War II days, immediately grasped the concept and made suggestions: We could interview the village metzger (sausage maker) in his quaint shop, school boys at the soccer field, foresters in a nearby hunting lodge, and children having a cook-out at a youth hostel in an 800-year-old castle. The German friend made all the arrangements ensuring that all the people to be interviewed spoke English.

The United States agricultural attaché in Copenhagen suggested a food research laboratory which might be willing to run tests on Frey ham and give an honest comparison. The food research lab personnel gave the product a thoughtful testimonial, charging the standard hourly research rate for their on-camera performances. . . .

TALENT FEE IS EISENHOWER SILVER DOLLAR

We insisted, of course, on getting talent releases that were written in the local language. For talent fees, I took along a pocketful of Eisenhower silver dollars, "souvenirs of America." The interviewees were delighted and our budget was preserved.

Communist-controlled Bologna, Italy, was the final location, and potentially the most difficult one. On my preliminary trip, I arrived in Bologna on the first day of May, an international holiday for Communists. The town was shut down while clench-fisted workers paraded with red flags. Few people spoke English, and obtaining the required police permits would take months. The local ad agency contact assured me that he could handle everything. But the problems persisted when the crew came prepared to shoot. I arrived in the ad agency's offices to find that my letter had arrived only a day earlier and no one spoke English. I communicated my urgent shooting schedule in pidgin French and on my way out was trapped for over thirty minutes in a phone-booth-size elevator with three gesticulating, shouting Italians.

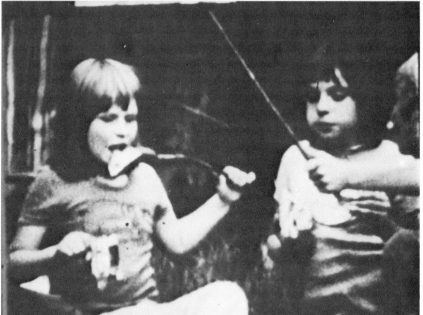

FIGURE 20-12

The intent of a unique series of television commercials was to ask bologna experts in Bologna, Italy, and frankfurter experts in Frankfurt, Germany, how American products compared with their own. The experts in these selected frames from two of a series of seven commercials happened to be a butcher in Bologna and a group of boys hosteling on the grounds of an 800-year-old castle in Germany, near Frankfurt.

That day we shot five commercials. The final touch of serendipity was learning that, although very few Italians speak English, the American announcer, John Pela of station WWL, New Orleans, had grown up in an Italian-speaking household. He handled the interviews in Italian, adding his own translation for the camera.

The production was handled by Asman-Todd Productions, a Louisville film house. After considering a European crew, we decided that Asman-Todd would not only be easier to communicate with, but less expensive. And they would be available for editing the footage as well.

The logistics of maneuvering seven people nearly 2,000 miles through Europe on a tight budget—of both time and money—held a large potential for trouble. Travel time as well as shooting time had been planned with no room for contingencies. Both came out perfectly. In two weeks, it never rained. There was no free time for sightseeing; we travelled from Louisville and back for $1,500 per person.

One reason the crew was able to adhere to the stringent shooting schedule was our insistence on credibility over technical perfection. We ended up after eight days of shooting with thirty-one very different and believable commercials (Figure 20-12).

QUESTIONS NEEDING ANSWERS

1 What do you think of the American ad agency's plan to use local ad agencies as contacts in each of the European cities?
2 If you were a copywriter assigned to the Frey meat commercials, which scenario-structure do you think would be most persuasive to American audiences? Why?
3 How would you have written the frankfurter commercial using the village sausage maker? Explain?

STUDENT PROJECT

The following radio commercial is one of a series of humorous creations selling a warehouse sale at a department store. Do you think it is an effective selling instrument? Explain in writing. Keep in mind that radio is a form of "theater of the mind," and so much of its effectiveness depends on voices, pacing, and sound effects.

BERT: And so, Shirley, welcome to the stenographic pool.

DICK: Thank you, sir.

BERT: Any questions?

DICK: Ah yes. May I be excused to go to Dayton's fabulous Warehouse sale?

BERT: Mr. Shirley, you've only been with the firm five minutes.

DICK: Well, I know, but Dayton's has this big sale.

BERT: No.

DICK: Appliances.

BERT: No

DICK: Furniture.

BERT: No. No. Just get to work, Shirley.

DICK: Right.

SFX: Door closing—BUZZ. BUZZ.

BERT: Yes, what?

DICK: Sir, I forgot my moth . . . my sister is getting . . . let's see married, so can I go to the . . .

BERT: No. No. No. No. You're going to Dayton's Warehouse Sale.

DICK: Oh great—thank you, sir.

BERT: Shirley, get to your shorthand.

DICK: Okay.

SFX: Door opens.

DICK: Ah, sir.

BERT: Yes.

DICK: I don't want to panic you or anything but I think an earthquake is due any second so could I possibly . . .

BERT: No.

DICK: RRRRR.

BERT: What now?

DICK: Oh, I think my appendix is back . . . oh my side.

BERT: Mr. Shirley, the only way you're going to get out of here to go to Dayton's fabulous Warehouse Sale is by being fired. Understand?

DICK: Yes sir.

BERT: Okay

DICK: Fathead.

BERT: You're fired.

DICK: Thank you. You won't regret this, sir.

(Courtesy of Grey Advertising, Inc.—Twin Cities, and Dayton's Department Stores).

THE CREATIVE CAMPAIGN

Update The company advertising manager and the ad agency account executive are responsible for planning the campaign. If, as someone once said, "love of *something* spurs creativity," then for these administrators, that something has to be a challenge—the challenge of making an obscure product a household word.

Webster calls a *campaign* a connected series of operations designed to bring about a particular result. An advertising campaign is just that. When The United States Treasury encourages you to "take stock in America—Buy U.S. Savings Bonds" in every ad it runs, it is following campaign strategy. Its ads are repeating the same message over and over in a variety of creative ways. Through sheer repetition, it achieves its major advertising objective (Figure

Bring home the bacon.

**Take stock in America.
Buy U.S. Savings Bonds.**

Winning Hand.

**Take stock in America.
Buy U.S. Savings Bonds.**

Feather your nest.

**Take stock in America.
Buy U.S. Savings Bonds.**

FIGURE 21-1
The "take stock in America" campaign theme is familiar to most Americans. We've seen the Treasury Department's ads for years. Overall, the message is simple—buy U.S. Savings Bonds—although from time to time, it resorts to cute techniques to attract attention. Media carry these campaign messages as a public service contribution.

21-1). On the other hand, a manufacturer who advertises hot dogs as "nutritious" one week and "fun food" the next is not producing a campaign.

Advertisers invest huge sums of money in campaigns. When Gillette opened its Trac II campaign, it allocated approximately $10 million for the first year's advertising. Succeeding years' budgets have been as high or higher. Considering that company money managers still look upon advertising as an "intangible asset," Gillette's investment is formidable. In many cases, the responsibility for this investment—no matter how large or small—lies with two administrators, the company advertising manager and the ad agency's account executive.

But their path is often thorny. They face both internal and external challenges. Inside the company, they are beset by rising prices of materials and labor, pressures for change in the product because of new technologies, and distribution realignments. Outside the company, they face competitive pricing strategies, new products, possible government regulations, the changing temperament of the mass market, and the innovations of other advertisers.

These administrators must know top management's objectives for a product or for the company before they can intelligently develop a campaign. In meeting specific company objectives, they must review consumption patterns of the total market (is the market growing or declining?), demographics of their audiences, present share of market and sales directions, media spending by most brands in their field, and major and minor selling points. Such a review produces hundreds of bits of information, from which the ad manager and account executive select what they consider the most meaningful and relevant—not necessarily what will lead to the cleverest ad campaign, but what will lead to the highest profits. During the evaluation period the administrators make their most critical decision. They decide on the product position.

POSITIONING

Positioning is an "against" strategy. Advertisers position their product for a particular job against competition. Volkswagen's Beetle positioned itself as a "small, low-cost, no-nonsense car" against plush American automobiles. The tourist department of Virginia positions the state as a "place for lovers" against those states that simply promote "relaxation, sports, and entertainment." Advertisers try to choose the position that will produce the best results over a period of time. They look for uniqueness of customer or of product.

When Burlington introduced a new men's sock with a built-in odor fighter (Biogard from Dow Chemical), it positioned it as a grooming and personal care essential. Freddie Laker positioned his group charter flights to London with, "Who says you can't get a reserved seat on my airline?" (Figure 21-2). Zayre, the retail general merchandise chain, positions itself around low prices: "Compare, you can't do better than Zayre!" (Figure 21-3). With the energy crisis, advertisers immediately repositioned their products: Firestone began a campaign showing how steel-belted radial tires can save gasoline. American Can Company's paper products division stressed backyard rather than away-from-home picnics and barbecues. Hefty Bags launched a "Backyard America Sweepstakes" (Figure 21-4). When Volvo's price went up, the Swedish manufacturer instructed its ad agency (Scali, McCabe, Sloves) to reposition the car as a luxury automobile. Previously, Volvo had been touted as a gas miser (Figures 21-5 and 21-6). Fortunately, for most creative staffs, most brand positions remain fairly consistent over time. If nothing else, a constant position is a matter of economy.

Richard Mercer, vice president and associate creative director of Batten, Barton, Durstine & Osborn (BBDO), a large multinational advertising agency, explained how his agency found a position for its client, Burger King. (The position was the slogan, "Have it your way," a reference to the fact that customers could now ask for their hamburgers prepared in different ways and not be forced to accept the standard fare.)

*Skytrain®
AIR PASSENGER SERVICE

FREDDIE LAKER MAKES NEWS AGAIN

"Now, the day you come to buy a ticket on Laker Skytrain Service, you'll get a ticket."

"We're delighted to tell you the latest development on our Skytrain Service to and from London. Thanks to Government Approval, the day you come to buy a ticket, you'll get a ticket and a confirmed seat on that day's flight. Or, if it's full, on the next available flight.

No disappointments or waiting.

Any one of our in-town offices will gladly sell you a ticket for our daily, spacious DC-10s. Every flight is staffed by multi-million-mile crews and eleven friendly cabin attendants. And you'll be assured a comfortable seat with

full in-flight services. You can buy hot meals, drinks, movies, stereo and duty-free goods, if you wish.

Don't stand by at any other airline. Surely, now Laker is your way to fly. The service is super and the price makes sense."

Sir Freddie Laker

Los Angeles to London $199
Return flight approx. $168

*Service Mark of Laker Airways, Ltd.
Diners Club, Master Charge, VISA, American Express

For up-to-the-hour seat availability call: (213) 646-9650
For complete information call: (213) 646-9600
Or see your travel agent.

Ticket sales locations:
L.A. International Airport, Int. Terminal 2
The Ambassador Hotel, 3400 Wilshire Blvd., L.A.
Disneyland Hotel, Travel Port, 1150 West Cerritos Ave., Anaheim
Van Nuys Flyaway Bus Terminal, 7610 Woodley Ave., Van Nuys
U.C.L.A. Travel Service, 308 Westwood Plaza, L.A.
Jet Exchange, 14513 East Whittier Blvd., Whittier

All offices open 4AM to 12 Noon. Airport office open 4AM to flight closing.

Laker AIRWAYS
The Scheduled Airline With A Difference—It's Cheaper!

FIGURE 21-2
"Who says you can't get a reserved seat on my airline?" is the price position Freddie Laker took for his low-cost group charter flights to London. (Courtesy Laker Airways Limited and Stiefel/Raymond Advertising, Inc.)

FIGURE 21-3

"Compare—you can't do better than Zayre," is the campaign position of this retail price discounter. A split-screen technique demonstrates the difference in prices paid by each shopper at different stores. Guess which one is the Zayre shopper. (Courtesy Ingalls Associates, Inc.)

FIGURE 21-4

Results of the Backyard America campaign over the previous year's campaign: volume increased substantially. Hefty used national print and television and Jonathan Winters as the presenter. (Courtesy Mobil Chemical Company.)

No matter which way you turn these days, you're bound to run into one of life's more unpleasant realities.

Which is why it pays to do your turning in a car that was designed to help you cope with them. The Volvo 164.

Latest government figures show the 164 gets about fifty percent more gas mileage than the most popular domestic cars in its price range. But not at the expense of spending the rest of your life in the right hand lane. Its aggressive 3-liter, fuel-injected engine is fast enough for any civilized man.

And should you run into an unending parade of cars and horns and unsightly billboards, you'll find the 164 a most congenial place to be. Its orthopedically-designed seats actually adjust to the needs of your spine. And such civilities as air-conditioning, power steering and leather are all standard equipment.

The Volvo 164

A CIVILIZED CAR BUILT FOR AN UNCIVILIZED WORLD.

When you run up against drivers less skillful than you, the 164 provides you with a staggering combination of safety features to call upon. Including a braking system we feel is one of the safest in the world.

To assist you in your struggle through big-city traffic, the 164 has a turning circle nearly as small as the Volkswagen Beetle's. A virtue you'll be particularly thankful for while tucking into one of those tight parking spaces other luxury cars are forced to pass by.

And if you glance at the picture above, you'll notice something else about the 164. It looks good. Just in case the going gets civilized.

VOLVO

© 1973 VOLVO OF AMERICA CORPORATION

FIGURE 21-5
Volvo's first introduction to the American market was as a gas miser (among other features).

LUXURY IS BUILT IN. NOT TACKED ON.

The luxury of a Volvo 164 isn't something you just see. It's something you feel. A sense of elegance that's not gaudily apparent. But very much real.

Inside, for example, there are no brocades or wood-grain veneers. Yet, in its own way, the interior of the 164 reeks of quality. You can smell the fine leather used to face the seats. And these seats are a luxury in themselves. Numerous automotive journals have pronounced them "among the most comfortable in the world."

On the dashboard, no fancy dials or gadgets. The only instrument you may be unfamiliar with is the tachometer. Which in the 164 bears watching. The three liter, fuel-injected engine is so smooth and quiet, the tachometer is sometimes the only way to tell if you're in second or fourth gear. (No extra charge for 4-speed manual with overdrive or automatic transmission.)

Exposed structural parts of the Volvo body are made of rustproof galvanized steel.

Rustproofing isn't just sprayed on. It's drawn into the metal with a powerful magnetic charge before Volvo receives its final exterior coats. The result is an exterior finish that surpasses any mere "paint job." Even the striking metallic finishes are included in the base price of the Volvo 164.

Its overall styling, like all the world's truly elegant cars, is if anything over understated. It cannot be confused with those so-called luxury cars whose arrival loudly proclaims, "dollars, dollars, dollars!"

The Volvo 164 simply states, "sense."

VOLVO 164

The luxury car for people who think.

© 1975 VOLVO OF AMERICA CORPORATION. LEASING AVAILABLE

FIGURE 21-6

Now Volvo has been repositioned as a luxury car. A major reposition poses a major creative challenge to the creative staff.

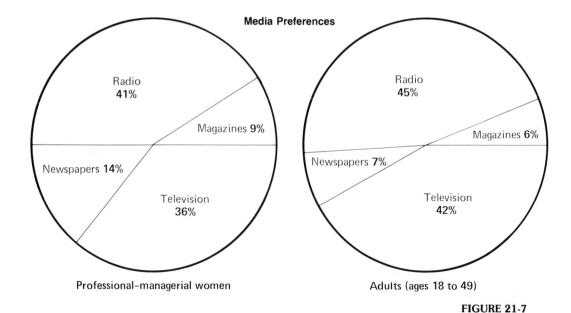

Media Preferences

Professional-managerial women

Radio 41%
Magazines 9%
Newspapers 14%
Television 36%

Adults (ages 18 to 49)

Radio 45%
Magazines 6%
Newspapers 7%
Television 42%

FIGURE 21-7

Media preferences also help in making positioning decisions.

"Problem Tracking"[1] clearly indicated that one of the most frequently occurring problems for fast-food customers (particularly our competitor's) was having to wait for special orders. . . . We learned . . . it would be well worth our while to advertise the fact that at Burger King you don't have to wait a long time for special orders. . . . We did concept tests—scores of them in key cities. . . . We did comparative studies among ourselves and our competitors. . . . Working together with all these inputs, Burger King's marketing people and BBDO's account group built a strategy and objectives, and we copywriters and art directors built some advertising. . . . We did many campaigns. . . . Then together Burger King and BBDO selected the one campaign which, according to all available evidence . . . best implemented the strategy.[2]

Positioning only makes economic sense if the target group or subgroup is large enough to justify a complete campaign (Figure 21-7). Because positioning can be expensive, deciding on it is an important management decision. Frequently, company officials, even the advertising administrators themselves, challenge a brand's established position. Should they continue with it? Should they alter its emphasis? Should they change it completely?

Administrators may argue for a position change if any or all of the following take place:

1 The position selected by a competitor is more successful than their own.

[1]"Problem Tracking" as invented by Batten, Barton, Durstine & Osborn (BBDO) is a research technique for determining the prime prospect's problems. It determines the frequency in which the problem occurs and whether the company can gain by advertising a solution to the problem.
[2]Speech given by Richard Mercer, "Burger King versus McDonald's," at Eastern Annual Conference of the AAAA, New York, November 19, 1974.

2 Total industry sales steadily decline.
3 Short- or long-term shortages force consumers to change their buying patterns.
4 Demographic changes cause consumption changes.
5 New technologies, new regulations, or new pricing suggest more exciting appeals.

Plan of Action

Having made the positioning decision, the advertising administrators develop a plan to guide the creative staff and media buyers. Generally, the plan includes advertising objectives, stated position, major selling points, budget, and hoped-for results. Here's how the Missouri-based Gardner Advertising Company, a large ad agency, set up its plan of action for Chuck Wagon dog food.

I General Creative Strategy

1 Advertising will convince consumers that Chuck Wagon is different from any other dry dog food because:

a It is a unique combination of three elements: red juicy chunks, golden crunchy nuggets, and rich savory broth.
b It is highly palatable and completely nutritious.

II New Creative Objectives

1 Maintain the highest interest, memorability, and involvement inherent in the brand's mnemonic (aid to memory) device, the miniature wagon.
2 Provide for a dramatic, meaningful, and unique product story. The primary theme is that Chuck Wagon is a highly palatable dog food *whether served wet or served dry*.
3 The target audience for Chuck Wagon continues to be defined as female heads of households in dog-owning households with an annual income of $10,000 plus.

III New Creative Strategy

1 Support for the new creative objectives will come from:

a the disclosure that Chuck Wagon (dry) will remain fresh and appetizing all day;
b the disclosure that Chuck Wagon (wet) is a unique combination of tender chunks and crunchy nuggets, all in a rich broth;
c the dog's obvious pleasure in the product (wet or dry).[3]

No two advertisers or ad agencies establish a plan of action in the same manner. Some plans, like the Chuck Wagon example, are terse and to the point. Others take the form of a comprehensive essay in which the advertiser states the strategic action plan in terms of the basic and secondary selling

[3]Gardner Advertising Company, "Chuck Wagon Campaign Strategy" statement.

arguments, the features and benefits of the product, and a concise definition of the target audience. The essential purpose of either kind of plan is the same, however. It's to stimulate the creative staff into developing the actual elements of the campaign.

THE IDEA PARADE

After studying the pertinent research on their consumer audience and product, the copywriters begin to develop the campaign. (For more on how copywriters work, see Chapter 18, "Creativity in Print Media Advertising: Copy.") There are a few popular ways to begin. Copywriters and artists believe that all ad layouts in a campaign should clearly resemble one another. Likewise, television storyboards should contain either an ongoing character such as Mr. Whipple (for Charmin) or Mrs. Olson (for Folger's Coffee), or a repeated claim such as "No single blade will do" for Gillette Trac II.

Copywriters may create a slogan that will better identify a position. Gillette's Trac II slogan does it very well, as does Burger King's "Have it your way." The copywriters ask questions: Do we use demonstrations for every ad? Is there one unique and simple way to get our position across? Shall we use illustrative art instead of the usual photography? Shall we use a corporate color? How about a new logo more in keeping with our new position? From these questions (and answers) the creative staff begins to shape concepts. The artists render countless thumbnail sketches. The copywriters doodle with headlines and dramatic ideas. From all this activity comes a campaign or two worth testing.

Meanwhile, these same people or others have also been at work on sales promotion and merchandising. If the campaign calls for a spokesperson such as Ol' Lonely (Maytag), for example, the copywriters and artists develop point-of-purchase retail-store displays and banners featuring the under-worked washer repairman. Sometimes a campaign requires informative booklets, films, samples, and coupons distributed through retailers, the newspapers, or the mail. The campaign may call for devising interesting sales meetings, audiovisual and trade promotions, direct mail to influence the sales force, publicity events, and so on. All these creative responses must reflect the general campaign theme.

While the creative staff has been at work, those charged with developing the media plan have been engrossed in matching the target audience with the most cost-effective media. The media planners also ask questions. Are the women we want to influence heavy magazine readers or heavy television viewers? Can we get spot-television availabilities in our top ten markets in prime time without shooting the budget? Is it wiser to spread our messages out over a year's time or concentrate on a quick media blitz? The answers to these and other questions end up in the media plan.

Finally, after the creative staff has finished and the media planners have submitted their detailed recommendations, the administrators tie it all together into a single, unified campaign. Some campaigns are relatively simple and may take less than a week to devise. Others may take months of hard work and a platoon of specialists.

Perpetuating the Campaign

Some advertisers change campaigns each year. There is never a second or third-generation look for them. They feel that the pressures of competition are such that they must change. Other campaigns roll along for years with essentially the same theme. It takes courage to stick with a theme when a company's competitors keep changing. Yet, if the company's analysis indicates that the campaign is effective and capable of warding off competitive assaults, why change? B. F. Goodrich has successfully used the same case history approach with big pictures and provocative headlines in its industrial advertising for over twenty-five years (Figure 21-8). It makes economic sense to continue with a successful campaign. Successful ads receive high readership and recall. They effectively meet consumer wants. And it's cheaper to continue a campaign in motion than to start all over again. Unfortunately, advertisers may push to change campaigns more in response to what competitors are doing than to the effectiveness of the established campaign. Schlitz abandoned its highly memorable research-backed "gusto" campaign aimed at the heavy beer drinkers to woo a wider audience. When the new campaign failed, Schlitz reinstituted its "gusto" theme only to discover that Miller High Life had initiated its own powerfully supported "macho" theme. Now both brewers are chasing the heavy beer drinkers.

Occasionally advertisers will introduce a campaign that appears to have all the elements of success and yet falls somewhat short of management's expectations. In these instances, it may be necessary to rework the strategy, maintaining what is effective and discarding the rest. To the untrained eye, the campaigns appear to be the same, yet the new emphasis delivers improved results. Aerovent, a supplier of ventilation systems for poultry and livestock, went through such a campaign change. Its new advertising agency suggested that even though Aerovent was in the ventilation systems business, its ads feature fans. When the new ads featured systems, the respondents were now interested in tailored systems, not a simple fan. The new campaign had at last matched the company's selling strategy with its communications strategy (Figure 21-9).

ACCOUNTABILITY

Accountability is simply management's way of holding people responsible for how they spend company advertising money. Accountability procedures help take some of the guesswork out of determining the effectiveness of advertising.

We have all seen clever, interesting, and entertaining campaigns that

Rubber brakes—for runaway cases

A typical example of B. F. Goodrich improvement in rubber

Here's where glass used to break as cases of bottles slid downstairs from second floor to first. The metal chute is slippery, so there'd be runaways and collisions.

Someone thought of using a conveyor belt on part of the chute, to act as a brake to slow up the cases. Fine, except that all too soon the rough belt cover became worn and smooth. Then it could no longer grip the cases; more breakage, more mess to clean up.

Then a B. F. Goodrich distributor saw the belt and had an idea. B. F. Goodrich had just developed the Ribflex belt to move cartons, bags, packages up steep inclines. Why couldn't it carry things *down* just as safely? This new belt is made with parallel ribs that are cross cut into thousands of flexible grip blocks, soft so they bend just enough to grip anything carried by the belt, and so hold it firmly. Yet the rubber is so tough that these belts will keep their gripping power long after rough-surface belts become worn and ineffective.

Now when a case hits the Ribflex belt, it stops and then rides down—smoothly, safely at belt speed. And not one bottle has broken since the B. F. Goodrich belt was put on.

The Ribflex belt is typical of B. F. Goodrich research which is constantly at work improving all kinds of belting, hose and other rubber products and finding new ways to use them better. Don't decide any rubber product you may buy is the best to be had without first finding out from your BFG distributor what B. F. Goodrich research may have done recently to improve it. *The B. F. Goodrich Company, Dept. M-217, Akron 18, Ohio.*

B.F. Goodrich
INDUSTRIAL PRODUCTS DIVISION

Job No. E-3699
Time—April 26, 1954—M-217

Proof from The Griswold-Eshleman Co., Cleveland
Business Week—May 1, 1954—M-216   Factory—June, 1954—M-218

Final Proof—SBH—3-19-54
Mill and Factory—June, 1954—M-219

FIGURE 21-8
One of the more consistent of industrial campaigns is this 1954 ad. Strong headlines and large, interesting pictures have been B. F. Goodrich's trademark for twenty-five years.

FIGURE 21-9
Examples of
Aerovent's
advertising
evolution:
first-generation ads
illustrated fans;
second-generation
ads began to stress
the systems
approach to
handling air; and the
current-generation
ads illustrate a
sophisticated section
of a total system.
(Courtesy Aerovent
Fan & Equipment
Co.)

unfortunately were also failures. They failed because they did not fulfill their advertising objectives. If management's goal was to establish a 50 percent brand recognition, the campaign failed if it achieved anything less, regardless of circumstances.

Some companies, maybe even most, stress actual sales increases over meeting advertising goals in their accountability evaluations. But there are better ways to hold campaigns accountable. Business advertisers can look for increases in the volume of inquiries from certain desired Standard Industrial Classification Groups (SICs), companies, and industries. Retailers can measure the increase in the number of customers over the campaign period. Retail-store audits done by research firms *before, during*, and *after* a campaign also help to establish advertising accountability. "Image attribution" tests (in which people are surveyed about their deeply held feelings) can also help to point out shifts in public attitudes toward products, brands, and causes.[4] Then there are readership studies, Arbitron and Nielsen Television and Radio ratings, inquiries, sales force reports on reactions of retailers and distributors, and finally, reaction from competitors. When advertisers notice that some of their copy platform starts to creep into the competition's ads, they can be sure they've touched a responsive chord.

INTRODUCING NEW PRODUCTS

The introduction of new products goes hand in hand with advertising campaigns because sooner or later the product will need planned, consistent, unified exposure. In fact, most observers of advertising become familiar with campaigns because they are almost synonymous with new product introductions. New products fuel business. For example, 75 percent of Procter & Gamble's sales volume of over $7 billion since World War II has come from new products. Each of these products has had a high-powered advertising campaign behind it. But most of these campaigns did not start out as a full-blown national operation. They began life, instead, as *test market* campaigns designed to find out whether they had the creative power to propel their products to success. A test market is a familiar and popular marketing tool used by consumer goods companies for determining the probable success of a product and its supporting advertising campaign within a restricted geographical area.

What makes a good test market? The theoretical answer is quite simple. A good test market is a city or region that is typical of many other cities and that contains the type of people who are prospects for a company's products.

---

[4] A New York research company, McCollum-Spielman, tested television viewers and discovered that a Chevron gasoline commercial persuaded 46 percent of the viewers to have a more favorable attitude toward the sponsor, an attitude shift more than three times as high as could normally be expected. Address by Harold M. Spielman, "The use of attitudinal measurements in the evaluation of television advertising," sixteenth Annual Advertising Research Conference, American Marketing Association, New York, May 16, 1978.

The purpose of a test market is to reduce risks. The intent is to tailor the new campaign so it is successful in several test markets. When it is successful, it goes national, thus considerably reducing the chances of a national (and expensive) fiasco.

Test cities should be independent of "fall out" or "spill off" from nearby cities or trading areas. They should be self-contained. Their economies should be stable. In other words, test marketers should avoid depressed as well as booming economies. They need a target city with: (a) typical consumers with average incomes[5], schooling, and family size, (b) isolated media sources, (c) sufficient retail outlets proportional to the number of such businesses in other cities (there should be enough stores available to the population should it decide to buy the test product), and (d) a large enough population to provide meaningful data.

Over the years, marketers have built a list of "safe" test market cities. The theory is that if the product and the advertising are effective there, they'll find acceptance everywhere. It doesn't always happen; however, enough companies have had success in these cities so that we feel free to list some of them:[6]

Minneapolis	Houston	Cincinnati
Atlanta	Milwaukee	Columbus (Ohio)
Buffalo	Kansas City	Spokane
Indianapolis	Memphis	Denver
Tampa-St. Petersburg	Salt Lake City	Phoenix
Seattle	Portland (Oregon)	
Nashville	Albany	

New product campaigns strain the creative team. In addition to a memorable, hard-selling campaign, the team is expected to include "immunity" to competition. Getting from product conception to sale in the marketplace once took many years: thirty for the zipper, sixteen for the automatic transmission. The pioneering company had years to earn back its large investment. It's different today. The ballpoint pen went from idea to market in just seven years, the videotape recorder in six years, the instant camera in only two years. No sooner were these products on the market (patents notwithstanding) than competitors appeared. Some companies, like Bic with its disposable butane lighters and ballpoint pens, wait for others to develop a market before they enter it, generally with similar products at lower prices. Blessed with a good product, a memorable campaign, and the necessary ad dollars, competitors and imitators can easily catch up with and even surpass pioneers.

[5]"Average" is defined as being typical of most of the people in the country.
[6]"Arbitron ADI Test Market Guide, 1977.

SOME CREATIVE CAMPAIGNS

Not all effective campaigns are expensive. In fact, success is all the sweeter when a low-cost campaign meets its objectives despite the presence of a better-financed competitor. Here are some examples of modest-budget campaign creativity. They are not all that unusual. You can find similar examples in almost every city.

Land O'Lakes Felco Recently Felco, a division of Land O'Lakes farmers cooperative, ran one of its typical glove sale promotions aimed at its co-op branch managers. Objectives: (1) To increase glove sales by 10 percent over the Fall & Winter Sale; (2) To increase the number of accounts on the primary glove mailing list (accounts having ordered in the past year); (3) to establish direct mail as a viable means for Land O'Lakes to sell gloves on the wholesale level. Strategies: (1) Develop a theme or artwork where all direct mail pieces tie in together to establish continuity; (2) Develop an easy-to-order catalog where discounts are easily seen; (3) Develop at least three flyers to be sent out every other week to the complete mailing list. Results: Sold 2,406 dozen ($58,000) or 34 percent over established goal. Expenses were $2,149 or 3.7 percent of sales. Another plus: many accounts ordered gloves that had never ordered them before from the company. (The theme "Booking Spring and Summer Glove Needs at a Great Price," was based on the knowledge that a well-stocked farm store will push ample supplies of what it has on its shelves and bins.)

Wisconsin Gas Using the old ant-and-the-grasshopper fable, the creative people at Wisconsin Gas and its ad agency came up with a memorable newspaper campaign. The ad manager for the Milwaukee-based utility, explained the reasoning behind the campaign theme: "When times are good, we tend to act like the grasshopper; when hard times arrive (like an energy crisis) we try and follow the example of the ant, busily preparing for what's ahead. Sometimes, it's too late. The tale of the ant and the grasshopper was tailored to the story we wanted to tell. . . . Newspapers were chosen as our prime medium because we needed a day-to-day message. . . . We placed large color cutouts of these two characters in our main offices and offered energy conservation booklets to our customers for the asking. So we were able to carry the story theme for an entire year."[7] The campaign cost $35,000 (Figure 21-10).

Qwip Systems Qwip facsimile machines enable the transmission of "hard copy"—words and pictures—over ordinary telephone lines.

While facsimile products have been on the market for years, it was unknown to most businesspeople—and also expensive to those who were aware of facsimile.

Qwip Systems came into being in 1974 after Richard L. Nelson invented a simple, efficient, and low-cost machine, which made possible the expanded use of facsimile by businesses of all sizes.

In 1977 Qwip Systems was ready to proceed with a national advertising

---

[7]"An Energy Conservation Story," *Business Building Bulletin*, May 1976, (No. 575).

Seven warm ideas for winter's coldest days.

Clean, natural gas heat is the most economical way to heat your home. Stretch your heating dollar further by using these tips from our industrious ant.

1. Change or clean furnace filters each month. **2.** Don't block heating registers or cold air returns with furniture or draperies. **3.** On sunny days, let the sun shine in. When it isn't shining, close draperies for added insulation. **4.** Close off unused rooms and shut the heating registers in those rooms. **5.** Close the damper on your fireplace when it's not in use. On very cold winter days, more warm air goes up the chimney than the fire gives off. **6.** Set your thermostat at the lowest comfortable temperature during the day and 5 degrees lower at night. For every degree over 70, heating costs increase approximately 3%. **7.** A humidifier will make your house feel warmer at lower temperatures.

Don't fiddle away precious gas energy or money like the silly grasshopper. Conserve and save like the industrious ant.

For more tips, write to your nearest Wisconsin Gas Company office for a free copy of our energy conservation story.

WISCONSIN GAS

Natural Gas is *Pure* Energy . . . Conserve it!

Wasting hot water is money down the drain.

You save fuel and money when you conserve hot water. Next to your furnace, your water heater is one of the largest users of energy in your home. It accounts for approximately 15% of your fuel bill.

HERE ARE FIVE TIPS FROM OUR INDUSTRIOUS ANT TO HELP YOU USE HOT WATER EFFICIENTLY.

1. Set your water heater thermostat between 140°-160°. A higher setting only wastes energy and increases your bill. **2.** Fix leaking faucets. A leaking faucet that fills a coffee cup in 10 minutes wastes 3,280 gallons of water a year. **3.** Take quick showers. **4.** Have a full load in your washer and dishwasher before you start the wash cycle. **5.** Take care of your water heater. Several times a year, drain a pail or two of water from the faucet near the bottom of the unit. This removes sediment and deposits that make your water heater work harder and waste fuel and money.

Don't fiddle money down the drain like the silly grasshopper. *Conserve* and *save money* like the industrious ant.

For more tips, write to your nearest Wisconsin Gas Company office for a free copy of our energy conservation story.

WISCONSIN GAS

Natural Gas is *Pure* Energy . . . Conserve it!

FIGURE 21-10
A utility uses the ant and grasshopper fable to convince Wisconsinites to imitate the industrious ant. The campaign also included small teaser ads with energy-saving tips from the busy ant.

campaign. The product had many unique selling features, such as low price, portability, and repair by replacement. But Qwip was beset by two problems:

1 The unorthodox spelling of the Qwip name hampered selling efforts and impeded the development of brand awareness.
2 There was confusion between the odd name Qwip and the petroleum-associated brand Exxon, its parent company. Sales reps found that they were confusing prospects by talking about Exxon . . . or by trying to explain the Qwip name.

Advertising man George Lois came up with a print campaign, using black and white ads with provocative headlines that took the "Qw" problem and turned it into a selling advantage.

Theme of the campaign was "Qwip qwazy." Ads were headlined: "America's sanest offices are going Qwip qwazy" . . . "Are you qwazy? Don't mail it. Use the Qwip." The phrase "Qwip qwazy" appeared in all ads as well as in collateral materials—lapel buttons, bumper stickers, T-shirts, mailing pieces.

The campaign ran for five months. Budget was $150,000. It successfully

"Some seqwitaries are better equipped than others!"

If you work in an office _not_ equipped with Qwip,® you should have no qwalms about qwickly inqwiring "Why not?"

Qwip is an incredibly simple machine that sends letters and practically anything else you can put down on paper (including pictures) right over the telephone. It's the simple, qwick way to get a message safely in someone's hands—just as written. With desk-to-desk delivery— crosstown or cross country—in four minutes flat.

So your boss is able to rush out all those urgent things people wanted yesterday. Like estimates, orders and invoices. Statements. Designs. Corrections on balance sheets, blueprints and manuscripts. Not to mention all those last minute letters.

Incidentally, you might also mention to your boss that while there may be other machines that work like Qwip, none have its exclusive features or its low, low rental (as little as $29 a month).

Why be an ordinary secretary when, with Qwip, you can be the best equipped seqwitary in the city!

Call Toll Free (800) 221-2222
In New York State (212) 398-5151   Or send coupon

A qwote from Qwentin Qwibble
"Miss Qwinn—it's qwazy to mail it, or fwy it, or desqwibe it. Use Qwip!"

Qwip SYSTEMS   DD
Division of **EXON** Enterprises Inc.
1270 Avenue of the Americas, New York, N.Y. 10020

○ Please have a Qwip representative
   visit me without obligation.
○ Please send me more information.

Name _____

Title _____

Company _____

Street _____ City _____

State _____ Zip _____ Tel. _____

Qwip is a trademark of **EXON** Corporation

FIGURE 21-11
Playing on words, Qwip sets its sights on the small-business market. George Lois, famed advertising innovator, set the stage for the campaign.

enabled Qwip salespeople to overcome the brand-name confusion of product and launched Qwip on the road to brand dominance of the facsimile field (Figure 21-11).

Manufactured Housing Institute   The message that this association carried to the American people was that "Livin's easier in a mobile home." Working through the Mobile Home Dealers National Association, the manufacturers created a complete promotional package for every dealer within the organization. The package included, among other things: customer handout fact cards, table tents, posters, bumper stickers, pens, key chains, mobile home buyer's guides, balloons, buttons, pennants, door mats, and matchbooks. Supporting the entire effort, the manufacturers' association created a short, public-interest nature film for television showing. The campaign cost for this first unified industry drive was approximately $180,000 (Figure 21-12).

Amchem Products   In structuring an ad campaign for Ethrel, an applied chemical plant regulator, Lewis & Gilman, a Philadelphia-based ad agency, positioned the new agricultural product to work on three major crops: tomatoes, apples, and cherries. The agency's research department studied the major crops and concluded that small pockets of consumers are located in diverse geographical areas, and that crop production practices for the same crop differ by geographical area. Ethrel's campaign included direct mail, publicity, print ads, and audiovisual materials (eight separate grower films to be used in meetings with farmers). The agency scheduled a series of visits between the Ethrel product manager and leading environmental writers in California.[8] To eliminate any possibility of adverse environmental sentiment before Ethrel advocates could tell its story, the company previewed its audiovisual materials before the agricultural subcommittee of the California state legislature. Introductory ads were full-color, two-page spreads in key grower publications. Ad emphasis was on efficient harvesting and premium crops.

At campaign's end, twenty-eight feature stories had appeared in leading grower journals. Ethrel became the dominant product in the growth regulator field. Sales goals were met for number of acres treated. Awareness among Ethrel users and nonusers was above 90 percent.

In the early stages of the Ethrel introduction, the agency and Amchem ad officials sought out key innovators among growers of the major crops. They were asked to experiment with the product under the supervision of Amchem's technical staff. The agency then used actual testimonials from these innovators to tell the Ethrel story around the country. Some statements from key growers: "It's the most exciting thing since the cannery tomato!" "Ethrel saved the field." "We'd pay $100 a gallon for it rather than do without it" (Figure 21-13). The campaign cost approximately $250,000.

J. Homestock   A small furniture chain, J. Homestock introduced itself to New England and the Middle Atlantic States with an ad showing a tiny Volkswagen with a household of merchandise strapped to its roof. Since that

---

[8]"Building a winning campaign for Amchem," *New Agriculture*, Fall 1976, pp. 9–13.

items

Description	Item No.	Lot Quantity	Price	Suggested Application
Fact Card — Handy pocket-size card with 9 Livin's Easier mobile home features	1A 1B 1C	200 400 1,000	$2.50 4.00 8.50	Let the FACTS sell mobile home living. Use as a customer handout, mailing stuffer or sales tool for your personnel.
Table Tents — 5 Attractive 2-sided table top displays. Highlighting 5 outstanding home benefits.	2	100 Assorted	3.85	Sell the benefits of mobile home living. These will point out *specific* features in your home.
17 x 22 Poster — Theme poster to accentuate 4 "Reasons to Purchase."	3	20	1.95	Place on window or wall to sell the advantages of mobile home living.
8½ x 22 Poster — Vertical Theme Poster (with pricing space).	4	20	1.45	Window or wall poster designed to instill in customer's mind that Livin's Easier in a Mobile Home.
22 x 8½ Poster — Horizontal Theme Poster	5	20	1.45	Window or wall poster designed to instill in customer's mind that Livin's Easier in a Mobile Home.
17 x 11 Hanger Poster — Horizontal over-wire hanger type poster	6	20	1.95	A constant reminder that Livin's Easier in a Mobile Home in your office, showroom, and service department.
Bumper Stickers — Theme Bumper Sticker (removable adhesive).	7A 7B 7C	100 300 500	3.85 9.55 15.25	Every vehicle in your organization should sport one and your customers will love 'em.

FIGURE 21-12

Highlighting outstanding benefits of owning a mobile home, this brochure helped to launch the first unified industry campaign for The Manufactured Housing Institute.

time, trendy advertising has played a role in appealing to the more affluent shoppers, among them the eighteen-to-thirty-five-year-old set. The Boston ad agency (Marvin & Leonard) explained the campaign this way: "Quite simply, we let the merchandise itself carry the store message. The ads are purposely designed that way. There are no brassy headlines, no fantastic statements, just clean, uncluttered sketches, right-to-the-point copy, and, of course, bold price points. The positioning itself is a problem for a store that carries full lines of virtually every style and taste and price of furniture and accessories. Therefore, the decision was to present a little bit of the store in each ad! Each ad carries the repetitive slogan, 'A surprisingly intelligent place to buy furniture' "[9] (Figure 21-14). The campaign costs per year are approximately 5 to 7 percent of sales.

If there is a common ground in all these successful campaigns, it's the

[9]"J. Homestock: Trendy ads build consumer base," *Business Building Bulletin*, Oct. 1977, (No. 592).

FIGURE 21-13

This Ethrel brochure was designed specifically to influence a major crop-grower audience. The company had earlier solicited innovative farmers to test its new product. These farmers later became testimonial givers and provided a big boost to the new product campaign.

advertisers' dependence on research. The Land O'Lakes Felco research pointed up the fact that managers with heavy inventories will push the sales of these items; Wisconsin Gas' information revealed that the average citizen was still unconvinced of an energy shortage; Qwip took advantage of competitors' weaknesses after it learned about them; the Manufactured Housing Institute knew of its own industry voices often working at cross-purposes and attempted to unify them; and Amchem's research discovered that crop production practices for the same crop differed by geographical region. Armed with knowledge, each of these companies was able to develop campaigns that made sense to target audiences. Without current knowledge of the marketplace, and the application of effective strategy, advertisers' campaigns risk failure no matter how brilliant the art and copy.

607
THE
CREATIVE
CAMPAIGN

IN SUMMARY

1 An ad campaign is a series of ads that repeat one basic message.

2 Supervision of the company's investment in advertising is the responsibility of the

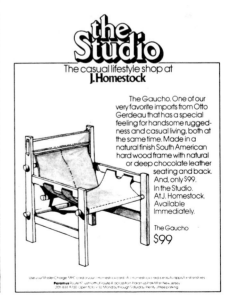

FIGURE 21-14
Trendy advertising using clean-cut line drawings and pointed copy attracted consumers in the New England Area to J. Homestock. The layouts all resemble one another.

company advertising manager and/or the ad agency account executive.

3   Positioning is an "against" strategy that ad administrators choose for a product in order to have a unique selling point and to produce maximum profits.

4   Whether to switch a position can be a difficult decision. A decision to change results from any of the following reasons: a competitor's position is better; product sales for the entire industry are declining; consumption patterns are changing because of shortages or changes in the population; and new technologies either improve the product or lower the price.

5   After deciding on the product's position, the advertising administrators develop a plan of action to present to their creative staffs. The plan includes the advertising objectives, the position, major selling points, the budget, and the hoped-for results.

6   Some campaigns run only for one year; others last for many. Those that change every year do so under the pressure of competition. Yet it makes economic sense to continue with a successful campaign.

7   Accountability is management's way of holding the advertising administrators responsible for the way they spend the company's advertising monies.

8   Some ways to determine the accountability of a campaign are the number of inquiries, customer traffic in retail stores, retail store audits, "image attribution" tests, readership studies, television and radio ratings, sales force reports, reactions of competitors, and relative sales performances. The latter is the easiest way of all, but it's not fair to the advertising staff because other marketing factors such as distribution, pricing, and the product itself may affect sales.

9   Advertising campaigns and the introduction of new products go hand in hand because sooner or later products need campaigns for public exposure.

10   The purpose of a test market is to reduce the risks of introducing a new product.

11   A good test market city has representative populations, isolated media sources, enough retail outlets for marketing the product, and enough people for the data to be significant. Consumers in the test market city should have average incomes, schooling, and family size.

12   Not all successful campaigns cost a lot of money.

CASE STUDY   Fighting the Fuel Crisis: The Homefoamers

Scientific Applications, Incorporated, is the parent company of the nation's largest network of foam insulation specialists, the Homefoamers. Begun in Iowa in 1971, the members of the Homefoamer network now reach from coast to coast, thanks to an unconventional insulating material, the energy shortage, and management's decision to employ advertising to grow.

First, the product. The foam, a urea formaldehyde resin and foaming agent, with an extremely high insulation value per cubic inch, is pumped into the sidewalls of a structure, where it flows around obstructions into cracks and crevices where heat would normally escape. Once in place, the foam delivers a substantial fuel saving. Scientific's first step toward success was to develop a network of dealers, called Homefoamers, to distribute and install its foam. Initially, the company made a bid for the retail market in seventeen Midwestern states in 1974. It solicited dealers by advertising in business

FIGURE 21-15

Recognizing that its success depended on aiding its 750 dealers nationwide, Homefoamers provided them with local newspaper ads, promotional booklets, and clever doorknob hangers.

ALL RIGHT, OWENS-CORNING.

WE BET YOU $100,000.00 THAT WE CAN INSULATE SIDEWALLS BETTER THAN YOU CAN.

There has been a lot of controversy and confusion about the value of your kind of insulation vs. our kind of insulation. So, we're asking you to put your money where your insulation is. Let's build 2 identical houses and insulate the walls of one with your product, and the walls of the other with ours. We'll even put your fine product in the attic of both houses because that's where we think it belongs. Then we'll see how much fuel both houses consume for a whole year.

We're betting $100,000.00 that the house we insulate will use less fuel than the house you insulate.

Anxiously awaiting your reply,

America's largest network of foam insulation specialists

FIGURE 21-16
As the company expanded, it entered the new construction market with a dramatic challenge to a competitor.

publications such as *Roofing, Siding, Insulating; Qualified Remodeler; Professional Builder; Home Improvement Contractor; Multi-Housing News; Builder;* and *Professional Remodeling.* The selection and attention to its dealers have made Homefoamers' advertising and promotion successful. Each installer must complete a rigorous, intensive training course in the proper techniques of installing the foam and must be recertified annually. All Homefoamer dealers must adhere to Homefoamer standards. These include guidelines set forth by the U.S. Department of Housing and Urban Development as well as those developed by the company. These points are emphasized in the consumer advertising.

The company also offers its dealer network advertising assistance through a Communications Planner, a manual providing each dealer with camera-ready ads; storyboards for television spots; radio commercials; tips for direct-mail, billboard, and Yellow Page advertising; and programs for public relations and co-op advertising. Other aids include sales and management training tapes, visual presentation books of consumer installations, and sales literature (Figures 21-15).

By mid-1977, Scientific had expanded nationwide with over 750 dealers. In 1971, sales totaled $5,594; in 1976, sales topped $6 million. Its effective consumer advertising approach has been to take an educational approach to this product. The target market consists of homeowners twenty-eight to forty-eight years of age, with homes built between 1940 and 1965 and family income of $15,000 to $30,000 annually. Research showed that the consumer is aware of the severity of the energy situation; will insulate when the heating-cooling bill gets out of hand; is favorably disposed toward insulation; and does not think of foam as readily as fiberglass. The homeowner who has already made insulation additions is just as likely to be a prospective customer as one who has not. This research became the basis for ads that ran in the following publications: *U.S. News & World Report, Business Week, Better Homes and Gardens, Popular Mechanics, Mechanics Illustrated, Sunset, Popular Science, Southern Living, Progressive Farmer, Farm Journal.* Later on, the company and its dealer network began to seek out new construction and commercial projects, and its advertising reflects this change (Figure 21-16).

Leads generated from the company's national advertising effort are passed along to the dealers. Whenever the company senses the need, it will supplement its advertising to consumers with some network television spots, notably on "The Today Show" and "The Tonight Show." The carefully planned advertising and promotional campaigns have helped Homefoamers insulate over 250,000 homes in the brief time it's been in business.

QUESTIONS NEEDING ANSWERS

1 Would Homefoamers have made faster progress had it gone to national television spots in 1971 to advertise for dealers? Explain.
2 If you were a Homefoamer dealer in your home town, which advertising medium would you use? Why?
3 How would you go about building a mailing list of homes built between 1940 and 1965?
4 What do you think led to the creation of the ad slogan "Genuine homefoamer?"

STUDENT PROJECT

You, Franklin Meats, are a manufacturer of meat products. You make most of the standard packaged luncheon meats. Your plant is in the Phoenix-Tucson area. Here are the consumption figures for that region.

Product	Market potential (millions)	Percent of total market
Wieners	$11.1	31.6
Bacon	10.3	29.3
Sliced luncheon meat	7.8	22.2
Canned hams	3.1	8.8
Boneless hams	2.8	8.0
	$35.1	99.9

But you have company in this market: Oscar Mayer, Armour, Swift, Hormel, Jimmy Dean, Bob Evans, Wilson, Rath, Corn King. Oscar Mayer uses a lot of magazines—$5,548,000 a year; Armour likes Sunday supplements—$2,867,000; Swift likes point-of-purchase (P.O.P.)—$2,023,000; Rath likes premiums—$806,000; Jimmy Dean uses coupons—$2,069,000. *Your budget is $500,000.* Keep in mind that you are able to concentrate more money on your specific market than any of the nationals whose budgets (listed) are spread out over the entire country.

Now, your specific problem. Franklin has just completed satisfactory testing of a new product, a wiener made of turkey meat. It calls it Hot Turks. Your job is to create an advertising campaign for the product in the Phoenix-Tucson area.

More data: Research shows that people who eat hot dogs are concerned over low nutrition, high fat, poor taste, poor appearance, nitrites, and freshness. Franklin's Hot Turks, on the other hand, have little fat, good taste, and good nutrition.

QUESTIONS ABOUT THE PROJECT

1 How will you invest your ad dollars? Explain.
2 What position will you take for Hot Turks?
3 Will you test-market the product? Explain.
4 Describe your plan of action. Include major selling points, consumer and trade promotions, publicity, and so on.
5 Describe your creative ad campaign approach: graphics, headlines, and so on.

Unit

6

THE PRODUCTION OF ADVERTISING

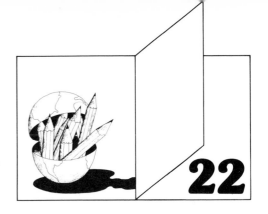

22

THE PRODUCTION
OF ADVERTISING

Update The countless hours of research—isolating demographic factors to pinpoint a target audience, evaluating the physical and psychological needs of that audience, searching for economical media for creative messages—all are a necessary prelude to the final television commercial, direct mailer, or magazine or newspaper ad. Now we can look at production because now we know what we want from our advertising—and we can make sure that we get it.

In 1884, a printer could handset 12,000 characters in a ten-hour work day. Phototypesetters today can do better in *a dozen seconds*. Computerized equipment can print 1,000 or more characters a second. Amazing? Mind-boggling? Of course. But what does any of this have to do with the photograph in a magazine or the person selling soap on television? Everything, because the visible part of an ad is the tip of the iceberg and depends on what is underneath and invisible. Part of the hidden support system underlying the ads we see and hear is the complex production process. And production is a heavily technological operation.

Production, as used within the context of advertising, is the process of converting a creative idea into a finished advertisement. In other words, production is only a means to an end—whether that end is a television image, sounds on the radio, or printed pages.

The people involved with production include company and ad agency personnel, as well as all independent suppliers of art, photography, television and radio commercials, printing, engravings, and typography. The company and the ad agency people are the buyers. The independent suppliers are the sellers. The job of the buyers is to make sure that the suppliers' finished product is as nearly imitative of the original concept as is humanly and mechanically possible.

Production of broadcast commercials appears to be more of a mystery to most people than print media production. Perhaps it's the relative newness of radio and television on the advertising stage. Or maybe it's the fact that people are awed by the miracles of electronics and modern photographic techniques. For that reason, we're going to take a look first at the production of television and radio commercials. Then, we'll move on to print.

TELEVISION AND RADIO COMMERCIALS

Recording the Storyboard

The artist's storyboard and the writer's copy provide necessary direction to the people who convert these conceptual preliminaries into final film or videotape. The television *director* takes charge of this production process. Ordinarily he or she works for a package house[1] that has had to bid competitively for the job. The director's immediate superior is the *producer*. The producer has overall responsiblity for making the commercial and is the strategic head who leaves the tactical details to the director. A producer may work for the package house, an advertising agency, or a local television station. Among other things, the producer establishes a schedule that the director implements. The schedule specifies the number of shooting days and details the design and building of scenery, the acquisition of costumes and properties, and the casting of those who appear in the commercial. The director is further responsible for integrating all the following into the commercial: music, movement, dialogue, lighting, sound, and makeup.

But others on the set add their talents: assistant director, camera and sound crew, electrician, makeup crew, and more. The camera crew shoots all

[1]"Package house" is a name given to an independent firm specializing in creating and producing television and radio commercials.

the action that takes place on the set at one time. If sequences must be shot elsewhere, the producer or the director schedules these so as to minimize costly waiting time. Preplanning is important in keeping costs down, especially in an inflationary economy in which, during a relatively short time, the cost of everything from union labor to floor tiles to car rentals, can go up sharply.

Experts claim the best-quality commercials are shot on 35 mm film that specialists later convert to 16 mm for television station use. (The same strip of film carries both sight and sound.) Film presents certain advantages for directors over videotape and live productions. It allows directors to get the sharpest images and the best color. It permits them to travel to any location and allows for smooth editing changes, as well as for the addition of sound at any time. Sound specialists record music and narration separately from the film shooting and "dub" these in their proper sequence on the film track. For example, if the copywriter has called for a musical background over the narration and images, the camera crew shoots the visuals first. This part of the commercial is called the *work print*. In cooperation with the director or the producer, an editor edits this print, adding, subtracting, and rearranging elements to meet the ad's pictorial objectives. Then the editor or the director orders the work print to be projected in a sound recording studio. Here sound specialists synchronize music and narration to the visual frames of the work print. This is called an *interlock screening*. For the first time, ad agency, producer, and director can pass judgment on the commercial.

If the work passes muster among this audience of insiders, editors can polish the commercial and add optical effects such as *fades* and *dissolves* where needed. The result is the *answer print*, the final and master print of the commercial. From this answer print come the release prints that go out to television stations.

Film is not the only medium of television commercials. *Videotape* is steadily growing in importance. A 1-inch wide ribbon of magnetic tape, videotape is an electronic medium. Videotape records picture and sound simultaneously and can replay the result almost instantly. Until recently, videotape machines were bulky and difficult to transport. but new, compact, hand-held cameras solve this handling problem. Videotape has an advantage over film in that it is far cheaper and less time-consuming to reshoot videotape sequences than it is to spend time in editing. Tape presents a colder, harsher appearance than full-color film, some experts claim. Yet videotape is perfectly satisfactory in many circumstances. Its major advantages over film are lower costs and quick release time (Figures 22-1 and 22-2).

Recording the Radio Spot

After the client approves the copywriter's radio script, the script may go out for bids to production houses specializing in radio commercials. A simple script may even begin right in the ad agency's or local radio station's own audio-recording studio. As in the case of television commercials, the

FIGURE 22-1
Shooting a television commercial is quite similar to filming a sequence in a movie. The skill of the production specialists (director, camera crew, lighting technicians, and film editors) makes the difference between an average commercial and an outstanding one. (Courtesy Standard Brands.)

advertising agency people meet with the producer to establish guidelines, confer on vocal and instrumental talent, and determine costs.

Talent fees, for example, are usually fixed by AFTRA (American Federation of Television and Radio Artists), a union whose members include radio and television announcers, actors, singers, news commentators, and others who perform over network or large-city stations. The union sets minimum talent fees for rehearsal time and commercial work. Local rates vary from city to city.

Most professional sound recording studios keep libraries of canned music and sound effects (prerecorded catalogs of various mood music and sounds) for almost any situation. Before they record, they play a selection of musical or sound effect "cuts" as a sort of audition for the producer and/or agency representative. If the music in the library is not satisfactory, the studio may arrange to record original music, using anything from a single instrumentalist to a full-blown symphony orchestra. In these instances, the advertiser may have to make financial arrangements with the copyright owners of the music, ASCAP (American Society of Composers, Authors and Publishers) or BMI (Broadcast Music Inc.), and the musical talent. In most cases, it is far less expensive to use the studio's canned music and sound effects. For example, if a commercial calls for "dogs barking," it might take considerable time and money before the proper sounds are located and recorded. A canned sound effects record will generally contain a wide variety of dog barks and allow the advertiser to select the appropriate one right in the studio and within minutes. Some tunes in the recording studio's canned music catalog are in the public domain and require no payment to a copyright owner.

Magnetic tape of the familiar black or brown reel-to-reel variety is what

FIGURE 22-2

Videotape is popular for its economy and its ability to record sight and sound at the same time. The 1-inch tape is standard in television broadcasting.

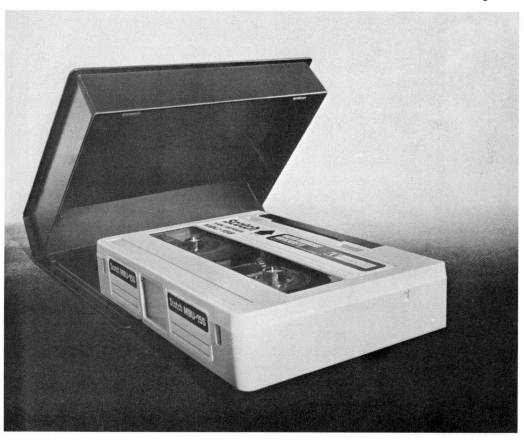

sound specialists use to record the finished commercial. It picks up the lowest (about 20 cycles) and the highest (about 20,000 cycles) perceptible musical notes. After the client has approved the taped commercial, it sometimes goes to a company that makes *electrical transcriptions* (ET). ETs are simply records. They play at 33⅓ rpm and are usually 16 inches in diameter. From tape to final record (sometimes called a *pressing* or a *disk*) can take from eight to thirty-six hours depending on how many pressings the advertiser requires. In the main, advertisers prefer to send tapes or cassettes of their commercials. If advertisers prefer a live reading of commercials, they'll ship the script alone.

PRINT PRODUCTION

Finished Art

An artist's layout of an ad is only a blueprint. Before it is printed, the ad will first be made into finished art and then into a printing plate. Artists prepare finished art that is suitable for reproduction. They draw it to size (exact or larger), render mechanically perfect drawings, and paste down proofread, smudge-free copy in the proper spots. To help in the paste-up process, artists use T-squares to "square up" all the elements of the ad. Printers and platemakers cannot realign crooked lines of copy unless they redo the work of the artist, a risky and expensive proposition.

When photographs are to appear in the ad, artists usually indicate their exact size and location by a ruled blank area called a *keyline* on the illustration board. If they don't keyline the area, they may indicate the space with a red acetate overlay. Many photographs need cleaning up or retouching so they will reproduce well. *Retouching* is a technique of emphasizing or deemphasizing certain pictorial elements. Artists also give instructions for enlarging, reducing, or cropping pictures on tissue overlays.

Throughout the preparation of final art, artists take into consideration the method of printing, the number of colors, and any special effects called for in the layout. All these affect the ad's final appearance.

Completed artwork usually moves on either to the platemaker or to the printer. But before we discuss platemaking, let's digress and examine typography. So many people take it for granted, and few ever realize its great potential.

Typography

The reading matter of advertising we call *type* or *typography*. There are over 1,000 different families of type available to the advertiser. These families are known as *fonts* or *faces*, complete assortments of any one style of type. (Figure 22-3).

Type affects the appearance of printed pieces and ads. It should first and foremost be legible. It should also convey the feeling—formality, antiquity, elegance—selected by the artist. (Figure 22-4).

Over the years, a loose system for classifying typefaces has evolved. It is not precise, but it does help the artist.

Oldstyle   Patterned after letter forms in Roman inscriptions, oldstyle faces are very legible, open, and round, with a good contrast between heavy and light strokes. Short cross strokes at the extremities of the letters form *serifs*.

Modern   Over 200 years old, the modern family shows extreme contrast between thick and thin strokes.

Sans Serif   An extremely popular series of typefaces, sans serif alphabets feature letters that have no serifs and ordinarily have little contrast between thick and thin strokes. The sans serif families have a clean and contemporary look.

Script   Script typefaces are designed to look like handwriting.

Decorative Faces   Most decorative faces are contemporary styles designed to command attention or to create moods.

Display Faces   Display faces are not so much a separate family of type as they are a distinct part of many typefaces. Their distinction rests on their large size. They are primarily designed for headlines, posters, and banners. With the new electronic machines they can be set in sizes up to 5 inches in height.

It takes several years before practicing artists can master the art of selecting advertising type faces. Along with this knowledge goes the ability to improve the legibility of copy by altering *leading*, the white space between lines of copy. However, artists' concern with typography for their ads is not ended when they have specified the type. Now they must be concerned with the fit.

Copyfitting

The selecting and specifying of type come to nought if the advertising message does not fit the allocated space. The artist must *copyfit*. Copyfitting is the practice of taking a specific space according to the layout, analyzing the copywriter's manuscript, and fitting one into the other.

Many companies that provide typography services to advertisers give out simplified copyfitting or typefitting cards or booklets. These devices greatly speed up the copyfitting job and have the added advantage of acting as a promotional piece for the typesetter. Without these devices, the artists must fall back on counting the characters in the words of the manuscript and converting these into the widths and depth of copy. (For example, the words *Copyfitting takes time* have twenty-two characters including the spaces between the words, which are always counted.) Then they count line after line. To hasten the *body type* counting operation, keep in mind that there is

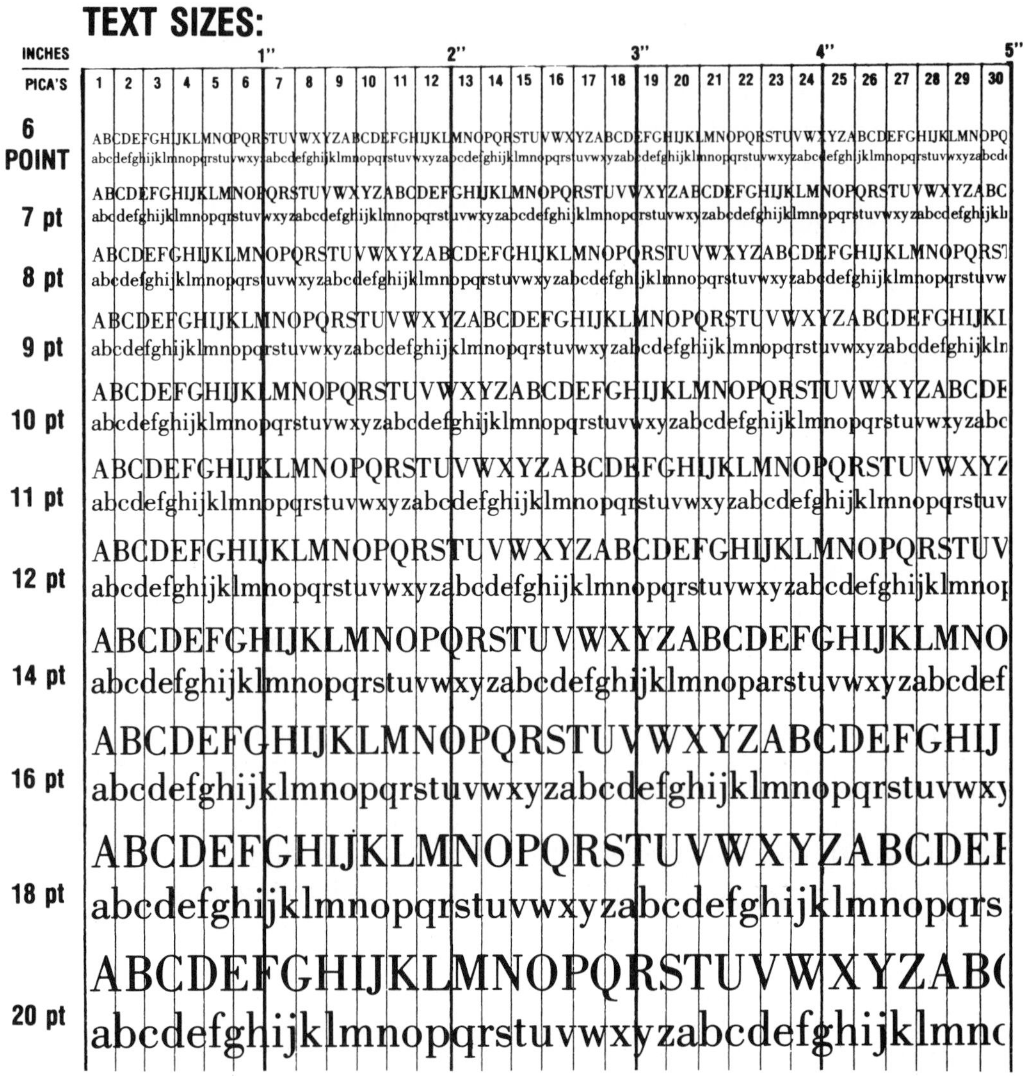

TEXT SIZES:

INCHES							1"						2"						3"						4"						5"
PICA'S	1	2	3	4	5	6	7	8	9	10	11	12	13	14	15	16	17	18	19	20	21	22	23	24	25	26	27	28	29	30

6 POINT
ABCDEFGHIJKLMNOPQRSTUVWXYZABCDEFGHIJKLMNOPQRSTUVWXYZABCDEFGHIJKLMNOPQRSTUVWXYZABCDEFGHIJKLMNOPQ
abcdefghijklmnopqrstuvwxyzabcdefghijklmnopqrstuvwxyzabcdefghijklmnopqrstuvwxyzabcdefghijklmnopqrstuvwxyzabcd

7 pt
ABCDEFGHIJKLMNOPQRSTUVWXYZABCDEFGHIJKLMNOPQRSTUVWXYZABCDEFGHIJKLMNOPQRSTUVWXYZABC
abcdefghijklmnopqrstuvwxyzabcdefghijklmnopqrstuvwxyzabcdefghijklmnopqrstuvwxyzabcdefghijklm

8 pt
ABCDEFGHIJKLMNOPQRSTUVWXYZABCDEFGHIJKLMNOPQRSTUVWXYZABCDEFGHIJKLMNOPQRST
abcdefghijklmnopqrstuvwxyzabcdefghijklmnopqrstuvwxyzabcdefghijklmnopqrstuvw

9 pt
ABCDEFGHIJKLMNOPQRSTUVWXYZABCDEFGHIJKLMNOPQRSTUVWXYZABCDEFGHIJKL
abcdefghijklmnopqrstuvwxyzabcdefghijklmnopqrstuvwxyzabcdefghijklmn

10 pt
ABCDEFGHIJKLMNOPQRSTUVWXYZABCDEFGHIJKLMNOPQRSTUVWXYZABCDE
abcdefghijklmnopqrstuvwxyzabcdefghijklmnopqrstuvwxyzabc

11 pt
ABCDEFGHIJKLMNOPQRSTUVWXYZABCDEFGHIJKLMNOPQRSTUVWXYZ
abcdefghijklmnopqrstuvwxyzabcdefghijklmnopqrstuvwxyzabcdefghijklmnopqrstuv

12 pt
ABCDEFGHIJKLMNOPQRSTUVWXYZABCDEFGHIJKLMNOPQRSTUV
abcdefghijklmnopqrstuvwxyzabcdefghijklmnopqrstuvwxyzabcdefghijklmnop

14 pt
ABCDEFGHIJKLMNOPQRSTUVWXYZABCDEFGHIJKLMNO
abcdefghijklmnopqrstuvwxyzabcdefghijklmnoparstuvwxyzabcdef

16 pt
ABCDEFGHIJKLMNOPQRSTUVWXYZABCDEFGHIJ
abcdefghijklmnopqrstuvwxyzabcdefghijklmnopqrstuvwxy

18 pt
ABCDEFGHIJKLMNOPQRSTUVWXYZABCDEF
abcdefghijklmnopqrstuvwxyzabcdefghijklmnopqrs

20 pt
ABCDEFGHIJKLMNOPQRSTUVWXYZABC
abcdefghijklmnopqrstuvwxyzabcdefghijklmnc

FIGURE 22-3
Above are examples of typeface classifications, point size, and pica widths. On the right, from top to bottom, Modern Didot (modern), Helvetica (sans serif), Spencerian (script), and LaSalle (decorative).

feature contemporary designs
MODERN DIDOT DESIGN 4D42

feature contemporary designs
HELVETICA DESIGN THO5C

Feature Contemporary Spencerian Designs 1543CC

Contemporary design LASALLE TPL 6C

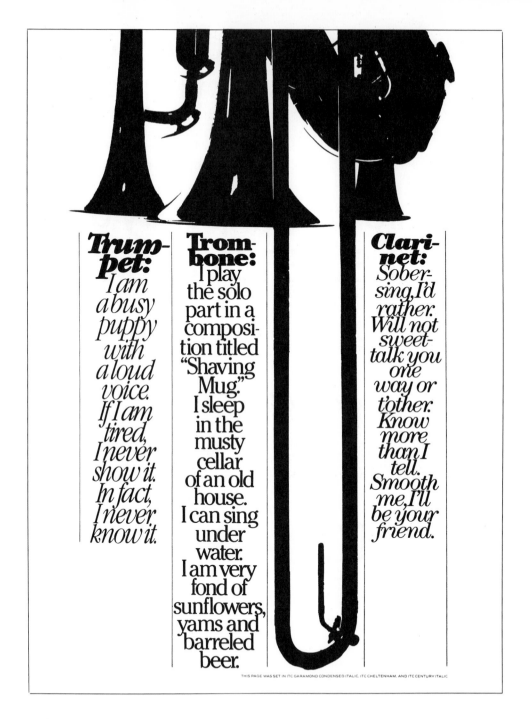

Trumpet: I am a busy puppy with a loud voice. If I am tired, I never show it. In fact, I never know it.

Trombone: I play the solo part in a composition titled "Shaving Mug." I sleep in the musty cellar of an old house. I can sing under water. I am very fond of sunflowers, yams and barreled beer.

Clarinet: Sober-sing, I'd rather. Will not sweet-talk you one way or t'other. Know more than I tell. Smooth me, I'll be your friend.

THIS PAGE WAS SET IN ITC GARAMOND CONDENSED ITALIC, ITC CHELTENHAM, AND ITC CENTURY ITALIC.

FIGURE 22-4

Very much a part of this eye-catching layout are the variety of typefaces and the manner in which the artist used them to develop a mood. Typography in the hands of an expert is truly a contemporary art form. (Courtesy u&lc—Herb Lubalin and Percy Seitlin.)

an average of thirty-one words to a square inch of solidly set 8-point type and twenty-three words if the type is leaded, that is, if space is inserted between the lines of copy. There are twenty words per square inch for 10-point type (solid) and sixteen words if lines are leaded. Or, standard pica typewriters— 12-point type—have ten characters to the running inch. Armed with any of these formulas, advertisers can calculate the number of characters in a desired type size provided they know the width of the line. A more precise method of copyfitting requires specific information about the pica width of *each* selected typeface. A complicating factor in copyfitting is the fact that each typeface has its own dimensional width. Thus, the space that does nicely for one typeface may not do as well for another of the exact same *point size*. (The height of type is measured in points.)

Generally, the decision on the width of the copy falls to the artists. They can design their layouts solely from an esthetic point of view, or they can remember Dr. Flesch's warning about too-wide lines of copy slowing readership. Some ad experts prefer line widths not to exceed 4 inches or 24 picas. (Lines widths are measured in picas; a pica is approximately one-sixth of an inch.)

The Typesetting Revolution

People used to set type in a hand-held metal device known as a composing stick. They put in each required letter of a specific typeface until they assembled a full line and repeated this process until all the copy was set. In its most basic form, this was the method used by Gutenberg in 1450. It is still used today on small printing jobs.

Hot Type   Then the faster linotype machines came along. These cast a full line of type at a time, using molten metal or "hot type" to form their characters. They actually produce the printing medium because the printer takes the metal type, places it in a form on the press, and runs it. Many of these hot-type machines are in daily use today.

Cold Type   It was inevitable that sooner or later the bother of handling type would lead to the development of cleaner, faster methods. *Direct impression composition* and *photographic typesetting* do not use hot type. Both these rapidly growing systems have begun to move the typesetter out of the typesetting plant and into the modern office. These cold-type systems are relatively easy to learn.

Typewriter/Direct-impression Composition   Ordinary typewriters produce type that can be pasted down and used for reproduction. But typewriter type is ordinary and fuzzy. Even if it is not enlarged, it simply does not make clean, sharp impressions. Several new machines that have typewriterlike keyboards can produce clean type proofs on paper suitable for reproduction. These direct-impression units form letters much as a typewriter does but faces have proportionately designed letters that imitate professional typography.

Computerized Photographic Typesetting A phototypesetting machine produces typography on film or photographic paper. Phototypesetters have a master font of characters, a light source, and a light-sensitive carrier material (film or special paper). The keyboard operator selects the master character negative and automatically moves it into position. Light then exposes the negative to the film or paper. Within minutes, the operator has a glossy proof of the type matter. The newest generation of these typesetters uses cathode ray tubes (CRT's) and can set over 1,000 lines a minute.[2]

Type Input If there is a typesetting output revolution, there is a similar upheaval taking place in the input end of the system. Through the use of optical character recognition (OCR) and video display terminals (VDTs), operators can "read" manuscripts at high speeds. The video display terminals are simply keyboard-operated devices. Editors see copy on the televisionlike screen, correct it right on the screen, and send a tape to the electronic typesetter. Joining the phototypesetters and VDTs are new machines that can readily manipulate large display type. One condenses, expands, backslants, italicizes, and alters proportions—truly a versatile design tool for the artist.

The growth of the cold-type technology is so rapid that it almost is hard to believe. But costs reflect the popularity of and trade enthusiasm for the machines. Back in 1970, an inexpensive VDT cost $17,000 or more. Today you can purchase one for $3,000 or less.[3]

But type houses haven't abandoned hot-metal composition. Many still offer a full spectrum of hot and cold type, because for many advertisers it is less expensive to set copy for a small job in hot metal—the automated typesetting start-up costs can be high. However, the more involved and lengthy the job, the more efficient automated photocomposition becomes.

Platemaking

The final art is completed, photos and illustrations keylined, and the specified type neatly pasted into place. Now comes the platemaking process. This converts the artist's and typographer's work into a *reproducible* printing pattern. Without this intermediate step there is no way to reproduce the artwork in quantity without some sort of carrier or, in printer's language, *a plate.*

The type of plate depends on the type of printing process. Although professional platemakers, often called *engravers,*[4] usually handle the details, a passing knowledge of platemaking will help advertisers to recognize why some plates reproduce better than others. To understand the specific function of each type of plate, they need to look at each method of printing. There are

[2]*Pocket Pal*, 12th ed. (New York: International Paper Company, 1978), p. 58.
[3]Donald Goldman, "The word: Copy processing/typesetting," *u&lc*, December 1977, p. 7.
[4]Even though technology has introduced us to printing processes that no longer use etched images (hence the word *engraving*), the graphics arts industry continues to refer to all printing carriers as plates or engravings.

three basic ways to print commercially: letterpress, offset, and gravure (intaglio).

Letterpress Printing Plates   People who use rubber stamps know that it is the raised portion of the rubber that does the printing. That's the principle of letterpress printing, except that letterpress prints from raised metal, not rubber. The metal in this case is either zinc (inexpensive), magnesium, or copper (more costly). The images on the raised portions of an ink-smeared metal plate transfer to paper under pressure of the printing press.

To make a letterpress plate, craftspeople use an old technique called *photoengraving*. The engravers photograph the finished artwork. Then they record this image on a metal plate in which all the picture and message areas are protected by a light-sensitive coating. During progressive acid baths known as "bites," the nonprotected areas are eaten away.

If the artwork includes photographs, the engravers produce a *halftone plate*. The halftone process reproduces all the tones *between* pure black and pure white by breaking up the masses of different-sized (but still tiny)dots. In other words, all the tones of the photograph are represented by a pattern of large, small, and medium-sized dots. These dots become the ink-carrying areas of the halftone plate (Figures 22-5 and 22-6).

FIGURE 22-5
A black-and-white halftone produced from a black-and-white glossy photo reproduces all the tones between pure black and pure white. The plate that carries this image may be zinc or the costlier copper. (Courtesy Eastman Kodak.)

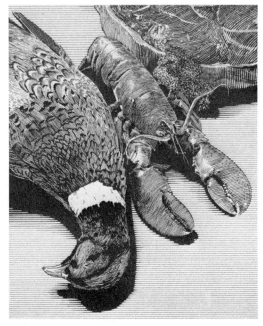

FIGURE 22-6
An artist's line sketch reproduces extremely well in newspapers and magazines. Solids, lines, and type matter are called "line art" and cost less to engrave than photographs. Their major drawback is their lack of realism. (Courtesy Eastman Kodak.)

FIGURE 22-7
Duotones mellow
subjects and
backgrounds. They
are favorite tools of
artists seeking
multicolor effects.
Sometimes unusual
effects can be created
by enlarging the dot
patterns and running
them as duotones.
(Courtesy Eastman
Kodak.)

To make these dots, engravers photograph the artwork (the photos) through a wire or glass screen. The screen breaks the rays of light into a sensitized dotted pattern on the metal plate. The finer the screen, the greater the detail. Halftones made with a 65-line-to-the-inch screen are coarse and appropriate for rough paper such as newsprint. Magazines often require screens up to 150 lines.

Color Reproduction Engravers make reproducible plates in four colors through the four-color halftone process. They make a separate halftone with filters for each of the primary colors. These are printed in yellow, magenta, and cyan (blue). They also add a black plate. When all the plates are put together and printed, the result should be as close to the original as possible.

The process doesn't always work perfectly, because of the inherent inadequacies of inks. Most color work is therefore done in a series of steps. Artists can compare these steps on *progressive proofs*, color proofs of each individual color plate as it appears alone and as it appears after the addition of each successive color.

In two-color printing, there must be a separate plate for each of the two colors. The engraver makes the black plate, for example, of only those parts of the original art that appear as black. There is also the *duotone halftone*, one of the more popular multicolor techniques and highly favored by artists. The engravers make two halftone plates from the same black-and-white photograph but in making one of them they turn the screen at a 30-degree angle. The dots of that plate thus appear *between* those of the other. When the plates are printed, one atop the other, the reader sees a harmonious and pleasing two-color effect. (Figure 22-7).

The great majority of letterpress printing of ads is not done from the original copper plates but from duplicate plates called *electrotypes* or *electros*. The purpose here is to save the originals in case they need to be used to reproduce other duplicates. Electros are often used as the "masters" to create *papier-mâché* mats, those lightweight ad reproductions favored by coop advertisers. In the newspaper business, duplicate plates are called *stereotypes*. They are cast from *papier-mâché* mats using a hot-metal process and are currently favored by large-city newspapers.

Offset Printing Plates The offset printing process, frequently called *lithography*, is based on the fact that water and grease don't mix. The chemically treated printing plates can be plastic, a light and flexible metal such as aluminum, or even paper. The chemically treated portion of the plate that carries the art and copy attracts greasy ink. The surrounding water-treated surface repels the ink. During the printing cycle, the inked image contacts a rubber-blanketed offset cylinder. This process transfers or "offsets" the image to the rubber blanket. When paper contacts the rubber blanket, it receives the image. There is no contact between the offset plate and the paper, as there is in letterpress printing.

In order to meet some of the competitive advantages of letterpress, such as clarity and definition, offset printers have greatly improved the platemaking techniques. Now the lightweight plates are deep-etched, or they are made of two metals joined together: copper and aluminum, for example. These techniques, borrowed from letterpress engraving, improve the ink-carrying capabilities of the offset plate as well as its ability to withstand long printing runs. The original offset plates of thin aluminum, plastic, or paper, called *surface plates*, are still in popular use, however. They are economical, and should any error occur during the platemaking process, they can be discarded and new ones put into use (Figures 22-8 and 22-9).

Gravure Printing Plates In gravure or intaglio printing, the photographic negative of the ad is etched in the form of a series of small pits on copper cylinders. The ink in the pits below the plate surface transfers to paper under pressure. The pits vary in depth but not in size. The deepest pits print the darkest parts of the ad, since the depth of the pit determines the amount of the ink—which is always thinner than in letterpress and offset—that transfers to the paper. Gravure printing provides a variety of shadings but no sharp, clean lines as in offset and letterpress. The familiar word *rotogravure* refers to gravure printing on a rotary press. For large-quantity printing runs, it is the fastest and cheapest method. The fact that it produces rich, deep colors and striking contrasts is another plus, but short runs are not economical. Currently, advertisements made from gravure plates are found mostly in newspapers and preprinted inserts. Lately, however, some quality magazines

FIGURE 22-8
Flexible offset plates
can be aluminum,
plastic, or paper.
Offset's great attraction
is economy, and
advertisers appreciate
the savings.

have begun offering the process to their advertisers, such as *National Geographic, Reader's Digest, Ladies Home Journal, Better Homes and Gardens, McCall's,* and *Redbook. The National Enquirer* also uses gravure.

Printing

The various printing presses used for letterpress operate according to a common principle. Rollers apply an even coating of ink to the raised printing surface of the plate. Then, paper is squeezed against the surface to pick up the ink. Letterpress presses are often classified according to the design of the part of the press holding the plates, the *bed*. There are *flat bed (platen)* presses, *vertical* presses, and presses with cylindrical beds, often called *rotary* presses. Paper is either sheet-fed or web-fed onto a rotary press, the web being a continuous roll of paper. Most large newspapers use rotary presses.

Offset printing utilizes rotary presses with three large cylinders, one above the other. In addition to its economical features (it requires less make-ready and preparation time), offset allows the advertiser to print on a

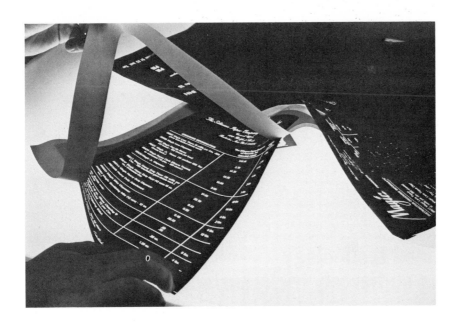

FIGURE 22-9
The film negative (top) is an essential component of the offset plate-making process. It is produced by photographing the art: keylines and paste-ups, photographs and illustrations. A specialist *strips* (mounts with cellophane tape) each art element—now on film—into one single negative assembly, which is mounted on an orange-colored, opaque sheet (bottom). The orange sheet blocks the light from nonprinting areas.

DISCOVERED BY UNIROYAL:

To demonstrate the softness of engravings made with a Uniroyal process, we hand printed on an egg. Yet soft Flex-Light plates can last as long as some metal plates —and are produced by a simple photographic process.

Printed with Uniroyal Flex-Light®

An advanced technology for printing on fiercely tricky surfaces

FIGURE 22-10
Offset printing on a fragile egg demonstrates the medium's versatility. (Courtesy Uniroyal.)

rough surface as well as on a smooth one—and even on flimsy foils and plastic films (Figure 22-10). The presses are sheet-fed or web-fed. Speed is by far the main advantage of the web offset press—with the paper moving up to 1,800 feet per minute.

In the gravure process, the most common presses are sheet-fed and rotary. The printing unit itself consists of a printing cylinder on which the flexible copper plate is mounted, a rubber roller cylinder that feeds the paper against the printing surface, and an inking system. Whereas the plate costs for gravure are high, the cost for paper is generally lower than for other printing methods. Most, if not all, of the large mail-order catalogs are printed on rotogravure presses.

Last but certainly not least among the more popular printing methods, is the *offset duplicator*, also known as the *multilith*. This is a small offset press primarily used for small runs: sales sheets, catalogs, price sheets, bulletins, letterheads, house organs, and the like.

Suppliers can show advertisers what a finished piece will look like *before* it is finished. The typographer, for example, presents type proofs for checking. The letterpress platemaker runs off engraver's proofs. Advertisers printing four-color by offset receive thin, cellophane-type proofs. For a black-and-white ad, advertisers will receive photostats of the artwork. For a small sum, advertisers can even have the offset plate run on a small-job press—100 or 200 pieces or so—to see how the ad will appear.

When advertisers are about to print a brochure, catalog or other print message, the printer provides them with a *brownprint* or a *blueline*. These are faded representations of all the elements of the finished piece exactly in place.

TABLE 22-1

635

THE PRODUCTION
OF ADVERTISING

ADVERTISERS' TROUBLESHOOTING GUIDE

Problem	Probable cause
Television	
Spots and/or smudges appear on film.	Haphazard film processing. Check original answer print.
Weak, flat color is seen on projector or videotape unit.	Poor film exposure, lighting, or processing; perhaps all three.
Prints show flat, undefined pictures or uninterrupted gray or color tone over everything.	Old film stock or poor lighting. Catch this at the work print stage.
There is poor lip synchronization between speakers and sound.	Check answer print.
Closeups and long shots are not in focus.	Poor camerawork. Check work print.
Sequences appear jerky.	Check work print and/or editing. Perhaps too many "cuts" were inserted.
Radio	
Sound is garbled, indistinct.	Poor recording, taping, or pressing.
Sound effects and music are too loud or too soft.	Poor sound studio work. Go back to original narration.
Hissing sound is heard.	Poor taping or pressing.
Print	
Photos are murky.	Check original art and compare. If art is good, the fault rests with either engraver, printer, or paper. If art is bad, reshoot photo or retouch to bring out highlights.
Blurry effect is seen near bright objects in photo portions of ad.	Check original photos. If highlights there are the problem, have platemaker remove halo effect on negative; otherwise retouch photo.
Dark splotches or spots appear on ad or literature.	Check to see whether all copies show same problem. If not, spots may indicate dirt, ink, or paper particles on press. Solution: printers must clean presses more often.
Color is indistinct or not precisely on subjects.	Printing press is off-register. Colors and images don't coincide.
Parts of ad are missing, such as photos, illustrations, words, letters.	Check original art. If okay, platemaker possibly "masked out" missing elements during negative assembly. Catch these errors in the brownprint or engraver proof stages or before.
All ads in a magazine appear weak.	Insufficient ink used during press run.
There is too much "showthrough" from the back side of the ad.	Paper lacks opacity. Printer may have to use an opaque ink.
Color photos appear weak, lacking in body.	Check original art. Sometimes a device called a densitometer is used to determine consistency of the colors throughout. Pastel colors can create problems.

All that is missing are the colors and some of the clarity. Advertisers note necessary changes.

Production, as we have said earlier, is only a means to an end. The advertiser's job is to give the highest quality final art to the production specialists. From that point onward, the production specialists take the job to completion. If their work is good, the advertiser will undoubtedly reward them with more. If it's not, the wise advertiser will look around for other suppliers. (See Table 22-1 for guidelines).

IN SUMMARY

1 Production is the conversion of a creative idea into a finished advertisement.
2 The person in charge of converting the artist's storyboard and the copywriter's words into a piece of film or videotape is the director. The director's superior, the producer, has the overall responsibility for making the commercial.
3 The major advantages of videotape over film are cost and short release time.
4 After radio commercials are recorded on reel-to-reel tape, they may be put on records called electronic transcriptions (ETs), tapes, or cassettes for distribution.
5 The artist pastes up and keylines print ads before their mechanical reproduction.
6 A font or typeface is a complete assortment of any one style of type.
7 Type should always be legible.
8 Typefaces are classified as old style (with serifs), modern, sans serif, script, decorative, and display.
9 There are various ways to set type: by hand, linotype, direct-impression typewriters, and the new generation of electronic typesetters.
10 Electronic phototypesetters have spawned input machines such as optical character recognition (OCR) units and video display terminals (VDTs), which can read and edit copy at high speeds.
11 Different kinds of plates are used for the various printing processes: letterpress, offset, and gravure. Letterpress is known for clarity; offset for economy; and gravure for deep, rich colors and long runs.
12 The mechanical trades advise advertisers about the final appearance of their print advertising by presenting them with type proofs, color and/or engravers' proofs, or brownprints. These are the advertisers' last chance to make corrections before final printing or publication.

CASE STUDY   Queen of the TV Food Cosmeticians. She Cooked 200 Pancakes that No One Ate! by Margaret Engel A person of ordinary patience might be able to spend hours filling an immense table with an Elizabethan-era feast: roasts, tarts, pies, suckling pigs, and the like, but who would be willing to outfit two additional tables as back-up intentionally, for television cameras?

Calm, adaptable Zenja Cary, that's who.

"If you don't have the temperament for that, you're in the wrong business," exclaims Miss Cary, a veteran of 25 years of creating "beauty" shots of food.

Cary is the queen of New York City's food stylists, spending her days preparing mass quantities of beautiful edibles no stomach will ever greet or digest.

Her food appeals to the eye, not the palate, and television viewers will find Miss Cary's food mouth-watering.

Art directors, advertising agencies, and photographers hire Miss Cary at $200 to $400 a day, plus expenses, to provide fresh supplies of client products for as many takes as the TV director orders.

On a recent day, Miss Cary scooped several freezers full of ice cream balls, until her arms ached. "It must have been a hundred or more scoops," she recalled, ruefully.

Her next day was spent baking pancakes, exhausting 10 packages of batter. She cooked over 200 pancakes in the director's search for the perfect shot. "Each time the actor poured the syrup, we had to have a new stack, and they poured about 45 to 50 times."

A day of shooting usually lasts 10 hours, beginning with crew calls at 8:30 A.M., although she will have been on the job an hour or two earlier. If the commercial is not being shot in her own studio (she has three fully equipped kitchens: modern, country, and traditional designs, in her Cary Kitchen overlooking Central Park), a messenger service will carry her food cartons and equipment (including two portable ovens) to the sound stage. "Many of the stoves you encounter are rented, and they're bad. I always carry an oven thermometer."

While lighting is being arranged, and the lines rehearsed by the actor, Miss Cary and members of her four-person crew are baking rapidly.

Serving food "on cue" requires the precision of a drill sergeant. Armed with her ever-present water spritzer, cotton swabs, and long bamboo skewers (to fluff up rice), she duplicates plate after plate of the product, keeping hot food steaming and cold food from melting.

The tight angles of a television shot demand a uniform product for each take to avoid reestablishing a shot. A script supervisor takes careful notes in order to help Miss Cary duplicate each setup. "If it's really complicated, we'll take a Polaroid."

Miss Cary likes to work with the ad in the planning stage. "I ask, Is this a good idea? Would this sell the product? Would I do this for my family? Sometimes people writing the ads have no idea of cooking, and it shows.

"Two or three days before a shoot, I review the storyboard. Then I speak to the production company and see in what order they're shooting, whether the close-ups are first or if they want a master shot of the whole table."

There are no routine assignments. "We expected to have an easy day with a canned pasta product that we only had to open, heat, and serve. But the little boy in the commercial could not say his lines. He got tired. Another actor had to leave to do a matinee performance of a play. We were there all day."

Food styling is long past the day of putting marbles in soup to make it look chunkier. (A Federal Trade Commission order put an end to that.) "No, you just open a can and hope the chunks are there. The critical rule is that all the food must be edible. Some of the companies have set their own guidelines." Miss Cary often must sign affidavits, attesting to the product's use.

She began preparing food for cameras when television was in its infancy, producing short cooking films for trade groups like the National Broiler Council and the Evaporated Milk Association. She has long realized not all foods are equal in the camera's eye.

"Salads are a dream, but cheese and pizza are very difficult to work with. They get oily. Chili, sausages, any mixture really, are hard to photograph."

When the director yells "Print" Miss Cary is still cooking. "You may think you're done, but they'll decide to reverse the shot. You always need a back-up. You have to anticipate."

The job requires resourcefulness and skill, but the greatest talent of all is patience.

"Frustration is handing an actor 'that perfect hamburger' and he misses the line. There's nothing to do but hand him another one".

QUESTIONS NEEDING ANSWERS

1 In shooting food for a television spot, would it make any difference if the commercial were done on videotape rather than film? Explain.
2 Miss Cary said, "Sometimes people writing the ads have no idea of cooking, and it shows." Explain how this might be true in the directions the copywriter includes on the script of the commercial, or in the way the artist has laid out the storyboard.
3 In a "pancake shoot" under the camera and the hot lights, who would most likely be watching to see that everything was going according to the storyboard?

STUDENT PROJECT

Visit a nearby printer and ask to borrow (or photocopy) a typical brownprint. Examine it and describe what changes in it you'd make if you were the advertiser. Perhaps you can compare it to the finished printed piece of advertising literature.

QUESTIONS ABOUT THE PROJECT

1 Was the printer at all surprised that you would ask to see a brownprint? Explain.
2 Were there any drastic changes between the brownprint and the finished piece? Explain the differences.
3 Is the brownprint a reasonable facsimile of the photographs? Could you have relied on it for giving the printer the go-ahead?
4 Did the printer insist on a written approval from the advertiser or the ad agency before running the job? Explain.

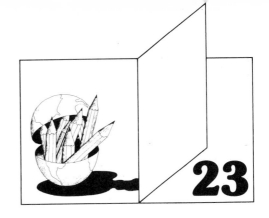

23

INTERNATIONAL ADVERTISING

Update In the previous chapter, we looked at a wide variety of production choices. We can select any of a thousand typefaces. We can print by letterpress, offset, or gravure and on coated paper, uncoated paper, newsprint, film, foil, cardboard, and even cloth. In the broadcast area, we employ sophisticated camera and electronic transmitting techniques. But in foreign countries markets are more restrictive. We'll learn more about production and other important aspects of international advertising in this chapter.

In our discussion of international advertising, we're going to be taking the point of view of an American exporter or a United States-based multinational company. Thus, for definition's sake, *international advertising* will mean

TABLE 23-1
PURCHASING POWER AROUND THE WORLD

(100 = purchasing power in Zurich)			
San Francisco	139	Johannesburg	72
Chicago	127	Dublin	67
Los Angeles	125	Milan	67
New York	119	Sao Paulo	63
Toronto	111	Paris	61
Montreal	107	Madrid	58
Geneva	102	Tokyo	57
Amsterdam	101	Rio de Janeiro	50
Zurich	100	Panama City	48
Copenhagen	98	Mexico City	45
Sydney	98	Athens	44
Luxembourg	95	Hong Kong	42
Stockholm	89	Istanbul	39
Oslo	81	Lisbon	34
Brussels	80	Tel Aviv	34
Vienna	78	Bogota	32
London	73	Manila	26
		Buenos Aires	19

(Compiled by the Union Bank of Switzerland)
Source: U.S. News & World Report, 1976

persuasive communications formulated by Americans (and their worldwide agencies) to sell goods and services overseas through foreign media.

We have earlier discussed several reasons why advertising flourishes in the United States but limps along in other countries. Another reason for the relative vitality of domestic advertising is the value we place on economic liberty, one aspect of which is the right of a company to make its wares and advertise them to the people.

In some countries where governments decide which goods and services its citizens will produce, open advertising is impossible. Even in certain countries where people are free to manufacture and sell, many are too poor to buy. On the whole, living standards in the United States are still above those in even the wealthiest European and Asiatic countries, including Japan.[1] Despite inflation, wage earners for example in San Francisco can buy considerably more for their incomes than people anywhere else in the world.[2] Because purchasing power is, in effect, advertising's launching pad, we can get a quick preview of the state of advertising throughout most of the world if we examine the purchasing power of the world's citizenry (Table 23-1).

Literacy and a unified people speaking a common language also contribute to the relative importance of the advertising function in any one country. In India, there are fourteen major languages and 135 dialects with an illiteracy rate of 70 percent.[3] How do we reach people who can't read or

[1]*Prices and Earnings Around the Globe,* Union Bank of Switzerland, Zurich, March 1976, p. 5.
[2]Ibid.
[3]Mahra Masani, "Broadcasting and the People," (New Delhi: National Book Trust, 1976), p. 7.

write? Literacy also reflects on the popularity of newspapers (and advertising) in nations around the world. Consider these newspaper facts: six printed newspaper copies were *sold* per 1,000 people in Laos, twenty-two per 1,000 in Cambodia, seven per 1,000 in Indonesia, thirty-five in the Philippines, six in Nigeria, four in Saudi Arabia, forty-six in Albania, forty-nine in Ecuador, 239 in Belgium, 201 in Singapore, 264 in the Union of Soviet Socialist Republics, 283 in the United States, 394 in Australia, 320 in Austria, 485 in Hong Kong, and 511 in Japan.[4]

THE NINETEEN INDUSTRIALIZED NATIONS

The people most frequently exposed to advertising are citizens of the industrialized nations. With few exceptions, the people of the industrialized nations are the prime targets for American advertising, because they are able to buy greater amounts of American-made goods. For this reason, most of this chapter will concentrate on those countries. Third-world countries are not ignored by the American exporter, however. They are constantly under evaluation for market potential and possible advertising commitments.

If American manufacturers know that the people of the industrialized countries are good advertising targets, so do foreign manufacturers. Their advertising, too, has been increasing in recent years, as can be seen in Table 23-2, a list of mass-media advertising expenditures of most Western nations.

In the Far East, Japan and Hong Kong spend relatively freely on advertising. Japan's per capita ad expenditure is $20.43, Hong Kong's $9.05.

[4]*Statistical Yearbook 1977*, Department of International Economic and Social Affairs, United Nations.

TABLE 23-2

MASS MEDIA EXPENDITURES IN MILLIONS OF DOLLARS ANNUALLY

Austria	185
Belgium	199
Denmark	161
Finland	164
France	1,103
Germany	2,337
Italy	440
Netherlands	556
Norway	135
Spain	379
Sweden	215
Switzerland	534
United Kingdom	643
United States	17,325
Argentina	170

Source: Michael Hook, "Media in Europe" presentation. (Courtesy Ogilvy & Mather, London.)

Compare these figures to Indonesia's per capita ad expenditure of $0.01.[5]

Yet even in countries with a high rate of illiteracy, some people are fully capable of buying American-made goods. For example, 5 percent of India's 550 million people have incomes equal to an average American's. This 5 percent is a market larger than the population of Canada. While India's overall per capita income is extremely low, the more affluent 5 percent represent a formidable sales volume—provided they can be advertised to economically.

THE CREATIVE APPROACH

By and large creative advertising people should write copy specifically tailored to the foreign market. Cultural and psychological differences among countries are often so wide than an ad that makes sense to us might bewilder or shock foreigners. For example, a common sight in American ads is a person soaping him or herself in the bathtub or shower. In Japan, this scene would be very strange indeed, because the Japanese soap themselves before they rinse with water. In Muslim countries, ads featuring swine would be considered an abomination.

Advertisers must make sure that they don't offend religious or other customs. Here is a tragic example of cultural ignorance. Throughout the third world, new mothers receive free sample tins of powdered milk when they leave hospital maternity wards. The samples come from, among other companies, Nestlé, reputed to be the largest infant-formula distributor in the third world.

> In an attempt to do what's best for their babies, they [new mothers] abandoned breast feeding. And they . . . try to reconstitute a powdered formula where they have no clean water, no suitable pot for sterilizing, insufficient fuel to boil their one bottle and nipple several times a day, and no refrigeration for the milk. . . . A laborer in Uganda would have to spend 33 percent of the average daily wage to feed an infant on powdered milk. In Pakistan, the figure is 40 percent. . . . The can contains a four-day supply. But 82 percent of the mothers (in Barbados) said they made it last anywhere from five days to three weeks.

> Some mothers who have run out of formula have been found mixing cornstarch with water to give the baby something that looked like milk. . . . The British Charity Organization, War on Want, found a Nigerian mother feeding her baby on water alone. She had seen the bottle and nipple pictured on a billboard and thought the manufactured items themselves provided the nourishment. Unsterilized and diluted bottle formula exacerbates the two most common causes of infant sickness and death around the world: malnutrition and diarrhea.[6]

[5]*Asian Press and Media Directory.* Estimates prepared by International Advertising Corporation (Seoul, Korea), 1974.
[6]Barbara Garson, "The Bottle Baby Scandal," *Mother Jones Magazine,* December 1977, p. 33.

The baby formula tragedy is an extreme example of modern technology and advertising creating problems instead of solutions. And the moral and ethical questions raised go far beyond marketing.

Many advertising departments of exporting companies follow a *centralized plan of creativity*. Under this arrangement, copywriters at the home office in the United States develop the same creative selling program for all countries. Only the language varies, and the translations are best made abroad because many translations made in the United States are too scholarly.

Other advertisers, however, prefer to operate under a *decentralized creative plan*. Under this arrangement, advertisers prepare company artwork and send it overseas on film negatives. These serve as a guide only. Each country's local agent has the authority to redo the artwork and copy to meet local conditions. If the finished art and copy are the responsibility of a United States-based ad agency, it will create the overall theme but leave specific ads and promotions to the local, overseas ad agencies who work under their direction.

For years, there has been an unresolved controversy over which arrangement (centralized or decentralized) is best for the United States-based advertiser. One method controls production and campaign unity more effectively. The other responds better to local conditions and may sacrifice creative continuity. There doesn't seem to be a single right answer for all companies. Each must choose in light of its own foreign situation.

The Local Ad Agency

Generally foreign ad agencies are just as knowledgeable about their markets as American agencies are about theirs. The better overseas ad agencies perform many of the same functions as their American counterparts: creating ads, selecting media, overseeing production, and so on. The better-known overseas agencies are often affiliated with large American agencies. These American companies not only invest in their overseas affiliates, but they also bring them American multinational clients with large budgets (Figure 23-1). Smaller American ad agencies also become affiliated with various overseas groups. For example, an American member of the IAA (International Advertising Association) is free to enlist the help of any of its members in order to better serve the American multinational client overseas. Gregory, Incorporated, an ad agency in Cleveland, Ohio, cooperates with affiliates in France, Germany, Spain, and other European nations through an international group called International Chain of Industrial and Technical Advertising Agencies (ICITA).

The American "master" agency develops the worldwide plan and sets the tone of the campaign. From then on, it's the local agency's responsibility to convey the general tone of the plan. When possible, the master agency requests engravers' proofs, tapes, and so on before publication or airing in order to check on local agencies' compliance (Figure 23-2). The master

agency may divide all media commissions with the overseas agencies who actually place the space "buys."[7] Another arrangement has the master agency receiving a set fee and each local agency taking the complete 15 percent commission. The latter method appears more equitable for all concerned.

There are, of course, many local ad agencies overseas that are unaffiliated with any American agency. Spain has over 800, England over 900, Ireland forty (Table 23-3). Not all are full-service agencies, but most can provide American companies with specialized marketing services.

Multinational companies should provide their satellite ad agencies with complete portfolios of their marketing goals and advertising, past and present. In addition, they need to send a constant flow of news releases, new-product announcements, and proofs of magazine, newspaper, and broadcast ads. They should insist that overseas agencies maintain close contact with the administrative group of the overseas sales force to ensure greater advertising efficiency. And multinationals shouldn't stifle creative ideas simply because

[7]Overseas ad agencies object to commission splitting because it suggests to their local clients that the agency can get along on a 7.5 percent commission instead of a 15 percent commission. Local clients may ask, "Why are you showing preference for Americans?"

FIGURE 23-2
Picker Corporation, an American manufacturer of medical x-ray equipment, exports to six key countries (among others) in Europe: England, Switzerland, Germany, Belgium, France, and the Netherlands. Media are specialized medical journals written for radiologists in up to five different languages. Advertising supervision rests with an American ad agency cooperating with ICITA members overseas. (Courtesy Gregory, Inc.)

TABLE 23-3

NUMBER OF AD AGENCIES IN WESTERN EUROPE

Austria	80
Belgium/Luxembourg	50
Denmark	100
Finland	49
France	300
Greece	200
Holland	180
Ireland	40
Italy	165
Norway	58
Portugal	30
Spain	822
Sweden	140
Switzerland	456
United Kingdom	900
West Germany	1,300

(Compiled by Stern Magazine, 1977)

they come from a small, local agency. Bigness does not guarantee great ideas.

When several agencies work for one multinational client, an agreeable *exclusivity rule* is necessary. This rule permits the client to own and use everything created for it by its agencies anywhere in the world. One good operating method is for all agencies to sign a client-agency agreement in exchange for the full 15 percent agency compensation and/or payment of other legitimate charges. Then clients have full use of advertising material without further residual charges.

GOVERNMENT RESTRICTIONS

National governments can severely restrict advertising. In the United States, the government interferes with advertising only when it is proved false or misleading (see Chapter 16).[8] The same situation does not hold true world wide. In Norway, for example, cigarette manufacturers cannot advertise *anywhere.* (In the United States, cigarettes can still be advertised everywhere except on television and radio.) Even cigarette point-of-purchase advertising displays are not allowed in retail stores. Nor does Norway permit the advertising of liquor. The government contends that permissible advertising must be informative: no hoopla. In fact, in each Norweigian ad agency a designated person is responsible for making sure advertisements comply with government code. Each layout has a place for this individual's signature, which attests to the agency's compliance (Figure 23-3).

Acceptable advertising practices in one country may not be allowable in

[8]Cigarette and liquor advertising are the American exceptions. When the United States government declared smoking a national health hazard, the FCC and the FTC forced the tobacco companies off the airwaves. The companies still advertise with the other privately owned media, however.

FIGURE 23-3

This McCullough chain-saw ad appeared in a Spanish-speaking daily tabloid. The ad describes the product's advantages and indicates there is a model for every purpose.

another. This suggests that multinational advertisers need to be aware of country-by-country ad restrictions to avoid problems with the authorities. Some multinationals make it a habit to check with the foreign embassies in the United States. Others rely on their overseas ad agency affiliates. We've selected a few more industrial countries to illustrate some of the problems an American advertiser can face overseas.

In 1971, Sweden enacted a Marketing Practices Act to protect the consumer against deceptive advertising practices. The Act banned trading stamps, return of box tops for special consideration, and merchandising gimmicks. If a manufacturer wants to give something away, it must be money. Manufacturers who offer premiums as an inducement for customers to buy their product must offer premiums that are related to the product. They cannot offer a pair of pantyhose for the purchase of a wristwatch. If they plan to run a contest, they must make sure that contestants work in order to win; the contestants cannot win by chance without effort. To put teeth into this regulation, the Swedish government established a consumer ombudsman charged with bringing action against anyone who engages in unfair advertising practices.

Swedish magazines carry few ads. Billboards are nonexistent. There may be an occasional posterboard in a public place such as a bus or train stop, and the government allows painted ads on building walls at certain corporate businesses. Denmark is more liberal in this regard. It also prohibits billboards, but it allows retailers to identify their businesses with gawdy signs and painted walls: Jolly Cola, Pilsener Beer, Mer Apple Juice, Colonel Sanders Kentucky Fried Chicken. There is no commercial television or radio.

In Germany, advertisers cannot say that their products are better than someone else's *unless they can back their claims with specific proof.* In Italy, jingles are against the law.

Leaving Europe, we find other governments are also active in restricting advertising. No moving lights for outdoor advertising is one of the restrictions placed on advertisers in Hong Kong; no billboards are allowed in Puerto Rico. In South Africa, there are no commercials on television. Radio time is so scarce there that it is booked up as much as a year ahead.

These are typical examples of how some governments insulate people from advertising. Yet many of these same governments permit ads to be run that would never make it in the United States. These are generally explicit ads selling toilet paper, birth control, and personal hygiene products.

Overseas ad specialists recommend that American companies selling to foreign markets learn what they can and cannot do in advertising *before* they proceed with any promotions. They point out that official first impressions are crucial.

THE MEDIA PICTURE

Analyzing the division of the media advertising investment is one way to learn what's going on overseas. Where television is in general use, the percent of

TABLE 23-4

MASS MEDIA EXPENDITURES IN PERCENTAGES, 1973–1974

	Television	Press	Cinema	Outdoor	Radio
Austria	23	65	1	3	8
Belgium	3	71	2	22	1
Denmark	0	95	2	3	0
Finland	16	79	1	4	0
France	14	56	2	11	17
Germany	12	79	1	5	4
Italy	17	62	5	8	8
Netherlands	10	83	1	5	1
Norway	0	94	3	3	0
Spain	28	49	3	10	9
Sweden	0	93	1	6	0
Switzerland	8	78	2	12	0
United Kingdom	23	72	1	4	1
United States	28	60	–	2	10
Argentina	23	51	3	8	15

(Compiled by Ogilvy & Mather, London)

European dollars spent on it approximates that in the United States (Table 23-4). The bulk of European ad dollars goes to the print media, especially to newspapers and magazines. In some third-world countries, the emphasis is on radio, movies, and village loudspeakers. A major reason for the difference is the degree of illiteracy in third-world countries. Iran reportedly has an illiteracy rate of 75 percent. Radio is a strong medium in that country, although there are pockets of affluence that are covered by newspapers and magazines. A magazine such as *Zan-E-Rooz* (Modern Woman) serves over 100,000 female readers in the same way as its American counterparts, *McCall's* or *Ladies Home Journal*.

Advertisers to underdeveloped countries sometimes have to fall back on generalized newspapers instead of consumer or trade journals—which may be nonexistent—to reach the target audiences they want. Compromises of this sort contribute to waste circulation and high cost. Yet advertisers must use whatever is available. In the United States, when advertisers face a situation in which neither newspapers nor magazines will reach a substantial number of customers and prospects, they usually resort to direct mail. But direct mail is not always the easy solution overseas. For one thing, people are not anxious to provide their names. For another, many consider unsolicited direct mail an invasion of their privacy. However, there is substantial direct-mail activity in certain countries: West Germany, Switzerland, Sweden, Denmark, and Holland. In most other countries of the world, direct mail plays a subordinate role within the international advertising media mix.

Television

Commercial television is available in all countries of Europe except Belgium, Denmark, Norway, and Sweden. Commercial spots run between breaks and at the termination of programs. But television is coming on strong on other continents. In 1973, Korean television advertising accounted for almost $16 million out of a total ad expenditure of $55 million.[9] Five of ten Koreans view it daily. In Latin America as well as in Africa, television antennae are becoming a more familiar sight. In Tunisia there was a 727 percent increase in the number of television sets per 1,000 people in a few years' time; in Mauritius an increase of 340 percent.[10] In Kenya, advertisers invest over $1 million a year in the new medium, although they still spend more on cinema advertising. In Iran, some advertisers consider television the second-best medium, behind the enduring favorite, radio. It is inevitable that television will take a greater proportion of the international advertising dollar as worldwide industrialization continues.

At the moment, it is not possible for a multinational company with product distribution throughout Africa and the Near East to buy *one spot* and expect it to reach a substantial number of households in those regions. In fact, this is not possible in Europe either.

Of all the European countries, Ireland, Austria, the United Kingdom, Spain, and Portugal spend the largest percentage of their total advertising dollars in commercial television.[11] Other countries would follow suit were it not for government policies. In most countries, strict government control of programming and airtime is the rule rather than the exception. Even in France, television spending only grew from 2 to 14 percent over a recent two-year period because of government restrictions. Factors that limit investment in European television appear to be varied. Strong government controls restrict the number of breaks for commercials, the number of advertisers, and the periods in which companies may advertise. Owners of print media also influence policy restricting television. (They learned from the example of the United States, where competing media owners did little or nothing to prevent television from growing.) A block system concentrates all spots into five to ten continuous commercials.

Finally, overdemand causes advertisers to reserve time as much as one year ahead of airing, *with no assurance they'll get the times they want.* Frequently, because of this overdemand, spots run beyond the seasons of the year in which companies really want to advertise. In Austria, for example, where television is the most important medium for brand advertising, only twenty minutes of advertising per day are allowed. Holland allows about fifteen minutes for each of its two stations per day. What is particularly frustrating for an American advertiser is the fact that while television commercial time is in short supply, actual coverage is excellent in many Western European countries: in France 90 percent, in Holland 82 percent, in Austria 90 percent, and in Greece 97 percent. Short of a radical change in government attitudes toward commercial advertising on television most

[9]"World Advertising Expenses," International Advertising Association/INRA, 1973.
[10]Ibid.
[11]*Commercial Television in Europe* (London: Benton & Bowles Ltd., 1973).

advertisers will have to continue using it as a supplemental rather than as a major medium. (For example, in the United Kingdom there are a maximum of six minutes per hour of advertising permitted during three equally spaced ad breaks.)

Radio

Radio is less popular among advertisers in Europe (except France) than in the third world. Although Europeans do listen to the radio, government restrictions have inhibited radio advertising. Only recently has commercial radio invaded the United Kingdom. Generally radio is more popular in Southern Europe, particularly in Spain, Portugal, and Italy. The overwhelming presence of radio in North and Latin America is simply not found in Europe.

In developing nations, radio listenership is highest among the lower classes. In Kenya, radio advertising is substantial. Yet in Nigeria, 1,700 miles to the west, commercial radio is nowhere as important as newspapers. In India, radio is basic. It reaches more people than any other medium. But the Indian advertiser's problem is not the medium itself, but the many languages and dialects needed to reach target audiences.

Many native distributors of American goods propose to manufacturers the percentage of the advertising budget they'd like to see spent on radio, magazines, newspapers, movies, and even village loudspeakers, a valuable media source in countries like Egypt. These recommendations are generally very helpful because the distributor "knows the territory." Sometimes, however, American manufacturers must check alternate recommendations. Distributors may have vested interests in certain media or they may sell other products to media owners and reward their patronage with advertising paid for by the absentee American advertiser.

Print

In many nations of the world, newspapers are strongly oriented to upper-class males. This is particularly true of developing countries. As an example, in Korea, 98 percent of businesspeople and 96 percent of students read the newspapers. Korean newspapers account for approximately a third of the total advertising investment. In Kenya, by far the greatest ad volume goes to newspapers; magazines and weekly papers follow.[12] Daily newspapers in Iran and other male-dominated countries become a selective medium, a role reserved for magazines in the United States. In industrialized nations, newspapers are more of a mass medium, however, and they traditionally receive the largest investment of advertising dollars. Thus they form the backbone of most ad campaigns directed to the consumer.

Western countries offer the advertiser magazines, also. *Der Spiegel* is a

[12]"World Advertising Expenses," International Advertising Association/INRA, 1973.

highly visible German weekly with a circulation of 900,000 and a high pass-along readership of over five readers per copy. Its counterpart in France is *L'Express. Paris Match* and Germany's *Epoca* and *Stern* are good family and general-interest magazines similar to *Time* and *Newsweek. Margriet* and *Story* are Dutch general-interest magazines that reach over 40 percent of Dutch women. In the United Kingdom, *The News of the World* is a Sunday newspaper-magazine that reaches 39 percent of all adults; the *Daily Mirror* reaches 33 percent (Figure 23-4).

In Switzerland—with its three national languages, German, French, and Italian—there is no one national magazine. Therefore advertisers must supplement magazine advertising with newspaper support in each of the major Swiss cities: Bern, Geneva, Basel, Lucerne, and Zurich. Media buyers in Switzerland and France find that enough different magazines are published in these countries to allow them to divide their markets. Among the sixty major magazines published in Switzerland, for example, there are those devoted to general interest, fashions, radio and television, home and garden, sports, business, and teen activities. In France, by using the two major Paris newspapers, *Le Monde* and *Le Figaro*, and employing strong regional newspapers in Lyon, Marseilles, and Bordeaux as support, an advertiser can devise a strong drive to reach most adults. Advertisers interested in the Swedish market have at least seventeen general interest and fashion magazines available. *Damernas Varld* is one of the best in terms of revenue brought in by advertising. To reach male readers in Sweden, advertisers have a selection of eleven publications. Many Swedish men and women read the strong national newspaper, *Expressen* (with a paid circulation of 545,000).

In the industrial and professional sector in Europe, excellent magazines are published in England, France, and Germany. In addition, copies of such internationally known magazines as *Time, Newsweek, International Management*, and *Business Week* are read by the corporate business community. *Reader's Digest* reaches speakers of at least thirteen different languages in Western Europe, Asia, and South America. Advertisers can even buy space in geographic editions of the publication—the Belgian-Flemish, the Belgian-French, or the combination of both, for example. Or they can buy space in copies reaching key city circulations in Europe, Latin America, Asia, Africa, Australia, and New Zealand. For the handyman or woman of Latin America, there's *Mecánica Popular*, with a total circulation over 160,000. Mexico, Argentina, and Columbia are responsible for the largest circulation bites. There's *Time Scandinavia, Time Common Market, Time Middle East/Africa, Time Israel*, and so on. Heavily oriented toward news events in South America, *Vision* also provides demographic breakdowns, like *Andean Group* and *Southern Zone*. Young, upscale, married Latin American women read *Bienhogar*, making a circulation package of about 285,000. Other well-known names appear: *Cosmopolitan En Español, Vanidades Continental*, and *Vogue* in Italian, English, and French. Brazil has several profusely illustrated periodicals, newsweeklies, picture magazines, and specialized trade

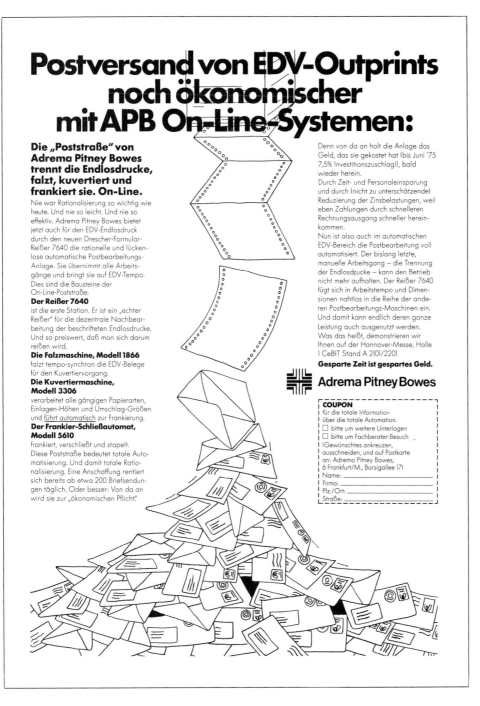

Postversand von EDV-Outprints noch ökonomischer mit APB On-Line-Systemen:

Die „Poststraße" von Adrema Pitney Bowes trennt die Endlosdrucke, falzt, kuvertiert und frankiert sie. On-Line.

Nie war Rationalisierung so wichtig wie heute. Und nie so leicht. Und nie so effektiv. Adrema Pitney Bowes bietet jetzt auch für den EDV-Endlosdruck durch den neuen Drescher-Formular-Reißer 7640 die rationelle und lückenlose automatische Postbearbeitungs-Anlage. Sie übernimmt alle Arbeitsgänge und bringt sie auf EDV-Tempo. Dies sind die Bausteine der On-Line-Poststraße:

Der Reißer 7640

ist die erste Station. Er ist ein „echter Reißer" für die dezentrale Nachbearbeitung der beschrifteten Endlosdrucke. Und so preiswert, daß man sich darum reißen wird.

Die Falzmaschine, Modell 1866

falzt tempo-synchron die EDV-Belege für den Kuvertiervorgang.

Die Kuvertiermaschine, Modell 3306

verarbeitet alle gängigen Papierarten, Einlagen-Höhen und Umschlag-Größen und führt automatisch zur Frankierung.

Der Frankier-Schließautomat, Modell 5610

frankiert, verschließt und stapelt. Diese Poststraße bedeutet totale Automatisierung. Und damit totale Rationalisierung. Eine Anschaffung rentiert sich bereits ab etwa 200 Briefsendungen täglich. Oder besser: Von da an wird sie zur „ökonomischen Pflicht".

Denn von da an holt die Anlage das Geld, das sie gekostet hat (bis Juni '75 7,5% Investitionszuschlag!), bald wieder herein.

Durch Zeit- und Personaleinsparung und durch (nicht zu unterschätzende) Reduzierung der Zinsbelastungen, weil eben Zahlungen durch schnelleren Rechnungsausgang schneller hereinkommen.

Nun ist also auch im automatischen EDV-Bereich die Postbearbeitung voll automatisiert. Der bislang letzte, manuelle Arbeitsgang – die Trennung der Endlosdrucke – kann den Betrieb nicht mehr aufhalten. Der Reißer 7640 fügt sich in Arbeitstempo und Dimensionen nahtlos in die Reihe der anderen Postbearbeitungs-Maschinen ein. Und damit kann endlich deren ganze Leistung auch ausgenutzt werden. Was das heißt, demonstrieren wir Ihnen auf der Hannover-Messe, Halle 1 CeBIT Stand A 2101/2201

Gesparte Zeit ist gespartes Geld.

Adrema Pitney Bowes

COUPON
für die totale Information über die totale Automation.
□ bitte um weitere Unterlagen
□ bitte um Fachberater-Besuch
(Gewünschtes ankreuzen, ausschneiden, und auf Postkarte an: Adrema Pitney Bowes, 6 Frankfurt/M., Borsigallee 17)
Name: _____
Firma: _____
Plz./Ort: _____
Straße: _____

FIGURE 23-4

Looking like its American original, this Pitney Bowes ad directs its message to German businesses. The ad appeared in the popular German newsweekly, *Der Spiegel*.

journals. As yet, magazines haven't taken hold in Japan, except for several colorful annuals used to promote the export trade.

By and large, companies can expect better-educated, more affluent audiences when they place their ads in overseas magazines and newspapers. This is not unlike the readership picture in the United States. The major difference appears to be in the quantity of readers, not the quality, although reader-profile information is spotty and uncertain at best. (Figure 23-5).

PRODUCTION PROBLEMS

Overseas advertisers can expect production problems that do not exist in the United States. For one, they must accept the fact that they'll be dealing with the customs service of every country in which they sell. It's time-consuming but necessary. Even sending business films back and forth requires special customs documents. Some national customs services exist simply to control the flow of good into their countries and their activities embrace advertising materials as well. Shipping advertising literature printed in the United States into Canada can be very expensive because of duties imposed by the receiving country. To reduce this cost, exporting companies may simply send the offset printing plate negatives to representatives overseas who turn them over to local printers. This effectively bypasses customs for bulk literature.

Films carry differing tariff rates according to their size in millimeters and whether they're exposed or unexposed. Some American companies employ "paperwork specialists," customs brokers, and international freight forwarders to expedite the sending overseas of all advertising materials. These specialists are experts on duties and tariffs all over the world. They can play an important role in helping American companies meet advertising deadlines and are generally listed in the Yellow Pages of large metropolitan *port* cities. It is also wise to check with the United States State Department or the Department of Commerce about restrictions on doing business in foreign countries. Advertisers who intend to do any overseas shooting for television commercials using local scenery (parks, castles, churches) must make certain that they get clearance from the proper government authorities.

There are other problems. Paper stock in magazines and newspapers is not always of the best quality. Good halftones or offset plates will have to compensate for that. Magazines produced in the Scandinavian countries, Germany, England, and Switzerland are usually better. Switzerland has a reputation for producing high quality in all printed matter. The Swiss reading public expects to see expertly rendered artwork and precise printing. Anything less can hurt the advertiser's image.

Advertisers who intend to conduct direct-mail campaigns to retailers and distributors throughout Europe should make certain that the material carries the postage of the country of the retailers. Sometimes advertisers must purchase goods or services from the country where they wish to place their advertising in order to get an import license. (An import license permits a

Volamos por el mundo como todo el mundo quiere volar.

Todos los días volamos por el mundo.

Llevamos italianos de Roma a Nueva York. Llevamos turistas de Venezuela a Florida y California. Hombres y mujeres de negocios de Río a Tokio y más latino-americanos a otros países que cualquier otra línea aérea del mundo.

Y como todo el mundo vuela con noso-tros, tenemos una idea muy clara de lo que sus clientes quieren de una línea aérea.

Quieren que los dejen tranquilos, pero que les brinden atención.

Quieren poner su confianza en una larga experiencia. Quieren ideas jóvenes.

Quieren una línea aérea que trata de poner sus vuelos al alcance de todos.

Por eso Pan Am vuela por América Latina con más 747 que cualquier otra línea. Y ofrece a sus clientes una tripulación con pericia adquirida mundialmente. Por eso todos los días en cinco continentes y en 71 ciu-dades de 47 países todo el mundo vuela con Pan Am. Les damos las gracias a sus clientes. Y a usted que les reco-mendó Pan Am.

FIGURE 23-5

Upscale readers in most industrialized countries are prime targets for Pan-Am ads in any language. Unfortunately, reader profile data is spotty at best, making specific print media selection more difficult.

foreign manufacturer to sell its goods in the host country). Some companies do this by having native printers run off advertising literature. It helps to create a reservoir of goodwill. Of course, in some countries, advertisers find they simply cannot get quality art, type, or printing, and they resign themselves to making the best of the local conditions. In these situations, they are no better or worse off than any other advertiser, foreign or domestic.

Advertising administrators of exported products need to remember that advertising, after all, is still part of the marketing mix. All other components need to be right, too, if the advertising is to work. Where there are no mass media, some of the selling burden will fall on point-of-purchase displays and signs, often the first and only advertising of the product that prospects have seen. For that reason, experienced administrators are careful to insist that their worldwide advertising plans include sales promotion and merchandising.

While we've concentrated in this chapter on the industrialized nations, we should also recognize that industry and capital is being exported in ever-increasing amounts to many underdeveloped countries. In the near future they, too, will become important markets to American advertisers. Who can doubt that there is a huge market across the seas and the borders for products of American companies, large and small? Despite worldwide inflation, shortages of resources, and political upheavals, millions of people in both industrialized and third-world countries are joining those who already enjoy the fruits of "the good life." The challenge for the American company is this: Can an American advertiser develop the insight to fully understand the problems of other peoples and other cultures, and thereby adopt the necessary strategies to sell goods?

IN SUMMARY

1 Citizens of the industrialized nations are the most frequently exposed to advertising.

2 In creating advertising for overseas countries, American copywriters and artists must make certain they don't offend religious and national customs.

3 Under a *centralized plan of creativity*, domestic copywriters develop one program for all countries where the product is sold. Under a *decentralized plan*, the authorized local agent in each country uses the United States-planned material as a guide but is not bound by it.

4 Better-known foreign ad agencies are often affiliated with large American advertising agencies. Smaller American ad agencies are affiliated with groups of cooperative agencies overseas and in the United States.

5 The preferred method for compensating several ad agencies working together for a single client is to pay the "Master agency" a set fee for masterminding the campaign and to allow each local agency its full 15 percent commission for the media it places advertising in.

6 National governments can be quite restrictive about what advertising they permit within their borders. Each country has its own rules and biases. Few are as liberal as the United States.

7 Most European ad dollars go into print media, especially newspapers and magazines.

8 Commercial television is available in all countries of Europe except Belgium, Denmark, Norway, and Sweden. The television medium is also growing on other continents.

9 Considering the many language and other kinds of barriers among nations of the world, it is hardly possible for an advertiser to buy one television spot and beam it to an entire global or continental market.

10 Of all European countries, Ireland, Austria, the United Kingdom, Spain, and Portugal spend the largest percentage of their total advertising dollars on commercial television.

11 Various factors limit investment in European television by advertisers: strong government controls restricting the numbers of commercials, advertisers, and commercial periods; owners of print media who influence governmental policies; and the overdemand of advertisers for available time slots.

12 Generally speaking, radio is more popular in Southern Europe than in Northern Europe. It is also the dominant medium in many third-world countries.

13 Daily newspapers are a selective medium in areas of the world where the male influence is dominant. In Europe, newspapers traditionally receive the largest percentage of invested ad dollars. They form the backbone of most ad campaigns.

14 There are numerous quality magazines available to the international advertiser. By and large, however, they require additional media support such as newspapers. Some of the best-known names in the magazine publishing world, such as *Reader's Digest, Time,* and *Newsweek,* offer geographic editions in a variety of countries.

15 International advertisers frequently deal with the customs service of every country in which they sell and promote. Some employ customs brokers and international freight forwarders to speed the flow of advertising materials from one country to another.

16 International advertisers may find that experience dictates purchasing advertising materials and services in countries where production skills are relatively unsophisticated, in order to obtain an import license for their exported goods as well as for their advertisements.

17 Where there are no mass media to speak of, international advertisers have to rely on point-of-purchase displays and signs in retail stores.

CASE STUDY "How Parker Gave the World a Name for Pens," by Phil W. Ritz, Director U.S. Export, The Parker Pen Company

Many companies are discovering only today what George S. Parker sensed soon after founding The Parker Pen Company: To be a leader in world markets demands that much of the manufacturing, product development, and marketing take place on foreign soil.

Parker made its first steps toward "giving the world a name for pens" about seventy-five years ago with the establishment of a Scandinavian distributorship. From these early roots, Parker has extended itself into every corner of the world as a multinational company with a combination of carefully selected distributors and patiently developed subsidiaries.

SIGNEZ PARKER!

FIGURE 23-6
Parker Pen ads are seen all over the world in 25 languages.

George S. Parker's methods for selecting overseas distributors worked so well that many appointed in the early 1920s still represent the company today. As Mr. Parker described it, "I went to a town like Bombay, for instance. I would first get acquainted with the American consul. Through the consul I would get acquainted with the bankers and businessmen. I would stay in the city long enough to get the atmosphere. By the time I got through, I pretty nearly had the idea who to sell." Parker now sells fully assembled products to about 115 exclusive-by-country distributors covering virtually every market in the world that allows writing instrument importation. In addition, there are some fifteen subsidiaries that perform both manufacturing and marketing activities. Some markets have established high tariff barriers to prevent or deter access. Other markets, like India, completely prohibit the importation of many consumer products like Parker pens. Smugglers are active in supplying Parker demand in these countries and counterfeiting also is encountered. Parker pens are sold legitimately in well over 100,000 retail outlets around the world.

All Parker marketing activities are decentralized to put decision makers closer to the marketplace. Primary responsibility for marketing rests with four area managers who manage Parker's four regions of the world: Asia/Pacific, Europe/Africa/Middle East, North America, and Latin America.

Parker has been an international advertiser of writing instruments since the opening of the Scandinavia distributorship in 1903. Currently fifty-seven advertising agencies present Parker's messages in more than 130 overseas markets using some twenty-five languages. Responsibility for handling advertising rests with the Parker market group manager, in conjunction with the distributor and the appointed local advertising agency. The language barrier is one of the greatest problems faced in the overseas market. Parker ensures the correctness of its translations by appointing local advertising agencies that have a first-hand knowledge of the subtleties of language and local idiom.

J. Walter Thompson Co., the world's largest advertising agency, represents Parker in several major markets: Canada, Mexico, the United States, Puerto Rico, Brazil, Venezuela, Guatemala, Malaysia, India, Japan, Korea, Australia, and New Zealand. Even these interrelated agencies approach the Parker account independently. Robin Restall, J. Walter Thompson's senior vice president for international coordination, says he found that among top international agencies, the secret of success is the local nature of their activities: "However professional and pragmatic creative people might be, they don't like receiving campaigns from other countries to adapt to their own markets. This can lead to a decline of interest and enthusiasm among the creative people who have to do the adapting."

Parker's four area managers are responsible for sharing their advertising strategies and tactics with each other by exchanging marketing plans, media schedules, and reprints. In addition, they meet at least twice yearly to discuss common concerns and plan worldwide introductions of new products. Parker plants in Mexico, Argentina, Brazil, Peru, Colombia, Rhodesia and South Africa produce primarily for domestic consumption. Plants in the United States, the United Kingdom, France, West Germany, Spain, Canada, and Australia produce for export, as well as home market consumption. Currently about 40 percent of Parker's United States exports goes to the Europe/Africa/Middle East area, another 40 percent to the Asia/Pacific area, and the remaining 20 percent goes to the Latin American area.

Selling gift-quality writing instruments overseas is different in many respects from selling them in the United States. Some examples of the differences are:

1   Nearly half Parker's United States exports (in value) are fountain pens. Inside the United States, fountain pens account for a very small percentage of sales.
2   Gold, silver, and other precious metals are in great demand for writing instruments overseas. In the United States plastics and stainless steel dominate.
3   Fine and extra-fine points are required in most Oriental markets. Medium points dominate in the United States.
4   In the United States market, conservative colors such as black and navy blue dominate. In some export markets bright colors such as red and bright blue dominate. Some cultures have taboos against certain colors such as white, which is often associated with death.

Parker's corporate headquarters are still located in Janesville, Wisconsin, where George S. Parker took up pen repairing part time when he was a telegrapher for the railroad. The company recently began construction of a multimillion dollar corporate headquarters in Janesville scheduled to be completed in 1980. A unique feature of Arrow Park, the manufacturing plant in Janesville, is the Path of Nations, a half-block long walkway featuring native stones and flags from the original eighty-five export markets served from Janesville. Each year thousands of people from around the world come to Janesville to see the Path of Nations and discover how Parker gave the world a name for pens (Figure 23-6).

QUESTIONS NEEDING ANSWERS

1   What advantages are there for Parker in permitting its overseas distributors to direct the activities of the local ad agencies? What disadvantages?
2   Why would some markets prohibit the importation of products like Parker pens? Explain.
3   Do you think there is a difference between the way a high school graduate in Nigeria looks upon a Parker pen and the way the product is viewed by a high

school graduate in the United States? Explain. Would you employ the same advertising strategy to reach both? Explain.

4 Do you think it is good competitive strategy to write ads in a sort of universal or "neutral" language that may not be the best local expression for Parker's selling points? Explain.

5 If you were developing the marketing strategy for Parker's international activities, what would you change? Explain.

STUDENT PROJECT

Contrast the volume and the types of advertising found in the United States' *Business Week* with those in the United Kingdom's *The Economist.*

QUESTIONS ABOUT THE PROJECT

1 Do you see any difference in the kinds of companies that advertise in these publications? Explain.

2 How would you compare the color reproduction of ads in both publications? The quality of the paper stock?

3 Which publication carries the most effective ads? Explain.

Unit

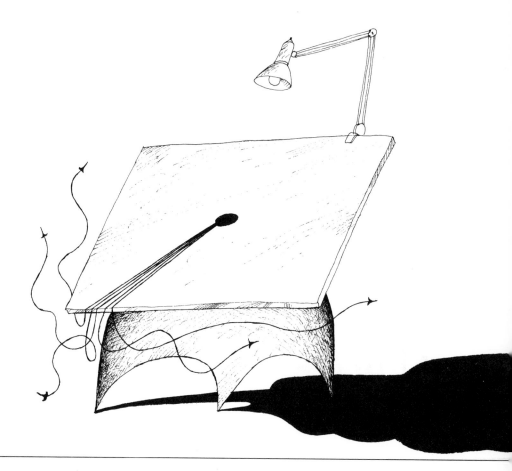

7

CAREERS IN ADVERTISING

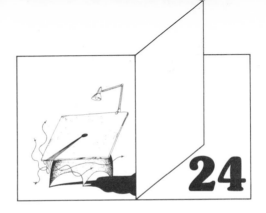

24

GETTING A JOB IN ADVERTISING

Update   For someone seeking a career in advertising, we can do no better than to repeat the summation provided by the American Association of Advertising Agencies: "If you're looking for a career at the core of business . . . if you enjoy working with quick, imaginative people . . . if the challenge of winning the public's attention and trust through bright, effective communication excites you . . . if you're resilient and have a knack for solving problems under pressure . . . if you're not afraid of assuming responsibility and making decisions . . . then consider advertising."[1]

Most job seekers are victims of circumstances. If the want ads happen to list openings in the steel industry, they may begin their career in steel. If the

---

[1]*A Guide to Careers in Advertising* (New York: American Association of Advertising Agencies, 1975), p. 17.

shoe industry is seeking people, they could end up in shoes. The want ads are one traditional way to get that first job. But that way fails to address itself to whether the applicants *want* to spend any time in steel or shoes. And once they accept a job, the chances are good that they'll remain in the field, particularly if they are successful and earn a good salary. It takes a lot of courage to leave a field in which you have experience to begin again in something new. The solution, of course, is to be the architect of your future and not let chance decide for you.

To prepare for a future in advertising, you need to decide in what section of the country you wish to live, in what industries you wish to work, and the kinds of jobs you want. With these conditions established, you now have a direction and a goal. If you know what they want *before* you start to look for that advertising job, you'll be closer to achieving it than someone who grabs any job willy-nilly.

Once you've set your sights on the kind of jobs you want, search out the help-wanted columns in current issues of *Advertising Age, Sales and Marketing Management Magazine, Industrial Marketing, Media Decisions, Public Relations Journal,* and/or the daily newspapers (Figure 24-1). If the pickings are slim, some ad experts recommend checking for job openings with the sales and advertising clubs found in most major cities. These clubs are close to the pulse of the business community and often are among the first to know of job opportunities. They can often provide important details about jobs that are not readily available from the classified ads.

However, even when neither of these job sources is fruitful, it may not mean that jobs do not exist. Companies often *make* jobs for disciplined, creative talent. They know that new talent can bring them income and prestige.

For people who are good but not creative stars, persistence and luck are important in finding a job. Persistence is a personal quality much admired by businesspeople. Luck or being in the right place at the right time can also land you a job. But luck seems to thrive in conjunction with hard work and talent. In the last analysis, despite peoples' inherent talent, getting a job depends on how well they sell themselves.

ADVERTISING'S FUTURE

Advertising, as we have said before, is an art and not a science, a field that depends on people and not machines. In economic terms, it's a labor-intensive business, one that will keep needing new people (Table 24-1). An analysis of the percentage changes in employment by industry over the last fifteen years shows that there are greater increases in the number of people employed in service businesses, such as advertising, than in most other industries, such as transportation, banking, and manufacturing.[2] Specifically,

[2]U.S. Department of Commerce, Survey of Current Business, January 1977, p. S-14.

JOBS AVAILABLE NOW

MKTG MGR. Pkg Gds. Midwest $29M
PRODUCT MGR—Food—N.J. . . 33M
AD MGR—Chem—Midwest . . . 30M
MKT RESCH—Food—N.J. 30M
MKTG MGR.—Cosmetics—N.J. 35M
MKTG RESCH—Banking—Phila 30M
MKT. RESCH—Food 30M
MKTG MGR.—Fast Food—Mass 25M
All fees paid by client companies.

CORWEN/MARCHANT ASSOC.,
527 Madison Ave.
New York, N.Y. 10022
(212) 753-0157

Marketing Product Managers $25M+ Consumer Packaged Goods.
JAR, an executive search firm used by select managements nationwide.
For confidential review re current or future opportunities, mail resume or phone Jim Roberts, President.

JAR & ASSOCIATES
Box 176
Westfield, NJ 07091
(201) 232-1585

MEDIA DIRECTOR

$20MM, Chicago-based agency needs an articulate presenter, solid administrator, and strong planner.
Send resume in full confidence to:

Box 296, ADVERTISING AGE
740 Rush St., Chicago, Ill. 60611

PRINT PRODUCTION MANAGER

Chicago Ad Agency wants take-charge person with 4-5 years of experience in print or graphic arts. Will be responsible for traffic and purchasing functions. Must type.
Send resume and salary requirements to:

Box 286, ADVERTISING AGE
740 Rush St., Chicago, Ill. 60611

WRITER

We are seeking a writing talent who can contribute a high degree of creativity in a diversity of areas including print advertising, product literature and sales promotion. Must have several years of good experience, be highly motivated, and desire to take charge and grow with our suburban Philadelphia agency. Great opportunity. Full benefits. Send resume and salary requirements.

Box 291, ADVERTISING AGE
708 Third Ave., New York, N.Y. 10017

MARKETING

PRODUCT MANAGEMENT
ACCOUNT MANAGEMENT
EXP. PACKAGED GOODS

Personal Involvement
Confidentiality
We would like to know you

CAMERON-WARD
Executive Search Consultants
333 East 49th St.,
New York, N.Y. 10017
212/688-1871

WANTED!

By one of America's largest Catalog Showroom Retailers an . . .

ASSISTANT ADVERTISING MANAGER

This aggressive, mature, creative, shirt-sleeve Ad Man will work with our Corporate Advertising Manager. He will have 2 to 3 years heavy retail advertising background and is not afraid of deadline pressure. He can create good layout and write appealing copy. A knowledge of paste-up, mechanicals, type specifications, color separation, catalog production and co-op procedures will surely give him away.
REWARD: We offer a challenge, an excellent salary and an outstanding benefit package to this person.
Please forward resume, detailing experience and salary history to:

SERVICE MERCHANDISE *Catalog Showrooms*

Charles T. Neill
2968 Foster Creighton Dr.
Nashville, TN 37204
An Equal Opportunity Employer M/F

ACCOUNT EXECUTIVE N.Y.-N.J. AREA

Our account is one of the top five computer companies in the country. You will have total responsibility for agency-client communications, campaign planning, and campaign implementation. At least 3 years of agency AE experience managing $500K+ accounts is essential as is a strong background in the business data processing, minicomputer, and peripherals markets. If you qualify, send a copy of your resume to:

Mark L. Nigberg
THE NIGBERG CORPORATION
10 Speen St., Framingham, MA 01701

ADVERTISING ASSISTANT

Immediate opening for self-starter with minimum 3 years experience in advertising and promotion. College degree required. Individual must have creative and administrative skills with the ability to effectively communicate with our staff, retail customers and creative services.
Excellent company benefits program including profit sharing, life and accident insurance, shared health and major medical insurance, pension plan, etc.
Salary open. Send resume to:
Mr. William E. Johnson
Corporate Personnel Director
JOCKEY INTERNATIONAL, INC.
2300 — 60th Street
Kenosha, Wisconsin 53140
An Equal Opportunity Employer M/F

ASSOCIATE BRAND MANAGER

Consumer products sales of $600-million makes our organization a leader in our industry. Our corporate headquarters, located in one of the fastest growing Sun Belt cities, has an opportunity for an Associate Brand Manager to join our professional marketing team. This is an opportunity for an individual with over three years experience in brand management with a major consumer package goods manufacturer, with food product background a plus. College degree required, MBA preferred.

Responsibilities entail managing all aspects of the marketing of a product line, including product packaging, positioning, creative coordination, media selection and spending levels, promotions, market research programs and sales forecasting for production and distribution requirements. The individual will coordinate with our Manufacturing Department to optimize short and long term profitability of products managed.

The person with a creative drive to produce rapid results without the usual organizational drag placed on key people in many large corporate environments will find an excellent salary and benefits package including relocation expenses. Please send resume and salary history. All inquiries will be held confidential.

Box 248, ADVERTISING AGE
740 Rush St., Chicago, Ill. 60611

An Equal Opportunity Employer M/F

ACCOUNT MANAGEMENT

(Branch Manager)

We have been retained by a $15mm full service agency (in business 20 yrs.) to bring on board a Branch Mgr. for a new Chgo. office. 5-10 yrs. exp. must include fast food and agency bkgrd. The successful candidate will have demonstrated creativity in promotional concepts, mkg. plan writing and sales ability, interpretation of research and solid media understanding. Competitive salary, fringe benefits and bonus. Call or write us 312/782-0235, Suite 4032, 55 East Monroe, Chicago 60603

THE EXECUTIVE PURSUIT

S. Wyle, President

Our consulting firm recruits only for communications and marketing needs of corporate and agency clients.

FIGURE 24-1
Every week ads similar to these fill the classified columns of the advertising industry's weekly, *Advertising Age*. Jobs range from advertising assistants and writers, artists, and designers to vice presidents. (Courtesy Advertising Age.)

TABLE 24-1

NUMBER OF EMPLOYEES PER $100,000 OF GROSS INVESTMENT
IN TWENTY-SIX INDUSTRIES*

Industry	Number of employees
Apparel and textile production	19.00
Contract construction	14.00
Leather and leather products	13.53
Furniture and fixtures	12.53
Services	10.85
Wholesale and retail trade	9.57
Textiles	8.84
Fabricated metals	7.91
Printing and publishing	7.76
Rubber and plastics	6.84
Miscellaneous manufacturing	6.52
Instruments and related products	6.04
Electrical equipment and supplies	5.61
Food and kindred products	5.48
Lumber and wood products	5.36
Nonelectrical machinery	5.17
Stone, clay, and glass	4.15
Transportation equipment	4.01
Paper and allied products	3.70
Primary metals	3.30
Chemicals and allied products	2.44
Mining	2.40
Tobacco	2.17
Finance, insurance, and real estate	0.98
Transportation, utility services	0.95
Petroleum and coal products	0.92

(Source: U.S. Department of Commerce, *Survey of Current Business,*
January 1977, p. S-14.)
*When we rank twenty-six American industry categories according to
how many persons are needed per $100,000 of gross investment, we
see that the most labor-intensive industries are apparel, construction,
leather, furniture, and services, in that order. Services include companies providing advertising counsel. The least labor-intensive industries
are transportation, communications, and petroleum and coal products.
Gross investment is measured in constant 1958 dollars.

there are more than 20,000 national and regional advertisers and over 7,000
advertising agencies, not to mention the thousands of community and
governmental groups currently employing or seeking advertising assistance.
The industry itself has moved from billings of $25 billion in 1973 to over $48
billion in 1978.[3] This increase is obviously more than outpacing inflation.

TYPES OF JOBS

Getting into advertising can be difficult. But it appears that a college
background is becoming more important, particularly in advertising agencies.

[3]Robert J. Coen, " Trends in Advertising Expenditures," The Interpublic Group of Companies,
Inc. Annual Report, 1977, p. 14.

A recent survey covering more than 300 agency people across the country shows that more than 75 percent have a bachelor's degree or better.[4] A number of advertising professionals concede that getting into the field may be difficult, but they seem to agree that people who make it find themselves with a well-paying lifetime career.

Most advertising jobs demand certain personal characteristics such as optimism, imagination, curiosity, adaptability, and cooperation. Here is a list of job titles people find in the business:

Corporate jobs: Copywriters, artists, writers, production specialists, ad managers, public relations administrators, market researchers, house organ editors and writers, audiovisual managers. (See Chapters 14 and 15 for job descriptions.)

Ad agency jobs: Copywriters, artists, media buyers, production specialists, market researchers, account executives, traffic specialists, office managers, treasurers, and film and television commercial producers. (See Chapter 15.)

Art studio jobs: Layout artists, illustrators, photographers, and sales representatives. (See Chapters 14, 15, and 17.)

Newspaper jobs: Layout artists, copywriters, sales representatives, advertising sales managers, classified ad salespersons, market researchers. (See Chapters 8, 14, and 15.)

Magazine jobs: Sales promotion specialists, space salespersons, advertising sales managers, and production specialists. (See Chapters 11, 14, and 15.)

Broadcast jobs: Continuity writers, sales promotion specialists, time-sales representatives, and advertising sales managers. (See Chapters 8, 14, and 15.)

Outdoor and transit jobs: Artists and salespersons. (See Chapters 7 and 15.)

Affiliated service jobs: Convention display artists and designers, public relations writers, premium promoters, photographers, typesetting specialists, platemakers, printers, market research, mailing-list brokers, film and videotape writers, directors, producers, jingle creators, and others. (See Chapters 13, 15, and 22.)

WHAT EMPLOYERS ARE LOOKING FOR

Corporate advertising managers and personnel directors of both media and ad agencies hire people of varying academic backgrounds. Throughout advertising, one finds people with majors in advertising, marketing, journalism, applied art, business, history, drama, sociology, psychology, economics, English, languages, engineering, chemistry, agriculture, home economics, and statistics. Although candidates without college degrees do find advertising jobs, their lack of a degree is a severe handicap, and they must have unusual talents to overcome it.

Public relations firms prefer prospective employees to have a strong background in newswriting, because so much of their work consists of doing

---

[4]*A Guide to Careers in Advertising*, p. 14.

just that. Contrary to myth, p.r. people do not spend their time in bars, golf courses, and country clubs flashing smiles and "glad-handing." Agencies favor college graduates with journalism, English, photography, business, and advertising backgrounds. Some employers prefer graduates with a wide knowledge of the world and are not concerned with a strict academic discipline of any sort. Recently, college graduates with agricultural, scientific, and industrial backgrounds have found that they are in demand if they possess communications skills. Their salaries, even at the entry level, are often several thousand dollars more than others.

The advertising industry—companies, agencies, media, and suppliers—has always demanded people who are socially and psychologically mature and who can get along with others. They want people with practical as well as theoretical intelligence, and good judgment along with academic degrees. Because advertising is a business of communication, the industry requires people who can think, write, speak, and *listen*. And they look for enthusiasm, an eagerness to get on the job and perform. Many companies would prefer to hire a rank beginner with enthusiasm and a willingness to learn than someone with actual experience but no drive.

How can interviewers detect whether job candidates are intelligent in practical affairs and show good judgment? Aside from reviewing college grades—not necessarily the best way to select an employee—they can observe the way candidates dress for the interview and the way they conduct themselves. Do candidates expand on their résumés and use language that reveals good reading habits and familiarity with the world? Do they respond to questions and then pose questions of their own? Often job candidates can help the interviewer if they bring along a portfolio of relevant advertising "roughs" of their work, done either in college or on the job somewhere. These samples go a long way toward revealing how the candidates' minds work.

THE JOB SEARCH

Narrowing the Field

Once you have decided what areas you may want to live in, look for companies whose needs match your qualifications. If you're interested in joining an advertising agency, you can locate most of the agencies in a region by referring to the agency red book (its official title is *Standard Directory of Advertising Agencies*). This large reference volume is found in public libraries, in ad agencies, and sometimes in the libraries of large daily newspapers. It contains pertinent data about most American advertising agencies: names, addresses, phone numbers, media credit affiliations, names of key personnel, and often a list of clients. The client list helps to classify the agency as oriented toward consumer, industrial, or agricultural products and services. Yellow Pages of phone books also list advertising agencies in each community.

If you prefer corporate advertising departments, however, a companion red book is available: *Standard Directory of Advertisers.*[5] This reference provides names, addresses, approximate yearly sales, approximate number of employees, products manufactured, top officials, name of the ad agency handling the account, name of the account executive, and advertising media used. The directory covers some 17,000 corporations. Sometimes the ad agency account executive will provide valuable details of the client's ad department.

Another way to learn about potential employers is to look through the *Standard & Poor's Index* available at most libraries. This reference provides business data about corporations.

Retail-minded job applicants should contact the ad departments of local newspapers and broadcasting stations; these can shed some light on what retail stores are within their spheres of influence. *Standard Rate & Data Service/Newspapers/Spot TV/Spot Radio* and *Editor & Publisher Year Book* list names, addresses, and other vital information about specific media.

Once you have decided where to apply for work, learn as much as you can about your targets. Try contacting persons who currently work for the company in other than an advertising capacity. This should provide another point of view as to the company's future. Sometimes it makes sense to discover what competitors have to say about the company. Your efforts to gather information will indicate that you have a genuine interest in the job and may also protect you from making a poor choice.

Dealing with an Employment Agency

Sometimes it's practical to seek the services of an employment agency, especially if you are moving into new and unfamiliar areas or if an agency knows of special job openings that are not usually advertised. If you do use an employment agency, it makes sense to go to one that specializes in advertising and marketing jobs. (If you are not familiar with the names of such agencies, ask the business editor of any large metropolitan daily newspaper, its classified ad manager, and/or the local chamber of commerce.) Employment agencies charge for their services, although many employers arrange to pay this fee.

Approach employment agencies as if they were potential employers. (Some agencies, in fact, have such excellent rapport with area employers that their recommendations carry a good deal of weight.) The agency interview is also an excellent opportunity to practice your skills of persuasion, because the interviewer at the employment agency must be impressed. Agency interviewers have seen many advertising and marketing people and can usually offer good advice.

Sometimes an employment agency will bargain for a higher entry salary for its clients than the clients might have been able to get for themselves. For

[5]Published by National Register Publishing Company, subsidiary of Standard Rate & Data, Skokie, Illinois, which also publishes the companion red book, *Standard Directory of Advertising Agencies.*

experienced and easily marketable creative advertising people, certain employment agencies direct mail résumés to selected companies around the country, thus broadening the exposure. This service is usually paid for by the job hunter. In all cases, you and the employment agency should agree—before the agency does any work—on what the fee is and who pays it.

THE RÉSUMÉ

Most prospective employers expect to see a résumé. This document is a typed or printed sheet, usually 8½ × 11 inches, listing your occupational history, talents, honors, awards, education, and professional and student organization affiliations (Figure 24-2). The résumé helps an employer to examine what applicants have done and what they hope to do and to compare job candidates. A mere résumé cannot hope to show the *real* person, but it helps employers decide who to ask for interviews. If a résumé reveals a candidate's lack of required credentials, the candidate will likely receive nothing more than a thank-you note.

Résumés are important and should be taken seriously. Compose yours carefully so that it reveals what is best about you. There are any number of ways to develop a personal résumé. One of the best is to remember that your target audience is a specific employer or a specific type of employer. You might list your accomplishments in the order of what that employer might consider most crucial. Here's a suggested format:

Name, address, and telephone number

Job experience with dates

Honors and awards

Professional organizations and memberships

Professional objectives (Be careful not to limit yourself.)

Education

Hobbies and activities

Once you have assembled this material, have it typed and mimeographed or typeset and printed. (It is always better to have a small oversupply of résumés.) Getting some jobs may depend on what you look like, so you may want to include a photo; a head shot will do. Send good photographs, never a Polaroid or a candid snapshot. Some enterprising job seekers supplement their résumés with direct mail, a tactic that separates them from the crowd and shows a prospective employer something of their creativity (Figure 24-3). Others actually rough out an ad and sell themselves as if they were a product. It's risky if you're not sure what makes a good ad, but if you do know, it shows a prospective employer that you do indeed have the creative qualities required of advertising people.

A word of caution. No matter what kinds of jobs you seek in advertising,

SCOTT WILLIAM KIRKPATRICK   AGE 29, MARRIED

DEGREES:

    M.B.A. Agribusiness, 1978, University of Santa Clara

    B.S. Animal science, 1974, Iowa State University

    B.S. Industrial Administration, 1971, Iowa State University

CURRICULUMS:

    Agribusiness...... Agricultural Marketing, Commodity and Futures Trading,
    U.S. Agricultural Policy, Financial Accounting, Quantitative Methods,
    International Trade and Development
    Animal Science...... Animal Nutrition, Reproduction, Meat Science, Agronomy

WORK EXPERIENCE:

    1977 - 1974, SELF-EMPLOYED FARMER...... A limited partner in a
    950-acre diversified farm in Iowa. Responsibilities included
    management of a cow-calf operation, a farrow-to-finish hog
    operation and 700 acres of corn and soybeans.

    1973 - 1972, SALES ENGINEER...... Royal Trane Air Conditioning
    Company, a dealership of the Trane Company, in Cincinnati,Ohio.
    Responsibilities were to design and sell air conditioning and
    heating systems to architects, general contractors and home
    owners.

    1971 - 1967, PART-TIME EMPLOYMENT...... Held a variety of jobs
    to pay half of college expenses. These jobs included: Pepsi-Cola
    delivery man, rural milkman for Flynn Dairy, assembly line worker
    at John Deere, sorority house waiter at I.S.U., dishwasher at
    Mary Greeley Hospital in Ames, maintenance man-janitor at Diamond
    Laboratories in Des Moines, self-employed painting house numbers
    on curbs.

ORGANIZATIONS:

    I have been or am presently affiliated with: American Simmental Association,
    Clarke County Iowa Extension Advisory Council, National Cattlemans Asso-
    ciation, Sigma Alpha Epsilon social fraternity, 4-H.

PRESENT ADDRESS:

    440 N. Winchester #95, Santa Clara, California, 95050
    408-243-8320

Additional resume information and references supplied upon request.

FIGURE 24-2
A typical résumé.

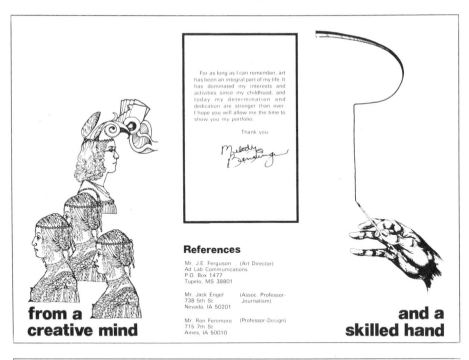

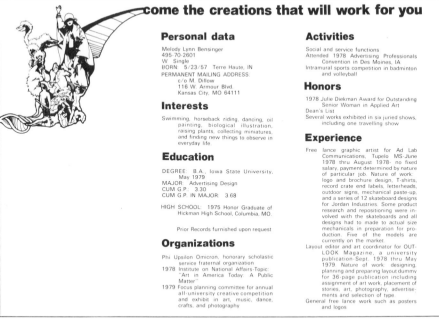

FIGURE 24-3
Unique presentations sell job applicants' experience as well as their creativity. (Courtesy Melody Bensinger and Neil Gadbury.)

Neil Gadbury:
Job Candidate

Promising job candidate
shows how his work and
dedication bring results.

Meet Neil Gadbury
and see for yourself
how he will produce for you.

Resume of
Neil Gadbury

Professional Objectives:
Account Executive
Advertising Manager
Marketing Manager

Education:

Candidate for the degree Masters of Journalism and Mass Communications in November, 1975, from Iowa State University, Ames, Iowa. Courses concentrate on advertising, communications through mass media, and researching the influence of mass media on audiences. Thesis topic is humor in advertising. The thesis attempts to study humor and one effect it may have on commercial messages. Activities and work at Iowa State include an Administrative Assistantship on the **Iowa State Daily** and the **Bomb**, National Advertising Manager for the **Iowa State Daily**, Photography lab assistant, staff writer for the **Iowa State Daily**. Played on the Journalism department's intramural basketball and softball teams.

Received a Bachelor of Arts degree in Business Administration in June of 1971, from Winona State College, Winona, Minnesota. Courses emphasize marketing, advertising and promotion. Historian for the Society for the Advancement of Management (SAM).

Attended Iowa Central Community College in Fort Dodge, Iowa from 1967 to 1969 majoring in liberal arts.

Work Experience:

Assistant Store Manager for the Woolworth Company. Responsibilities included merchandise selection and buying for a portion of the store, advertising and promotion, display, clerk supervision and training.

Administrative Assistant for the **Iowa State Daily** and the **Bomb**. The **Daily** is Iowa State University's student newspaper, duties included promoting linage from national advertisers, billing, collecting and bookkeeping of the national advertising accounts. The **Bomb** is Iowa State University's student yearbook, duties included bookkeeping and budget control.

Painting Contractor during the summer of 1974. Placed competitive bids on interior and exterior painting.

Address:
160 C University Village
Ames, Iowa 50010
Phone 515/292-6596

Summer jobs held while in high school and college: retail sales clerk for two men's clothing stores, construction laborer on prefabricated steel buildings, short-order cook.

Activities:

Avocations are the study of photography and camping. I enjoy many sports, among them are tennis, racket ball, handball, golf, all forms of aquatic sports and hiking. I have been a member of the P.B.O. Elks for four years.

References:
Jack Engel
Iowa State Daily Business Office
129 Press Building
Iowa State University
Ames, Iowa 50010

Jerome Nelson
Asst. Professor of Journalism
118 Press Building
Iowa State University
Ames, Iowa 50010

Dale E. Boyd
Asst. Professor of Journalism
211 Press Building
Iowa State University
Ames, Iowa 50010

Personal Data:
Born February 2, 1949, in Fort Dodge, Iowa.
Graduated from Fort Dodge Senior High in 1967.
Height; 5'7", weight; 135 lbs.
Married Donette Enfield of Humboldt, Iowa, on December 27, 1969.
We have two children: Richard, 5, and Nichole, 3.

remember that businesspeople are conscious of mistakes in spelling and grammar! Carefully proofread your résumé and any supporting material you send. Wise applicants have a friend proofread the materials also, so that carelessness doesn't rob them of their reward: the personal interview.

THE INTERVIEW: EYEBALL TO EYEBALL

The name of the interviewing game is preparation. First of all, you should have checked the company in some of the reference books listed earlier in the chapter. Know what the company manufactures or, if it's an ad agency, what types of accounts it handles. Some applicants even write out a career plan for themselves: where they want to be five years from now, what type of job they'll want, and so on. Also be prepared to tell the interviewer what brought you to advertising in the first place. Career-related questions are frequently asked by interviewers; you should know the answers before the questions are asked and you should practice giving them.

Often job applicants prepare a portfolio of things that they have done that they think will interest a prospective employer: tearsheets, proofs, or rough layouts and copy of ads, news, creative stories, or publicity items published anywhere. Some ad professionals suggest that applicants keep any rough rewrites they have worked with, since ad managers and creative directors of agencies may want to see their progress from a project's start to its finish. Portfolios should be neat. If you need to redo some of the work, do it ahead of time. It doesn't make sense to spend precious interviewing time apologizing for mistakes. It is often a good idea to provide a short explanation for each ad, brochure, p.r. release, or broadcast commercial presented. "This ad is designed to reach men over fifty. Their problem was——. Here's how I approached the creative challenge:——."

Dressing conservatively makes sense for most interviews. Greet the interviewer with a firm handshake when you enter the office and look him or her in the eye. Allow your enthusiasm to shine through honestly and avoid the bubbly, the gushy, the sugary in anything you say. If you have prepared yourself for the interview, your answers will be to the point and will reflect your command of the situation. It's wise to show an interest in what advertising the company is doing. Some applicants ask questions about company objectives and competition. Such professional inquiries reveal to the interviewer that the applicant has done homework on the company. They'll help to move the applicant to the head of the class of job seekers.

The job of the interviewer is to try to assess whether the applicant fits into company plans. Smart applicants make it easy by telling what they've done before that is relevant to what the company is doing now. For example, if they've worked for a veterinarian during vacations and they know that the ad agency interviewing them has a dog food account, they'll tell the agency about their valuable background.

When the interview is over, be sure to thank the interviewer for his or her interest and time. Follow this up with a letter or phone call several days later saying how pleased you were to meet the interviewer and to see the company at first hand. Don't be afraid to ask for the job, either, at the conclusion of the interview or in your follow-up. Employers expect it.

WHAT'S THE PAY?

As with most other jobs in this country, people get paid according to the law of supply and demand. In advertising, the supply of artists, for example, is large, but the supply of creative people and copywriters is small. Thus, the entry-level salary for artists is usually below that for copywriters. Here are some rough estimates of what job applicants can expect to earn yearly in the

TABLE 24-2

SELECTED AVERAGE SALARIES 1978 (ALL AGENCY SIZES COMBINED)

Advertising agency:[6]	High	Average
Chief executive officer	$107,500	$69,700
Account supervisor	57,300	35,300
Account executive	36,100	22,700
Creative director	64,200	41,500
P.r. director	35,500	26,400
P.r. account executive	25,500	17,400
Art director	32,000	21,400
Layout artist, senior	21,700	16,000
Layout artist, junior	15,000	11,000
Copy chief	41,800	28,300
Copywriter, senior	31,000	20,900
Copywriter, junior	17,800	12,800
Broadcast/producer	32,600	22,600
Associate producer	22,600	15,300
Media director	39,300	26,500
Media supervisor	25,500	18,400
Buyer-space/time	18,100	12,700
Research director	41,600	29,300
Research analyst	20,000	15,000
Production manager	26,900	19,100
Production assistant	17,300	12,000
Traffic manager	16,200	12,000

Corporate ad department:		
Entry-level copywriter	$10,000	
Entry-level artist	8,500	
Experienced copywriter	14,000+	
Experienced artist	13,000+	
Advertising manager	from 17,000	
Entry-level p.r. writer	9,600	
Experienced p.r. writer	14,000+	
Manager, public relations	17,000+	

[6]Rubel and Humphrey, "1978 Advertising Agency Salary Study," Spring 1978, vol. 21, no.4, pp. 14-21.

TABLE 24-3

RATE OF INCREASE FOR FIVE MAJOR AD AGENCY FUNCTION GROUPS,
1978 (ALL SIZE GROUPS COMBINED)

Function group	Rate of increase over 1975 (percent)
Administrative	17.2
Contact (incl. p.r.)	16.8
Creative (incl. broadcast)	15.9
Media and research	17.1
Print production and traffic	14.0

Source: The Rubel Service, "1978 Advertising Agency Salary Study," Spring
1978 (Vol. 1, No. 4), p. 5.

various jobs in advertising (add 2 to 7 percent a year depending on the vigor
of inflation).

A number of the larger ad agencies prefer entry-level employees with a
master of business (MBA) degree who can be steered into account
management positions. Some entry-level salaries for top MBA holders may
begin at $20,000. As a rule, job candidates for either companies or ad
agencies can expect to earn less if they work for a very small firm than if they
work for a large corporation. On the other hand, they may do better still over
the long run if they work for a medium-sized company, or if they work for an
ad agency and are responsible for client contact and for influencing the size of
budgets. According to a study by Rubel & Humphrey,[7] *contact* personnel got
better salary increases than most other agency employees (Table 24-3).

Little has been said in this chapter about the opportunities for self-
employment in the advertising industry even though a large portion of the
nonadvertising population is self-employed. Operating as a freelance advertising consultant is difficult because success usually depends on experience;
most companies are reluctant to try the ideas of persons new to the field.
However, if self-employment is to be a practical course of action for an
advertising newcomer, it will more than likely begin at the retail level where
budgets are low.

It is estimated that about a third of the people in advertising work in
agencies. The others work in media, in company ad departments, or with
suppliers. The road from the first entry-level job to the top in any of these
three areas is not much different from that in any business or profession. It
depends on a goodly amount of ambition, knowledge, and talent.

Good luck!

CASE STUDY   Advertising People   The advertising

industry provides an assortment of jobs, none without problems. Yet, as in most
occupations, superior people manage to rise to the top despite obstacles. We conclude
this chapter, and the book, with a brief look at some persons who are making their
mark in the field, hoping that they will serve as an inspiration to a new generation of
achievers.

[7]Ibid.

FIGURE 24-4
Reva Korda, *Ogilvy & Mather*, New York City.

FIGURE 24-5
Louis F. Kutscher, *Architectural Record*, Stamford, Conn.

REVA KORDA, *Executive Vice President/Creative Head, Ogilvy & Mather, New York.* Reva entered advertising as a copywriter for Gimbels' department store. She later joined Macy's, where her creative copy attracted the attention of an advertising legend, David Ogilvy. He hired her as a junior copywriter, and she was on her way. She has written and supervised work for Avon, Campbell, General Foods, Hershey Foods, Lever Bros., Mattel, Bristol-Myers, Sears, and many other important companies. She has taught classes of Ogilvy & Mather creative people on five continents. In 1975 Reva became the first woman elected to the Board of O&M International; she's also on the OMI Creative Council, reviewing creative work produced by offices all over the world. She says "I believe the best preparation for a job in advertising is a good liberal arts education—as it probably is for most jobs" (Figure 24-4).

LOUIS F. KUTSCHER, *District Manager*, Architectural Record, *Stamford, Connecticut.* Lou Kutscher has spent his entire working life selling advertising space for one magazine, *Architectural Record.* Educated at Andover and Yale, Lou earned his way through both schools selling products and services of one kind or another. He regards advertising space as simply a "salesperson in print" who can most efficiently communicate a multitude of vital messages to potential buyers, known and unknown. Lou has been active in the leadership of business advertising associations in Cleveland, New York, and Stamford. A history major at Yale, he finds liberal arts subjects, such as history, the most helpful in bringing seemingly disjointed and unrelated facts together in a meaningful way. Media buyers throughout the country consider Lou one of the top professional space salesmen of the decade because of his ability to translate marketing information to advertisers (Figure 24-5).

GLORIA ALEFF, *President, Gloria Aleff and Associates, Waverly, Iowa.* "I like people. And I have had the opportunity to work with especially good people—smart, experienced business associates. It is through this contact with some of the best minds in the advertising/marketing fields that I have benefited most. Daily I learn something new from my clients, and it is to them that I attribute my growth.

FIGURE 24-6
Gloria Aleff, *Gloria Aleff and Associates*, Waverly, Iowa.

FIGURE 24-7
Les Anderson, *Bozell & Jacobs*, Omaha, Nebraska.

"Growth is important in advertising because advertising is a dynamic field. Clients' needs change. Products change. Media requirements change. The only element that remains the same is the challenge: to produce quality work. It's that simple.

"Sound reasoning is important. My advice to any student of advertising has always been, listen to your common sense. You know more than you give yourself credit for. It's true. We're all the same . . . just people. You know as well as anybody what will work and what won't. A good ad sells a product without sacrificing creativity. Creativity is totally wasted unless your product is believable. Know your product. Know your market. Present the benefit. It's simple, right? Almost.

"Advertising would be simple if you had to please only yourself. Add another person and you add another opinion.

"Together, my staff and I form an agency team—combining efforts to produce the quality work that best meets clients' needs. Separating our jobs into specific roles, I see my job as a management one. I generate new business, handle the accounts, and generally manage the agency.

"We specialize in agricultural and industrial advertising and have chosen to base ourselves in the Midwest where many such accounts are located. We are a support agency for John Deere and Company and the Maytag Company, and a full service agency for Waterloo Industries, as well as for small, successful businesses in the area. Yet it all began, after weeks of door knocking, when we received our first job from the Maytag Company—a $350 card to fit in the lid of an automatic washer. A small job, but an important one. It cost us over $400 to produce, but it was one terrific lid card! We billed the company only the predetermined $350 and "ate" the rest . . . we were growing." (Figure 24-6).

LES ANDERSON, *Vice President/Executive Art Director, Bozell & Jacobs, Omaha, Nebraska.* Mr. Anderson has been with Bozell & Jacobs since 1961. He received his professional training at the Art Center College of Design, Los Angeles, California where he majored in Advertising Illustration.

He has been involved in nearly every phase of agency operation. His client experience includes dairy foods, utilities, banks, industrial development, farm machinery, seed, feed, chemicals, fertilizer, animal health, and many other areas. Creatively, he has been involved in the preparation and supervision of many extremely successful advertising campaigns that appear in all media.

During his career, Mr. Anderson has been the recipient of many awards of excellence won in both regional and national advertising competitions.

New business activity is also one of his primary responsibilities. His involvement in this area has contributed greatly to the growth of the Bozell & Jacobs Agricultural Division, now the nation's largest agri-business advertising group (Figure 24-7).

JOE ROSE, *Manager, Hog and Beef Chows Advertising and Sales Promotion, Ralston Purina, St. Louis.* Joe first became interested in advertising when—as an older-than-average-student—he switched from courses leading to a veterinary medicine degree to a major in journalism. When he enrolled in a beginning course in advertising and loved it, he knew he had found something he enjoyed doing. Nine months *before* be completed his course work at Iowa State University, Joe applied for a job with Creswell, Munsell, Schubert and Zirbel, Iowa's largest ad agency and a subsidiary of Young & Rubicam. His persistence, his animal science background, and the quality of his school advertising projects impressed the agency's management. Joe was hired upon graduation as an assistant account executive for several agricultural accounts.

Hard field work and six months later, he moved up to become an account executive, where he soon came to the attention of Ralston Purina, which hired him at a substantial increase in salary. From student to product ad manager took less than two years!

Joe gathers testimonials on products and writes and produces sales aids, technical papers, radio spots, and multimedia shows for dealers and farmers. Says Joe: "Some people think that photographing cattle and hogs and farm machinery is not as glamorous and exciting as photographing models for toothpaste commercials or the new sportscar models. Don't you believe it. Maybe some of the Hollywood glamour is missing, but it can get very exciting when a cow decides that the photo session is over and charges." Joe's one-word creed for success is *persistence*. He was thirty-one when when he graduated from college (Figure 24-8).

FIGURE 24-8
Joe Rose, *Ralston Purina*, St. Louis, Mo.

REID MILES, *photographer and film director, Los Angeles.* "Sure I have a reputation for being difficult. I can't work with guys who say cover this and cover that. . . . There's no difference between stills and film. One moves, the other doesn't. . . . I've always been certain. I know I'm good talent."[8] This is Reid Miles

[8]Mickey Mulligan Twohy, "Reid Miles," *Communication Arts*, January/February, 1977, p. 58.

FIGURE 24-9

FIGURE 24-10

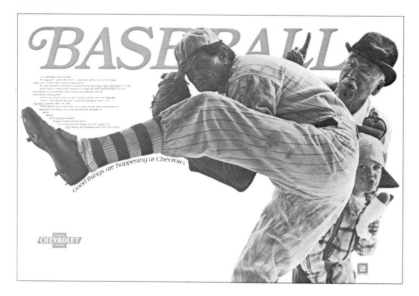

FIGURE 24-11
Reid Miles,
photographer and film
director, Los Angeles.

talking to writer Mickey Twohy[9] about what makes him tick. Reid has had a major
hand in the artistic success of leading blue-chip advertising accounts (Kawasaki,
Raleigh, Buick, Dole Pineapple, Kellogg Cereals, Polaroid, Du Pont, and more). Reid
shoots both still and film in his Hollywood studio whenever possible. Precise sets,
faithful to mood and period, are built for the camera.

"For me, the ad is designed in front of the lens. . . . I shoot heavily on vitality,
animation, and humor. In order to get comedy, the action has to be exaggerated to get
the look I want. . . ."[10] Reid likes to shoot real people with real faces who can be
believable in front of a camera. He uses actors, about forty-five of them: old, fat, ugly,
skinny—all kinds of people. He puts them in front of the product and recreates vintage
Norman Rockwell imagery. Reid's Rockwellian series for Kawasaki won him national
acclaim, and he has used the same approach for other advertisers (Figures 24-9 and
24-10).

"For me, work is my thing. It could be a combination of creative drive and the
Puritan work ethic. I was going to school and holding a full-time job when I was 14. I
sold *Liberty Magazine*, watered lawns, worked in a fish cannery, as a busboy and
waiter . . . work is my world"[11] (Figure 24-11).

[9]Twohy, op. cit., p. 58.
[10]Twohy, op. cit., p. 61.
[11]Twohy, op. cit., p. 64.

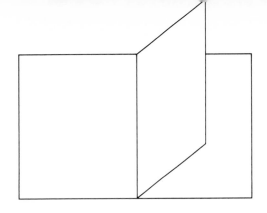

GLOSSARY

Account executive See *account group*.

Account group Those persons within an ad agency who manage and supervise the client's advertising.

Accountability A management term meaning responsibility for the manner in which employees invest company advertising dollars.

Administrators Among the top officials of a company are the administrators: presidents, vice presidents, and comptrollers.

Advertising Council, The A nonprofit organization of advertisers, AAAA agencies, and media owners formed to produce and present public service advertising.

Advertising cycle Marketers divide the life of a product into three advertising cycles: pioneering, competitive, and retentive. Each follows the distinct stages in the theoretical sales history of a product—its introduction, its move to maturity, and its decline.

Advertising goals (objectives) A specific statement of measurable and attainable goals that depend on the tools of advertising, and not on other elements of the marketing mix, for success.

Advertising specialties Low-cost gift items imprinted with the advertiser's name and given free to selected customers and prospects.

Affiliates Local outlets of the broadcasting networks.

Agate line rate In newspapers a basic measurement of advertising space, $\frac{1}{14}$ inch deep and one column wide. Also referred to as *line rate* and *open line rate*.

Agency network A string of widely dispersed ad agencies voluntarily cooperating with each other for their mutual benefit.

American Advertising Federation (AAF) The largest association of advertising people, ad clubs, and other advertising associations.

American Association of Advertising Agencies (AAAA) An association of prominent advertising agencies. Sometimes called the *AAAA* or the *4As*.

American Business Press (ABP) A centralized organization of business publications devoted to the economic welfare of its individual member magazines.

American Federation of Television and Radio Artists (AFTRA) A union of radio and television personalities and others who perform over network or large city stations at wage rates set by the union.

American Newspaper Publishers Association (ANPA) The trade association of daily and Sunday newspaper publishers.

American Society of Composers, Authors, and Publishers (ASCAP) An organization of copyright owners and creators of original music and books.

Amplitude modulated signal (AM) A long, direct radio wave that travels the earth's surface. An AM signal can travel up to several hundred miles.

Annual report A printed booklet detailing the highlights of the preceding financial year for the issuing company.

Answer print The final composite print of a filmed television\ commercial in which sound has been added to the visuals and the entire commercial has been correctly timed. Often called *final print* or *master print*.

Arbitron reports A system of obtaining ratings for television and radio programs developed by the Arbitron Company.

Area of dominant influence (ADI) A geographical area definition of television markets based on the principle of allocating individual counties to one market area that enjoys a 50 percent or better share of viewing hours. Developed by the Arbitron Company and used in media scheduling.

Art or artwork A general term describing any or all of the following visual parts of an advertisement: layout, photographs, illustrations, line drawings, and typography.

Association of National Advertisers (ANA) Among the oldest operating advertising trade associations whose members include leading national advertisers.

Asymmetrical layout An informal arrangement of the elements in a piece of advertising.

Audimeter An electronic device for recording when the television set in a household is on. Used by the A. C. Nielsen Company in its research operations.

Audio The sound portion of a television commercial.

Audit Bureau of Circulations (ABC) Organized in 1914 by advertisers, their agencies, and publishers, ABC established standard measurements to verify media circulation claims.

Audited publications Magazines and newspapers whose circulations are verified by an independent auditing firm such as Audit Bureau of Circulations (ABC).

Availability The time period available for purchase in broadcasting.

Bait-and-switch advertising An insincere retail offer to sell a product when the intention is to sell something else, generally at a higher price.

Barter A traditional practice of selling advertising space or time in exchange for merchandise or other valuable assets, such as is done on a television serial or game show.

Barter House An organization that buys large blocks of advertising time or space that it resells to advertisers in exchange for money or merchandise.

Bed The surface of a printing press on which the plates are laid.

Billboards Large, outdoor, upright structures on which advertising is placed. Also called outdoor boards, poster boards, or bulletins.

Billings Amounts of gross business developed by an advertising agency, which includes media and production commissions and fees.

Black & white In terms of magazine advertising rates, a one color ad. Most magazine ad rates are listed as black & white with a separate listing for additional colors.

Bleed ads Any illustration or type matter that goes beyond the standard dimensions of a publication for its conventional ads. Bleed ads are generally charged a premium.

Bounceback card A card or enclosure designed to get an additional response or business.

Boutique agencies A specialty advertising agency devoted primarily, if not exclusively, to providing copy and art services.

Brainstorming A technique of developing ideas by encouraging open discussion.

Broadside An overly large folder generally sent out as a direct-mail piece.

Brownprint A facsimile (in faded brown) of the way the final printed advertising piece will look. It is made by the printer and sent to the advertiser as a final check before the job is run.

Bulk mail A lower-priced class of United States mail usually delivered to the post office already sorted according to ZIP Code.

Bulletin See *billboards*.

Business media see *business publications*.

Business/Professional Advertising Association National organization of advertising professionals working for industrial companies, their ad agencies, and their media. Once known as the Association of Industrial Advertisers.

Business publications Specialized magazines designed for business, industrial, and professional readers. Also called *business media*.

Business Publications Audit (BPA) The best-known independent auditing organization for business publications.

Cable television Private businesses operating in various localities that pick up television signals from other nearby or distant transmitters and relay them to subscribers (tied in by means of cable connections) for a monthly fee. Also known as *Community Antenna Television System* (CATV).

Camera-ready After the illustrative and copy elements of a piece of advertising have been arranged in their final form, they are camera-ready, or ready for print reproduction by means of the camera.

Campaign All the advertising efforts in support of a product or service directed toward achieving an advertising or public relations goal.

Canned spots Radio ads prepared and supplied by manufacturers. Canned spots may be on a script, on tape, or on a record and are usually part of a cooperative advertising program.

Case history A popular type of industrial advertisement that features an application at a specific company.

Cathode ray tube (CRT) A vacuum tube that generates a focused beam to reproduce images and/or type characters on a screen.

Centralized plan of creativity In reference to international advertising, a single creative selling program for all countries, the only change being that of language.

Circulation In print advertising, the number of copies of a magazine or newspaper distributed on a regular basis to households, plants, or individuals. In broadcasting, the cumulative audience. See *reach*.

City magazines Metropolitan magazines devoted to hometown and urban concerns.

Classified ads Generally appearing in a special section of a newspaper, classified ads are also known as "the want ads." A variation, *display classified*, allows for illustrations and a wider typeface selection.

Closing date The time by which advertising material for publication and broadcast must be in the hands of the media in order to be included in a specific issue or program.

Clutter A state in which there are many commercial messages within a short period of time or space, with the result that too few are remembered.

Cold Type The machine process of setting type by means of a camera arrangement using film or sensitized paper. Also known as *photocomposition*.

Collateral material Non-commissionable projects developed by ad agencies for their clients: brochures, sales sheets, catalogs, films, and sales promotion materials. Usually paid for by negotiated fees or as an add-on percentage of the job cost.

Column inch A unit of newspaper advertising display space 1 inch deep and one column wide.

Commercial The advertiser's sales message on either radio or television.

Commercial marketing association An organization of producers of a commodity (such as wool) who band together in order to market their products. Activities generally include selling and advertising.

Commissionable media Media that pay recognized advertising agencies the standard commission for business directed to them by the agencies, usually 15 percent.

Community Antenna Television System see *cable television*.

Comp layout See *layout*.

Composition See *type*.

Computerized photographic typesetting Computer-directed electronic typesetting using character storage, an optical system, and light-sensitive paper.

Consumer advertising Defines the type of advertising calling public attention to products and services by paid announcements through the mass media. It differs from industrial, professional, and trade advertising in that the target of the advertising is the ultimate consumer. It is the most visible of all types of advertising.

Consumer magazines Publications written for the general public.

Consumer ombudsman In some countries, a person responsible for taking action against anyone using deceptive advertising.

Contact personnel (account group) A term used to describe junior and senior ad agency account executives.

Continuity The regularity with which messages appear in advertising media over a protracted period of a year or more. Also, repetition of the same basic idea, format, and/or strategy. In broadcasting, the script that provides the stations with a continuous flow of spoken words.

Controlled circulation The circulation of business publications, generally restricted to only that audience of qualified interest to the publishers and their advertisers.

Cooperative advertising An agreement between a manufacturer and a retailer to share the costs of running a local ad placed by the retailer but featuring the manufacturer's product. Also a joint advertising venture by groups of manufacturers, wholesalers, or retailers.

Copy Printed or verbal messages in advertisements.

Copy chief The head of a group of copywriters in either an ad agency or an advertising department.

Copy platform See *strategy platform.*

Copy testing A method of measuring the effectiveness of advertising.

Copyfitting The technique of fitting copy of a specified size and style into a given space.

Copywriter A person who creates the ideas and the text of advertisements.

Corrective advertising Since the mid-1960s, the FTC has the assumed power to demand that companies responsible for deceptive advertising erase false impressions by running "corrective" ads.

Cost per impression A measure of the cost of any medium to reach a viewer, listener, or reader.

Cost per thousand (CPM) A standard measurement benchmark of the efficiency of media as they compare to each other. CPM represents the cost of a medium to reach 1,000 readers, viewers, or listeners.

Council of Better Business Bureaus (CBBB) A business-supported organization designed to protect the public against fraudulent business practices.

Cover date The date that appears on the cover of a magazine.

Cover positions Premium-priced positions of a magazine issue. The second cover is the inside front cover; third cover is the inside back cover; fourth cover is the back page of the publication. Front covers are generally not sold for advertising.

CPM See *cost per thousand.*

CU Television slang for a camera close-up.

Cumes The shortened form of cumulative audience. See *reach.*

Customized profit systems An innovative manufacturer's sales tool that appraises retailers' shelf allocations by profits and product lines.

Customs brokers Paperwork specialists who expedite the shipment of advertising and other materials between countries. Also known as *international freight forwarders.*

Cut In engraving, a photoengraving or electrotype. In television and movie slang, directions for the camera to jump from one scene to another. In a recording studio, to reproduce sounds on a record.

Daniel Starch See *Starch INRA Hooper, Inc.*

Day-parts In broadcasting, times of telecast programs described as morning, afternoon, early evening, night, and late night.

Dealer imprint The name and address of a dealer printed or stamped on ads and sales literature.

Decentralized plan (of creativity) A creative selling plan designed to meet the needs of each country and its conditions.

Decorative faces A series of novelty typefaces designed with the intent of commanding attention.

Demographics A statistical study of human populations citing numbers, ages, income, education, sex, and other factors. Advertisers are particularly interested in these characteristics of their customers and prospects.

Depth interview An unstructured technique of interviewing respondents designed to bring out more than casual answers. *See psychographics.*

Design engineer The person in a plant whose primary job is to draw the plans and specifications for manufacturing a product.

Diary A research method used to record consumer listening, viewing, purchasing, and other habits of interest to advertisers. Best-known diaries are those distributed by A.C. Nielsen Company and the Arbitron Company.

Die-cut A shape or pattern cut into a direct-mail piece by a special cutting press using a die.

Direct-impression composition Type matter created by typewriterlike machines.

Direct mail A form of advertising that is sent through the mail.

Direct-mail format The physical appearance of a piece of direct-mail advertising.

Direct marketing The marketing of goods or services directly to the consumer by the manufacturer. It may include direct-response ads and/or door-to-door selling.

Direct response A form of advertising that expects a responsive action on the part of the reader, listener, or viewer. Also called *mail order* if sent through the mail.

Disk See *pressing.*

Display ads A newspaper term to describe ads fourteen lines and more and generally illustrated.

Display advertising A method of attracting customers by imprinting product information on pieces of cardboard, plastic, or light metals placed in windows, on counters, and on floors. Display advertising may also be called *point-of-purchase (P.O.P.) advertising.*

Display faces (type) Display faces are common to many typefaces; their main distinction is their size, 18 points or larger. Sometimes called *display type.*

Dissolve A gradual scene change in television or movies.

Dolly in or back Television camera directions for moving the camera backward or forward.

Drive time The same as *traffic time,* a radio term. The morning and afternoon hours when listeners drive to and from work.

Dub To insert visual and/or audio elements into a film sequence.

Duotone (halftone) Popular multicolor technique of engraving in which two halftone plates are made from the same black-and-white photograph.

Duplication of readership A situation in which the same subscribers receive competitive magazines and/or newspapers.

ECU In television slang, an extreme camera close-up.

Editor and Publisher Year Book An annual that lists basic information about daily, weekly, and triweekly newspapers.

Electronic transcriptions (ETs) Another name for records.

Electrotypes (electros) Duplicate plates made from an original engraving plate, copper or zinc.

Engraver's proofs A number of glossy reproductions of an advertisement sent to the advertiser for use in merchandising. Sometimes called *preprints* if they are run before the ad appears in a publication or *reprints* after the ad has run.

Engraving See *platemaking.*

Exclusivity rule A tacitly accepted rule in international advertising whereby a multinational advertising client owns and can use everything created for it by any or all of its agencies anywhere in the world.

Fairness Doctrine A government regulation requiring broadcasting stations to allow advocates of both sides of a controversial public issue to present their views.

Federal Communications Commission (FCC) The federal agency that has authority over radio and television transmission systems. Broadcasting systems must apply to the commission for a license and assignment of a wave-length over which they may broadcast.

Federal Election Campaign Act Under this law passed in 1974, major-party presidential candidates receive lump sum grants from the United States Treasury for advertising and promotion.

Food and Drug Administration (FDA) An agency within the Department of Health, Education and Welfare charged with enforcing federal laws barring the sale of impure foods, drugs, and cosmetics.

Federal Trade Commission (FTC) An independent commission of the United States government established in 1914 to prevent, among other things, false and deceptive advertising of goods. In recent years, the Commission has taken stands against companies that advertise to children and has challenged the broadcast industry code that limits the amount of advertising sold on television.

Field experimentation In terms of budget allocations, a method of actually assigning a budget to a test project and discovering its adequacy under real conditions.

First Amendment The First Amendment of the United States Constitution states, among other things, that "Congress shall make no law . . . abridging the freedom of speech, or of the press." The Supreme Court has held that this protection covers advertising.

Fixed budgeting A budgeting technique for advertising that provides the same relative dollars year after year.

Fixed position A television or radio spot bought for a specific time.

Fixed rate The costliest spot in broadcasting, because it cannot generally be displaced by someone offering more for the time. See *preemptible rate*.

Flat-bed press A printing press in which a moving flat surface holds the printing plates while an impression cylinder applies the pressure. Sometimes called *flat-bed cylinder press*. Compare *vertical press*.

Flight The period of time an ad schedule runs without interruption. Generally the term refers to broadcast media scheduling and is expressed in days, weeks, and months.

Focus group survey Generally a market research procedure based on in-depth interviews with a small group of individuals having some common interests. Their opinions, while valuable, cannot be assumed to represent those of masses of people.

Fonts or faces A family of one style of type.

Food days For most supermarkets, the days their ads appear in the local newspapers, generally Wednesdays and Thursdays.

Four-color process A means of reproducing full-color ads by use of a variety of plates. One set prints everything that is to appear in yellow, another everything appearing in red, the third everything in blue (cyan), and the fourth everything in black. The plates are sometimes called *four-color process plates*.

Fourth cover See *cover positions*.

Frequency The number of times a household (or individual) is exposed to an advertisement within a given time period. Time of measurement is generally shorter for the broadcast media than for print.

Frequency-modulated signal (FM) A straight broadcast signal that travels only as far as the horizon, about 40 to 50 miles.

Full-service agency An advertising agency that provides a full range of client services: marketing, media buying, public relations, copywriting, art, and broadcasting production, all from within its own organization.

Gatefold Any folded insert within a magazine larger in width dimensions than the conventional page. Gatefolds are usually found within the first few pages.

Gross impressions The total number of people or households exposed to an advertisement (or program), measured without regard for duplication.

Gross rating points (GRP) A measurement of the viewing (or listening) audience of specific programs, generally expressed on a weekly basis. Also a measurement used in the outdoor industry to describe reach and frequency. See *rating point*.

Gravure printing (rotogravure) A method of printing in which the design is sunk below the surface of the plate to hold varying amounts of ink. In gravure platemaking, an etched cylinder is made from the photo negative of a piece of advertising.

Guideline budgeting A method of budgeting for advertising that is based on what the company has been spending in previous years.

Halftone Halftone photography makes it possible to reproduce a photograph with a broad range of tones from light to dark.

Headline (or head) A caption, generally in large type, designed to attract a reader's attention quickly.

Hi-Fi A brilliant full-color printing process for newspaper pages usually done by an outside printing plant. The ads appear as a continuous design so they can be fed into the newspaper press and cut to fit the page size. The ad is on one side only, leaving the other side available for printing by the newspaper. Somewhat similar to *Spectacolor.*

Horizontal publication A business publication designed to be read by people with similar job functions throughout a broad spectrum of industries. Compare *vertical publication.*

Hot type Machine-set type that is cast by using molten metal.

House organ A newspaper or magazine published by an advertiser for internal or external use.

Image attribution Tests in which people reveal their deeply held feelings about products and brands.

Industrial advertising A type of advertising for nonretail goods and services aimed at buyers who work in manufacturing, process, construction, and service industries.

Industrial buyers A wide assortment of people in various industries who buy industrial products from manufacturers, distributors, and manufacturers' reps.

Industrial distributor An industrial intermediary between the manufacturer and the industrial buyer.

Industrial road show An extravaganza featuring music, dialog, and actors to present a new line of products to distributors, dealers, and salespeople. Sometimes called an "industrial."

In-house agency (house agency) An advertising agency wholly owned by an advertiser, the agency's only client. In-house agencies may provide full or limited service.

Inquiry publications Sometimes called *inquiry books,* these are generally tabloid-size business publications devoted exclusively to showing new products and encouraging reader inquiries.

Insert In magazines, a special preprinted page produced by the advertiser and sent to the publisher who binds it into the magazine at an extra charge. Also an advertising piece placed inside a newspaper and delivered as part of the paper.

Insertion order An ad agency form notifying media and the client about an upcoming ad.

Institutional advertising A type of advertising designed to build the image of the advertiser rather than to sell specific products or services. Also meant to build favorable attitudes toward the advertiser.

International advertising Advertising used overseas.

International Advertising Association (IAA) A group of individuals active in the business of advertising internationally.

Interlock screening (interlock) An early production stage of a filmed television commercial in which the edited workprint and a separate magnetic sound track are played together for the first review of what the final commercial will look and sound like.

International Chain of Industrial and Technical Advertising Agencies (ICITA) An organization made up of advertising agencies in different countries who are affiliated to provide services to multinational and/or domestic advertisers.

Island-half position In print media, a premium-priced advertisement surrounded entirely by editorial matter rather than by other ads.

Iteration A method of using the law of diminishing returns for ranking media according to their reach and cost.

Keyline (mechanical) The pasteup assembly of all elements in a print advertisement, brochure, or catalog, showing the way they will appear in the finished piece.

King-size poster An outside transit display advertisement.

Labor-intensive In economics, a term that describes an operation heavily dependent on manual labor.

Layout A drawing or sketch of a proposed print advertisement, brochure, sales sheet, or catalog. If carefully done it is called a *comprehensive (comp) layout*; otherwise it is called a *rough layout* or *rough*.

lc Lowercase letters.

Leading (pronounced ledding) The amount of space allowed between lines of type, always expressed in points.

Letterpress A method of printing from raised metal that transfers images to paper under pressure of the printing press.

Line drawing Artwork that can be reproduced without the use of a halftone screen. Sometimes called *line art*.

Line rate See *agate line rate*.

Lithography Originally, a printing process using a flat stone specially prepared with some greasy substance to repel water but accept ink. Today a thin metal sheet takes the place of the stone. See *offset*.

Local rate A reduced line rate offered to local newspaper advertisers; usually lower than that offered to out-of-towners and national advertisers.

Logo or logotype A unique trademark, company name, or device used as an identifying symbol on products, packages, ads, and letterheads.

LS A long shot in television camera language.

Lucy See *projection machine*.

Magazine sections A special newspaper supplement of a highly pictorial nature inserted in Sunday newspapers. Sometimes called *newspapers within newspapers*.

Mail order See *direct response*.

Mailing list broker A person or company that rents the names and addresses of one advertiser's direct-mail list to another advertiser for a commission.

Maintenance engineer A plant official who is responsible for keeping equipment running smoothly and efficiently.

Make-good In print advertising, a free repeat insertion of an advertisement to make up for an error in the original insertion. In broadcasting, a rescheduling of a commercial previously preempted.

Manufacturer's representative An independent agent of the manufacturer's sales department who is paid earned commissions.

Market A geographical area or persons buying and selling. A market can be wholesale, retail, or industrial. Markets are sometimes referred to according to the kinds of goods that are sold in them. For example, the life insurance market, the military market, the automotive market.

Market research The study of market characteristics and audiences in order to make sound marketing decisions.

Market share A company's part of the total industry sales on a dollar, unit, or percentage basis.

Marketing An umbrellalike description for the activities of people involved in the transfer of goods from producer to consumer. It includes distribution, brand decisions, pricing, sales, and advertising.

Marketing goals (objectives) A specific statement of measurable goals relating to a product in terms of dollar sales, profit, units sold, and/or market share.

Marketing mix A combination of variables involved in the marketing process: distribution, brand policies, pricing, the product, sales, and advertising.

Marketing Practices Act (Sweden) A 1971 Swedish law protecting the consumer against deceptive advertising practices.

Mats Papier mâché reproductions of ads created for letterpress newspapers.

MCC Media Data Form The name of the standardized format made available to business publication owners by the Media Comparability Council.

Mechanical See *keyline and camera-ready*.

Media The means of transmitting information to large groups of people: newspapers, magazines, radio, billboards, and so on.

Media buyer (director) The person in charge of selecting, evaluating, and buying media at an advertising agency.

Media-buying service An independent agency offering advertisers one service only, the selection, evaluation, and buying of media according to established advertising objectives.

Media commission Compensation, usually 15 percent of billing, paid by media to ad agencies for placing business with them.

Media Comparability Council (MCC) An organization that provides a standard format for publishers to present advertisers with important media information.

Media contract A legal agreement between a medium and an ad agency concerning space and/or time purchased on behalf of a client.

Merchandising In retailing, the planning and supervising involved in marketing goods or services at the time, place, price, and quantity necessary to meet marketing objectives. Also pro-

moting, advertising, and publicity to an advertiser's target audience, sales force, channels of distribution, and suppliers.

Milline rate A formula for comparing the advertising line rates of newspapers.

Model simulation Enacting theoretical business situations to determine the results of certain courses of action, usually accomplished with a computer.

Modern Despite its name, a 200-year-old typeface with extreme contrasts between thick and thin strokes.

Monthly declining balance A budgetary control system applicable to advertising budgets in which all monthly expenditures are regularly subtracted from a previous balance.

MS A medium shot in television camera language.

Multimedia presentation A dramatic presentation technique using combinations of slides, film, and sound to deliver a promotional message.

National Advertising Division (NAD) The makers of policy for the National Advertising Review Board.

National Advertising Review Board (NARB) Currently the ad industry's most effective organization for detecting, preventing, and publicizing misleading ads.

National media The informational means to reach a nationwide audience.

National Newspaper Association (NNA) The trade association of weekly newspaper publishers.

Network A number of television or radio stations joined together to broadcast simultaneously. NBC for example, is a national network.

Newspaper Advertising Bureau A service group funded by the American Newspaper Publishers Association (ANPA) to encourage advertisers to use newspapers to reach customers and prospects.

Nielsen reports Various reports by the

A. C. Nielsen Company providing measurements of audience size for television and radio stations and advertisers. Other reports by Nielsen chart consumer goods movements in and out of retail outlets.

Nonaudited publications Newspapers and magazines whose circulations are not surveyed by an auditing firm but that rely on other means of verification, such as a statement from the publisher.

Offset (lithography) In printing, a flat-surface method in which ink is *offset* from a plate to a rubber blanket, and then from the blanket to paper. Offset is the fastest-growing of the major printing methods. In platemaking, a thin metal or plastic sheet that carries the printing image and text and is run on offset printing presses.

Offset duplicator A small offset printing press.

Oldstyle A typeface patterned after letter forms found in Roman inscriptions.

On-sale date The date a magazine issue goes on sale, which is generally before the date printed on the cover (perhaps as much as two to three weeks).

One-time rate In print advertising, the rate for a single insertion during a calendar year, usually at the highest price, before frequency or bulk discounts begin. Sometimes called *open rate*.

Open line rate See *agate line rate*.

Optical character recognition (OCR) A computer process for distinguishing typeface characters and converting the information to electric impulses.

Outdoor See *billboards*.

Outdoor Advertising Association of America (OAAA) The outdoor advertising industry's trade association.

Package house In television and radio, an organization that produces commercials from ad agency scripts and storyboards.

Package plan (television or radio) Combinations of spots to serve varying needs of broadcast advertisers over a particular period of time.

Painted bulletin A billboard ad that is painted by an artist instead of being printed on a press.

Pan Direction given to the person running the television camera; the camera eye moves slowly and evenly, horizontally or vertically.

Pass-along readership A term magazine publishers use to describe people other than subscribers who read their magazines. Media buyers consider this kind of readership a bonus since it is not generally included as a basis for determining the price of an advertising page.

Per-unit budgeting Ad budgets set by allocating a specific dollar amount for one or a number of units sold or manufactured.

Percentage-of-sales budgeting A popular method of allocating an annual advertising budget, based on a selected percentage of the company's total sales for the previous year.

Photocomposition See *cold type*.

Photoengraving A photographic process of preparing printing plates for printing.

Photographic typesetting See *cold type*.

Pica A linear measurement of type. There are 6 picas to an inch. The length and depth of copy is specified in picas, for example, 18 picas wide by 30 picas deep.

Plant engineer A technically trained individual responsible for maintaining the physical structure of a plant and overseeing its efficient functioning.

Plate The end result of a process that transfers and duplicates artwork and text onto a printing surface of either metal or plastic. See *platemaking*.

Platemaking The general term given to converting pictures, illustrations, and text into a reproducible printing pattern on metal, plastic, or a similar hard material that is then fed into a printing press. In letterpress printing, also referred to as *engraving*.

Point   A unit of measurement describing the size of type, about $\frac{1}{72}$ inch in depth (technically 0.0138 inch). There are 72 points to the inch. The most common range of point sizes is 4 to 144.

Point-of-purchase advertising (P.O.P.)   A type of advertising found in retail stores, which is the point where the sale to the consumer is made. P.O.P. is regarded as the advertiser's "last chance" to give a sales message to the shopper. P.O.P. materials include window displays, signs, and banners. Also known as *point-of-sale*.

Point-of-sale advertising   See *point-of-purchase advertising*.

Positioning   Creating a distinct identity for a product through advertising or public relations that makes it appear more interesting to the consumer, even though its physical properties remain unchanged from the way in which it was portrayed earlier.

Post Office statement   The claimed circulation of a newspaper or magazine made on a formal Post Office form and deposited with the Post Office annually.

Poster panel   See *billboards*.

PR   See *public relations*.

Preemptible rate   A term that applies to pricing broadcast commercials. A preemptible rate is subject to cancellation if another advertiser pays a higher rate.

Preferred position   A special place within a publication, more desirable because of greater audience traffic. Preferred positions carry higher rates and are usually in great demand by advertisers.

Premium position   See *preferred position*.

Premiums   Items of value given free or at a reduced price as an inducement to purchase another product.

Preprints   See *engraver's proofs*.

Presenter   A person who represents a company in its advertising.

Press agentry   The initiating of stunts and events so they will be reported on by the media.

Press conference   A convening of media editors and reporters to hear news about a specific company product or event.

Press kit   Publicity materials handed out at press conferences, conventions, and trade shows, usually in elaborate folders.

Press release   A typewritten document providing news about a product, service, person or event.

Pressing   The process of making a record or disc from a tape.

Prime prospect   A specific type of individual of great sales interest to an advertiser.

Prime time   In television broadcasting, the hours between 7:30 P.M. and 11:00 P.M..

Problem tracking   A research technique attributed to an ad agency, BBD&O, that helps to discover the prime prospect's problem.

Production   In advertising, the process of converting a creative idea into finished advertising.

Production add-ons   An agency charge added to the cost of production work (art, type, and so on.) done on behalf of a client. The charge may run from 17.65 percent to 20 percent and repays the agency for handling and supervising the work.

Production engineer   A person responsible for overseeing the many facets involved in the direct manufacture of a product, from raw materials to finished goods.

Progressive proofs (progs)   A set of photoengraving proofs in color, some separate and others combined to help the advertiser determine what the final reproduction will look like. See *four-color process*.

Project engineer   Versatile engineers

whose knowledge enables them to see a product through planning, designing, and manufacturing.

Projection machine (Lucy) A device used to enlarge and/or reduce artwork.

Proof A printed trial impression of an advertisement developed for client and/or agency approval.

Psychographics The study of people's real needs and wants.

Public relations A planned strategy aimed at influencing public understanding. Often called p.r.

Public Relations Society of America (PRSA) The name of the professional organization representing public relations people throughout the country. PRSA establishes standards of performance for its members.

Public service announcement (PSA) A nonprofit or public-agency radio or television commercial run by broadcast stations at no charge because it is in the public interest.

Publicity A tool for providing commercially significant news about goods and services to the media without having the sponsor pay for it.

Publics Target audiences of public relations people.

Publisher's statement A statement signed by a publisher attesting to the circulation of a magazine or newspaper.

Purchase order A document indicating intent to buy certain specified merchandise and equipment.

Purchasing agent (PA) A person in a plant or commercial enterprise or institution whose primary job is buying goods and services.

Rate card An advertising medium's printed document listing prices and related information. Sometimes called the *card rate* to describe the price paid by an advertiser for time or space.

Rating points In broadcasting, the percentage of households in any given market reached by a television or radio program at a certain time. See *gross rating points*. In outdoor advertising, the number of people exposed to an outdoor sign over a specified period of time.

Ratings The percentage of television or radios tuned to a specific program at a specific time. Ratings are determined by surveys made by research organizations such as Nielsen and Arbitron.

Reach The number of different, or unduplicated, homes reached by a particular medium at a specific time and sometimes called a *cumulative audience*. The specific time for a broadcast program is generally one to four weeks. For example, if 10 million people watch "MASH" each week for four weeks (total audience of 40 million) and 50 percent of them watch it twice while 50 percent watch it only once, its reach is 30 million.

Release A legal, signed statement by a person photographed or represented in an ad permitting the advertiser to use the photograph. Sometimes called a *photo release*.

Release prints Copies of the final film print.

Reprints See *engraver's proofs*.

Research engineer A plant official with long-range responsibilities for solving theoretical and practical engineering problems.

Residuals The money paid to talent used in a television commercial according to a formula developed by AFTRA.

Respondent A person who answers a questionnaire or is the subject of an interview conducted for market research purposes.

Retail advertising A type of advertising done by local retail stores.

Retail display allowance Funds paid to retailers by manufacturers for providing a premium location within the store for the manufacturer's displays.

Retainer fee A negotiated annual fee between ad agency and advertiser in payment of the agency's work. The fee is usually paid in monthly installments.

Retouching   An artistic technique used to make changes in photographs.

Reverse   A part of a piece of advertising in which the original colors are reversed; the white background appears as black and the conventional black letters appear as white.

Rifle approach   In direct mail, a direct appeal from a manufacturer to a specific consumer. Compare *shotgun approach*.

Roman type   An upright style of letter types dating from the Roman school of design.

Rotary press   A long-run press in which the impression and the printing surfaces are cylindrical, although the printed matter is on a flat plane. A sheet is printed with every revolution of the impression cylinder.

Rotogravure   Gravure printing on a rotary press.

Rough layout   See *layout*.

Rule of 2 percent   In direct-response advertising, the anticipated return on a conventional mailing.

Run of book (ROB)   An advertisement position controlled by the magazine publisher and usually lower in price than a preferred position.

Run of paper (ROP)   The position of a newspaper advertisement over which the advertiser has no control, as contrasted with preferred position.

Run of schedule (ROS)   A broadcaster's term to indicate a commercial run at a time of the station's own choosing, and usually at a lower price.

Sales force   The entire selling arm of a company.

Sales promotion   Specific marketing activities that stimulate sales, such as special offers, contests, and price discounts.

Sampling   The act or process of selecting a representative group of people for testing. In advertising, the term refers to the selection of individuals at random. Also the distribution of miniature products by mail or through retail stores.

Sans serif   A typeface with no serifs (the short lines drawn at an angle to the upper and lower ends of the strokes of a letter).

Satellite   A receiving station for communication signal transmissions, usually in cable broadcasting systems. Also called *satellite earth station.*.

Saturation   A media strategy employing wide coverage and/or frequency on a stepped-up scale in order to achieve maximum impact.

Scenario   The outline of a television commercial or movie.

Screen   In photoengraving, the precisely ruled glass or contact screen with a given number of lines per linear inch. The number of lines per inch gives the screen its number, such as 100-line or 133-line. Halftone photography is done through the grid pattern of a halftone screen. Also refers to the gradations of color tones, for example, a 50 percent screen of black.

Script   Typefaces designed to imitate handwriting.

Second cover   See *cover positions*.

Selective couponing   A form of currency, backed by a manufacturer having a specific "cents off" value and distributed to a particular consumer group.

Selective perception   In psychology, a process of tuning out or tuning in events according to individual bias.

Self-liquidators   Promotional premium offers paid for by the consumer rather than the sponsor.

Self-mailer   A direct-mail piece that carries an address and therefore requires no covering envelope.

Serif faces   A series of typefaces having short cross-lines angling from the ends of the main strokes of letters.

Service industries   Companies that provide a wide range of assistance and technical help to manufacturing and processing plants, commercial businesses, construction firms, and institutions.

Set fee An agency-designated *fee* established as a minimum for each client based on the amount of estimated client service delivered by the ad agency.

Sets in use A percentage of radio or television households tuned in at a specific time.

SFX An abbreviation for sound effects.

Sheet-fed Printing presses designed for printing individual flat sheets of paper. Compare *web-fed*.

Shopper A weekly newspaper-type tabloid made up of mostly classified ads and distributed free over a wide geographical area. Shoppers compete with newspapers for advertisers' dollars.

Short rate The difference between the contracted rate of advertising and the earned rate.

Shotgun approach A means of carrying an ad message to a general audience with no particular person in mind. Compare *rifle approach*.

Showing The impact resulting from the numbers of outdoor boards rented in a given geographical area, such as a 100 showing or a 50 showing. In recent years, showings have been tied in with gross rating points so that a 50 GRP showing delivers a daily exposure to half the adult population of an area. A 100 showing can be almost any number of boards depending on the population density and geographical spread of an area.

Simmons reports Reports by a research organization (W. R. Simmons & Associates) well known for providing information about media demographics and product usage.

Spectacolor A full-color newspaper printing process similar to HiFi and also printed by an outside printing plant. It differs from Hi-Fi in that there is no

need for a continuous design because pages come out with registration marks to fit a newspaper page.

Split runs In direct mail, a method of comparing the pulling power of different ad approaches aimed at the same audience. In newspaper and magazine advertising, a service made available for advertisers so they can run different ads in alternate copies of the same magazine issue.

Spot The purchase of broadcast time on a market-by-market basis as contrasted with showing a commercial simultaneously throughout the country. Also the name given to a broadcast commercial.

Square halftone A square or rectangular reproduction of a photograph that appears as part of an ad. See *halftone*.

Standard & Poor's Index A source book containing business data about American corporations.

Standard Directory of Advertisers (Red Book) An annual reference book listing major American advertisers and key corporate officials, including ad managers.

Standard Directory of Advertising Agencies (Red Book) An annual reference book of the majority of the leading American advertising agencies, their management officials and their clients.

Standard Industrial Code (SIC) Category numbers assigned by the government to all industries and businesses to identify the types of products each plant manufactures or the types of services provided.

Standard Metropolitan Statistical Areas (SMSA) An area with a central city of at least 50,000 inhabitants or more and defined by the government along county lines. Responsibility for defining SMSAs rests with the Office of Management and Budget of the federal government. Each area includes the entire county as well as adjacent counties tied in socially and economically with the central city.

Standard Rate & Data Service (SRDS) A subscription service for buyers of magazine, television, radio, newspaper, and transit advertising space and time. The company also publishes a semiannual directory for renters of consumer and business direct-mail lists.

Starch INRA Hooper, Inc. Producer of newspaper and magazine readership studies including advertising and public opinion research. The organization operates domestically as well as internationally.

Station posters Scaled-down billboards designed for bus, railroad, subway, and air terminals.

Stereotype mats See *mats*.

Storyboard A series of drawings or sketches of the key scenes in a television commercial.

Straight project fee A negotiated fee paid to an ad agency for a special project.

Strategy platform A guide for copywriters to keep them aware of the objectives of the advertising they are creating. Also called *copy platform*.

Stratified sample A method of sampling that divides the population into subgroups and then determines how many from each subgroup will be selected to develop a random sample.

Superimposition (super) An image from one television camera placed over the image from another.

Surface plates Offset printing plates.

Symmetrical layout A formal arrangement of all the elements in a piece of advertising.

Syndicated art services Companies that sell advertising illustrations, ideas, and campaigns to newspapers on a subscription basis.

Tab sections A tabloid-size newspaper section usually carrying features and complimentary advertising. A favored promotional device of weekly newspapers.

Target Group Index (TGI) A copyrighted report by Axiom Market Research Bureau, based on surveys of selected media audiences and including demographic and product usage information.

Task budgeting A means whereby companies allocate the amount of advertising dollars they anticipate it will take to bring about a desired result.

Tear sheets Copies of ads clipped from newspapers and magazines and sent to advertisers as proof of publication.

Test mailing The testing of a direct-mail program in a predetermined area or in sufficient numbers to preview its degree of success before a major advertising investment is made.

Test market A city or region containing a typical cross-section of the people who are normally prospects for a company's products. Also to test goods and services in selected markets prior to making a national advertising investment.

Test market profiles A compilation of media and marketing statistics for 199 market areas in the United States as provided by A. C. Nielsen Company.

Tf "Till forbid." Instructions to a publisher to continue to run an ad until advised to stop. Also the name of an association of magazine space representatives who would like to have their advertisers run ads in their publications on a tf basis.

Third cover See *cover positions*.

Throwaways Inexpensively printed sales messages, often called *circulars*.

Thumbnail sketches Unusually small layouts rendered by artists during the creative process.

Trade association Like-minded businesspeople banding together to protect the economic welfare of the group.

Trade show A major gathering place where buyers and sellers meet to examine new and existing products and to learn how to improve their marketing operations.

Trademark A device, a word, or a piece of art that is part of a company brand and thus gives its owner legal protection to its exclusive use because it is sufficiently distinctive from competitors'.

Traffic (traffic control) That section of an ad agency whose function it is to keep reproducible advertising (tapes, film, engravings) moving to the proper media before closing dates.

Traffic time See *drive time.*

Transit advertising Advertising carried by buses, taxicabs, and subway trains.

Translator station A television station that picks up programs from another station and rebroadcasts them. Translator stations are not permitted to originate programs locally.

Television director (package house) The person responsible for the actual casting, rehearsal, performance, and shooting of a television commercial.

Television producer (commercials) The person in an ad agency or package house with overall responsibility for making television commercials, including the hiring of the director.

Two-page spread A print ad consisting of two pages side-by-side.

Two-tiered rate structure system In newspaper advertising, the traditional pricing method whereby a higher rate is charged to national advertisers and a lower (local) rate to hometown retailers.

Type or typefaces Distinctive designs of printed letters, numbers, and punctuation marks that appear in advertisements.

Typography A style or arrangement of printed letters usually sold by a commercial company called a *typographer* or *type house.*

uc Upper-case letters.

UHF transmission Ultrahigh frequency waves, television transmission waves able to travel only in straight paths from the transmitter. Because waves are sent out more frequently (hence the name UHF), they cover a shorter distance.

Universe A term used by market researchers to define large groups of people from whom are drawn representative samples in order to determine the opinions of the larger group.

Vertical press A printing press in which the bed is in a vertical position. Compare *flat-bed press.*

Vertical publication A business magazine designed to be read by members of a single industry. Compare *horizontal publication.*

VHF transmission Very high frequency waves are transmitted in a straight line, generally from horizon to horizon. Unlike ultrahigh frequency waves, VHF waves are favored by commercial stations because they require fewer auxiliary transmitters to reach their audience.

Video The visual portion of a television commercial.

Video display terminal (VDT) A screen used to show words so typesetting operators can create, add, delete, or change copy.

Videotape A magnetic tape made for television on which both picture and sound can be recorded and played.

Waste circulation Readers of a print medium who are not prospects for a particular advertised product because they are uninterested in the product, they reside in an area where the product is not distributed, or they are unable to purchase the product.

Web-fed Printing presses fed by a continuous roll of paper. Compare *sheet-fed.*

Web printing See *web-fed.*

White space The unprinted area of an ad used by artists to highlight another element of the ad.

Wipe A television direction that cleans the screen.

Word of mouth The unsolicited passing on of information about a product or service by an individual.

Work print In filming a television commercial, the visual portion of the first assemblage of scenes in their proper sequence. Sometimes known as a *rough cut.*

Zinc plate A photoengraving made in zinc. Also called a *zinc etching.*

Zoned delivery A method developed by newspapers, magazines, and direct-mail houses for dividing their total circulations into precise ZIP Code zones.

Zoom An optical effect used in television and movies to shift quickly from one extreme camera angle to another—from an extreme closeup to a long shot, and vice versa.

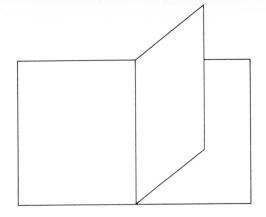

BIBLIOGRAPHY

Ashford, Gerald: *Everyday Publicity* (New York: Law Arts, 1970).

Barton, Roger: *Media in Advertising* (New York: McGraw-Hill, 1964).

Bedell, Clyde: *How to Write Advertising That Sells,* 2d ed. (New York: McGraw-Hill, 1952).

Bockus, H. William, Jr.: *Advertising Graphics,* 3d ed. (New York: Macmillan, 1979).

Caples, John: *Tested Advertising Methods* (New York: Harper & Row, 1961).

Cutlip, Scott and Allen Center: *Effective Public Relations* (Englewood Cliffs, N.J.: Prentice-Hall, 1978).

Dalbey, Homer M., Irwin Gross, and Yoram Wind: *Advertising Measurement and Decision Making* (Boston: Allyn and Bacon, 1968).

Flesch, Rudolph: *The Art of Plain Talk* (New York: Harper & Row, 1946).

Hoge, Cecil C., Sr.: *Mail Order Moonlighting* (Berkeley: Ten Speed Press, 1976).

Lendt, David, ed.: *The Publicity Process,* 2d ed. (Ames: Iowa State University Press, 1978).

Lois, George, and Bill Pitts: *The Art of Advertising: George Lois on Mass Communication* (New York: Abrams, 1977).

Marston, John E.: *The Nature of Public Relations* (New York: McGraw-Hill, 1963).

Nelson, Roy Paul: *The Design of Advertising,* 3d ed. (Dubuque, Iowa: Wm. C. Brown, 1979).

Norins, Hanley: *The Compleat Copywriter* (New York: McGraw-Hill, 1966).

Ogilvy, David: *Confessions of an Advertising Man* (New York: Dell Publishing Company, 1963).

Reeves, Rosser: *Reality in Advertising* (New York: Knopf, 1961).

Riso, Ovid: *Sales Promotion Handbook* (Chicago: Dartnell, 1973).

Schiller, Robert D., ed.: *Market and Media Evaluation* (New York: Macmillan, 1969).

Seiden, Hank: *Advertising Pure and Simple* (New York: American Management Association, 1977).

Still, Richard and Edward Cundiff: *Sales Management Decisions, Policies and Cases,* 2d ed. (Englewood Cliffs, N.J.: Prentice-Hall, 1969).

Young, James W.: *A Technique for Producing Ideas* (Chicago: Crain Books, 1975).

INDEX

Page numbers in *italic* indicate illustrations, tables, or ads.

727